# Window on Humanity

## A Concise Introduction to Anthropology

### Ninth Edition

**Conrad Phillip Kottak**
*University of Michigan*

Mc
Graw
Hill

WINDOW ON HUMANITY: A CONCISE INTRODUCTION TO ANTHROPOLOGY, NINTH EDITION

2 3 4 5 6 7 8 9 LCR 24 23 22 21 20 19

ISBN 978-1-260-07147-4
MHID 1-260-07147-2

Executive Portfolio Manager: *Claire Brantley*
Product Development Manager: *Dawn Groundwater*
Marketing Manager: *Nancy Baudean*
Content Project Managers: *Rick Hecker/Katie Reuter*
Senior Buyer: *Laura M. Fuller*
Designer: *Egzon Shaqiri*
Content Licensing Specialist: *Carrie Burger*
Cover Image: © *golero/GettyImages*
Compositor: *Aptara®, Inc.*

**Library of Congress Cataloging-in-Publication Data**

Names: Kottak, Conrad Phillip author.
Title: Window on humanity : a concise introduction to anthropology / Conrad Phillip Kottak, University of Michigan.
Description: Ninth Edition. | New York : McGraw-Hill Education, [2019] | Audience: Age: 18+ | Eighth edition: 2018.
Identifiers: LCCN 2019021810| ISBN 9781260071474 (Hard Cover : acid-free paper) | ISBN 1260071472 (Hard Cover : acid-free paper)
Subjects: LCSH: Anthropology.
Classification: LCC GN25 .K68 2019 | DDC 301–dc23 LC record available at https://lccn.loc.gov/2019021810

mheducation.com/highered

To my wife,
Isabel Wagley Kottak

**Also available from McGraw-Hill by Conrad Phillip Kottak:**

*Mirror for Humanity: A Concise Introduction to Cultural Anthropology,* 12th ed. (2020)

*Anthropology: Appreciating Human Diversity,* 18th ed. (2019)

*Cultural Anthropology: Appreciating Cultural Diversity,* 18th ed. (2019)

*CULTURE, 2nd ed. (2014) (Lisa Gezon and Conrad Phillip Kottak)*

*On Being Different: Diversity and Multiculturalism in the North American Mainstream,* 4th ed. (2012) (with Kathryn A. Kozaitis)

# Brief Contents

# Contents

## Chapter 4

## Evolution, Genetics, and Human Variation   72

## Chapter 5

## The Primates   100

## Chapter 6

## Early Hominins   127

# Anthropology Today Boxes

# Preface

*Window on Humanity* is intended to provide a concise, readable introduction to general (four-field) anthropology. Its shorter length increases the instructor's options for assigning additional reading—case studies, readers, and other supplements—in a semester course. *Window* also can work well in a quarter system, for which traditional texts may be too long.

Just as anthropology is a dynamic discipline that encourages new discoveries and explores the profound changes now affecting people and societies, this edition of *Window on Humanity* makes a concerted effort to keep pace with changes in the way students read and learn core content today. Our digital program, **Connect Anthropology,** includes assignable and assessable quizzes, exercises, and interactive activities, organized around course-specific learning objectives. **Connect** also includes **SmartBook,** the adaptive reading experience. The tools and resources provided in Connect Anthropology are designed to engage students and enable them to improve their performance in the course. This 9th edition has benefited from feedback from more than 2,000 students who worked with these tools and programs while using the 8th edition of *Window* or one of my other recent texts. We were able to respond to specific areas of difficulty that students encountered, chapter by chapter. I used this extensive feedback to revise, rethink, and clarify my writing in almost every chapter. In preparing this edition, I benefited tremendously from both students' and professors' reactions to my book.

As I work on each new edition, it becomes ever more apparent to me that while any competent and useful text must present anthropology's core, that text also must demonstrate anthropology's relevance to the 21st-century world we inhabit. Accordingly, each new edition contains content changes as well as specific features relevant to our changing world. One of my primary goals is to help students make connections between what they read and their own lives. Accordingly, the "Anthropology Today" boxes placed near the end of each chapter examine recent developments in anthropology as well as contemporary topics and issues that are clearly related to anthropology's subject matter. Each chapter also contains a feature that I call "Think Like an Anthropologist," which attempts to get students to do just that—to apply their critical thinking skills as an anthropologist might.

I realize that most students who read this book will not go on to become anthropologists, or even anthropology majors. For those who do, this book should provide a solid foundation to build on. For those who don't—that is, for most of my readers—my goal is to instill a sense of understanding and appreciation of human diversity and of anthropology as a field. May this course and this text help students think differently about, and achieve greater understanding of, their own culture and its place within our globalizing world.

# McGraw-Hill Connect Anthropology

Connect Anthropology is a premier digital teaching and learning tool that allows instructors to assign and assess course material. Connect Anthropology includes assignable and assessable quizzes, exercises, and interactive activities, organized around course-specific learning objectives. **NewsFlash** activities, which are updated regularly, bring in articles on current events relevant to anthropology with accompanying assessment.

The system is praised by users—faculty and students alike—for helping to make both teaching and learning more efficient, saving time and keeping class time and independent study time focused on what is most important and only those things that still need reinforcing, and shifting the teaching/learning process away from memorization and cramming. The result is better grades, better concept retention, more students staying in class and passing, and less time spent preparing classes or studying for tests.

# Provide a Smarter Book and Better Value with SmartBook

**SMARTBOOK** Available within Connect, SmartBook makes study time as productive and efficient as possible by identifying and closing knowledge gaps. SmartBook identifies what an individual student knows and doesn't know based on the student's confidence level, responses to questions and other factors.

SmartBook builds an optimal, personalized learning path for each student, so students spend less time on concepts they already understand and more time on those they don't. As a student engages with SmartBook, the reading experience continuously adapts by highlighting the most impactful content a student needs to learn at that moment in time. This ensures that every minute spent with SmartBook is returned to the student as the most value-added minute possible. The result? More confidence, better grades, and greater success.

New to this edition, SmartBook is now optimized for phones and tablets and accessible for students with disabilities using interactive features.

# Chapter-by-Chapter Changes

The 9th edition of *Window on Humanity* was extensively informed by student data, collected anonymously by McGraw-Hill Education's SmartBook. This data graphically illustrated "hot spots" where students struggle the most—at both the sentence and paragraph level—which yielded a plan for revision and improvement centered on the content that is toughest for students.

In addition to revisions and updates throughout the book, the following are this edition's major or significant changes:

### Chapter 1: What Is Anthropology?
- Updated "Anthropology Today" box, "School of Hope."

## Chapter 2: Culture

- Expanded discussion of cultural appropriation.
- Revised and expanded section on globalization.
- Updates throughout, especially in the "Anthropology Today" box, "Preserving Cultural Heritage."

## Chapter 3: Doing Anthropology

- New information on the use of LiDAR ("Light Detection and Ranging") technology as a tool for understanding the past, specifically in the Maya area.
- New discussion of fluorine dating and its role in uncovering the Piltdown hoax.
- A new "Anthropology Today" box, "A Workshop in Genomics for Indigenous Peoples," has been added.

## Chapter 4: Evolution, Genetics, and Human Variation

- The "Evolution" section now discusses A. R. Wallace's role in recognizing natural selection as the prime mechanism of biological evolution.
- The "Human Biological Adaptation" section includes a rewritten subsection, "Genes and Disease."

## Chapter 5: The Primates

- Rewritten "Our Place among Primates" section, with two new subheads: "Apes Are Our Closest Relatives" and "Zoological Taxonomy."
- New discussion of *Nyanzapithecus alesi* in the "Miocene Hominoids" section.

## Chapter 6: Early Hominins

- The Piltdown hoax is now part of an expanded discussion of bipedalism versus brain size as a key marker of "What Makes Us Human?"
- Expanded discussion of *Au. sediba* as one of "The Varied Australopiths."
- New "Anthropology Today" box, "3-D Bone Scans Suggest Lucy's Climbing Ability and Cause of Death".

## Chapter 7: The Genus *Homo*

- This chapter has been extensively revised and updated, reflecting new discoveries, and condensed to fit in the new information.
- New section, "Neandertals, Denisovans, and Anatomically Modern Humans."
- A new section, "Asian Island Anomalies," updates the discussion of *H. floresiensis* (Indonesia) and discusses the more recently reported find of *H. luzonensis* (Philippines).
- New discussions of the 2017 discovery of the earliest AMH fossils in Jebel Irhoud, Morocco; AMH migrations out of Africa; and AMH skulls found in Israel in the "Modern Humans" section.
- New material on the 2017 Madjedbebe discoveries in Australia.

- New discussion of a monumental 2018 report based on DNA analysis of American fossil finds, and detailing the branching of ancestral Native Americans as they settled the Americas.

## Chapter 8: The First Farmers

- A new major subhead titled "American First?" exposes the foreign roots of key features of our daily lives.
- There is a new discussion of recent evidence, from a Jordanian desert, for the world's earliest bread.

## Chapter 9: The First Cities and States

- The discussion of Maya civilization has been expanded and updated, based on information from the recent LiDAR survey of northern Guatemala.
- The "Anthropology Today" box on "The Fantastic Claims of Pseudo-Archaeology" has been revised.

## Chapter 10: Language and Communication

- New discussion of Jane Hill's research into the mixed use of Spanish and English in Mexican-themed restaurants in the "Sociolinguistics" section.
- Updated "Anthropology Today" box, "Words of the Year".

## Chapter 11: Making a Living

- There is a new "Anthropology Today" box: "When the Mills Shut Down: An Anthropologist Looks at Deindustrialization."
- The author paid special attention to clarifying writing and Learn Smart probes for this chapter.

## Chapter 12: Political Systems

- The "Anthropology Today" box, "The Illegality Industry: A Failed System of Border Control," has been updated.

## Chapter 13: Families, Kinship, and Marriage

- The "Families" section has been thoroughly updated, including a new discussion of the extended families of the Moso people of southwestern China and updated statistics concerning changes in North American kinship.
- A new section, "It's All Relative," examines the definition of close family relations in light of the Trump administration's Muslim travel ban.
- The "Same-Sex Marriage" section has been significantly updated.
- Recent research and a new Figure 13.4, "Why Americans Marry" have been incorporated within the "Arranged Marriages versus Romance Marriages" section.
- The introduction to the "Plural Marriages" section has been rewritten to clarify the difference between polygyny and polyandry.
- The "The Online Marriage Market" section incorporates new research.

- The author paid special attention to clarifying writing and SmartBook probes for this chapter.

## Chapter 14: Gender

- The "Gender in Industrialized Societies" section has been heavily revised and updated.
- The "Beyond Male and Female" section has been revised substantially to clarify American gender categories in flux.

## Chapter 15: Religion

- The "World Religions" section has been revised to incorporate the latest statistics.
- A new section on "Religious Changes in the United States" has been added.
- Content of the previous "Anthropology Today" box, "Newtime Religion," has been moved into the text.
- The new "Anthropology Today" box, "Great Expectorations," brings back (by popular demand) a discussion of baseball magic.

## Chapter 16: Ethnicity and Race

- All sections have been substantially revised, with new photos and statistics.
- Newly available data from the 2016 census now informs the discussion of Canadian ethnic diversity.
- A new discussion of biracial Japanese has been added.
- Results of a new study of cultural/ethnic/linguistic diversity among 180 countries have been added.
- Also added are new demographic projections for the United States through 2060, including significant growth in the dependency ratio.
- Recent election results now inform the "Backlash to Multiculturalism" section.

## Chapter 17: Applying Anthropology

- A new section, "Can Change Be Bad," applies this chapter's key point—that innovation succeeds best when it is culturally appropriate—to the international spread of programs aimed at social and economic change as well as of businesses.
- The author paid special attention to clarifying writing and Learn Smart probes for this chapter.

## Chapter 18: The World System, Colonialism, and Inequality

- "The Persistence of Inequality" section, including discussion of the water crisis in Flint, Michigan, has been updated, and a new section on exposure to risks that reduce life expectancy has been added.
- The "Development/Neoliberalism" sections include an updated discussion on tariffs and trade agreements, including NAFTA (now USMCA).
- "The World System Today" and the "Anthropology Today" box have been revised and updated.
- The author paid special attention to clarifying writing and SmartBook probes for this chapter.

## Chapter 19: Anthropology's Role in a Globalizing World

- Updated statistics on energy consumption and an updated and expanded Table 19.1, Total Energy Consumption, 2017, Top Twelve Countries (in MTOE—Million Tons of Oil Equivalent) + Current Share of World Energy Consumption + Annual Percentage Increase + Per Capita Energy Consumption by Country.

- The "Global Climate Change" section incorporates the latest statistics, has two new subheads: "Emissions and Global Warming" and "Climate Change," and adds a discussion of the implications of the devastating 2017 hurricanes (Harvey, Irma, and Maria).

- The "Interethnic Contact" section adds new information and statistics on media penetration and impact in Brazil and the Middle East.

- The author paid special attention to clarifying writing and SmartBook probes for this chapter.

# Content and Organization

No single or monolithic theoretical perspective orients this book. My e-mail, along with reviewers' comments, confirms that instructors with a very wide range of views and approaches have been pleased with *Window* as a teaching tool.

- In Chapter 1, anthropology is introduced as an integrated four-field discipline, with academic and applied dimensions, that examines human biological and cultural diversity in time and space. Anthropology is discussed as a comparative and holistic science, featuring biological, social, cultural, linguistic, humanistic, and historical approaches. Chapter 2 examines the central anthropological concept of culture, including its symbolic and adaptive features. Chapter 3 is about doing anthropology—the methods and ethics of research in anthropology's subfields.

- The chapters focusing on biological anthropology and archaeology (4, 5, 6, 7, 8, and 9) offer up-to-date answers to several key questions: When did humans originate, and how did we become what we are? What role do genes, the environment, society, and culture play in human variation and diversity? What can we tell about our origins and nature from the study of our nearest relatives—nonhuman primates? When and how did the primates originate? What key features of their early adaptations are still basic to our abilities, behavior, and perceptions? How did hominids develop from our primate ancestors? When, where, and how did the first hominins emerge and expand? What about the earliest real humans? How do we explain biological diversity in our own species, *Homo sapiens?* What major transitions have taken place since the emergence of *Homo sapiens?*

- Chapters 8 and 9 discuss the Neolithic, especially the domestication of plants and animals, as a major adaptive change, with profound implications for human lifeways. The spread and intensification of farming and herding are tied to the appearance of the first towns, cities, and states, as well as the emergence of social stratification and major social inequalities.

- The chapters on linguistic and sociocultural anthropology (10, 11, 12, 13, 14, 15, 16, 17, 18, and 19) are organized to place related content close together—although they are sufficiently independent to be assigned in any order the instructor might select. Thus, "Political Systems" (Chapter 12) logically follows "Making a Living" (Chapter 11). Chapters 13 and 14 ("Families, Kinship, and Marriage" and "Gender," respectively) also form a coherent unit. The chapter on religion (15) covers not just traditional religious practices but also contemporary world religions and religious movements. It is followed by four chapters (16, 17, 18, and 19) that form a natural unit exploring sociocultural transformations and expressions in today's world.

- Those last four chapters address several important questions: How are race and ethnicity socially constructed and handled in different societies, and how do they generate prejudice, discrimination, and conflict? How and why did the modern world system emerge and expand? How has world capitalism affected patterns of stratification and inequality within and among nations? What were colonialism, imperialism, and Communism, and what are their legacies? How do people today actively interpret and confront the world system and the products of globalization? What factors threaten continued human diversity? How can anthropologists work to ensure the preservation of that diversity?

- Let me also single out two chapters present in *Window on Humanity* but not found consistently in other anthropology texts: "Ethnicity and Race" (Chapter 16) and "Gender" (Chapter 14). I believe that systematic consideration of race, ethnicity, and gender is vital in an introductory anthropology text. Anthropology's distinctive four-field approach can shed special light on these topics. We see this not only in Chapter 16 ("Ethnicity and Race") but also in Chapter 4 ("Evolution, Genetics, and Human Variation"), in which race is discussed as a problematic concept in biology. Race and gender studies are fields in which anthropology always has taken the lead. I'm convinced that anthropology's special contributions to understanding the biological, social, cultural, and linguistic dimensions of race, ethnicity, and gender should be highlighted in any introductory text.

## Teaching Resources

The following instructor resources can be accessed through the Library tab in **Connect Anthropology:**

- Instructor's manual
- PowerPoint lecture slides
- Computerized test bank
- Word version of the test bank

# Create

 Design your ideal course materials with McGraw-Hill Education's
Create: http://www.create.mheducation.com

Rearrange or omit chapters, combine materials from other sources, and/or upload any other content you have written to make the perfect resource for your students. You can even personalize your book's appearance by selecting the cover and adding your name, school, and course information. When you order a Create book, you receive a complimentary review copy. Get a printed copy in three to five business days or an electronic copy (eComp) via e-mail in about an hour. Register today at http://www.create.mheducation.com and craft your course resources to match the way you teach.

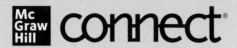

## You're in the driver's seat.

Want to build your own course? No problem. Prefer to use our turnkey, prebuilt course? Easy. Want to make changes throughout the semester? Sure. And you'll save time with Connect's auto-grading too.

# 65%

### Less Time Grading

Laptop: McGraw-Hill Education

## They'll thank you for it.

Adaptive study resources like SmartBook® help your students be better prepared in less time. You can transform your class time from dull definitions to dynamic debates. Hear from your peers about the benefits of Connect at **www.mheducation.com/highered/connect**

## Make it simple, make it affordable.

Connect makes it easy with seamless integration using any of the major Learning Management Systems— Blackboard®, Canvas, and D2L, among others—to let you organize your course in one convenient location. Give your students access to digital materials at a discount with our inclusive access program. Ask your McGraw-Hill representative for more information.

Padlock: Jobalou/Getty Images

## Solutions for your challenges.

A product isn't a solution. Real solutions are affordable, reliable, and come with training and ongoing support when you need it and how you want it. Our Customer Experience Group can also help you troubleshoot tech problems— although Connect's 99% uptime means you might not need to call them. See for yourself at **status. mheducation.com**

Checkmark: Jobalou/Getty Images

SUPPORT AT
*every step*

## Effective, efficient studying.

Connect helps you be more productive with your study time and get better grades using tools like SmartBook, which highlights key concepts and creates a personalized study plan. Connect sets you up for success, so you walk into class with confidence and walk out with better grades.

## Study anytime, anywhere.

Download the free ReadAnywhere app and access your online eBook when it's convenient, even if you're offline. And since the app automatically syncs with your eBook in Connect, all of your notes are available every time you open it. Find out more at www.mheducation.com/readanywhere

> *"I really liked this app—it made it easy to study when you don't have your text-book in front of you."*
>
> - Jordan Cunningham, Eastern Washington University

## No surprises.

The Connect Calendar and Reports tools keep you on track with the work you need to get done and your assignment scores. Life gets busy; Connect tools help you keep learning through it all.

## Learning for everyone.

McGraw-Hill works directly with Accessibility Services Departments and faculty to meet the learning needs of all students. Please contact your Accessibility Services office and ask them to email accessibility@mheducation.com, or visit **www.mheducation.com/about/accessibility** for more information.

# Acknowledgments

I'm grateful to many colleagues at McGraw-Hill. I offer particular thanks to product developer Bruce Cantley, who helped me plan and implement this revision, and worked with me to complete and submit the manuscript. I am privileged to be working with Claire Brantley, executive portfolio manager, and Dawn Groundwater, product development manager. Thanks as well to McGraw-Hill's entire team of sales reps and regional managers for the work they do in helping professors and students gain access to my books. I also acknowledge Michael Ryan, vice president for portfolio and learning content, for his support.

As usual, Rick Hecker has done a great job as content project manager, guiding the manuscript through production and keeping everything moving on schedule. Laura Fuller, buyer, worked with the printer to make sure everything came out right. Thanks, too, to Charlotte Goldman, freelance photo researcher, and to Scott Lukas, Lake Tahoe Community College, who originally created the content for the Connect products for this book. I also thank Amy Marks for copyediting, Marlena Pechan for proofreading, and Egzon Shaqiri for executing the design.

I'm grateful to the reviewers of previous editions and others for their enthusiasm and their suggestions for changes, additions, and deletions (sometimes in very different directions!). Very, very special thanks as well to the more than 2,000 students who have used SmartBook and helped me pinpoint content and writing that needed clarification. Never have so many voices contributed to a revision as to this one. My readers also share their insights about *Window* via e-mail. Anyone—student or instructor—can reach me at the following e-mail address: ckottak@bellsouth.net.

As usual, my family provides me with understanding, support, and inspiration in my writing projects. Dr. Nicholas Kottak and Dr. Juliet Kottak Mavromatis regularly share their insights with me, as does Isabel Wagley Kottak, my long-term companion in the field and in life, to whom this book is dedicated.

During my long academic career, I've benefited from the knowledge, help, and advice of so many friends, colleagues, teaching assistants (graduate student instructors—GSIs), and students that I can no longer fit their names into a short preface. I hope they know who they are and accept my thanks. I do especially thank my co-authors of other books: Lara Descartes (*Media and Middle Class Moms*), Lisa Gezon (*Culture*), and Kathryn Kozaitis (*On Being Different*). Kathryn (with whom I have worked on four editions), Lisa (two editions), and Lara are also prized former students of mine. Today they all are accomplished anthropologists in their own right, and they continue to share their wisdom with me.

I'm very grateful to my Michigan colleagues who've offered insights and suggested ways of making my books better. Thanks especially to a 101 team that has included Tom Fricke, Stuart Kirsch, Holly Peters-Golden, and Andrew Shryock. Special thanks as well to Joyce Marcus and Kent Flannery for continuing to nurture the archaeologist in me. Most recently, I've benefited from the knowledge and cutting-edge research of my colleagues in Section 51 (Anthropology) of the National Academy of Sciences. Special thanks to Dolores Piperno for granting us use of her teosinte photo in Chapter 8.

Feedback from students and from my fellow anthropologists, along with teaching forums and workshops, keeps me up-to-date on the interests, needs, and views of the people for whom *Window* is written. I also benefit from my long-term and ongoing participation in the General Anthropology Division (GAD) of the American Anthropological Association and my co-editorship (with Chris Furlow and Kathryn Kozaitis) of the GAD Bulletin *General Anthropology*. I continue to believe that effective anthropology textbooks are based in the enjoyment of teaching, respect for students, and appreciation of anthropology as a holistic and humanistic science. I hope this product of my experience will continue to be helpful to others.

*Conrad Phillip Kottak*

*Seabrook Island, South Carolina*

*ckottak@bellsouth.net*

# About the Author

The author at Bayon temple, Angkor Thom, Cambodia in February 2018. Courtesy Isabel Wagley Kottak

**Conrad Phillip Kottak,**

who received his AB and PhD degrees from Columbia University, is the Julian H. Steward Collegiate Professor Emeritus of Anthropology at the University of Michigan, where he served as anthropology department chair from 1996 to 2006. He has been honored for his teaching by the university and the state of Michigan and by the American Anthropological Association. He is an elected member of the American Academy of Arts and Sciences and the National Academy of Sciences, where he chaired Section 51, Anthropology, from 2010 to 2013. He co-edits *General Anthropology,* the biannual bulletin of the General Anthropology Division of the American Anthropological Association.

Professor Kottak has done ethnographic fieldwork in Brazil, Madagascar, and the United States. His general interests are in the processes by which local cultures are incorporated—and resist incorporation—into larger systems. This interest links his earlier work on ecology and state formation in Africa and Madagascar to his more recent research on globalization, national and international culture, and media, including new media and social media.

Kottak's popular case study *Assault on Paradise: The Globalization of a Little Community in Brazil* (2006, reissued and updated by Waveland Press in 2018) describes his long-term and continuing fieldwork in Arembepe, Bahia, Brazil. His book *Prime-Time Society: An Anthropological Analysis of Television and Culture* (2009) is a comparative study of the nature and impact of television in Brazil and the United States.

Kottak's other books include *The Past in the Present: History, Ecology and Cultural Variation in Highland Madagascar* (1980), *Researching American Culture: A Guide for Student Anthropologists* (1982), *Madagascar: Society and History* (1986), and *Media and Middle Class Moms: Images and Realities of Work and Family* (with Lara Descartes, 2009). The most recent editions (18th) of his texts *Anthropology: Appreciating Human Diversity* and *Cultural Anthropology: Appreciating Cultural Diversity* were published by McGraw-Hill in 2019. He also is the author of *Mirror for Humanity: A Concise Introduction to Cultural Anthropology* (12th ed., McGraw-Hill, 2020) and of this book—*Window on Humanity: A Concise Introduction to Anthropology* (9th ed., McGraw-Hill, 2020).

Kottak's articles have appeared in academic journals, including *American Anthropologist, Journal of Anthropological Research, American Ethnologist, Ethnology, Human Organization,* and *Luso-Brazilian Review.* He also has written for more popular journals, including *Transaction/SOCIETY, Natural History, Psychology Today,* and *General Anthropology.*

In other research projects, Professor Kottak and his colleagues have investigated ecological awareness in Brazil, biodiversity conservation in Madagascar, and media use by modern American families. Most recently, he has collaborated with Professor Richard Pace and several graduate students on research investigating "The Evolution of Media Impact: A Longitudinal and Multi-Site Study of Television and New Electronic/Digital Media in Brazil," a project supported by the National Science Foundation.

Conrad Kottak appreciates comments about his books from professors and students. He can be reached at the following e-mail address: ckottak@bellsouth.net.

# Chapter 1

# What Is Anthropology?

## The Cross-Cultural Perspective

"That's just human nature." "People are pretty much the same all over the world." Opinions like these, which we hear in conversations, in media, and in other scenes in daily life, promote the erroneous idea that people in other countries have the same desires, feelings, values, and aspirations that we do. Such statements imply that because people are essentially the same, they are eager to receive the ideas, beliefs, values, institutions, practices, and products of an expansive North American culture. Often this assumption turns out to be wrong.

Anthropology offers a broader view—a distinctive comparative, cross-cultural perspective. Most people think that anthropologists study nonindustrial societies, and they do. My research has taken me to remote villages in Brazil and Madagascar, a large island off the southeast coast of Africa. In Brazil I sailed with fishers in simple sailboats on Atlantic waters. Among Madagascar's Betsileo people, I worked in rice fields and took part in ceremonies in which I entered tombs to rewrap the corpses of decaying ancestors.

However, anthropology is much more than the study of nonindustrial peoples. It is a comparative science that examines all societies, ancient and modern, simple and complex. Most of the other social sciences tend to focus on a single society, usually an industrial nation such as the United States or Canada. Anthropology offers a unique cross-cultural perspective, constantly comparing the customs of one society with those of others.

Today's anthropologists work in varied roles and settings. Nory Condor Alarcon (top photo) is an anthropologist who works for the Forensic Laboratory of the Public Ministry of Ayacucho, Peru. Here she comforts a young woman as she confirms that the lab's forensic team has identified the remains of several of her close relatives. In the bottom photo, a group of experts including anthropologist Mac Chapin (left), hold a press conference at UN Headquarters in New York introducing a new high-tech map of Indigenous Peoples of Central America. (top): Robin Hammond/ IDRC/Panos Pictures/Redux Pictures; (bottom): Eduardo Munoz Alvarez/AFP/Getty Images

Among scholarly disciplines, anthropology stands out as the field that provides the cross-cultural test. How much would we know about human behavior, thought, and feeling if we studied only our own kind? What if our entire understanding of human behavior were based on analysis of questionnaires filled out by American college students? That question should make you think about the basis for statements about what humans are like, individually or as a group. A primary reason anthropology can uncover so much about what it means to be human is that the discipline is based on the cross-cultural perspective. A single culture simply cannot tell us everything we need to know about what it means to be human. We need to compare and contrast.

To become a cultural anthropologist, one typically does *ethnography* (the firsthand, personal study of local settings). Ethnographic fieldwork usually entails spending a year or more in another society, living with the local people and learning about their way of life. No matter how much the ethnographer discovers about that society, he or she remains an alien there. That experience of alienation has a profound impact. Having learned to respect other customs and beliefs, anthropologists can never forget that there is a wider world. There are normal ways of thinking and acting other than our own.

## Human Adaptability

Anthropologists study human beings wherever and whenever they find them—in a Turkish café, a Mesopotamian tomb, or a North American shopping mall. Anthropology is the exploration of human diversity in time and space. Anthropology studies the whole of the human condition: past, present, and future; biology, society, language, and culture. Of particular interest is the diversity that comes through human adaptability.

Humans are among the world's most adaptable animals. In the Andes of South America, people wake up in villages 16,000 feet above sea level and then trek 1,500 feet higher to work in tin mines. Tribes in the Australian desert worship animals and discuss philosophy. People survive malaria in the tropics. Men have walked on the moon. The model of the *Star Trek* starship *Enterprise* in Washington's Smithsonian Institution is a symbol of the *Star Trek* mission "to seek out new life and new civilizations, to boldly go where no one has gone before." Wishes to know the unknown, control the uncontrollable, and create order out of chaos find expression among all peoples. Creativity, adaptability, and flexibility are basic human attributes, and human diversity is the subject matter of anthropology.

Students often are surprised by the breadth of **anthropology**, which is the study of humans around the world and through time. Anthropology is a uniquely comparative and **holistic** science. *Holism* refers to the study of the whole of the human condition: past, present, and future; biology, society, language, and culture.

People share **society**—organized life in groups—with other animals, including baboons, wolves, mole rats, and even ants. Culture, however, is more distinctly human. **Cultures** are traditions and customs, transmitted through learning, that form and guide the beliefs and behavior of the people exposed to them. Children learn such a tradition by growing up in a particular society, through a process called *enculturation.* Cultural traditions include customs and opinions, developed over the generations, about proper and improper behavior. These traditions answer such questions as: How should we do things? How do we make sense of the world? How do we tell right from wrong? A culture produces a degree of consistency in behavior and thought among the people who live in a particular society.

The most critical element of cultural traditions is their transmission through learning rather than through biological inheritance. Culture is not itself biological, but it rests on certain features of human biology. For more than a million years, humans have had at least some of the biological capacities on which culture depends. These abilities are to learn, to think symbolically, to use language, and to employ tools and other products in organizing their lives and adapting to their environments.

Anthropology confronts and ponders major questions of human existence as it explores human biological and cultural diversity in time and space. By examining ancient bones and tools, we unravel the mysteries of human origins. When did our ancestors separate from those remote great-aunts and great-uncles whose descendants are the apes? Where and when did *Homo sapiens* originate? How has our species changed? What are we now, and where are we going? How have changes in culture and society influenced biological change? Our genus, *Homo,* has been changing for more than 2 million years. Humans continue to adapt and change both biologically and culturally.

## Adaptation, Variation, and Change

**Adaptation** refers to the processes by which organisms cope with environmental forces and stresses, such as those posed by climate and *topography* or terrains, also called landforms. How do organisms change to fit their environments, such as dry climates or high mountain altitudes? Like other animals, humans use biological means of adaptation. But humans are unique in also having cultural means of adaptation.

Mountainous terrains pose particular challenges, those associated with high altitude and oxygen deprivation. Consider four ways (one cultural and three biological) in which humans may cope with low oxygen pressure at high altitudes. Illustrating cultural (technological) adaptation would be a pressurized airplane cabin equipped with oxygen masks. There are three ways of adapting biologically to high altitudes: genetic adaptation, long-term physiological adaptation, and short-term physiological adaptation. First, native populations of high-altitude areas, such as the Andes of Peru and the Himalayas of Tibet and Nepal, seem to have acquired certain genetic advantages for life at very high altitudes. The Andean tendency to develop a voluminous chest and lungs probably has a genetic basis. Second, regardless of their genes, people who grow up at a high altitude become physiologically more efficient there than genetically similar people who have grown up at sea level would be. This illustrates long-term physiological adaptation during the body's growth and development. Third, humans also have the capacity for short-term or immediate physiological adaptation. Thus, when lowlanders arrive in the highlands, they immediately increase their breathing and heart rates. Hyperventilation increases the oxygen in their lungs and arteries. As the pulse also increases, blood reaches their tissues more rapidly. All these varied adaptive responses—cultural and biological—achieve a single goal: maintaining an adequate supply of oxygen to the body. Table 1.1 summarizes the cultural and biological means that humans use to adapt to high altitudes.

TABLE 1.1    **Forms of Cultural and Biological Adaptation (to High Altitude)**

| Form of Adaptation | Type of Adaptation | Example |
| --- | --- | --- |
| Technology | Cultural | Pressurized airplane cabin with oxygen masks |
| Genetic adaptation (occurs over generations) | Biological | Larger "barrel chests" of native highlanders |
| Long-term physiological adaptation (occurs during growth and development of the individual organism) | Biological | More efficient respiratory system, to extract oxygen from "thin air" |
| Short-term physiological adaptation (occurs spontaneously when the individual organism enters a new environment) | Biological | Increased heart rate, hyperventilation |

As human history has unfolded, the social and cultural means of adaptation have become increasingly important. In this process, humans have devised diverse ways of coping with a wide range of environments. The rate of cultural adaptation and change has accelerated, particularly during the past 10,000 years. For millions of years, hunting and gathering of nature's bounty—*foraging*—was the sole basis of human subsistence. However, it took only a few thousand years for **food production** (the cultivation of plants and domestication of animals), which originated some 12,000–10,000 years ago, to replace foraging in most areas. Between 6000 and 5000 B.P. (before the present), the first civilizations arose. These were large, powerful, and complex societies, such as ancient Egypt, that conquered and governed large geographic areas.

Much more recently, the spread of industrial production and the forces of globalization have profoundly affected human life. Throughout human history, major innovations have spread at the expense of earlier ones. Each economic revolution has had social and cultural repercussions. Today's global economy and communications link all contemporary people, directly or indirectly, in the modern world system. People must cope with forces generated by progressively larger systems—region, nation, and world. The study of such contemporary adaptations generates new challenges for anthropology: "The cultures of world peoples need to be constantly rediscovered as these people reinvent them in changing historical circumstances" (Marcus and Fischer 1986, p. 24).

## Cultural Forces Shape Human Biology

Anthropology's comparative, biocultural perspective recognizes that cultural forces constantly mold human biology. (**Biocultural** refers to using and combining both biological and cultural perspectives and approaches to analyze and understand a particular issue or problem.) Culture is a key environmental force in determining how human bodies grow and develop. Cultural traditions promote certain activities and abilities, discourage others, and set standards of physical well-being and attractiveness. Consider how this works in sports. North American girls are encouraged to pursue, and therefore do well in, competition involving figure skating, gymnastics, track and field, swimming, diving, and many other sports. Brazilian girls, although excelling in the team sports of basketball and volleyball, haven't fared nearly as well in individual sports as have their American and Canadian counterparts.

Cultural standards of attractiveness and propriety influence participation and achievement in sports. Americans run or swim not just to compete but also to keep trim and fit. Brazil's beauty standards traditionally have accepted more fat, especially in female buttocks and hips. Brazilian men have had significant international success in swimming and running, including at the Olympics. Brazilian women have been less successful in those competitive individual sports. One reason why Brazilian women may avoid competitive swimming in particular may be that sport's effects on the body. Years of swimming sculpt a distinctive physique: an enlarged upper torso, a massive neck, and powerful shoulders and back. Successful female swimmers tend to be big, strong, and bulky. The nations that have produced them most consistently are the United States, Canada, Australia, Germany, the Scandinavian nations, the Netherlands, and former Soviet countries, especially Russia. In those countries, this body type isn't as stigmatized as it is in Latin countries. For women, Brazilian culture traditionally has preferred developed hips and buttocks to a muscled upper body. Many young female swimmers in Brazil choose to abandon the sport rather than their culture's "feminine" body ideal.

Athletes primed for the start of the 10 kilometer women's marathon swim at the 2016 Summer Olympics in Rio de Janeiro. Years of swimming sculpt a distinctive physique—an enlarged upper torso and neck, and powerful shoulders and back. Tim de Waele/Corbis/Getty Images

When you grew up, which sport did you appreciate the most—soccer, swimming, football, baseball, tennis, golf, or some other sport (or perhaps none at all)? Is this because of "who you are" or because of the opportunities you had as a child to practice and participate in this particular activity? When you were young, your parents might have told you that drinking milk and eating vegetables would help you grow up "big and strong." They probably didn't as readily recognize the role that *culture* plays in shaping bodies, personalities, and personal health. If nutrition matters in growth, so, too, do cultural guidelines. What toys and games are appropriate for boys and girls? What kinds of work should men and women do? Where should people live? What are proper uses of their leisure time? What role should religion play? How should people relate to their family, friends, and neighbors? Although our genetic attributes provide a foundation for growth and development, human biology is fairly plastic—that is, it is malleable. Culture is an environmental force that affects our development as much as nutrition, heat, cold, and altitude do. Culture also guides our emotional and cognitive growth and helps determine the kinds of personalities we have as adults.

## General Anthropology

The academic discipline of anthropology, also known as **general anthropology** or "four-field" anthropology, includes four main subdisciplines, or subfields. They are sociocultural anthropology, anthropological archaeology, biological anthropology, and linguistic anthropology. (From here on, the shorter term *cultural anthropology* will be used as a synonym for *sociocultural anthropology*.) Of the subfields, cultural anthropology has the largest membership. Most departments of anthropology teach courses in all four subfields.

There are historical reasons for the inclusion of four subfields in a single discipline. The origin of anthropology as a scientific field, and of American anthropology in particular, can be traced to the 19th century. Early American anthropologists were concerned especially with the history and cultures of the native peoples of North America. Interest in the origins and diversity of Native Americans brought together studies of customs, social life, language, and physical traits. Anthropologists still are pondering such questions as these: Where did Native Americans come from? How many waves of migration brought them to the New World? What are the linguistic, cultural, and biological links among Native Americans and between them and Asia? (Note that a unified four-field anthropology did not develop in Europe, where the subfields tend to exist separately.)

Early American anthropology was especially concerned with the history and cultures of Native North Americans. Ely S. Parker, or Ha-sa-no-an-da, was a Seneca Indian who made important contributions to early anthropology. Parker also served as commissioner of Indian affairs for the United States. Source: National Archives and Records Administration

There also are logical reasons for the unity of American anthropology. Each subfield considers variation in time and space (that is, in different geographic areas). Cultural anthropologists and anthropological archaeologists study changes in social life and customs (among many other topics). Archaeologists use studies of living societies to imagine what life might have been like in the past. Biological anthropologists examine evolutionary changes in human biology. Linguistic anthropologists may reconstruct the basics of ancient languages by studying modern ones.

The subfields influence each other as anthropologists talk to each other, read books and journals, and meet in professional organizations. General anthropology explores the basics of human biology, society, and culture and considers their interrelations. Anthropologists share certain key assumptions. Perhaps the most fundamental is the idea that sound conclusions about "human nature" cannot be derived from studying a single population, nation, society, or cultural tradition. A comparative, cross-cultural approach is essential.

# The Subdisciplines of Anthropology

## Cultural Anthropology

**Cultural anthropology** is the study of human society and culture. This subfield describes, analyzes, interprets, and explains social and cultural similarities and differences. To study and interpret cultural diversity, cultural anthropologists engage in two kinds of activity: ethnography (based on fieldwork) and ethnology (based on cross-cultural comparison). **Ethnography** provides an account of a particular culture, society, or community. During ethnographic fieldwork, the ethnographer gathers data that he or she organizes, analyzes, and interprets to develop that account, which may be in the form of a book, an article, or a film. Traditionally, ethnographers have lived in small communities and studied local behavior, beliefs, customs, social life, economic activities, politics, and religion (see Galman 2018; Okely 2012; Vivanco 2017; Wolcott 2008).

An anthropological perspective derived from ethnographic fieldwork often differs radically from that of economics or political science. Those fields focus on national and official organizations and policies and often on elites. However, the groups that anthropologists traditionally have studied usually have been relatively poor and powerless. Ethnographers often observe discriminatory practices directed toward such people, who experience food shortages, dietary deficiencies, and other aspects of poverty. Political scientists tend to study programs that national planners develop, whereas anthropologists discover how these programs work on the local level.

Communities and cultures are less isolated today than ever before. As noted by Franz Boas (1940/1966) many years ago, contact between neighboring tribes always has existed and has extended over enormous areas. "Human populations construct their cultures in interaction with one another, and not in isolation" (Wolf 1982, p. ix). Villagers increasingly participate in regional, national, and world events. Exposure to external forces comes through education, the mass media, migration, and modern transportation. (The "Anthropology Today" box at the end of this chapter examines the role of a residential school in eastern India in bridging barriers between cultures.) City and nation increasingly

TABLE 1.2 **Ethnography and Ethnology—Two Dimensions of Cultural Anthropology**

| Ethnography | Ethnology |
|---|---|
| Requires fieldwork to collect data | Uses data collected by a series of researchers |
| Is often descriptive | Is usually synthetic |
| Is specific to a group or community | Is comparative and cross-cultural |

invade local communities with the arrival of teachers, tourists, development agents, government and religious officials, and political candidates. Such linkages are prominent components of regional, national, and international systems of politics, economics, and information. These larger systems increasingly affect the people and places anthropology traditionally has studied. The study of such linkages and systems is part of the subject matter of modern anthropology.

**Ethnology** examines, compares, analyzes, and interprets the results of ethnography—the data gathered in different societies. Ethnologists use such data to compare, contrast, and generalize about society and culture. Looking beyond the particular to the more general, they attempt to identify and explain cultural differences and similarities, to test hypotheses, and to build theory to enhance our understanding of how social and cultural systems work. Ethnology gets its data for comparison not only from ethnography but also from the other subfields, particularly from anthropological archaeology, which reconstructs social systems of the past. (Table 1.2 summarizes the main contrasts between ethnography and ethnology.)

## Anthropological Archaeology

**Anthropological archaeology** (more simply, "archaeology") reconstructs, describes, and interprets human behavior and cultural patterns through material remains. At sites where people live or have lived, archaeologists find artifacts—material items that humans have made, used, or modified—such as tools, weapons, campsites, buildings, and garbage. Plant and animal remains and ancient garbage tell stories about consumption and activities. Wild and domesticated grains have different characteristics, which allow archaeologists to distinguish between gathering and cultivation. Examination of animal bones reveals the ages of slaughtered animals and provides other information useful in determining whether species were wild or domesticated.

Analyzing such data, archaeologists answer several questions about ancient economies: Did the group get its meat from hunting, or did it domesticate and breed animals, killing only those of a certain age and sex? Did plant food come from wild plants or from sowing, tending, and harvesting crops? Did the residents make, trade for, or buy particular items? Were raw materials available locally? If not, where did they come from? From such information, archaeologists reconstruct patterns of production, trade, and consumption.

Archaeologists have spent considerable time studying potsherds, fragments of earthenware. Potsherds are more durable than many other artifacts, such as textiles and wood. The quantity of pottery fragments allows estimates of population size and density. The discovery that potters used materials that were not available locally suggests systems of trade. Similarities in manufacture and decoration at different sites may be proof of cultural connections. Groups with similar pots may share a common history. They might have common cultural ancestors. Perhaps they traded with each other or belonged to the same political system.

Many archaeologists examine paleoecology. *Ecology* is the study of interrelations among living things in an environment. The organisms and environment together constitute an *ecosystem,* a patterned arrangement of energy flows and exchanges. Human ecology studies ecosystems that include people, focusing on the ways in which human use "of nature influences and is influenced by social organization and cultural values" (Bennett 1969, pp. 10–11). *Paleoecology* looks at the ecosystems of the past.

In addition to reconstructing ecological patterns, archaeologists may infer cultural transformations, for example, by observing changes in the size and type of sites and the distance between them. A city develops in a region where only towns, villages, and hamlets existed a few centuries earlier. The number of settlement levels (city, town, village, hamlet) in a society is a measure of social complexity. Buildings offer clues about political and religious features. Temples and pyramids suggest that an ancient society had an authority structure capable of marshaling the labor needed to build such monuments. The presence or absence of certain structures, like the pyramids of ancient Egypt and Mexico, reveals differences in function between settlements. For example, some towns were places where people went to attend ceremonies. Others were burial sites; still others were farming communities.

Anthropological archaeologists from the University of Pennsylvania work to stabilize the original plaster at an Anasazi (Native American) site in Colorado's Mesa Verde National Park. George H.H. Huey/Alamy Stock Photo

Archaeologists also reconstruct behavior patterns and lifestyles of the past by excavating. This involves digging through a succession of levels at a particular site. In a given area, through time, settlements may change in form and purpose, as may the connections between settlements. Excavation can document changes in economic, social, and political activities.

Although archaeologists are best known for studying prehistory, that is, the period before the invention of writing, they also study the cultures of historical and even living peoples (see Sabloff 2008). Studying sunken ships off the Florida coast, underwater archaeologists have been able to verify the living conditions on the vessels that brought ancestral African Americans to the New World as enslaved people. In a well-known research project in Tucson, Arizona, archaeologist William Rathje learned a great deal about contemporary life by studying modern garbage (Zimring 2012). The value of "garbology," as Rathje called it, is that it provides "evidence of what people did, not what they think they did, what they think they should have done, or what the interviewer thinks they should have done" (Harrison, Rathje, and Hughes 1994, p. 108). What people report may contrast strongly with their real behavior as revealed by garbology. For example, the three Tucson neighborhoods that reported the lowest beer consumption actually had the highest number of discarded beer cans per household (Rathje and Murphy 2001; Zimring 2012)!

## Biological Anthropology

**Biological anthropology** is the study of human biological diversity through time and as it exists in the world today. There are five specialties within biological anthropology:

1. Human biological evolution as revealed by the fossil record (paleoanthropology)
2. Human genetics
3. Human growth and development
4. Human biological plasticity (the living body's ability to change as it copes with environmental conditions, such as heat, cold, and altitude)
5. Primatology (the study of monkeys, apes, and other nonhuman primates)

A common thread that runs across all five specialties is an interest in biological variation among humans, including their ancestors and their closest animal relatives (monkeys and apes).

These varied interests link biological anthropology to other fields: biology, zoology, geology, anatomy, physiology, medicine, and public health. Knowledge of osteology—the study of bones—is essential for anthropologists who examine and interpret skulls, teeth, and bones, whether of modern-day humans or of our fossilized ancestors. *Paleontologists* are scientists who study fossils. *Paleoanthropologists* study the fossil record of human evolution. Paleoanthropologists often collaborate with archaeologists, who study artifacts, in reconstructing biological and cultural aspects of human evolution. Fossils and tools often are found together. Different types of tools provide information about the habits, customs, and lifestyles of the ancestral humans who used them.

More than a century ago, Charles Darwin noticed that the variety that exists within any population permits some individuals (those with the favored characteristics) to do better than others at surviving and reproducing. Genetics, which developed after Darwin, enlightens us about the causes and transmission of the variety on which evolution depends. However, it isn't just genes that cause variety. During any individual's lifetime, the environment works along with heredity to determine biological features. For example, people with a genetic tendency to be tall will be shorter if they have poor nutrition during childhood. Thus, biological anthropology also investigates the influence of environment on the body as it grows and matures. Among the environmental factors that influence the body as it develops are nutrition, altitude, temperature, and disease, as well as cultural factors, such as the standards of attractiveness that were discussed previously.

Biological anthropology (along with zoology) also includes primatology. The primates include our closest relatives—apes and monkeys. Primatologists study their biology, evolution, behavior, and social life, often in their natural environments. Primatology assists paleoanthropology, because primate behavior and social organization may shed light on early human behavior and human nature.

## Linguistic Anthropology

We don't know (and probably never will) when our ancestors acquired the ability to speak, although biological anthropologists have looked to the anatomy of the face, skull, and vocal tract to speculate about the origin of language. Primatologists have described the communication systems of monkeys and apes. We do know that grammatically complex languages have existed for thousands of years. Linguistic anthropology offers further illustration of anthropology's interest in comparison, variation, and change. **Linguistic anthropology** studies language in its social and cultural context, throughout the world and over time. Some linguistic anthropologists make inferences about universal features of language, linked perhaps to uniformities in the human brain. Others reconstruct ancient languages by comparing their contemporary descendants. Still others study linguistic differences to discover varied perceptions and patterns of thought in different cultures (see Bonvillain 2012, 2016).

Historical linguistics considers variation in time, such as the changes in sounds, grammar, and vocabulary between Middle English (spoken from approximately C.E. [formerly A.D.] 1050 to 1550) and modern English. **Sociolinguistics** investigates relationships between social and linguistic variation: How do different speakers use a given language? How do linguistic features correlate with social factors, including class and gender differences (Coates 2016; Eckert and McConnell-Ginet 2013)? One reason for variation is geography, as in regional dialects and accents. Linguistic variation also is expressed in the bilingualism of ethnic groups. Linguistic and cultural anthropologists collaborate in studying links between language and many other aspects of culture, such as how people reckon kinship and how they perceive and classify colors.

## Applied Anthropology

What sort of man or woman do you envision when you hear the word *anthropologist*? Although anthropologists have been portrayed as quirky and eccentric, bearded and bespectacled, anthropology is not a science of the exotic carried on by quaint scholars in ivory towers. Rather, anthropology has a lot to tell the public. Anthropology's foremost professional organization, the American Anthropological Association (AAA), has formally acknowledged a public service role by recognizing that anthropology has two dimensions: (1) academic anthropology and (2) practicing, or **applied, anthropology**. The latter refers to the application of anthropological data, perspectives, theory, and methods to identify, assess, and solve contemporary social problems. As American anthropologist Erve Chambers (1987) has stated, applied anthropology is "concerned with the relationships between anthropological knowledge and the uses of that knowledge in the world beyond anthropology" (p. 309). More and more anthropologists from the four subfields now work in "applied" areas such as public health, family planning, business, market research, economic development, and cultural resource management.

Because of anthropology's breadth, applied anthropology has many applications. For example, applied medical anthropologists consider both the sociocultural and the biological contexts and implications of disease and illness. Perceptions of good and bad health, along with actual health threats and problems, differ among societies. Various ethnic groups recognize different illnesses, symptoms, and causes and have developed different health care systems and treatment strategies.

Applied archaeology, usually called *public archaeology*, includes such activities as cultural resource management, public educational programs, and historic preservation. Legislation requiring evaluation of sites threatened by dams, highways, and other construction

Applied anthropology in action. Professor Robin Nagle of New York University is also an anthropologist-in-residence at New York City's Department of Sanitation. Nagle studies curbside garbage as a mirror into the lives of New Yorkers. Here she accompanies sanitation worker Joe Damiano during his morning rounds in August 2015. Richard Drew/AP Images

TABLE 1.3   **The Four Subfields and Two Dimensions of Anthropology**

| Anthropology's Subfields (General Anthropology) | Examples of Application (Applied Anthropology) |
|---|---|
| Cultural anthropology | Development anthropology |
| Anthropological archaeology | Cultural resource management (CRM) |
| Biological anthropology | Forensic anthropology |
| Linguistic anthropology | Study of linguistic diversity in classrooms |

activities has created an important role for public archaeology. To decide what needs saving, and to preserve significant information about the past when sites cannot be saved, is the work of **cultural resource management** (CRM). CRM involves not only preserving sites but also allowing their destruction if they are not significant. The *management* part of the term refers to the evaluation and decision-making process. Cultural resource managers work for federal, state, and county agencies and other clients. Applied cultural anthropologists sometimes work with public archaeologists, assessing the human problems generated by proposed changes and determining how they can be reduced. Table 1.3 relates anthropology's four subfields to its two dimensions.

# Anthropology and Other Academic Fields

As mentioned previously, one of the main differences between anthropology and the other fields that study people is anthropology's unique blend of biological, social, linguistic, cultural, historical, and contemporary perspectives. Paradoxically, while distinguishing anthropology, this breadth is what also links it to many other disciplines. For instance, techniques used to date fossils and artifacts have come to anthropology from physics, chemistry, and geology. Because plant and animal remains often are found with human bones and artifacts, anthropologists collaborate with botanists, zoologists, and paleontologists.

## A Humanistic Science

As a discipline that is both scientific and humanistic, anthropology has links with many other academic fields. Anthropology is a **science**—a "systematic field of study or body of knowledge that aims, through experiment, observation, and deduction, to produce reliable explanations of phenomena, with references to the material and physical world" (*Webster's New World Encyclopedia* 1993. College Edition. Englewood Cliffs, NJ: Prentice Hall. p.937). The chapters that follow present anthropology as a humanistic science devoted to discovering, describing, understanding, and explaining similarities and differences in time and space among humans and our ancestors. Clyde Kluckhohn (1944) described anthropology as "the science of human similarities and differences" (p. 9). His statement of the need for such a field still stands: "Anthropology provides a scientific basis for dealing with the crucial dilemma of the world today: how can peoples of different appearance, mutually unintelligible languages, and dissimilar ways of life get along peaceably together?" (p. 9). Anthropology has compiled an impressive body of knowledge, which this textbook attempts to encapsulate.

Besides its links to the natural sciences (e.g., geology, zoology) and social sciences (e.g., sociology, psychology), anthropology also has strong links to the humanities. The humanities include English, comparative literature, classics, folklore, philosophy, and the arts. These fields study languages, texts, philosophies, arts, music, performances, and other forms of creative expression. Ethnomusicology, which studies forms of musical expression on a worldwide basis, is especially closely related to anthropology. Also linked is folklore, the systematic study of tales, myths, and legends from a variety of cultures. One might well argue that anthropology is among the most humanistic of all academic fields because of its fundamental respect for human diversity. Anthropologists listen to, record, and represent voices from a multitude of nations and cultures. Anthropology values local knowledge, diverse worldviews, and alternative philosophies. Cultural anthropology and linguistic anthropology in particular bring a comparative and non-elitist perspective to forms of creative expression, including language, art, narratives, music, and dance, viewed in their social and cultural context.

## Cultural Anthropology and Sociology

Students often ask about how anthropology differs from sociology, which is probably the discipline closest to anthropology, specifically to sociocultural anthropology. Like anthropologists, particularly cultural anthropologists, sociologists study society—consisting of human social behavior, social relations, and social organization. Key differences between sociology and anthropology reflect the kinds of societies traditionally studied by each discipline. Sociologists typically have studied contemporary Western, industrial societies. Anthropologists, by contrast, traditionally focused on nonindustrial and non-Western societies. Sociologists and anthropologists developed different methods to study these different kinds of society. To study contemporary Western societies, which tend to be large-scale, complex nations, sociologists have relied on surveys and other means of gathering quantifiable data. Sociologists must use sampling and statistical techniques to collect and analyze such data, and statistical training has been fundamental in sociology. Working in much smaller societies, such as a village, anthropologists can get to know almost everyone and have less need for sampling and statistics. However, because anthropologists today are working increasingly in modern nations, use of sampling and statistics is becoming more common.

Traditionally, ethnographers studied small and nonliterate (without writing) populations and developed methods appropriate to that context. An ethnographer participates directly in the daily life of another culture and must be an attentive, detailed observer of what people do and say. The focus is on a real, living population, not just a sample of a population. During ethnographic fieldwork, the anthropologist takes part in the events she or he is *observing*, describing, and analyzing. Anthropology, we might say, is more personal and less formal than sociology.

## Anthropology Today   *School of Hope*

A school is one kind of community in which culture is transmitted—a process known as enculturation. A boarding school where students reside for several years is fully comparable as a enculturative setting to a village or another local community. You've all heard of Hogwarts. Although fictional, is it not a setting in which enculturation takes place?

Often, schools serve as intermediaries between one cultural tradition and another. As students are exposed to outsiders, they inevitably change. In today's world, opportunities to become bilingual and bicultural—that is, to learn more than one language and to participate in more than one cultural tradition—are greater than ever before.

The Kalinga Institute of Social Sciences (KISS) is a boarding school in Bhubaneswar, India, whose mission is to instill in indigenous students a "capacity to aspire" to a better life (Finnan 2016). KISS is the world's largest residential school for tribal children. Located in Odisha, one of India's poorest states, KISS supports 25,000 students from first grade through graduate training. Its students represent 62 of India's tribal groups. Children as young as age 6 travel to KISS by bus or train, sometimes from hundreds of miles away. They leave their families for up to 10 months at a time, returning to their villages only during the summer.

During six months of research at KISS in 2014–2015, anthropologist Christine Finnan gathered stories and personal accounts about the school and its effects. Working with three Indian research partners, she interviewed 160 people: students, former students, parents, staff, teachers, administrators, and visitors. Her team observed classes, meals, celebrations, and athletic competitions. They also visited several tribal villages to find out why parents send their children so far away to school. Finnan wanted to determine what children gained and lost from growing up at KISS. (For a fuller account of the research described here, see Finnan 2016 at www.sapiens.org).

KISS students at an assembly for visiting foreign dignitaries. KISS officials use such events not only to showcase the school to visitors but also to help build solidarity among students. Courtesy of Christine Finnan

Acceptance to KISS is based on need, so that the poorest of the poor are chosen to attend. The school offers cost-free room and board, classes, medical care, and vocational and athletic training to all its students. The value system at KISS encourages responsibility, orderliness, and respect. Children learn those behaviors not only from KISS employees but also from each other—especially from older students. Students are repeatedly reminded that they are special, that they can rise out of poverty and become change agents for their communities. Many students hope to return to their villages as teachers, doctors, or nurses.

KISS receives no government support. Most of its funding comes from its profitable sister institution, the Kalinga Institute of Industrial Technology (KIIT), a respected private university. By targeting indigenous children, KISS meets an educational need that is unmet by the government. In India's tribal villages, the presence of teachers is unreliable, even when there are village schools. At KISS, in sharp contrast, teachers don't just instruct; they also serve in loco parentis, living in the dormitories or in nearby housing, and viewing many of their students as family members.

During her fieldwork, Finnan found attitudes about KISS among all parties to be overwhelmingly positive. Students contrasted their KISS education with the poor quality of their village schools. Teachers mentioned their shared commitment to poverty reduction. Parents were eager for their children to be admitted. Although KISS encourages students to take pride in their native language and culture, both students and parents understand that change is inevitable. Students will adopt new beliefs, values, and behaviors, and they will learn Odia, the state language used at KISS. They will become bilingual and bicultural.

When Finnan began her research, she was aware of the now-notorious boarding schools for indigenous students that were established during the 19th and 20th centuries in the United States and Australia. Native American and Aboriginal children were forcibly removed from their families, required to speak English and accept Christianity, and taught that their native cultures were inferior. The educational style was authoritarian, and its goal was forced assimilation. Finnan found KISS's positive educational philosophy and respect for indigenous cultures to be very different from those archaic institutions.

To more fully evaluate KISS's success in meeting its goals, Finnan has retained her connection with the school. She recently (2018) received data indicating that KISS's promise of improved employment opportunities is being realized. A survey of 10,023 former students indicates that approximately 85 percent have jobs that are likely a result of their KISS education. In addition, whereas over 80 percent of tribal students drop out of district schools before completing 10th grade, only about 20 percent of KISS students do so. Those who stay at KISS score higher than the state average on state-mandated tests, and considerably higher than averages for tribal children. KISS also can point to a series of successful scholars, ambassadors, and athletes among its graduates. Each year, 5 percent of its graduating class is admitted tuition-free to KIIT. At that highly selective university, students can study engineering, medicine, and law, among other subjects.

This chapter examined the difference between applied and academic anthropology. Think about whether Finnan's research was academic or applied, and whether there is a sharp distinction between these two dimensions of anthropology. Even if Finnan did not intend her work to be applied anthropology, her findings certainly suggest educational lessons that can be applied beyond this case. What are some of those lessons?

In today's interconnected world, however, the interests and methods of anthropology and sociology have converged—come together—as they study many of the same topics and areas. For example, many sociologists now work in non-Western countries, smaller communities, and other settings that used to be mainly within the anthropological orbit. As industrialization and urbanization have spread across the globe, anthropologists now work increasingly in industrial nations and cities, rather than villages. Among the many topics studied by contemporary cultural anthropologists are rural-urban migration and transnational (from one country to another) migration, inner-city life, religious/ethnic conflict, crime, and warfare. Contemporary anthropologists are as likely as sociologists to study race, ethnicity, gender, inequality, power, and globalization.

## Summary

1. Anthropology is the holistic, biocultural, and comparative study of humanity. It is the systematic exploration of human biological and cultural diversity across time and space. Examining the origins of, and changes in, human biology and culture, anthropology provides explanations for similarities and differences among humans and their societies.

2. The four subfields of general anthropology are (socio)cultural anthropology, anthropological archaeology, biological anthropology, and linguistic anthropology. All consider variation in time and space. Each also examines adaptation—the process by which organisms cope with environmental stresses. Anthropology's biocultural perspective is a particularly effective way of approaching interrelations between biology and culture. Cultural forces mold human biology, including our body types and images.

3. Cultural anthropology explores the cultural diversity of the present and the recent past. Archaeology reconstructs cultural patterns, often of prehistoric populations. Biological anthropology documents diversity involving fossils, genetics, growth and development, bodily responses, and nonhuman primates. Linguistic anthropology considers diversity among languages. It also studies how speech changes in social situations and over time. Anthropology has two dimensions: academic and applied. Applied anthropology is the use of anthropological data, perspectives, theory, and methods to identify, assess, and solve contemporary social problems.

4. Concerns with biology, society, culture, and language link anthropology to many other fields—sciences and humanities. Sociologists traditionally study Western, industrial societies, whereas anthropologists have focused on rural, nonindustrial peoples.

## Think Like an Anthropologist

1. If, as Franz Boas illustrated early on in American anthropology, cultures are not isolated, how can ethnography provide an account of a particular community, society, or culture? Note: There is no easy answer to this question! Anthropologists continue to deal with it as they define their research questions and projects.

2. The American Anthropological Association has formally acknowledged a public service role by recognizing that anthropology has two dimensions: (1) academic anthropology and (2) practicing, or applied, anthropology. What is applied anthropology? Based on your reading of this chapter, identify examples from current events where an anthropologist could help identify, assess, and solve contemporary social problems.

**Key Terms**

adaptation, *4*
anthropological
  archaeology, *9*
anthropology, *3*
applied
  anthropology, *13*
biocultural, *5*
biological
  anthropology, *11*

cultural
  anthropology, *8*
cultural resource
  management
  (CRM), *14*
culture, *3*
ethnography, *8*
ethnology, *9*
food production, *5*

general
  anthropology, *7*
holistic, *3*
linguistic
  anthropology, *12*
science, *14*
society, *3*
sociolinguistics, *12*

# Chapter 2

# Culture

## What Is Culture?

In Chapter 1 we saw that humans share *society*, organized life in groups, with social animals, such as apes, monkeys, wolves, and ants. Although other animals, especially apes, have rudimentary cultural abilities, only humans have fully elaborated cultures—distinctive traditions and customs transmitted over the generations through learning and through language.

The concept of culture has long been basic to anthropology. Well over a century ago, in his book *Primitive Culture*, the British anthropologist Edward Tylor proposed that cultures, systems of human behavior and thought, obey natural laws and therefore can be studied scientifically. Tylor's definition of culture still offers an overview of the subject matter of anthropology, and it is widely quoted.

"Culture . . . is that complex whole which includes knowledge, belief, arts, morals, law, custom, and any other capabilities and habits acquired by man as a member of society" (Tylor 1871/1958, p. 1). The crucial phrase here is "acquired . . . as a member of society."

Tylor's definition focuses on attributes that people acquire not through biological inheritance but by growing up in a particular society in which they are exposed to a specific cultural tradition. **Enculturation** is the process by which a child *learns* his or her culture.

## Culture Is Learned

The ease with which children absorb their cultural tradition rests on the uniquely elaborated human capacity to learn. Other animals may learn from experience, so that, for example, they avoid fire after discovering that it hurts. Social animals also learn from other members of their group. Wolves, for example, learn hunting strategies from other pack members. Such social learning is particularly important among monkeys and apes, our closest biological relatives. But our own *cultural learning* depends on the uniquely developed human capacity to use **symbols**, signs that have no necessary or natural connection to the things they stand for, or signify.

Through cultural learning, people create, remember, and deal with ideas. They understand and apply specific systems of symbolic meaning. Anthropologist Clifford Geertz (1973) described cultures as sets of "control mechanisms—plans, recipes, rules, instructions" and likens them to computer programs that govern human behavior (p. 44). During enculturation, people gradually absorb and internalize their particular culture—a previously established system of meanings and symbols that helps guide their behavior and perceptions throughout their lives.

Every person begins immediately, through a process of conscious and unconscious learning and interaction with others, to internalize, or incorporate, a cultural tradition through the process of enculturation. Sometimes culture is taught directly, as when parents tell their children to say "thank you" when someone gives them something or does them a favor.

We also acquire culture through observation. Children pay attention to the things that go on around them. They modify their behavior not just because other people tell them to do so, but also because of their own observations and growing awareness of what their culture considers right and wrong. Many aspects of culture are absorbed unconsciously. North Americans acquire their culture's notions about how far apart people should stand when they talk, not by being told directly to maintain a certain distance but through a gradual process of observation, experience, and conscious and unconscious behavior modification. No one tells Brazilians or Italians to stand closer together than North Americans do; they learn to do so as part of their cultural tradition.

## Culture Is Symbolic

Symbolic thought is unique and crucial to humans and to cultural learning. A symbol is something verbal or nonverbal, within a particular language or culture, that comes to stand for something else. There need be no obvious, natural, or necessary connection between a symbol and the thing that it symbolizes. The familiar pet that barks is no more naturally a *dog* than it is a *chien*, *Hund*, or *mbwa*, the words for "dog" in French, German, and Swahili, respectively. Language is one of the distinctive possessions of *Homo sapiens*. No other animal has developed anything approaching the complexity of language, with its multitude of symbols.

There also is a rich array of nonverbal symbols. Flags, for example, stand for various countries, as arches do for a hamburger chain. Holy water is a potent symbol in Roman

Children acquire culture through instruction, observation, and participation. Here we see diverse American kids participating in a national tradition, as they celebrate Independence Day (July 4). Ariel Skelley/Getty Images

Catholicism. As is true of all symbols, the association between water and what it stands for (holiness) is arbitrary and conventional. Water probably is not intrinsically holier than milk, blood, or other natural liquids. Nor is holy water chemically different from ordinary water. Holy water is a symbol within Roman Catholicism, which is part of an international cultural system. A natural thing has been associated arbitrarily with a particular meaning for Catholics, who share beliefs and experiences that are based on learning and transmitted across the generations. Our cultures immerse us in a world of symbols that are both linguistic and nonverbal. Particular items and brands of clothing, such as jeans, shirts, or shoes, can acquire symbolic meanings, as can our gestures, posture, and body decoration and ornamentation.

All humans possess the abilities on which culture rests—the abilities to learn, to think symbolically, to manipulate language, and to use tools and other cultural products in organizing their lives and coping with their environments. Every contemporary human population has the ability to use symbols and thus to create and maintain culture. Our nearest relatives—chimpanzees and gorillas—have rudimentary cultural abilities. However, no other animal has elaborated cultural abilities to the extent that *Homo* has.

## Culture Is Shared

Culture is an attribute not of individuals per se but of individuals as members of *groups*. Culture is transmitted in society. We learn our culture by observing, listening, talking, and interacting with other people. Shared beliefs, values, memories, and expectations link people who grow up in the same culture. Enculturation unifies people by providing us with common experiences. Today's parents were yesterday's children. If they grew up in North America, they absorbed certain values and beliefs transmitted over the generations. People become agents in the enculturation of their children, just as their parents were for them. Although a culture constantly changes, certain fundamental beliefs, values, worldviews, and child-rearing practices endure. One example of enduring shared enculturation is the American emphasis on self-reliance and independent achievement.

Despite characteristic American notions that people should "make up their own minds" and "have a right to their opinion," little of what we think is original or unique. We share our opinions and beliefs with many other people—nowadays not just in person but also via new media. Think about how often (and with whom) you share information or an opinion via texting, Facebook, Instagram, Twitter, and other apps. Illustrating the power of shared cultural background, we are most likely to agree with and feel comfortable with people who are socially, economically, and culturally similar to ourselves. This is one reason Americans abroad tend to socialize with each other, just as French and British colonials did in their overseas empires. Birds of a feather flock together, but for people, the familiar plumage is culture.

## Culture and Nature

Culture takes the natural biological urges we share with other animals and teaches us how to express them in particular ways. People have to eat, but culture teaches us what, when, and how. In many cultures, people have their main meal at noon, but most North Americans prefer a large dinner. English people eat fish (e.g., kippers—kippered herring) for breakfast, but North Americans prefer hot cakes and cold cereals. Brazilians put hot milk into strong coffee, whereas many North Americans pour cold milk into a weaker brew. Midwesterners dine at 5 or 6, Spaniards at 10.

Cultural habits, perceptions, and inventions mold "human nature" into many forms. People have to eliminate wastes from their bodies. But some cultures teach people to defecate squatting, while others tell them to do it sitting down. Peasant women in the Andean highlands squat in the streets and urinate, getting all the privacy they need from their massive skirts. All these habits are parts of cultural traditions that have converted natural acts into cultural customs.

Culture influences how we perceive nature, human nature, and "the natural," and cultural advances have overcome many "natural" limitations. We can prevent and cure diseases, such as polio and smallpox, that felled our ancestors. We can use pills to enhance or restore sexual potency. Through cloning, scientists have challenged the way we think about biological identity and the meaning of life itself. Culture, of course, does not always protect us. Hurricanes, earthquakes, tsunamis, floods, and other natural forces regularly thwart our efforts to modify the environment through building, development, and expansion.

## Culture Is All-Encompassing and Integrated

For anthropologists, culture includes much more than refinement, good taste, sophistication, education, and appreciation of the fine arts. Not only college graduates but all people are "cultured." The most interesting and significant cultural forces are those that affect people every day of their lives, particularly those that influence children during enculturation.

*Culture*, as defined anthropologically, encompasses features that sometimes are considered trivial or unworthy of serious study, such as those of "popular" culture. To understand contemporary North American culture, we must consider holidays, mass media, the Internet, fast food, sports, and games. As a cultural manifestation, a rock star may be as interesting as a symphony conductor (or vice versa); a comic book may be as significant as a book-award winner.

The term **popular culture** encompasses aspects of culture that have meaning for many or most people within the same national culture. American examples include July 4th, Halloween, Thanksgiving, football, homecoming dances, dinner-and-a-movie dates, and retirement parties. Although popular culture is available to us all, we use it selectively, and its meaning varies from one person to the next. For example, the World Cup, the Super Bowl, Taylor Swift, *Star Wars*, and *The Simpsons* mean something different to each of their fans. All of us creatively consume and interpret print media, music, television, films, theme parks, celebrities, politicians, and other popular culture products.

Cultures are not haphazard collections of customs and beliefs. Cultures are integrated, patterned systems. If one part of the system (e.g., the economy) changes, other parts also change. For example, during the 1950s, most American women planned domestic careers as homemakers and mothers. Since then, an increasing number of American women, including wives and mothers, have entered the workforce. Only 32 percent of married American women worked outside the home in 1960, compared to about 60 percent today.

What are some of the social repercussions of this particular economic change? Attitudes and behavior regarding marriage, family, and children have changed. Late marriage, "living together," and divorce have become more common. Work competes with marriage and family responsibilities and reduces the time available to invest in child care.

Cultures are integrated not simply by their dominant economic activities and related social patterns but also by sets of values, ideas, symbols, and judgments. Cultures train their individual members to share certain personality traits. A set of characteristic **core values** (key, basic, central values) integrates each culture and helps distinguish it from others. For instance, the work ethic and individualism are core values that have integrated American culture for generations. Different sets of dominant values influence the patterns of other cultures.

## Culture Is Instrumental, Adaptive, and Maladaptive

Culture is the main reason for human adaptability and success. Other animals rely on biological means of adaptation (such as fur or blubber, which are adaptations to cold). Humans also adapt biologically—for example, by shivering when we get cold or sweating when we get hot. But in addition to biological responses, people also have cultural ways of adapting. To cope with environmental stresses, we habitually use technology, or tools. We hunt cold-adapted animals and use their fur coats as our own. We turn the thermostat up in the winter and down in the summer. In summer, we have a cold drink, jump in a pool, or travel to someplace cooler. In winter, we drink hot chocolate, seek out a sauna, or vacation in warmer climates. People use culture *instrumentally*, that is, to fulfill their basic biological needs for food, drink, shelter, comfort, and reproduction.

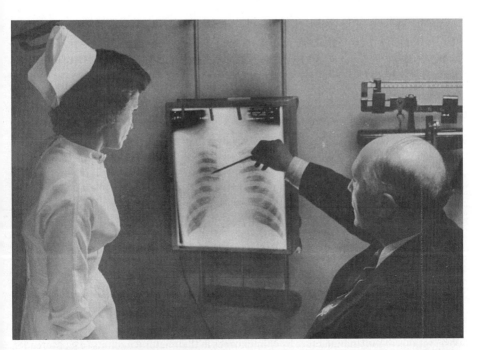

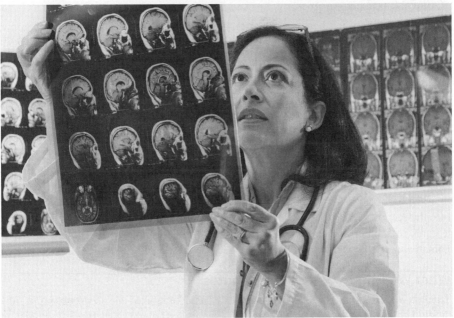

In the top photo (circa 1950), a male doctor points out features of an X-ray to a female nurse. In the bottom photo, a contemporary doctor holds up and studies MRI scans. Nowadays, female college graduates aged 30 to 34 are just as likely to be doctors, dentists, lawyers, professors, managers, and scientists as they are to be working in traditionally female professions, as teachers, nurses, librarians, secretaries, or social workers. (top): Walter Sanders/The LIFE Picture Collection/Getty Images; (bottom): Ron Levine/Getty Images

People also use culture to fulfill psychological and emotional needs, such as friendship, companionship, approval, and sexual desirability. People seek *informal support*—help from people who care about them—as well as *formal support* from associations and institutions. To these ends, individuals cultivate ties with others on the basis of common experiences, political interests, aesthetic sensibilities, or personal attraction.

On one level, cultural traits (e.g., air conditioning) may be called *adaptive* if they help individuals cope with environmental stresses. But on a different level, such traits can also be *maladaptive*. That is, they may threaten a group's continued existence. Thus, chlorofluorocarbons (e.g., as found in old air conditioners) have been banned in the United States because they deplete the ozone layer and, by doing so, can harm humans and other life. Many modern cultural patterns may be maladaptive in the long run. Some examples of maladaptive aspects of culture are policies that encourage overpopulation, poor food-distribution systems, overconsumption, and environmental degradation.

# Culture's Evolutionary Basis

The human capacity for culture has an evolutionary basis that extends back perhaps 3 million years, the date of the earliest evidence of tool manufacture in the archaeological record. Tool making by our distant ancestors may extend even farther back, based on observations of tool manufacture by chimpanzees in their natural habitats (e.g., Mercader, Panger, and Boesch 2002).

Similarities between humans and apes, our closest relatives, are evident in anatomy, brain structure, genetics, and biochemistry. Most closely related to us are the African great apes: chimpanzees and gorillas. *Hominidae* is the zoological family that includes fossil and living humans, as well as chimps and gorillas. We refer to members of this family as **hominids**. The term **hominins** is used for the group that leads to humans but not to chimps and gorillas and that encompasses all the human species that ever have existed.

Many human traits are part of an ancestral arboreal heritage that we share with monkeys and apes. These traits developed as our ancestors adapted to life in the trees millions of years ago. They include (1) grasping ability and manual dexterity (especially opposable thumbs), (2) depth and color vision, (3) learning ability based on a large, visually oriented brain, and (4) substantial parental investment in a limited number of offspring (see the section "Primate Adaptations" in Chapter 5). All these traits continue to be key features of human adaptation. Manual dexterity, for example, is essential to a major human adaptive capacity: tool making.

## What We Share with Other Primates

There is a substantial gap between primate *society* (organized life in groups) and fully developed human *culture*, which is based on symbolic thought. Nevertheless, studies of nonhuman primates reveal many similarities with humans, such as the ability to learn from experience and change behavior as a result. Monkeys, and especially apes, learn throughout their lives. In one group of Japanese macaques (land-dwelling monkeys), for example, a 3-year-old female started washing sweet potatoes before she ate them. First her mother, then her age peers, and finally the entire troop began washing sweet potatoes as well. The ability to benefit from experience confers a tremendous adaptive advantage, permitting the avoidance of fatal mistakes. Faced with environmental change, humans and other primates don't have to wait for a genetic or physiological response. They can modify learned behavior and social patterns instead.

Although humans employ tools much more than any other animal does, tool use also turns up among several nonhuman species, including birds, beavers, sea otters, and especially apes (see Campbell 2011). Humans are not the only animals that make tools with a specific purpose in mind. Chimpanzees living in the Taï forest of Ivory Coast make and use stone tools to break open hard, golf-ball-sized nuts (Mercader et al. 2002; Wilford 2007b). Nut cracking is a learned skill, with mothers showing their young how to do it. In 1960, Jane Goodall began observing wild chimps—including their tool use and hunting behavior—at Gombe Stream National Park in Tanzania, East Africa (see Goodall 2010). The most studied form of ape tool making involves "termiting," in which chimps make tools to probe termite hills. They choose twigs, which they modify by removing leaves and peeling off bark to expose the sticky surface beneath. They carry the twigs to termite hills, dig holes with their fingers, and insert the twigs. Finally, they pull out the twigs and dine on termites that were attracted to the sticky surface. Given what is known about ape tool use and manufacture, it is unsurprising that early hominins shared this ability; currently, the earliest evidence for hominin stone tool making dates back 3 million years. Bipedalism (moving around upright on two legs) would have allowed early hominins to carry and wield tools and weapons against predators and competitors in an open grassland habitat.

The apes have other abilities on which culture depends. Wild chimpanzees and orangutans aim and throw objects. Gorillas build nests, and they throw branches, grass, vines, and other objects. Hominins have elaborated the capacity to aim and throw, without which we never would have developed projectile technology and weaponry—or baseball.

As with tool making, anthropologists once considered hunting to be a distinctive human activity not shared with the apes. Again, however, primate research shows that other primates, especially chimpanzees, are habitual hunters. For example, in Uganda's Kibale National Park, chimps form large hunting parties, including an average of 26 individuals (almost always adult and adolescent males). Most hunts (78 percent) result in at least one prey item being caught—a much higher success rate than that among lions (26 percent), hyenas (34 percent), or cheetahs (30 percent). Chimps' favored prey there is the red colobus monkey (Mitani and Watts 1999).

It is likely that human ancestors were doing some hunting by at least 3 million years ago, based on the existence of early stone tools designed to cut meat. Given our current understanding of chimp tool making and hunting, we can infer that hominids may have been hunting much earlier than the first archaeological evidence attests. Because chimps typically devour the monkeys they kill, leaving few remains, we may never find archaeological evidence for the first hominid or hominin hunt, especially if it proceeded without stone tools.

Different forms of tool use by chimps. Top photo shows a Liberian chimp using a hammer stone to crack palm nuts. The bottom photo shows chimps using prepared twigs to "fish" for termites from a termite hill. (top): Clive Bromhall/Oxford Scientific/Getty Images; (bottom): Stan Osolinski/Oxford Scientific/Getty Images

## How We Differ from Other Primates

Although chimps often share meat from a hunt, apes and monkeys (except for nursing infants) tend to feed themselves individually. Cooperation and sharing are much more characteristic of humans. Until fairly recently (12,000 to 10,000 years ago), all humans were hunter-gatherers who lived in small social groups called bands. In some world areas, the hunter-gatherer way of life persisted into recent times, permitting study by ethnographers. In such societies, men and women take resources back to the camp to share. Everyone shares the meat from a large animal. Nourished and protected by younger band members, elders live past reproductive age and are respected for their knowledge and experience. Humans are among the most cooperative of the primates—in the food quest and other social activities. As well, the amount of information stored in a human band is far greater than that in any other primate group.

Another difference between humans and other primates involves mating. Among baboons and chimps, most mating occurs when females enter **estrus**, during which they ovulate. In estrus, the vaginal area swells and reddens, and receptive females form temporary bonds with, and mate with, males. Human females, by contrast, lack a visible estrus cycle, and their ovulation is concealed. Not knowing when ovulation is occurring, humans maximize their reproductive success by mating throughout the year. Human pair bonds for mating are more exclusive and more durable than are those of chimps. Related

TABLE 2.1   **Cultural Features of Chimpanzees (Rudimentary) and Humans (Fully Developed)**

|  | Chimpanzees | Humans |
|---|---|---|
| *Cultural learning* | Rudimentary | Fully developed |
| *Tool use* | Occasional | Habitual |
| *Tool manufacture* | Occasional: hammer stones, termiting | Habitual and sophisticated |
| *Aimed throwing* | Occasional objects, not tools | Projectile technology |
| *Hunting* | Significant, but no tools | Basic hominin subsistence strategy, with tools |
| *Food sharing* | Meat sharing after hunt | Basic to human life |
| *Cooperation* | Occasional in hunting | Basic to human life |
| *Mating and marriage* | Female estrus cycle, limited pair bonds | Year-round mating, marriage, and exogamy |
| *Kin ties* | Limited by dispersal at adolescence | Maintained through sons and daughters |

to our more constant sexuality, all human societies have some form of marriage. Marriage gives mating a reliable basis and grants to each spouse special, though not always exclusive, sexual rights in the other.

Marriage creates another major contrast between humans and other primates: exogamy and kinship systems. Most cultures have rules of exogamy requiring marriage outside one's kin or local group. Exogamy confers adaptive advantages because it creates ties between the spouses' kin groups. Their children have relatives, and therefore allies, in two kin groups rather than just one. Such ties of affection and mutual support between members of different local groups tend to be absent among primates other than *Homo*. Other primates tend to disperse at adolescence. Among chimps and gorillas, females tend to migrate, seeking mates in other groups. Humans also choose mates from outside the natal group, and usually at least one spouse moves. However, *humans maintain lifelong ties with sons and daughters.* The systems of kinship and marriage that preserve these links provide a major contrast between humans and other primates (see Bergendorff 2016; Chapais 2008; Hill et al. 2011). Table 2.1 lists differences in the cultural abilities of humans and chimpanzees, our nearest relatives.

## Universality, Generality, and Particularity

Anthropologists agree that cultural learning is uniquely elaborated among humans and that all humans have culture. Anthropologists also agree that although *individuals* differ in their emotional and intellectual tendencies and capacities, all human *populations* have equivalent capacities for culture. Regardless of their genes or their physical appearance, people can learn *any* cultural tradition. To understand this point, consider that contemporary North Americans are the genetically mixed descendants of people from all over the world. Our ancestors were biologically varied, lived in different countries and continents, and participated in hundreds of cultural traditions. However, successive waves of immigrants and their descendants now share a national culture.

In studying human diversity in time and space, anthropologists distinguish among the universal, the generalized, and the particular. Certain biological, psychological, social, and cultural features are **universal**, found in every culture. Others are merely **generalities**, common to several but not all human groups. Still other traits are **particularities**, unique to certain cultural traditions.

## Universals and Generalities

Biologically based universals include a long period of infant dependency; year-round (rather than seasonal) sexuality; and a complex brain that enables us to use symbols, languages, and tools. Among the social universals is life in groups and in some kind of family. Generalities occur in certain times and places but not in all cultures. They may be widespread, but they are not universal. One cultural generality that is present in many but not all societies is the nuclear family, a kinship group consisting of parents and children. Many middle-class Americans still view the "traditional" nuclear family, consisting of a married man and woman and their children, as a proper and "natural" group. This view persists despite the fact that nuclear families now comprise only about 20 percent of all American households. Cross-culturally, too, this kind of "traditional" family is far from universal. Consider the Nayars, who live on the Malabar Coast of India. Traditionally, the Nayars lived in female-headed households, and husbands and wives did not live together. In many other societies, the nuclear family is submerged in larger kin groups, such as extended families, lineages, and clans (see Chapter 13).

Societies can share beliefs and customs because of borrowing or through (cultural) inheritance from a common cultural ancestor. Speaking English is a generality shared by North Americans and Australians because both countries had English settlers. Another reason for generalities is domination, as in colonial rule, when a more powerful nation imposes its customs and procedures on another group. In many countries, use of the English language reflects colonial history. More recently, English has spread through **diffusion** (cultural borrowing) to many other countries, as it has become the primary language used in business and travel.

## Particularity: Patterns of Culture

A cultural particularity is a trait or feature of culture that is not generalized or widespread; rather, it is confined to a single place, culture, or society. Yet because of cultural borrowing, which has accelerated through modern transportation and communication systems, traits that once were limited in their distribution have become more widespread. Traits that are useful, that have the capacity to please large audiences, and that don't clash with the cultural values of potential adopters are more likely than others to be borrowed. Nevertheless, certain cultural particularities persist—for example, foods such as the pork barbecue with a mustard-based sauce available only in South Carolina and the "pasty," beef stew baked in pie dough, characteristic of Michigan's Upper Peninsula. Besides diffusion (which, for example, has spread McDonald's food outlets, once confined to San Bernardino, California, across the globe), there are other reasons that cultural particularities are increasingly rare. Many cultural traits are shared as cultural universals and as a result of independent invention. Facing similar problems, people in different places have come up with (independently invented) similar solutions. Again and again, similar cultural causes have produced similar cultural results.

At the level of the individual cultural trait or element (e.g., bow and arrow, hot dog, Netflix), particularities may be getting rarer. At a higher level, however, particularity is more obvious. Different cultures emphasize different things. *Cultures are integrated and patterned differently and display tremendous variation and diversity.* When cultural traits are borrowed, they are modified to fit the culture that adopts them. They are *reintegrated*—patterned anew—to fit their new setting. Patterned beliefs, customs, and practices lend distinctiveness to particular cultural traditions.

Consider the universal life-cycle events, such as birth, puberty, marriage, parenthood, and death, that many cultures observe and celebrate. The occasions (e.g., marriage, death) may be the same and universal, but the patterns of ceremonial observance may be dramatically different. Cultures vary in just which events merit special celebration. Americans, for example, regard expensive weddings as more socially appropriate than lavish funerals. The Betsileo of Madagascar take the opposite view. The marriage ceremony is a minor event that brings together just the couple and a few close relatives. However, a funeral is a measure of the deceased person's social position and lifetime achievement, and it may attract a thousand people. Why use money on a house, the Betsileo say, when one can use it on the tomb where one will spend eternity in the company of dead relatives? Cremation, an increasingly common option in the United States, would horrify the Betsileo, for whom ancestral bones and relics are important ritual objects.

Cultures vary tremendously in their beliefs, practices, integration, and patterning. By focusing on and trying to explain alternative customs, anthropology forces us to reappraise our familiar ways of thinking. In a world full of cultural diversity, contemporary American culture is just one cultural variant, more powerful perhaps but no more natural than the others.

## Culture and the Individual

Generations of anthropologists have theorized about the relationship between the "system" on one hand and the "person" or "individual" on the other. *System* can refer to various concepts, including culture, society, or social structure. Individual human beings always make up, or constitute, the system. Within that system, however, humans also are constrained (to some extent, at least) by its rules and by the actions of other individuals. Cultural rules provide guidance about what to do and how to do it, but people don't always do what the rules say should be done. People use their culture actively and creatively, rather than blindly following its dictates (see Handwerker 2009). Cultures are dynamic and constantly changing. People learn, interpret, and manipulate the same rule in different ways—or they emphasize different rules that better suit their interests. Culture is *contested*: Different groups in society struggle with one another over whose ideas, values, goals, beliefs, interests, and causes will prevail. Even common symbols may have radically different *meanings* to different individuals and groups in the same culture. Golden arches may cause one person to salivate, while someone else plots a vegetarian protest. Different people may wave the same flag to support or oppose a particular war or political candidate. Behavior as the U.S. national anthem is played at an NFL game may symbolically pledge allegiance or protest police brutality.

Symbolic acts at a public event, such as this NFL game, may be used to convey very different messages. In the top photo, as the national anthem is played, players Eli Harold #58, Colin Kaepernick #7, and Eric Reid #35 take a knee to protest racism and brutality against blacks. In the bottom photo, hearing the same music, fans display the American flag and stand with hands over heart. (top): Michael Zagaris/Getty Images Sport/Getty Images; (bottom): Jonathan Daniel/Getty Images Sport/Getty Images

Even when they agree about what should be done, people don't always do as their culture directs or as other people expect. Many rules are violated, some very often (e.g., automobile speed limits). Some anthropologists find it useful to distinguish between ideal and real culture. The *ideal culture* consists of what people think or say they *should* do and what they *say* they do (such as how much beer they consume). *Real culture* refers to their actual behavior as observed by the anthropologist (e.g., the evidence from garbage, as described in Chapter 1.)

Culture is both public and individual, both external and internal, both in the world and in people's heads. Anthropologists are interested not only in public and collective behavior but also in how *individuals* think, feel, and act. The individual and culture are linked because human social life is a process in which individuals internalize the meanings of *public* (i.e., cultural) messages. Then, alone and in groups, people influence culture by converting their private (and often divergent) understandings into public expressions (D'Andrade 1984).

Conventionally, culture has been seen as social glue transmitted across the generations, binding people through their common past, rather than as something being continually created and reworked in the present. The tendency to view culture as an entity rather than as a process is changing. Contemporary anthropologists now emphasize how day-to-day action, practice, or resistance can make and remake culture (Gupta and Ferguson 1997b). *Agency* refers to the actions that individuals take, both alone and in groups, in forming and transforming cultural identities.

The approach to culture known as *practice theory* (Bourdieu 1977; Ortner 1984) recognizes that individuals within a society or culture have diverse motives and intentions and different degrees of power and influence. Such contrasts may be associated with gender, age, ethnicity, class, and other social variables. Practice theory focuses on how such varied individuals—through their actions and practices—manage to influence, create, and transform the world they live in. Practice theory appropriately recognizes a reciprocal relation between culture (the system) and the individual. The system shapes how individuals experience and respond to events, but individuals also play an active role in how society functions and changes. Practice theory recognizes both constraints on individuals and the flexibility and changeability of cultures and social systems.

## Levels of Culture

Anthropologists also recognize cultural systems—levels of culture—that are larger and smaller than nation-states. **National culture** encompasses those beliefs, learned behavior patterns, values, and institutions that are shared by citizens of the same nation. **International culture** extends beyond and across national boundaries. Because culture is transmitted through learning rather than genetics, cultural traits can spread through borrowing, or diffusion, from one group to another.

Because of diffusion, migration, colonialism, and globalization, many cultural traits and patterns have acquired international scope. The contemporary United States, Canada, Great Britain, and Australia share cultural traits they have inherited from their common linguistic and cultural ancestors in Great Britain. Roman Catholics in many countries share beliefs, symbols, experiences, and values transmitted by their church. The World Cup has become an international cultural event, as people in many countries know the rules of, play, and follow soccer.

Cultures also can be smaller than nations. Although people who live in the same country share a national cultural tradition, all cultures also contain diversity. Individuals, families, communities, regions, classes, and other groups within a culture have different learning experiences, as well as shared ones. **Subcultures** are different symbol-based patterns and traditions associated with particular groups in the same complex society. In large or diverse nations such as the United States or Canada, a variety of subcultures originate in region, ethnicity, language, class, and religion. The religious backgrounds of American Jews, Baptists, and Roman Catholics create subcultural differences among them. While sharing a national culture, U.S. northerners and southerners also differ in their beliefs, values, and customary behavior as a result of national and regional history. Italian Americans have ethnic traditions different from those of Irish, Polish, Hispanic, or African Americans.

Nowadays, many anthropologists are reluctant to use the term *subculture*. They feel that the prefix *sub-* is offensive because it means "below." Subcultures thus may be perceived as "less than" or somehow inferior to a dominant, elite, or national culture. In this discussion of levels of culture, I intend no such implication. My point is simply that nations may contain many different culturally defined groups. As mentioned earlier, culture is contested. Various groups may strive to promote the correctness and value of their own practices, values, and beliefs in comparison with those of other groups or the nation as a whole. Politicians may claim to be putting their country first, even as their policies disproportionately benefit certain groups within that nation.

## Ethnocentrism, Cultural Relativism, and Human Rights

**Ethnocentrism** is the tendency to view one's own culture as superior and to apply one's own cultural values in judging the behavior and beliefs of people raised in other cultures (see Bizumic 2018). We hear ethnocentric statements all the time. Ethnocentrism can contribute to social solidarity, a sense of value and community, among people who share a cultural tradition. People everywhere think that the familiar explanations, opinions, and customs are true, right, proper, and moral. They regard different behavior as strange, immoral, or savage. Often other societies are not considered fully human. Their members may be castigated as cannibals, thieves, rapists, or people who do not bury their dead.

Opposing ethnocentrism is **cultural relativism**, the viewpoint that behavior in one culture should not be judged by the standards of another culture. This position also can present problems. At its most extreme, cultural relativism argues that there is no superior, international, or universal morality, that the moral and ethical rules of all cultures deserve equal respect. In the extreme relativist view, Nazi Germany would be evaluated as nonjudgmentally as Athenian Greece.

In today's world, human rights advocates challenge many of the tenets of cultural relativism. For example, several societies in Africa and the Middle East have traditions of female genital modification (FGM). *Clitoridectomy* is the removal of a girl's clitoris.

*Infibulation* involves sewing the lips (labia) of the vagina, to constrict the vaginal opening. Both procedures reduce female sexual pleasure and, it is believed in some cultures, the likelihood of adultery. Such practices have been opposed by human rights advocates, especially women's rights groups. The idea is that the tradition infringes on a basic human right—disposition over one's body and one's sexuality. Some African countries have banned or otherwise discouraged the procedures, as have Western nations that receive immigration from such cultures. Similar issues arise with circumcision and other male genital operations. Is it proper to require adolescent boys to undergo collective circumcision to fulfill cultural tradition, as has been done in parts of Africa and Australia? Is it right to circumcise a baby boy without his permission, as has been done routinely in the United States and as is customary among Jews and Muslims?

Some would argue that the problems with relativism can be solved by distinguishing between methodological and moral relativism (see Kellenberger 2008). In anthropology, cultural relativism is not a moral position but a methodological one. It states: To understand another culture fully, you must try to determine how the people in that culture see things. What motivates them—what are they thinking—when they do the things they do? Such an approach does not preclude making moral judgments or taking action. When faced with Nazi atrocities, a methodological relativist would have a moral obligation to stop doing anthropology and take action to intervene. In the FGM example, we can best understand the motivations for the practice by considering the perspective of those who engage in it. Having done this, one then faces the moral question of whether to intervene to stop it. We should also recognize that different people and groups living in the same society—for example, women and men, old and young, the more and less powerful—can have widely different views about what is proper, necessary, and moral (see Hunt 2007).

The idea of **human rights** invokes a realm of justice and morality beyond and superior to the laws and customs of particular countries, cultures, and religions (see Donnelly 2013). Human rights include the rights to speak freely; to hold religious beliefs without persecution; and not to be murdered, injured, or enslaved or imprisoned without charge. Such rights are seen as *inalienable* (nations cannot abridge or terminate them) and international (larger than and superior to individual nations and cultures). Four United Nations documents describe nearly all the human rights that have been recognized internationally. Those documents are the UN Charter; the Universal Declaration of Human Rights; the International Covenant on Economic, Social and Cultural Rights; and the International Covenant on Civil and Political Rights.

Alongside the human rights movement has arisen an awareness of the need to preserve cultural rights. Unlike human rights, **cultural rights** are vested not in individuals but in *groups*, such as religious and ethnic minorities and indigenous societies (see Chow 2018). Cultural rights include a group's ability to preserve its culture, to raise its children in the ways of its forebears, to continue its language, and not to be deprived of its economic base by the nation in which it is located. The related notion of indigenous **intellectual property rights (IPR)** has arisen in an attempt to conserve each society's cultural base—its core beliefs, knowledge, and practices. Much traditional cultural knowledge has commercial value. Examples include ethnomedicine (traditional medical knowledge and techniques), cosmetics, cultivated plants, foods, folklore, arts, crafts, songs, dances, costumes, and rituals. Anthropologist George Nicholas (2018) defines **cultural appropriation**

Top: A Maori haka. Maori men dressed as warriors perform their traditional haka during a festival celebrating Maori heritage in January 2016 in Auckland, New Zealand. Bottom: Illustrating cultural appropriation, members of New Zealand's Kiwis rugby team enact their version of the haka prior to an October 2016 match against England. The notion of indigenous property rights states that any society has a fundamental right to preserve and manage its cultural base. Does the rugby team have the right to perform the haka? (top): Hannah Peters/Getty Images News/Getty Images; (bottom): Jan Kruger/Getty Images Sport/Getty Images

as taking or using, without permission or recompense, an aspect of someone else's heritage in inappropriate, harmful, or unwelcome ways. Harmful appropriation occurs when cultural features that are considered special or sacred are not treated as such, or when they are commercialized. According to the IPR concept, a particular group should determine how indigenous knowledge and its products may be used and distributed and the level of compensation required. (This chapter's "Anthropology Today" discusses the related concept of "cultural heritage.")

The notion of cultural rights is related to the idea of cultural relativism, and the problem discussed previously arises again. What does one do about cultural rights that interfere with human rights? I believe that anthropology's main job is to present accurate accounts and explanations of cultural phenomena. The anthropologist doesn't have to approve infanticide, cannibalism, or torture to record their existence and determine their causes and the motivations behind them. However, each anthropologist has a choice about where he or she will do fieldwork. Some anthropologists choose not to study a particular culture because they discover in advance or early in fieldwork that behavior they consider morally repugnant is practiced there. Anthropologists respect human diversity. Most ethnographers try to be objective, accurate, and sensitive in their accounts of other cultures. However, objectivity, sensitivity, and a cross-cultural perspective don't mean that anthropologists have to ignore international standards of justice and morality. What do you think?

## Mechanisms of Cultural Change

Why and how do cultures change? One way is through diffusion, or borrowing, of traits between cultures. Such exchange of information and products has gone on throughout human history because cultures never have been truly isolated. Contact between neighboring groups has always existed and has extended over vast areas (Boas 1940/1966). Diffusion is *direct* when two cultures trade with, intermarry among, or wage war on one another. Diffusion is *forced* when one culture subjugates another and imposes its customs on the dominated group. Diffusion is *indirect* when items or traits move from group A to group C via group B without any firsthand contact between A and C. In this case, group B might consist of traders or merchants who take products from a variety of places to new markets. Or group B might be geographically situated between A and C, so that what it gets from A eventually winds up in C, and vice versa. In today's world, much international diffusion is indirect—culture spread by the mass media and advanced information technology.

**Acculturation**, a second mechanism of cultural change, is the ongoing exchange of cultural features that results when groups have continuous firsthand contact. This contact may change the cultures of either or both groups, but each group remains distinct. In situations of acculturation, cultures have exchanged and blended foods, recipes, music, dances, clothing, tools, languages, and technologies.

One example of acculturation is a *pidgin*, a mixed language that develops to ease communication between members of different societies in contact. This usually happens in situations of trade or colonialism. Pidgin English, for example, is a simplified form of English that blends English grammar with the grammar of a native language. Pidgin English first developed to facilitate commerce in Chinese ports. Similar pidgins developed later in Papua New Guinea and West Africa.

**Independent invention**—the process by which humans innovate, creatively finding solutions to problems—is a third mechanism of cultural change. Faced with comparable problems and challenges, people in different societies have innovated and changed in similar ways, which is one reason cultural generalities exist. One example is the independent invention of agriculture in the Middle East and Mexico. Often a major invention, such as agriculture, triggers a series of subsequent, interrelated changes. Thus, in both Mexico and the Middle East, agriculture led to many social, political, and legal changes, including notions of property and distinctions in wealth, class, and power.

## Globalization

The term **globalization** encompasses a series of processes that work transnationally to promote change in a world in which nations and people are increasingly interlinked and mutually dependent. The forces of globalization include international commerce and finance, travel and tourism, transnational migration, and the media—including the Internet and other high-tech information flows (see Friedman and Friedman 2008; Haugerud, Stone, and Little 2011; Stoddard and Collins 2017). New economic unions (which have met considerable resistance in their member nations) have been created through the World Trade Organization (WTO), the International Monetary Fund (IMF), and the European Union (EU).

It's important to distinguish between two different meanings of the term *globalization.* As used in this book, the primary meaning of globalization is *worldwide connectedness.* Modern systems of production, distribution, consumption, finance, transportation, and communication are global in scope. A second meaning of globalization is *political* and has to do with ideology, policy, and free trade (see Kotz 2015). In this more limited sense, globalization refers to efforts by international financial powers to create a global *free market* for goods and services. This second, political, meaning of globalization has generated, and continues to generate, significant opposition. In this book, *globalization* is a neutral term for the fact of global connectedness and linkages, rather than any kind of political position (see also Eriksen 2014; Ervin 2014).

The media, including the Internet and satellite and digital transmissions, play a key role in globalization (Kjaerulff 2010; Lule 2018). Long-distance communication is faster and easier than ever, and it now covers most of the globe. The media help propel a transnational culture of consumption, by spreading information about products, events, lifestyles, and the perceived benefits (and sometimes costs) of globalization. Emigrants transmit information and resources transnationally, as they maintain their ties with home (phoning, Skyping, FaceTiming, Facebooking, WhatsApping, tweeting, texting, e-mailing, visiting, sending money). People increasingly live their lives across borders, maintaining social, financial, cultural, and political connections with more than one nation-state (see Lugo 1997; Staudt 2018). Examples of such "multiplaced" people include business and intellectual leaders, development workers, and members of multinational corporations, as well as migratory domestic, agricultural, and construction workers.

The Internet and cell phones have made possible the very rapid global transmission of money, resources, and information. Transactions that once involved face-to-face contact now proceed across vast distances. For example, when you order something using the Internet, the only human being you might speak to is the delivery driver, and a drone may soon replace that human. The computers that process your order from Amazon can be on different continents, and the products you order can come from a warehouse anywhere. The average food product now travels 1,300 miles and changes hands a dozen times before it reaches an American consumer (Lewellen 2010).

The effects of globalization are broad and often unwelcome. An army of outsiders and potential change agents now intrudes on people everywhere. Tourism has become the world's number-one industry. Airbnb, VRBO, and other short-term rental sites are transforming residential neighborhoods in many cities. Economic development agents and the media promote the idea that work should be for cash rather than mainly for subsistence. Local people have devised various strategies to deal with threats to their autonomy, identity, and livelihood (Maybury-Lewis, Macdonald, and Maybury-Lewis, 2009). New forms of cultural expression and political mobilization, including the rights movements discussed previously, are emerging from the interplay of local, regional, national, and international cultural forces.

# Anthropology Today  *Preserving Cultural Heritage*

*Heritage* refers to something that has been passed on from previous generations. *Cultural heritage*—the culture, values, and traditions of a particular group—includes not only such material things as artifacts, artwork, and buildings but also intangibles such as language, music, dances, and stories. Every human group has a shared heritage. Members of that group are its proper guardians. Heritage becomes a matter of international concern when one group seizes it from another, or destroys it for political or religious purposes.

As the world system has expanded, heritage items often have been collected, purchased, and stolen from indigenous people for museums and private collections. Many times they were sold by people (e.g., explorers or colonial officials) who had no right to sell them. Among the world's most famous items of cultural heritage are the Parthenon Sculptures, also known as the Elgin Marbles, on display at—and one of the most prized possessions of—London's famed British Museum. Lord Elgin, the British ambassador to the Ottoman empire, acquired these sculptures in the early 19th century in Athens, Greece. Their ownership remains a point of contention between Greece and the United Kingdom.

Some items are recognized as important to the shared heritage of humanity as a whole. This is what UNESCO (the United Nations Educational, Scientific and Cultural Organization) has in mind when it designates sites as having "*World* Heritage" value. Their significance extends beyond their particular geographic location. The disappearance or destruction of such sites would deprive future generations of key aspects of our shared history. Surveying the globe, UNESCO has designated (as of this writing) 1,092 World Heritage sites (see http://whc.unesco.org/en/list/). Of those, 209 were chosen because of their natural resources, such as waterfalls, glaciers, rivers, flora, and fauna. However, the overwhelming majority (845 sites) are cultural heritage sites, so chosen because of their archaeological or historical value. The final 38 sites are mixed cultural and natural, such as the Tikal National Park in Guatemala, which is an archaeological site in a rain forest. Fifty-four of the World Heritage sites are currently considered endangered. Many of those are in areas of war and instability, including six sites in Syria, five in Libya, and three each in Iraq and Mali (see http://whc.unesco.org/en/list/?&danger=1).

In 2012, Islamic extremists occupied and wreaked havoc on Timbuktu, Mali, one of those endangered sites, where they destroyed mausoleums and other heritage items, which they considered to be objects of idolatry. One of the perpetrators, Ahmad al-Faqi al-Mahdi, was successfully prosecuted in 2016 by the International Criminal Court, where he pleaded guilty and was sentenced to nine years in prison.

In 2015, members of the Islamic State (known variously as ISIS, IS, ISIL, and Daesh) destroyed architectural ruins—and murdered a prominent Syrian archaeologist—at Palmyra, Syria, a major cultural center of the ancient world and another endangered UNESCO World Heritage site. The structures destroyed included Palmyra's almost 2,000-year-old Arch of Triumph and Temple of Baalshamin. In both cases, items of cultural heritage were intentionally destroyed, in violation of The Hague's 1954 Convention for the Protection of Cultural Property in the Event of Armed Conflict.

Responding to ongoing threats to cultural preservation, local activists, cultural historians, anthropologists, and others have taken various steps to ensure that indigenous groups maintain or recover items of cultural heritage. The United Nations has enacted a number of measures,

*continued*

## Anthropology Today   *continued*

including those mentioned previously, as well as the 1972 Convention Concerning the Protection of the World Cultural and Natural Heritage and its 2007 Declaration on the Rights of Indigenous Peoples. Both affirm that indigenous peoples have the right to keep, control, protect, and develop their particular cultural heritage, traditional knowledge, and cultural expressions. An American example is the Native American Graves Protection and Repatriation Act (NAGPRA), which affirms that Native American remains belong to Native Americans. NAGPRA requires American museums to return remains and artifacts to any tribe that requests them and can prove a "cultural affiliation" between itself and the remains or artifact.

Different groups may value cultural heritage sites, artifacts, and remains for different reasons (see Barker 2018). For example, anthropologists value the skeleton known as "Kennewick Man" for its scientific importance—what this early fossil from Oregon can tell us about the peopling of North America. Native American tribes in Oregon, by contrast, value Kennewick Man as "the Ancient One," an ancestor whose remains needed to be buried in a culturally appropriate manner. For Lord Elgin, the Parthenon friezes were a valuable commodity that he could (and did) sell to the British government. For the British Museum, the Elgin Marbles are prized works of art proudly displayed in a chamber far from their point of origin. Athenians value the Marbles as a creation of their classic civilization that should be returned to Greece, where descendants of their makers can determine their use. Khaled al-Asaad, an 81-year-old Syrian archaeologist known for his work in preservation, died in Palmyra at the hands of ISIS, who view ancient buildings as objects of idolatry, but who also view ancient artifacts as commodities that can be traded for money. Cultural heritage items, then, can be viewed in multiple ways—as a source of identity, as a commodity, or as a threat to be destroyed.

On March 31, 2016, in Palmyra, Syria, a photographer holds up his photo of the Temple of Bel taken two years earlier. Members of ISIS destroyed this historic temple in September 2015. Joseph Eid/AFP/Getty Images

Multinational corporations lay off workers in their home country when they auto-mate, move, or outsource their operations to places where labor and materials are cheaper. Automation and the globalization of labor create unemployment "back home." Financial globalization means that nations have less control over their own economies. Institutions such as the World Bank, the IMF, the European Union, and the European Central Bank routinely constrain and dictate the national economic policies of countries like Greece and Spain.

Sovereign nations resist. The British vote to withdraw from the European Union ("Brexit") is one example of political mobilization against globalization, as are regular protests at meetings of the principal agencies concerned with international trade. Dem-onstrators continue to show their disapproval of policies of the WTO, the IMF, and the World Bank. Anti-globalization activists fault those organizations for policies that, they say, promote corporate wealth at the expense of farmers, workers, and others at or near the bottom of the economy. Protesters also include environmentalists seeking tougher environmental regulations and trade unionists advocating global labor standards. Re-lated to these protests was the 2011 Occupy movement, which spread quickly from Wall Street to other American (and Canadian) cities. That movement protested growing in-equality—between the top 1 percent and everyone else (see Hickel 2017). Similar senti-ments motivated Bernie Sanders's 2016 presidential campaign. Anti-globalism also figured in the 2016 election of Donald J. Trump as president of the United States and his actions once elected (e.g., withdrawal from international agreements, and imposi-tion of tariffs).

## Summary

1. *Culture*, which is distinctive to humanity, refers to customary behavior and beliefs that are passed on through enculturation. Culture rests on the human capacity for cultural learning. Culture encompasses rules for conduct internalized in human beings, which lead them to think and act in characteristic ways.

2. Although other animals learn, only humans have cultural learning, dependent on symbols. Humans think symbolically—arbitrarily bestowing meaning on things and events. By convention, a symbol stands for something with which it has no necessary or natural relation. Symbols have special meaning for people who share memories, values, and beliefs because of common enculturation.

3. Cultural traditions mold biologically based desires and needs in particular direc-tions. Everyone is cultured, not just people with elite educations. Cultures may be integrated and patterned through economic and social forces, key symbols, and core values. Cultural rules don't rigidly dictate our behavior. There is room for creativity, flexibility, diversity, and disagreement within societies. Cultural means of adaptation have been crucial in human evolution. Aspects of culture also can be maladaptive.

4. The human capacity for culture has an evolutionary basis that extends back perhaps 3 million years—to early toolmakers whose products survive in the archaeological

record (and most probably even farther back—based on observation of tool use and manufacture by apes). Humans share with monkeys and apes such traits as manual dexterity (especially opposable thumbs), depth and color vision, learning ability based on a large brain, substantial parental investment in a limited number of offspring, and tendencies toward sociality and cooperation.

5. Many hominin traits are foreshadowed in other primates, particularly in the African apes, which, like us, belong to the hominid family. The ability to learn, basic to culture, is an adaptive advantage available to monkeys and apes. Chimpanzees make tools for several purposes. They also hunt and share meat. Sharing and cooperation are more developed among humans than among the apes, and only humans have systems of kinship and marriage that permit us to maintain lifelong ties with relatives in different local groups.

6. Using a comparative perspective, anthropology examines biological, psychological, social, and cultural universals and generalities. There also are unique and distinctive aspects of the human condition (cultural particularities). North American cultural traditions are no more natural than any others. Levels of culture can be larger or smaller than a nation. Cultural traits may be shared across national boundaries. Nations also include cultural differences associated with ethnicity, region, and social class.

7. Ethnocentrism describes judging other cultures by using one's own cultural standards. Cultural relativism, which anthropologists may use as a methodological position rather than a moral stance, is the idea of avoiding the use of outside standards to judge behavior in a given society. Human rights are those based on justice and morality beyond and superior to particular countries, cultures, and religions. Cultural rights are vested in religious and ethnic minorities and indigenous societies, and intellectual property rights, or IPR, apply to an indigenous group's collective knowledge and its applications.

8. Diffusion, migration, and colonialism have carried cultural traits and patterns to different world areas. Mechanisms of cultural change include diffusion, acculturation, and independent invention. Globalization comprises a series of processes that promote change in a world in which nations and people are interlinked and mutually dependent.

## Think Like an Anthropologist

1. Our culture—and cultural changes—affect how we perceive nature, human nature, and "the natural." This theme continues to fascinate science fiction writers. Recall a recent science fiction book, movie, or TV program that creatively explores the boundaries between nature and culture. How does the story develop the tension between nature and culture to craft a plot?

2. What are some issues about which you find it hard to be culturally relativistic? If you were an anthropologist with the task of investigating these issues in real life, can you think of a series of steps that you would take to design a project that would, to the best of your ability, practice methodological cultural relativism?

## Key Terms

# Chapter 3

# Doing Anthropology

## What Do Anthropologists Do?

"Been on any digs lately?" Ask your professor how many times she or he has been asked this question. Then ask how often he or she actually has been on a dig. Remember that anthropology has four subfields, only two of which (archaeology and biological anthropology) require much digging—in the ground, at least. Even among biological anthropologists, it's mainly paleoanthropologists (those concerned with the fossil record) who must dig. Students of primate behavior in the wild, such as Jane Goodall, don't do it.

Nor, most of the time, is it done by forensic anthropologists, such as the title character in the old TV series *Bones*.

To be sure, cultural anthropologists "dig out" information about lifestyles, as linguistic anthropologists do about the features and use of language. Traditionally, cultural anthropologists have done a variant on the *Star Trek* theme of seeking out, if not new, at least different "life" and "civilizations," sometimes boldly going where no scientist has gone before.

Despite globalization, the cultural diversity under anthropological scrutiny right now may be as great as ever before, because the anthropological universe has expanded to modern nations. Today's cultural anthropologists are as likely to study artists in Miami or bankers in Beirut as indigenous Australians in the outback or Polynesians in outrigger canoes. Still, we can't forget that anthropology did originate in non-Western, nonindustrial societies. Its research techniques, especially those subsumed under the label "ethnography," were developed to deal with small populations. Even when working in modern nations, anthropologists still consider ethnography with small groups to be an excellent way of learning about how people live their lives and make decisions.

Before this course, did you know the names of any anthropologists? If so, which ones—real or fictional? For the general public, biological anthropologists and archaeologists tend to be better known than cultural anthropologists because of what they study and discover—making them attractive subjects for the Discovery Channel. You're more likely to have seen film of Jane Goodall with chimps or a paleoanthropologist holding a skull than a linguistic or cultural anthropologist at work. Archaeologists occasionally appear in the media to describe a new discovery or to debunk pseudo-archaeological arguments about, say, how visitors from space have left traces on Earth. One cultural anthropologist was an important public and media figure for much of the 20th century. Margaret Mead, famed for her work on teen sexuality in Samoa and gender roles in New Guinea, may well be the most famous anthropologist who ever lived. Mead, one of my own professors at Columbia University, appeared regularly on NBC's *Tonight Show* and wrote a column for *Redbook* magazine. In all her venues, including teaching, museum work, television, anthropological films, popular books, and magazines, Mead helped Americans appreciate the relevance of anthropology to understanding their daily lives. That's a worthy goal that more contemporary anthropologists should emulate.

This chapter is about what anthropologists do. It focuses on archaeology, biological anthropology, and cultural anthropology. Linguistic methods are discussed in Chapter 10; applied anthropology in Chapter 17. (Given space limitations in a brief introductory textbook such as this, only some of the many methods and techniques employed by anthropologists can be covered here.)

## Research Methods in Archaeology and Biological Anthropology

Recall from Chapter 1 that archaeology and biological anthropology are two of anthropology's four subfields. Anthropological archaeology reconstructs human behavior through the analysis of material remains (and other sources, including written records, if available). Biological anthropologists study biological attributes of living humans (e.g., their genetics, growth, development, and physiological adaptation) and other primates, as well as ancient ones. Within biological anthropology, paleoanthropology is the study of ancient humans and human evolution through bones, skulls, teeth, and other material remains. In studying the past, biological anthropologists share many research interests and techniques with archaeologists. Members of both subfields must collaborate with many other kinds of scientists to do their work effectively.

## Multidisciplinary Approaches

Scientists from diverse fields—e.g., soil science and **paleontology** (the study of ancient life through the fossil record)—collaborate with anthropologists in the study of sites where artifacts or fossils have been found. *Palynology*, the study of ancient plants through pollen samples, can be used to determine a site's former environment. Physicists and chemists help archaeologists and biological anthropologists with dating techniques. By examining human skeletons, *bioarchaeologists* can reconstruct their physical traits, health status, and diet (Larsen 2015; Martin, Harrod, and Perez 2013; Perry 2012). Evidence for difference in social status may endure through the ages in hard materials, such as bones, jewels, and buildings. The chemical composition of bones at a site may reflect dietary contrasts between elites and less privileged commoners.

To reconstruct ancient human biological and cultural features, anthropologists and their collaborators analyze the remains of humans, plants, and animals, as well as such artifacts (manufactured items) as ceramics, casts, and metals. Visible remains found at archaeological sites include bones, charcoal from ancient fires, burials, and storage pits. Archaeologists also can draw on microscopic evidence, including fossil pollen, *phytoliths* (plant crystals), and starch grains. A phytolith is a microscopic crystal found in wheat, rice, maize, manioc (cassava), and other early domesticates. Because phytoliths are inorganic and don't decay, they can reveal which plants were present even when no other plant remains survive. Phytoliths can be recovered from teeth, tools, containers, ritual objects, and garden plots.

Starch grain analysis recovers microfossils of food plants from the stone tools used to process them. Starch grains preserve well in areas, such as the humid tropics, where other organic remains typically decay. These grains have been recovered from stone tools, pottery fragments, and basketry, as well as human coprolites (fossilized feces) (Bryant 2003, 2007a, 2007b). Vaughn Bryant (2007b, 2013) stresses the importance of microscopic evidence in understanding the past. One example he cites is Bonnie Williamson's analysis of Middle to Late Stone Age tools from a cave site in South Africa. Examining hundreds of stone tools, Williamson found that many still had residues stuck to their cutting edges. Previously, it had been assumed that these tools were used by men to hunt and butcher animals, but Williamson found that over 50 percent of all the residues were from plants. Williamson's analysis suggested an important role for women (in gathering and processing plant foods) in these early cultures.

Anthropologists also work with geologists, geographers, and other scientists in using satellite images to find ancient footpaths, roads, canals, and irrigation systems, which can then be investigated on the ground. Aerial photos (taken from airplanes) and satellite images are forms of *remote sensing* used in site location. Anthropologists have used satellite imagery to identify, and then investigate on the ground, regions where deforestation

In the Mosquitia region of Honduras, an archaeologist consults a handheld GPS device loaded with data from an aerial survey using an imaging technique called LIDAR (see next photo).
Dave Yoder/National Geographic Image Collection/Alamy Stock Photo

is especially severe and where people and biodiversity, including nonhuman primates, may be at risk (Green and Sussman 1990; Kottak 1999).

A new technology known as LiDAR (light detection and ranging) has enabled scientists to map more than 800 square miles (2,100 square kilometers) of the Maya Biosphere Reserve in the Petén region of Guatemala. This LiDAR dataset is the largest ever obtained for archaeological research. LiDAR allowed scientists to digitally remove the tree canopy from aerial images of this now-unpopulated landscape to reveal the ruins of a Maya civilization that was much larger in scale and population than most Maya specialists had imagined previously (Clynes 2018).

## Studying the Past

Archaeologists and biological anthropologists share techniques that enable them to reconstruct the human past. The field of **paleoanthropology** focuses on the fossil record of human evolution. **Fossils** are remains (e.g., bones), traces, or impressions (e.g., footprints) of ancient life forms. Typically, a team composed of scientists, students, and local workers participates in a paleoanthropological or archaeological study. Such teams may also include paleontologists, geologists, palynologists, paleoecologists, physicists, and chemists. Paleontologists help locate fossil beds containing remains of animals that can be dated and that are known to have coexisted with hominins at particular times. Good preservation of faunal (animal) remains may suggest that hominin fossils have survived as well. Sometimes it's impossible to date the hominin fossils and artifacts found at a given site by using the most

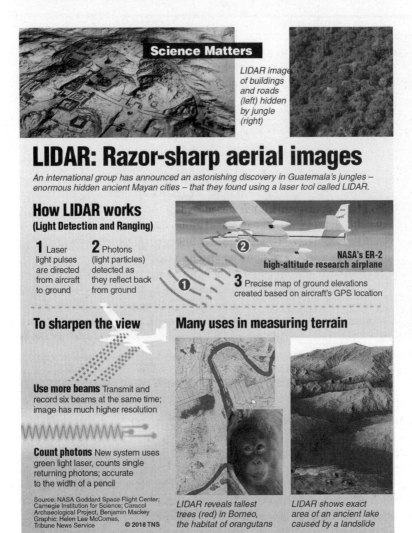

## Science Matters

LIDAR image of buildings and roads (left) hidden by jungle (right)

# LIDAR: Razor-sharp aerial images

*An international group has announced an astonishing discovery in Guatemala's jungles – enormous hidden ancient Mayan cities – that they found using a laser tool called LIDAR.*

## How LIDAR works
### (Light Detection and Ranging)

**1** Laser light pulses are directed from aircraft to ground

**2** Photons (light particles) detected as they reflect back from ground

NASA's ER-2 high-altitude research airplane

**3** Precise map of ground elevations created based on aircraft's GPS location

## To sharpen the view

**Use more beams** Transmit and record six beams at the same time; image has much higher resolution

**Count photons** New system uses green light laser, counts single returning photons; accurate to the width of a pencil

Source: NASA Goddard Space Flight Center; Carnegie Institution for Science; Caracol Archaeological Project, Benjamin Mackey
Graphic: Helen Lee McComas, Tribune News Service    © 2018 TNS

## Many uses in measuring terrain

LIDAR reveals tallest trees (red) in Borneo, the habitat of orangutans

LIDAR shows exact area of an ancient lake caused by a landslide

LIDAR explained.
McComas/TNS/Newscom

accurate and direct (radiometric) methods. In this case, comparison of the faunal remains at that site with similar, but more securely dated, fauna at another site may suggest a date for those animal fossils and the hominins and artifacts associated with them.

## Survey and Excavation

Once potential sites have been identified, more intensive surveying begins in the search for hominin traces—bones or tools. Some early hominin sites are strewn with thousands of tools. Typically, archaeologists, paleoanthropologists, and paleontologists combine both local (excavation) and regional (systematic survey) perspectives. They recognize that sites may not be discrete and isolated, but parts of larger systems.

*Systematic Survey*

**Systematic survey** provides a regional perspective by gathering information on settlement patterns over a large area. *Settlement patterns* refers to the distribution of sites within a region. Regional surveys reconstruct settlement patterns by addressing several questions: Where were sites located? How big were they? What kinds of buildings did they have? How old are the sites? Ideally, a systematic survey involves walking over the entire survey area and recording the location and size of all sites. From artifacts found on the surface, the surveyor estimates when each site was occupied.

*Excavation*

During an **excavation**, scientists dig through the layers of deposits that make up a site. These layers, or strata, are used to establish the time order of materials. This relative chronology is based on the principle of *superposition*: In an undisturbed sequence of strata, the oldest layer is on the bottom. Each successive layer above is younger than the one below. This relative time ordering of material lies at the heart of archaeological, paleoanthropological, and paleontological research.

The archaeological and fossil records are so rich, and excavation is so labor intensive and expensive, that nobody digs a site without a good reason. Sites are excavated because they are endangered, or because they answer specific research questions (see Sabloff 2008). Cultural resource management (CRM) focuses on managing the preservation of archaeological sites that are threatened by modern development. Many countries require archaeological impact studies before construction can take place. If a site is at risk and the development cannot be stopped, CRM archaeologists are called in to salvage what information they can from the site (see King 2011; McManamon, 2017).

## Kinds of Archaeology

Archaeologists pursue diverse research topics, using a wide variety of methods (see Renfrew and Bahn 2016). Experimental archaeologists try to replicate ancient techniques and processes (e.g., tool making) under controlled conditions. Historical archaeologists use written records as guides and supplements to archaeological research. They work with remains that are more recent—often much more recent—than the advent of writing. Colonial archaeologists are historical archaeologists who use written records as guides to locate and excavate postcontact sites in North and South America, and to verify or question the written accounts. Classical archaeologists usually are affiliated with university departments of classics or the history of art, rather than with anthropology departments. These classical scholars tend to focus on the literate civilizations of the Old World, such as Greece, Rome, and Egypt. Classical archaeologists often are more interested in styles of architecture and sculpture than in the social, economic, and political features that typically interest anthropological archaeologists. Underwater archaeology is a growing field that investigates submerged sites, most often shipwrecks. Special techniques, including remotely operated vehicles, are used, but divers also do underwater survey and excavation.

# Dating the Past

The archaeological record hasn't revealed every ancient society that has existed on Earth; nor is the fossil record a representative sample of all the plants and animals that ever have lived. Some body parts and some species are better represented than others are, for many reasons. Bones and teeth preserve better than do soft parts, such as flesh and skin. The chances of fossilization increase when remains are buried in silt, gravel, or sand. Good places for bone preservation include swamps, floodplains, river deltas, lakes, and caves. Species living in such areas have a better chance to be preserved than do animals in other habitats. Fossilization also is favored in areas with volcanic ash. Once remains do get buried, chemical conditions must be right for fossilization to occur. If the sediment is too acidic, even bones and teeth will dissolve. The study of all the processes that affect the remains of dead animals is called **taphonomy**, from the Greek *taphos*, which means "tomb." Those processes include scattering by carnivores and scavengers, distortion by various forces, and the possible fossilization of the remains.

The conditions that lead to a fossil discovery also influence the fossil record. For example, fossils are more likely to be uncovered through erosion in arid areas than in wet areas. Sparse vegetation allows wind to scour the landscape and uncover fossils. The fossil record has been accumulating longer in Europe than in Africa because civil engineering projects and fossil hunting have been going on longer in the former than in the latter. A world map showing where fossils have been found does not indicate the true range of ancient life. Such a map tells us more about ancient geological activity, modern erosion, or recent human activity—such as paleontological research or road building. In considering the fossil record in later chapters, we'll see that certain areas provide more abundant fossil evidence for particular time periods. This doesn't necessarily mean that primates or hominins were living only in that area at that time. Nor does failure to find a fossil species in a particular place always mean the species didn't live there.

Documenting stratigraphy, one archaeologist diagrams layers (strata) of rock at La Pineta, a southern Italian Paleolithic site, while another archaeologist scrapes the rock using a trowel. The oldest stratum here is 600,000 years old. Pasquale Sorrentino/Science Source

## Relative Dating

Scientists use many techniques to date fossils. These methods offer different degrees of precision and are applicable to different periods of the past. Dating may be relative or absolute. **Relative dating** provides a time frame in relation to other strata or materials rather than absolute dates in numbers. Many dating methods are based on the geological study of **stratigraphy**, the science that examines the ways in which earth sediments accumulate in strata (singular, *stratum*). Soil that erodes from a hillside into a valley covers, and is younger than, the soil already deposited there. Stratigraphy permits relative dating. That is, the fossils in a given stratum are younger than those below them and older than those above them. We may not know the exact or absolute dates of the fossils, but we can place them in time relative to remains in other layers. Remains of animals and plants that lived at the same time are found in the same stratum. When fossils are found in a particular stratum, the associated geological features (such as frost patterning) and remains of particular plants and animals offer clues about the climate at the time of deposition.

Besides stratigraphy, a second type of relative dating is fluorine absorption analysis. Bones fossilizing in the same ground for the same length of time absorb the same proportion of fluorine from the local groundwater. Fluorine analysis uncovered a famous hoax involving the so-called Piltdown man, once considered an unusual and perplexing human ancestor (Maxwell 2012; Stringer 2012b; Weiner 2003). The Piltdown "find," from England, turned out to be the jaw of a young orangutan attached to the skull of a modern human. Fluorine analysis showed the association to be false. The skull had much more fluorine than the jaw—impossible if they had come from the same individual and had been deposited in the same place at the same time. Someone had fabricated Piltdown man in an attempt to muddle the interpretation of the fossil record. (The attempt was partially successful—it did fool some scientists.)

## Absolute Dating

Fossils can be dated more precisely, with dates in numbers (**absolute dating**), by using several methods. For example, the $^{14}C$, or carbon-14, technique is used to date organic remains. This is a *radiometric* technique (so called because it measures radioactive decay). $^{14}C$ is an unstable radioactive isotope of normal carbon, $^{12}C$. Cosmic radiation entering the Earth's atmosphere produces $^{14}C$, and plants take in $^{14}C$ as they absorb carbon dioxide. $^{14}C$ moves up the food chain as animals eat plants and as predators eat other animals.

With death, the absorption of $^{14}C$ stops. This unstable isotope starts to break down into nitrogen ($^{14}N$). It takes 5,730 years for half the $^{14}C$ to change to nitrogen; this is the half-life of $^{14}C$. After another 5,730 years, one-quarter of the original $^{14}C$ will remain. After yet another 5,730 years, one-eighth will be left. By measuring the proportion of $^{14}C$ in organic material, scientists can determine a fossil's date of death, or the date of an ancient campfire. However, because the half-life of $^{14}C$ is short, this dating technique is less dependable for specimens older than 40,000 years than it is for more recent remains.

Fortunately, other radiometric dating techniques are available for earlier periods. One of the most widely used is the potassium-argon (K/A) technique. $^{40}K$ is a radioactive isotope of potassium that breaks down into argon-40, a gas. The half-life of $^{40}K$ is far longer than that of $^{14}C$—1.3 billion years. With this method, the older the specimen, the more reliable the dating. Furthermore, whereas $^{14}C$ dating can be done only on organic remains, K/A dating can be used only for inorganic substances: rocks and minerals. $^{40}K$ in rocks gradually breaks down into argon-40. That gas is trapped in the rock until the rock is heated intensely (as with volcanic activity), at which point it may escape.

TABLE 3.1    **Absolute Dating Techniques**

| Technique | Abbreviation | Materials Dated | Effective Time Range |
|---|---|---|---|
| Carbon-14 | $^{14}C$ | Organic materials | Up to 40,000 years |
| Potassium-argon | K/A and $^{40}K$ | Volcanic rock | Older than 500,000 years |
| Uranium series | $^{238}U$ | Minerals | Between 1,000 and 1,000,000 years |
| Thermoluminescence | TL | Rocks and minerals | Between 5,000 and 1,000,000 years |
| Electron spin resonance | ESR | Rocks and minerals | Between 1,000 and 1,000,000 years |

When the rock cools, the breakdown of potassium into argon resumes. Dating is done by reheating the rock and measuring the escaping gas.

In Africa's Great Rift Valley, which runs down eastern Africa and in which early hominin fossils abound, past volcanic activity permits K/A dating. In studies of strata containing fossils, scientists find out how much argon has accumulated in rocks since they were last heated. They then determine, using the standard $^{40}K$ deterioration rate (half-life), the date of that heating. Considering volcanic rocks at the top of a stratum with fossil remains, scientists establish that the fossils are older than, say, 1.8 million years. By dating the volcanic rocks below the fossil remains, they determine that the fossils are *younger than,* say, 2 million years. Thus, the age of the fossils is set at between 2.0 million and 1.8 million years. Note that absolute dating is "absolute" in name only; it may give ranges of numbers rather than exact dates.

Many fossils were discovered before the advent of modern stratigraphy. Often we can no longer determine their original stratigraphic placement. Furthermore, fossils aren't always discovered in volcanic layers. Like $^{14}C$ dating, the K/A technique applies to a limited period of the fossil record. Because the half-life of $^{40}K$ is so long, the technique cannot be used with materials less than 500,000 years old.

Other radiometric dating techniques can be used to cross-check K/A dates, again by using minerals surrounding the fossils. One such method, *uranium series dating,* measures fission tracks produced during the decay of radioactive uranium ($^{238}U$) into lead. Two other radiometric techniques are especially useful for fossils that can't be dated by $^{14}C$ (up to 40,000 B.P.–before the present) or $^{40}K$ (more than 500,000 B.P.). These methods are *thermoluminescence (TL)* and *electron spin resonance (ESR).* Both TL and ESR measure the electrons that are constantly being trapped in rocks and minerals. Once a date is obtained for a rock found associated with a fossil, that date also can be applied to that fossil. Table 3.1 summarizes the time spans for which the various absolute dating techniques are applicable.

## Molecular Anthropology

**Molecular anthropology** analyzes genomes (a *genome* is the total genetic makeup of an organism, including all its DNA) to establish when ancient species lived, and when they diverged from other species. What is the basis for such a *genetic clock*? Differences in

DNA arise from mutations—changes in genetic structure that are passed on through heredity. Through time, more and more mutations occur, so that the DNA of descendants differs increasingly from the DNA of their ancestors. Molecular anthropologists assume that mutations occur at a predictable rate. They can multiply that rate by the number of DNA differences to estimate the number of years that have passed between the ancestor and the descendant. Similarly, molecular anthropologists can multiply the mutation rate by the number of differences in DNA among species to estimate how many years they have been diverging from a common ancestor. Such DNA analysis and comparison enables molecular anthropologists to determine and date evolutionary relationships between ancient human ancestors and other primate ancestors. For example, molecular anthropology suggests that the common ancestors of humans and chimps probably lived around 7 million years ago (m.y.a.), whereas the common ancestor of humans, chimps, and gorillas lived about 8 m.y.a.

## Kinds of Biological Anthropology

The interests of biological anthropologists are varied and encompass recent and living as well as ancient and deceased humans and other primates. This chapter describes many, but far from all, of the topics and methods within contemporary biological anthropology.

### Bone Biology

Central to biological anthropology is **bone biology** (skeletal biology)—the study of bone as a biological tissue, including its genetics; cell structure; growth, development, and decay; and patterns of movement (*biomechanics*) (White, Black, and Folkens 2012). Bone biologists study skeletal characteristics of living and deceased humans and hominins. **Paleopathology** is the study of disease and injury in skeletons from archaeological sites (see Buikstra and Roberts 2012; Cohen and Armelagos 2013; Larsen 2018; Weiss 2015).

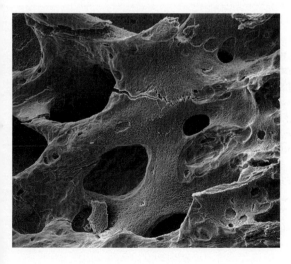

Bone affected by osteoporosis (brittle bone disease). Steve Gschmeissner/Science Photo Library RF/Science Source

Some forms of cancer leave evidence in the bone. Breast cancer, for example, may spread (metastasize) skeletally, leaving lesions in the bones and skull. Certain infectious diseases (e.g., syphilis and tuberculosis) also mark bone, as do injuries and nutritional deficiencies (e.g., rickets, a vitamin D deficiency that deforms the bones). In *forensic anthropology*, biological anthropologists work in a legal context, assisting coroners, medical examiners, and law enforcement agencies in recovering, analyzing, and identifying human remains and determining causes of death (Byers 2017; Langley and Tersigni-Tarrant, 2017; Nafte 2016).

## Anthropometry

Biological anthropologists use various techniques to study nutrition, growth, and development. **Anthropometry** is the measurement of human body parts and dimensions, including skeletal parts (*osteometry*). Anthropometry is done on living people as well as on skeletal remains from sites. Body mass and composition provide measures of nutritional status in living people. *Body mass index* ($kg/m^2$) is the ratio of weight in kilograms to height in meters squared. An adult body mass above 30 is considered at risk of overweight, while one below 18 is at risk of underweight or malnutrition.

## Primatology

Primatology is another subfield of biological anthropology. Primate behavior has been observed in zoos and through experiments, but the most significant studies have been done in natural settings, among free-ranging apes, monkeys, and lemurs. Since the 1950s, when primatologists began their shift from zoos to natural settings, numerous studies have been done of apes (chimps, gorillas, orangutans, and gibbons), monkeys (e.g., baboons, macaques), and lemurs. Studies of primate social systems and behavior, including their mating patterns, infant care, and patterns of contact and dispersal, suggest hypotheses about behavior that humans may share with our nearest relatives—as well as with our hominid ancestors.

# Research Methods in Cultural Anthropology

Early students of society, such as the French scholar Émile Durkheim, were among the founders of both sociology and anthropology. Durkheim studied the religions of Native Australians (Durkheim 1912/2001), as well as mass phenomena, such as suicide rates, in countries like France (Durkheim 1897/1951). Key differences between anthropology and sociology would eventually emerge based on the kinds of societies each studied. Sociologists focused on the industrial West; anthropologists, on nonindustrial societies. Different methods of data collection and analysis were developed to deal with those different kinds of societies. To study large-scale, complex nations, sociologists came to rely on questionnaires and other means of gathering masses of quantifiable data. For many years, sampling and statistical techniques have been basic to sociology, whereas statistical training has been less common in anthropology (although this is changing somewhat as anthropologists increasingly work in modern nations).

Traditional ethnographers studied small, nonliterate (without writing) populations and relied on ethnographic methods appropriate to that context. According to Marcus and Fischer (1986), "[e]thnography is a research process in which the anthropologist closely observes, records, and engages in the daily life of another culture—an experience labeled as the fieldwork method—and then writes accounts of this culture, emphasizing descriptive detail" (p. 18).

# Ethnography: Anthropology's Distinctive Strategy

Traditionally, the process of becoming a cultural anthropologist has required a field experience in another society. Early ethnographers studied small-scale, relatively isolated societies with simple technologies and economies and little social differentiation (see Konopinski 2014; Moore 2012). Traditionally, ethnographers have tried to understand the whole of a particular culture (or, more realistically, as much as they can, given limitations of time and perception). To pursue this goal, ethnographers adopt a free-ranging research strategy, moving from setting to setting, person to person, and place to place to discover the totality and interconnectedness of social life. By expanding our knowledge of the range of human diversity, ethnography provides a foundation for generalizations about human behavior and social life. Ethnographers draw on varied techniques to piece together a picture of otherwise alien lifestyles (see Bernard 2018; Bernard and Gravlee 2014; Gmelch and Gmelch 2018; Vivanco 2017). We turn now to a consideration of those techniques.

## Observation and Participant Observation

Ethnographers must pay attention to hundreds of details of daily life, seasonal events, and unusual happenings. They should record what they see as they see it. Things never will seem quite as strange as they do during the first few weeks in the field. Often anthropologists experience culture shock—a creepy and profound feeling of alienation—on arrival at a new field site (see Cohen 2015). Although anthropologists study human diversity, the actual field experience of diversity takes some getting used to. The ethnographer eventually grows accustomed to, and accepts as normal, cultural patterns that initially were alien. Staying a bit more than a year in the field allows the ethnographer to repeat the season of his or her arrival, when certain events and processes may have been missed because of initial unfamiliarity and culture shock.

Many ethnographers record their impressions in a personal diary, or notebook, which is kept separate from more formal field notes. Later, this record of early impressions will help point out some of the most basic aspects of cultural diversity. Such aspects include distinctive smells, noises people make, how they cover their mouths when they eat, and how they gaze at others. These patterns, which are so basic as to seem almost trivial, are part of what Bronislaw Malinowski (1922/1961) called "the *imponderabilia* of native life and of typical behavior" (p. 20). These features of culture are so fundamental that people take them for granted. They are too basic even to talk about, but the unaccustomed eye of the fledgling ethnographer picks them up. Thereafter, becoming familiar, they fade to the edge of consciousness. Initial impressions are valuable and should be recorded.

Bronislaw Malinowski (1884–1942), who was born in Poland but spent most of his professional life in England, did fieldwork in the Trobriand Islands from 1914 to 1918. Malinowski is generally considered to be the father of ethnography. Does this photo suggest anything about his relationship with Trobriand villagers? Mary Evans Picture Library/The Image Works

First and foremost, ethnographers should try to be accurate observers, recorders, and reporters of what they see in the field.

Ethnographers strive to establish *rapport*, a good, friendly working relationship based on personal contact, with their hosts. Fundamental to ethnography is **participant observation**— taking part in community life, participating in the events one is observing, describing, and analyzing. As human beings living among others, ethnographers cannot be totally impartial and detached observers. By participating, ethnographers may learn why people find various events meaningful, as they see how those events are organized and conducted.

In Arembepe, Brazil, I learned about fishing by sailing on the Atlantic with local fishers. I gave Jeep rides to malnourished babies and their parents, to pregnant mothers, and once to a teenage girl possessed by a spirit. All those people needed to consult specialists outside the village. I danced on Arembepe's festive occasions, drank libations commemorating new births, and became a godfather to a village girl. Most anthropologists have similar field experiences. The common humanity of the student and the studied, the ethnographer and the research community, makes participant observation inevitable.

## Conversation, Interviewing, and Interview Schedules

Participating in local life means that ethnographers continually talk to people and ask questions. As their knowledge of the local language and culture increases, they understand more. There are several stages in learning a field language. First is the naming phase— asking name after name of the objects around them. Later they are able to pose more complex questions and understand the replies. They begin to understand simple

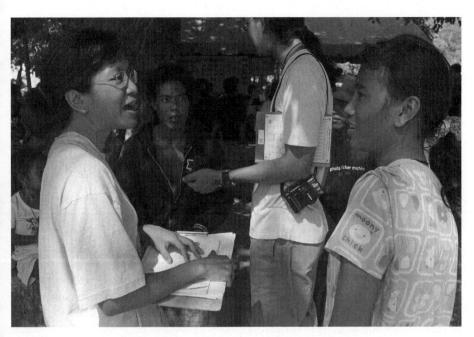

A month after the devastating Indian Ocean earthquake and tsunami of December 2004,
Thai anthropologist Narumon Hinshiranan (left) helped guide the relief effort among the
Moken, a maritime people who live on the Surin Islands along Thailand's Andaman coast.
Dr. Hinshiranan had done prior fieldwork among the Moken people and speaks their language.
Aroon Thaewchatturat/Alamy Stock Photo

conversations between two villagers. With improving language expertise, they eventually
become able to comprehend rapid-fire public discussions and group conversations.

One data-gathering technique I have used in both Arembepe and Madagascar involves
an ethnographic survey that includes an interview schedule. Soon after I began research
in Arembepe, my fellow field workers and I attempted to complete an interview schedule
in each of Arembepe's then 160 households. We entered almost every household (fewer
than 5 percent refused to participate) to ask a set of questions on a printed form. Our
results provided us with a census and basic information about the village. We wrote down
the name, age, and gender of each household member. We gathered data on family type,
religion, present and previous jobs, income, expenditures, diet, possessions, and many
other items on our eight-page form.

Although we were doing a survey, our approach differed from the survey research design routinely used by sociologists and other social scientists working in large, industrial
nations. That survey research, discussed later in the chapter, involves sampling (choosing
a **sample**—a small, manageable study group from a larger population). We did not select a
partial sample from the total population. Instead, we tried to interview in all households
in the community (that is, to have a total sample). We used an interview schedule rather
than a questionnaire. With the **interview schedule**, the ethnographer talks face to face
with people, asks the questions, and writes down the answers. Questionnaire procedures

tend to be more impersonal; often the respondent fills in the form. Think of how many times in the recent past you have been asked to fill out some kind of the survey, usually online, frequently using a service known as Survey Monkey. Calls to customer service frequently lead to a request that a survey be completed at the end of the call. The ostensible purpose of such surveys is to improve customer service. During the survey process, however, no one ever sees another human being.

Our goal of getting a total sample allowed us to meet almost everyone in the village and helped us establish rapport. Decades later, Arembepeiros still talk warmly about how we were interested enough in them to visit their homes and ask them questions. We stood in sharp contrast to the other outsiders the villagers had known, who considered them too poor and backward to take seriously.

Like survey research, however, our interview schedule did gather comparable quantifiable information. It gave us a basis for assessing patterns and exceptions in village life. Our schedules included a core set of questions that were posed to everyone. However, some interesting side issues often came up during the interview, which we pursued then or later.

We followed such leads into many dimensions of village life. One woman, for instance, a midwife, became our go-to person when we wanted detailed information about local childbirth. Another woman had done an internship in an Afro-Brazilian cult (*candomblé*) in the city. She still went there regularly to study, dance, and get possessed. She became our candomblé expert.

Thus, our interview schedule provided a structure that directed but did not confine us as researchers. It enabled our ethnography to be both quantitative and qualitative. The quantitative part consisted of the basic information we gathered and later analyzed statistically. The qualitative dimension came from our follow-up questions, open-ended discussions, pauses for gossip, and work with key consultants.

## The Genealogical Method

Many of us learn about our own ancestry and relatives by tracing our genealogies. Computer programs, websites, and DNA testing services allow us to fill in our "family trees." The **genealogical method** is a well-established ethnographic technique. Early ethnographers developed notation and symbols to deal with kinship, descent, and marriage. Genealogy is a prominent building block in the social organization of nonindustrial societies, where people live and work each day with their close kin. Indeed, another term for such cultures is *kin-based societies*, because everyone is related and spends most of his or her time with relatives. Anthropologists need to collect genealogical data to understand current social relations and to reconstruct history. Rules of behavior attached to particular kin relations are basic to everyday life. Marriage also is crucial in organizing nonindustrial societies, because strategic marriages between villages, tribes, and clans create political alliances.

## Key Cultural Consultants

Every community has people who by accident, experience, talent, or training can provide the most complete or useful information about particular aspects of life. These people are **key cultural consultants**, also called *key informants*. In Ivato, the

Betsileo village in Madagascar where I spent most of my time, a man named Rakoto was particularly knowledgeable about village history. However, when I asked him to work with me on a genealogy of the 50 to 60 people buried in the village tomb, he called in his cousin Tuesdaysfather, who knew more about that subject. Tuesdaysfather had survived an epidemic of influenza that ravaged Madagascar, along with much of the world, around 1919. Immune to the disease himself, Tuesdaysfather had the grim job of burying his kin as they died. He kept track of everyone buried in the tomb. Tuesdaysfather helped me with the tomb genealogy. Rakoto joined him in telling me personal details about the deceased villagers.

## Life Histories

In nonindustrial societies—as in our own—individual personalities, interests, and abilities differ. Some villagers prove to be more interested in the ethnographer's work and are more helpful, interesting, and pleasant than others are. Anthropologists develop likes and dislikes in the field, just as they do at home. Often when they find someone unusually interesting, they collect his or her **life history.** This recollection of a lifetime of experiences provides a more intimate and personal cultural portrait than would be possible otherwise. Life histories, which may be audio- or video-recorded for later review and analysis, reveal how specific people perceive, react to, and contribute to changes that affect their lives. Many ethnographers include the collection of life histories as an important part of their research strategy.

## Local Beliefs and Perceptions, and the Ethnographer's

One goal of ethnography is to discover local (native) views, beliefs, and perceptions, which may be compared with the ethnographer's own observations and conclusions. In the field, ethnographers typically combine two research strategies, the emic (local-oriented) and the etic (scientist-oriented). These terms, derived from linguistics, have been applied to ethnography by various anthropologists. Marvin Harris (1968/2001) popularized the following meanings of the terms: An **emic** approach investigates how local people think. How do they perceive and categorize the world? What are their rules for behavior? What has meaning for them? How do they imagine and explain things? Operating emically, the ethnographer relies on local people to explain things and to say whether something is significant or not. The term **cultural consultant**, or informant, refers to individuals the ethnographer gets to know in the field, the people who teach him or her about their culture, who provide the emic perspective.

The **etic** (scientist-oriented) approach shifts the focus from local observations, categories, explanations, and interpretations to those of the anthropologist. The etic approach acknowledges that members of a culture often are too involved in what they are doing to interpret their cultures impartially. Operating etically, the ethnographer emphasizes what he or she (the observer) notices and considers important. As a trained scientist, the ethnographer should try to bring an objective and comprehensive viewpoint to the study of other cultures. Of course, the ethnographer, like any other scientist, is also a human being with cultural blinders that prevent complete objectivity. As in other sciences, proper training can reduce, but not totally eliminate, the observer's bias. But anthropologists do have special training to compare behavior between different societies.

What are some examples of emic versus etic perspectives? Consider our holidays. For North Americans, Thanksgiving Day has special significance. In our view (emically), it is a unique cultural celebration that commemorates particular historical themes. But a wider, etic, perspective sees Thanksgiving as just one more example of the postharvest festivals held in many societies. Another example: Local people give folk explanations for illnesses caused by germs and other pathogens. Emic agents that cause illness include angry or envious spirits, ancestors, witches, and sorcerers. *Illness* refers to a culture's (emic) perception and explanation of bad health, whereas *disease* refers to the scientific (etic) explanation of poor health, involving known pathogens.

Ethnographers typically combine emic and etic strategies in their fieldwork. The statements, perceptions, categories, and opinions of local people help ethnographers understand how cultures work. Local beliefs are also interesting and valuable in themselves. However, people often fail to admit, or even recognize, certain causes and consequences of their behavior. This is as true of North Americans as it is of people in other societies.

## Problem-Oriented Ethnography

Although anthropologists remain interested in the totality of people's lives in a particular community or society, it is impossible to study everything. As a result, contemporary ethnographic fieldwork generally is aimed at investigating one or more specific topics or problems (see Galman 2018; Murchison 2010; Sunstein and Chiseri-Strater 2012). Topics that an ethnographer might choose to investigate include marriage practices, gender roles, religion, and economic change. Examples of problem-oriented research include various impact studies done by anthropologists, such as the impact of television, the Internet, education, drought, a hurricane, or a change in government on a particular community or society.

In researching a specific problem, anthropologists often need to look beyond local people for relevant data. Government agencies or international organizations may have gathered information on such matters as climate and weather conditions, population density, and settlement patterns. Often, however, anthropologists have to do their own measurements of such variables as field size, yields, dietary quantities, or time allocation. Information of interest to ethnographers extends well beyond what local people can and do tell us. In an increasingly interconnected and complicated world, local people lack knowledge about many factors that may affect their lives—for example, international terrorism, warfare, or the exercise of power from regional, national, and international centers (see Sanjek 2014).

## Longitudinal Studies, Team Research, and Multisited Ethnography

Geography limits anthropologists much less now than in the past, when it could take months to reach a field site and return visits were rare. Modern transportation systems allow anthropologists to return to the field repeatedly. Ethnographic reports now routinely include data from two or more field stays. We can even follow the people we study as they move from village to city, cross the border, or travel internationally. **Longitudinal research** is the long-term study of an area or a population, usually based on repeated visits.

One example is the study of Gwembe District, Zambia. This study, planned in 1956 as a longitudinal project by Elizabeth Colson and Thayer Scudder, continued with Colson, Scudder, and their associates and successors of various nationalities. As is often the case with longitudinal research, the Gwembe study also illustrates *team research*—coordinated research by multiple ethnographers (Scudder and Colson 1980). Researchers studied four villages in different areas for 60 years. Periodic censuses provided basic data on population, economy, kinship, and religious behavior. Censused people who had moved were interviewed to see how their lives compared with those of people who stayed behind. The initial focus of study was the impact of a large hydroelectric dam, which subjected the Gwembe people to forced resettlement. Thereafter, Scudder and Colson (1980) examined how education provided access to new opportunities, even as it also widened a social gap between people with different educational levels. The anthropologists next focused on a change in brewing and drinking patterns, including a rise in alcoholism (Colson and Scudder 1988). When Colson, who died in 2016 at the age of 99, retired from the University of California at Berkeley, she moved to Gwembe district and is buried where she spent her last days.

As mentioned, longitudinal research often is team research. My own field site of Arembepe, Brazil, first entered the world of anthropology as a field-team village in the 1960s. It was one of four sites for the now-defunct Columbia-Cornell-Harvard-Illinois Summer Field Studies Program in Anthropology. For at least three years, that program sent a total of about 20 undergraduates annually, the author included, to do summer research abroad. The teams were stationed in rural communities in four countries: Brazil, Ecuador, Mexico, and Peru. Since my wife, Isabel Wagley Kottak, and I began studying it in 1962, Arembepe has become a longitudinal field site. Generations of researchers have monitored various aspects of change and development. The community has changed from a village into a town and illustrates the process of globalization at the local level. Its economy, religion, and social life have been transformed (see Kottak 2018).

Brazilian and American researchers worked with us on team research projects during the 1980s (on the impact of television) and the 1990s (on environmental risk perception). Students from various universities have drawn on our baseline information from the 1960s in their recent studies in Arembepe. Their topics have included standards of physical attractiveness, family planning, conversion to Protestantism, changing food habits, and the influence of the Internet and social media. Arembepe is thus a site where various field workers have worked as members of a longitudinal, multigenerational team. The more recent researchers have built on prior contacts and findings to increase knowledge about how local people manage new circumstances. In 2016, a team completed new fieldwork in Arembepe and other Brazilian communities, updating our study of media impact, which began during the 1980s.

Traditional ethnographic research focused on a single community or "culture," treated as more or less isolated and unique in time and space. In recent years, ethnography has shifted toward studies of change and of contemporary flows of people, technology, images, and information. Reflecting today's world, fieldwork must be more flexible and on a larger scale. Ethnography increasingly is *multitimed* and *multisited*. That is, it studies people through time and in multiple places. Malinowski could focus on Trobriand culture and spend most of his field time in a particular community. Nowadays we cannot afford

Janet Dunn, one of many anthropologists who have worked in Arembepe. Where is Arembepe, and what kinds of research have been done there? Christopher M. O'Leary

to ignore, as Malinowski did, the outside forces that increasingly impinge on the places we study. Integral to our analyses now are the external entities (e.g., governments, corporations, nongovernmental organizations, new social movements, the drug trade) that interact with and influence local communities throughout the world.

Anthropologists increasingly study people in motion. Examples include people living on or near national borders, nomads, seasonal migrants, homeless and displaced people, immigrants, and refugees (see Andersson 2014; De Leon 2015; Lugo 1997). As fieldwork changes, with less and less of a spatially set field, what can we take from traditional ethnography? Gupta and Ferguson (1997a) correctly cite the "characteristically anthropological emphasis on daily routine and lived experience" (p. 5). The treatment of communities as discrete entities may be a thing of the past. However, "anthropology's traditional attention to the close observation of particular lives in particular places" has an enduring importance (Gupta and Ferguson 1997b, p. 25). The method of close observation helps distinguish cultural anthropology from sociology and survey research, to which we now turn.

## Survey Research

Working increasingly in large-scale societies, anthropologists have developed innovative ways of blending ethnography and survey research (Fricke 1994; Kottak 2009; Pace and Hinote 2013). Before examining such mixed field methods, let's consider the main differences between survey research and ethnography. Sociologists have developed and refined the **survey research** design, which involves sampling, impersonal data collection, and statistical analysis. Survey research draws a sample (a manageable study group) from a much larger population. A properly selected and representative sample permits accurate inferences about the larger population.

In small communities, ethnographers can get to know almost everyone. Given the greater size and complexity of nations, survey research can't help being more impersonal. Survey researchers call the people they study *respondents*—those who respond to questions during a survey. Sometimes survey researchers interview their sample of respondents personally or by phone. Sometimes they ask them to fill out a questionnaire, often online.

Probably the most familiar example of survey research and sampling is the polling that is done to predict political races. An ever-increasing number of organizations now gather information designed to estimate outcomes and to determine what kinds of people voted for which candidates. During sampling, researchers gather information about age, gender, religion, occupation, income, and political party preference. These characteristics (**variables**—attributes that vary among members of a sample or population) are known to influence political decisions. Polling then leads to pronouncements about the voting tendencies and behavior of such categories as "soccer moms," college-educated women, and blue-collar men.

Many more variables affect social identities, experiences, and activities in a modern nation than in the small communities where ethnography grew up. In contemporary North America, hundreds of factors influence our behavior and attitudes. These *social predictors* include age; religion; level of education; the region of the country we grew up in; whether we come from a town, suburb, or city; and our parents' professions, ethnic origins, and income levels. In any large nation, many predictor variables (social indicators) influence behavior and opinions. Because we must be able to detect, measure, and compare the influence of social indicators, many contemporary anthropological studies have a statistical foundation. Even in rural fieldwork, more anthropologists now draw samples, gather quantitative data, and use statistics to interpret them (see Bernard 2013, 2018; Bernard and Gravlee 2014). Statistical analysis can support and round out an ethnographic account of local social life.

In the best studies, however, the hallmark of ethnography remains: Anthropologists enter the community and get to know the people. They participate in local activities, networks, and associations. They observe and experience social conditions and problems. They watch the effects of national policies and globalization on local life. The ethnographic method and the emphasis on personal relationships in social research are valuable gifts that cultural anthropology brings to the study of any society.

# Doing Anthropology Right and Wrong: Ethical Issues

Science exists in society and in the context of law and ethics. Anthropologists can't study things simply because they happen to be interesting or of value to science. We must consider ethics as well (see Gonzalez-Ruibal 2018; Radin 2018). Anthropologists typically have worked abroad, outside their own society. In the context of international contacts and cultural diversity, different ethical codes and value systems will meet, and often compete.

Archaeologists and biological anthropologists, in particular, often work as members of international teams. These teams typically include researchers from several countries, including the host country—the place (e.g., Ethiopia) where the research takes place.

Anthropologists must inform officials and colleagues in the host country about the purpose, funding, and likely results, products, and impacts of their research. They need to negotiate the matter of where the materials produced by the research will be analyzed and stored—in the host country or in the anthropologists' country—and for how long. To whom do research materials such as bones, artifacts, and blood samples belong? What kinds of restrictions will apply to their use?

Anthropologists must obtain **informed consent** from research participants. This means that they must agree (consent) to take part in the research, after being informed about its nature, procedures, and possible impacts. Informed consent should be obtained from anyone who provides information or who might be affected by the research. Although nonhuman primates can't give informed consent, primatologists still must take steps to ensure that their research doesn't endanger the animals they study (see Riley and Bezanson 2018). Either government agencies or nongovernmental organizations (NGOs) may be in charge of protecting primates. If so, the anthropologist will need to obtain informed consent from a representative of the responsible agency or NGO to conduct research.

With living humans, informed consent is a necessity, not only in gathering information but especially in obtaining biological samples, such as blood, urine, or DNA (see this chapter's "Anthropology Today"). The research subjects must be told how the samples will be collected, used, and identified and about the potential costs and benefits to them. Informed consent is needed from anyone providing data or information, owning materials being studied, or otherwise having an interest that might be affected by the research.

It is appropriate for North American anthropologists working in another country to (1) include host country colleagues in their research planning and requests for funding; (2) establish truly collaborative relationships with those colleagues and their institutions before, during, and after fieldwork; (3) include host country colleagues in dissemination, including publication, of the research results; and (4) ensure that something is "given back" to host country colleagues. For example, research equipment and technology can remain in the host country. Additionally, funding can be provided for host country colleagues to conduct research, attend international meetings, or visit foreign institutions—especially those where their international collaborators work.

## Ownership Issues

Even with efforts to respect different value systems and acknowledge the contributions of the host country and its colleagues, ethical issues continue to arise. Recently, several disputes have arisen over the ownership of human remains, artifacts, and heritage items (see Barker 2018). Lawsuits against museums by groups seeking the repatriation of remains and artifacts have become common (see Rothstein 2006). Peru, for instance, sued Yale University to recover objects removed during the exploration of Machu Picchu (an important Peruvian archaeological and tourist site) by Yale explorer Hiram Bingham in 1912. Native Australians have argued that images of native Australian fauna, such as the emu and kangaroo, belong exclusively to the Aboriginal people (Brown 2003). Michael F. Brown (2003) describes efforts by Hopi Indians to control and restrict historic photos of secret religious ceremonies.

Many anthropologists have worked to represent or assist indigenous groups, for example, when disasters strike or when disputes arise with external agents. Sometimes, however, issues involving access to, or ownership of, physical and archaeological remains place anthropologists and indigenous people in opposing camps. The Native American Graves Protection and Repatriation Act (NAGPRA) gives ownership of Native American remains to Native Americans. Hundreds of thousands of Native American remains are said to be in American museums (see Skeates 2017). NAGPRA requires museums to return remains and artifacts to any tribe (nation) that requests them and can prove a "cultural affiliation" between itself and the remains or artifact.

The 1996 discovery in Washington state (on federal land) of a skeleton dubbed "Kennewick Man" led to a legal case between anthropologists and five Native American nations with homelands in the area where Kennewick Man was discovered. The anthropologists wanted to conduct a thorough scientific study of the skeleton, which is one of the oldest (between 9,500 and 8,500 years old) and best preserved human remains ever discovered in North America. What might its anatomy and DNA reveal about the early settlement of the Americas? The Umatilla Indians and their allies in four other Native American nations believe they have always occupied the region where the skeleton was found. In their view, Kennewick Man, whom they call "the Ancient One," was their ancestor, and they sought to rebury him with dignity and without contamination from scientific testing.

In 2002, U.S. Magistrate Judge John Jelderks ruled that the Kennewick remains could be studied scientifically, finding little initial evidence linking the find to any identifiable contemporary group or culture. His ruling, later backed by a federal appeals court, cleared the way for scientists to begin their study (see Burke et al. 2008; Owsley and Jantz 2014; Walker and Owsley 2012). One result of that study was the discovery that an identifiable genetic connection did exist between the Ancient One and one of the tribes that claimed him as their ancestor.

Analysis by Danish scientists of DNA extracted from a finger fragment revealed the closest known genetic relatives of the Ancient One to be members of the Confederated Tribes of the Colville Reservation, one of the claimant tribes, located just 200 miles from the burial site. Admirably, the geneticists who analyzed the Ancient One's DNA worked with those tribes, seeking their consent and collaboration. Colville tribal members donated their own DNA, which helped establish their connection to the Ancient One. On December 19, 2016, President Barack Obama signed an act directing the return of the Ancient One to the five Native American nations living in the area where the skeleton was found 20 years earlier (Colwell 2017).

## The Code of Ethics

To guide its members in making decisions involving ethics and values, the American Anthropological Association (AAA) offers a Code of Ethics (http://ethics.americananthro.org/category/statement/.) The most recent code, approved in 2012, points out that anthropologists have obligations to their scholarly field, to the wider society and culture, and to the human species, other species, and the environment. Like physicians who take the Hippocratic oath, the anthropologist's first concern should be to *do no harm* to the people, animals, or artifacts being studied (see Borofsky and Hutson 2016). The stated aims of the AAA code are to offer guidelines and to promote discussion and education, rather than to investigate possible misconduct. The code addresses several contexts in which anthropologists work. Some of its main points are highlighted in the next paragraph.

Anthropologists should be open and honest about their research projects with all parties affected by the research. Those parties should be informed about the nature, procedures, purpose(s), potential impacts, and source(s) of support for the research. Researchers should pay attention to proper relations between themselves as guests and the host nations and communities where they work. The AAA does not advise anthropologists to avoid taking stands on issues. Indeed, seeking to shape actions and policies may be as ethically justifiable as inaction.

## Anthropologists and the Military

The AAA has deemed it of "paramount importance" that anthropologists study the causes of terrorism and violence. How should such studies be conducted? What ethical issues might arise?

Consider a Pentagon program, Project Minerva, initiated late in the George W. Bush administration, designed to draw on social science expertise to combat national security threats. Project Minerva sought scholars to translate documents captured in Iraq, study China's shifting political scene, and explain ongoing violence in Afghanistan (Cohen 2008). Project Minerva and related programs raised concerns that governments might use anthropological research in ethically problematic ways.

More recently, anthropologists have been especially critical of the Pentagon's Human Terrain System (HTS) program. Launched in February 2007, HTS embedded anthropologists and other social scientists in military teams in Iraq and Afghanistan (see Jaschik 2015; Sims 2016). On October 31, 2007, the AAA Executive Board issued a statement of disapproval of HTS—outlining how HTS violates the AAA Code of Ethics (see https://www.americananthro.org/ConnectWithAAA/Content.aspx?ItemNumber=1626). The board noted that HTS had placed anthropologists, as contractors with the U.S. military, in war zones, where they were expected to collect cultural and social data for use by the military. The ethical concerns raised by these activities include the following:

1. It may be impossible for anthropologists in war zones to identify themselves as anthropologists, as distinct from military personnel. This constrains their ethical responsibility as anthropologists to disclose who they are and what they are doing.
2. HTS anthropologists were asked to negotiate relations among several groups, including local populations and the military units in which they (the anthropologists) were embedded. Responsibilities to their units might conflict with their obligations to their local consultants. This could interfere with the obligation, stipulated in the AAA Code of Ethics, to do no harm.
3. In an active war zone, it is difficult for local people to give "informed consent" without feeling coerced to provide information. As a result, "voluntary informed consent" (as stipulated by the AAA Code of Ethics) is compromised.
4. Information supplied by HTS anthropologists to military field commanders could help target specific groups for military action. Such use of fieldwork-derived information would violate the AAA Code of Ethics stipulation that those studied not be harmed.
5. The identification of anthropology and anthropologists with the U.S. military could indirectly (through suspicion of "guilt by association") endanger the research, and even the personal safety, of other anthropologists and their consultants throughout the world.

How do you think anthropologists should study warfare, conflict, and terrorism?

## Anthropology Today *A Workshop in Genomics for Indigenous Peoples*

The "Anthropology Today" box on cultural heritage in Chapter 2 discussed how every human group has a shared heritage, and that members of that group are its proper guardians. The same applies to a group's biological heritage, including its DNA and physical (ancestral) remains. Historically, indigenous peoples, including Native Americans, lost their lands and sovereignty and often were forced to give up their religion, language, and cultural practices. Their cultural sites, artifacts, and practices, as well as their physical remains, were appropriated and treated as part of the public domain, to be used freely by others, for example, in museums. Contemporary Native American communities properly want to assert and ensure that they control access to their heritage (Nicholas 2018).

Today, some indigenous communities, including the Navajo Nation, refuse to participate in any genetic research, and many tribes prohibit research on ancestral remains. Suspicion of science is understandable, given the history of scientists' collaboration with U.S. expansion at the expense of Native Americans. Kim TallBear, an anthropologist at the University of Alberta in Edmonton, Canada, and a member of the Sisseton Wahpeton Oyate in the Dakotas, recounts how, during westward expansion, grave robbers would collect Native bodies from battlefields, boil them down to bone, and send those bones to scientists and collectors in the eastern United States. Many of those skeletons ended up in museums, often curated by researchers who believed in the biological inferiority of non-White people (Wade 2018a). Indigenous communities still see science as part of that power structure.

In 1996, Ripan Malhi, then a graduate student in molecular anthropology at the University of California, Davis, was eager to use new genetic techniques to study the origins and population history of Native American groups (see Wade 2018). Malhi began by analyzing DNA from previously collected blood samples, but he needed additional samples for comparison. He began his quest to collect more genetic samples by giving a lecture about DNA to a group of Native Americans on a reservation in Northern California. From them, he hoped to gather dozens of DNA samples (using cheek swabs). When he finished his lecture, however, the first question he was asked was "Why should we trust you?" With suspicion of scientists permeating the room, Malhi was unable to collect samples.

Native Americans are well aware that scientists previously have used their biological samples without permission and have resisted returning samples, data, artifacts, and human remains to those who claim them. Many indigenous communities, like the Navajo, have responded by severely restricting scientists' access to their bodies and remains.

Malhi, now a molecular anthropology professor at the University of Illinois, hopes to remedy the problematic relationship between science and indigenous communities. He cofounded (with Kim TallBear and others) the Summer Internship for Indigenous Peoples in Genomics (SING), an annual weeklong program funded by (among others) the National Institutes of Health (NIH) and the National Science Foundation (NSF). The program, which instructs indigenous scientists in genomics, has trained more than 100 graduates since its inception in 2011 (see Wade 2018a).

*continued*

## Anthropology Today *continued*

Members of the Havasupai tribe pray over blood samples at Arizona State University in Tempe, Arizona on April 20, 2010. The university returned the blood samples, previously taken without consent, and agreed to pay $700,000 and provide other forms of assistance to Havasupai tribe members. The Havasupai had to fight for access to their samples, in an episode that fueled suspicion between scientists and several Native American communities. Jim Wilson/The New York Times/Redux Pictures

As described on SING's website (https://sing.igb.illinois.edu/), the annual workshop promotes discussions of the uses, misuses, and limitations of genomics as a tool for indigenous communities. It also helps train indigenous peoples in concepts and methods currently used in genomics. At a typical SING workshop, each day begins and ends with indigenous stories, songs, and prayers. At the 2018 workshop, a major activity was for participants to extract and analyze their own mitochondrial DNA (mtDNA). They also examined and critiqued informed consent forms used by researchers, and considered the range of questions that DNA can and cannot answer (Wade 2018a).

A key role of SING has been to raise awareness of indigenous concerns and how to prioritize them in research. In 2018, SING alumni and faculty published ethical guidelines for genomic studies. Those guidelines call for intense community engagement, especially in identifying research questions, determining publication goals, and deciding how to collect and handle samples and data (Wade 2018a).

SING has also helped forge new research partnerships. Through the program, Deborah Bolnick, an anthropological geneticist at the University of Connecticut, has established a collaborative research project with indigenous partners in the southern United States. One goal of that project is to see how mtDNA, which is inherited only through women, lines up with the communities' matrilineal clans (in which descent is traced only through women). The hope is that mtDNA analysis may help restore clan identities to community members whose knowledge of clan ties and history has been lost (see Wade 2018).

As a final illustration of a fruitful collaboration between scientists and Native Americans, consider the case of Spirit Cave, Nevada. As reported in November 2018, the recent extraction and analysis of ancient DNA from a burial in Spirit Cave confirmed a line of kinship that spans more than 10,000 years. The genome of the man buried in Spirit Cave (11,000 B.P.) proved to be closely related to remains from the nearby Lovelock Cave (dated to a mere 600 B.P.). The local tribe, the Fallon Paiute-Shoshone, had first learned of the Spirit Cave body (which had been unearthed in 1940 and stored in a museum) in 1996. The new genetic information prompted the Bureau of Land Management to turn over the skeleton to the tribe, which had sought its repatriation for years. The tribe buried their ancestor at an undisclosed location in 2016 (Wade 2018b; Zimmer 2018b).

## Summary

1. As they study the past, archaeologists and biological anthropologists may share research topics and methods and work together in multidisciplinary teams. Remote sensing may be used to locate ancient footpaths, roads, canals, and irrigation systems, which can then be investigated on the ground. Archaeologists combine both local (excavation) and regional (systematic survey) perspectives. Sites are excavated because they are in danger of being destroyed or because they address specific research interests. There are many kinds of archaeology, such as historical, classical, and underwater archaeology.

2. The fossil record is not a representative sample of all the plants and animals that have ever lived. Hard parts, such as bones and teeth, preserve better than soft parts, such as flesh and skin. Stratigraphy and radiometric techniques are used to date fossils. Carbon-14 ($^{14}$C) dating is most effective with fossils less than 40,000 years old. Potassium-argon (K/A) dating can be used for fossils older than 500,000 years. Molecular anthropology uses genetic analysis (of DNA sequences) to assess and date evolutionary relationships.

3. Within biological anthropology, bone biology is the study of bone genetics; cell structure; growth, development, and decay; and patterns of movement. Paleopathology is the study of disease and injury in skeletons from archaeological sites. Anthropometry, the measurement of human body parts and dimensions, is done on living people and on skeletal remains from sites. Studies of primates suggest hypotheses about behavior and adaptations that humans do or do not share with our nearest relatives—as well as with our hominid ancestors.

4. Ethnographic methods include firsthand and participant observation, rapport build-ing, interviews, genealogies, work with key consultants or informants, the collection of life histories, the discovery of local beliefs and perceptions, problem-oriented and longitudinal research, and team research. Ethnographers work in communities and form personal relationships with local people as they study their lives.

5. An interview schedule is a form an ethnographer completes as he or she visits a se-ries of households. Key consultants, or informants, teach us about particular areas of local life. Life histories document personal experiences with culture and culture change. Genealogical information is particularly useful in societies in which princi-ples of kinship and marriage organize social and political life. Emic approaches fo-cus on native perceptions and explanations. Etic approaches give priority to the ethnographer's own observations and conclusions. Longitudinal research is the sys-tematic study of an area or a population over time. Longitudinal, team, and multi-sited ethnographic research are increasingly common.

6. Traditionally, anthropologists worked in small-scale societies; sociologists, in modern nations. Different techniques developed to study these different kinds of societies. Anthropologists do their fieldwork in communities and study the totality of social life. Sociologists use surveys and study samples to make inferences about a larger population. Anthropologists may employ ethnographic procedures to study cities, towns, or rural areas.

7. Because science exists in society, and in the context of law and ethics, anthropolo-gists can't study things simply because they happen to be interesting or of scientific value. Anthropologists have obligations to their scholarly field, to the wider society and culture (including that of the host country), and to the human species, other species, and the environment. The AAA Code of Ethics offers ethical guidelines for anthropologists. Ethical problems often arise when anthropologists work for govern-ments, especially the military.

## Think Like an Anthropologist

1. Imagine yourself as a biological anthropologist working as part of a team at an African site. What other academic disciplines might be represented on your team? What kinds of jobs would there be for team members, and where would the members be recruited? What might happen to the fossils and other materials that were recov-ered? Who would be the authors of the scientific papers describing any discovery made by the team?

2. What do you see as the strengths and weaknesses of ethnography compared with survey research? Which provides more accurate data? Might one be better for find-ing questions, while the other is better for finding answers? Or does it depend on the context of research?

3. Many of the ethical issues that affect the work of anthropologists have some legal dimension, whether in their own country, in another country, or even among several nations. Have you thought about law as a possible future career? (If not, think of a friend who has.) Write a convincing argument about why anthropology could be a valuable tool for a lawyer.

## Key Terms

absolute dating, *51*
anthropometry, *54*
bone biology, *53*
cultural consultant, *59*
emic, *59*
etic, *59*
excavation, *49*
fossils, *47*
genealogical method, *58*
informed consent, *64*

interview schedule, *57*
key cultural consultants, *58*
life history, *59*
longitudinal research, *60*
molecular anthropology, *52*
paleoanthropology, *47*
paleontology, *46*
paleopathology, *53*

participant observation, *56*
relative dating, *50*
sample, *57*
stratigraphy, *51*
survey research, *62*
systematic survey, *49*
taphonomy, *50*
variables, *63*

# Chapter 4

# Evolution, Genetics, and Human Variation

## Evolution

Compared with other animals, humans have uniquely varied ways—cultural and biological—of adapting. Exemplifying *cultural* adaptation, we manipulate our artifacts and behavior in response to environmental conditions. We turn up thermostats or travel to Florida in the winter. We use air conditioning or visit the mountains to escape the summer's heat. Although such reliance on culture has increased during human evolution, people haven't stopped adapting biologically. As in other species, human populations adapt genetically in response to environmental forces, and individuals react physiologically to stresses. Thus, when we work in the sun, sweating occurs spontaneously, cooling the skin and reducing the temperature of subsurface blood vessels. We are ready now for a more detailed look at the principles that determine human biological adaptation, variation, and change.

# Natural History before Darwin

During the 18th century, many scholars became interested in biological diversity, human origins, and our place among life forms. At that time, the commonly accepted explanation for the origin of species came from Genesis, the first book of the Bible: God created all life during six days of Creation. According to **creationism**, biological similarities and differences originated at the Creation. Characteristics of life forms were seen as immutable; they could not change. Through calculations based on genealogies in the Bible, the biblical scholars James Ussher and John Lightfoot even purported to trace the Creation to a very specific time: October 23, 4004 B.C., at 9 A.M.

The 18th-century Swedish naturalist Carolus Linnaeus developed the first comprehensive (and still influential) classification, or taxonomy, of plants and animals, based on similarities and differences in their physical characteristics. He used traits such as the backbone to distinguish vertebrates from invertebrates and mammary glands to distinguish mammals from birds. Linnaeus viewed the differences between life forms as part of the Creator's orderly plan. He thought that biological similarities and differences had been set at the time of Creation and had not changed.

Fossil discoveries during the 18th and 19th centuries raised doubts about creationism. Fossils showed that different kinds of life once had existed. If all life had originated at the same time, why weren't ancient species still around? Why weren't contemporary plants and animals found in the fossil record? A modified explanation combining creationism with **catastrophism** arose to replace the original doctrine. In this view, fires, floods, and other catastrophes, including the biblical flood involving Noah's ark, had destroyed ancient species. After each destructive event, God had created again, leading to contemporary species. To explain certain clear similarities between fossils and modern animals, the catastrophists argued that some ancient species had managed to survive in isolated areas. For example, after the biblical flood, the progeny of the animals saved on Noah's ark spread throughout the world.

The alternative to creationism and catastrophism was *transformism*, better known as **evolution**. Evolutionists believe that new species arise from old ones through a long and gradual process of transformation, or *descent with modification* over the generations. Charles Darwin became the best known of the evolutionists. However, he benefited from the work of earlier scholars, including his own grandfather. In a book called *Zoonomia,* published in 1794, Erasmus Darwin had proclaimed the common ancestry of all animal species.

Another major influence on Charles Darwin was Sir Charles Lyell, the father of geology (see Eldredge and Pearson 2010). During Darwin's famous voyage to South America aboard the *Beagle,* he read Lyell's influential book *Principles of Geology* (1837/1969), which exposed him to Lyell's principle of **uniformitarianism**. Uniformitarianism states that the present is the key to the past. Thus, in the present we observe natural forces at work all around us. Given enough time, those same forces can produce major changes. Such natural forces as rainfall, mudslides, earthquakes, and volcanic action have gradually built and modified geological features such as mountain ranges. The Earth's structure has been transformed gradually through natural forces operating for millions of years.

Uniformitarianism was a necessary building block for evolutionary theory. It cast serious doubt on the belief that the world was only 6,000 years old. It would take much longer for such ordinary forces as rain and wind to produce major geological changes. The longer time span also allowed enough time for the biological changes that fossil discoveries were revealing. Darwin applied the ideas of uniformitarianism and long-term transformation to living things. He argued that all life forms are ultimately related and that the number of species has increased over time.

## Evolution: Theory and Fact

Darwin proposed a *theory of evolution* in the strict sense. A **theory** is a set of logically connected ideas formulated to explain something. A theory suggests patterns, connections, and relationships that future research may confirm.

Evolution as a scientific theory is a central organizing principle of modern biology and anthropology. Evolution, however, is both a theory and a fact. Factually, there is absolutely no doubt that biological evolution has occurred and is still occurring. To be sure, scientists do debate the *details* of particular evolutionary processes and events. Nevertheless, they accept certain facts, as the following examples illustrate. Fact: Our Earth with liquid water is more than 3.6 billion years old. Fact: Cellular life has been around for at least half that time. Fact: Multicellular life is at least 800 million years old. Facts: All life forms arose from ancestral forms that were different. Birds arose from nonbirds, and humans arose from nonhumans (see Moran 1993). Fact: Viruses and other microorganisms mutate all the time, posing a problem for public health officials seeking to control disease transmission (see this chapter's "Anthropology Today").

Although the *fact* that evolution has occurred was recognized before Charles Darwin, for example, by Erasmus Darwin, the *theory* of evolution, through natural selection (*how* evolution occurred), was Charles Darwin's major contribution. Actually, natural selection was not Darwin's unique discovery. Working independently, the British naturalist Alfred Russel Wallace had reached a similar conclusion (Costa 2014; Shermer 2011; Smith and Beccaloni 2010). In a joint paper read to London's Linnaean Society in 1858, Darwin and Wallace made their discovery public. Darwin's book *On the Origin of Species (by Means of Natural Selection)* (1859/2018) offered much fuller documentation of natural selection as the prime mechanism of biological evolution.

**Natural selection** is the process by which the life forms that are best suited to survive and reproduce in a particular environment do so in greater numbers than other members of the same population. Natural selection is most obvious when there is competition for strategic resources among members of a population. Such resources include those that are necessary for the survival of the individual, such as food and space, along with those that are necessary for the survival of the species—that is, mates. Members of a population compete not only for food but also for mates—for the right to reproduce. More than survival of the fittest, natural selection is differential reproductive success. You can win the competition for food and space, but without a mate, you have no impact on the future of the species.

For natural selection to work on any population, there must be variety within that population, as there always is. The giraffe's neck can illustrate how natural selection works on variety within a population. In any group of giraffes, there always is variation

Charles Darwin (1809–1882), the English naturalist who is famous for his theory of evolution by means of natural selection, as developed in his 1859 book *On the Origin of Species (by Means of Natural Selection)*, whose title page is shown here with Darwin's photo.
duncan1890/Getty Images

in neck length. When food is adequate, the animals have no problem feeding themselves. But when dietary foliage is not as abundant, giraffes with longer necks have an advantage. They can feed off the higher branches. If this ability permits longer-necked giraffes to survive and reproduce even slightly more effectively than shorter-necked ones, giraffes with longer necks will transmit more of their genetic material to future generations.

An incorrect alternative to this (Darwinian) explanation would be the inheritance of acquired characteristics. That is the idea that in each generation individual giraffes strain their necks to reach just a bit higher. This straining somehow modifies their genetic material. Over generations of strain, the average neck gradually gets longer through the accumulation of small increments of neck length acquired during the lifetime of each generation of giraffes. This is *not* how evolution works. If it did work in this way, weight lifters could expect to produce especially muscular babies. Evolution works as the process of natural selection takes advantage of the variety that already is present in a population.

Evolution through natural selection continues today. One classic recent example of natural selection is the change in the coloring of the peppered moth that occurred in England following industrialization. The peppered moth naturally occurs in both light or dark variations (in either case with black speckles, thus the name "peppered"). Before the Industrial Revolution in Great Britain, the light-colored variety, which

A speckled (peppered) moth and a black one. Which environment would favor each of these variants? The Natural History Museum/The Image Works

camouflaged effectively against the light color of most tree bark, was prevalent. During the 1800s, as industrial pollution increased, soot covered buildings and trees, which turned darker as a result. The lighter moths now stood out against these darker backgrounds and were easily visible to their predators, creating a major selective disadvantage. The dark moths, by contrast, blended in with the soot. As a result, the darker moths survived and reproduced in greater numbers than lighter moths, and became the dominant moth for the industrial age. In the 20th century, the air quality in Great Britain improved, the soot disappeared from trees and buildings, and the lighter moths once again became the predominant species. We see here how natural selection favors darker moths in polluted environments and lighter-colored moths in nonindustrial or less polluted environments.

The purpose of evolutionary theory is to provide explanations. Explanations rely on associations and theories. An association is an observed relationship between two or more variables, such as the length of a giraffe's neck and the number of its offspring, or an increase in the frequency of dark moths as industrial pollution spreads. A theory is more general; it suggests associations and attempts to explain them. Something, such as the giraffe's long neck, is explained if it illustrates a general principle or an association, such as the concept of adaptive advantage. The truth of a scientific statement (e.g., evolution occurs because of differential reproductive success due to variation within the population) is confirmed by repeated observations.

## Genetics

Charles Darwin recognized that for natural selection to work there must be variety in the population undergoing selection. Documenting and explaining variety among humans—human biological diversity—is one of anthropology's major concerns.

Genetics, a science that emerged after Darwin, helps us understand the causes of biological variation. We now know that DNA (deoxyribonucleic acid) molecules make up genes and chromosomes, which are the basic hereditary units. Biochemical changes (mutations) in DNA provide much of the variety on which natural selection operates. Through sexual reproduction, recombination of the genetic traits of mother and father in each generation leads to new arrangements of the hereditary units received from each parent. Such genetic recombination also adds variety on which natural selection may operate.

## Mendel's Experiments

In 1856, in a monastery garden, the Austrian monk Gregor Mendel began a series of experiments that were to reveal the basic principles of genetics. Mendel studied the inheritance of seven traits in pea plants. For each trait there were only two forms. For example, plants were either tall (6–7 feet) or short (9–18 inches), with no intermediate forms. The ripe seeds could be either smooth and round, or wrinkled. The peas could be either yellow or green, with no intermediate colors.

When Mendel began his experiments, one of the prevailing beliefs about heredity was what has been called the "paint-pot" theory. According to this theory, the traits of the two parents blended in their children, much as two pigments are blended in a can of paint. Children therefore were a unique mixture of their parents, and when those children reproduced, their traits would blend inextricably with those of their mates. However, prevailing notions about heredity also recognized that occasionally the traits of one parent might swamp those of the other. If children looked far more like their mother than their father, people might say that her "blood" was stronger than his. Occasionally, too, there would be a "throwback," a child who was the image of his or her grandparent or who possessed a distinctive chin or nose characteristic of a whole line of descent.

Through his experiments with pea plants, Mendel discovered that heredity is determined by discrete particles or units. Although traits could disappear in one generation, they reemerged in their original form in later generations. For example, Mendel crossbred pure strains of tall and short plants. Their offspring were all tall. This was the first descending, or first filial, generation, designated $F_1$. Mendel then interbred the plants of the $F_1$ generation to produce a generation of grandchildren, the $F_2$ generation. In this generation, short plants reappeared. Among thousands of plants in the $F_2$ generation, there was approximately one short plant for every three tall ones.

From similar results with the other six traits, Mendel concluded that although a **dominant** form could mask the other form—the **recessive**—in *hybrid*, or mixed, individuals, the recessive trait was not destroyed; it wasn't even changed. Recessive traits would appear in unaltered form in later generations because genetic traits were inherited as discrete units.

These basic genetic units that Mendel described were factors (now called genes or alleles) located on **chromosomes**. Chromosomes are arranged in matching (homologous) pairs. Humans have 46 chromosomes, arranged in 23 pairs, one chromosome in each pair from the father and the other from the mother. The genetic testing service 23andMe takes its name from these 23 chromosome pairs.

**FIGURE 4.1**
**Simplified Representation of a Normal Chromosome Pair**
Letters indicate genes; superscripts indicate alleles.

McGraw-Hill Education

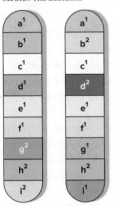

For simplicity, a chromosome may be pictured as a surface with several positions (see Figure 4.1), to each of which we assign a lowercase letter. Each position is a **gene**. Each gene determines, wholly or partially, a particular biological trait, such as whether one's blood is type A, B, or O. **Alleles** (e.g., $b^1$ and $b^2$ in Figure 4.1) are biochemically different forms of a given gene. In humans, A, B, AB, and O blood types reflect different combinations of alleles of a particular gene.

In Mendel's experiments, the seven contrasting traits were determined by genes located on seven different pairs of chromosomes. The gene for height occurred in one of the seven pairs. When Mendel crossbred pure tall and pure short plants to produce his $F_1$ generation, each of the offspring received an allele for tallness (T) from one parent and one for shortness (t) from the other. These offspring were mixed, or **heterozygous**, with respect to height; each had two dissimilar alleles of that gene. Their parents, in contrast, had been **homozygous**, possessing two identical alleles of that gene (see Hartl 2014).

In the next generation ($F_2$), after the mixed plants were interbred, short plants reappeared in the ratio of one short to three talls. Knowing that shorts produced only shorts, Mendel could assume that they were genetically pure. Another fourth of the $F_2$ plants produced only talls. The remaining half, like the $F_1$ generation, were heterozygous; when interbred, they produced three talls for each short (see Figure 4.2).

Dominance produces a distinction between **genotype**, one's hereditary makeup, and **phenotype**, one's expressed physical characteristics. Genotype is what is written in your genes; phenotype is how you appear. Mendel's peas had three genotypes—TT, Tt, and tt—but only two phenotypes—tall and short. Because of dominance, the heterozygous plants were just as tall as the genetically pure tall ones.

Although some human genetic traits follow Mendelian laws, with only two forms—dominant and recessive—other traits are determined differently. For instance, three alleles determine whether our blood type is A, B, AB, or O. People with two alleles for type O have that blood type. However, if they received an allele for either A or B from one parent

**FIGURE 4.2    Punnett Squares of a Homozygous Cross and a Heterozygous Cross**
These squares show how genotypic and phenotypic ratios of the $F_1$ and $F_2$ generation are generated.

McGraw-Hill Education

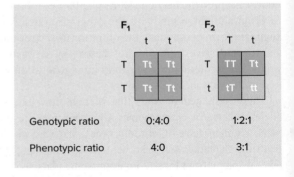

and one for O from the other, they will have blood type A or B. In other words, A and B are both dominant over O. A and B are said to be *codominant*. If people inherit an allele for A from one parent and one for B from the other, they will have type AB blood, which is chemically different from the other varieties, A, B, and O. These three alleles produce four phenotypes—A, B, AB, and O—and six different genotypes—OO, AO, BO, AA, BB, and AB (see Figure 4.3). There are fewer phenotypes than genotypes because O is recessive to both A and B.

**FIGURE 4.3** **Determinants of Phenotypes (Blood Groups) in the ABO System**
The four phenotypes—A, B, AB, and O—are indicated in parentheses and by color.

McGraw-Hill Education

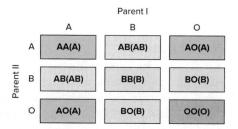

## Independent Assortment

Through additional experiments, Mendel also formulated his law of **independent assortment**. He discovered that traits are inherited independently of one another. For example, he bred pure round, yellow peas with pure wrinkled, green ones. All the $F_1$ generation peas were round and yellow, the dominant forms. But when Mendel interbred the $F_1$ generation to produce the $F_2$, four phenotypes turned up. Round greens and wrinkled yellows had been added to the original round yellows and wrinkled greens. The independent assortment and recombination of genetic traits provide one of the main ways by which variety is produced in any population.

An organism develops from a fertilized egg, or *zygote*, created by the union of two sex cells, one from each parent. The zygote grows rapidly through **mitosis**, or ordinary cell division, which continues as the organism grows. The process by which sex cells are produced is called **meiosis**. Unlike ordinary cell division, in which two cells emerge from one, in meiosis four cells are produced from one. Each has half the genetic material of the original cell. In human meiosis, four cells, each with 23 individual chromosomes, are produced from an original cell with 23 pairs.

With fertilization of egg by sperm, the father's 23 chromosomes combine with the mother's 23 to re-create the pairs in every generation. However, the chromosomes sort independently, so that a child's genotype is a random combination of the DNA of its four grandparents. It is conceivable that one grandparent will contribute very little to his or her grandchild's heredity. Independent assortment of chromosomes is a major source of variety because the parents' genotypes can be assorted in $2^{23}$, or more than 8 million, different ways.

# Population Genetics and Mechanisms of Genetic Evolution

**Population genetics** studies the genetic attributes of populations within which breeding normally takes place (see Archibald 2018; Brooker 2019; Hartl 2014; Nielsen and Slatkin 2013). The term **gene pool** encompasses all the DNA, alleles, genes, chromosomes, and genotypes within a breeding population—the "pool" of genetic material available. When population geneticists use the term *evolution*, they have a more specific definition in mind than the one given earlier ("descent with modification over the generations"). Geneticists define **genetic evolution** as change in gene frequencies (i.e., in the frequency of alleles in a breeding population) over time, across the generations. The four principal forces or mechanisms that cause genetic evolution are natural selection, mutation, genetic drift, and gene flow (see Relethford 2012; Templeton 2019).

## Natural Selection

Natural selection remains the first and best explanation for evolution, including genetic evolution. Essential to understanding evolution through natural selection is the distinction between genotype and phenotype. *Genotype* refers just to hereditary factors—genes and chromosomes. Phenotype—an organism's evident or manifest biological characteristics—develops over the years as environmental forces influence that organism. (See the photo of the identical twins, below. Identical twins have exactly the same genotype, but their actual biology, their phenotypes, will differ if they grow up in different environments.) Furthermore, because of dominance, individuals with different genotypes may

Separated at birth, identical twin sisters Anais Bordier and Samantha Futerman found each other 25 years later, via Facebook. Here they tell their story on a British morning TV show. Ken McKay/ITV/REX/Shutterstock

have identical phenotypes (like Mendel's tall pea plants). Natural selection can operate only on phenotype—on what is exposed, not on what is hidden. For example, a harmful recessive gene cannot be eliminated from the gene pool if it is masked by a favored dominant.

Phenotype includes not only outward physical appearance but also internal organs, tissues, and cells and physiological processes and systems. Many biological reactions to foods, disease, heat, cold, sunlight, and other environmental factors are not automatic, genetically programmed responses but the product of years of exposure to particular environmental stresses. Human biology is not totally set at birth; rather, it has considerable *plasticity*. That is, it is changeable, being affected by the environmental forces, such as diet and altitude, that we experience as we grow up (see Beckett 2019; Cameron and Bogin 2012).

The environment works on the genotype to build the phenotype, and certain phenotypes do better in some environments than other phenotypes do. However, remember that favored phenotypes can be produced by different genotypes. Because natural selection works only on genes that are expressed, maladaptive recessives can be eliminated only when they occur in homozygous form. When a heterozygote carries a maladaptive recessive, its effects are masked by the favored dominant. The process of perfecting the fit between organisms and their environment is gradual.

## Directional Selection

After several generations of selection, gene frequencies will change. Adaptation through natural selection will have occurred. Once that happens, those traits that have proved to be the most **adaptive** (favored by natural selection) in that environment will be selected again and again from generation to generation. Given such *directional selection*, or long-term selection of the same trait(s), maladaptive recessive alleles will be eliminated from the gene pool.

Directional selection will continue as long as environmental forces stay the same. However, if the environment changes, new selective forces start working, favoring different phenotypes. This also happens when part of the population colonizes a new environment. Selection in the changed, or new, environment continues until a new equilibrium is reached. Then there is directional selection until another environmental change or migration takes place. Over millions of years, such a process of successive adaptation to a series of environments has led to biological modification and branching. The process of natural selection has led to the tremendous array of plant and animal forms found in the world today.

Selection also operates through competition for mates. Males may openly compete for females, or females may choose to mate with particular males because they have desirable traits. Obviously, such traits vary from species to species. Familiar examples include color in birds; male birds, such as cardinals, tend to be more brightly colored than females are. Colorful males have a selective advantage because females like them better. Over the generations, as females have opted for colorful mates, the alleles responsible for color have built up in the species. **Sexual selection**, based on differential success in mating, is the term for this process in which certain traits of one sex are selected because of advantages they confer in winning mates.

Selection operates *only* on traits that are present in a population. A favorable mutation *may* occur, but a population doesn't normally come up with a new genotype or phenotype just because one is needed or desirable. Many species have become extinct because they weren't sufficiently varied to adapt to environmental shifts.

## Stabilizing Selection

We've seen that natural selection *reduces* variety in a population through directional selection—by favoring one trait or allele over another. Selective forces also can work to *maintain* variety through *stabilizing selection*, by favoring a **balanced polymorphism**, in which the frequencies of two or more alleles of a gene remain constant from generation to generation. This may be because the phenotypes they produce are neutral, or equally favored, or equally opposed, by selective forces. Sometimes a particular force favors (or opposes) one allele, while a different but equally effective force favors (or opposes) the other allele.

One well-studied example involves two alleles, $Hb^A$ and $Hb^S$, that affect the production of the beta strain (Hb) of human hemoglobin. Hemoglobin, which is located in our red blood cells, carries oxygen from our lungs to the rest of the body via the circulatory system. The allele that produces normal hemoglobin is $Hb^A$. Another allele, $Hb^S$, produces a different hemoglobin. Individuals who are homozygous for $Hb^S$ suffer from *sickle-cell anemia*. Such anemia, in which the red blood cells are shaped like crescents, or sickles, is associated with a disease that usually is fatal. This condition interferes with the blood's ability to store oxygen. It increases the heart's burden by clogging the small blood vessels.

Given the fatal disease associated with $Hb^S$, geneticists were surprised to discover that certain populations in Africa, India, and the Mediterranean had very high frequencies of $Hb^S$. In some West African populations, that frequency is around 20 percent. Researchers eventually discovered that both $Hb^A$ and $Hb^S$ are maintained because selective forces in certain environments favor the heterozygote over either homozygote.

Initially, scientists wondered why, if most $Hb^S$ homozygotes died before they reached reproductive age, the harmful allele hadn't been eliminated. Why was its frequency so high? The answer turned out to lie in the heterozygote's greater fitness. Only people who were homozygous for $Hb^S$ died from sickle-cell anemia. Heterozygotes suffered very mild anemia, if any. On the other hand, although people homozygous for $Hb^A$ did not suffer from anemia, they were much more susceptible to *malaria*—a killer disease that continues to plague *Homo sapiens* in the tropics.

The heterozygote, with one sickle-cell allele and one normal one, was the fittest phenotype for a malarial environment. Heterozygotes have enough abnormal hemoglobin, in which malaria parasites cannot thrive, to protect against malaria. They also have enough normal hemoglobin to fend off sickle-cell anemia. The $Hb^S$ allele has been maintained in these populations because heterozygotes survived and reproduced in greater numbers than did either homozygote.

This example demonstrates the relativity of evolution through natural selection: Adaptation and fitness are in relation to specific environments. Traits are not adaptive or maladaptive for all times and places. Even harmful alleles can be selected if heterozygotes have an advantage. Moreover, as the environment changes, favored phenotypes and gene frequencies can change. In malaria-free environments, normal-hemoglobin homozygotes reproduce more effectively than heterozygotes do. With no malaria, the frequency of $Hb^S$ declines, because $Hb^S$ homozygotes can't compete in survival and reproduction with the other types. This has happened in areas of West Africa where malaria has been reduced through drainage programs and insecticides. Selection against $Hb^S$ also has occurred in the United States among Americans descended from West Africans.

## Mutation

The second force or mechanism of genetic evolution is **mutation**–a change in the DNA molecules from which genes and chromosomes are made. Mutations are the most important source of variety on which natural selection operates. If a mutation occurs in a sex cell that joins with another in a fertilized egg, the new organism will carry that mutation in every cell. Because DNA directs protein building, a protein (such as a hemoglobin) that differs from that of the parent may be produced in the child. The form of hemoglobin associated with sickle-cell anemia is caused by a genetically minor (but phenotypically major) difference between normal individuals and those with the disease.

Another form of mutation is *chromosomal rearrangement*. Pieces of a chromosome can break off, turn around and reattach, or migrate somewhere else on that chromosome. A mismatch of chromosomes resulting from rearrangement can lead to speciation (the formation of new species). Chromosomes also may fuse. When the ancestors of humans split off from those of chimpanzees around 7-6 million years ago, two ancestral chromosomes fused together in the human line. Humans have 23 chromosome pairs, versus 24 for chimps.

Evolution depends on mutations as a major source of genetically transmitted variety, raw material on which natural selection can work. Alterations in genes and chromosomes may result in entirely new types of organisms, which may demonstrate some new selective advantage. Variants produced through mutation can be especially significant if there is a change in the environment. They may prove to have an advantage they lacked in the old environment, as is illustrated by the spread of the $Hb^S$ allele in malarial environments (see also this chapter's "Anthropology Today" for an example of how a disease microorganism mutates and spreads).

## Random Genetic Drift

A third mechanism of genetic evolution is **random genetic drift**. This term refers to random changes in gene frequencies, most typically seen in small populations. The changes happen by chance rather than because of natural selection. To illustrate how genetic drift works, let's compare the sorting of genes to a game involving a bag of only 12 marbles, 6 red and 6 blue. In step 1, you randomly draw 6 marbles from the bag. Statistically, your chances of drawing 3 reds and 3 blues are less than those of getting 4 of one color and 2 of the other. Step 2 is to fill a new bag with 12 marbles based on the ratio of marbles drawn in step 1. Let's say that in step 1 you drew 4 reds and 2 blues: The step 2 bag will have 8 red marbles and 4 blue ones. Step 3 is to randomly draw 6 marbles from the new bag. Your chances of drawing blues in step 3 are lower than they were in step 1, and the probability of drawing all reds increases. If you do draw all reds, the next bag (step 4) will have only red marbles.

This game is analogous to random genetic drift operating over a few generations. The blue marbles were lost purely by chance. Alleles of a gene also can be lost by chance rather than because of any disadvantage they confer.

Contrast this example with the discussion of how, because of natural selection, dark-colored moths replaced light-colored ones in industrial England. Dark replaced light because of a selective advantage. With our simulation of drift, however, red marbles replaced blue ones by chance, not because either color conferred any selective advantage or disadvantage. *Fixation* refers to the total replacement of blue by red. Imagine a human example in which everyone with brown eyes happens to die in an accident, and all the survivors have blue eyes. Blue has replaced brown merely by chance, not because of natural selection. The history of the human line features a series of small populations, migrations, and fixation due to genetic drift. One cannot understand human origins, human genetic variation, and a host of other important anthropological topics without recognizing the importance of genetic drift.

## Gene Flow

A fourth mechanism of genetic evolution is **gene flow**, the exchange of genetic material between populations of the same species. Gene flow, like mutation, works in conjunction with natural selection by providing variety on which selection can work. Gene flow may consist of direct interbreeding between formerly separated populations of the same species (e.g., Europeans, Africans, and Native Americans in the United States), or it may be indirect.

Consider the following hypothetical case (see Figure 4.4). In a certain part of the world live six local populations of a certain species. $P_1$ is the westernmost of these populations. $P_2$, which interbreeds with $P_1$, is located 50 miles to the east. $P_2$ also interbreeds with $P_3$, located 50 miles east of $P_2$. Assume that each population interbreeds with, and

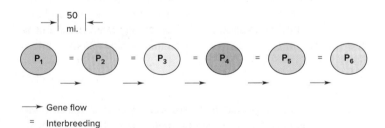

→ Gene flow

= Interbreeding

**FIGURE 4.4    Gene Flow between Local Populations**
$P_1$–$P_6$ are six local populations of the same species. Each interbreeds ($=$) only with its neighbor(s). Although members of $P_6$ never interbreed with $P_1$, $P_6$ and $P_1$ are linked through gene flow. Genetic material that originates in $P_1$ eventually will reach $P_6$, and vice versa, as it is passed from one neighboring population to the next. Because they share genetic material in this way, $P_1$–$P_6$ remain members of the same species. In many species, local populations distributed throughout a larger territory than the 250 miles depicted here are linked through gene flow.

McGraw-Hill Education

only with, the adjacent populations. $P_6$ is located 250 miles from $P_1$ and does not directly interbreed with $P_1$, but it is tied to $P_1$ through the chain of interbreeding that ultimately links all six populations.

Assume further that some allele exists in $P_1$ that isn't particularly advantageous in its environment. Because of gene flow, this allele may be passed on to $P_2$, by it to $P_3$, and so on until it eventually reaches $P_6$. In $P_6$ or along the way, the allele may encounter an environment in which it does have a selective advantage. If this happens, it may serve, like a new mutation, as raw material on which natural selection can operate.

In the long run, natural selection works on the variety within a population, whatever its source—mutation or gene flow. Selection and gene flow have worked together to spread the $Hb^S$ allele in Central Africa. Frequencies of $Hb^S$ in Africa reflect not only the intensity of malaria but also the length of time gene flow has been going on.

Gene flow is important in the study of the origin of species. A **species** is a group of related organisms whose members can interbreed to produce offspring that can live and reproduce. A species has to be able to reproduce itself through time. We know that horses and donkeys belong to different species because their offspring cannot meet the test of long-term survival. A horse and a donkey may breed to produce a mule, but mules are sterile. So are the offspring of lions with tigers. Gene flow tends to prevent **speciation**—the formation of new species—unless subgroups of the same species are separated for a sufficient length of time.

When gene flow is interrupted, isolating the formerly connected subgroups, new species may arise. Imagine that an environmental barrier arises between $P_3$ and $P_4$, so they no longer interbreed. If over time, as a result of isolation, $P_1$, $P_2$, and $P_3$ become incapable of interbreeding with the other three populations, speciation will have occurred.

## Race: A Discredited Concept in Biology

Historically, scientists have approached the study of human biological diversity in two main ways: (1) racial classification (now largely abandoned) versus (2) the current explanatory approach, which focuses on understanding specific differences. *Biological differences are real, important, and apparent to us all.* Modern scientists find it most productive to seek explanations for this diversity, rather than trying to pigeonhole people into categories called races. First we'll consider problems with **racial classification** (the attempt to assign humans to discrete categories—races—based on common ancestry). Then we'll offer some explanations for specific aspects of human biological diversity.

What is race, anyway? In theory, a biological race is a geographically isolated subdivision of a species. Such a *subspecies* would be capable of interbreeding with other subspecies of the same species, but it would not actually do so because of its geographic isolation. Some biologists also use *race* to refer to "breeds," as of dogs or roses. Thus, a pit bull and a Chihuahua would be different races of dogs. Such domesticated "races" have been bred by humans for generations. Humanity (*Homo sapiens*) lacks such races because human populations have not been isolated enough from one another to develop into such discrete groups. Nor have humans experienced controlled breeding like that which has created the various kinds of dogs and roses.

The photos in this chapter illustrate only a small part of the range of human biological diversity. This woman wearing a sun hat is from Emerald Valley, Huangshan, Anhui Province, China. Rodrigo A Torres/Glow Images

A Quechua woman in Macha, Bolivia. Leonid Plotkin/Alamy Stock Photo

A boy at the Pushkar livestock fair, Rajasthan, India. Conrad P. Kottak

A Polynesian boy from Bora Bora, Society Islands, French Polynesia. Tom Cockrem/ Lonely Planet Images/Getty Images

A Native Australian girl from East Arnhem Land, Northern Territory, Australia. Lynn Gail/ Lonely Planet Images/Getty Images

A race is supposed to reflect shared *genetic* material (inherited from a common ancestor), but early scholars instead used phenotypical traits (usually skin color) for racial classification. Recall that an organism's phenotype is its "manifest biology"—anatomy and physiology. Humans display hundreds of evident (detectable) physical traits. They range from skin color, hair form, eye color, and facial features (which are visible) to blood groups, color blindness, and enzyme production (which become evident through testing) (see Anemone 2011).

Racial classifications based on phenotype raise the problem of deciding which trait(s) should be primary. Should races be defined by height, weight, body shape, facial features, teeth, skull form, or skin color? Like their fellow citizens, early European and American scientists gave priority to skin color. Many schoolbooks and encyclopedias still proclaim the existence of three great races: the white, the black, and the yellow. This overly simplistic classification was compatible with the political use of race during the colonial period of the late 19th and early 20th centuries. Such a tripartite scheme kept white Europeans neatly separate from their African and Asian subjects. Colonial empires began to break up, and scientists began to question established racial categories, after World War II (see DeSalle and Tattersall 2018; Tattersall and DeSalle 2011).

## Races Are Not Biologically Distinct

History and politics aside, one obvious problem with classifying people by skin color is that the terms *white*, *black*, and *yellow* do not accurately describe human skin colors. So-called "white" people are more pink, beige, or tan than white. "Black" people are various shades of brown, and "yellow" people are tan or beige. It does not make the tripartite division of human races any more accurate when we use the more scientific-*sounding* synonyms—*Caucasoid*, *Negroid*, and *Mongoloid*—rather than white, black, and yellow.

Another problem with classifying people by skin color is that many populations don't fit neatly into any one of the three "great races." For example, where would one put the Polynesians? *Polynesia* is a triangle of South Pacific islands formed by Hawaii to the north, Easter Island to the east, and New Zealand to the southwest. Does the "bronze" skin color of Polynesians connect them to the Caucasoids or to the Mongoloids? Some scientists, recognizing this problem, enlarged the original tripartite scheme to include the Polynesian "race." Native Americans presented a similar problem. Were they red or yellow? Some scientists added a fifth race—the "red," or Amerindian—to the major racial groups.

Many people in southern India have dark skin, but scientists have been reluctant to classify them with "black" Africans because of their Caucasoid facial features and hair form. Some, therefore, have created a separate race for these people. What about the Australian Aborigines, hunters and gatherers native to what has been, throughout human history, the most isolated continent? By skin color, one might place some Native Australians in the same race as tropical Africans. However, similarities to Europeans in hair color (light or reddish) and facial features have led some scientists to classify them as Caucasoids. But there is no evidence that Australians are closer genetically or historically to either of these groups than they are to Asians. Recognizing this problem, scientists often regard Native Australians as a separate race.

Finally, consider the San ("Bushmen") of the Kalahari Desert in southern Africa. Scientists have perceived their skin color as varying from brown to yellow. Some who regard San skin as "yellow" have placed them in the same category as Asians. In theory, people of the same race share more recent common ancestry with each other than they do with any others. But there is no evidence for recent common ancestry between San and Asians. Somewhat more reasonably, some scholars assign the San to the Capoid race (from the Cape of Good Hope), which is seen as being different from other groups inhabiting tropical Africa.

Similar problems arise when any single trait is used as a basis for racial classification. An attempt to use facial features, height, weight, or any other phenotypical trait is fraught with difficulties. For example, consider the Nilotes, natives of the upper Nile region of Uganda and South Sudan. Nilotes tend to be tall and to have long, narrow noses. Certain Scandinavians are also tall, with similar noses. Given the distance between their homelands, to classify them as members of the same race makes little sense. There is no reason to assume that Nilotes and Scandinavians are more closely related to each other than either is to shorter and nearer populations with different kinds of noses.

Would racial classifications be better if we based them on a combination of physical traits rather than a single trait such as skin color, height, or nose form? To do so would avoid some of the problems raised using a single trait, but other problems would arise. The main problem is that physical features do not go together in a consistent bundle. Some tall people have dark skin; others are lighter. Some short people have curly hair; others have straight hair. Imagine the various possible combinations of skin color, stature, and skull form. Add to that facial features such as nose form, eye shape, and lip thickness. People with dark skin may be tall or short and have hair ranging from straight to very curly. Dark-haired populations may have light or dark skin, along with various skull forms, facial features, and body sizes and shapes. The number of combinations is very large, and the amount that heredity (versus environment) contributes to such phenotypical traits is often unclear (see also Anemone 2011; Beall 2014). Using a combination of physical characteristics would not solve the problem of constructing an accurate racial classification scheme.

## Genetic Markers Don't Correlate with Phenotype

The analysis of human DNA indicates that fully 94 percent of human genetic variation occurs *within* so-called races. Considering conventional geographic "racial" groupings such as Africans, Asians, and Europeans, there is only about 6 percent variation in genes from one group to the other. In other words, there is much greater variation within each of the traditional "races" than between them. Humans are much more alike genetically than are any of the living apes. This suggests a recently shared common ancestor (perhaps as recent as 70,000 to 50,000 years) for all members of modern *Homo sapiens*. Sampling the mitochondrial DNA (mtDNA) of various populations, Rebecca Cann, Mark Stoneking, and Allan C. Wilson (1987) concluded that humans are genetically uniform overall, suggesting recent common ancestry. The fact that African populations are the most diverse genetically provides evidence that Africa was where the human diaspora originated (see also Fairbanks 2015).

Contemporary work in genomics has allowed scientists to construct regional and global phylogenetic trees based on shared genetic markers. Such trees can be based on mtDNA (which pertains to females) and the Y chromosome (which pertains to males). As the human genome becomes better known, molecular anthropologists refine their models of genetic relationships among human groups (see Stoneking 2015). A **haplogroup** is a lineage, or branch, of such a genetic tree marked by one or more specific genetic mutations. For example, the global mtDNA tree includes branches known as M and N. The Y chromosome tree includes branches known as C and F. Those four branches (either M or N for mtDNA and either C or F for the Y chromosome) are known to be associated with the spread of modern humans out of Africa between 70,000 and 50,000 B.P. Because Native Australians share those four branches, they are known to be part of that diaspora.

Although long-term genetic markers do exist, they do not correlate neatly with phenotypical similarities and differences. Because of changes in the environment that affect individuals during growth and development, the range of phenotypes characteristic of a population may change without any genetic change whatsoever. There are several examples. In the early 20th century, the anthropologist Franz Boas (1940/1966) described changes in skull form (e.g., toward rounder heads) among the children of Europeans who had migrated to North America. The reason for this was not a change in genes, for the European immigrants tended to marry among themselves. Also, some of their children had been born in Europe and merely raised in the United States. Something in the environment, probably in the diet, was producing this change. Changes in average height and weight produced by dietary differences in a few generations are common and may have nothing to do with race or genetics.

# Human Biological Adaptation

Traditional racial classification assumed that biological characteristics such as skin color were determined by heredity and that they were stable over many generations. We now know that a biological similarity does not necessarily indicate recent common ancestry. Tropical Africans and southern Indians, for example, can share dark skin color for reasons other than common ancestry. Scientists have made considerable progress in *explaining* variation in human skin color, along with many other features of human biological diversity (see Relethford 2009). We shift now from racial classification to those scientific explanations, in which natural selection plays a key role.

## Explaining Skin Color

The role that natural selection plays in producing variation in skin color will illustrate the explanatory approach to human biological diversity. Comparable explanations have been provided for many other aspects of human biological variation. Skin color is a complex biological trait—influenced by several genes. Just how many genes is not known. **Melanin**, the primary determinant of human skin color, is a chemical substance manufactured in the epidermis, or outer skin layer. The melanin cells of darker-skinned people produce more and larger granules of melanin than do those of lighter-skinned people.

By screening out ultraviolet (UV) radiation from the sun, melanin offers protection against a variety of maladies, including sunburn and skin cancer.

Before the 16th century, most of the world's very dark-skinned peoples lived in the *tropics*, a belt extending about 23 degrees north and south of the equator, between the Tropic of Cancer (north) and the Tropic of Capricorn (south). The association between dark skin color and a tropical habitat existed throughout the Old World, where humans and their ancestors have lived for hundreds of thousands of years. The darkest populations of Africa evolved in sunny, open grassland, or savanna, country.

Outside the tropics, skin color tends to be lighter. Moving north in Africa, for example, there is a gradual transition from dark brown to medium brown. Average skin color continues to lighten as one moves through the Middle East, into southern Europe, through central Europe, and to the north. South of the Tropic of Capricorn skin color also is lighter. In the Americas, by contrast, tropical populations don't have very dark skin. This is because the settlement of the New World by light-skinned Asian ancestors of Native Americans was relatively recent, probably dating back no more than 20,000 years.

How, aside from migrations, can we explain the geographic distribution of human skin color? Natural selection provides an answer. In the tropics, intense UV radiation poses a series of threats, including severe sunburn, that make light skin color an adaptive disadvantage (Table 4.1 summarizes those threats). By damaging sweat glands, sunburn reduces the body's ability to perspire and thus to regulate its own temperature (thermoregulation). Sunburn also can increase susceptibility to disease. Melanin, nature's own sunscreen, confers a selective advantage (i.e., a better chance to survive and reproduce) on darker-skinned people living in the tropics. Another disadvantage of having light skin color in the tropics is that exposure to UV radiation can cause skin cancer.

When and why might light skin color be advantageous? Years ago, W. F. Loomis (1967) focused on the role of UV radiation in stimulating the synthesis of vitamin D by the human body. The unclothed human body can produce its own vitamin D when exposed to sufficient sunlight. However, in a cloudy environment that also is so cold that

Before the 16th century, almost all the very dark-skinned populations of the world lived in the tropics, as do these Samburu girls from Kenya. Bartosz Hadyniak/Getty Images

Very light skin color, illustrated by these German children, maximizes absorption of ultraviolet radiation by those few parts of the body exposed to direct sunlight during northern winters. Robert Niedring/Alloy/ Getty Images

**TABLE 4.1  Advantages and Disadvantages (Depending on Environment) of Dark and Light Skin Color**

Also shown are cultural alternatives that help overcome biological disadvantages, and examples of natural selection (NS) operating today in relation to skin color.

| | | Cultural Alternatives | NS in Action Today |
|---|---|---|---|
| **DARK SKIN COLOR** Advantage | Melanin is natural sunscreen. In tropics: screens out UV. Reduces susceptibility to folate destruction and thus to neural tube defects (NTDs), including spina bifida. Prevents sunburn and thus enhances sweating and thermoregulation. Reduces disease susceptibility. Reduces risk of skin cancer. | | |
| Disadvantage | Outside tropics: reduces UV absorption. Increases susceptibility to rickets, osteoporosis. | Foods, vitamin D supplements | East Asians in northern U.K. Inuit with modern diets |
| **LIGHT SKIN COLOR** Advantage | No natural sunscreen. Outside tropics: admits UV. Body manufactures vitamin D and thus prevents rickets and osteoporosis. | | |
| Disadvantage | Especially in tropics: increases susceptibility to folate destruction and thus to NTDs, including spina bifida. Impairs spermatogenesis. Increases susceptibility to sunburn and thus to impaired sweating and poor thermoregulation. Increases disease susceptibility. Increases susceptibility to skin cancer. | Folic acid/folate supplements Shelter, sunscreens, lotions, etc. | Whites still have more NTDs |

people have to wear clothing much of the year (such as northern Europe, where very light skin color evolved), clouds and clothing impede the body's manufacture of vitamin D. Vitamin D deficiency diminishes the absorption of calcium in the intestines. A nutritional disease known as *rickets*, which softens and deforms the bones, may develop (see Brickley 2018). In women, deformation of the pelvic bones from rickets can interfere with childbirth. In cold northern areas, light skin color maximizes the absorption of UV radiation and the synthesis of vitamin D by the few parts of the body that are exposed to direct sunlight. There has been selection against dark skin color in northern areas because melanin screens out UV radiation.

This natural selection continues today: East Asians living in northern areas of the United Kingdom have a higher incidence of rickets and osteoporosis (also related to vitamin D and calcium deficiency) than the general British population. A related illustration involves Eskimos (Inuit) and other indigenous inhabitants of northern Alaska and northern Canada. According to Nina Jablonski (quoted in Iqbal 2002), "Looking at Alaska, one would think that the native people should be pale as ghosts." One reason they are not pale is that they haven't lived in this region very long in terms of geological time. Even more important, their traditional diet, which is rich in seafood, including fish oils, supplies sufficient vitamin D so as to make a reduction in pigmentation unnecessary. However, again illustrating natural selection at work today, when these people abandon their traditional diets based on fish and sea mammals, they suffer from high rates of childhood rickets and adult osteoporosis. Far from being stable and unchanging, skin color can become an evolutionary liability very quickly.

Another key factor explaining the geographic distribution of skin color involves the effects of UV on folate, an essential nutrient that the human body manufactures from folic acid (Jablonski 2012). Pregnant women require large amounts of folate to support rapid cell division in the embryo, and there is a direct connection between folate and individual reproductive success. Folate deficiency causes neural tube defects (NTDs) in human embryos. NTDs are marked by the incomplete closure of the neural tube, so the spine and spinal cord fail to develop completely. One NTD, anencephaly (with the brain an exposed mass), results in stillbirth or death soon after delivery. With spina bifida, another NTD, survival rates are higher, but babies have severe disabilities, including paralysis. NTDs are the second most common human birth defect after cardiac abnormalities. Today, women of reproductive age are advised to take folate supplements to prevent serious birth defects such as spina bifida.

Natural sunlight and UV radiation destroy folate in the human body. Because melanin, as we have seen, protects against UV hazards, such as sunburn and its consequences, dark skin coloration is adaptive in the tropics. Now we see that melanin also is adaptive because it conserves folate in the human body and thus protects against NTDs, which are much more common in light-skinned than darker-skinned populations (Jablonski 2006, 2012; Jablonski and Chaplin 2000). Africans and African Americans rarely demonstrate severe folate deficiency, even among individuals with marginal nutritional status. Folate also plays a role in another key reproductive process, spermatogenesis—the production of sperm. In mice and rats, folate deficiency can cause male sterility; it may well play a similar role in humans.

Today, of course, cultural alternatives to biological adaptation permit light-skinned people to survive in the tropics and darker-skinned people to live in the far north. People can clothe themselves and seek shelter from the sun; they can use artificial sunscreens if they lack the natural protection that melanin provides. Dark-skinned people living in the north can, indeed must, get vitamin D from their diet or take supplements. Today, pregnant women are routinely advised to take folic acid or folate supplements as a hedge against NTDs. Even so, light skin color still is correlated with a higher incidence of spina bifida.

Jablonski and Chaplin (2000) explain variation in human skin color as resulting from a balancing act between the evolutionary needs to (1) protect against all UV hazards (thus favoring dark skin in the tropics) and (2) have an adequate supply of vitamin D (thus favoring lighter skin outside the tropics). We see that common ancestry, the presumed basis of race, is not the only reason for biological similarities. Natural selection, still at work today, also plays an important role.

## Genes and Disease

There is abundant evidence for human genetic adaptation and thus for evolution (change in gene frequency). Remember that adaptation and evolution go on in specific environments. There is no generally or ideally adaptive allele and no perfect phenotype. Furthermore, we have seen that even an apparently maladaptive allele like $Hb^S$—which produces a lethal anemia—has a selective advantage in the heterozygous form in malarial environments. Also, alleles that once were maladaptive can lose their disadvantage if the environment shifts. For example, medical advances now allow many people with genetic disorders to live normal lives.

Let's consider now some examples of how microbes have been selective agents for humans, particularly before the advent of modern medicine. As food production (farming and herding) began to spread about 10,000 years ago, infectious diseases posed a mounting risk. Food production supports larger, denser populations and a more sedentary lifestyle than does hunting and gathering. People live closer to each other and to their own wastes, making it easier for microbes to survive and to find hosts. Domesticated animals also transmit diseases to people.

Smallpox, which mutated from cowpox, has been a particularly important selective agent. Until 1979, when the last case was reported, smallpox had been a major threat to humans (Diamond 1990, 1997/2017). Smallpox epidemics have played important roles in world history, often killing one-fourth to one-half of the affected population.

Having a particular blood type appears to protect against certain microbes, including smallpox. In the ABO system, blood is typed according to compounds on the surface of the red blood cells. Different compounds distinguish between type A and type B blood. The compounds on type A cells trigger the production of *antibodies* in type B blood, so that A cells clot in B blood (and vice versa). The different compounds work like chemical passwords; they help us distinguish our own cells from invading cells, including microbes we ought to destroy. The surfaces of some microbes have compounds similar to ABO blood group compounds. We don't produce antibodies to compounds similar to those that we have on our own blood cells.

People with A or AB blood are more susceptible to smallpox than are people with type B or type O. Presumably this is because a compound on the smallpox virus is similar to the type A compound, permitting the virus to slip by the defenses of a type A individual. By contrast, type B and type O individuals recognize the smallpox virus as an intruder and produce antibodies to combat it.

The relation between type A blood and susceptibility to smallpox was first suggested by the low frequencies of the A allele in areas of India and Africa where smallpox was once endemic. A comparative study done in rural India during a virulent smallpox epidemic did much to confirm this relationship. Drs. F. Vogel and M. R. Chakravartti analyzed blood samples from smallpox victims and their uninfected siblings (Diamond 1990). The researchers focused on 415 infected children, none ever vaccinated against smallpox. The results of the study were clear: Someone with type A or type AB blood had a seven times greater chance of getting smallpox than did an O or B person.

In most human populations, the O allele is more common than A and B combined. Type A is most common in Europe; type B frequencies are highest in Asia. Since smallpox was once widespread in the Old World, we might wonder why natural selection did not eliminate the A allele entirely. The answer appears to be this: Other diseases spared the type A people and penalized those with other blood groups.

For example, type O people seem to be especially susceptible to bubonic plague. Type O people also are more likely to get cholera, which has killed as many people in India as smallpox has. On the other hand, the O allele may protect against syphilis, which probably originated in the New World (see this chapter's "Anthropology Today"). Frequencies of type O blood are very high among the native populations of Central and South America. The distribution of human blood groups appears to represent an evolutionary compromise based on susceptibility to a variety of different diseases.

In the case of diseases for which there still are no known cures, genetic resistance maintains its significance (see Hartigan 2013). There is genetic variation in susceptibility to the HIV virus, for example. Longitudinal studies have shown that people exposed to HIV vary in their risk of developing AIDS and in the rate at which the disease progresses.

As an interesting case of what we might call fortuitous preadaptation, consider the *CCR5* gene. This gene codes for a receptor protein on the surface of white blood cells. The viral infection HIV uses the *CCR5* receptor to invade and infect cells. However, individuals who are homozygous for an allele known as *CCR5-Δ32* (*delta 32*) are resistant to this invasion. This HIV immunity illustrates preadaptation or preselection, because the original selection for this allele had nothing to do with HIV. Rather, the allele was originally adaptive and spread because it conferred resistance to pathogens that caused deadly epidemics in earlier European history.

This *CCR5-Δ32* allele is found in between 3 and 14 percent of Europeans, but it is absent in Africans, East Asians, and Native Americans. The allele is most common in Scandinavia and Russia. Susan Scott and Christopher Duncan (2004) argue that a series of lethal epidemics that ravaged Europe between 1347 and 1660 were caused by a virus that produced a deadly hemorrhagic fever. This virus used the *CCR5* receptor gene to invade (and usually kill) its human hosts. Outbreaks of this hemorrhagic fever continued longest, through 1800, in Sweden, Denmark, Russia, Poland, and Hungary. Given the persistent hemorrhagic plague threat, selection for *CCR5-Δ32* (which conferred resistance) continued in those countries, where it has its highest frequencies (see Relethford 2012, p. 368). It is merely by lucky chance that *CCR5-Δ32* also confers resistance to HIV and AIDS. (See the section "Emerging Diseases" in Chapter 19).

## Lactose Tolerance

Many biological traits that illustrate human adaptation are not under simple genetic control. Genetic determination of such traits may be only partial, or several genes may work or interact to influence the trait in question. Sometimes there is a known genetic component but the trait also responds to stresses encountered during growth. We speak of **phenotypical adaptation** when adaptive changes occur during an individual's lifetime. Phenotypical adaptation is made possible by *biological plasticity*—our ability to change in response to the environments we encounter as we grow (see Cameron and Bogin 2012).

One genetically determined biochemical difference among human groups involves the ability to digest large amounts of milk—an adaptive advantage when other foods are scarce and milk is available. Milk contains a complex sugar called *lactose*, and the digestion of milk depends on an enzyme called *lactase*, which works in the small intestine. Among all mammals except humans and some of their pets, lactase production ceases after weaning, so that these animals can no longer digest milk.

A 44-year-old Fulani farmer-herder enjoys fresh milk from the family cows in Sabgu village, Cameroon. Per-Anders Pettersson/Getty Images News/Getty Images

## Anthropology Today    *Disease Evolution: A Case Study*

The same processes (e.g., mutation and environmental adaptation) that operate in the evolution of life in general also apply to the evolution of disease microorganisms. Consider syphilis, a sexually transmitted infection (STI) that appears to have originated as a childhood infection transmitted through skin contact. The syphilis bacterium (*Treponema pallidum*), which most probably originated in the Americas, mutated and spread rapidly when it reached Europe via the return voyage of Christopher Columbus and his crew in 1493. In just a few years, the mutated bacterium—as the STI syphilis—spawned an epidemic and became a major killer during the European Renaissance. Although the New World origin of syphilis has been widely accepted, some observers believe that syphilis already existed in Europe before Columbus but did not become a major threat until the Renaissance, when it erupted in epidemic form, perhaps in response to environmental and social changes, including the growth of cities.

What kinds of evidence can help us solve the puzzle of the origin and evolution of syphilis? Anthropologists Kristin Harper, Molly Zuckerman, and (the late) George Armelagos (2014) have considered bone biology, genetics, and nonhuman primates in their studies of syphilis and its close cousins, yaws and bejel (known together as treponemal diseases). Like syphilis, yaws and bejel are chronic, debilitating diseases, but neither spreads sexually. Yaws, found in tropical regions, spreads via skin-to-skin contact. Bejel, found in arid areas like the Middle East, spreads via contaminated utensils. All three diseases often leave skeletal evidence, including crater-like markings on the skull, bone lesions, and shinbones that are swollen and pitted.

Bone biology provides evidence of *Treponema pallidum* infection throughout the Americas prior to Columbus. Many of the affected skeletons are of juvenile individuals, suggesting nonsexual transmission. By contrast, the skeletal evidence for pre-Columbian treponemal infection in the Old World is spotty and ambiguous. Based on an extensive review, Harper, Zuckerman, and Armelagos (2014) could find no European skeleton with both a confirmed diagnosis of *Treponema* and a reliable pre-Columbian date. For this reason, those researchers were not convinced that the pathogen existed in Europe before Columbus. They do recognize, however, that *Treponema* may have existed in Africa, where monkeys and apes continue to experience treponemal infections.

The scourge of syphilis: This historic (1497) woodcut depicts a bedridden woman and a young man seated on a stool—both covered with the lesions or skin pustules that are characteristic of the disease. The first European syphilis epidemics occurred in 1494. What is significant about that date? INTERFOTO/Alamy Stock Photo

Genetics is another important tool for studying the origin and evolution of syphilis. When researchers compared *T. pallidum* strains from around the world, the closest genetic match to syphilis was a yaws-causing strain of *T. pallidum* found in South America. This strain infects children in indigenous communities in Guyana. Those children develop sores on their shins that resemble both yaws and syphilis. In terms of its genetics and clinical symptoms, this South American strain occupied a space midway between yaws and syphilis. The close genetic and clinical similarity of syphilis to this South American strain strongly suggests that syphilis descends from a non-sexually-transmitted yaws-like pathogen in the Americas. However, genetic comparisons also suggest that some forms of treponemal disease were present in the pre-Columbian Old World as well, most probably in Africa.

Researchers working in national parks in Tanzania in the 1980s and 1990s reported a gruesome treponemal disease that attacked the genitals of baboons. One strain from these baboons was indistinguishable from a group of human yaws strains, suggesting the possibility of cross-species transmission. Researchers are examining the risk of the bacterium jumping from animals to humans. The human diseases that are easiest to wipe out are those that cannot jump back and forth between animals and people. We can seem to eradicate a disease such as yaws among humans, only to have it jump back later from its animal hosts.

We see in this account how biological anthropologists can combine the study of genetics, skeletons, clinical manifestations, and nonhuman primates to understand the origin, evolution, and spread of syphilis and its cousins (see also Gibbens 2018 and Romm 2016). Anthropologists use a similar multipronged approach to study the evolution of other life forms, especially humans.

Lactase production and the ability to tolerate milk vary among human populations. About 90 percent of northern Europeans and their descendants are lactose tolerant; they can digest several glasses of milk with no difficulty. Similarly, about 80 percent of two African populations, the Tutsi of Rwanda and Burundi in East Africa and the Fulani of Nigeria in West Africa, produce lactase and digest milk easily. Both of these groups traditionally have been herders. However, such nonherders as the Yoruba and the Igbo in Nigeria, the Baganda in Uganda, the Japanese and other Asians, Inuit, South American Indians, and many Israelis cannot digest lactose (Kretchmer 1972/1975).

Recent genetic studies have helped clarify when and how humans developed lactose tolerance (see Mielke, Konigsberg, and Relethford 2011). An allele known to favor adult lactose tolerance existed, but still was uncommon, in central and eastern Europe as recently as 3,800 years ago (Burger et al. 2007). Sarah Tishkoff and her associates found that the alleles that confer lactose tolerance in East Africans differ from those of lactose-tolerant Europeans. Her genetic studies of 43 East African groups suggested that three different mutations favoring lactose tolerance arose in Africa between 6,800 and 2,700 years ago (Tishkoff et al. 2007). Again we see that the same phenotype—in this case, lactose tolerance—can be produced by different genotypes. It also should be noted that the variable human ability to digest milk seems to be a difference of degree. Some populations can tolerate very little or no milk, but others are able to metabolize much greater quantities. People who move from no-milk or low-milk diets to high-milk diets can increase their lactose tolerance; this suggests some phenotypical adaptation.

Human biology changes constantly, even without genetic change. In this chapter, we've considered several ways in which humans adapt biologically to their environments, and the effects of such adaptation on human biological diversity. Modern biological anthropology seeks to explain specific aspects of human biological variation. The explanatory framework encompasses the same mechanisms—selection, mutation, drift, gene flow, and plasticity—that govern adaptation, variation, and evolution among other life forms.

## Summary

1. In the 18th century, Carolus Linnaeus developed biological taxonomy. He viewed differences and similarities among organisms as part of God's orderly plan rather than as evidence for evolution. In the mid-19th century, Charles Darwin proposed that natural selection could explain the origin of species, biological diversity, and similarities among related life forms. Natural selection requires variety in the population undergoing selection.

2. Through breeding experiments with peas in 1856, Gregor Mendel discovered that genetic traits pass on as units. These are now known to be chromosomes, which occur in homologous pairs. Alleles—some dominant, some recessive—are the chemically different forms that occur at a given genetic locus. Mendel also formulated the law of independent assortment. Each of the seven traits he studied in peas was inherited independently of all the others. Independent assortment of chromosomes and their recombination provide some of the variety needed for natural selection. But the major source of such variety is mutation, a chemical change in the DNA molecules of which genes are made.

3. Population genetics studies gene frequencies in stable and changing populations. Natural selection is the most important mechanism of evolutionary change. Others are mutation, random genetic drift, and gene flow. Given environmental change, nature selects among traits already present in the population. New types don't appear just because they are needed.

4. One well-documented case of natural selection in contemporary human populations is that of the sickle-cell allele. In homozygous form, the sickle-cell allele, $Hb^S$, produces an abnormal hemoglobin. This clogs the small blood vessels, impairing the blood's capacity to store oxygen. The result is sickle-cell anemia, which is usually fatal. Homozygotes for normal hemoglobin are susceptible to malaria and die in great numbers. Heterozygotes get only mild anemia and are resistant to malaria. In a malarial environment, the heterozygote has the advantage.

5. Other mechanisms of genetic evolution complement natural selection. Random genetic drift operates most obviously in small populations, where pure chance can easily change allele frequencies. Gene flow and interbreeding keep subgroups of the same species genetically connected and thus impede speciation.

6. Because of a range of problems involved in classifying humans into racial categories, contemporary biologists focus on specific differences and try to explain them.

Because of extensive gene flow and interbreeding, *Homo sapiens* has not evolved sub-species or distinct races. Biological similarities between groups may reflect—rather than common ancestry—similar but independent adaptations to similar natural selective forces, such as degrees of ultraviolet radiation from the sun in the case of skin color.

7. Differential resistance to infectious diseases such as smallpox has influenced the distribution of human blood groups. There are genetic antimalarials, such as the sickle-cell allele. *Phenotypical adaptation* refers to adaptive changes that occur in an individual's lifetime in response to the environment the organism encounters as it grows. Lactose tolerance is due partly to phenotypical adaptation. Biological simi-larities between geographically distant populations may be due to similar but inde-pendent genetic changes rather than to common ancestry. Or they may reflect similar physiological responses to common stresses during growth.

## Think Like an Anthropologist

1. How does the scientific meaning of "theory" differ from the common one? Can evolution be both a theory and a fact?

2. Consider the American Anthropological Association Statement on Race. What is its main argument? If race is a problematic concept when applied to humans, what has replaced, or should replace, it?

3. Choose three to five people in your classroom who contrast phenotypically. Which of their features vary most evidently? How might you explain this variation with reference to one of the evolutionary mechanisms discussed in this chapter? To what extent does the variation you observe in your classmates reflect culture rather than biology?

## Key Terms

adaptive, *81*
alleles, *78*
balanced
   polymorphism,
   *82*
catastrophism, *73*
chromosomes, *77*
creationism, *73*
dominant, *77*
evolution, *73*
gene, *78*
gene flow, *84*
gene pool, *79*
genetic evolution,
   *80*

genotype, *78*
haplogroup, *89*
heterozygous, *78*
homozygous, *78*
independent
   assortment, *79*
meiosis, *79*
melanin, *89*
mitosis, *79*
mutation, *83*
natural selection,
   *74*
phenotype, *78*
phenotypical
   adaptation, *95*

population
   genetics, *79*
racial classification,
   *85*
random genetic
   drift, *83*
recessive, *77*
sexual selection, *81*
speciation, *85*
species, *85*
theory, *74*
uniformitarianism,
   *73*

# Chapter 5

# The Primates

## Our Place among Primates

**Primatology** is the study of nonhuman **primates**—fossil and living apes, monkeys, tarsiers, lemurs, and lorises—including their behavior and social life (see Campbell 2011; Strier 2014). Primatology is fascinating in itself, but it also helps anthropologists make inferences about the early social organization and adaptive strategies of *hominids* (members of the zoological family that includes fossil and living humans). Of particular relevance to humans are two kinds of primates:

1. Those whose ecological adaptations are similar to our own: **terrestrial** monkeys and apes—that is, primates that live on the ground rather than in the trees.
2. Those that are most closely related to us: the great apes, specifically the chimpanzees and gorillas (see King 2016; Muller, Wrangham, and Pilbeam 2017; Schaik 2016; Stanford 2018).

## Apes Are Our Closest Relatives

Similarities between humans and apes are evident in physiology, anatomy, brain structure, and DNA. The physical similarities between humans and apes are recognized in zoological **taxonomy**—the assignment of organisms to categories (*taxa*; singular, *taxon*) according to their relatedness and resemblance. Taxonomy is an important way of representing evolutionary, or phylogenetic, relationships. Many similarities between organisms reflect their common *phylogeny*—their genetic relatedness based on common ancestry. Related organisms share features they have inherited from the same ancestor. Humans and apes belong to the same taxonomic superfamily, Hominoidea (hominoids). Monkeys belong to two other superfamilies (Ceboidea and Cercopithecoidea). Humans and apes share a more recent common ancestry with each other than either does with monkeys.

Although apes are more similar to humans than to monkeys, in the popular imagination, humans associate apes with monkeys, rather than with themselves. At zoos, human parents say to their kids, "Look at the monkey," when they are seeing a chimp, a gorilla, or an orangutan. The national tabloids use phrases like "monkeying around" or "monkey see, monkey do" when reporting on stories that involve apes. We easily appreciate the monkey in the ape but not the ape in ourselves.

Still, the apes do fascinate us to some degree, precisely because of their humanlike qualities. Zoo gorillas are especially popular when they are displayed in "family" groups. The antics of orangutans and especially of chimps have been featured in movies and TV shows. The *Planet of the Apes* movies recognize both that apes are not monkeys and that apes are quite similar to us. Imagine a live-action film called *Planet of the Monkeys*. Where could a director find human actors who could locomote on four limbs for an entire movie?

## Zoological Taxonomy

Figure 5.1 summarizes the levels of classification used in zoological taxonomy. Each lower-level unit belongs to the one above it. Starting near the bottom of the figure, we see

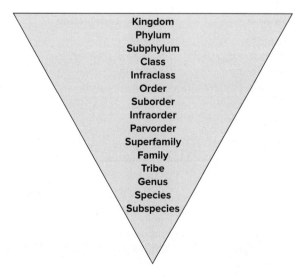

**FIGURE 5.1   The Principal Classificatory Units of Zoological Taxonomy**
Moving down the figure, the classificatory units become more exclusive, so that "kingdom" at the top is the most inclusive unit and "subspecies" at the bottom is the most exclusive.

McGraw-Hill Education

Kingdom
Phylum
Subphylum
Class
Infraclass
Order
Suborder
Infraorder
Parvorder
Superfamily
Family
Tribe
Genus
Species
Subspecies

that similar species belong to the same genus (plural, *genera*). Similar genera make up the same family, and so on through the top of the figure, where similar phyla (plural of *phylum*) are included in the same kingdom. The highest (most inclusive) taxonomic level is the *kingdom*. At that level, animals are distinguished from plants.

At the lowest level of taxonomy, a species may have subspecies. These are its more or less—but not yet totally—isolated subgroups. Subspecies can coexist in time and space. For example, the Neandertals, who lived between 130,000 and perhaps 39,000 years ago, sometimes are assigned not to a separate species but merely to a different subspecies of *Homo sapiens*. Just one subspecies of *Homo sapiens* survives today.

The similarities used to assign organisms to the same taxon are called **homologies**, similarities they have inherited jointly from a common ancestor. Table 5.1 summarizes the place of humans in zoological taxonomy. We see in the table that we are mammals, members of the class Mammalia. This is a major subdivision of the kingdom Animalia. Mammals share certain traits, including mammary glands, that set them apart from other taxa, such as birds, reptiles, amphibians, and insects. Mammalian homologies indicate that all mammals share more recent common ancestry with each other than they do with any bird, reptile, or insect.

Humans are mammals that, at a lower taxonomic level, belong to the *order* Primates, which also includes monkeys and apes. Another mammalian order is Carnivora—the carnivores (dogs, cats, foxes, wolves, badgers, weasels). Rodentia (rats, mice, beavers, squirrels) form yet another mammalian order. The primates share structural and biochemical homologies that distinguish them from other mammals. These resemblances were inherited from their common ancestors after those early primates became reproductively isolated from the ancestors of the other mammals.

TABLE 5.1    **The Place of Humans (*Homo sapiens*) in Zoological Taxonomy**
*Homo sapiens* can be classified using these common names: animal, chordate, vertebrate, mammal, eutherian, primate, haplorrhine, simian, catarrhine, hominoid, hominid, and hominin. (Figure 5.2 summarizes the taxonomic placement of the other primates.)

| Taxon | Scientific (Latin) Name | Common (English) Name |
|---|---|---|
| Kingdom | Animalia | Animals |
| Phylum | Chordata | Chordates |
| Subphylum | Vertebrata | Vertebrates |
| Class | Mammalia | Mammals |
| Infraclass | Eutheria | Eutherians |
| Order | Primates | Primates |
| Suborder | Haplorrhini | Haplorrhines |
| Infraorder | Simiiformes | Simians ("anthropoids") |
| Parvorder | Catarrhini | Catarrhines |
| Superfamily | Hominoidea | Hominoids |
| Family | Hominidae | Hominids |
| Tribe | Hominini | Hominins |
| Genus | *Homo* | Humans |
| Species | *Homo sapiens* | Recent humans |
| Subspecies | *Homo sapiens sapiens* | Anatomically modern humans |

# Homologies and Analogies

Organisms are assigned to the same taxon on the basis of homologies. The extensive biochemical homologies between apes and humans confirm our common ancestry and support our traditional joint classification as hominoids (see Figure 5.3). Recent sequencing of ape genomes has shown that chimps and humans share approximately 99 percent of their DNA, with gorillas trailing at 98 percent (Wong 2014).

Common ancestry isn't the only reason for physical similarities between species. Similar traits also can arise if species experience similar selective forces and adapt to them in similar ways. We call such similarities **analogies**. The process by which analogies are produced is called **convergent evolution**. For example, fish and porpoises (dolphins) share many analogies resulting from convergent evolution to life in the water. Like fish, porpoises, which are mammals, have fins. They are also hairless and streamlined for efficient locomotion. Analogies between birds and bats (wings, small size, light bones) illustrate convergent evolution to flying.

In theory, only homologies should be used in taxonomy. In the past, however, a reluctance to lump apes and humans too closely together resulted in placing chimps, gorillas, and orangutans all together in the family *Pongidae* (the pongids). This placement, however, violates the rule that taxonomy should be based on recent common ancestry. There is absolutely no doubt that humans, gorillas, and chimpanzees are more closely related to each other than any of the three is to orangutans, which are Asiatic apes. As discussed,

FIGURE 5.2   **Classification of Primates**
Names within parentheses are common names.

McGraw-Hill Education

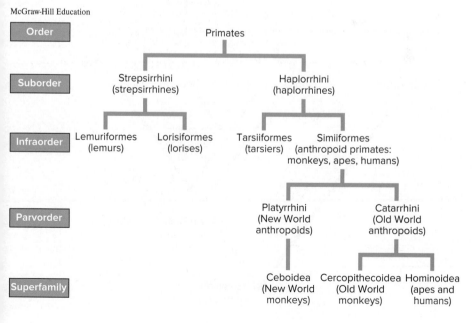

Hominidae is the name of the zoological family that includes hominids—fossil and living humans. Because chimps and gorillas share a more recent common ancestor with humans than they do with orangutans, most scientists now also place gorillas and chimps in the hominid family. *Hominid* would then refer to the zoological family that includes fossil and living humans, chimpanzees, gorillas, and their common ancestors. This leaves the orangutan (genus *Pongo*) as the only member of the pongid family (Pongidae).

## FIGURE 5.3   Humans and the Apes

The top drawing shows the evolutionary (phylogenetic) relationships among the living great apes and humans. Note that humans and the African apes are more closely related to each other (as hominids) than either is to the orangutan (a pongid). The bottom drawing shows the same phylogeny, along with estimated dates of divergence and last common ancestor (represented by dots). It is based on the extent of shared DNA among these groups.

McGraw-Hill Education

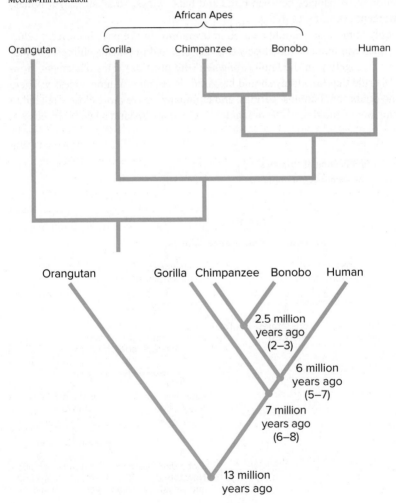

If chimps and gorillas are classified as hominids, what do we call the group that leads to humans but not to chimps and gorillas? For that group, scientists insert a taxonomic level called *tribe* between family and genus. The tribe *hominini* (hominins) describes all the human species that ever have existed (including the extinct ones) and excludes chimps and gorillas. Figure 5.2 summarizes primate taxonomy, and Figure 5.3 illustrates our degree of relatedness to the living great apes.

# Primate Adaptations

There are between 400 and 500 species of primates, which have adapted to varied ecological niches (see Fleagle 2013). Some primates are active during the day; others, at night. Some eat insects; still others, fruits; others, shoots, leaves, and bulk vegetation; and still others, seeds, roots, or gums. *Terrestrial* primates live on the ground; **arboreal** primates live in trees, and there are intermediate adaptations. Many trends in primate evolution are best exemplified by monkeys, apes, and humans, and those trends can be summarized briefly. Together they constitute a heritage that humans share with monkeys and apes.

1. *Grasping.* Primates have five-digited feet and hands that are suited for grasping (e.g., of tree branches) and manipulating objects (e.g., food items). Facilitating manual dexterity is the fact that humans and many other primates have **opposable thumbs**: The thumb can touch the other fingers. Some primates also have grasping feet. Proficiency in grasping is an adaptive advantage in the arboreal niches in which many primates live or once lived. However, in adapting to **bipedal** (two-footed) locomotion, humans eliminated most of the foot's grasping ability.

2. *Smell to sight.* Several anatomical changes reflect the shift from smell to sight as the primates' most important means of obtaining information. Primates have excellent *stereoscopic* (able to see in depth) and color vision. The portion of the brain devoted to vision expanded, while the area concerned with smell shrank.

3. *Nose to hand.* The sense of touch, conveyed by *tactile organs*, also provides information. Some nonprimates, including cats and dogs, have sensitive tactile skin on their noses. Cats' facial whiskers also serve a tactile function. In primates, however, the main touch organ is the hand, specifically the sensitive pads of the "fingerprint" region.

4. *Brain complexity.* The proportion of brain tissue concerned with memory, thought, and association has increased in primates. The primate ratio of brain size to body size exceeds that of most mammals.

5. *Parental investment.* Most primates give birth to a single offspring rather than a litter. Because of this, growing primates receive more attention and have more learning opportunities than do other mammals. Learned behavior is an important part of primate adaptation.

6. *Sociality.* Primates tend to be social animals that live with others of their species. The need for longer and more attentive care of offspring places a selective value on support by a social group.

Think about how our primate heritage is reflected in how we use our senses—vision, hearing, touch, taste, and smell. Which are you using right now? Which do you most depend on to navigate the world?

Like almost all other **anthropoids** (humanlike primates)—a group that includes monkeys, humans, and apes—humans are diurnal, or active during the day. If we were night animals, we'd sense things differently. Our eyes might be bigger, like those of an owl or a tarsier. Maybe we'd have biological radar systems, as bats do. Perhaps we'd develop a more acute sense of hearing or smell to penetrate the dark. Many animals rely on scents and odors to help them interpret the world. Humans, by contrast, use an array of products to cover up or eliminate even the faint odors our limited olfactory apparatus permits us to smell. Consider as well the structure of your hand—especially your opposable thumb and sensitive finger pads. Imagine a cat or dog trying to light a match or send a text message. The sensory shifts that occurred in primate evolution explain something fundamental about ourselves.

## The Primate Suborders

In primate evolution there was an early separation of two groups: (1) the ancestors of lemurs and lorises and (2) the ancestors of tarsiers, monkeys, apes, and humans. The lemur-loris group and their ancestors compose the suborder **Strepsirrhini** or strepsirrhine primates. The suborder **Haplorrhini**, the haplorrhine primates, includes tarsiers, monkeys, apes, and humans (see Masters, Gamba, and Génin 2013). Strepsirrhine nostrils, like those of a dog, are surrounded by moist, naked skin, in contrast to the dry, often hairy skin that surrounds haplorrhine nostrils. Another distinguishing strepsirrhine feature is a layer of the eye that reflects light and provides better night vision.

Based on certain analogies in the appearance and adaptation of these primates, scientists used to lump together tarsiers, lemurs, and lorises as *prosimians*, meaning "pre-monkeys," in contrast to *anthropoids*, meaning "humanlike" (and also encompassing monkeys and apes). Some researchers still use the term *prosimian* colloquially to refer to these primates, but it does not reflect phylogeny. Based on their evolutionary history, tarsiers belong with monkeys, apes, and humans rather than with the lemurs.

The split between haplorrhines and strepsirrhines took place over 60 million years ago. The early history of the primates is limited to lemurlike and tarsierlike animals known through the fossil record. By 50 million years ago, several genera of tarsierlike primates were living in Asia, North America, and Europe, which were much warmer than they are now. Tarsiers survive today only in Indonesia, Malaysia, and the Philippines. Active at night (nocturnal), tarsiers do not compete directly with monkeys, apes, and humans, which are diurnal. Lorises also survive as nocturnal primates in parts of Asia.

The lemurs of Madagascar are the best known nonhuman primates other than monkeys and apes. Ancestral lemurs were able to survive, multiply, and diversify on the isolated island of Madagascar, where they had no primate competitors until

A ring-tailed lemur (*Lemur catta*). This variety of lemur lives in the dry forests and bush of southern and southwestern Madagascar. Gudkov Andrey/Shutterstock

humans arrived on that island around 2,000 years ago. In their behavior and biology, Madagascar's lemurs, which include some 50 species, show adaptations to an array of environments. Their diets and times of activity differ. Lemurs eat fruits, other plant foods, eggs, and insects. Some are nocturnal; others are active during the day. Some are totally arboreal; others spend some time in the trees and some on the ground. Like all nonhuman primates, they are endangered today, primarily as a result of human activity.

## Monkeys

The haplorrhine suborder has two infraorders, one consisting of living and fossil tarsiers; the other includes all the anthropoid, or humanlike, primates. The term *anthropoid* refers to monkeys, apes, and humans, as distinct from tarsiers and all other primates.

There are two groups of monkeys—New World monkeys (platyrrhines) and Old World monkeys (catarrhines). The catarrhines also include apes and humans, all of which originated in the Old World. *Catarrhine* means sharp-nosed, and *platyrrhine* means flat-nosed. These names come from Latin terms that describe the placement of the nostrils.

Catarrhines (Latin, *Catarrhini*) is the taxonomic name for the group that includes all Old World monkeys, apes, and humans. Because taxonomy reflects phylogeny, this placement together means that Old World monkeys, apes, and humans are more closely related to each other than they are to New World monkeys. In other words, one kind of monkey (Old World) is more like a human than it is like another kind of monkey (New World). The New World monkeys were reproductively isolated from the catarrhines before the latter diverged into the Old World monkeys, apes, and humans. This is why New World monkeys belong to a different taxon.

All New World monkeys and many Old World monkeys are arboreal. Whether in the trees or on the ground, however, monkeys move differently than apes and humans. Their arms and legs move parallel to one another, as dogs' legs do. This contrasts with the tendency toward *orthograde posture*, the straight and upright stance of apes and humans. Unlike apes, which have longer arms than legs, and humans, who have longer legs than arms, monkeys have arms and legs of about the same length. Most monkeys also have tails, which help them maintain balance in the trees. Apes and humans lack tails.

## New World Monkeys

New World monkeys live in the forests of Central and South America. Unlike Old World monkeys, many New World monkeys have *prehensile*, or grasping, tails. Sometimes the prehensile tail has tactile skin, which permits it to work like a hand, for instance, in conveying food to the mouth. Old World monkeys, however, have developed their own characteristic anatomical specializations. They have rough patches of skin on the buttocks, adapted to sitting on hard, rocky ground and rough branches. If the primate you see in the zoo has such patches, it's from the Old World. If it has a prehensile tail, it's a New World monkey. There's only one nocturnal monkey, a New World monkey appropriately called the night monkey or owl monkey. All other monkeys and apes, and humans, too, of course, are diurnal—active during the day.

Shown here in Brazil's Atlantic rain forest is a muriqui (or woolly spider monkey)—the largest New World monkey. Note the prehensile tail. BrazilPhotos.com/Alamy Stock Photo

## Old World Monkeys

The Old World monkeys include both terrestrial and arboreal species. They range over areas of Africa and Asia, and even extend into Europe's Rock of Gibraltar, where they are commonly known by the misnomer "Barbary apes." They should be called "Barbary monkeys" (macaques), rather than apes. Along with baboons, macaques are terrestrial monkeys.

Arboreal primates tend to be smaller than their terrestrial cousins. Small size enables them to reach a wider range of foods at the ends of branches. Arboreal monkeys are lithe and agile. They escape from the few predators in their environment—snakes and monkey-eating eagles—through alertness and speed. Large size, by contrast, is advantageous for terrestrial primates in dealing with their predators, which are more numerous on the ground.

A nature male mandrill (*Papio sphinx*) ambles through gallery forest in Lope National Park, Gabon, Africa. These (mainly) terrestrial Old World monkeys are related to baboons. Curioso/Shutterstock

Another contrast between arboreal and terrestrial primates is in sexual dimorphism—marked differences in male and female anatomy and temperament. Sexual dimorphism tends to be more marked in terrestrial than in arboreal species. Baboon and macaque males are larger and fiercer than are females of the same species. However, it's hard to tell, without close inspection, the sex of an arboreal monkey.

Terrestrial monkeys have specializations in anatomy, psychology, and social behavior that enable them to cope with terrestrial life. Adult male baboons, for example, are fierce-looking animals that can weigh 100 pounds (45 kilograms). They display their long, projecting canines to intimidate predators and when confronting other baboons. A male baboon also can puff up his ample mane of shoulder hair, so that a would-be aggressor perceives him as larger than he actually is.

Near the time of puberty, baboon and macaque males typically leave their home troop for another. Because males move in and out, females form the stable core of the terrestrial monkey troop (Cheney and Seyfarth 1990). By contrast, among chimpanzees and gorillas, females are more likely to emigrate and seek mates outside their natal social groups (Chapais 2008; Wilson and Wrangham 2003). Among terrestrial monkeys, then, the core group consists of females; among apes, it is composed of males.

## Apes

Humans and the apes together compose the **hominoid** superfamily (Hominoidea). Among the hominoids, the so-called great apes are orangutans, gorillas, and chimpanzees. The lesser (smaller) apes are the gibbons and siamangs of Southeast Asia and Indonesia.

Apes and humans share several traits that distinguish them from monkeys and other primates. Body size tends to be larger. The lifespan is longer, and there is a longer interval between births. There is a tendency toward upright posture, although habitual upright bipedalism is characteristic only of hominins. The brain is larger, the face is shorter and less projecting, and all hominoids are tailless.

Apes live in forests and woodlands, and almost all apes are threatened or endangered today because of human encroachment. Gibbons are light, agile, and completely arboreal, and they are skilled brachiators. **Brachiation** is hand-over-hand movement through the trees. The heavier gorillas, chimpanzees, and adult male orangutans spend considerable time on the ground. Nevertheless, ape behavior and anatomy reveal past and present adaptation to arboreal life. For example, apes still build nests to sleep in trees. Apes have longer arms than legs, which is adaptive for brachiation (see Figure 5.4). The structure of the shoulder and clavicle (collarbone) of the apes and humans suggests that we had a brachiating ancestor. In fact, young apes still brachiate. Adult apes tend to be too heavy to brachiate safely. Their weight is more than many branches can withstand. Gorillas and chimps now use the long arms they have inherited from their more arboreal ancestors for life on the ground. The terrestrial locomotion of chimps and gorillas is called *knuckle-walking*. In it, long arms and callused knuckles support the trunk as the apes amble around, leaning forward.

FIGURE 5.4    **The Limb Ratio of the Arboreal Gibbon and Terrestrial *Homo***
How does this anatomical difference fit the modes of locomotion used by gibbons and humans?

McGraw-Hill Education

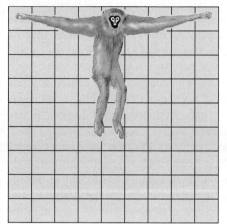
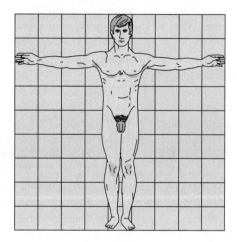

## Gibbons

Gibbons are widespread in the forests of Southeast Asia, especially in Malaysia. Smallest of the apes, male and female gibbons have about the same average height (3 feet, or 1 meter) and weight (12 to 25 pounds, or 5 to 10 kilograms). Gibbons spend most of their time just below the forest canopy (treetops). For efficient brachiation, gibbons have long arms and fingers, with short thumbs. Slenderly built, gibbons are the most agile apes. They use their long arms for balance when they occasionally walk erect on the ground or along a branch. Gibbons are the preeminent arboreal specialists among the apes. They subsist on a diet mainly of fruits, with occasional insects and small animals. Gibbons and siamangs, their slightly larger relatives, tend to live in *primary groups*, which are composed of a permanently bonded male and female and their preadolescent offspring.

## Orangutans

There are two surviving, but critically endangered, species of orangutan, Asiatic apes that belong to the genus *Pongo*. Orangutans once were found throughout Southeast Asia, but today they are confined to two Indonesian islands—Borneo and Sumatra. Researchers estimate the number of orangutans left on Borneo at between 70,000 and 100,000, meaning their population was more than halved over the study period, which ran between 1999 and 2015 (Sample 2018). No more than 7,500 survive on Sumatra (Isaacson 2012). Historically, orangutans existed throughout Sumatra, but today they are restricted to the north of the island.

Orangutan sexual dimorphism is striking. Weighing more than twice as much as females, adult males are intermediate in size between chimp and gorilla males. Orang males can weigh up to 300 pounds (135 kilograms), but they usually weigh around 200 pounds (90 kilograms). Less bulky than gorillas, male orangs can be more arboreal than male gorillas, although they typically climb, rather than swing through, the trees. The smaller size of females and young permits them to make fuller use of the trees. Orangutans have a varied diet of fruits, bark, leaves, and insects. Because they live in jungles and feed in trees, orangutans are difficult to study. Still, field reports about orangs in their natural setting (Schaik 2004) have clarified their behavior and social organization. They are the least sociable of the great apes (see Isaacson 2012; Schaik 2004). Often they are solitary, with their tightest social units formed by females and preadolescent young, and males foraging alone.

Since 1971 Biruté Mary Galdikas has studied wild orangutans in central Borneo. She is one of three prominent primatologists—all women—encouraged by famed paleoanthropologist Louis B. Leakey to study and protect the great apes. Leakey wanted them to study apes specifically because he felt their research would offer insights about ourselves and our extinct ancestors (as indeed they have). The others are Jane Goodall (working with chimpanzees) and the late Dian Fossey (who worked with mountain gorillas). As Galdikas (2007) reports, economic globalization has fueled worldwide demand for pulp, paper, palm oil, and precious metals, leading to the destruction of Indonesia's tropical forests and endangering the orang. By now, over 80 percent of the orang habitat has been either depopulated or totally destroyed (Galdikas 2007). Dr. Galdikas has urged Indonesia to impose a tax on multinational companies that profit from rain forest destruction and to use the revenues for forest and orangutan

Dr. Biruté Mary Galdikas joins orangutans on a feeding platform in Tanjung Puting National Park in Indonesia. In addition to her decades of work with orangs, Dr. Galdikas has established Camp Leakey, named for her mentor, Louis Leakey, as a research and education center within this national park. Orangutan Foundation International

conservation. Indonesia, however, is a large, populous country with millions of people suffering from poverty. The temptation to exploit natural resources to feed people, and to expand the economy, is great. Is there a realistic chance that the orangutan will survive in the wild?

## Gorillas

Within just one species, *Gorilla gorilla*, there are three subspecies of gorilla. The western lowland gorilla is the one usually seen in zoos. This subspecies, the smallest, lives mainly in forests in the Central African Republic, Congo, Cameroon, Gabon, Equatorial Guinea, and Nigeria. The eastern lowland gorilla, of which there are only four in captivity, is slightly larger and lives in eastern Congo. There are no mountain gorillas, the third subspecies, in captivity. These are the largest gorillas with the longest hair (to keep them warm in their mountainous habitat). They are also the rarest gorillas, which Dian Fossey (1983) and other scientists have studied in Rwanda, Uganda, and eastern Congo.

The eastern lowland gorilla has recently been classified as "critically endangered" by the International Union for Conservation of Nature (IUCN). Its population has declined by more than 70 percent in 20 years, to fewer than 5,000 individuals. An accurate count has been impossible for many years because of violence in the region. The cause of this decline is mainly hunting, which, although illegal, happens anyway. The eastern mountain

Mountain gorillas are the rarest and most endangered kind of gorilla. Dian Fossey (shown here) and other scientists have studied them in Rwanda, Uganda, and eastern Congo. Here, Fossey (now deceased) observes a young gorilla in Rwanda's Virunga Mountains. Liam White/Alamy Stock Photo

gorilla—a major tourist attraction—also is critically endangered; about 1,000 individuals remain (Aldred 2012).

Full-grown male gorillas may weigh 400 pounds (180 kilograms) and stand 6 feet tall (183 centimeters). Like most terrestrial primates, gorillas show marked sexual dimorphism. The average adult female weighs half as much as the male. Gorillas spend little time in the trees, where it's hard for an adult male to move his bulk. When gorillas sleep in trees, they build nests, which usually are no more than 10 feet (3 meters) off the ground. By contrast, the nests of chimps and female orangs may be 100 feet (30 meters) above the ground.

Gorillas spend most of their time moving through the jungle, eating ground plants, leaves, bark, fruits, and other vegetation (see Rothman, Raubenheimer, and Chapman 2011). Like most primates, gorillas live in social groups. The troop is a common unit of primate social organization, consisting of multiple males and females and their offspring. Although troops with up to 30 gorillas have been observed, most gorillas live in smaller groups, with 10 to 20 members. Gorilla troops tend to have fairly stable memberships, with little shifting between troops (Fossey 1983). Each troop has a silverback male, named for the strip of white hair extending down his back. This is the physical sign of full maturity among the male gorillas. The silverback is usually the only breeding male in the troop, which is why gorilla troops are sometimes called "one-male groups." However, a few younger, subordinate males may also adhere to such a one-male group.

## Chimpanzees

Chimpanzees belong to the genus *Pan*, which has two species: *Pan troglodytes* (the common chimpanzee) and *Pan paniscus* (the bonobo or "pygmy" chimpanzee) (Arcadi 2018; De Waal 2013; Stanford 2018). Like gorillas, chimps live in tropical Africa, but they span a larger area and more varied environments than gorillas do. The common chimp, *Pan troglodytes*, lives in western central Africa (Gabon, Cameroon), as well as in western Africa (Ivory Coast, Sierra Leone, Liberia, Gambia) and eastern Africa (Congo, Uganda, and Tanzania). Bonobos live in remote and densely forested areas of just one country—the Democratic Republic of the Congo (DRC). Common chimps live mainly in tropical rain forests but also in woodlands and mixed forest-woodland-grassland areas, such as the Gombe Stream National Park, Tanzania, where Jane Goodall and other researchers began to study them in 1960 (see Goodall 2009, 2010).

Chimps prefer fruits but are actually omnivorous, adding animal protein to their diet by hunting small mammals (especially monkeys), birds' eggs, and insects. Chimps are lighter and more arboreal than gorillas are. The adult male's weight—between 100 and 200 pounds (45 to 90 kilograms)—is about half that of the male gorilla. There is much less sexual dimorphism among chimps than among gorillas. Females approximate 88 percent of the average male height. This is similar to the ratio of sexual dimorphism in *Homo sapiens*.

Several scientists have studied wild chimps, and we know more about the full range of their behavior and social organization than we do about the other apes (see Goodall 2009; Matsuzawa 2011; Nishida 2012). The long-term research of Jane Goodall (2010) and others at Gombe provides especially useful information. Approximately

Chimpanzees live mainly in tropical rain forests but also in woodlands and mixed forest-woodland-grassland areas, such as the Gombe Stream National Park, Tanzania, where Jane Goodall began to study them in 1960. Shown here 30 years after her first visit to Gombe, Goodall continues her lifelong commitment to these endangered animals. Michael Nichols/National Geographic/Getty Images

150 chimpanzees range over Gombe's 30 square miles (80 square kilometers). Goodall has described communities of about 50 chimps, all of which know one another and interact from time to time. Communities regularly split up into smaller groups: a mother and her offspring; males, females, and young; a few males; and occasionally solitary animals. Females are more likely than males to migrate and mate outside their natal group.

When chimps, which are very vocal, meet, they greet one another with gestures, facial expressions, and calls. They hoot to maintain contact during their daily rounds. Males habitually cooperate in hunting parties (see Hart and Sussman 2009; Mitani et al. 2012; Nishida 2012). Like baboons and macaques, chimps exhibit dominance relationships through attacks and displacement.

As with all the apes, chimp survival is threatened today, mainly by human activities. In one study, Carroll (2008) found that Ivory Coast's chimpanzee populations had fallen by 90 percent over an 18-year period. That country had been considered home to about half of all West African chimps. Scientists found just 800 to 1,200 chimps there in 2008, compared with 8,000 to 12,000 in 1990. The 1990 survey itself had confirmed a significant decline from the 1960s, when Ivory Coast was home to an estimated 100,000 chimps. Between 1990 and 2008, Ivory Coast's human population increased by 50 percent, resulting in more hunting and deforestation. These threats to wildlife remain, augmented by civil unrest and political instability.  For the latest information, see the Save the Chimps website: https://www.savethechimps.org/about-us/chimp-facts/.

## Bonobos

Ancestral chimps eventually spread out of the forests and into woodlands and more open habitats (see Choi 2011; Hare and Yamamoto 2017). Bonobos, which belong to the species *Pan paniscus,* apparently never left the protection of the trees. Up to 10,000 bonobos survive in the humid forests south of the Zaire River, in the DRC. Despite their common name—the *pygmy* chimpanzee—bonobos can't be distinguished from chimpanzees by size. Adult males of the smallest subspecies of chimpanzee average 95 pounds (43 kilograms), and females average 73 pounds (33 kilograms). These figures are about the same for bonobos (De Waal 2013).

Although smaller than the males, female bonobos seem to rule. De Waal (2013) characterizes bonobo communities as female-centered, peace-loving, and egalitarian. The strongest social bonds are among females, although females also bond with males. The male bonobo's status reflects that of his mother, to whom he remains closely bonded for life.

The frequency with which bonobos have sex—and use it to avoid conflict—makes them exceptional among the primates. Despite frequent sex, the bonobo reproductive rate doesn't exceed that of the chimpanzee. A female bonobo gives birth every five or six years. Then, like chimps, female bonobos nurse and carry around their young for up to five years. Bonobos reach adolescence at around 7 years of age. Females, which first give birth at age 13 or 14, are full grown by 15 years.

## Endangered Primates

Deforestation poses a special risk for the primates, because 90 percent of surviving nonhuman primate species live in tropical forests—in Africa, Asia, South America, and Central America. As the Earth's human population swells, all nonhuman primates have become endangered. The Primates in Peril report lists and discusses the 25 most endangered primates.

Although deforestation is the main reason primates are disappearing, it isn't the only threat. Another is human hunting. Primates are a major food source in Amazonia and West and Central Africa, where people kill thousands of monkeys annually. Hunting poses less of a threat in Asia. In India, Hindus avoid monkey meat because the monkey is sacred, whereas Muslims avoid it because monkeys are considered unclean and unfit for human consumption.

People also hunt primates for their skins and pelts; poachers sell their body parts as trophies and ornaments. Africans use the skins of black-and-white colobus monkeys for cloaks and headdresses, and tourists buy coats and rugs made from colobus pelts. In Amazonia, ocelot and jaguar hunters shoot monkeys to bait the traps they set for the cats. Primates also are killed when they are agricultural pests. In some areas of Africa and Asia, mandrills and baboons (Africa) and macaques (Asia) raid crops, resulting in drives to kill the monkeys that interfere with human subsistence.

A final threat to primates is their capture for use in labs or as pets. Although this threat is minor compared with deforestation and hunting, it does pose a serious risk to certain endangered species in heavy demand. One of the species most hurt by this trade has been the chimpanzee, which has been widely used in biomedical research. Fortunately, the use of chimpanzees in such research has been curbed significantly in recent years (see this chapter's "Anthropology Today").

## Primate Evolution

The fossil record gives us barely a glimpse of the diverse bioforms—living beings—that have existed on Earth, including only a small fraction of all the extinct types of primates. With reference to the primate fossil record, we'll see that different geographic areas provide more abundant fossil evidence for different time periods. This doesn't necessarily mean that primates were not living elsewhere at the same time. Discussions of primate and human evolution must be tentative, because the fossil record is limited and spotty (see Fleagle 2013; Tuttle 2014). Much is subject to change as knowledge increases. A key feature of science is to recognize the tentativeness and uncertainty of knowledge. Scientists, including fossil hunters, continually seek out new evidence and devise new methods, such as DNA comparison, to improve their understanding, in this case of primate and human evolution.

## Chronology

We learned in Chapter 3 that the remains of animals and plants that lived at the same time are found in the same stratum. Based on fossils found in stratigraphic sequences, the history of vertebrate life has been divided into three main eras. The *Paleozoic* (544–245 **m.y.a.**—million years ago) was the era of ancient life—fishes, amphibians, and primitive reptiles. The *Mesozoic* (245–65 m.y.a.) was the era of middle life—reptiles, including the dinosaurs. The *Cenozoic* (65 m.y.a.-present) is the era of recent life—birds and mammals. Each era is divided into periods, and the periods are divided into epochs.

Anthropologists are concerned with the Cenozoic *era* (Figure 5.5), which includes two *periods:* Tertiary and Quaternary. Each of these periods is subdivided into *epochs.* The Tertiary had five epochs: Paleocene, Eocene, Oligocene, Miocene, and Pliocene. The Quaternary includes just two epochs: Pleistocene and Holocene, or Recent. Figure 5.5 gives the approximate dates when each of these epochs began.

Sediments from the Paleocene epoch (65–54 m.y.a.) have yielded fossil remains of diverse small mammals, including, by the late Paleocene, the earliest known primate. Lemurlike and tarsierlike fossils abound in strata dating from the Eocene (54–34 m.y.a.). Haplorrhine fossils also date to the Eocene, becoming more abundant (as proto-monkeys, or monkey precursors) during the ensuing Oligocene (34–23 m.y.a.). Hominoids (proto-apes) became widespread during the Miocene (23–5 m.y.a.). Hominins first appeared in the late Miocene, just before the Pliocene (5–2.6 m.y.a.).

FIGURE 5.5   **Periods and Epochs of the Cenozoic Era**
The geological time scale is based on stratigraphy. Eras are subdivided into periods, and periods
into epochs. In what era, period, and epoch did *Homo* originate?

McGraw-Hill Education

| Era | Period | Epoch | Climate and Life Forms |
|---|---|---|---|
| Cenozoic | Quaternary | Holocene<br>11,700 B.P. | Transition to agriculture; emergence of states |
| | | Pleistocene<br>2.6 m.y.a. | Climatic fluctuations, glaciation; spread of *Homo*, extinction of (hyper) robust australopiths |
| | Tertiary | Pliocene<br>5 m.y.a. | *Au. africanus, Au. afarensis, Au. anamensis, Ardipithecus* |
| | | Miocene<br>23 m.y.a. | Cooler and drier grasslands spread in middle latitudes; Africa collides with Eurasia (16 m.y.a.); proto-apes (ape precursors) diverse and abundant |
| | | Oligocene<br>34 m.y.a. | Cooler and drier in the north; proto-monkeys (monkey precursors) in Africa (Fayum); separation of catarrhines and platyrrhines; separation of hylobatids (gibbons) from pongids and hominids |
| | | Eocene<br>54 m.y.a | Warm tropical climates become widespread; modern orders of mammals appear; strepsirrhine and tarsierlike primates are abundant; simians appear later |
| | | Paleocene<br>65 m.y.a | First major mammal radiation; first primates; separation of strepsirrhines and haplorrhines |

## Early Primates

When the Mesozoic era ended, and the Cenozoic era began, around 65 m.y.a., North America was connected to Europe but not to South America. (The Americas joined together just 3 million years ago.) Over millions of years, the continents have "drifted" to their present locations, carried along by the gradually shifting plates of the Earth's surface (see Figure 5.6).

The Mesozoic era ended with a massive worldwide extinction of plants and animals, including the dinosaurs. Thereafter, mammals eventually replaced reptiles as the dominant large land animals. The spread of angiosperms (flowering plants) created a rich new ecological niche in which early primates could thrive, spread, and diversify (see Sussman, Rasmussen, and Raven 2013). Facilitating the expansion of flowering plants was a long period of global warming that began around 56 m.y.a. With the rising temperatures, tropical forests spread throughout North America, Europe, and Asia. (Africa and South America were island continents at that time.) Primates adapted to this expanding

FIGURE 5.6    **Placement of Continents at the End of the Mesozoic**
When the Mesozoic era ended, and the Cenozoic began, some 65 m.y.a., North
America was connected to Europe, but not to South America.

McGraw-Hill Education

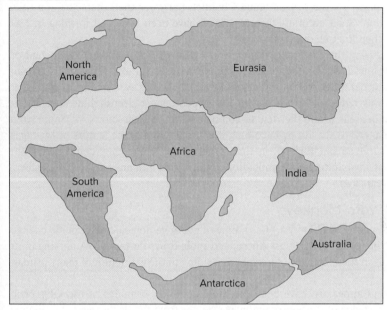

niche—widespread tropical forests and the flowering trees within them. Manual dexterity, including a good grasping ability, would have helped early primates reach, and feed near, the ends of delicate branches. This is where the most abundant fruits, flowers, gums, and nectars were located, along with the insects that pollinate flowering plants.

## Early Cenozoic Primates

A tiny, complete skeleton from China, first described in 2013, is the earliest definite primate so far discovered. Named *Archicebus achilles* because of its prominent ankle and heel, this early Chinese primate has been tentatively assigned to the tarsier lineage. *Archicebus achilles* weighed no more than 1 ounce, and it had a 5-inch (13-centimeter) tail that was longer than its 4-inch (10-centimeter) body. It lived 55 m.y.a., when Earth was a natural greenhouse, with rain forests everywhere and palm trees growing in what is now Alaska. Unlike today's tarsiers, *Archicebus* had very small eyes and was not nocturnal. Being so small and metabolically active, it probably spent its days frantically leaping around in the humid tropical forest it inhabited (Ni et al. 2013; Wilford 2013). This find supports the view that the first primates evolved in Asia—not too long after the dinosaurs went extinct (66 m.y.a.). Somehow primates crossed open water to reach Africa by 38 m.y.a. (Africa remained an island continent until 16 m.y.a.).

*Archicebus achilles* lived during the late Paleocene (65–54 m.y.a.), the first epoch of the Cenozoic era. A variety of primate species inhabited Europe and North America during the Cenozoic's second epoch, the Eocene (54–34 m.y.a.). The primates of the Eocene were early strepsirrhines and tarsierlike haplorrhines, with at least 60 genera living in Asia, North America, and Europe, and reaching Africa by the late Eocene. By the end of the Eocene, ancestral lemurs had reached Madagascar. They must have traveled from East Africa across the Mozambique Channel—narrower then than now—on thick mats of vegetation. Such naturally formed "rafts" have been observed forming in East African rivers, then floating out to sea.

It was also during the Eocene that ancestral simians (proto-monkeys) branched off from the tarsier line. These proto-monkeys were diurnal (see Schultz, Opie, and Atkinson 2011). In this diurnal niche, vision was favored over smell. The eyes and brain got bigger, and the snout was reduced. By the end of the Eocene, most strepsirrhine species had become extinct in areas where they had to compete with the proto-monkeys. Some strepsirrhines did manage to survive by becoming nocturnal. Others, the lemurs of Madagascar, not only survived but thrived on that large island, where they could adapt and diversify without any haplorrhine competition until the first humans reached Madagascar around 2,000 years ago.

## Oligocene Proto-Monkeys

The Oligocene epoch (34–23 m.y.a.) was a time of major geological and climatic change. The Great Rift Valley formed in East Africa, and India drifted into Asia. A cooling trend began, especially in the Northern Hemisphere, leading to the extinction of many primate species.

Proto-monkeys appear to have been the most common primates of the Oligocene. Most of our knowledge of those proto-monkeys comes from fossils discovered in Egypt's Fayum region. This area is a desert today, but 34–31 m.y.a. it was a swampy area, where conditions were favorable for fossilization. The Fayum proto-monkeys lived in trees and ate fruits and seeds. Compared with earlier primates, they had larger brains, reduced snouts, and more forward-looking eyes.

The split between New World monkeys and Old World monkeys was already under way. One group of the Fayum proto-monkeys was plausibly ancestral to the New World monkeys. Members of this group were small (2–3 pounds, or 0.9–1.4 kilograms), with similarities to living marmosets and tamarins, which are small South American monkeys. Like living New World monkeys, members of this group retained the dental formula of earlier primates. That formula, also shared with lemurs, lorises, and tarsiers, is 2.1.3.3, meaning two incisors, one canine, three premolars, and three molars. (The formula is based on one-fourth of the mouth, either the right or left side of the upper or lower jaw.)

The other group of Fayum proto-monkeys had a new and different dental formula (2.1.2.3), indicating the loss of a premolar, and a total of 32 teeth, versus 36 in the earlier primates. This formula is shared by all later Old World monkeys, apes, and humans. This group of Fayum fossils is plausibly ancestral to Old World monkeys, apes, and humans.

Evidence for another important evolutionary split comes from Tanzania's Rukwa Rift Basin. In 2013, researchers working there reported their discovery of two late Oligocene finds, dated to 25.2 m.y.a. One find seems to be a hominoid (a proto-ape, plausibly ancestral to apes and humans), while the other is an Old World monkey. The proto-ape fossil is a lower right jaw with teeth, and the Old World monkey find is a jaw fragment with a single tooth (Bower 2013; Stevens et al. 2013). Proto-apes became the most common primate during the Miocene epoch, which followed the Oligocene.

Exactly when did the hominoid (ape-human) line diverge from the Old World monkeys? Molecular dating based on DNA comparisons suggests that proto-apes split from the Old World monkey line between 30 and 25 m.y.a. The fact that these Tanzanian fossils date back 25.2 m.y.a. suggests that the split occurred earlier in that range of dates—perhaps 30 m.y.a. In addition to Egypt and Tanzania, primate bones have been found in Oligocene deposits in other parts of North Africa, West Africa, southern Arabia, China, Southeast Asia, and North and South America.

## Miocene Hominoids: The Proto-Apes

### Planet of the Proto-Apes

Hominoid fossils become abundant during the Miocene epoch (23–5 m.y.a.), which is divided into three parts: lower, middle, and upper. The early or lower Miocene (23–16 m.y.a.) was a warm and wet period, when forests covered East Africa. Recall that Hominoidea is the superfamily that includes fossil and living apes and humans. For simplicity's sake, the earliest hominoids are here called proto-apes, or simply *apes*. Although some of these may be ancestral to living apes, none is identical, or often even very similar, to modern apes.

During the early (lower) Miocene (23–16 m.y.a.), water separated Africa from Europe and Asia. During the middle Miocene, however, Arabia drifted into Eurasia, providing a land connection between Africa, Europe, and Asia. Migrating both ways—out of and into Africa—after 16 m.y.a. were various animals, including proto-apes, the most common primates of the middle Miocene (16–10 m.y.a.). Over 20 species have been discovered in Europe, Africa, and Asia.

### *Gigantopithecus*

The most remarkable Miocene ape was *Gigantopithecus*—almost certainly the largest primate that ever lived. Confined to Asia, it persisted for millions of years, from the late Miocene until 400,000 years ago, when it coexisted with members of our own genus, *Homo erectus*. Some people think *Gigantopithecus* is not extinct yet, that we know it today as the yeti and Bigfoot (Sasquatch). With a fossil record consisting only of jawbones and teeth, it is difficult to say for sure just how big *Gigantopithecus* was. Based on ratios of jaw and tooth size to body size in other apes, estimates of its weight range from 600 pounds (272 kilograms) to twice that, with a height between 9 and 10 feet (2.7 to 3 meters). There were at least two species of *Gigantopithecus*: One coexisted with *H. erectus* in China and Vietnam, and the other, much earlier (5 m.y.a.), lived in northern India.

### *Nyanzapithecus alesi*

The 2014 discovery in northern Kenya of a lemon-sized fossil ape skull—that of an infant that lived 13 m.y.a.—reveals what the common ancestor of living African apes and humans may have looked like (see Nengo et al. 2017). A volcano had buried the forest where the baby ape lived, preserving the fossil while providing volcanic minerals that permitted its dating. Ape fossils from this time period (the middle Miocene) are scarce and consist

This drawing imagines a day in the life of Gigantopithecus, the largest ape ever to have lived. What would be the likely environmental effects of a population of such large apes? Sibbick/Fortean/TopFoto/The Image Works

Nyanzapithecus alesi is the most complete extinct ape skull known in the fossil record. Isaiah Nengo

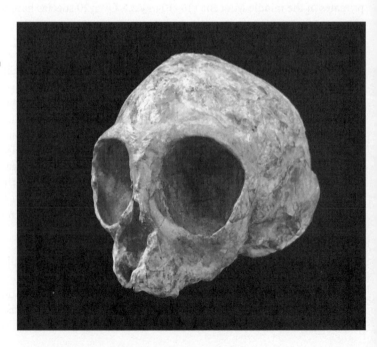

mainly of isolated teeth and jaw fragments. This tiny skull, nicknamed Alesi by its discoverers (full name *Nyanzapithecus alesi*), is the most complete extinct ape skull known in the fossil record. The teeth allowed placement of the specimen as a new species, *Nyanzapithecus alesi*, within the established genus *Nyanzapithecus*, previously known only from teeth. This discovery supports the idea that the common ancestor of humans and the African apes lived in Africa. (See Wang 2017 for a video of the skull, including the teeth and the inner ear.)

## An Evolutionary Timetable

In the current timetable of primate evolution, the lineage of Old World monkeys diverged from the hominoid line around 30 m.y.a. The ancestors of the lesser apes (gibbons and siamangs) separated from those of the great apes perhaps 16 m.y.a. Sometime thereafter, perhaps as early as 13 m.y.a., the orangutan line diverged from that leading to the African apes and humans (see Figure 5.3). Yet another split took place when the gorilla line branched off from the line leading to chimpanzees and hominins. Around 7–6 m.y.a., another split in the lineage led to the various early hominins. Some intriguing fossils dating from that critical time period have been discovered recently and are examined in Chapter 6.

Such evolutionary timetables are based on a combination of DNA and fossil evidence. We know that chimps, bonobos, and gorillas are our closest surviving cousin species. We do not, however, know much about the specific ancestry of gorillas and chimps. This is primarily because those apes tend to live in humid forests, where conditions are not favorable to preservation and fossilization. Ancient hominins, however, tended to live in less humid environments, so we are fortunate to have a larger, and constantly growing, hominin fossil record, which we consider in Chapters 6 and 7.

## Anthropology Today  *Should Apes Have Human Rights?*

In Africa and Asia, the dwindling populations of great apes face extinction due to human warfare, oil exploration, deforestation, deliberate hunting, and other threats. Continents away, animal rights activists work to conserve apes, even to grant them legal rights. In 2000, the U.S. Congress enacted the Great Ape Conservation Act, which authorized $5 million annually over five years to protect apes in the wild. In 2005, Congress reauthorized that act, which matched public with private funding, for another five years. The money would help protect habitats, battle poachers, and educate local populations about the importance of the apes. (Reauthorization bills introduced in Congress since 2010 have not passed.)

What did the Great Ape Conservation Act accomplish? In Indonesia, funding helped slow the conversion of forests to commercial plantations. In Congo, one of the few countries in which the mountain gorilla survives, promotion of alternative fuels has helped reduce deforestation for charcoal production. By 2010, when it ended, the Great Ape Conservation Fund had helped fund more than 50 programs in 7 Asian and 12 African countries.

*continued*

## Anthropology Today  *continued*

The humanlike characteristics of the great apes are evident to anyone who has seen the various *Planet of the Apes* movies, especially the most recent ones, featuring the intelligent, speaking chimpanzee named Caesar and his companions. Scientific knowledge confirms that apes are close to humans in their cognitive abilities and emotional states. Experiments teaching sign language to chimps and gorillas, described in Chapter 10, demonstrate that apes are capable of learning hundreds of meaningful signs and of communicating with humans and other signing apes. DNA confirms the close relationships among humans, chimps, and gorillas. Scientists know that the great apes have complex mental abilities, which elevate their capability for suffering. On that basis alone, say rights advocates, apes deserve basic protections from the pain, isolation, and arbitrary imprisonment inflicted by medical experiments or captivity in zoos.

In 1993, philosophers Peter Singer and Paola Cavalieri published *The Great Ape Project*, a book that argued that chimpanzees, gorillas, bonobos, and orangutans should have the same basic rights as human beings. In fact, in December 2014, an Argentine court did extend legal rights to a 28-year-old orangutan named Sandra, a captive ape born in Germany and taken to the Buenos Aires zoo, where she lived for 20 years. As the world's first animal legally recognized as a "nonhuman person," Sandra's new status facilitated her transfer to a sanctuary in Brazil. A month earlier, in North America, a New York state court had denied an appeal put forth on behalf of a pet chimp named Tommy. The court argued that, regardless of their intelligence or feelings, chimpanzees cannot fulfill the social obligations expected of a person with rights. In 2017, the New York Supreme Court's appellate division affirmed the lower court's decision, saying there was no legal precedent for chimpanzees being considered people, and that their cognitive capabilities did not mean they could be held legally accountable for their actions.

In addition to promoting legal rights for apes, advocates have urged governments and the United Nations to ban ape captivity in zoos and circuses and their use in scientific research, especially medical testing. Several nations, including New Zealand, the United Kingdom, Sweden, Austria, Belgium, and the Netherlands have banned research on apes for ethical reasons. In January 2013, the U.S. National Institutes of Health (NIH) accepted a committee recommendation to curtail the use of chimpanzees in research. Of the 450 chimpanzees then under NIH control, 400 would be retired and moved to sanctuaries. NIH did retain 50 chimps for possible future research use, but they, too, were transferred to a sanctuary in November 2015. Today, NIH no longer uses chimps for research; its former research chimps are enjoying their freedom in animal sanctuaries. Almost 300 of them were moved to Chimp Haven near Shreveport, Louisiana, where they live in large social groups on 200 acres of parkland (see http://www.chimphaven.org/).

How do you feel about animal rights in general and ape rights in particular? Because the great apes are so close to humans genetically, physically, and temperamentally, do they merit special treatment among the animals?

**Source:** Associated Press (2017), Becker (2013), Collins (2015), Eldred (2013), Kahn (2011), Keim (2014), Mitani (2011), and *The Week* (2013).

# Summary

1.  Humans, apes, monkeys, tarsiers, lemurs, and lorises are primates. The primate order is subdivided into suborders, infraorders, parvaorders, superfamilies, families, tribes, genera, species, and subspecies. Organisms in any subdivision (taxon) of a taxonomy are assumed to share more recent ancestry with each other than they do with organisms in other taxa. But it's sometimes hard to tell the difference between homologies, which reflect common ancestry, and analogies, biological similarities that develop through convergent evolution.

2.  The primate order has two suborders: Strepsirrhini (lemurs and lorises) and Haplorrhini (tarsiers, monkeys, apes, and humans). The strepsirrhine and haplorrhine lines had split by 60 m.y.a. By the end of the Eocene, early simians (proto-monkeys) had adapted to a diurnal (daytime) ecological niche. Tarsiers and lorises survived by adapting to nocturnal life. Lemurs survived on the island of Madagascar.

3.  The infraorder Simiiformes includes the anthropoid or "humanlike" primates—monkeys, apes, and humans. All share a common dental formula (2.1.2.3) and fully developed primate features, such as depth and color vision, and a shift in tactile areas to the fingers. All New World monkeys are arboreal. Old World monkeys include both terrestrial species (e.g., baboons and macaques) and arboreal ones. The great apes are orangutans, gorillas, chimpanzees, and bonobos. The lesser apes are gibbons and siamangs.

4.  Gibbons and siamangs live in Southeast Asian forests. These apes are slight, arboreal animals whose mode of locomotion is brachiation. Sexual dimorphism, slight among gibbons, is marked among orangutans, which are confined to two Indonesian islands. Sexually dimorphic gorillas, the most terrestrial apes, are vegetarians confined to equatorial Africa. Two species of chimpanzees live in the forests and woodlands of tropical Africa. Chimps are less sexually dimorphic, more numerous, and more omnivorous than gorillas are.

5.  Primates have lived during the past 65 million years, the Cenozoic era, with seven epochs: Paleocene, Eocene, Oligocene, Miocene, Pliocene, Pleistocene, and Holocene, or Recent.

6.  The earliest known primate, discovered in China 55 m.y.a., dates to the late Paleocene epoch (65-54 m.y.a.). Thereafter, lemurlike and tarsierlike primates proliferated during the Eocene (54-34 m.y.a.). During the Oligocene (34-23 m.y.a.), proto-monkeys became the most common primates. The split between ancestral platyrrhines (New World monkeys) and catarrhines (Old World monkeys, apes, and humans) occurred during the Oligocene, as did the split between Old World monkeys and hominoids.

7.  The earliest known hominoid (proto-ape) dates to 25.2 m.y.a., just before the Miocene (23-5 m.y.a.). Proto-apes proliferated during the middle and late Miocene. Since the middle Miocene (16-10 m.y.a.), Africa, Europe, and Asia have been connected. Proto-apes spread to all three continents and became the most common primates of the middle Miocene. Asia's *Gigantopithecus*, the largest primate ever to live, persisted for millions of years, finally coexisting with *Homo erectus*.

## Think Like an Anthropologist

1. There have been reported sightings of Bigfoot in the Pacific Northwest of North America and of the yeti (abominable snowman) in the Himalayas. What facts about apes might lead you to question such reports?
2. Our cultural background affects the ways in which we perceive nature, human nature, and "the natural." Can you think of aspects of your culture that have affected the way you think about humans' relationship to other primates?

**Key Terms**

analogies, *103*
anthropoids, *106*
arboreal, *105*
bipedal, *105*
brachiation, *110*
convergent
   evolution, *103*

Haplorrhini, *106*
hominoid, *110*
homologies, *102*
m.y.a., *117*
opposable
   thumb, *105*
primates, *100*

primatology, *100*
Strepsirrhini, *106*
taxonomy, *101*
terrestrial, *100*

# Chapter  6

# Early Hominins

## What Makes Us Human?

In trying to determine whether a fossil is a human ancestor, should we look for traits that make us human today? Sometimes yes, sometimes no. We do look for similarities in DNA, including mutations shared by certain lineages but not others. But what about such key human attributes as bipedal locomotion, a long period of childhood dependency, big brains, and the use of tools and language? Some of these key markers of humanity are fairly recent—or have origins that are difficult to date.

In 1924, the Australian anatomist Raymond Dart, who was working in South Africa, announced the discovery there of *Australopithecus africanus* as an early *bipedal* human ancestor. Dart's fellow scientists, however, found it hard to accept this small-brained, primitive creature as a hominin. It looked too apelike, and besides, it came from Africa. The ethnocentrism associated with colonialism dismissed Africa as a proper place to look for human origins. Furthermore, scientists back then assumed erroneously that a key early hominin marker would be a large brain, and certainly not the ape-sized cranium of Dart's South African fossil.

Piltdown man, ostensibly found in a gravel pit in Piltdown, East Sussex, England, in 1912, seemed a more proper human ancestor. It had a large, modern-looking skull, and it came from Europe. Its apelike jaw, however, was hard to explain. What was one to make of this unusual and perplexing mixture? Amazingly, it took over 40 years for Piltdown man to be debunked as a forgery. Fluorine absorption analysis applied to the skull and jaw in 1953 turned Piltdown man into the now infamous "Piltdown hoax." The skull had much more fluorine than the jaw—impossible if they had come from the same individual and had been deposited in the same ground at the same time. Someone had attached the jaw of a young orangutan to the skull of a modern human, then buried the "fossil" in an attempt to muddle the interpretation of the fossil record. The hoax survived longer than its perpetrator probably imagined. Even big-brained scientists can be fooled by the biases of their time.

We know now that bipedalism, rather than a big brain, is the key attribute that distinguishes early hominins from the apes, and upright bipedal locomotion remains fundamental to human existence.

## Bipedalism

Skeletal material from ***Ardipithecus***, the earliest widely accepted hominin genus (5.8–4.4 m.y.a.), indicates a capacity—albeit an imperfect one—for upright bipedal locomotion—the key feature differentiating early hominins from the apes. The *Ardipithecus* pelvis is transitional between one suited for arboreal climbing and one modified for bipedalism. Ethiopia's *Ardipithecus* shows that bipedalism goes back more than 5 million years. Some scientists see even earlier evidence of bipedalism in two other fossil finds, described later in the chapter—one from Chad (*Sahelanthropus tchadensis*) and one from Kenya (*Orrorin tugenensis*).

Bipedalism traditionally has been viewed as an adaptation to open grassland or savanna country, although *Ardipithecus* appears to have lived in a humid woodland habitat. Perhaps bipedalism developed in the woodlands but became even more adaptive out on the savanna (see Choi 2011). Scientists have suggested several advantages of bipedalism: the ability to see over tall grass and scrub vegetation, to carry items back to a home base, and to reduce the body's exposure to solar radiation (see Ferraro et al. 2013). Studies with scale models of primates suggest that quadrupedalism (four-footed locomotion) exposes the body to 60 percent more solar radiation than does bipedalism. Based on the fossil and archaeological records, upright bipedal locomotion preceded stone tool manufacture and the expansion of the brain. However, although early hominins could move bipedally on the ground, they also preserved enough of an apelike anatomy to make them good climbers (see the later description of *Ardipithecus* as well as of "Lucy's baby"). They could take to the trees to sleep and to escape terrestrial predators.

## Brains, Skulls, and Childhood Dependency

Early hominins had small brains. *Australopithecus afarensis*, a bipedal hominin that lived more than 3 million years ago, had a cranial capacity (430 cm³—cubic centimeters) that barely surpassed the chimp average (390 cm³). The form of the *afarensis* skull also is like that of the chimpanzee, although the ratio of brain to body size may have been larger. Brain size has increased during hominin evolution, especially with the advent of the genus *Homo*. But this increase had to overcome the problem of giving birth to big-brained babies. Larger skulls require larger birth canals, but the requirements of upright bipedalism impose limits on the expansion of the human pelvic opening. If the opening is too

*Australopithecus afarensis* (3.8–3.0 m.y.a.) striding bipedally. A key part of being human, bipedalism evolved among hominins long before the big brain. *Encyclopaedia Britannica*/UIG/Getty Images

large, the pelvis doesn't provide sufficient support for the trunk. Locomotion suffers, and posture problems develop. If, by contrast, the birth canal is too narrow, mother and child (without the modern option of Cesarean section) may die. Natural selection has struck a balance between the structural demands of upright posture and the tendency toward increased brain size—the birth of immature and dependent children whose brains and skulls grow dramatically after birth.

## Tools

Given what is known about tool use and manufacture by the great apes, it is likely that early hominins shared this ability as a homology with the apes. We'll see later that the first firm evidence for hominin stone tool manufacture is dated to 3.3 m.y.a. Upright bipedalism would have permitted the use of tools and weapons against predators and competitors. Bipedal locomotion also allowed early hominins to carry things, including scavenged parts of carnivore kills, back to a home base (see Ferraro et al. 2013).

## Teeth

Ironically, some of the physical markers that have led scientists to identify certain early fossils as hominins rather than apes are features that have been lost during subsequent human evolution. Consider one prominent example: big back teeth. (Indeed, a pattern of overall dental reduction has characterized human evolution.) In adapting to the savanna, with its gritty, tough, and fibrous vegetation, it was advantageous for early hominins to have large back teeth and thick tooth enamel. This permitted thorough chewing of tough, fibrous vegetation and mixture with salivary enzymes to permit digestion of foods that otherwise would not have been digestible.

The churning, rotary motion associated with such chewing also favored reduction of the canines and first premolars (bicuspids). These front teeth are much sharper and longer in the apes than in early hominins. For early hominins, reduced canines and large back teeth with thick enamel became key adaptive features in a savanna habitat.

## Chronology of Hominin Evolution

Recall that the term *hominin* is used to designate the human line after its split from ancestral chimps. *Hominid* refers to the taxonomic family that includes humans and the African apes and their immediate ancestors. In this book, *hominid* is used when there is doubt about the hominin status of the fossil (e.g., with Toumai, as described later). Although recent fossil discoveries have pushed the hominin lineage back to almost 6 million years, humans actually haven't been around too long when the age of the Earth is considered. If we compare Earth's history to a 24-hour day (with one second equaling 50,000 years),

Earth originated at midnight.

Life originated at 4:00 A.M.

The earliest fossils were deposited at 5:45 A.M.

The first vertebrates appeared at 9:02 P.M.

The first dinosaurs, at 10:56 P.M.

The earliest mammals, at 11:39 P.M.

The earliest primates, at 11:40 P.M.

The earliest hominins, at 11:58 P.M.

And *Homo sapiens* arrives 6 seconds before midnight.

Although the first hominins appeared late in the Miocene epoch, for the study of hominin evolution, the Pliocene (5-2.6 m.y.a.), Pleistocene (2.6 m.y.a.-11,700 B.P.), and Recent (11,700 B.P.-present) epochs are most important.

## Who Were the Earliest Hominins?

Decades of important, and continuing, discoveries of fossils and tools have increased our knowledge of hominid and hominin evolution. The most significant recent discoveries have been made in Africa—Kenya, Tanzania, Ethiopia, Chad, and South Africa. These finds come from different sites and may be the remains of individuals that lived hundreds of thousands of years apart. Furthermore, geological processes operating over thousands or millions of years inevitably distort fossil remains. Table 6.1 summarizes the major events in hominid and hominin evolution. You should consult it throughout this chapter and the next one.

TABLE 6.1   Dates and Geographic Distribution of Major Hominoid, Hominid, and Hominin Fossil Groups

| Fossil Group | Dates, m.y.a. | Known Distribution |
|---|---|---|
| **Hominoid** | | |
| *Nyanzapithecus alesi* | 13 | Kenya |
| **Hominid** | | |
| Common ancestor of hominids | 8? | East Africa |
| *Sahelanthropus tchadensis* | 7–6 | Chad |
| *Orrorin tugenensis* | 6 | Kenya |
| **Hominins** | | |
| *Ardipithecus kadabba* | 5.8–5.5 | Ethiopia |
| *Ardipithecus ramidus* | 4.4 | Ethiopia |
| **Gracile australopiths (*Australopithecus*)** | 4.2–1.78 | Ethiopia, East and South Africa |
| *Au. anamensis* | 4.2–3.9 | Kenya |
| *Au. afarensis* | 3.8–3.0 | East Africa (Laetoli, Hadar) |
| *Au. garhi* | 2.6–2.5 | Ethiopia |
| *Au. africanus* | 3.5–2.5 | South Africa |
| *Au. sediba* | 1.98–1.78 | South Africa |
| **Robust australopiths (*Paranthropus*)** | 2.6–1.0 | East and South Africa |
| *P. aethiopicus* | 2.6 | Kenya |
| *P. robustus* | 1.9–1.0 | South Africa |
| *P. boisei* | 2.3–1.4 | East Africa |
| ***Homo*** | | |
| *H. rudolfensis* | 2.03–1.78 | East Africa |
| *H. habilis* | 1.9–1.44 | East Africa |
| *H. erectus* | 1.9–0.5 | Africa, Asia, Europe |
| *H. heidelbergensis* | 0.8–0.2 | Africa, Asia, Europe |
| Neandertals | 0.13–0.039 (130,000–39,000) | Europe, Middle East, Central Asia, Siberia |
| **Anatomically modern humans** | 0.3–present (300,000–present) | Worldwide (after 15,000 B.P.) |

## *Sahelanthropus tchadensis*

In July 2001, anthropologists working in Central Africa—in northern Chad—unearthed the 7- to 6-million-year-old skull of the oldest possible human ancestor yet found. This discovery consists of a nearly complete skull, two lower jaw fragments, and three teeth. It dates to the time period when humans and chimps could have been diverging from a recent common ancestor. The discovery was made by a multinational team led by the French paleontologist Michel Brunet. The actual discoverer was the university undergraduate Ahounta Djimdoumalbaye, who spied the skull embedded in sandstone. The new fossil was dubbed *Sahelanthropus tchadensis*, referring to the northern Sahel region of Chad where it was found. The fossil also is known as Toumai, a local name meaning "hope of life."

The skull, an apparent adult male, had a chimp-sized brain (320-380 cm$^3$), heavy brow ridges, and a relatively flat, humanlike face. Toumai's habitat included savanna, forests, rivers, and lakes—and abundant animal life such as elephants, antelope, horses, giraffes, hyenas, hippopotamuses, wild boars, crocodiles, fish, and rodents. The animal species enabled the team to date the site where Toumai was found (by comparison with radiometrically dated sites with similar fauna).

Toumai blends apelike and hominin characteristics. Although the brain was chimp-sized, the tooth enamel was thicker than a chimp's enamel, suggesting a diet that included not just fruits but also tougher vegetation. Also, Toumai's snout did not protrude as far as a chimp's, making it more humanlike, and the canine tooth was shorter than those of other apes.

The skull is nearly complete, despite having been crushed and distorted by geological processes. The placement of its *foramen magnum* (the "big hole" through which the spinal cord joins the brain) farther forward than in apes suggests that *Sahelanthropus* moved bipedally. Its discovery in Chad indicates that early hominid (and possibly hominin) evolution was not confined to East Africa's Rift Valley. The abundant early hominin fossil record that has come out of the Rift Valley may well reflect geology, preservation, and modern exposure of fossils rather than the actual geographic distribution of species in the past. The discovery of *Sahelanthropus* in Chad is the first proof of a more widespread distribution of early hominids.

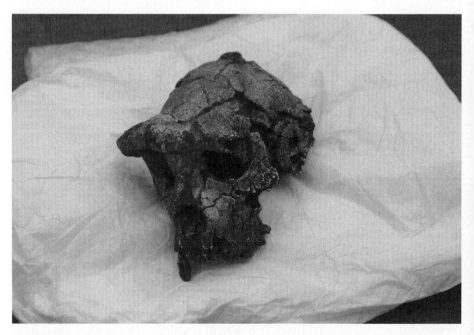

The skull of Toumai, or *Sahelanthropus tchadensis*, discovered in northern Chad in 2001 and dated to 7-6 m.y.a. Is Toumai a possible hominin ancestor? Patrick Robert/Corbis Historical/Getty Images

## Orrorin tugenensis

In January 2001, Brigitte Senut, Martin Pickford, and others reported the discovery, near the village of Tugen in Kenya, of possible early hominin fossils they called *Orrorin tugenensis* (Aiello and Collard 2001; Senut et al. 2001). The find consisted of 13 fossils from at least five individuals. The fossils include pieces of jaw with teeth, isolated upper and lower teeth, arm bones, and a finger bone. *Orrorin* appears to have been a chimp-sized or smaller creature that climbed easily and walked on two legs when on the ground. The fossilized left femur (thigh bone) suggests upright bipedalism, while the thick right humerus (upper arm bone) suggests tree-climbing skills. Associated animal remains indicate that *Orrorin* lived in a wooded environment.

    *Orrorin*'s upper incisor, upper canine, and lower premolar are more like the teeth of a female chimpanzee than like human teeth. But other dental and skeletal features, especially bipedalism, led the discoverers to assign *Orrorin* to the hominin lineage. *Orrorin* lived after *Sahelanthropus tchadensis* but before *Ardipithecus kadabba*, discovered in Ethiopia, also in 2001, and dated to 5.8–5.5 m.y.a. The hominin status of *Ardipithecus* is more generally accepted than is that of either *Sahelanthropus* or *Orrorin*.

## Ardipithecus

*Ardipithecus* had two known species—*Ardipithecus kadabba* (5.8–5.5 m.y.a.) and *Ardipithecus ramidus* (4.4 m.y.a.). The later (*ramidus*) fossils were discovered first, in 1992–1994 in Ethiopia by Berhane Asfaw, Gen Suwa, and Tim White. Dating to 4.4 m.y.a., those *ramidus* fossils are the remains of some 17 individuals, with cranial, facial, dental, and upper limb bones. Subsequently, much older *Ardipithecus* (*kadabba*) fossils, dating back to the Miocene epoch, were found in Ethiopia. The *kadabba* find consists of 11 specimens,

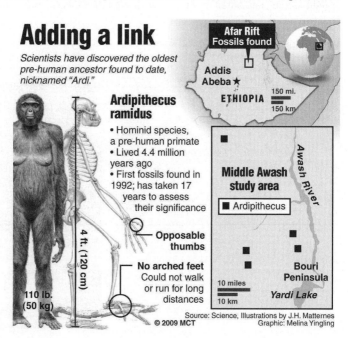

*Ardipithecus ramidus:* Representations of "Ardi," including its skeleton and a map of the discovery area. Living 4.4 million years ago, Ardi was both a hominid and a hominin. What's the difference between those terms? Yingling/MCT/Newscom

**Adding a link**

Scientists have discovered the oldest pre-human ancestor found to date, nicknamed "Ardi."

Afar Rift Fossils found

Addis Abeba ★

ETHIOPIA

150 mi.
150 km

**Ardipithecus ramidus**

• Hominid species, a pre-human primate
• Lived 4.4 million years ago
• First fossils found in 1992; has taken 17 years to assess their significance

4 ft. (120 cm)

Opposable thumbs

No arched feet
Could not walk or run for long distances

110 lb. (50 kg)

**Middle Awash study area**

■ Ardipithecus

Awash River

10 miles
10 km

■

■

■
Bouri Peninsula

*Yardi Lake*

Source: Science, Illustrations by J.H. Matternes
© 2009 MCT    Graphic: Melina Yingling

including a jawbone with teeth, hand and foot bones, fragments of arm bones, and a piece of collarbone. At least five individuals are represented. These creatures were apelike in size and anatomy. As of this writing, because of its likely bipedalism, *Ardipithecus kadabba* is recognized as the earliest known hominin, with the *Sahelanthropus* find from Chad, dated to 7–6 m.y.a., and *Orrorin* from Kenya, dated to 6 m.y.a., as possibly even older hominins.

In 2009, a newly reported find—a fairly complete skeleton dubbed "Ardi"—was heralded on the front page of the *New York Times* and throughout the media (Wilford 2009). Ardi (4.4 m.y.a.), a member of *Ardipithecus ramidus*, replaces Lucy (3.2 m.y.a.—see the section on *Australopithecus afarensis*) as the earliest known hominin skeleton. Scientists infer that Ardi was female, based on its small, slight skull and small canine teeth compared with others at the site. However, at 4 feet (1.2 meters) tall and 120 pounds (54 kg), Ardi stood about a foot taller than and weighed twice as much as Lucy.

Ardi's pelvis appears to be transitional between one suited for climbing and one modified for bipedal locomotion. Although Ardi's lower pelvis remains primitive, the structure of her upper pelvis allowed her to walk on two legs with a straightened hip. Still, she probably could neither walk nor run as well as Lucy and later hominins. Her feet lacked the archlike structure of later hominin feet, and she had a divergent big toe, like an ape (see Ward, Kimbel, and Johanson 2011). Ardi's apelike lower pelvis indicates retention of powerful hamstring muscles for climbing. Her hands, very long arms, and short legs all recall those of extinct apes, and her brain was no larger than that of a modern chimp.

Based on associated animal and plant remains, *Ardipithecus* lived in a humid woodland habitat. The size, shape, and wear patterns of the teeth suggest an omnivorous diet of plants, nuts, and small mammals. Although *Ardipithecus* probably fed both in trees and

The Ethiopian paleoanthropologist Yohannes Haile-Selassie was a key member of the multinational, multidisciplinary team responsible for the "Ardi" discovery and analysis. AFP/Getty Images

on the ground, the smaller canines suggest less of a fruit diet than is characteristic of living apes. *Ardipithecus* canines resemble modern human canines more than the tusklike, piercing upper canines of chimps and gorillas. The ancestral relationship of *Ardipithecus* to later hominins has not been determined, but Ardi has been called a plausible ancestor for *Australopithecus* (see Wilford 2009).

## The Varied Australopiths

Some Miocene hominins evolved into a varied group of Pliocene-Pleistocene hominins known collectively as the **australopiths**—for which there is an abundant fossil record. Two genera are generally recognized within the australopiths: *Australopithecus* (*Au.*) and *Paranthropus*. The various species (with the oldest at the bottom of each group) are as follows:

**Genus *Australopithecus***

*Au. sediba* (1.98–1.78 m.y.a.)

*Au. garhi* (2.6–2.5 m.y.a.)

*Au. africanus* (3.5–2.5 m.y.a.)

*Au. afarensis* (3.8–3.0 m.y.a.)

*Au. anamensis* (4.2–3.9 m.y.a.)

**Genus *Paranthropus***

*Paranthropus robustus* (1.9–1.0 m.y.a.)

*Paranthropus boisei* (2.3–1.4 m.y.a.)

*Paranthropus aethiopicus* (2.6 m.y.a.)

The date ranges given for these species are approximate, with some fossils dated more precisely than others. The earliest South African australopith fossils (*Au. africanus* and *Paranthropus robustus*), for example, were found in a nonvolcanic area where radiometric dating could not be done until recently (see Braga and Thackeray 2016). The hominin fossils from the volcanic regions of East Africa usually have radiometric dates.

### *Australopithecus anamensis*

*Ardipithecus* may (or may not) have evolved into *Au. anamensis*, a bipedal hominin from northern Kenya, whose fossil remains were first reported by Meave Leakey and Alan Walker in 1995. *Au. anamensis* consists of 78 fragments from two sites: Kanapoi and Allia Bay. The fossils include upper and lower jaws, cranial fragments, and a partial shin bone (tibia). The Kanapoi fossils date to 4.2 m.y.a., and those at Allia Bay to 3.9 m.y.a. Members of this species had apelike canines, along with strong jaws and heavily enameled teeth, suggesting they may at times have eaten hard, abrasive foods. They probably preferred the fruits and nuts available in their habitat—one of lakes surrounded by forests and woodlands. Based on the tibia, *anamensis* weighed about 110 pounds (50 kg). This would make it larger than either the earlier *Ardipithecus* or the later *Au. afarensis*. Because of its date and its location in the East African Rift Valley, *Au. anamensis* may be ancestral to *Au. afarensis* (3.8–3.0 m.y.a.), which usually is considered ancestral to all the later australopiths, as well as to *Homo* (see Figure 6.1).

## Australopithecus afarensis

*Au. afarensis* fossils come from two sites, Laetoli in northern Tanzania and Hadar in the Afar region of Ethiopia. Laetoli is earlier (3.8–3.6 m.y.a.). The Hadar fossils date to

**FIGURE 6.1    Phylogenetic Tree for African Apes, Hominids, and Hominins**
The presumed divergence date for ancestral chimps and hominins was between 6 and 8 m.y.a. Branching in later hominin evolution is also shown. For more exact dates, see the text and Table 6.1.

McGraw-Hill Education

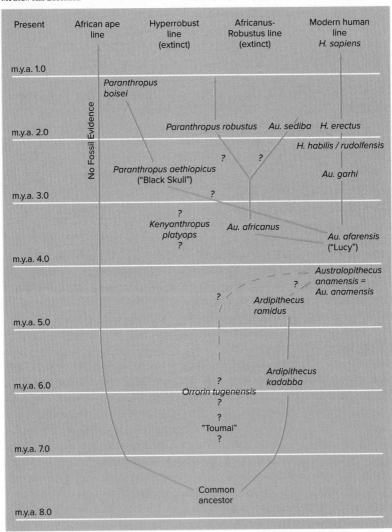

between 3.3 and 3.0 m.y.a. All told, *Au. afarensis* existed for about 800,000 years, from 3.8 to 3.0 m.y.a. Mary Leakey (Meave's mother-in-law) directed the research that led to the Laetoli finds. D. C. Johanson and M. Taieb led the international expedition that made the discoveries at Hadar. The two sites have yielded significant samples of *afarensis* fossils. From Laetoli we have two dozen specimens; and from Hadar, between 35 and 65 individuals. The Laetoli remains are mainly teeth and jaw fragments, along with some very informative fossilized footprints. The Hadar sample includes skull fragments and postcranial material, most notably 40 percent of the skeleton of a tiny hominin female, dubbed "Lucy," who lived around 3 m.y.a.

Although the hominin remains at Laetoli and Hadar were deposited half a million years apart, their many resemblances explain their placement in the same species. *Au. afarensis,* although clearly a hominin, was still similar in many ways to chimps and gorillas (*Ardipithecus* and *Au. anamensis* were even more apelike).

From the same general area of northern Ethiopia as Lucy comes another important member of *Au. afarensis* (Owen 2006, 2012). This toddler, the world's oldest fossil child, soon was dubbed "Lucy's Baby"—despite having lived a hundred thousand years before Lucy (3.3 m.y.a. for the child versus 3.2 m.y.a. for Lucy). The child is an amazingly complete find, with a more intact skull and much more skeletal material than exists for Lucy. Unearthed in 2000, the child probably was female and about 3 years old when she died. The remains include a well-preserved skull with a monkey-sized face, a mandible (jawbone), baby teeth, tiny fingers, a torso, a foot, and a kneecap. Not surprisingly, given what we already know about *Au. afarensis*, the skull and upper body are apelike, while the lower body confirms bipedalism. Despite bipedalism, the skeleton's upper body includes two complete shoulder blades similar to a gorilla's, suggesting that it was an adept climber (see Owen 2012). The climbing ability of *Au. afarensis* is the subject of this chapter's "Anthropology Today."

If Lucy's Baby had lived, she would have developed rapidly, reaching adulthood earlier than modern humans, and her lifespan would have been much shorter than ours. The *afarensis* growth cycle was more similar to the chimpanzee pattern than to the modern human pattern. The shorter growth period would have allowed less time for guidance and socialization.

How did the dentition of *Au. afarensis* compare with ape and human dentitions? The *afarensis* canines were longer and sharper than in *Homo* and projected beyond the other teeth. Compared with an ape's tusklike canines, however, the *afarensis* canines were reduced. More like an ape's than a human's premolar, the *afarensis* lower premolar was pointed and projecting. It had one long cusp and only a tiny bump that hints at the bicuspid premolar that eventually developed in hominin evolution (see Figure 6.2).

The *afarensis* diet was mainly vegetarian, including leaves, seeds, fruits, and nuts. Lucy and her kind probably also ate insects and small vertebrates, such as lizards. Dental microwear studies show that *afarensis* ate soft, sugar-rich foods (such as fruits), but their tooth size and shape confirm that they could also process hard, brittle foods. These may have been fallback foods, which they ate when more desirable foods were unavailable. *Au. afarensis* molars are large. The lower jaw (mandible) is thick and is buttressed with a bony ridge behind the front teeth. The cheekbones are large and flare out to the side for the attachment of chewing muscles.

**FIGURE 6.2   Comparison of Dentition in Ape, *Au. afarensis*, and Human Palates**
Teeth of chimpanzee, *Au. afarensis*, and modern human. In (a), note the parallel tooth rows in the chimpanzee, as compared to those of the modern human. In (b), note the sharply pointed premolar of the chimpanzee, the pointed premolar of *Au. afarensis*, and the bicuspid premolar of the modern human.

McGraw-Hill Education

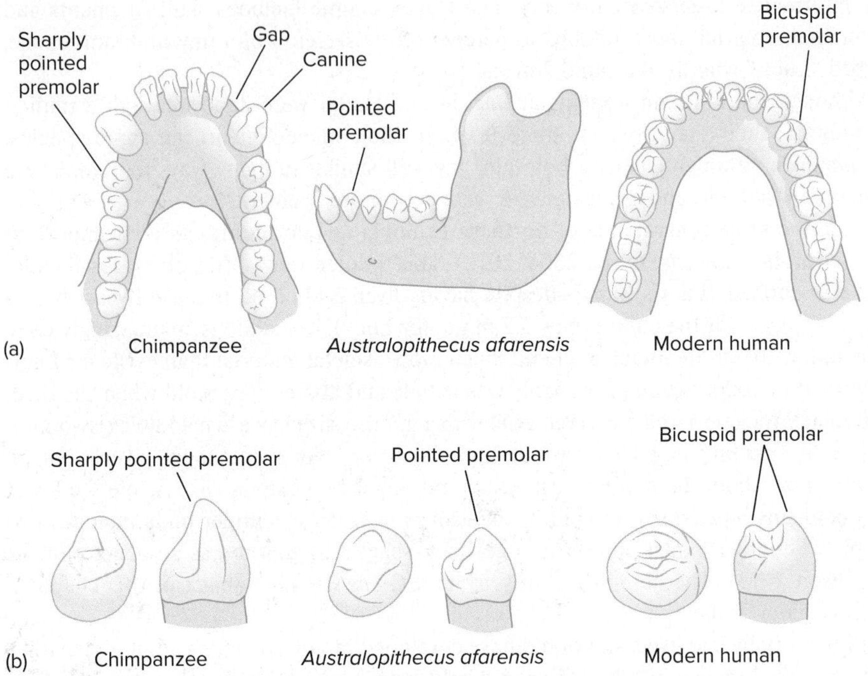

(a)   Chimpanzee   *Australopithecus afarensis*   Modern human

(b)   Chimpanzee   *Australopithecus afarensis*   Modern human

The small *Au. afarensis* skull contrasts with those of later hominins. Its cranial capacity (430 cm³) barely surpasses the chimp average (390 cm³). Although bidepal, *Au. afarensis* still contrasts in many ways with later hominins. For example, sexual dimorphism is marked. *Au. afarensis* females, such as Lucy, stood between 3 and 4 feet (0.9 and 1.2 meters) tall; males might have reached 5 feet (1.5 meters). Adult males may have weighed almost twice as much as the females did. Table 6.2 includes data on the various australopiths, including mid-sex body weight and brain size. *Mid-sex* means midway between the male average and the female average.

Lucy and her kind were far from dainty. Her muscle-engraved bones are much more robust than ours are. With only rudimentary tools and weapons, early hominins needed powerful and resistant bones and muscles. Lucy's apelike arms are longer and stronger than those of later hominins; she probably spent significant time in the trees (Klein 2016). Canines, premolars, and skulls were apelike as well, but the molars, chewing apparatus, and cheekbones foreshadowed later hominin trends, and the pelvic and limb bones were indisputably hominin. The hominin pattern was being built from the ground up.

**TABLE 6.2    Facts about Selected Australopiths Compared with Chimps and *Homo***

| Species | Dates (m.y.a.) | Known Distribution | Important Sites | Body Weight (Mid-Sex) | Brain Size (Mid-Sex) (cm³) |
|---|---|---|---|---|---|
| Anatomically modern humans (AMHs) | 0.3–present (300,000–present) | Worldwide | Beijing, Mumbai, Nairobi, New York, Paris, Rio de Janeiro, Sydney | 132 lb/60 kg | 1,350 |
| *Pan troglodytes* (chimpanzee) | Modern | Tropical Africa | Gombe (Tanzania), Ivory Coast | 93 lb/42 kg | 390 |
| *Au. sediba* | 1.98–1.78 | South Africa | Malapa | Insufficient data | 420 |
| *Paranthropus boisei* | 2.3–1.4 | East Africa | Olduvai, East Turkana | 86 lb/39 kg | 490 |
| *Paranthropus robustus* | 1.9–1.0 | South Africa | Kromdraai, Swartkrans | 81 lb/37 kg | 540 |
| *Au. africanus* | 3.5–2.5 | South Africa | Taung, Sterkfontein, Makapansgat | 79 lb/36 kg | 490 |
| *Au. afarensis* | 3.8–3.0 | East Africa | Hadar, Laetoli | 77 lb/35 kg | 430 |
| *Au. anamensis* | 4.2–3.9 | Kenya | Kanapoi, Allia Bay | Not enough data | No published skulls |
| *Ardipithecus* | 5.8–4.4 | Ethiopia | Aramis | Not enough data | Not enough data |

Important evidence of striding bipedalism by *Au. afarensis* comes from Laetoli. Volcanic ash, which can be dated by the K/A (potassium/argon) technique, covered a trail of footprints of two or three hominins walking to a water hole. (For more on fossilized footprints, see Curry 2018.) These prints confirm that a striding biped lived in Tanzania by 3.6 m.y.a. The structure of the pelvic, hip, leg, and foot bones all indicate that upright bipedalism was *Au. afarensis*'s mode of locomotion (see Choi 2012; Ward et al. 2011). Accordingly, australopith (*afarensis* and later) pelvises are much more similar to the human pelvis than to an ape pelvis. With bipedalism, the pelvis forms a sort of bowl that balances the weight of the trunk and supports that weight with less stress. The *afarensis* spine also had the lower spine (lumbar) curve characteristic of *Homo*. This curvature helps transmit the weight of the upper body to the pelvis and the legs. The head balanced directly on top of the neck, with the foramen magnum located right underneath the skull rather than at the back, as in a quadruped. In apes, the thigh bone (femur) extends straight down from the hip to the knees. In *Australopithecus* and *Homo*, however, the thigh bone angles into the hip, permitting the space between the knees to be narrower than the pelvis during walking.

Although the pelvises of the australopiths were similar to those of *Homo*, they were not identical. The most significant contrast is a narrower australopith birth canal. Expansion of the birth canal is a trend in hominin evolution. Undoubtedly, australopith skulls

An ancient trail of hominin footprints fossilized in volcanic ash. Mary Leakey found this 230-foot (70-meter) trail at Laetoli, Tanzania, in 1979. It dates from 3.6 m.y.a. and confirms that *Au. afarensis* was a striding biped. John Reader/Science Source

grew after birth to accommodate a growing brain, but human skulls and brains grow much more. Nevertheless, young australopiths must have depended on their parents and kin for nurturance and protection. Those years of childhood dependency would have provided time for observation, teaching, and learning. This may provide indirect evidence for a rudimentary cultural life.

## Gracile and Robust Australopiths

Raymond Dart (in 1924) coined the term *Australopithecus africanus* to describe the first fossil representative of this species, the skull of a juvenile that was found accidentally in a quarry at Taung, South Africa. The many australopith fossils found subsequently in South Africa appear to have lived between 3.5 and 1 m.y.a. The most recent South African *Australopithecus* find, *Au. sediba*, has been dated to between 1.98 and 1.78 m.y.a.

*Smithsonian* magazine named *Australopithecus sediba* as the number one hominid (and hominin) fossil discovery of 2011. (It was actually discovered between 2008 and 2010, but first described in 2011.) The original find was by Matthew Berger, the nine-year-old (at the time) son of paleoanthropologist Lee Berger. That first find (Malapa Hominin 1) is an almost complete skull and partial skeleton of an 11- to 12-year-old boy who stood 4'3" (1.3 m.) tall. Remains of a second representative of the species (Malapa Hominin 2), an adult, were found a few weeks later. This late australopith species, which lived a bit less than 2 million years ago, offers a unique blend of hominin features (see Morin 2013; Williams et al. 2018).

The South African australopiths fall into two groups: **gracile** (*Au. africanus* and *Au. sediba*) and **robust** (*Paranthropus robustus*). "Gracile" indicates that the australopiths in that category were slighter and less rugged, with smaller teeth and faces, than were members of *Paranthropus*. Based on recent advances in dating techniques, *Au. africanus* appears to have lived between 3.5 and 2.5 m.y.a. *Au. sediba*, also gracile and a likely descendant of *africanus*, has been dated to 1.98–1.78 m.y.a.

Three species names are associated with *Paranthropus*: one from South Africa—*Paranthropus robustus* (1.9–1.0 m.y.a.), and two from East Africa—*Paranthropus boisei* (2.3–1.4 m.y.a.) and *Paranthropus aethiopicus* (2.6 m.y.a.). Both *Au. africanus* and *Paranthropus* probably descend from *Au. afarensis*, which itself was gracile in form, or from an (as yet undiscovered) South African version of *Au. afarensis*.

The South African australopiths still had skulls that were more ape-sized than human. The average brain size of *Au. africanus* was 490 cm$^3$, compared with 540 cm$^3$ for *Paranthropus robustus*. These figures can be compared with an average cranial capacity of 430 cm$^3$ in *Au.* afarensis and 1,350 cm$^3$ in *Homo sapiens*. The cranial capacity of chimps (*Pan troglodytes*) averages 390 cm$^3$ (see Table 6.2). The brains of gorillas (*Gorilla gorilla*) average around 500 cm$^3$, which is within the australopith range, but gorilla body size is much greater.

As in earlier hominins, sexual dimorphism within each South African species remained much more pronounced than it is in *Homo sapiens*. Australopith females, whether gracile or robust, were shorter, weighed much less, and had smaller canines than males of the same species. The dimorphism in body size exceeded that in chimpanzees but probably was less than in gorillas.

The teeth, jaws, and skulls of these australopiths leave no doubt that their diet was mainly vegetarian, although they did eat meat from time to time. They captured small and slow-moving game, and they scavenged, bringing home parts of kills made by large cats and other carnivores. Natural selection modifies the teeth and surrounding structures to conform to the stresses associated with a particular diet (see Ungar 2017). Large back teeth, jaws, and associated facial and cranial structures confirm a diet requiring extensive grinding and crushing. The cheekbones of the South African australopiths (especially *Paranthropus*) were elongated structures that anchored large chewing muscles running up the jaw. Another set of robust chewing muscles extended from the back of the jaw to the sides of the skull. Their canines, however, are reduced, and their premolars are fully bicuspid.

Compared with the graciles, *Paranthropus* had larger skulls and back teeth. They also had thicker faces and more rugged skull features and muscle markings on the skeleton. *Paranthropus* had chewing muscles that were strong enough to produce a *sagittal crest*, a bony ridge on the top of the skull. Such a crest forms as the bone grows. It develops from the pull of the chewing muscles as they meet at the midline of the skull and serves to anchor those muscles.

Members of *Paranthropus boisei* had the largest back teeth of all the australopiths. Their females had bigger back teeth than did earlier australopith males. In adapting to very arid areas, *Paranthropus* became ever more specialized as they processed vegetation

(Left) Profile view of *Paranthropus boisei* skull—Olduvai Hominid (OH) 5, originally called *Zinjanthropus boisei*. This skull of a young male, discovered by Mary Leakey in 1959 at Olduvai Gorge, Tanzania, dates back to 1.8 m.y.a. (Right) Profile view of an *Au. africanus* (gracile) skull (Sterkfontein 5). The cranium, discovered by Dr. Robert Broom and J. T. Robinson in April 1947, dates back to 3.5–2.5 m.y.a. (Left): The Natural History Museum/Alamy Stock Photo; (Right): The Natural History Museum/Alamy Stock Photo

that was harder to chew than for any previous hominin. They became hyperrobust, with huge back teeth, jaws, and associated areas of the face and skull. *Paranthropus boisei* persisted in East Africa until about 1.4 m.y.a., when it finally became extinct, as did *Paranthropus robustus* in South Africa around 1 m.y.a. (see Braga and Thackeray 2016). Figure 6.3 is a drawing of the skulls of four species of *Australopithecus*.

**FIGURE 6.3    Four Types of Early Hominins** What are the main differences you notice?

McGraw-Hill Education

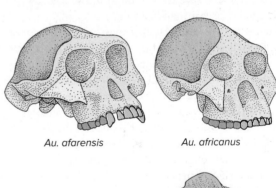

*Au. afarensis*          *Au. africanus*

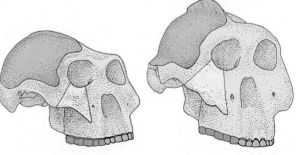

*Paranthropus robustus*          *Paranthropus boisei*

A possible third species, *Paranthropus aethiopicus*, was discovered in 1985 in northern Kenya. This discovery is commonly called the "black skull" because of the blue-black sheen it bore from the minerals surrounding it. The jaw was apelike and the brain was small, but there was a massive bony crest atop the skull (as in *Paranthropus boisei*). Scientists disagree about whether the black skull, dated to 2.6 m.y.a., is merely a very early member of *Paranthropus boisei*, or whether it merits its own species name, *Paranthropus aethiopicus*. Whatever its designation, the black skull shows that some of the anatomical features of the genus *Paranthropus* (2.6–1.0 m.y.a.) did not change very much during about 1.5 million years.

# Early Stone Tools

The simplest obviously manufactured stone tools were discovered in 1931 by L. S. B. and Mary Leakey at Olduvai Gorge, Tanzania. That locale gave the tools their name—**Oldowan tools.** The oldest tools from Olduvai are about 1.8 million years old, but older Oldowan tools (from 2.6–2.0 m.y.a.) have been found in other parts of Africa.

For example, recent discoveries at Ain Boucherit in Algeria confirm that early hominins were using Oldowan-like stone tools (and eating meat) in North as well as East Africa by 2.4 m.y.a. Ain Boucherit shows that hominins had reached the Mediterranean fringe in North Africa earlier than formerly believed. Either stone tool manufacture and use dispersed early from East Africa, or hominins independently invented tool making in both North and East Africa (Sahnouni et al. 2018).

The purpose of flaking stone in the Oldowan tradition was not so much to make core tools (choppers) as to create the sharp stone flakes that were the mainstay of the Oldowan tool kit (Figure 6.4). The chopper was a by-product of flaking that was probably used for food processing—for pounding, breaking, and bashing. Flakes probably were used mainly as cutters, for example, to dismember game carcasses. Crushed fossil animal bones indicate that stones were used to break open marrow cavities. Also, Oldowan deposits include pieces of bone or horn with scratch marks suggesting they were used to dig up tubers or insects.

## Surprisingly Early Stone Tools

In 1999 an international team reported the discovery, in Ethiopia, of a new australopith species, dated to 2.6–2.5 m.y.a. Surprised by the combination of skeletal and dental features in this new hominin, they named it ***Australopithecus garhi*** (*Au. garhi*). The word *garhi* means "surprise" in the Afar language. Associated with these hominin fossils is evidence, the earliest yet found, of animal butchery (Asfaw, White, and Lovejoy 1999). *Au. garhi* (or whoever did the butchering) used early stone tools to butcher, and extract marrow from, the bones of the antelopes and horses found at the site.

In 1997 the Ethiopian archaeologist Sileshi Semaw had found stone tools dating to 2.6 m.y.a. at the nearby Ethiopian site of Gona. Did *Au. garhi* make these tools? If not, who did? Based on what we know about chimpanzee stone tool use, combined with discoveries of even older stone tools, it becomes increasingly likely that the australopiths were toolmakers, with some capacity for culture.

## FIGURE 6.4   **Making Oldowan Tools**

The toolmaker strikes a hard stone (the core) in just the right place to remove thin, sharp flakes.

McGraw-Hill Education

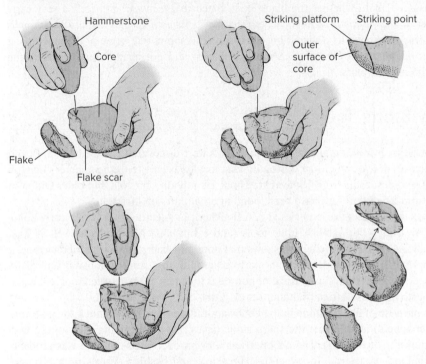

The year 2015 was a particularly important one for announcements about hominin evolution. A hard-to-reach cave in South Africa yielded a treasure trove of fossils (see Chapter 7). The earliest member of the genus *Homo*, dated to 2.8 m.y.a., was found in Ethiopia, and the earliest stone tools were discovered in Kenya. Dated to 3.3 m.y.a., these tools are 700,000 years older than the previously recognized earliest stone tools. Sonia Harmand of Stony Brook University led the team that discovered these tools, scattered in a dry river bed near the western shore of Kenya's Lake Turkana. At this site, Lomekwi 3, the ancient toolmakers knapped stone intentionally, breaking off sharp pieces from a core with quick, hard strikes. Much larger and cruder than the Oldowan tools that came later, the Lomekwi tools bear scars from the rudimentary techniques used to make them. The toolmakers probably used two hands and rested the stone core on an anvil while hitting it with a hammer stone, as wild chimps still do today when cracking open nuts (see Wilford 2015).

## Oldowan Hominins at the Kanjera Site

Comparisons with chimps and bonobos suggest that hominins always have lived in social groups composed of multiple males and females. In such a group, a chimp female in

Associated with *Australopithecus garhi*, which lived 2.6–2.5 m.y.a., is evidence, the earliest yet found, of animal butchery. This drawing imagines meat-eating by members of *Au. garhi.* Kennis & Kennis/MSF/Science Source

estrus will mate with multiple males, and males mate with multiple females. At some point in their evolution, hominins developed pair bonding (Lukas and Clutton-Brock 2013; Opie et al. 2013; Zimmer 2013). A male and a female would pair off, bond, and mate exclusively or mainly with each other for a significant length of time. Such a bond would increase the likelihood that the offspring of the female were also those of the male. Both parents would do all they could to ensure the child's survival and well-being. At some point, especially as hominins became dependent on hunting, a gender-based division of labor developed. Men who hunted took meat home to share with their mates, their children, and other members of their social group.

Anthropologists have found excellent evidence for hunting around 2 million years ago at a very rich site in Kenya–the Kanjera South; or KJS, site, located on the shores of Lake Victoria (Ferraro et al. 2013). The archaeologists analyzed thousands of tools and animal bones (many showing marks of cutting or cracking) from the site. Using Oldowan stone tools, the ancient hominins who occupied the site were acquiring and processing meat— from hunting and scavenging. The animal bones at the site reveal that these Oldowan hominins hunted and butchered numerous small antelopes. The archaeologists could tell this because bones of the entire animal were present at the site—indicating that carcasses had been brought back whole. Cut marks show that hominins used their simple stone tools to remove animal flesh. They also used fist-sized stones to crack open animal bones to get at the marrow. The Oldowan hominins also ate larger antelopes, which they almost certainly scavenged. These antelopes were represented by only part of the skeleton and skull, suggesting that hominins brought back remainders from the kills of other preda-tors, which could not as easily get at the brains and bone marrow of their prey.

## Anthropology Today    *3-D Bone Scans Suggest Lucy's Climbing Ability and Cause of Death*

One of the key discoveries for the understanding of hominin evolution continues to be Lucy, the 3.5-foot-tall exemplar of *Au. afarensis* discovered by Donald Johanson in Ethiopia in 1974. Lucy's skeleton came to the United States in 2007–2008 as part of a traveling museum exhibit on Ethiopia. As part of her nationwide tour, Lucy spent 10 days at the University of Texas, where scientists launched a detailed study of her bones. John Kappelman, a paleoanthropologist, and other members of the Texas team used a high-resolution CT scanner to X-ray Lucy's entire skeleton (see Kappelman 2016; Zimmer 2016a). Next, they converted those bone scans into three-dimensional models for closer study. Those 3-D images are now available for all to see, download, and study at the website https://elucy.org/.

To determine how Lucy habitually used her bones, the researchers analyzed the 3-D digital models built from scans of the fossil. Bone width (cortical thickness) indicates its strength. For example, a professional baseball pitcher's throwing arm and shoulder are more developed than the other arm and shoulder. Lucy's thick arm bones suggest strength, which the researchers attribute to climbing (see Klein 2016; Ruff 2016).

Although bipedalism was her preferred means of locomotion, Lucy probably used the trees to avoid predators; gather fruits, nuts, and honey; and perhaps sleep. Bones strengthen or weaken through patterns of everyday use. The researchers compared the internal structure of Lucy's upper right arm and her leg bones with the same bones of chimps and modern humans. The ratio of strength between Lucy's arms and legs turned out to be slightly more chimplike than human, suggesting

that she did more climbing than modern humans do (see Klein 2016; Ruff 2016).

Her lower body leaves no doubt that Lucy and her kind were bipedal. How, then, do we explain her long and strong arms, her curved fingers and toes, and her apelike shoulder blades. Do these features indicate continued arboreal adaptation, or are they merely homologies retained from more arboreal ancestors. Johanson, Lucy's discoverer, argues the latter. The Texas scientists stress the former—that Lucy, although bidepal, still spent significant time in the trees.

But not always successfully. Could Lucy have died by falling from a tree? What do the bones say? Like most ancient fossils, Lucy's skeleton was damaged after her death by taphonomic and geological processes. Some of her skeletal damage, however, seemed to reflect compressive bone-to-bone fractures that occurred near the time of her death. The Texas team showed these images to orthopedic surgeons, who found the breaks consistent with bone fractures resulting from a fall from a high place. Specifically, Lucy's fractures suggested that she landed feet-first, then fell forward, holding out her arms for protection. Fractures to her rib cage suggest internal injuries that would have killed her. Kappelman and his colleagues conclude that a fall from a tree caused Lucy's death (Kappelman 2016; Zimmer 2016a).

Living in a wooded environment near a stream, Lucy may have split her time between the ground and the trees. She may even have slept in nests, as chimpanzees do, on average about 40 feet above the ground (Zimmer 2016a). A fall from such a height could very well prove fatal. Next time you dream of falling from a tree, think of Lucy, and be happy you sleep at ground level.

The Kanjera site provides the earliest, and very complete, evidence for what the anthropologists call "persistent" reliance on meat within the hominin diet. We don't know the genus or species of these hominins, but we do know the significance of a meat-laden diet. Among the likely social changes associated with such a diet were a gender-based division of labor, pair bonding, and increased parental (especially male) investment in children. Meat supported population increase and territorial expansion among homi-nins. We hear so much today about the dangers of too much red meat that we forget that meat is an excellent and concentrated source of calories, protein, and fat. Its inclusion in the ancient hominin diet supported an increase in the size of the human body and brain, which is a very expensive organ in terms of its energy needs. To summarize, a regular diet of red meat was a key factor allowing the growth of the hominin body and brain and the spread of hominins within and beyond Africa, a story told in Chapter 7.

## Summary

1. A skull found in northern Chad, dated at 7-6 million years old, officially named *Sahelanthropus tchadensis*, more commonly called "Toumai," may or may not be the earliest hominin yet known, as may the somewhat less ancient *Orrorin tugenensis*, found in Kenya in 2001.

2. Hominins have lived during the late Miocene, Pliocene (5.0-2.6 m.y.a.), and Pleis-tocene (2.6 m.y.a-11,700 B.P.) epochs. The australopiths had appeared by 4.2 m.y.a. (as *Au. anamensis*). The australopiths include two genera: *Australopithecus* and *Paranthropus*. The known species of *Australopithecus* are as follows: *Au. anamensis* (4.2-3.9 m.y.a.), *Au. afarensis* (3.8-3.0 m.y.a.), *Au. africanus* (3.5-2.5 m.y.a.), *Au. garhi* (2.6-2.5 m.y.a.), and *Au. sediba* (1.98-1.78 m.y.a.). The species of *Paran-thropus* are as follows: *Paranthropus robustus* (1.9-1.0 m.y.a.), *Paranthropus boisei* (2.3-1.4 m.y.a.), and *Paranthropus aethiopicus* (2.6 m.y.a.). The earliest definite hom-inin remains, from Ethiopia, are classified as *Ardipithecus kadabba* (5.8-5.5 m.y.a.) and *ramidus* (4.4 m.y.a.). Next comes *Au. anamensis*, then a group of fossils from Hadar, Ethiopia, and Laetoli, Tanzania, classified as *Au. afarensis*.

3. These earliest hominins shared many primitive (apelike) features, including upper bodies adapted for climbing; elongated premolars; a small, apelike skull; and marked sexual dimorphism. Still, *Au. afarensis* and its predecessors were definite hominins. In *Au. afarensis* this is confirmed by abundant skeletal evidence for upright bipedalism.

4. Remains of two later groups, *Au. africanus* (graciles) and *Paranthropus robustus* (robusts), were found in South Africa. Both groups show the australopith trend toward a powerful chewing apparatus. They had large molars and premolars and large and robust faces, skulls, and muscle markings. All these features are more pronounced in the robusts than they are in the graciles. The basis of the australopith diet was savanna vegetation.

5. *Paranthropus boisei*, the hyperrobust australopiths, became extinct around 1.4 m.y.a., as did *Paranthropus robustus* around 1 m.y.a. *Paranthropus* became increasingly spe-cialized, dependent on tough, coarse, gritty, fibrous savanna vegetation.

6. Oldowan tools (flakes and choppers) dated to 1.8 m.y.a. were first found at Olduvai Gorge in Tanzania, hence, their name. Earlier Oldowan tools (some as old as 2.6 m.y.a.) have been found subsequently at other African sites. Even earlier stone tools (3.3 m.y.a.) come from a recent discovery at the Lomekwi 3 site in Kenya. A regular diet of red meat was a key factor allowing the growth of the hominin body and brain and the spread of hominins within and beyond Africa. Among the likely social changes associated with the new diet were a gender-based division of labor, pair bonding, and increased parental (especially male) investment in children.

## Think Like an Anthropologist

1. If you found a new hominid fossil in East Africa, dated to 5 m.y.a., would it most likely be an ape ancestor or a human ancestor? How would you tell the difference?
2. Compare the significance of the *Ardipithecus* and *Au. afarensis* finds (i.e., Ardi and Lucy, respectively). Which do you consider to be more important, and why?

## Key Terms

*Ardipithecus, 128*
*Au. afarensis, 136*
*Au. africanus, 141*
*Au. anamensis, 135*
*Au. garhi, 143*

australopiths, *135*
gracile, *141*
Oldowan tools, *143*
*Paranthropus*
  *boisei, 141*

*Paranthropus*
  *robustus, 141*
robust, *141*

# Chapter 7

# The Genus *Homo*

## Early *Homo*

This chapter surveys the biological and cultural features associated with the various species of *Homo* known through the fossil record: *H. rudolfensis, H. habilis, H. erectus, H. heidelbergensis*, the Neandertals, their cousins the Denisovans, and the diminutive species known as *H. floresiensis*. The chapter concludes with a discussion of the advent of anatomically modern humans (AMHs). Also considered is a recent and highly significant discovery known as *H. naledi*.

## Recent Discoveries

Chapter 6 reported on the discovery of the earliest known stone tools (dated to 3.3 m.y.a.) at the Lomekwi 3 site in Kenya. This was one of three very important early hominin discoveries in Africa announced in 2015. The second is the discovery in Ethiopia of a hominin jawbone fragment with five teeth dated to 2.8 m.y.a.–close to the end of the *Au. afarensis* time span (3 m.y.a.) This fossil is the earliest known member of the *Homo* lineage (Villmoare et al. 2015). It's unclear whether this fossil, known as LD 350-1, belongs to a known early species of *Homo*, or whether it deserves its own species name. Linking the fossil to *Homo* are its slim molar teeth, its cusp pattern, and the shape of the mandible (lower jaw). The front of the jaw, however, has a more primitive look, including a receding chin line, like *Au. afarensis*.

The third key 2015 announcement was one of the most exciting fossil finds of the 21st century. The discovery site was South Africa's Rising Star cave, located in an area known as the "Cradle of Humankind," because of the important hominin fossil discoveries made there during the first half of the 20th century. So far, the Rising Star cave has yielded the remains of at least 15 individuals, ranging in age from infants and juveniles to older adults. Paleoanthropologist Lee Berger, the leader of the discovery team, dubbed the fossils *Homo naledi*, after the word (*naledi*) for "star" in the local Sotho language. Based on their mix of primitive and modern features, these fossils, originally undated, could have lived between 3 and 2 m.y.a. However, *H. naledi* recently has been assigned a surprisingly late date—of merely 335,000 to 236,000 B.P. (see Berger and Hawks 2017).

Among their primitive, apelike features are curved fingers on an otherwise humanlike hand, apelike shoulders adapted to climbing, and flaring iliac blades in the upper pelvis. As in other early hominins, the skeleton gets more human as it gets closer to the ground, reflecting bipedalism. The lower pelvis, lower legs, and feet are very human. The teeth, too, especially the reduced molars, are more modern and belong with *H. erectus*, Neandertals, and modern humans rather than with australopiths.

One of *H. naledi*'s most noticeable primitive characteristics is its tiny brain. The remains include four skulls, two males and two females. Cranial capacity was small in both sexes, averaging just 560 cm$^3$ for the males and 465 cm$^3$ for the females (compared with an average of 1,350 cm$^3$ for modern humans). As expected, sexual dimorphism shows up not only in the skulls but also in body size. The males were about 5 feet (1.5 meters) tall, weighing about 100 pounds (45 kg); females were somewhat shorter and lighter.

The members of Berger's team who did the actual work of collecting and excavating the bones were all young, slender women (see this chapter's "Anthropology Today"). Such a body frame was necessary to navigate the extremely narrow passages leading to the chamber where the fossils were located. Many of the bones were simply lying on the cave floor; others had to be dug out. The researchers removed more than 1,500 bones during an initial three weeks of intensive work. These fossils, which include bones, teeth, and skulls, provide an unusually complete picture of the hominins buried there. The bones range from skulls, ribs, and long bones, to remains as tiny as the bones of the inner ear. There also are complete hands and feet. The range of ages present spans the entire length of the *H. naledi* life cycle.

Some paleoanthropologists, while recognizing the importance of this find, doubt that *H. naledi* represents a new species. Tim White, a member of the Ardi team, suggested assignment of *H. naledi* to *H. erectus*. Watch the news for further developments on *H. naledi* and the Rising Star cave.

## *H. rudolfensis*

In 1972, in an expedition led by Richard Leakey, Bernard Ngeneo unearthed a skull designated KNM-ER 1470. The name comes from its catalog number in the Kenya National Museum (KNM) and its discovery location (East Rudolph—ER)—east of Lake Rudolph, at a site called Koobi Fora. The 1470 skull attracted immediate attention because of its unusual combination of a large brain (775 cm$^3$) and very large molars. Its brain size was more human than that of the australopiths, but its molars recalled those of the hyper-robust australopiths. Some paleoanthropologists attributed the large skull and teeth to a very large body, assuming that this had been one *really big* hominin. But no postcranial remains were found with 1470, nor have they been found with any later discovery of a 1470-like specimen. How does one interpret 1470 when its brain size suggests *Homo*, while its back teeth resemble those of an australopith? In 1986, 1470 received its own species name, *Homo rudolfensis*, from the lake near which it was found.

Note the contrasts between the two skulls in the photo below. KNM-ER 1470, on the right, is *H. rudolfensis*; KNM-ER 1813, on the left, is a skull of *H. habilis*. (*H. habilis*, discussed in the next section, is a species of early *Homo* discovered and named in 1960 by L. S. B. and Mary Leakey, parents of Richard.) The *habilis* skull has a more marked brow ridge and a depression behind it, whereas 1470 has a less pronounced brow ridge and a longer, flatter face.

For decades after finding 1470, the Leakey family and others scoured deposits near Lake Turkana for fossils similar to 1470. Between 2007 and 2009 they found them, near the 1470 discovery site (see Gibbons 2012; Leakey et al. 2012). In 2012 Meave Leakey (Richard's wife) and her associates announced the discovery at Koobi Fora of a face and two jawbones, showing that 1470 was not unique. These new fossils, dating to 2.03–1.78 m.y.a., confirmed that *H. rudolfensis* lived in the same area and at the same time as at least two other species of *Homo*—*habilis* and *erectus*. Note that *Paranthropus* also existed at this time. The bushy tree of hominin evolution had produced at least four species living in Africa at the same time but no doubt separated in space or by adaptation to different ecological niches.

Meet two kinds of early *Homo*: on the left KNM-ER 1813, on the right KNM-ER 1470. The latter (1470) has been classified as *H. rudolfensis*. What's the classification of 1813? Kenneth Garrett

The face of the new *H. rudolfensis* skull—that of a juvenile—was well preserved and included upper teeth. It was a smaller version of the 1470 skull, both featuring an unusually flat face that contrasts with the more jutting upper jaw of *H. habilis*. The lower jaw bones, one of which was remarkably complete, provided new information, because the 1470 fossil lacked a lower jaw. *H. rudolfensis* had an unusual, U-shaped palate, with canines facing the front of the jaw rather than placed on the sides in a V-shaped palate, as in *H. habilis*. The new jaws also had smaller molars than expected, based on those of 1470.

## *H. habilis* and *H. erectus*

A team headed by L. S. B. and Mary Leakey discovered the first representative of ***H. habilis*** (OH7–Olduvai Hominid 7) at Olduvai Gorge in Tanzania in 1960. We now know that *H. habilis* was a contemporary of *H. erectus* and lived from about 1.9 to 1.44 m.y.a. The original *H. habilis* find was from Olduvai's oldest layer, Bed I, which dates to 1.8 m.y.a. This layer has yielded both small-brained *Paranthropus boisei* fossils (average 490 cm$^3$) and *H. habilis* skulls, with cranial capacities between 600 and 700 cm$^3$. (Table 7.1 gives cranial capacities for the various forms of *Homo* discussed in this chapter.) The Leakeys chose the name *Homo habilis* (which means "*able* man" in Latin), because they assumed that *H. habilis* had tool-making *ability* and was responsible for the Oldowan tools also found in Bed I. We now know, however, that tool making preceded *H. habilis* and dates back to 3.3 m.y.a.

Another important *habilis* find was made in 1986 by Tim White of the University of California, Berkeley. OH62 is the partial skeleton of a female *H. habilis* from Olduvai Bed I. This was the first find of an *H. habilis* skull with a significant amount of skeletal material. OH62, dating to 1.8 m.y.a., consists of parts of the skull, the right arm, and both legs.

This photo shows the early (1.6 m.y.a.) *H. erectus* WT15,000, or Nariokotome boy, found in 1984 near Lake Turkana, Kenya. This is the most complete *H. erectus* ever found. Kenneth Garrett/National Geographic Creative

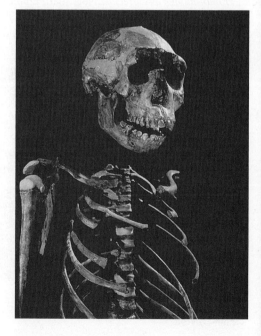

TABLE 7.1   **Summary of Data on *Homo* Fossil Groups**

Fossil representatives of the genus *Homo,* compared with anatomically modern humans (AMHs) and chimps (*Pan troglodytes*)

| Species | Dates | Known Distribution | Important Sites | Brain Size (in cm³) |
|---------|-------|--------------------|-----------------|--------------------|
| Anatomically modern humans (AMHs) | 300,000 B.P.–present | Worldwide | Jebel Irhoud (Morocco), Omo Kibish and Herto (Ethiopia), Border Cave and Klasies River (South Africa), Misliya cave, Skhūl and Qafzeh (Israel), Cro-Magnon (France) | 1,350 |
| Neandertals | 130,000–39,000 B.P. | Europe, southwestern Asia | La Chapelle-aux-Saints | 1,430 |
| Denisovans | 400,000–50,000 B.P. | Asia | Denisova cave | ? |
| *H. floresiensis* | 700,000–60,000 B.P. | Flores island, Indonesia | Liang Bua cave | 400 |
| *H. heidelbergensis* | 800,000–200,000 B.P. | Africa, Europe, Asia | Kabwe, Petralona, Dali | 1,135 |
| *H. erectus* | 1.9 m.y.a.–500,000 B.P. | Africa, Asia, Europe | East/West Turkana, Olduvai, Dmanisi, Zhoukoudian, Java, Ceprano | 900 |
| *H. habilis* | 1.9–1.44 m.y.a. | East Africa | Olduvai, East Turkana | 650 |
| *H. rudolfensis* | 2.03–1.78 m.y.a. | East Africa | East Africa, East Turkana | 775 |
| Pan troglodytes | Modern | Central Africa | Gombe, Mahale | 390 |

OH62 was surprising because of its small size (3 feet, or 0.9 meter) and long, apelike limb bones. The limb proportions suggested greater tree-climbing ability than later hominins had. *H. habilis* may still have sought occasional refuge in the trees.

The small size and primitive proportions of *H. habilis* were unexpected, given what was known about early *H. erectus* in East Africa. In deposits near Lake Turkana, Kenya, Richard Leakey had uncovered two *H. erectus* skulls dating to 1.6 m.y.a. By that date, *H. erectus* (males, at least) had already attained a cranial capacity of 900 cm³, along with a modern body shape and height. An amazingly complete young male *H. erectus* fossil (WT15,000) found at West Turkana in 1984 by Kimoya Kimeu, a collaborator of the Leakeys, has confirmed this. WT15,000, also known as the Nariokotome boy, was a 12-year-old male who had already reached 5 feet 5 inches (1.67 meters). He might have grown to 6 feet had he lived.

## Sister Species

Two more recent hominin fossil finds from Ileret, Kenya (east of Lake Turkana), are very significant for two main reasons; they show that (1) *H. habilis* and *H. erectus* overlapped in time rather than being ancestor and descendant, as had been thought, and (2) sexual dimorphism in *H. erectus* was much greater than expected (see Spoor et al. 2007; Wilford 2007a).

One of these finds (KNM-ER 42703) is the upper jawbone of a 1.44-million-year-old *H. habilis*. The other (KNM-ER 42700) is the almost complete but faceless skull of a 1.55-million-year-old *H. erectus*. Their names come from their catalog numbers in the Kenya National Museum–East Rudolph, and their dates were determined from volcanic ash deposits.

These Ileret finds negated the previous view (held since the Leakeys described the first *habilis* in 1960) that *habilis* and then *erectus* evolved one after the other. Instead, they apparently split from a common ancestor prior to 2 m.y.a. Then they lived side by side in eastern Africa for perhaps half a million years. According to Meave Leakey, one of the authors of the report (Spoor et al. 2007), the fact that they remained separate species for so long "suggests that they had their own ecological niche, thus avoiding direct competition" (quoted in Wilford 2007a, p. A6). *Habilis* and *erectus* coexisted in the same general area (an ancient lake basin), much as gorillas and chimpanzees do today.

Given these finds, the fossil record for early *Homo* in East Africa now stands as follows: *H. rudolfensis* (2.03–1.78 m.y.a.), *H. habilis* (1.9–1.44 m.y.a), and *H. erectus* (1.9–0.5? m.y.a). The oldest definite *H. habilis* (OH24) dates to 1.9 m.y.a., as does the oldest *erectus*.

What about sexual dimorphism in *H. erectus*? As the smallest *erectus* find ever, KNM-ER 42700 also may be the first female *erectus* yet found, most probably a young adult or late subadult. Its small skull suggests that the range in overall body size among *H. erectus* may have been greater than previously thought, with greater sexual dimorphism than among chimps or contemporary humans. Another possibility is that the (as yet undiscovered) *H. erectus* males that lived in this area along with the female also were smaller than the typical *erectus* male.

## Hunting, Tools, and Teeth

The ecological niche that separated *H. erectus* from earlier hominins involved greater reliance on hunting, along with improved cultural means of adaptation. Significant changes in technology occurred during the 200,000-year period between Bed I (1.8 m.y.a.) and Lower Bed II (1.6 m.y.a) at Olduvai. Out of the crude Oldowan tools in Bed I evolved more varied tools. The earliest (1.76 m.y.a.) tools of the *Acheulean* type (see the next section) associated with *H. erectus* come from a site near Lake Turkana in Kenya (Wilford 2011c). These tools show signs of symmetry, uniformity, and functional differentiation. *H. erectus* was making and using tools for different jobs, such as smashing bones or digging for tubers. The new technology allowed *H. erectus* to acquire meat more reliably and to dig and process tubers, roots, nuts, and seeds more efficiently. New tools that could batter, crush, and pulp coarse vegetation also reduced chewing demands.

Dietary changes eased the burden on the chewing apparatus, so that chewing muscles developed less. Supporting structures, such as jaws and cranial crests, also were reduced. Smaller jaws had less room to fit large teeth. The size of teeth, which form before they erupt, is under stricter genetic control than jaw size and bone size are (see von

Cramon-Taubadel 2011). Natural selection began to operate against the genes that produced large teeth, which now caused dental crowding, impaction, pain, sickness, fever, and sometimes death (there were no dentists).

# Out of Africa I: *H. erectus*

There were multiple migrations of *Homo* out of Africa (see Lee 2018). First to expand was *H. erectus*, whose spread occurred between 2 and 1 m.y.a. Much later, populations of **anatomically modern humans (AMHs)** left Africa. The first of those migrations may have occurred around 300,000 B.P., but the main wave of AMH expansion was much later—around and after 80,000 B.P. That last wave included the ancestors of all humans on Earth today (see Hoffecker 2017).

*H. erectus* initiated the expansion of hominins beyond Africa—to Asia and Europe. Small groups broke off from larger ones and moved a few miles away. They foraged new tracts of edible vegetation and carved out new hunting territories. Through population growth and dispersal, *H. erectus* gradually spread. Fueling this expansion was commitment to an essentially human lifestyle based on hunting and gathering. This basic pattern survived until recently in certain parts of the world, although it now is fading rapidly.

## Acheulean Tools

The stone-tool-making techniques that evolved out of the Oldowan tradition, and that lasted until about 15,000 years ago, are described by the term **Paleolithic** (from Greek roots meaning "old" and "stone"). The Paleolithic, or Old Stone Age, has three divisions: Lower (early), Middle, and Upper (late). Stone tools were made from rocks, such as flint, that fracture sharply and in predictable ways when hammered. Quartz, quartzite, chert, and obsidian also are suitable. Each of the three main divisions of the Paleolithic had its typical *tool-making traditions*—coherent patterns of tool manufacture.

The main Lower Paleolithic tool-making tradition used by *H. erectus* was the **Acheulean**, named after the French village of St. Acheul, where it was first identified. Recent finds in Kenya date the oldest Acheulean hand axes to 1.76 m.y.a. With Oldowan tools, flaking was done simply to produce sharp flakes. A fundamental difference shows up in the Acheulean tradition, in which the core was chipped bilaterally and symmetrically. This type of chipping converted the core from a round piece of rock into a flattish, oval hand ax about 6 inches (15 cm) long. The Acheulean hand ax embodies a predetermined shape created from a template in the toolmaker's mind, suggesting a cognitive leap between earlier hominins and *H. erectus*.

Analysis of their wear patterns suggests that hand axes were versatile tools used for many tasks, from butchering and cutting to woodworking and vegetable preparation. Cleavers—core tools with a straight edge at one end—were used for heavy chopping and hacking at the sinews of larger animals. Stone picks probably were used for digging. Acheulean toolmakers also used flakes, with finer edges, as light-duty tools—to make incisions and for finer work. Dating back at least 1.76 m.y.a., the Acheulean tradition illustrates trends in the evolution of technology: the manufacture of more varied tools with predetermined forms, designed for specific tasks.

## Adaptive Strategies of *H. erectus*

More sophisticated tools helped *H. erectus* expand its range. Biological changes also increased hunting efficiency. *H. erectus* had a rugged but essentially modern, long-legged skeleton that permitted long-distance stalking and endurance during the hunt. There is archaeological evidence of *H. erectus*'s success in hunting elephants, horses, rhinos, and giant baboons.

In both body and brain, *H. erectus* was closer to *H. sapiens* than to the australopiths. Increasing cranial capacity has been a trend in human evolution. The average *H. erectus* brain (about 1,000 cm$^3$) doubled the australopith average and ranged between 800 and 1,250 cm$^3$, well above the modern minimum. Still, several anatomical contrasts, particularly in the cranium, distinguish *H. erectus* from modern humans. *H. erectus* had a lower and more sloping forehead accentuated by a large brow ridge above the eyes. Skull bones were thicker; the brain case was lower and flatter than in *H. sapiens,* with spongy bone development at the lower rear of the skull. Seen from behind, the *H. erectus* skull resembles a half-inflated football or a hamburger bun. The face, teeth, and jaws were larger than in contemporary humans but smaller than those of the australopiths. The front teeth were especially large, but molar size was well below the australopith average.

Hearths at various sites confirm that fire was part of the adaptive kit controlled by *H. erectus.* Early evidence for human control over fire has been found in Israel, dating back to almost 800,000 years ago. The newest early evidence of fire, dated at 1 m.y.a., comes from Wonderwerk Cave, South Africa, where microscopic plant ashes and burned bits of bone have been found in soil that previously yielded dozens of stone tools (Berna 2012). However, no remains of a hearth or campfire area, where fires would repeatedly have been lit, have been found in Wonderwerk Cave. The first hearths date back no more than 500,000 years. Fire provided protection against predators. It permitted *H. erectus* to occupy cave sites and widened the range of climates open to human colonization. Its warmth enabled people to survive winter cold in temperate regions. Human control over fire offered other advantages, such as cooking, which breaks down vegetable fibers and tenderizes meat. Cooking kills parasites and makes meat more digestible, thus reducing strain on the chewing apparatus.

## The Evolution and Expansion of *H. erectus*

Let's review some of the *H. erectus* fossil finds, whose geographic distribution is mapped in Figure 7.1. The most important early out-of-Africa site is Dmanisi in the former Soviet Republic of Georgia, at the easternmost edge of Europe. Discoveries there include one fairly complete skull, one large mandible, and two partial skulls—one of a young adult male (780 cm$^3$) and one of an adolescent female (650 cm$^3$). Note the small cranial capacities, at the lower end of the *H. erectus* range of variation. These fossils are dated to 1.77–1.7 m.y.a. There are notable similarities between the two partial skulls and that of the Nariokotome boy from Kenya (1.6 m.y.a.). Tools associated with the Kenyan and Georgian fossils also are similar (see Vekua, Lordkipanidze, and Rightmire 2002). The Dmanisi finds suggest a rapid spread, by 1.77 m.y.a., of early *Homo* out of Africa and into Eurasia.

The Dmanisi fossils are the most ancient undisputed hominin finds outside Africa. What led early hominins to spread so far? The most probable answer is "in pursuit of meat." Once hominins developed stronger bodies and high-protein meat diets, they

FIGURE 7.1    Location of Some Major *H. erectus* Sites

McGraw-Hill Education

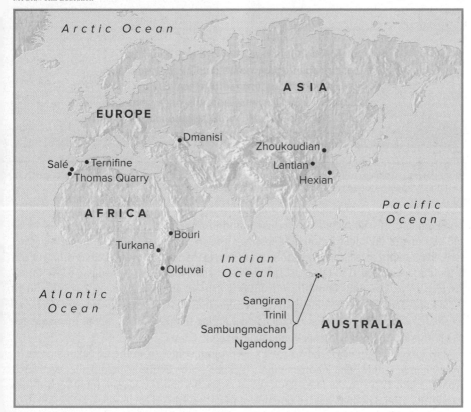

could—indeed had to—spread out. They expanded their home ranges in accordance with those of the animals they hunted. The quest for meat eventually led them out of Africa, into Eurasia (Georgia) and eventually Asia. More recent fossil finds at Dmanisi— four skeletons—show an advanced spine and lower limbs that would have facilitated mobility.

If the country of Georgia provides the earliest evidence for *H. erectus* outside of Africa, the country of Indonesia provided the very first fossil evidence for *H. erectus* as a species. In 1891, the Indonesian island of Java yielded the first (although not the most ancient) *H. erectus* fossil find, popularly known as "Java man." Eugene Dubois, a Dutch army surgeon, had gone there specifically to discover a transitional form between apes and humans. Of course, we now know that the transition to hominin had taken place much earlier than the *H. erectus* period and occurred in Africa. However, Dubois's good luck did lead him to the most ancient human fossils then known—parts of an *H. erectus* skull and a thigh bone. Later excavations in Java uncovered additional remains. The various Indonesian *H. erectus* fossils date back at least 700,000, and perhaps as much as 1.6 million, years.

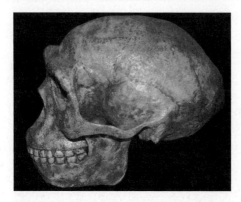

Meet *Homo erectus*. On the left is a reconstruction of one of the *H. erectus* skulls from Zhoukoudian, China; on the right, an attempt to render *H. erectus* in the flesh. (left): CM Dixon/ Heritage Image/age fotostock; (right): Tom McHugh/Science Source

Fragments of a skull and a lower jaw found in northern China at Lantian may be as old as some of the older Indonesian fossils. Other *H. erectus* remains, of uncertain date, have been found in Algeria and Morocco in North Africa. *H. erectus* remains have been found in Upper Bed II at Olduvai, Tanzania, in association with Acheulean tools. Other African *H. erectus* finds come from Ethiopia, Eritrea, and South Africa (in addition to Kenya and Tanzania). The time span of *H. erectus* in East Africa was long. Later *H. erectus* fossils have been found in Bed IV at Olduvai, dating to 500,000 B.P., about the same age as an important group of fossils found near Beijing, China.

The largest group of *H. erectus* fossils ever found comes from the Zhoukoudian cave, near Beijing, China. The Zhoukoudian ("Peking"—now Beijing—"man") site, excavated from the late 1920s to the late 1930s, was a major find for the human fossil record (see Lee 2018). Zhoukoudian yielded remains of tools, hearths, animal bones, and more than 40 hominins, including five skulls. The Zhoukoudian group lived between 780,000 and 500,000 years ago, when the Chinese climate was colder and moister than it is today. The people at Zhoukoudian hunted venison; seed and plant remains show they gathered as well.

What about Europe? No definite *H. erectus* remains have been found in western or northern Europe, whose earliest fossil hominins are now generally assigned to a Middle Pleistocene group known as *Homo heidelbergensis* (see the next section).

## Middle Pleistocene Hominins

The geological epoch known as the **Pleistocene** is considered the epoch of early human (as opposed to merely hominin) life. Its subdivisions are the Lower Pleistocene (2.6 m.y.a.–781,000 B.P.), the Middle Pleistocene (781,000–126,000 B.P.), and the Upper Pleistocene (126,000–11,7000 B.P.). These subdivisions refer to the placement of geological strata containing, respectively, older (lower), intermediate, and younger (upper) fossils. The Lower Pleistocene extends from the start of the Pleistocene through the advent of the ice ages in the Northern Hemisphere.

## Ice Ages of the Pleistocene

The Earth has experienced several ice ages, or **glacials**, major advances of continental ice sheets. These periods were separated by **interglacials**, long warm periods. With each glacial advance, the world climate cooled and continental ice sheets—massive glaciers—covered the northern parts of Europe and North America. Climates that are temperate today were arctic during the glacials.

The ice sheets advanced and receded several times during the last glacial period, the *Würm* (75,000–12,000 B.P.). Brief periods of relative warmth during the Würm (and other glacials) are called *interstadials*, in contrast to the longer interglacials. Hominin fossils found in association with animals known to occur in cold or warm climates, respectively, permit us to date them to glacial or interglacial (or interstadial) periods.

## *H. heidelbergensis*

Africa, which was center stage before and during the australopith period, is joined by Asia and Europe during later hominin evolution. In fact, European fossils and tools have contributed disproportionately to interpretations of later hominin evolution. This doesn't mean that our own species, *H. sapiens*, evolved in Europe. Far from it! There is no doubt that modern *H. sapiens*, like *H. erectus* before it, originated in Africa, reaching Europe only around 45,000 years ago (Benazzi et al. 2011; Higham et al. 2011). There probably were many more anatomically modern humans in the tropics than in Europe during the ice ages. We merely *know more* about recent human evolution in Europe because archaeology and fossil hunting—not human evolution—have been going on longer there than in Africa and Asia. (See Table 7.1 and Figure 7.2 for a summary and timeline of species within the genus *Homo*.)

The human skull and brain continued to increase after *H. erectus* and eventually overlapped with the modern range. (The modern average, remember, is about 1,350 cm$^3$.) A rounding out of the brain case was associated with the increased brain size. As Jolly and White (1995) put it, evolution was pumping more brain into the cranium—like filling a football with air.

A massive hominin jaw was discovered in 1907 in a gravel pit at Mauer, near Heidelberg, Germany. Dubbed "Heidelberg man," or *Homo heidelbergensis,* the jaw appears to be around 500,000 years old. The deposits that yielded this jaw also contained fossil remains of several animals, including bear, bison, deer, elephant, horse, and rhinoceros. The species name *H. heidelbergensis* is now commonly used to refer to the Middle Pleistocene hominins that lived between *H. erectus* and the Neandertals. This group includes fossil hominins that lived in Europe, Asia, and Africa between (very roughly) 800,000 and 200,000 B.P. (see Mounier, Condemi, and Manzi 2011).

A hominin jaw that is more than 1 million years old, found in Spain, is the oldest known hominin fossil in Europe and may be ancestral to *H. heidelbergensis*. Some of the earliest likely members of *H. heidelbergensis* come from northern Spain's Atapuerca Mountains, where the site of Gran Dolina has yielded the remains of 780,000-year-old hominins. The Spanish researchers who excavated them call this group *Homo antecessor*, but others include them in *H. heidelbergensis*. Another early possible *H. heidelbergensis* fossil is a cranial fragment found at Ceprano, near Rome, Italy, dated to around 800,000 B.P. (see Mounier et al. 2011). Other European fossils now assigned to *H. heidelbergensis* have

FIGURE 7.2    **Timeline of Species within the Genus *Homo* in Increments of 100,000 Years, from 2.5 m.y.a. through the Present (Oldest *Homo*, which as yet lacks a species name, is 2.8 million years old.)**

McGraw-Hill Education

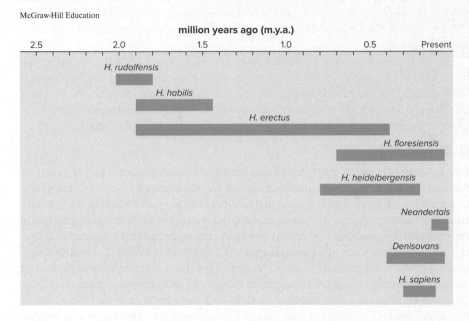

been found in England (at Swanscombe), Germany (at Steinheim as well as Mauer), and Greece (at Petralona).

*H. heidelbergensis* lived during the *Mindel* (second) glacial, the interglacial that followed it, and the following *Riss* (third) glacial. Hominins (probably late members of *H. heidelbergensis*) occupied the Arago cave in southeastern France during the Riss glacial– a time when Europe was bitterly cold. Arago is the only Riss glacial site with hominin facial material. The fossils from this cave consist of a partially intact skull, two jawbones, and teeth from a dozen individuals, with an apparent date of about 200,000 B.P. The geographic distribution of *H. heidelbergensis* extended well beyond Europe. African representatives have been found in Ethiopia (at Bodo), Tanzania (at Ndutu), and Zambia (at Broken Hill/Kabwe). Asian representatives have been found at the Chinese sites of Dali and Maba.

In addition to the fossil record, there also is ample archaeological evidence for the presence of Middle Pleistocene hominins in Europe. An English site in Suffolk, bordering the North Sea, shows that humans first reached northern Europe by 700,000 years ago during an interglacial period (Gugliotta 2005). At the site of Terra Amata, overlooking Nice in southern France, archaeologists have documented human activity dating back 300,000 years. Small bands of hunter-gatherers (15–25 people) made annual visits, during late spring–early summer, to Terra Amata, then a sandy cove on the Mediterranean coast, where they established camps, depending on the year, on a sand bar, the beach, or a sand dune (deLumley 1969/1976).

From a camp atop the dune, these people looked down on a river valley where animals were abundant. Bones found at Terra Amata show that their diet included red deer, young elephants, wild boars, wild mountain goats, an extinct variety of rhinoceros, and wild oxen. The Terra Amata people also hunted turtles and birds, fished, and collected oysters and mussels. The arrangement of postholes shows that these people used saplings to support temporary huts. There were hearths within the shelters. Tools were made from locally available rocks and beach pebbles. Thus, at Terra Amata, hundreds of thousands of years ago, people were already pursuing a lifestyle that survived in certain coastal regions until very recently.

# The Neandertals

Neandertals were first discovered in western Europe. The first one was found in 1856 in a German valley called Neander Valley—*tal* is the German word for "valley." Scientists at that time had trouble interpreting the discovery. It was clearly human, yet different enough from modern Europeans to be considered strange and abnormal. This was, after all, 35 years before Dubois found the first *H. erectus* fossils in Java and almost 70 years before the first australopith was found in South Africa. Darwin's *On the Origin of Species*, published in 1859, had not yet appeared. There was no framework for understanding human evolution. Over time, the fossil record filled in, along with evolutionary theory. There have been numerous subsequent discoveries of **Neandertals** in Europe and the Middle East, and extending eastward to central Asia and even Siberia.

In 2007 Svante Pääbo and his colleagues at Germany's Max Planck Institute for Evolutionary Anthropology announced their identification of Neandertal DNA in bones found at two sites in central Asia and Siberia. One of them, Teshik-Tash, in Uzbekistan, previously had been seen as the easternmost limit of Neandertal territory. However, bones from the second site, the Okladnikov cave in the Altai Mountains, place the Neandertals much farther (1,250 miles) east, in southern Siberia. The DNA sequence at these sites differs only slightly from that of European Neandertals. The Neandertals may have reached these areas around 127,000 years ago, when a warm period made Siberia more accessible than it is today.

## Cold-Adapted Neandertals

By 75,000 B.P., after an interglacial interlude, western Europe's hominins (Neandertals, by then) again faced extreme cold as the Würm glacial began. To deal with this environment, they wore clothes, made more elaborate tools, and hunted reindeer, mammoths, and woolly rhinos (see Conard 2011).

The Neandertals were stocky, with large trunks relative to limb length—a phenotype that minimizes surface area and thus conserves heat. Another adaptation to extreme cold was the Neandertal face, which has been likened to a *H. erectus* face that has been pulled forward by the nose. This extension increased the distance between outside air and the arteries that carry blood to the brain and was adaptive in a cold climate. The brain is sensitive to temperature changes and must be kept warm. The massive nasal cavities of Neandertal fossils suggest long, broad noses that would expand the area for warming and moistening air.

FIGURE 7.3    **Examples of Mousterian Tools: (a) Scraper, (b) Point, (c) Scraper, (d) Point, (e) Hand Ax**
The Neandertals' manufacture of diverse tool types for special purposes confirms Neandertal sophistication.

McGraw-Hill Education

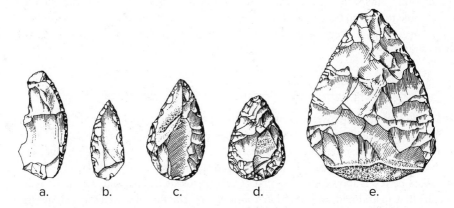

a.        b.        c.        d.        e.

Other Neandertal characteristics include huge front teeth, broad faces, and large brow ridges, as well as ruggedness of the skeleton and musculature. Neandertal teeth probably did many jobs later done by tools. The front teeth show heavy wear, suggesting that they were used for varied purposes, including chewing animal hides to make soft winter clothing out of them. The massive Neandertal face showed the stresses of constantly using the front teeth for holding and pulling.

Neandertal technology, a Middle Paleolithic tradition called **Mousterian**, included a variety of tools designed for different jobs. The Neandertals elaborated on a revolutionary technique of flake-tool manufacture (the *Levallois* technique) invented in southern Africa around 200,000 years ago, which spread widely throughout the Old World. Uniform flakes were chipped off a specially prepared core of rock. Additional work on the flakes produced the special-purpose tools shown in Figure 7.3. Scrapers were used to prepare animal hides for clothing. Larger points were attached to spears. Other special tools were designed for sawing, gouging, and piercing (Conard 2011).

## The Neandertals and Modern People

Generations of scientists have debated whether and to what extent the Neandertals may have been ancestral to anatomically modern humans, especially those of the Middle East and Europe, where fossils of both groups have been found. The current prevailing view proposes that *H. erectus* split into separate groups: one ancestral to the Neandertals, the other ancestral to AMHs. Current evidence leaves little doubt that modern humans evolved in Africa and eventually colonized Europe, displacing, or at least replacing, the Neandertals there.

Like *H. erectus* before them, the Neandertals had heavy brow ridges and slanting foreheads. However, average Neandertal cranial capacity (more than 1,400 cm$^3$) actually surpassed the modern average. Neandertal jaws were large, providing support for huge

**FIGURE 7.4**    **Drawings of *H. erectus*, *H. heidelbergensis*, Neandertal, and an Anatomically Modern Human (AMH)**
What are the main differences you notice? Is the Neandertal more like *H. erectus* or the AMH?

McGraw-Hill Education

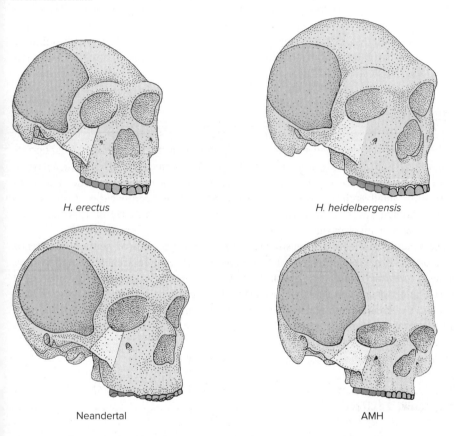

*H. erectus*                                         *H. heidelbergensis*

Neandertal                                           AMH

front teeth, and their faces were massive. The bones and skull were generally more rugged and had greater sexual dimorphism—particularly in the face and skull—than do those of AMHs. In some western European Neandertals, the contrasts with AMHs were particularly marked. The interpretation of one such fossil helped create the popular stereotype of the slouching cave dweller. This was the complete human skeleton discovered in 1908 at La Chapelle-aux-Saints in southwestern France. This was the first Neandertal to be discovered with the whole skull, including the face, preserved (Figure 7.4).

The La Chapelle skeleton was given for study to the French paleontologist Marcellin Boule. His analysis helped create an inaccurate stereotype of Neandertals as brutes who had trouble walking upright. Boule suggested that the Neandertal head was slung forward like an ape's. To round out the primitive image, Boule proclaimed that the Neandertals were incapable of straightening their legs for fully erect locomotion. However, a series of subsequent fossil discoveries show that the La Chapelle fossil wasn't a typical Neandertal but an extreme one. This much-publicized Neandertal "cave man" turned out to be an aging man whose skeleton had been distorted by osteoarthritis. Hominins, after all, have been erect bipeds for millions of years. European Neandertals were a variable population. Other Neandertal finds lack La Chapelle's combination of extreme features.

Based on his reconstruction of the complete Neandertal genome, Svante Pääbo and his colleagues found that between 1 and 4 percent of Neandertal DNA has been incorporated within the DNA of living Europeans and Asians (but not Africans). This finding suggests that Neandertals did some interbreeding with AMHs soon after the latter left Africa (see also Posth et al. 2017).

## The Denisovans

In 2010, scientists identified the Denisovan group as distant cousins of Neandertals (Callaway 2010; Jones 2019; Zimmer 2010). The name comes from Denisova, a cave in southern Siberia where five hominin traces (including a finger fragment, a wisdom tooth, and a small skull fragment) have been found. More recently (May, 2019), a fragmentary human jawbone, with two teeth, found in a Tibetan cave in 1980 has been identified as a Denisovan that lived about 160,000 years ago (Zimmer 2019).

The wisdom tooth from Denisova cave resembles the teeth of neither AMHs nor Neandertals. It has bulging sides and large, flaring roots. Remarkably, scientists have managed to extract the entire Denisovan genome from that single finger fragment and tooth. The genome sequencing suggests that the phenotype included brown skin, hair, and eyes. The **Denisovans** apparently lived in Asia from roughly 400,000 to 50,000 years ago. The DNA suggests that the split between ancestral Neandertals and Denisovans occurred around 400,000 years ago.

## Neandertals, Denisovans, and Anatomically Modern Humans

Recent analyses of fossil DNA suggest that the common ancestor of Neandertals, Denisovans, and AMHs lived around 660,000 B.P. The first split in that group occurred around 460,000 years ago, when it separated into two lineages, one jointly ancestral to Neandertals and Denisovans, the other ancestral to AMHs (Zimmer 2017b). The Neandertal-Denisovan group spread across Europe and Asia, with the split between ancestral Neandertals and Denisovans taking place around 400,000 B.P. The Neandertals spread to the west, eventually reaching the Middle East and Europe. The Denisovans headed east (while AMHs remained for a time in Africa).

Based on the most recent fossil evidence, very early AMHs were living in North Africa (Morocco) by 300,000 years ago. A recent DNA analysis suggests that an early group of AMHs (perhaps that of the Moroccan fossil) reached Europe sometime prior to 270,000 B.P. Once there, some of them mated with ancestral Neandertals. Eventually, this particular group of early AMHs disappeared, but some of their DNA survived in later Neandertals (Posth et al. 2017).

TABLE 7.2    **Evidence for Hominins Migrating out of Africa**

| Hominin group | Date | Migration to? | Nature of Evidence |
|---|---|---|---|
| Modern *H. sapiens* | After 80,000 B.P. | Worldwide | Fossil, DNA |
| Early AMHs | 194,000–177,000 B.P. | Israel, on to? | Fossil |
| Very early AMHs | 300,000–270,000 B.P. | Morocco, on to Europe? | Fossil, DNA |
| *H. erectus* | 2–1 m.y.a. | Asia, Europe? | Fossil |

Fossil and DNA evidence together now suggest at least four hominin migrations out of Africa: (1) that of *H. erectus* between 2 and 1 m.y.a.; (2) that of an early (now extinct) AMH group sometime before 270,000 years ago, (3) that of an AMH whose fossilized jawbone found in an Israeli cave dates to between 194,000 and 177,000 B.P.; and (4) that of the AMHs who spread throughout the world and gave rise to all living humans, starting around 80,000 years ago. (Table 7.2 summarizes evidence for hominin migrations out of Africa.)

# Asian Island Anomalies

Until about 20 years ago, anthropologists had assumed that anatomically modern humans had displaced all other members of the genus *Homo*, except for the Neandertals, by 100,000 B.P. Discoveries made during the past 20 years cast serious doubt on that belief. Particularly important have been hominin fossil finds on two Asian islands, one of them (Flores) part of Indonesia, the other (Luzon) of the Philippines. These hominins lived at the same time as AMHs but were sufficiently different to be classified as members of two previously unknown species—*Homo floresiensis* (on Flores) and *Homo luzonensis* (on Luzon). These are their stories.

## *Homo floresiensis*

From 700,000 to around 60,000 B.P,. a group of tiny humans lived in caves on Flores, an Indonesian island 370 miles east of Bali (see Zimmer 2016a). At 3.5 feet (a bit over 1 meter) tall, these tiny hominins, known as ***H. floresiensis***, made their living by hunting and gathering. They had surprisingly small skulls, about 370 cm$^3$—slightly smaller than the chimpanzee average. Their lower limbs and feet also were apelike. The big toe, for example, was stubby, like a chimp's. The feet were large, more than 7.5 inches (20 cm) long, out of proportion to the short lower limbs. These proportions, similar to those of some African apes, had never before been seen in hominins.

Before modern people reached Flores, which is very isolated, the island was inhabited only by a distinctive group of animals that had managed to reach it. These animals, including *H. floresiensis*, faced unusual evolutionary forces that pushed some toward gigantism and some toward dwarfism. Large carnivorous lizards known as Komodo dragons now are confined mainly to the nearby island of Komodo. Elephants, which are excellent swimmers, also reached Flores, where they evolved to a dwarf form the size of an ox.

*H. floresiensis* must have been influenced by the same evolutionary forces that reduced the size of the elephants.

The first specimen of *H. floresiensis*, an adult female, was uncovered in 2003 from a cave floor. Paleoanthropologists identified her as a very small but otherwise normal individual—a diminutive version of *H. erectus*. Because the downsizing was so extreme, she and her fellows were assigned to a new species. Remains of six additional individuals from that cave date from 100,000 to 60,000 B.P. Stone tools found with these remains appear more sophisticated than any known to have been made by *H. erectus*. Among those tools were small blades that might have been mounted on wooden shafts and used to hunt elephants.

A pair of apparent AMH teeth dated to 46,000 B.P. were unearthed in 2010 and 2011 in the same cave (Callaway 2016). The fact that these teeth are dated not too long (in geological time) after the last known members of *H. floresiensis* suggests that the arrival of AMHs may have contributed to the demise of the diminutive species. Other recent evidence suggests that AMHs used fire in that cave between 41,000 and 24,000 B.P. (Morley et al. 2016). A date of 41,000 B.P. is one of the earliest for AMHs in Southeast Asia. There is no evidence for the prior use of fire by *H. floresiensis*.

In fact, we do not know how long *H. floresiensis* managed to survive. The Ngadha people of central Flores and the Manggarai people of west Flores still tell stories about little people who lived in caves until the arrival of the Dutch traders in the 16th century (Wade 2004).

## Homo luzonensis

Announced on April 10, 2019, fossil bones and teeth found in the Philippines have revealed another long-lost and late-surviving cousin of modern people. These non-AMH fossils date to 67,000-50,000 100,000 B.P., a time when AMHs were spreading beyond Africa into Europe, Asia, and Australia (see Détroit, Mijares, et al, 2019; Gomez 2019; Ritter 2019).

The fossils consist of seven teeth and six bones from the feet, hands and thigh of at least three individuals. They were recovered from Callao Cave on the island of Luzon. Analysis of the bones and teeth led the discovery team to conclude that they belonged to a previously unknown species of *Homo*, which they named *Homo luzonensis*. The shapes and sizes of the teeth and a toe bone differ from other known members of *Homo*. The small teeth may suggest a small body size. Filipino archaeologist Armand Salvador Mijares led the discovery team, which included both foreign and local archaeologists. He plans to continue excavating and hopes to find larger fossil bones and associated stone tools.

There is no evidence that AMHs reached the Philippines until thousands of years after these dates for *H. luzonensis*. However, the previous discovery on Luzon of stone tools and butchered rhino bones confirm that hominins had reached the island more than 700,000 years ago. How might *H. luzonensis* be related to other species of *Homo*? Might it be an evolved descendant of *H. erectus*, as has been suggested for *H. floresiensis*? Or could it descend from an as-yet-unknown or unrecognized early hominin group that also spread out of Africa? Both *H. luzonensis* and *H. floresiensis* show a combination of modern features, and primitive traits that differ from those of *H. erectus*.

# Modern Humans

Anatomically modern humans (AMHs) evolved from an African version of *H. heidelbergensis* by as early as 300,000 years ago. Eventually (most probably after 80,000 B.P.), a wave of successful and adaptable AMHs began its spread from Africa to other areas, including Europe, where they replaced the Neandertals.

## Out of Africa: AMH Edition

### Ethiopian Discoveries

Considerable fossil and archaeological evidence supports the African origin of AMHs. A major fossil find was announced in 2003: the discovery, in an Ethiopian valley near a village called Herto, of three AMH skulls—two adults and a child. The skulls had been detached from their bodies and used—perhaps ritually—after death. Layers of volcanic ash allowed geologists to date the skulls to 160,000 to 154,000 B.P. The people represented by the skulls had lived by an ancient lake; they hunted and fished, using blades and hand axes. Except for a few primitive characteristics, the **Herto** skulls are anatomically modern—long with broad midfaces, featuring tall, narrow nasal bones. The cranial vaults are high, falling within modern dimensions.

Omo Kibish is one of several sites along the Omo River in southwestern Ethiopia. Excavating there between 1967 and 1974, Richard Leakey and his colleagues from the Kenya National Museum recovered AMH remains originally considered to be about 125,000 years old. The specimens now appear to be much older, with an estimated date of 195,000 B.P. (McDougall, Brown, and Fleagle 2005). The Omo remains include two partial skulls (Omo 1 and Omo 2), four jaws, a leg bone, and about 200 teeth. The Omo 1 site (Omo Kibish) also yielded a nearly complete skeleton of an adult male. The Omo 1 skull and skeleton have a modern human morphology with some primitive features. The Omo 2 skull is more primitive.

### Jebel Irhoud, Morocco, the Earliest Known AMHs

In June 2017, scientists announced the discovery and surprisingly early dating (300,000 B.P.) of several apparent AMH skull bones and tools, and evidence for cooking, at the desert site of Jebel Irhoud in Morocco (Hublin et al. 2017; Zimmer 2017c). These fossils are now the earliest known members of our species.

Since 2004, the paleoanthropologist Jean-Jacques Hublin and his colleagues have been working through layers of rock on a desert hillside at Jebel Irhoud. So far, they have unearthed skull bones from five ancient humans, all of whom died around the same time. The researchers also found flint blades in the same sedimentary layer as the skulls. Many of those blades had been burned. The cooking fires of these ancient humans probably heated blades that had been discarded and somehow buried in the ground under their hearths. The researchers determined that the blades had last been heated about 300,000 years ago. The skulls, discovered in the same rock layer as the blades, would share that same age.

The ancient humans of Jebel Irhoud shared a general resemblance among themselves, and with living humans. They had heavier brows, smaller chins, and wider and flatter faces than people today. But they were not so different that, if properly dressed, they would stand out in a crowd. Their cranial capacity was as large as in modern humans, but their skulls were long and low, like those of earlier hominins. The people at Jebel Irhoud were smart enough to make complex tools, including wooden-handled, flint-bladed spears used in hunting. Interestingly, their source of flint is located 20 miles south of Jebel Irhoud. These ancients clearly knew how to find and use distant resources. One wonders whether they also participated in regional alliances and trade networks.

### Israel's Misliya Cave

On January 25, 2018, scientists announced the discovery of a fossilized human jawbone in a collapsed cave in Israel. The fossil, an upper jawbone with seven intact teeth and one broken incisor, has been dated between 194,000 and 177,000 B.P. If that dating is correct, this is the earliest member of *Homo sapiens* yet found outside of Africa. The Israeli paleoanthropologist Israel Hershkovitz led the team that excavated the fossil from Misliya Cave on the western slopes of Mount Carmel. The jawbone had been discovered in 2002, but it took 16 additional years to complete the analysis and dating (Hershkovitz et al. 2018; St. Fleur 2018).

**FIGURE 7.5    Skhūl V**
This AMH with some archaic features was recently redated to 100,000 B.P. This is one of several fossils found at Skhūl, Israel.

McGraw-Hill Education

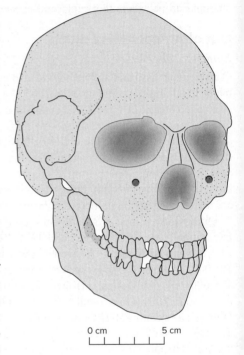

0 cm                    5 cm

This discovery provides support for genetic studies suggesting that some modern humans ventured out of Africa earlier than the migration that would eventually give rise to all living humans. To characterize this jawbone as "modern human" doesn't mean that its owner looked much like a living human. In form, it simply resembles other AMHs more than Neandertals. The *H. sapiens* population to which its owner belonged may have become extinct after leaving Africa (St. Fleur 2018).

### Other Early AMHs

Early AMHs also have been found at South African sites, including Border Cave, where AMH fossils and tools date back 150,000 years. A complex of South African caves near the Klasies River mouth was occupied by a group of hunter-gatherers some 120,000 years ago. Anatomically modern specimens, including the skull shown in Figure 7.5, have been found at Skhūl, a site on Mount Carmel in Israel. The Skhūl fossils date to 100,000 B.P. Another group of modern-looking and similarly dated (92,000 B.P.) skulls comes from the Israeli site of Qafzeh.

## "Mitochondrial Eve" and the Spread of AMHs

In 1987, geneticists at the University of California at Berkeley gathered evidence supporting the hypothesis that modern humans (AMHs) arose fairly recently in Africa, then spread to the rest of the world. Rebecca Cann, Mark Stoneking, and Allan C. Wilson (1987) analyzed genetic samples from 147 women whose ancestors came from Africa, Europe, the Middle East, Asia, New Guinea, and Australia. The researchers focused on mitochondrial DNA (mtDNA), which is located in the cytoplasm (the outer part, rather than the nucleus) of cells. Ordinary DNA, which makes up the genes that determine most physical traits, is found in the nucleus and comes from both parents. Only the mother, however, can transmit mtDNA to her offspring (Figure 7.6). The father plays no part in mtDNA transmission, just as the mother has nothing to do with the transmission of the Y chromosome, which comes from the father (and determines the sex of the child).

The Berkeley researchers counted, then compared, the number of mutations in the mtDNA in each of their 147 tissue samples. Based on the number of mutations shared, the researchers drew an evolutionary, or phylogenetic, tree. That tree started in Africa, then branched in two. One group remained in Africa, while the other one split off, carrying its mtDNA to the rest of the world. The Berkeley researchers concluded that everyone alive today has mtDNA that descends from a woman (they called her "Mitochondrial Eve") who lived in sub-Saharan Africa around 200,000 years ago. Eve was not the only woman alive then; she was just the only one whose descendants have included a daughter in each generation up to the present. Because mtDNA passes exclusively through females, mtDNA lines disappear whenever a woman has no children or has only sons. The nature of the branches in the phylogenetic tree suggests that Eve's descendants left Africa no more than 135,000 years ago.

Other evidence suggests a major migration of AMHs out of Africa between 80,000 and 50,000 years ago. As reported in *Nature* magazine in September 2016, three separate teams of geneticists studied a total of 787 DNA samples collected from human populations around the world (see Malaspinas et al. 2016; Mallick et al. 2016; Tucci and Akey 2016; Zimmer 2016b). Unlike previous studies, based mainly on Europeans and Asians, these genetic studies sampled multiple indigenous populations. Included, among many others, were the following: Basques, African pygmies, Mayans, Bedouins, Sherpas, and Cree Indians. Analysis of these genomes confirmed that all non-Africans today trace their ancestry to a single dispersal out of Africa between 80,000 and 50,000 B.P. This was not the first spread of AMHs out of Africa; it was merely the only one that appears to have left descendants that survive today (Zimmer 2016b).

FIGURE 7.6    **How mtDNA Is Inherited. Only the women shaded black transmit the mtDNA of the woman at the top of the genealogy.**

Norway DNA Norgesprosjektet

**Inheritance pattern of mtDNA**
(males carry their mother's mtDNA, but only females pass it on to their children)

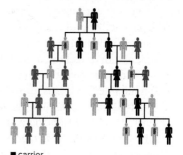

■ carrier

## AMHs on the Move

In January 2015, scientists announced the discovery in Israel of a 55,000-year-old AMH skull that may be closely related to the first modern humans to colonize Europe (Hershkovitz et al. 2015). The partial skull is that of a small adult of undetermined sex. The area where the skull was found would have been a likely corridor for AMHs expanding out of Africa into Eurasia. Designated Manot 1 after Israel's Manot Cave, where it was found, this fossil dates to a time when AMHs are likely to have been expanding beyond Africa. Some features of Manot 1 suggest that its ancestors, although mainly African AMHs, may also have included a few Neandertals, which are known to have occupied several nearby caves between 65,000 and 50,000 B.P. During the last (Würm) glacial period, which began around 75,000 years ago, Neandertals appear to have spread from western Europe into the Middle East, as part of a general southward expansion of cold-adapted fauna (Bar-Yosef 1987). Manot 1 provides the first evidence that Neandertals and moderns were living in this area around 55,000 B.P. This suggests that whatever interbreeding did take place between Neandertals and moderns may have occurred in the Middle East, prior to the AMH colonization of Europe.

The Neandertals may (or may not) have coexisted with modern humans in the Middle East for thousands of years. The overlap in Europe apparently spanned the period between around 45,000 B.P. and Neandertal extinction around 39,000 B.P. Redatings of a piece of modern jawbone with three teeth from England and of two baby teeth from Italy provide the oldest known skeletal evidence for AMHs in Europe (Wilford 2011a). The baby teeth from Italy were dated at 43,000 to 45,000 years old (Benazzi et al. 2011). The jawbone, from Kents Cavern in Devon, England, was 41,500 to 44,200 years old. Prior to these dates, the earliest reliably dated European AMH came from Romania (42,000–37,800 B.P.).

## The Advent of Behavioral Modernity

Scientists agree that (1) around 6 million years ago, our hominin ancestors originated in Africa, and as apelike creatures they became habitual bipeds; (2) by 3.3 million years ago, still in Africa, hominins were making crude stone tools; (3) by 1.7 million years ago, hominins had spread from Africa to Asia and eventually Europe; and (4) sometime around 300,000 years ago, anatomically modern humans evolved from ancestors who had remained in Africa. Like *Homo erectus* more than a million years earlier, AMHs spread out from Africa. Eventually they replaced nonmodern human types, such as the Neandertals in Europe and the successors of *H. erectus* in Asia.

There is disagreement, however, about when, where, and how AMHs achieved **behavioral modernity**—relying on symbolic thought, elaborating cultural creativity, and as a result becoming fully human in behavior as well as in anatomy. Was it as much as 200,000 or even 300,000, or as little as 45,000, years ago? Was it in Africa, the Middle East, or Europe? What triggered the change: a genetic mutation, population increase, competition with nonmodern humans, or some other cause?

The traditional (and increasingly unlikely) argument has been that modern behavior originated fairly recently, perhaps around 45,000 years ago, and only after *Homo sapiens* pushed into Europe. This theory of a "creative explosion" is based on finds such as the impressive cave paintings at Lascaux, Chauvet Cave, and other sites in France, Spain, and Romania (Balter 2010). However, recent discoveries outside Europe point to a much older, more gradual evolution of modern behavior.

A series of discoveries in Africa and the Middle East provide substantial evidence for earlier (than in Europe) modern behavior, in the form of finely made stone and bone tools, self-ornamentation, and abstract carvings. Surveying African archaeological sites dating to between 300,000 and 30,000 years ago, Sally McBrearty and Alison Brooks (2000) concluded that what might appear to be a sudden event in Europe actually rested on a slow process of cultural accumulation within Africa, where *H. sapiens* became fully human long before 45,000 years ago. At South Africa's Blombos Cave, for example, an archaeological team led by Christopher Henshilwood found evidence that AMHs were making bone awls and weapon points more than 70,000 years ago. Three points had been shaped with a stone blade and then finely polished. Henshilwood thinks these artifacts indicate symbolic behavior and artistic creativity—people trying to make beautiful objects.

Representing an even earlier occupation of Blombos Cave, Henshilwood's team has excavated a 100,000-year-old workshop, where early AMHs mixed the world's earliest known paint. Those AMHs used stones to grind colorful chunks of dirt, transported to Blombos from several miles away, into a red powder, known as ochre. The Blombos people collected their ochre in large abalone shells, where they liquefied and stirred it, then scooped it out as paint, using a bone spatula (Wilford 2011b). They may have applied the mixture to their skin, perhaps as decoration for a special event.

Even earlier evidence (dating back to 164,000 B.P.) for behavioral modernity comes from a cave site at Pinnacle Point, South Africa. The cave yielded small stone bladelets, which could be attached to wood to make spears, as well as red ochre.

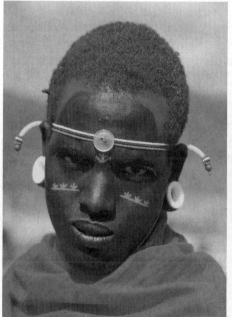 

Body ornamentation is a sign of behavioral modernity. On the left is a young Samburu man from Kenya in traditional makeup and costume. On the right, the "Kandi kid" from San Francisco, California, has bright blue hair, color contact lenses, facial piercings and gauged ears. What are the social functions of such ornamentation? Are such features markers of distinctive cultures? (left): Barry Lewis/Alamy Stock Photo; (right): Tristan Savatier/Getty Images

Cultural advances would have facilitated the spread of AMHs out of Africa. By 43,000 years ago, such advances had reached the Middle East, where, in Turkey and Lebanon, Steven Kuhn, Mary Stiner, and David Reese (2001) found evidence that coastal people made and wore beads and shell ornaments. Some of the shells were rare varieties, white or brightly colored. Such body ornaments could have been part of a system of communication, signaling group identity and social status.

Archaeological discoveries in many world areas confirm that neither anatomical modernity nor behavioral modernity was a European invention. Africa's role in the origin and development of humanity has been prominent for millions of years of hominin evolution (see Stringer 2012a and Wilford 2012; for the contrary, traditional view, see Klein 2013).

## Advances in Technology

Anatomically modern humans made tools in a variety of traditions, collectively known as **Upper Paleolithic** because of the tools' location in the upper, or more recent, layers of sedimentary deposits. The Upper Paleolithic traditions all emphasized **blade tools**. Blades were hammered off a prepared core. A blade is longer than a flake—its length is more than twice its width. Blades were chipped off cores 4-6 inches (10-15 cm) high by hitting a punch made of bone or antler with a hammerstone. Blades were then modified to produce a variety of special-purpose implements. Some were composite tools that were made by joining reworked blades to other materials.

Faster, more efficient, and more productive than previous stone tool making, Upper Paleolithic technology may have been especially valued by people whose economy depended on cooperative hunting of mammoths, woolly rhinoceroses, bison, wild horses, bears, wild cattle, wild boars, and—principally—reindeer. It has been estimated that approximately 90 percent of the meat eaten by western Europeans between 25,000 and 15,000 B.P. came from reindeer.

Trends observable over the course of the archaeological record continue with the Upper Paleolithic. First, the number of distinct tool types increased. This trend reflected functional specialization—the manufacture of special tools for particular jobs. A second trend was increasing standardization in tool manufacture. The form and inventory of tools reflect several factors: the jobs tools are intended to perform, the physical properties of the raw materials from which they are made, and distinctive cultural traditions about how to make tools.

Other trends include growth in *Homo*'s total population and geographic range and increasing local cultural diversity as people specialized in particular economic activities. Illustrating increasing economic diversity are the varied special-purpose tools made by Upper Paleolithic populations. Scrapers were used to hollow out wood and bone, scrape animal hides, and remove bark from trees. Burins, the first chisels, were used to make slots in bone and wood and to engrave designs on bone. Awls, which were drills with sharp points, were used to make holes in wood, bone, shell, and skin. Upper Paleolithic bone tools have survived: knives, pins, needles with eyes, and fishhooks. The needles suggest that clothes sewn with thread—made from the sinews of animals—were being worn. Fishhooks and harpoons confirm an increased emphasis on fishing.

# Glacial Retreat

Western Europe provides one well-studied example of the consequences of glacial retreat. The Würm glacial ended between 17,000 and 12,000 years ago. As the ice retreated, the tundra and steppe vegetation grazed by reindeer and other large herbivores gradually moved north. Some people moved north, too, following their prey.

Shrubs, forests, and more solitary animals appeared in southwestern Europe. With most of the big-game animals gone, western Europeans were forced to use a greater variety of foods. To replace specialized economies based on big game, more generalized adaptations developed during the 5,000 years of glacial retreat.

As water flowed from melting glacial ice, sea levels all over the world started rising. Today, off most coasts, there is a shallow-water zone called the *continental shelf*, over which the sea gradually deepens until the abrupt fall to deep water, which is known as the *continental slope*. During the ice ages, so much water was frozen in glaciers that most continental shelves were exposed. Dry land extended up to the slope's edge. The waters right offshore were deep, cold, and dark. Few species of marine life could thrive in this environment.

As seas rose, conditions more encouraging to marine life developed in the shallower, warmer offshore waters. The quantity and variety of edible species increased tremendously in waters over the shelf. Furthermore, because rivers now flowed more gently into the oceans, fish such as salmon could ascend those rivers to spawn. Flocks of birds that nested in seaside marshes migrated across Europe during the winter. Even inland Europeans could take advantage of new resources, such as migratory birds and springtime fish runs, which filled the rivers of southwestern France.

Although hunting remained important, southwestern European economies became less specialized. A wider range, or broader spectrum, of plant and animal life was being hunted, gathered, collected, caught, and fished. This was the beginning of what anthropologist Kent Flannery (1969) has called the *broad-spectrum revolution*. It was revolutionary because, in the Middle East, it led to food production—human control over the reproduction of plants and animals, a process to be examined in Chapter 8.

# Settling New Continents

During the major glacial advances, with so much water frozen in ice, land bridges formed, aiding human colonization of new areas. People spread from Africa into Europe and Asia, eventually reaching Australia and, much later, the Americas and the Pacific islands.

When did humans first settle Australia? Recent genetic dating suggests around 50,000 B.P. (Tobler et al. 2017; Zimmer 2017a), but archaeology tells a different story. In a northern Australian rock shelter called Madjedbebe, an excavation team has found evidence of a much older occupation, dating back at least 65,000 years (Clarkson et al. 2017; Marean 2017; St. Fleur 2017). This is the earliest reliable date for a human presence in Australia.

## Beringia and Beyond: Genetic Evidence

After Australia, *H. sapiens* had two more continents (North and South America) to settle. A vast land bridge known as *Beringia* once connected North America and Siberia. Submerged today under the Bering Sea, Beringia was once an expanse of dry land several hundred miles wide. The original settlers of the Americas came from Northeast Asia. Spreading across Beringia thousands of years ago, ancestors of Native Americans didn't realize they were embarking on the colonization of a new continent. They were merely big-game hunters who, over the generations, moved gradually eastward as they spread their camps and followed their prey—woolly mammoths and other tundra-adapted herbivores. Other ancient hunters would enter North America along the shore by boat, fishing and hunting sea animals.

In January 2018, scientists reported their analysis of the ancient genome of a 6-week-old baby girl who lived briefly and died 11,500 years ago in what is now central Alaska. Archaeologists had found her remains in 2010 buried beneath a hearth on a bed of antler points and red ocher. They named her Xach'itee'aanenh T'eede Gaay, which means "sunrise girl-child" in Middle Tanana, the language of the local community. Analysis of her DNA showed that she belonged to a previously unknown cousin branch that separated from ancestral Native Americans about 20,000 years ago. Scientists named her people **ancient Beringians**, after their homeland. They apparently remained in Beringia and Alaska for thousands of years, eventually disappearing, leaving no known living descendants (Moreno-Mayar 2018a, 2018b; Zimmer 2018). In November 2018, scientists reported

Woolly-mammoth hunters in Beringia, the vast stretch of land between Siberia and North America that was exposed during the ice ages.
North Wind Picture Archives/Alamy Stock Photo

on the discovery (in western Alaska) and genetic analysis of a second ancient Beringian, this one dated around 9,000 B.P. (Moreno-Mayar 2018b; Wade 2018b).

As far as we know, the ancient Beringians never ventured south of Alaska. Another group of early migrants from Siberia—ancestral Native Americans—did journey southward. Around 16,000 B.P., they split into two main branches—a northern branch and a southern branch. The northern branch includes the Athabaskans and other indigenous groups in Canada and Alaska, along with the Navajo and Apache in the southwestern United States (Moreno-Mayer 2018; Zimmer 2018). The second—the southern branch—expanded rapidly, perhaps in mere centuries, throughout North America and South America, starting around 14,000–13,000 years ago (Moreno-Mayer 2018b; Wade 2018b; Zimmer 2018).

Representing this southern, expansive branch are an 11,000-year-old burial from Spirit Cave, Nevada, as well as the 12,700-year-old remains of a boy (known as the Anzick child) from Montana. Both are linked genetically to 10,400-year-old skeletal remains from Brazil and a 10,900-year-old skeleton from Chile. These similarities suggest a quick dispersal of this southern branch from North into South America. Finally, around 9,000 B.P., two additional waves of people (later offshoots of the southern branch) began moving from North or Central America into South America. Over time, they mixed with and *eventually completely replaced*, South America's previous settlers (Posth et al. 2018; Zimmer 2018).

## Archaeological Evidence

This was truly a "new world" to its earliest colonists, as it would be to the European voyagers who rediscovered it thousands of years later. Its natural resources, particularly its big game, never before had been exploited by humans. On North America's rolling grasslands, early Native Americans, *Paleoindians*, hunted horses, camels, bison, elephants, mammoths, and giant sloths. The **Clovis tradition**—a sophisticated stone technology based on points that were fastened to the end of a hunting spear (see Figure 7.7)— flourished, widely but very briefly, in the Central Plains, on their western margins, and in what is now the eastern United States (Green 2006; Largent 2007a, 2007b).

$C^{14}$ (radiocarbon) dating suggests that the Clovis tradition lasted no more than 450 years (13,250–12,800 B.P.) and perhaps a mere 200 years (13,125–12,925 B.P.) (Waters and Stafford 2007). During this short time span, Clovis technology spread throughout North America. Unknown is whether this spread involved the actual movement of big-game hunters or the very rapid diffusion of a superior technology from group to group (Largent 2007b).

FIGURE 7.7    **A Clovis Spear Point**
Such points were attached to spears used by Paleoindians of the North American plains between 13,250 and 12,800 B.P. Are there sites with comparable ages in South America?

McGraw-Hill Education

## Anthropology Today    *The Rising Stars of a South African Cave*

Lee Berger is an American paleoanthropologist who has worked at South Africa's Witwatersrand University since the 1990s. Prior to the discovery of *H. naledi*, as described here, Berger was best known for the discovery of *Au. sediba*, another important recent find, which was described in Chapter 6.

Cavers Rick Hunter and Steve Tucker first drew Berger's attention to the Rising Star cave, located about 30 miles northwest of Johannesburg. When Hunter and Tucker entered that cave in October 2013, they weren't expecting to make a new discovery. Cavers had explored there for decades. Tucker made the discovery by accident when, after wedging himself into a crevice, he found that his feet didn't touch the bottom. That crevice, it turned out, led to a very narrow shaft, which descended for 40 feet (12 meters) before opening into a chamber. Tucker and Hunter dropped into that chamber and found its floor covered with bones. Tucker took snapshots to show Berger, who had asked Tucker and Hunter to look out for bones during their caving.

Once he saw the photos, Berger knew he was dealing with a hominin site. As a National Geographic explorer-in-residence, he persuaded that organization to fund a research expedition. His most immediate need was for researchers who could navigate the cave's ups, downs, and narrow passages to reach the floor where the bones were located. Berger used social media to recruit his ideal candidates: researchers who had a slim or thin build, a background in paleoanthropology or archaeology, and some caving and climbing experience. In response to his Facebook post, he received 57 applications and chose six young, fit, well-trained women—Canadian Marina Elliott; Australian Elen Feuerriegel; and Americans Lindsay Eaves, Alia Gurtov, Hannah Morris, and Becca Peixotto.

The fossil chamber containing the bones lies just 100 yards from the cave entrance, but that distance is a tortuous one, with three daunting obstacles. The first is a narrow space, a mere 10 inches wide, called "Superman's Crawl," because one can best squeeze through it by extending one arm in front while holding the other arm tightly against one's side, like Superman in flight. The next challenge is to climb a sharp ridge called the Dragon's Back, with steep falls on either side. The final obstacle is the 40-foot chute, barely 8 inches wide. (Tucker and Hunter were wiry enough to make the descent; Berger and most of his male associates were not.) At the bottom of the chute lies the Landing Zone (as the team members dubbed it), which leads into the Dinaledi ("many stars") chamber where the fossils were located.

For three weeks, the six young women, whom Berger described as "underground astronauts," traversed this daunting route each day, working in teams of three for alternating shifts. They wore hat torches to light their way. Prior to their arrival, cavers had threaded communication cables down to the fossil chamber. The young women's mission was to collect the bones scattered on the cave floor and to excavate fossils embedded in that floor. In 21 days, they brought up more than 1,500 bones, representing at least 15 individuals—a treasure trove of hominin fossils unsurpassed in the history of paleoanthropology.

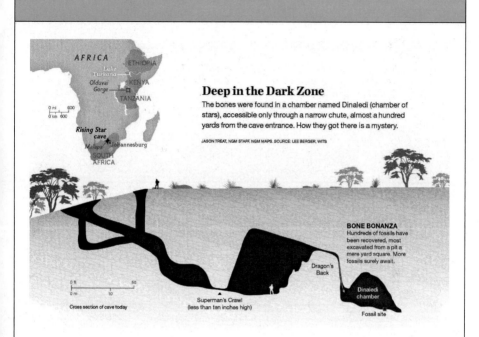

**Deep in the Dark Zone**

The bones were found in a chamber named Dinaledi (chamber of stars), accessible only through a narrow chute, almost a hundred yards from the cave entrance. How they got there is a mystery.

JASON TREAT, NGM STAFF. NGM MAPS. SOURCE: LEE BERGER, WITS

**BONE BONANZA**
Hundreds of fossils have been recovered, most excavated from a pit a mere yard square. More fossils surely await.

Dragon's Back

Dinaledi chamber

Superman's Crawl
(less than ten inches high)

Cross section of cave today

Fossil site

Location of the Rising Star cave in South Africa, and a cross-section showing the Dinaledi chamber within the cave and the tortuous path leading to that chamber—the fossil site.
Jason Treat/National Geographic Creative

While the six underground astronauts worked below the surface, other team members were busy examining and analyzing the bones being brought out of the cave. Eventually, Berger would host an analytic workshop at Witwatersrand University, attended not only by members of his *Au. sediba* team but also by young paleoanthropologists from around the world invited to help interpret this enigmatic new hominin.

Berger's approach to analyzing and publicizing the *H. naledi* fossils posed a sharp contrast to what was usual in paleoanthropology. Typically a discovery team spends years working on its analysis before announcing the discovery and its presumed significance. Berger's team immediately made the information widely available in the media, including a PBS program based on filming done during the excavation and analysis (see also Berger and Hawks 2017). The team also made images of the fossils available worldwide for study by other scientists and their students. Some paleoanthropologists were peeved (or worse) at Berger's departure from tradition and, particularly, his release of information about the *naledi* find before dating was

*continued*

## Anthropology Today *continued*

The six "underground astronauts" who excavated the fossil trove known as *Homo naledi* from the inner recesses of South Africa's Rising Star cave. From left to right: Becca Peixoto, Alia Gurtov, Elen Feuerrigel, Marina Elliott, Lindsay Eaves, and Hannah Morris.
Courtesy Dr. John Hawks, University of Wisconsin-Madison

established for the fossils. Berger's initial description of the find as a possible burial site drew specific criticism. Most scientists doubted that such small-brained hominins would have been capable of that type of behavior. The fossils themselves are described more fully in the text. It is likely that additional information on this find will be available by the time you read this.

In addition to the recent DNA evidence discussed previously, we know from archaeology that the Clovis people were not the first inhabitants of the Americas. One pre-Clovis find is a bone projectile point, embedded in a mastodon rib, from the Manis site in Washington state, dated to 13,800 B.P. (Waters et al. 2011). Sites in Wisconsin have yielded non-Clovis tools and butchered mammoth remains dating to 13,500 B.P. and 12,500 B.P. In Oregon's Paisley Caves, scientists have uncovered 13,200-year-old non-Clovis projectile points and human *coprolites* (fossilized feces) (Jenkins et al. 2012). The oldest pre-Clovis site is in South America, at the northern Patagonia settlement of Monte Verde, Chile, dating to 14,800 B.P. Adapting to different environments as they expanded through the Americas, Native Americans developed a variety of cultures. Some continued to rely on big game. Others became broad-spectrum foragers, and eventually farmers, as we shall see in Chapter 8.

# Summary

1. Key recent early hominin fossil discoveries include (a) a jaw fragment found in Ethiopia, dating to 2.8 m.y.a., that appears to be the earliest known member of the genus *Homo*, and (b) finds at South Africa's Rising Star cave of more than 1,500 bones, representing at least 15 individuals, which have been assigned to a new species, *H. naledi*. With a surprisingly recent date of 335,000 to 236,000 B.P., the *naledi* finds show a mixture of apelike and human characteristics.

2. Four hominin species coexisted in Africa around 2 m.y.a. They were *Paranthropus* (2.4-1.0 m.y.a.), *H. rudolfensis* (2.03-1.78 m.y.a.), *H. habilis* (1.9-1.44 m.y.a.), and *H. erectus* (1.9-0.5 m.y.a.). Compared with the australopiths, dental, facial, and cranial robustness was reduced in early *H. habilis* (1.9-1.44 m.y.a.) and *H. erectus* (1.9?-0.5? m.y.a.). *H. erectus* was the first hominin to achieve modern body size and form. *H. erectus*'s average cranial capacity doubled the australopith average. Tool complexity and archaeological evidence for cooperative hunting suggest a long period of enculturation and learning. *H. erectus* extended the hominin range beyond Africa to Asia and Europe.

3. Ancient *H. erectus* skulls have been found in Kenya and Georgia (in Eurasia), dating back some 1.77-1.6 million years. *H. erectus* persisted for more than a million years, evolving into *H. heidelbergensis* by the Middle Pleistocene. Fire allowed *H. erectus* to expand into cooler areas, to cook, and to live in caves.

4. *H. heidelbergensis* lived in Europe, Africa, and Asia between about 800,000 and 200,000 years ago. An African version of *H. heidelbergensis* gave rise to anatomically modern humans (AMHs) by 300,000 years ago.

5. The Neandertals (130,000-39,000 B.P.) who inhabited western Europe during the early part of the Würm glacial, were among the first hominin fossils found. With no examples of the australopiths or *H. erectus* yet discovered, the differences between them and modern humans were accentuated. The last common ancestors of Neandertals and AMHs lived about 660,000 years ago. There is genetic evidence that Neandertals in western Europe did some interbreeding with AMHs.

6. The Denisovans were cousins of the Neandertals who lived in Asia between about 400,000 and 50,000 years ago. After their split from the Denisovans around 400,000 B.P., the ancestral Neandertals spread westward, to the Middle East and Europe, while the Denisovans headed east.

7. *H. floresiensis* is the name of a species of tiny humans that managed to survive on the isolated island of Flores in Indonesia between 700,000 and 60,000 B.P. A probable descendant of *H. erectus*, *H. floresiensis* is marked by the unusually small size of its body and its chimp-sized skull.

8. An African version of *H. heidelbergensis* gave rise to anatomically modern humans by 300,000 years ago. The earliest AMH fossil finds come from Jebel Irhoud, Morocco (300,000 B.P.). Other early AMHs have been found at the Ethiopian sites of Omo Kibish (195,000 B.P.) and Herto (160,000-154,000 B.P.), and various South African sites, along with three Israeli sites, Misliya cave (194,000-177,000 B.P.), Skhūl (100,000 B.P.) and Qafzeh (92,000 B.P.). The Neandertals (130,000-39,000 B.P.)

and AMHs overlapped in Europe (from 45,000 B.P. to 39,000 B.P.) and in the Middle East even earlier. AMHs made Upper Paleolithic blade tools in Europe, and Middle and Late Stone Age flake tools in Africa.

9. When and where did human behavioral modernity originate? Mounting evidence now tends to favor an African origin. In western Europe, as glacial ice melted and the Upper Paleolithic ended, a broad-spectrum economy that incorporated fish, fowl, and plant foods supplemented, then replaced, the diminishing big-game supply.

10. Humans probably entered the Americas no more than 18,000 years ago. Pursuing big game in and across Beringia, or entering North America along the Pacific coast by boat, fishing and hunting sea animals, they gradually occupied a new continent. The Clovis (spear point) tradition flourished, widely but very briefly (13,250–12,800 B.P.), in a wide area of North America. The Clovis people were not the first inhabitants of the Americas. Adapting to different environments, Native Americans developed a variety of cultures. Some continued to rely on big game. Others became broad-spectrum foragers.

## Think Like an Anthropologist

1. As anatomically modern humans, we make up a variable population, yet we are all one species. When looking at the fossil record, how have scientists confronted the issue of variability and speciation? Consider the Neandertals and AMHs. Remembering the definition of species given in Chapter 4, should these hominins be placed in the same or different species?

2. What does *behavioral modernity* mean? What are the competing theories that attempt to explain the advent of behavioral modernity in AMHs? Is behavioral modernity a quality of individual humans or of humans as part of a social group? (Perhaps the answer is not one or the other but an interaction between the two, which some anthropologists might argue are inseparable.)

## Key Terms

Acheulean, *155*
anatomically modern humans (AMHs), *155*
ancient Beringians, *174*
behavioral modernity, *170*
blade tool, *172*
Clovis tradition, *175*
Denisovans, *164*
glacials, *159*
H. (Homo) erectus, *153*
H. (Homo) floresiensis, *165*
H. (Homo) habilis, *152*
H. (Homo) heidelbergensis, *159*
Herto, *167*
interglacials, *159*
Mousterian, *162*
Neandertals, *161*
Paleolithic, *155*
Pleistocene, *158*
Upper Paleolithic, *172*

# Chapter

# 8

# The First Farmers

## Broad-Spectrum Economies

In Chapter 7, we saw that, as the glaciers receded, foragers developed a more diversified economy, focusing less on large animals. This was the beginning of what Kent Flannery (1969) has called the **broad-spectrum revolution**. This refers to the period beginning around 15,000 B.P. in the Middle East and 12,000 B.P. in Europe, during which a wider range, or broader spectrum, of plant and animal life was hunted, gathered, collected, caught, and fished. It was revolutionary because, in the Middle East, it led to food production—human control over the reproduction of plants and animals.

### The Mesolithic in Europe

The broad-spectrum revolution in Europe includes the late Upper Paleolithic and the **Mesolithic**, which followed it. The Mesolithic had a characteristic tool type—the *microlith* (Greek for "small stone"). Among such small stone tools were arrowheads, spear points, and fish hooks. Of interest to anthropologists is what an abundance of such small and delicately shaped stone tools tells us about the way of life of the people who made them. The key aspect of the Mesolithic economy was the shift away from big game to the pursuit of a much broader spectrum of plant and animal species.

By 10,000 B.P., the human range in Europe had expanded to the formerly glaciated British Isles and Scandinavia. The reindeer herds had gradually retreated to the far north, with some human groups following (and ultimately domesticating) them. Forests replaced treeless steppe and tundra. People still hunted, but they stalked solitary forest animals rather than herd species. Coasts and lakes were fished intensively. Some important Mesolithic sites are Scandinavian shell mounds—the garbage dumps of prehistoric oyster collectors. Microliths were used as fishhooks and in harpoons. Dugout canoes were used for fishing and travel. For woodworking, Mesolithic carpenters used new kinds of axes, chisels, and gouges. The process of preserving meat and fish by smoking and salting grew increasingly important. (Meat preservation had been less of a problem previously, in a subarctic environment.) The bow and arrow became essential for hunting waterfowl in swamps and marshes. Dogs served as retrievers and as hunting companions in a forested environment (see Grimm 2016).

A recent genomic analysis of dogs and wolves suggests that there were two phases of domestication leading to dogs (see Arnold 2015). The first phase began, long before the Mesolithic, in China around 33,000 years ago. The second phase began around 15,000 years ago, when dogs began to spread out from Asia to other parts of the world. The first dogs may have arrived in Europe no more than 10,000 years ago, where they would have been useful as helpmates to humans in the Mesolithic economy.

## Developments in Asia, including Early Pottery

By 15,000 B.P., foragers in other world areas, including Japan, were also pursuing a broad-spectrum foraging economy. Consider the Japanese site of Nittano (Akazawa 1980), located on an inlet near Tokyo. Nittano was occupied several times between 6000 and 5000 B.P. by members of the widespread *Jomon* culture (16,000–2500 B.P.). The Jomon people hunted deer, pigs, bears, and antelope; gathered plants and nuts; and ate fish and shellfish. Their sites have yielded the remains of more than 300 species of shellfish and 180 species of edible plants, including berries, nuts, and tubers (Akazawa and Aikens 1986; Habu et al. 2011).

Based on their knowledge of Middle Eastern prehistory, archaeologists once assumed that pottery (ceramics) would have been invented after, rather than well before, the advent of food production (domestication). This assumption turns out to be false: The world's earliest pottery was made by foragers rather than farmers. Jomon clay pots date back 15,300 years. In the burnt fragments of large clay pots made by those broad-spectrum foragers, scientists have found traces of fat from fish and shellfish (Craig 2013; Subbaraman 2013). Not only did the Jomon people stew their fish, they also feasted on it in groups. Their large pots weren't just utilitarian cooking vessels; they brought people together to socialize, too (Craig 2013; Subbaraman 2013).

Even older—in fact, the world's oldest known—pottery comes from Jiangxi Province, southern China (Wu et al. 2012). Dated to 20,000 B.P., these pots were simple cooking vessels. Pottery making began in China 20,000 years ago and never stopped. Chinese cuisine always has featured cooking and steaming, which ceramics facilitate. As in Japan, a group of hunter-gatherers made the earliest pots; plant cultivation did not reach China for another 10,000 years.

In the Middle East, by contrast, the first pottery appeared 3,000–2,000 years *after*, rather than before, farming. Harvard archaeologist Ofer Bar-Yosef suggests that the earliest farmers/herders in the Middle East had a diet based on barbecued meats and pita breads and didn't need pottery (see Wu et al. 2012). In their cooking style, one simply ground the seeds, mixed them with water, and then cooked the dough right on the fire. Chinese cooking, by contrast, needed pots to cook and steam foods, and pottery appeared thousands of years earlier.

## The Neolithic

The term *Neolithic Revolution*, sometimes called the Agricultural Revolution, refers to the widespread transition, beginning at least 12,000 years ago, of human societies from lifestyles based entirely on foraging to lifestyles that included food production—farming and herding. The Neolithic is considered revolutionary because, in just a few thousand years, it transformed small, mobile groups into larger societies living in permanent settlements—villages, towns, and eventually cities. Neolithic economies fueled population growth, expansion, and the settlement of new environments. The many repercussions, including the advantages and disadvantages of food production, are examined in the section "Costs and Benefits" later in this chapter.

The transition from Mesolithic to Neolithic occurred when groups became dependent on domesticated foods for more than 50 percent of their diet. This happened gradually, after a long period of experimenting with and using domesticates as

The term *Neolithic* was coined to refer to techniques of grinding and polishing stone tools, such as this hammer head and two polished axes found in England. Was the new tool-making style the most significant thing about the Neolithic? CM Dixon/age fotostock

supplements to broad-spectrum foraging. Neolithic cultures (which are called *Formative* in the Americas) are identifiable archaeologically by their combination of dependence on cultivation, sedentary (settled) life, and use of ceramic vessels. The term **Neolithic** was coined to refer to new techniques of grinding and polishing stone tools (see Saville 2012). However, the primary significance of the Neolithic was the new total economy based on the domestication of plants and animals, rather than just its characteristic artifacts.

## The First Farmers and Herders in the Middle East

The Neolithic was revolutionary, but how did it all begin? Geologists date the start of the geological epoch known as the **Holocene**, which followed the Pleistocene, to 11,700 B.P. By that time, the shift toward the Neolithic was under way in the Middle East (Turkey, Iraq, Iran, Syria, Jordan, and Israel). No longer simply hunting, gathering, and fishing, people started managing and modifying the characteristics of familiar plants and animals. By 10,000 B.P., domesticates were an established part of the broad spectrum of resources used by Middle Easterners. By 7500 B.P., most Middle Easterners had abandoned broad-spectrum foraging for more specialized, fully Neolithic economies based on fewer species, which were domesticates (Bar-Yosef and Valla 2013; Bellwood 2005; Simmons 2007).

Archaeologist Kent Flannery (1969) laid out a series of stages or eras during which the Middle Eastern transition to farming and herding took place. First, the era of seminomadic hunting and gathering (12,000–11,000 B.P.) encompassed the last stages of broad-spectrum foraging. This was the period just before domesticated plants (wheat and barley) and animals (goats and sheep) were added to the diet. Next came the era of early dry farming (of wheat and barley) and caprine domestication (11,000–7500 B.P.). *Dry farming* refers to farming without irrigation; such farming depended on rainfall. *Caprine* (from *capra*, Latin for "goat") refers to goats and sheep, which were domesticated during this era.

During the era of increasing specialization in food production (7500–5500 B.P.), new crops were added to the diet, along with more productive varieties of wheat and barley. Cattle and pigs were fully domesticated (Simmons 2007). Table 8.1 highlights these stages, or eras, in the transition to food production. By 5500 B.P., agriculture had spread into the alluvial plain of the Tigris and Euphrates Rivers (see Figure 8.1), where early Mesopotamians lived in walled towns, some of which grew into cities.

TABLE 8.1    **The Transition to Food Production in the Middle East**

| Era | Dates (B.P.) |
| --- | --- |
| Origin of state (Sumer) | 5500 |
| Increasing specialization in food production | 7500–5500 |
| Early dry farming and caprine domestication | 11,000–7500 |
| Seminomadic hunting and gathering (e.g., later Natufians) | 12,000–11,000 |

FIGURE 8.1    **The Vertical Economy of the Ancient Middle East**
Geographically close but contrasting environments were linked by seasonal movements and trade patterns of broad-spectrum foragers. Traded resources included copper, obsidian, and asphalt, located in particular zones. As people traveled and traded, they moved plants from the hilly flanks where they grew wild into adjacent zones. In this way, humans became agents of selection.

McGraw-Hill Education

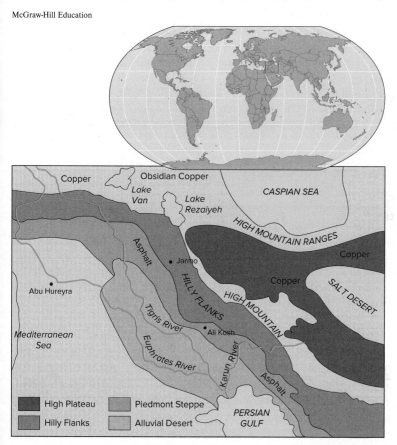

## The Environmental Setting: A Vertical Economy

Middle Eastern food production arose in the context of four distinct but linked environmental zones. From highest to lowest, they are as follows: (1) high plateau (5,000 feet, or 1,500 meters), (2) hilly flanks, (3) piedmont steppe (treeless plain), and (4) alluvial desert—the low-lying area watered by the Tigris and Euphrates Rivers. The **hilly flanks** is a woodland zone that flanks those rivers to the north (see Figure 8.1). *Alluvial* describes rich, fertile soil deposited by rivers and streams.

For thousands of years, the Middle East has had a *vertical economy*. Such an economy exploits environmental zones that, although close together in space, contrast with one another in altitude, rainfall, overall climate, vegetation, and other resources. This close juxtaposition of varied environments allowed foragers to follow game from zone to zone. In winter they hunted on the piedmont steppe, which had winter rains that provided pasture for game animals. When winter ended, the steppe dried up. Foragers followed their game up to the hilly flanks and high plateau country as the snow melted and pasture land became available. They also gathered as they climbed, harvesting wild grains that ripened successively as altitude increased.

The environmental zones also were linked through trade. Certain resources were confined to specific zones. Asphalt, used as an adhesive in the manufacture of sickles, came from the steppe. Copper and turquoise sources were in the high plateau. The zones were linked in two ways: by foragers' seasonal migration and by trade. The movement of people, animals, and products between zones was a precondition for the emergence of food production (Bouquet-Appel and Bar-Yosef 2008). As they moved, foragers carried seeds into new habitats, where mutations, genetic recombinations, and human selection eventually led to domestication.

## Steps toward Food Production

The Middle Eastern climate became warmer and moister during the late Pleistocene and early Holocene. This climate change favored the expansion of wild plants and animals. (See this chapter's "Anthropology Today" for the effects of contemporary climate change on archaeology.) Foragers could harvest wild grains as they ripened in the spring at low altitudes, in the summer at middle altitudes, and in the fall at high altitudes. Certain areas, particularly the hilly flanks zone, became so rich in wild plants and animals that foragers could adopt **sedentism**—sedentary (settled) life in villages—long before they became farmers and herders.

### Natufian Sedentism

A prime example of early sedentism is the widespread Natufian culture (15,000–11,700 B.P.), which was based on broad-spectrum foraging. The **Natufians** built their villages, which they occupied year-round, near the densest stands of wild wheat and barley, but also located centrally enough to permit foraging in adjacent zones. Kent Flannery (1973) has calculated that a family of experienced Natufian plant collectors could harvest enough ripening grain (over a three-week period)—2,200 pounds (1,000 kilograms)—to feed themselves for a year (see also Harlan and Zohary 1966). Having harvested all that grain, they would need a place to store it (e.g., a granary or storage pit). Furthermore, they could no longer maintain a fully nomadic lifestyle, because they'd need to stay close to their grain supply. Furthermore, wild sheep and goats could graze on the stubble that remained after people had harvested the grain. Plants and animals were available and co-dependent in the same area.

Natufian settlements show permanent architectural features and evidence for the processing and storage of wild grains. One such site is Abu Hureyra, Syria (see Figure 8.1), which initially was occupied by Natufian foragers prior to 11,000 B.P. Then it was abandoned—to be reoccupied later by food producers, between 9500 and 8000 B.P. From its Natufian period, Abu Hureyra has yielded the remains of grinding stones, wild plants, and gazelle bones.

## The Earliest Bread Making

Evidence for the world's earliest known bread comes from another Natufian site, Shubayqa 1 in Jordan. A team from the University of Copenhagen, Denmark, did a series of digs at Shubayqa 1 between 2012 and 2015 (see Richter and Arranz-Otaegui 2018). They excavated two circular buildings with stone floors, occupied between 14,500 and 11,700 B.P. From a fireplace dug into one of those floors, the researchers extracted more than 60,000 charred plant remains. Some of those remains were very similar to 9,000-year-old microscopic particles of bread and porridge from the Turkish Neolithic site of Çatalhöyük (see Chapter 9). Residents of Shubayqa 1 were making bread some 5,000 years earlier than the Neolithic occupants of Çatalhöyük.

Those ancient Natufian bread makers made flour by grinding wild barley, wheat, and oat, along with tubers from an aquatic plant belonging to the papyrus family. They ground those tubers into flour, which they mixed with cereal flour, and then baked, probably on a hot stone, to produce a multigrain flatbread. Archaeologists once assumed that bread making began during, rather than before, the Neolithic. We now know that bread making, along with the world's oldest stone houses, grinding tools, and sickle blades, predates the Neolithic, extending back into the Natufian period.

## Beyond the Optimal Zone

Long ago, the archaeologist Robert J. Braidwood (1975) assumed (erroneously it turns out) that food production began in the hilly flanks, where wild grains were so abundant. In 1948, Braidwood's team found evidence for early food production at Jarmo, a village in the hilly flanks inhabited between 9000 and 8500 B.P. Subsequently, however, archaeologists have found farming villages older than Jarmo (see Figure 8.1) in zones *adjacent to*, rather than in, the hilly flanks. One example is Ali Kosh, a village in the piedmont steppe (Hole, Flannery, and Neely 1969).

In the view of many scholars, the people most likely to adopt a new subsistence strategy, such as cultivation, would be those having the hardest time maintaining their traditional subsistence base (Binford 1968; Flannery 1973; Wenke and Olszewski 2007). This suggests that those ancient Middle Easterners who lived in areas where wild foods were scarcer would be *more* likely to experiment with new subsistence strategies than people living in the optimal zone. Why should people start farming when their wild grain supply was assured—and available at a lower labor cost? Recent estimates suggest that the productivity of early farmers (calories produced per work hour) was below that of the foragers they eventually replaced (see Bowles 2011; Bowles and Choi 2013). Indeed, we know now that Middle Eastern food production did begin in *marginal areas*, such as the piedmont steppe, rather than in the optimal zones, such as the hilly flanks. The sparser supply of wild foods outside the hilly flanks provided more of an incentive for foragers to experiment with early domestication (Binford 1968; Bouquet-Appel and Bar-Yosef 2008; Flannery 1969).

Around 11,000 B.P., the Middle Eastern climate turned drier, and the optimal zone for foraging shrank. People had fewer choices for village sites, which needed a permanent water source. Early experiments with domestication—planting the seeds of wild plants outside the optimal zone—may have taken place in well-watered areas outside the hilly flanks. The ensuing process of human selection and genetic change in plants and animals eventually led to cultivation. In either case—whether pushed by climate change or merely the need to subsist in marginal areas—necessity seems to have been the mother of invention.

## Genetic Changes and Domestication

What are the main differences between wild and domesticated plants? Domesticated plants are known as **cultivars**; their seeds, and often the entire plant, are larger. Compared with wild plants, cultivars tend to produce a higher yield per unit of area. They also lose their natural seed dispersal mechanisms. Domesticated beans, for example, have pods that hold together, rather than shattering as they do in the wild. Domesticated cereals have tougher connective tissue holding the seedpods to the stem.

Grains of wheat, barley, and other cereals occur in bunches at the end of a stalk (see Figure 8.2). The grains are attached to the stalk by an *axis* (plural *axes*). In wild cereals, this axis is brittle. Sections of the axis break off one by one, and a seed attached to each section falls to the ground. This is how wild cereals spread their seeds and propagate their species. But a brittle axis is a problem for people. Imagine the annoyance experienced by broad-spectrum foragers as they tried to harvest wild wheat, only to have the grain fall off or be blown away.

In very dry weather, wild wheat and barley ripen—their axes totally disintegrating—in just three days (Flannery 1973). The brittle axis must have been even more irritating to people who planted the seeds and waited for the harvest. Fortunately, certain stalks of wild wheat and barley happened to have tough axes. These were the ones whose seeds people saved to plant the following year.

Another problem with wild cereals is that the edible portion is enclosed in a tough husk. This husk was too tough to remove with a pounding stone. Foragers had to roast the grain to make the husk brittle enough to come off. However, some wild plants happened to have genes for brittle husks. Humans chose the seeds of these plants (which would have germinated prematurely in nature) because they could be more effectively prepared for eating.

People also selected traits in animals (Diamond 1997/2017; Miller, Zeder, and Arter 2009). Plants got larger with domestication, while animals got smaller, probably because smaller

**FIGURE 8.2   A Head of Wheat or Barley**
In the wild, the axis comes apart as its parts fall off one by one. The connecting parts (interstices) are tough and don't come apart in domesticated grains. In wild grains, the husks are hard. In domestic plants, they are brittle, which permits easy access to the grain. How did people deal with hard husks before domestication?

McGraw-Hill Education

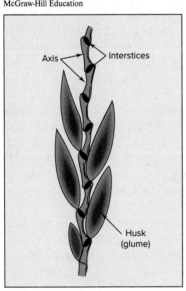

animals are easier to control. Wild sheep aren't woolly; wool coats were products of domestication. Although it's hard to imagine, a wool coat protects against extreme heat. Skin temperatures of domesticated sheep in very hot areas are much lower than temperatures on the surface of their wool. Woolly sheep, but not their wild ancestors, could survive in hot, dry alluvial lowlands. Wool had an additional advantage: its use for clothing.

Archaeological evidence for herd management predates anatomical evidence (e.g, in size) for full animal domestication. For example, certain early sites indicate a focus on killing 2- to 3-year-old males, which suggests a concern with preserving female breeding stock. Those ancient herd managers realized that a steady stream of young immigrant males from surrounding territories would replace slaughtered local males. By selectively culling wild animal populations, ancient Middle Easterners were gradually converting their prey animals into herd animals. In doing so, in a process that lasted more than a thousand years, they also were transforming themselves from hunters into herders (Zeder 2008).

## The Coevolution of Farming and Property Rights

Samuel Bowles and Jung-Kyoo Choi (2013) have proposed that a transition from common to private property rights accompanied (*coevolved* with) the transition from foraging to food production. Property notions vary depending on how easy it is to demarcate a society's key resources. When resources are wild, dispersed, and mobile, as among foragers, a common property system works best. No doubt prehistoric foragers, like recent foragers, made food sharing a habit. When a game animal was killed, its meat was shared widely, as was access to plant foods, which were scattered and only available seasonally. Things changed with food production, as individuals and families began to work, claim, and exclude others from fields and livestock.

We know that mature Neolithic economies out-produce foraging economies. Why, then, don't foragers immediately adopt farming when the opportunity presents itself? Multiple factors may constrain them. First is the fact that *early* farming was *not* more productive than broad-spectrum foraging, particularly when wild resources were as abundant as they were in the hilly flanks. Another constraint is a worldview—typical of foragers—that values sharing and common property. Individual foragers who want to try farming may have their innovative efforts thwarted by the value system of their traditional society. Bowles and Choi (2013) describe two Batek men, members of a Southeast Asian foraging society, who decided to try planting rice. When harvest time arrived, the novice farmers could not prevent other group members from harvesting their rice and sharing it with the entire group. Such a sharing ethos is incompatible with the disproportionate individual labor invested in farming. A change from common to more restrictive property rights was needed for farming and herding.

Sedentism made it easier to demarcate resources, such as dwellings and storage pits. Once a family of foragers had harvested and stored a ton of wheat, they would want to stay close enough to consume it—perhaps excluding those who did not help with the work involved. Individual labor was even more apparent when people started clearing land and planting and tending crops. A new system of property rights emerged—one that ensured a family's claim and control over the food they produced, excluding others.

Within the emerging Neolithic economy, the old ethos of sharing was replaced by a system in which fields, crops, dwellings, storage sites, and animals were recognized as the property of individuals or families. There is archaeological evidence that domesticated animals and cereals were stored within particular dwellings—making their ownership apparent. Once a critical mass of people adopted both the new property rights and the Neolithic economy, communities of farmers could out-produce foragers and spread widely as a result (Bowles and Choi 2013).

## Food Production and the State

Over time, Middle Eastern economies became more specialized, geared more exclusively toward crops and herds. The former marginal zones became centers of the new economy and of population increase and emigration. Some of the increasing population spilled back into the hilly flanks, where people eventually had to intensify production by cultivating. Domesticated crops could now provide a bigger harvest than could the grains that grew wild there. Thus, in the hilly flanks, too, farming eventually replaced foraging as the economic mainstay.

Farming colonies spread down into drier areas. By 7000 B.P., simple irrigation systems had developed, tapping springs in the foothills. By 6000 B.P., more complex irrigation techniques made agriculture possible in the arid lowlands of southern Mesopotamia. In the alluvial desert plain of the Tigris and Euphrates Rivers, a new economy based on

Simple irrigation systems like this one (in a **rice paddy in Chandbali, Orissa, India**) were being used in the Middle East by 7000 B.P. By **6000 B.P.,** more complex irrigation techniques had made agriculture possible in the arid lowlands of southern Mesopotamia. Lindsay Brown/Lonely Planet Images/Getty Images

irrigation and trade fueled the growth of an entirely new form of society. This was the *state*, a social and political unit featuring a central government, extreme contrasts of wealth, and social classes. The process of state formation is examined in Chapter 9.

# Other Old World Farmers

The path from foraging to farming was one that people followed independently in at least seven world areas. As we'll see later in this chapter, at least three were in the Americas. At least four were in the Old World. In each of these seven centers, people invented domestication independently—albeit of different sets of crops and animals. (Figure 8.3 is a map highlighting those seven areas.)

In the Old World, food production soon began to expand beyond the Middle East. This happened through trade, through the spread of domesticated plants and animals, and through the migration of farmers. Middle Eastern domesticates spread westward to northern Africa, including northern Egypt, and eventually into Europe (Zeder 2008). Those domesticates also spread eastward to India and Pakistan. In Egypt, the agricultural economy based on those domesticates gave rise to pharaonic civilization.

## The Neolithic in Africa

Excavations at the Nabta Playa site in southern Egypt have revealed considerable complexity in its early Neolithic economy and social system, along with very early pottery and cattle. Nabta Playa is a basin in the eastern Sahara Desert that, during prehistoric summers, filled with water. Over several millennia this temporary lake attracted people who used it for social and ceremonial activities (Wendorf and Schild 2000). The earliest settlements there (11,000–9300 B.P.) were small camps of herders. (Note the very early, and

**FIGURE 8.3** **Seven World Areas Where Food Production Was Invented Independently**
Do any of these areas surprise you?

Source: Bruce D. Smith, *The Emergence of Agriculture*. New York, NY: W H Freeman & Co, 1999, p. 12.

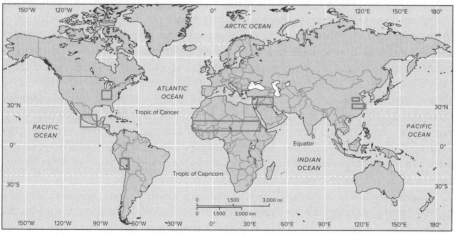

perhaps independent, domestication of cattle here.) Nabta was occupied only seasonally, as people came over from the Nile or from better-watered areas to the south. They returned to those areas in the fall.

By 9000 B.P., people were living at Nabta Playa year round. To survive in the desert, they dug large, deep wells and lived in well-organized villages, with huts arranged in straight lines. They collected sorghum, millet, legumes (peas and beans), tubers, and fruits. These were wild plants, and so the economy was not fully Neolithic. By 8800 B.P., these people were making their own pottery, possibly the earliest pottery in Egypt. By 8100 B.P., domesticated sheep and goats had arrived from the Middle East.

Around 7500 B.P., new settlers occupied Nabta Playa, introducing a more sophisticated social and ceremonial system. They sacrificed young cattle, which they buried in clay-lined chambers covered with stone slabs. They also built Egypt's earliest astronomical measuring device: a "calendar circle" used to mark the summer solstice. Nabta had become a regional ceremonial center: a place where groups gathered for ceremonies and to socialize. The site also is notable for an alignment of nine large, upright stone slabs. This formation, probably dating between 7500 and 5500 B.P., recalls similar large stone (*megalithic*) alignments, such as Stonehenge, found in western Europe. To construct such structures is a major effort requiring work parties—perhaps organized by a religious or civil authority. The findings at Nabta Playa reveal an elaborate and previously unsuspected ceremonialism, as well as social complexity, during the African Neolithic (see also Sadig 2010).

## The Neolithic in Europe

How did the Neolithic reach Europe? Did Middle Eastern farmers colonize Europe, or did their ideas, techniques, and domesticates spread there without any actual migration? We have good evidence now that the Neolithic was spread by the migration of farmers. Scandinavian scientists compared DNA from two sets of Swedish burials, both 5,000 years old. One burial represented a hunter-gatherer group; the other, a farmer group about 250 miles (400 kilometers) away. The ancient hunter-gatherer DNA linked them to living northern Europeans, especially Finns, while the farmer genome resembled that of contemporary southeastern Europeans. The researchers concluded that migrating farmers expanded across Europe from the Mediterranean beginning around 8,500 years ago. It took them about 3,000 years to reach northwestern Europe (Skoglund et al. 2012).

Excavations on Cyprus show that the island had been colonized by 10,600 B.P.—the early Neolithic—with village life and farming well under way. This confirms that migration from the mainland Middle East began—by boat—shortly after the beginning of farming (Vigne et al. 2012). Sailing about 40 miles (60 kilometers) from the mainland to Cyprus, Neolithic colonists carried with them all four major livestock species (domesticated sheep, goats, cattle, and pigs). To Cyprus they introduced the full Neolithic package: farming and herding, technologies, and, most likely, the social networks and belief systems they brought from their original homeland. The colonization of Cyprus can serve as a model of how the Neolithic spread across the rest of the Mediterranean basin—by boat and seafaring colonists (Zeder 2008).

The Mediterranean basin experienced a diaspora—slowly at first, then more rapidly—of Neolithic people and their lifestyle westward from the Middle East and Cyprus to the shores of the Atlantic (Zeder 2008). Expansion from Cyprus to Greece and its islands may have taken as long as 2,000 years. Thereafter, only 500 years were required for seafaring colonists to reach Italy, then just 500–600 years to travel the much greater distance from Italy to the Atlantic. Reaching southern France by 7700–7600 B.P., Neolithic colonists established a site that has yielded pottery, the remains of domestic sheep, and wheat. Thereafter, southern France experienced a marked geographic, ecological, and cultural break between its interior Mesolithic settlements and its coastal Neolithic colonies. Initially, the Neolithic colonists were confined to scattered coastal communities (Zeder 2008). By 6000 B.P., however, Europe had thousands of farming villages, from as far east as Russia to as far west as northern France (see Fowler 2015).

Modern Europeans get their DNA from three main sources (Zimmer 2015). First is that of the pre-Neolithic hunter-gatherers of the Upper Paleolithic and Mesolithic periods. Second was a wave of farmers who started arriving from Anatolia (in what is now Turkey) around 8500 B.P. They share DNA with contemporary Middle Easterners. The third source, reaching Europe around 4500 B.P., was a population of nomads from the Russian steppes known as the Yamnaya.

The DNA of Europeans changed significantly after the introduction of farming (Zimmer 2015). Those changes affected digestion, skin color, and height. A team led by David Reich, a geneticist at Harvard Medical School, analyzed genomes from remains of 230 Europeans who lived between 8,500 and 2,300 B.P. They found that certain genetic changes were adaptations to the new diet based on farming and herding. One such change made it easier to absorb nutrients from wheat and other crops. Another involved a gene that aids milk digestion, useful among herders, which became increasingly common after 4500 B.P.

Reich's team also identified changes in Europeans' skin color. Europe's original hunter-gatherers, as descendants of people who had come from Africa, retained dark skin as recently as 9,000 years ago. Apparently they did not need to reduce the melanin in their skin because their meat-rich diet was a sufficient source of vitamin D. The Anatolian farmers who colonized Europe after 8500 B.P. had lighter skin, and a new gene variant that emerged later lightened European skin even more. The widespread shift to farming, which reduced the intake of vitamin D compared with a meat diet, may have triggered the reduction in epidermal melanin.

Finally, the DNA of the Anatolian farmers made them relatively tall, with the Yamnaya even taller. Northern Europeans have inherited a larger amount of Yamnaya DNA, making them taller, too. The average height of southern Europeans, however, declined after the advent of farming, probably because of reduced animal protein in their diet (Zimmer 2015).

## The Neolithic in Asia

Archaeological research confirms the presence of Middle Eastern domesticates, including goats, sheep, cattle, wheat, and barley in Pakistan by 8000 B.P. A regional trade network must have extended from the Middle East to the Indus Valley of Pakistan and India.

Unlike the Indus Valley, which owed its Neolithic economy to diffusion from the Middle East, China developed farming on its own—and twice, with one farming system based on millet and another based on rice. Millet, a tall, small-seeded cereal still grown in northern China, is used in contemporary North America mainly as birdseed. Millet

Rice, originally domesticated in Asia, became a key caloric staple within mixed economies, including domesticated animals. This Vietnamese woman is herding ducks near a rice paddy.
Christophe Boisvieux/Corbis NX/Getty Images

was first domesticated in northern China around 10,000 B.P. By 7500 B.P., two varieties of that grain supported early farming communities in northern China, along the Huang He (Yellow River). Millet cultivation paved the way for widespread village life and eventually for Shang dynasty civilization, based on irrigated agriculture, between 3600 and 3100 B.P. The northern Chinese also domesticated dogs, pigs, and possibly cattle, goats, and sheep by 7000 B.P.

Rice is the main caloric staple for more than half the people on Earth today. The crop is central to the diets and agricultural economies of East Asia, Southeast Asia, and South Asia. Mediterranean cultures, by contrast, are primarily based on wheat (as bread). Of the three species of cultivated rice, the first was domesticated in China as early as 10,000 B.P. (Cambridge 2015). The second was domesticated in India around 4500 B.P., and the third, in west Africa beginning around 3500 B.P. (Hirst 2018).

Rice was domesticated in central to southern China at about the same time that millet was being domesticated in northern China. The crop was being cultivated in the Yangtze River corridor of southern China by 8400 B.P. (Jiao 2007). Southern Chinese farming was rice aquaculture in rich subtropical wetlands. Southern winters were mild, and summer rains, reliable. Northern China, by contrast, had harsh winters, with unreliable rainfall during the summer growing season. Still, food production was supporting large and stable villages in both areas by 7500 B.P. Based on the archaeological evidence, early Chinese villagers lived in substantial houses, made elaborate ceramic vessels, and had rich burials.

TABLE 8.2    Seven World Areas Where Food Production Was Invented Independently

| World Area | Major Domesticated Plants/Animals | Earliest Date (B.P.) |
| --- | --- | --- |
| Middle East | Wheat, barley<br>Sheep, goats, cattle, pigs | 11,000–10,000 |
| Northern China<br>(Yellow River) | Millet<br>Dogs, pigs, chickens | 10,000 |
| Southern China<br>(Yangtze River corridor) | Rice<br>Water buffalo, dogs, pigs | 10,000–6500 |
| Sub-Saharan Africa | Sorghum, pearl millet, African rice<br>Cattle | 10,000–4000 |
| Andean Region | Squash, potato, quinoa, beans<br>Camelids (llama, alpaca), guinea pigs | 10,000–5000 |
| Mesoamerica | Maize, beans, squash<br>Dogs, turkeys, guinea fowl | 8000–4700 |
| Eastern United States | Goosefoot, marsh elder, sunflower,<br>squash | 4500 |

Northern and southern China are two of the seven areas where food production was invented independently. (The others, recall, were the Middle East, Africa, and three areas of the New World—see the next section.) A different set of major foods was domesticated, at different times, in each area, as is shown in Table 8.2. Some grains, such as millet and rice, were domesticated more than once. Millet grows wild in China and Africa, where it became an important food crop, as well as in Mexico, where it did not. Indigenous African rice, grown only in West Africa, belongs to the same genus as Asian rice. Pigs and probably cattle were domesticated independently in the Middle East, China, and sub-Saharan Africa. We turn now to archaeological sequences in the Americas.

# The First American Farmers

Humans are relative newcomers to the Western Hemisphere. Never have fossils of Neandertals or earlier hominins been found in North or South America. The settlement of the Americas was one of the major achievements of anatomically modern humans. Spreading gradually through the Americas, early Native Americans occupied a variety of environments. Their descendants would independently invent food production, paving the way for the emergence of states based on agriculture and trade in Mexico and Peru.

## Key Aspects of Food Production in the Americas

The most significant contrast between Old and New World food production involved animal domestication, which was much more important in the former than the latter. The animals that were hunted during the early American big-game tradition either became extinct before people could domesticate them or were not domesticable. The largest animal ever domesticated in the New World (in Peru, around 4500 B.P.) was the llama. Early Peruvians and Bolivians ate llama meat and used that animal as a beast of burden. They bred the llama's relative, the alpaca, for its wool. Peruvians also added animal protein to their diet by raising and eating guinea pigs and ducks. The turkey was domesticated in the southwestern United States and in Mesoamerica. (**Mesoamerica** includes Mexico, Guatemala, and Belize.) The dog is the only animal that was domesticated throughout the New World. There were no cattle, sheep, or goats in the areas of the Americas where food production began. As a result, neither herding nor the kinds of relationships that developed between herders and farmers in many parts of the Middle East, Europe, Asia, and Africa emerged in the precolonial Americas.

The New World crops were different, although staples as nutritious as those of the Old World were domesticated from native wild plants. Three key caloric staples, major sources of carbohydrates, were domesticated by Native American farmers. **Maize**, or corn, was first domesticated in the tropical lowlands of southwestern Mexico. It became the major source of calories in Mesoamerica and Central America and eventually reached coastal Peru. The two other starchy staples domesticated in the Americas were root crops (potatoes and manioc). White ("Irish") potatoes were first domesticated in the Andes. **Manioc**, or cassava, was domesticated in the South American lowlands, where other root crops such as yams and sweet potatoes also were important. Secondary crops, especially beans and squash, added variety and essential proteins, vitamins, and minerals to the diet.

Food production was invented independently in at least three areas of the Americas: Mesoamerica, the eastern United States, and the south central Andes. Food plants known as goosefoot and marsh elder, along with the sunflower and a species of squash, were domesticated in the eastern United States by 4500 B.P. Those crops supplemented a diet based mainly on hunting and gathering. They never became caloric staples like maize, wheat, rice, millet, manioc, and potatoes. Eventually, maize spread to what is now the United States, where it was grown in areas of the Southwest, the central Plains, the eastern area just mentioned, and even parts of Canada. Domestication of several other species was under way in the south central Andes of Peru and Bolivia by 5000 B.P. They were the potato, quinoa (a cereal grain), beans, llamas, alpacas, and guinea pigs.

## The Tropical Origins of New World Domestication

New World farming began in the tropical lowlands of South America and then spread to Central America, Mexico, and the Caribbean islands. In Chapter 3, we learned about new techniques that allow archaeologists and botanists to recover and analyze microscopic evidence from pollens, starch grains, and phytoliths (plant crystals) (Bryant 2007a, 2013). Dolores Piperno and Karen Stothert (2003) found that phytoliths from cultivated squashes and gourds are substantially larger than those from wild species. They then used phytolith size to confirm that domesticated squash and gourds (*Cucurbita*) were grown in the lowlands of coastal Ecuador as far back as 10,000–9,000 years ago.

Farming in the tropical lowlands of South and Central America began at roughly the same time as early food production in the Middle East—around 10,000 years ago (Piperno and Pearsall 1998). By that time, people in Ecuador, Peru, Colombia, and Panama were growing plants in garden plots near their homes. Between 9000 and 8000 B.P., changes in seed form and phytolith size suggest that farmers were selecting certain characteristics in plants. By 7,000 years ago, farmers had expanded their plots into nearby forests, which they cleared using slash-and-burn techniques. By that time also, early farming ideas and techniques were diffusing from tropical lowlands into drier regions at higher elevations (Bryant 1999, 2003; Piperno and Pearsall 1998).

Maize was first domesticated in the lowlands of southwestern Mexico. The immediate ancestor of maize is a wild grain called **teosinte** (or teocentli) that is native to that region's Río Balsas watershed (Holst, Moreno, and Piperno 2007). Scientists have been puzzled by the fact that teosinte does not look much like corn. The teosinte that grows today in southwestern Mexico is a wild grass with hard kernels and no central stalk. What would have made this plant attractive to proto-farmers?

Could it be that teosinte had different characteristics when domestication began than it does now? Smithsonian researcher and archaeobotanist Dolores Piperno decided to experiment by growing teosinte in a glass chamber under environmental conditions (temperatures and $CO_2$ levels) mimicking those that existed in southwestern Mexico between 13,000 and 10,000 years ago. The teosinte that she grew resembled modern corn, including a central stalk, much more closely than does modern teosinte. It turns out that teosinte has significant phenotypical plasticity, which made it much more attractive to proto-farmers than the modern wild grain would be (see Fawcett 2014).

Teosinte grown in a glass chamber (shown here), replicating the environment of southwestern Mexico between 13,000 and 10,000 years ago, resembles modern corn, including a central stalk, much more closely than does modern teosinte. Courtesy of Dolores R. Piperno

Although evidence for exactly how maize evolved from its wild ancestor has yet to be found, we can infer some of the likely steps. The process would have included increases in the number of kernels per cob, the cob size, and the number of cobs per stalk. The kernels would need to ripen simultaneously rather than serially, as in wild teosinte. After its initial domestication in southwestern Mexico, around 8000 B.P., maize began to spread throughout first the lowlands, then the highlands of Mexico and Central America, and eventually well beyond.

## Explaining the Neolithic

Several factors had to converge to make domestication happen and to promote its spread. Most plants, and especially animals, aren't easy—or particularly valuable—to domesticate. Thus, of some 148 large animal species that seem potentially domesticable, only 14 have been domesticated. A mere dozen among 200,000 known plant species account for 80 percent of the world's farm production. Those 12 caloric staples are wheat, corn (maize), rice, barley, sorghum, soybeans, potatoes, cassava (manioc), sweet potatoes, sugarcane, sugar beets, and bananas.

Domestication resulted from a combination of conditions that had not come together previously. The development of a full-fledged Neolithic economy required settling down. Sedentism, such as that adopted by ancient Natufian hunter-gatherers, was especially attractive when several species of plants and animals were available locally for foraging and eventual domestication. The Middle East had such species, along with a Mediterranean climate favorable to the Neolithic economy. Among those species were the easiest wild plants to domesticate, including wheat, which required few genetic changes. The Natufians, as we've seen, adopted sedentism prior to farming. They lived off abundant wild grain and the animals attracted to the stubble left after the harvest. Eventually, with climate change and the need for people to sustain themselves in the marginal zones, hunter-gatherers started cultivating. In Mesoamerica, the shift from teosinte to maize required more genetic changes, so the domestication process took longer. The paucity of domesticable animals in Mesoamerica also slowed the transition to a full-fledged Neolithic economy.

When the Neolithic began, the Middle East had the world's largest Mediterranean climate with the highest species diversity. As we saw previously, this was an area of diverse environments concentrated in a limited area. This setting offered a multiplicity of plant species, as well as goats, sheep, pigs, and cattle. The first farmers eventually domesticated several crops: two kinds of wheat, barley, lentils, peas, and chickpeas (garbanzo beans). As in Mesoamerica, where corn (supplying carbohydrate) was supplemented by squash and beans (supplying protein), the Neolithic diet of the Middle East combined caloric staples such as wheat and barley with protein-rich pulses such as lentils, peas, and chickpeas.

A full-fledged Neolithic economy requires a minimal set of nutritious domesticates. Some world areas, such as North America (north of Mesoamerica), managed independently to invent domestication, but the inventory of available plants and animals was too meager to maintain a Neolithic economy. The early domesticates—squash, sunflower, marsh elder, and goosefoot—had to be supplemented by hunting and gathering. A full

Neolithic economy and sedentism did not develop in the east, southeast, and southwest of what is now the United States until maize diffused in from Mesoamerica—more than 3,000 years after the first domestication in the eastern United States.

As Jared Diamond (1997/2017, ch. 10) observes convincingly, the geography of the Old World facilitated the spread of plants, animals, technology (e.g., wheels and vehicles), and information (e.g., writing) (Ramachandran and Rosenberg 2011). Most crops in Eurasia were domesticated just once and spread rapidly in an east-west direction. The first domesticates spread from the Middle East to Egypt, North Africa, Europe, India, and eventually China (which had its own domesticates, as we have seen).

Figure 8.4 shows that Eurasia has a much broader east-west expanse than do Africa and the Americas, which are arranged north-south. This is important because climates are more likely to be similar moving across thousands of miles east to west than north to south. In Eurasia, plants and animals could easily spread east to west because of common day lengths and similar seasonal variations. More radical climatic contrasts have hindered north-south diffusion. In the Americas, for example, although the distance between the Mexican highlands and the South American highlands is just 1,200 miles, those two similar zones are separated by a low, hot, tropical region, which supports very different plant species than the highlands. Such environmental barriers to diffusion kept the Neolithic societies more separate and independent in the Americas (i.e., in Mesoamerica and South America) than they were in Eurasia. It took some 3,000 years for maize to reach what is now the United States, where productive Neolithic economies eventually did develop.

FIGURE 8.4    **Major Axes of the Continents**
Note the breadth of the east-west axis in Eurasia, compared with the much narrower east-west spreads in Africa, North America, and South America. Those three continents have north-south as their major axis.

McGraw-Hill Education

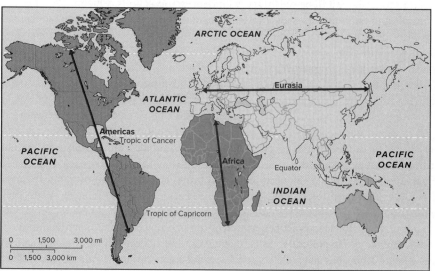

# Costs and Benefits

Food production brought advantages (benefits) and disadvantages (costs). Among the advantages were discoveries and inventions. People learned to spin and weave; to make pottery, bricks, and arched masonry; and to smelt and cast metals. They developed trade and commerce by land and sea. By 5500 B.P., Middle Easterners were living in vibrant cities with markets, streets, temples, and palaces. They created sculpture, mural art, writing systems, weights, measures, mathematics, and new forms of political and social organization.

Because it increased economic production and led to new social, scientific, and creative forms, food production often is considered an evolutionary advance. But the new economy also brought hardships. For example, food producers typically work harder than foragers do—and for a less adequate diet.

Herds, fields, and irrigation systems need care. Weeding can require hours of arduous bending. Pens and corrals must be built and maintained for livestock. Trade takes men, and sometimes women, away from home, leaving burdens for those who stay behind. For several reasons, food producers tend to have more children than foragers do. This means greater child care demands, but child labor also tends to be more needed and valued than it is among foragers. Many tasks in farming and herding can be done by children. The division of economic labor grows more complex, so that children and older people have assigned economic roles.

Public health declined in food-producing societies. Diets based on crops and dairy products tend to be less varied, less nutritious, and less healthful than foragers' diets, which usually are higher in proteins and lower in fats and carbohydrates. With the shift to food production, the physical well-being of the population often declines. Communicable diseases, protein deficiency, and dental caries increase (Cohen and Armelagos 2013).

Food producers tend to be sedentary, with denser populations, which makes it easier to transmit and maintain diseases. Malaria, sickle-cell anemia, and smallpox all spread along with food production. Population concentrations, especially cities, are breeding grounds for pathogens. Compared with farming villagers and urbanites, foragers were relatively disease free, stress free, and well nourished.

Other hardships and stresses accompanied food production. Poverty and social inequality increased (see Flannery and Marcus 2012). Elaborate systems of social stratification eventually replaced the egalitarianism of the past. Resources were no longer common goods, open to all, as they tend to be among foragers. Slavery and other forms of human bondage eventually were invented. Crime, war, and human sacrifice became widespread.

Population increase and the need to expand farming spurred deforestation. Farmers and herders often burn trees, brush, and pasture. Farmers burn to remove weeds; they also use the ashes for fertilizer. Herders burn to promote the growth of new, tender shoots for their livestock. But such practices, as well as the smelting of metals, have environmental costs, including air pollution. Salts, chemicals, and microorganisms accumulate in irrigated fields. Pathogens and pollutants that were nonissues during the Paleolithic endanger growing human populations. To be sure, food production has benefits. But its costs are just as evident. Is "progress" an appropriate word to describe food production and its consequences?

## American First?

Over the past 10,000 years, the products of domestication have diffused widely. They pervade our daily lives, prompting us to think about what, if anything, was American first. What could be more American than McDonald's, hamburgers, hot dogs, or apple pie? More American, in other words, than a now global fast-food chain, a sandwich and a sausage named for German cities, or a fruit first grown in the Middle East baked in a pastry crust from wheat, domesticated there as well. What we think of as truly American usually has foreign roots. Consider just McDonald's Big Mac as a world system in miniature. It consists of two all-beef patties (from cattle, an Old World domesticate), special sauce (similar to mayonnaise, invented in France), lettuce (Egypt), cheese (from cow's milk—Old World), pickles (India), and onions (Iran and West Pakistan), and it comes on a sesame seed (India) bun (wheat—the Middle East). The Egg McMuffin is only slightly less cosmopolitan. Eggs are from chickens, domesticated in Southeast Asia. Cheese comes from cow's milk (cows were domesticated in India, the Middle East, and Africa's eastern Sahara). Canadian bacon is from pork (western Asia), and the muffin is made of wheat (the Middle East). If you crave "real American" food—that is, food of New World origin—have some turkey or beans on a taco or tortilla (from maize or corn) and chocolate for dessert.

We have seen that the first domesticated food crops appeared about 11,000 years ago in both the Old World and the Americas. Such crops as wheat, barley, rice, and millet became key caloric staples in the Old World, just as maize (corn), manioc (cassava), and potatoes did in the Americas. Animal domestication, however, was to become significantly more important in the Old World than in the New World, where the Peruvian llama was the only large domesticated animal. A mutually supportive relationship developed between farming and herding in the Old World, where crops sustained sheep, goats, and eventually cattle, pigs, horses, and donkeys. No such relationship developed in the pre-Columbian Americas.

This leads to a second (deceptive) question: What could be more American than the habit of using your own wheels to get to your favorite restaurant? Wheels? Only in Old World prehistory were animals harnessed to wheeled vehicles. Ancient Mexicans also invented the wheel, but only for toys. Their homeland lacked the appropriate animals to pull plows, oxcarts, chariots, and carriages. How could a dog, turkey, or duck match a horse, a donkey, or an ox as a beast of burden? The absence of large-animal domestication in ancient Mexico is a key factor in world history, helping us understand the divergent development of societies on different sides of the oceans. Wheels fueled the growth of transport, trade, and travel in the Old World. Thousands of years after the origin of food production, advantages in transport would fuel an "Age of Discovery" and enable the European conquest of the Americas. Again, a key feature of contemporary American life turns out to have foreign roots.

## Anthropology Today *Global Climate Change and Other Threats to Archaeology*

Global climate change (GCC) involves not only global warming but also weather patterns that are becoming more extreme and less predictable. GCC threatens archaeological sites. Andrew Curry (2009) has described some of those threats, which are summarized here, in locales as diverse as the Swiss Alps, coastal Peru, Greenland, the Eurasian steppes, California's Channel Islands, and Africa's Sahara Desert.

The Alps: Recent heat waves have melted Alpine snow and glaciers. This has been both good and bad for archaeology—good because new sites have been uncovered, bad because thawing can rot remains. In summer 2003, after a record European heat wave, a hiker high in the Alps spotted a leather quiver left there by a Neolithic hunter almost 5,000 years ago.

The next summer, that hiker guided archaeologists back up the mountain, where they found a melting ice patch 260 feet (80 meters) long and 100 feet (30 meters) wide. As that ice pack shrank over two summers of fieldwork, archaeologists recovered both prehistoric and Roman remains. The finds show that people have been crossing the Alps for millennia, despite bitter cold and ice (Curry 2009).

Coastal Peru: When Spanish conquistadors arrived in Peru, they noticed a weather phenomenon that occasionally occurred around Christmas. They called it El Niño, or "little boy," after the Christ child. El Niño occurs every 3 to 10 years, as currents in the Pacific Ocean shift, changing global weather patterns. In Peru, El Niño brings warmer water and heavy rainfall

The Peruvian village of Aguas Calientes was flooded by the Vilcanota River in January 2010. Heavy rains and mudslides that year blocked the train route to the nearby ancient Inca citadel of Machu Picchu, leaving nearly 2,000 tourists stranded. AFP/Getty Images

along the coast. Peru's deserts typically get just over an inch of rain annually. In 1998, a particularly severe El Niño season, however, the region got 120 inches (3 meters) and serious flooding. Excess water can threaten archaeological sites, many of which are located along rivers or on easily eroded slopes (Curry 2009). Severe flooding in 2010 closed Machu Picchu, Peru's most famous ancient site, to tourism. If GCC leads to more frequent El Niño years, Peru's archaeological treasures may be further damaged.

Greenland: Violent wave action linked to GCC is destroying early coastal sites. Traditionally in summer, Greenland's coasts have been surrounded by an ice belt 30 to 40 miles (48 to 64 kilometers) wide. This drifting ice serves as a shock absorber, dampening the strength of the North Atlantic. In the past decade, however, this ice shield has virtually vanished, and Greenland's coasts are being pounded by huge waves. Most threatened are sites associated with the Thule culture, likely ancestors of the Inuit, whose members reached Greenland about 2,000 years ago. Supported by hunting and fishing, Thule villages were built close to the shore. Today, their ancient homes are disappearing, along with buried tools and artifacts (Curry 2009).

In some other cases, however, wave action has produced new information of interest to archaeologists. For example, storms in Wales in 2012 uncovered the fossilized footprints of a child who lived, or at least spent some time, alongside a prehistoric sea. In 2013, on an English beach, researchers found footprints of children and adults who lived around 800,000 years ago. A year later, researchers on Calvert Island in British Columbia discovered human footprints dating back to the earliest occupation of the Americas. All these prints were located near an ocean (Curry 2018).

Scythian tombs: Between 3,000 and 2,200 years ago, Scythian nomads dominated the Eurasian steppes from the Black Sea in the west to China in the east. Huge Scythian burial mounds, called kurgans, have been rich resources for archaeologists. Found from Ukraine to Kazakhstan, some of the best preserved kurgans are located in the Altai Mountains, near Siberian permafrost, where the cold has protected the graves for millennia. The tombs have yielded well-preserved mummies, often with clothing, burial goods, horses, and even stomach contents intact. With GCC, as the mountains warm up and the permafrost melts, the tombs are in danger of thawing and rotting away (Curry 2009).

California's Channel Islands: Some of the early settlers of the Americas came by boat, island-hopping from Siberia down to the California coast. Some of the best evidence for this comes from the Channel Islands, which were occupied at least 13,000 years ago by settlers who hunted pygmy mammoths, elephant seals, and sea lions. Human bones found on Santa Rosa Island, radiocarbon-dated to 13,000 B.P., are the oldest human bones yet found in the Americas. At that time, the world was much colder, and the oceans much lower, than today. Rising sea levels now threaten shell middens and coastal rock shelters. As well, coastal winds, waves, storm surges, and even seals can damage coastal sites. GCC now threatens to wipe out clues about how early humans settled the Americas just as researchers have begun to focus on the likelihood of coastal migration (Curry 2009).

Sudan desertification: Encroaching desert sands increasingly threaten historic artwork at Musawwarat es-Sufra, Sudan.

*continued*

## Anthropology Today *continued*

More than 2,000 years ago, the rulers of Meroe—a desert kingdom linked to ancient Egypt—constructed a temple complex and pilgrimage site 20 miles (32 kilometers) east of the Nile. Built of soft yellow sandstone, the walls and columns of the complex featured hieroglyphs and elaborate painted reliefs. Dominating the site was the 50-foot-long Temple of the Lion God, decorated with reliefs dedicated to the Meroitic god of fertility. Rising temperatures and overuse have killed off the area's vegetation, and Saharan sands creep ever closer. The reliefs suffer heavily from wind erosion, because the soft sandstone abrades easily (Curry 2009).

GCC is not, of course, the only current threat to archaeological sites and research. Political events also pose risks. In 2001 in Afghanistan the Taliban destroyed a series of pre-Islamic figures, including two monumental stone Buddhas, in an attempt to stop the worship of false idols. In 2013, a group of ancient Islamic manuscripts in Mali's historic city of Timbuktu were threatened by a fire caused by fighting between Islamist militants and

French troops. In 2015, members of the Islamic State destroyed architectural ruins—and murdered a prominent Syrian archaeologist—at Palmyra, Syria, a major cultural center of the ancient world (see "Anthropology Today" in Chapter 2).

Politics and regime change also can limit archaeological research. Iran and Iraq have been dangerous or off-limits for decades. For on-site investigation of emerging food production and state formation in the Middle East, archaeologists turned increasingly to Syria and Turkey. The former country, too, now is off-limits because of political unrest. Fortunately, previously assembled museum collections of human and animal remains outside those countries allow continuing analysis and new insights, even when national borders are closed to new fieldwork. However, archaeologists who manage museum collections increasingly encounter requests from nations and cultural groups that wish to repatriate remains collected, often a century ago or more, and sometimes without proper legal authorization. Can you think of other threats to archaeological sites and research?

## Summary

1. After 15,000 B.P., as the big-game supply diminished, Mesolithic foragers sought out new foods. By 11,000 B.P., domesticated plants and animals were part of a broad spectrum of resources used by Middle Easterners. By 7500 B.P., most Middle Easterners were moving away from broad-spectrum foraging toward more specialized food-producing economies. *Neolithic* refers to the period when the first signs of domestication appeared.

2. Braidwood proposed that food production began in the hilly flanks zone. Others questioned this: The abundant wild grain supply there already provided an excellent diet for the Natufians and other ancient Middle Easterners, who adopted sedentism before farming. There would have been no incentive to domesticate.

3. Ancient Middle Eastern foragers migrated seasonally in pursuit of game. They also collected wild plant foods that ripened at different altitudes. As they moved about, these foragers took grains from the hilly flanks zone, where they grew wild, to adjacent areas. Humans became agents of selection, preferring plants with certain attributes. Population spilled over from the hilly flanks into adjacent areas like the piedmont steppe. In such marginal zones, people started cultivating plants. They were trying to duplicate the dense wild grains of the hilly flanks.

4. After the harvest, sheep and goats fed off the stubble of these wild plants. Animal domestication occurred as people started selecting certain features and behavior and guiding the reproduction of goats, sheep, cattle, and pigs. Gradually, food production spread into the hilly flanks. Later, with irrigation, it spread down into Mesopotamia's alluvial desert, where the first cities, states, and civilizations developed by 5500 B.P. Food production then spread west from the Middle East into North Africa and Europe and east to Pakistan and India.

5. Excavations at Nabta Playa in southern Egypt provide evidence for the very early (11,000–9300 B.P.) domestication of cattle, and for ceremonialism and social complexity during the African Neolithic. The Neolithic reached Europe through the migration of farmers. Modern Europeans get their DNA from three main sources: pre-Neolithic European hunter-gatherers, farmers from Anatolia (8500 B.P.), and Yamnaya nomads from the Russian steppes (4500 B.P.). The Indus Valley (Pakistan and India) owed its Neolithic economy to diffusion from the Middle East. China developed farming on its own around 10,000 B.P. This happened twice, in northern China based on millet and in southern China based on rice.

6. There were at least seven independent inventions of food production: in the Middle East, sub-Saharan Africa, northern and southern China, Mesoamerica, the south central Andes, and the eastern United States.

7. In the New World, the most important domesticates were maize, potatoes, and manioc. The llama of the central Andes was the largest animal domesticated in the New World, where herding traditions analogous to those of the Old World did not develop. Economic similarities between the hemispheres must be sought in foraging and farming.

8. New World farming started in the tropical lowlands of South America, then spread to Central America, Mexico, and the Caribbean islands. Cultivation in South America began at about the same time that food production arose in the Middle East—around 10,000 years ago. By 7000 B.P., farming was diffusing from tropical lowlands into drier regions at higher elevations. The specific ancestor of maize, teosinte, grows wild in tropical southwestern Mexico, where maize was domesticated sometime before 8000 B.P.

9. Several factors, including a diversity of useful plant and animal species and early sedentism, combined to promote early domestication in the ancient Middle East. The first domesticates spread rapidly across Eurasia, facilitated by climatic similarities across a broad territorial expanse. In the Americas, food production spread less rapidly because of north-south climatic contrasts. Another factor that slowed the

Neolithic transition in the Americas was the lack of large animals suitable for domestication.

10. Food production and the social and political system it supported brought advantages and disadvantages. The advantages included discoveries and inventions. The disadvantages included harder work, poorer health, crime, war, social inequality, and environmental degradation.

11. Key features of contemporary North American life, including our most common foods and wheeled transport, have foreign roots.

## Think Like an Anthropologist

1. Considering that the transition from broad-spectrum foraging to a full Neolithic economy took thousands of years, do you think it's appropriate to use the word *revolution* to describe either the Neolithic or the broad-spectrum economy? Can you think of a better word to use?

2. In this chapter, what are some examples of the role geography plays in key events in human history? Geography also affects how we come to know about the past. How so?

## Key Terms

| | | |
|---|---|---|
| broad-spectrum revolution, *181* | maize, *196* | Neolithic, *184* |
| cultivars, *188* | manioc, *196* | sedentism, *186* |
| hilly flanks, *185* | Mesoamerica, *196* | teosinte, *197* |
| Holocene, *184* | Mesolithic, *181* | |
| | Natufians, *176* | |

# Chapter

9

# The First Cities and States

## State Formation

As Neolithic economies spread, diversified, and became more productive, new political entities, or **polities** (singular, *polity*), developed to manage them. The major new political forms were chiefdoms and states. A **chiefdom** is a polity with hereditary leaders and a permanent political structure. Some of its people and some of its settlements are ranked above others, and people with higher rank are favored in their access to resources. Often in chiefdoms, individuals are ranked in terms of their genealogical distance from the chief. The closer one is to the chief, the greater one's social importance, but the status distinctions are of degree rather than of kind. Chiefdoms are not divided into clearly defined social classes. Such social *stratification* is, however, a key feature of the state.

A **state** is a polity that has a formal, central government and *social stratification*—a division of society into classes. The first states had formed in Mesopotamia by 5500 B.P. and in Mesoamerica about 3,000 years later. Chiefdoms were precursors to states, with privileged and effective leaders—chiefs—but lacking the sharp class divisions that characterize states. By 7000 B.P. in the Middle East and 3200 B.P. in Mesoamerica, there is evidence for what archaeologists call the *elite level* of social and political organization, indicating a chiefdom or a state.

How and why did these new polities originate? The development and spread of Neolithic economies fueled population growth and established large settlements. New tasks, activities, and functions emerged in the larger and denser populations. Systems of political authority and control typically develop to handle regulatory problems that arise as the population grows, social groups proliferate, and the economy increases in scale and diversity.

**Primary states** are states that arose on their own, rather than through contact with already-established state societies (Wright 1994). Primary states are also known as archaic states or first-generation states. They formed in the context of competition among chiefdoms, as one of those chiefdoms conquered its neighbors and brought them into a larger political unit—a primary state (Stanish and Levine 2011). Such a process of primary state formation took place in *at least* six world areas: Egypt, Mesopotamia, the Indus River Valley, northern China, Mesoamerica, and the Andes (Millaire 2010). Primary states emerged after generations of interaction among competing polities (Stanish and Levine 2011). Multiple factors always contribute to state formation, with the effects of one magnifying those of the others. What are some of those factors?

## Regulation of Hydraulic Economies

One such factor has been the need to regulate hydraulic (water-based, e.g., irrigation and drainage) systems in societies with agricultural economies (Wittfogel 1957). In arid areas, such as ancient Egypt and Mesopotamia, a key role of state officials was to manage systems of irrigation, drainage, and flood control (see Scarre and Fagan 2016). Because it can feed more people, while requiring more labor, irrigated agriculture sustains and fuels population growth, which in turn promotes expansion of the system. The potential grows for conflict over access to water and arable land.

Political authorities arise to regulate production. They mobilize crews to maintain the hydraulic system. They also settle disputes about access to water. Such vital functions bolster the authority of state officials. Thus, growth in hydraulic systems is often (as in Mesopotamia, Egypt, and the Valley of Mexico) but not always associated with state formation.

## Regional Trade

All states have well-developed trade networks, and regional trade is a key factor that contributes to primary state formation (Stanish and Levine 2011). States may arise to control and regulate key nodes in regional trade networks. Examples include crossroads of caravan routes and places (e.g., mountain passes and river narrows) situated to threaten trade between centers. Long-distance trade has been important in the formation of many states, including those of Mesopotamia, Mesoamerica, and Peru (Hirth and Pillsbury 2013). Long-distance trade also exists, however, in areas where no primary states developed, such as in Papua New Guinea.

## Population, War, and Circumscription

Robert Carneiro (1970) saw three key factors as interacting to promote state formation: environmental circumscription, population increase, and warfare. An environment is *circumscribed* when it has definite boundaries that cut it off from surrounding areas and confine it. Environmental circumscription may be physical or social. Physically circumscribed environments include small islands and, in arid areas, river plains, oases, and valleys with streams—areas surrounded by some sort of physical or geographic boundary. Social circumscription exists when neighboring societies block expansion, emigration, or access to resources. When resources are concentrated in a limited area—even when no obstacles to migration exist—the effects are similar to those of circumscription.

Coastal Peru, an extremely arid area, illustrates the interaction of environmental circumscription, warfare, and population increase. The earliest cultivation there was limited to valleys with springs. Each valley was circumscribed by the Andes Mountains to the east, the Pacific Ocean to the west, and desert regions to the north and south (see Millaire 2010). Early farming triggered population increase, leading to bigger villages in each valley. Colonists split off from the old villages and founded new ones. With more villages and people, a scarcity of land developed. Rivalries and raiding arose among villages in the same valley.

Because the valleys were circumscribed, when one village conquered another, the losers had to submit to the winners—they had nowhere else to go. Conquered villagers were allowed to keep their land only by paying tribute to their conquerors. To do this, they had to intensify production, using new techniques to produce more food. By working harder, they managed to pay tribute while meeting their own subsistence needs. Villagers brought new areas under cultivation by means of irrigation and terracing.

Those early Peruvians didn't work harder because they chose to do so. They were forced to pay tribute, accept political domination, and intensify production by factors beyond their control. Once established, all these trends accelerated. Population continued to grow, warfare intensified, and villages eventually were incorporated into chiefdoms. Remember that primary states emerge in the context of competition among chiefdoms. State formation occurred when one chiefdom in a valley succeeded in conquering and incorporating the others (Carneiro 1990; Stanish and Levine 2011). Eventually, the states based in different valleys began to fight. The winners brought the losers into growing states and empires, which eventually expanded from the coast to the highlands. (An **empire** is a mature state that is large, multiethnic, militaristic, and expansive.) By the 16th century, from their capital, Cuzco, in the high Andes, the Inca ruled one of the major empires of the tropics.

The combination of population increase, warfare, and circumscription does not always lead to state formation. In highland Papua New Guinea, for example, valleys that were socially or physically circumscribed had population densities close to those of many states. Warfare also was present, but no states emerged. Whether states would have formed eventually will never be known, because European conquest truncated autonomous development there.

Whenever state formation occurred, the interacting causes, such as irrigation, population increase, or regional trade, magnified each other's effects. Key aspects of state formation are (1) changes in patterns of control over and access to resources, resulting in social stratification, and (2) increasing regulatory concerns, fostering management by state machinery. Different agencies arise to handle particular tasks and concerns. We must also remember that the changeover to a farming economy did not always lead to chiefdoms and states. Many societies with Neolithic economies never developed even chiefdoms. Similarly, there are chiefdoms that never developed into states, just as certain foragers never adopted food production, even when they knew about it.

## Attributes of States

The following attributes (from Fagan 1996) distinguish states from earlier forms of society:

1. Early states arose from competition among chiefdoms, as the most powerful chiefdom conquered the others, extended its rule over a larger territory, and managed to hold on to, and rule, the land and people acquired through conquest. Any state controls a specific regional territory, such as the Nile Valley or the Valley of Mexico. The regional expanse of a state contrasts with the smaller territories controlled by villages, kin groups, and chiefdoms in prestate societies.

2. Early states had productive agricultural economies, supporting dense populations, often in cities. Those economies usually featured some form of water control or irrigation.

3. Early states used tribute and taxation to accumulate, at a central place or treasury, resources needed to support hundreds, or thousands, of specialists. Among the specialists supported by that treasury were the state's rulers, its military, and other government officials.

Early states had hereditary rulers and a military, with the rulers often playing a military role. Rulers stayed in power by combining personal ability, religious authority, economic control, and the privileged use of force. Shown here is a detail from the painted casket of Egypt's Tutankhamun, the famous "King Tut," who ruled between 1332 and 1323 B.C.E. Roger Wood/Corbis/VCG/Getty Images

4. States are stratified into social classes. In the first states, the non-food-producing population consisted of a tiny elite, plus artisans, officials, priests, and other specialists. Most people were commoners. Slaves and prisoners constituted the lowest rung of the social ladder. Rulers stayed in power by combining personal ability, religious authority, economic control, and force.

5. Early states had imposing public buildings and monumental architecture, including temples, palaces, and storehouses.

6. Early states developed some form of record-keeping system, frequently a written script.

# State Formation in the Middle East

In Chapter 8, we saw that Neolithic economies emerged in the Middle East between 12,000 and 10,000 B.P. In the ensuing process of change, the center of population growth shifted from the zone where wheat and barley grew wild to adjacent areas where those grains were first domesticated. By 6000 B.P., population was increasing most rapidly in the alluvial plain of southern Mesopotamia. (**Mesopotamia** refers to the area between the Tigris and Euphrates Rivers in what is now southern Iraq and southwestern Iran.) This growing population supported itself through irrigation and intensive river valley agriculture. The first Middle Eastern towns had appeared around 10,000 B.P. By 5500 B.P., towns had grown into cities. The earliest city-states were Sumer (southern Iraq) and Elam (southwestern Iran), with their capitals at Uruk (Warka) and Susa, respectively (see Potts 2015).

## Urban Life

In the earliest settlements, homes of mud brick were built and rebuilt in the same place over the generations. Substantial *tells*, or mounds, arose from the debris of a succession of such houses (see Menez and Ur 2012). These sites have yielded remains of ancient community life, including streets, buildings, terraces, courtyards, wells, and other artifacts.

### Jericho

The earliest known town was Jericho, located in what now is Israel, at a well-watered oasis near the Dead Sea (see Figure 9.1). From the lowest (oldest) level, we know that around 11,000 years ago Jericho was first settled by Natufian foragers. Occupation continued thereafter, through and beyond biblical times (Laughlin 2006).

Soon after the Natufian period, Jericho developed into an unplanned, densely populated town with round houses and about 2,000 people. Surrounding that town was a sturdy wall with a massive tower. The wall may have been built initially as a flood barrier rather than for defense. Around 9000 B.P., Jericho was destroyed, but it was rebuilt later as a town with square houses. Its people buried their dead beneath their homes, a pattern seen at other early sites, such as Çatalhöyük in Anatolia, Turkey (see the following paragraph). Pottery reached Jericho around 8000 B.P.

FIGURE 9.1   **Sites in Middle Eastern State Formation**

McGraw-Hill Education

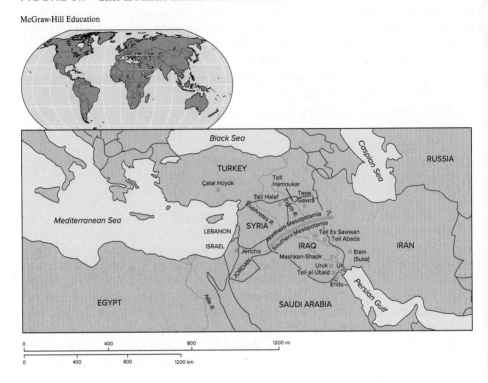

## *Çatalhöyük*

Long-distance trade, especially of obsidian, a volcanic glass used to make tools and orna-ments, became important in the Middle East between 9500 and 7000 B.P. One town that prospered from that trade was Çatalhöyük (Fowler 2011; Hodder 2013). A grassy mound 65 feet (20 meters) high holds the remains of this 9,000-year-old town, probably the largest settlement of the Neolithic age. Çatalhöyük was located on a river, which deposited rich soil for crops, created a lush environment for animals, and was harnessed for irrigation by 7000 B.P. Over the mound's 32 acres (12.9 hectares), up to 10,000 people once lived in crowded mud-brick houses packed so tightly that residents entered from their roofs.

Shielded by a defensive wall, Çatalhöyük flourished between 8000 and 7000 B.P. Its small mud-brick homes had separate areas for ritual and secular uses. In a given home, the ritual images (wall paintings) were placed along the walls that faced north, east, or west, but never south. That area was reserved for cooking and other domestic tasks. The wall paintings depicted bulls surrounded by stick figures running, dancing, and some-times throwing stones. Sometimes vultures were shown attacking headless humans. These images and their placement are reminiscent of Paleolithic cave art. The dwellings at Çatalhöyük were entered through the roof, and people had to crawl through holes from room to room, somewhat like moving between chambers in a cave. The deeper down one went, the richer the art became. The town's spiritual life seems to have revolved around a

Houses at Çatalhöyük, Turkey, featured ritual images on the walls facing north, east, and west. These wall paintings, including the one shown here, depicted bulls surrounded by stick figures running, dancing, and sometimes throwing stones. These images, which recall Paleolithic cave art, may reflect the site's hunter-gatherer past. Images & Stories/Alamy Stock Photo

preoccupation with animals, danger, and death, perhaps related to the site's hunter-gatherer past.

Two or three generations of a family were buried beneath their homes. In one dwelling, archaeologists found remains of 17 individuals, mostly children. After two or three generations of family burials, the dwelling was burned. The site was then covered with fine dirt and a floor laid for a new dwelling.

Çatalhöyük's residents, although they lived in a town, acted independently in family groups without any apparent control by a priestly or political elite. The town never became a full-fledged city with centralized organization. Just as it lacked priests, Çatalhöyük never had leaders who controlled or managed trade and production. Food was stored and processed not collectively but on a smaller, domestic scale (Fowler 2011; Hodder 2013).

## An Early Ritual Center

Göbekli Tepe is a remarkable archaeological site in southeastern Turkey that has become a major tourist attraction, despite its proximity to a crossing point for Syrian refugees fleeing into Turkey. Dated to 11,600 B.P., Göbekli Tepe provides the world's earliest evidence for monumental architecture. The site, a ceremonial center, which remains only partially excavated, was discovered in 1994, but the most significant findings have been published since 2008 (see Curry 2008, 2016; Flannery and Marcus 2012).

Göbekli Tepe was a ritual center, rather than a village or town. Located atop a high limestone ridge, the site apparently was chosen so that massive limestone blocks could be

Dated to 11,600 B.P., Göbekli Tepe is an important archaeological site in southeastern Turkey. Built by hunter-gatherers, Göbekli Tepe, a ritual center, provides the world's earliest evidence for monumental architecture. Courtesy of German Archaeological Institute/Deutsches Archäologisches Institut, Klaus Schmidt

quarried from the ridgetop and used to make upright posts or pillars for ritual houses. The site is particularly remarkable because it was built by hunter-gatherers. Other known prehistoric megalithic (massive stone) sites, such as Stonehenge, Easter Island, and the Olmec centers (see later in this chapter), were built much later than Göbekli Tepe, and by chiefdoms rather than foragers.

Göbekli Tepe's ancient architects looked out onto a well-watered riverine plain that offered an abundance of resources to broad-spectrum foragers. There for the taking were herds of gazelles, cattle, and other wild game; fruit and nut trees; migratory water fowl; and dense stands of wild wheat. Somehow those ancient foragers marshaled the labor to construct and reconstruct these ritual houses over the centuries—from about 11,600 B.P. until around 8200 B.P. They used flint tools to carve massive T-shaped limestone pillars, the tallest of which stood 18 feet (5.5 meters) high and weighed 16 tons (14.5 metric tons).

The buildings at Göbekli Tepe may have been maintained by multiple clans or descent groups, each of which built its own ritual house. The earliest buildings were round or oval; later they would become rectangular. The lower half of each building was subterranean, with stone masonry walls. A sitting bench ran the length of the interior. The most distinctive feature of each building was the pair of huge T-shaped pillars that supported the roof. Those two pillars were set in the center of the floor, with a ring of slightly smaller pillars set into the walls. Many of the pillars were carved in low relief with images of animals: boars, cattle, ducks, foxes, herons, lions, scorpions, and snakes. Some of the pillars have carvings of what may have been mythical human ancestors. The animal carvings may refer to origin myths. Some pillars showed signs of having had earlier images ground off, so that new ones could be carved. The owners of these ritual houses

eventually abandoned them, filling them in with dirt—perhaps to preclude their appropriation by outsiders (Flannery and Marcus 2012). The marshaling of human labor
demonstrated at Göbekli Tepe foreshadows processes and events that would become
much more common in chiefdoms and states.

## The Halafian and Ubaid Periods

The first Middle Eastern pottery (ceramics) dates back a bit more than 8,000 years, and
by 7000 B.P., pottery had become widespread. Archaeologists consider pottery shape,
finishing, decoration, and type of clay as features used for dating. Wide geographic distribution of a given pottery style may indicate trade, alliance, or a polity spanning a large
area at a particular time.

An early widespread pottery style, the **Halafian**, was first found at Tell Halaf in northern
Syria. *Halafian* (7500–6000 B.P.) refers to a delicate ceramic style. It also describes the period during which the first chiefdoms emerged (by 7000 B.P.). The low number of Halafian
ceramics at each site suggests they were luxury goods associated with a social hierarchy.

The partially overlapping Ubaid period (7000–6000 B.P.) is named for a southern
Mesopotamian pottery type first discovered at a small site, Tell el-'Ubaid, near the major
city of Ur in southern Iraq. Ubaid pottery is associated with advanced chiefdoms and
perhaps the earliest states. It diffused rapidly over a large area, becoming much more
widespread than the Halafian style.

Archaeological research focusing on the Ubaid period farther north, in northern
Syria, has found evidence for emerging urbanism dating back more than 6,000 years. At
a site known as Tell Zeidan, American and Syrian investigators uncovered an array of
artifacts from an ancient town on the upper Euphrates River. People occupied this site
for two millennia, until 6000 B.P. The site featured houses with mud-brick walls, floors
with hearths, painted pottery, stone seals, kilns, and obsidian blades. There also is evidence suggesting the emergence of irrigated agriculture, long-distance trade, political
leadership, and social differentiation (Wilford 2010).

For a time, although blocked by war and politics from Iraq and Iran (with their prime
sites of Mesopotamian antiquity), archaeologists could still work in Syria. They turned
their attention to the upper river valleys, across the border from Iraq in Syria and southern Turkey (see Hodder 2006; Wilford 2010). Unfortunately, recent political chaos has
impeded further archaeological research in Syria, leaving Turkey as today's prime locus
for research on Neolithic transformations and the emergence of social complexity in the
Middle East (see Özdoğan, Başgelen, and Kuniholm 2011).

## Social Ranking and Chiefdoms

The anthropologist Morton Fried (1960) defined three kinds of societies, based on the
degree of status differentiation within each type. An **egalitarian society**, most typically
found among foragers, has few status distinctions. It makes those distinctions based only
on age, gender, and individual talents or achievements. Thus, depending on the society,
adult men, elder women, talented musicians, or ritual specialists might have somewhat
higher status because of their activities or knowledge. In egalitarian societies, status distinctions are not usually inherited. Children of a respected person get no special recognition because of their parent; they have to earn it on their own.

Fried's second type of society, the **ranked society**, does have hereditary inequality, but it lacks stratification—clearly defined social classes. In a ranked society, individuals often are ranked according to their genealogical distance from the chief. Refining Fried's typology, Carneiro (1991) points out that we should distinguish between *two kinds of ranked society*. In type 1, individuals are ranked, but villages are independent (autonomous) of one another. In type 2, both individuals and villages are ranked, and there is loss of village autonomy. Smaller villages, no longer independent, have come under the authority of leaders who live in larger, higher-ranked, villages. According to Kent Flannery (1999), *only this second type of ranked society, featuring loss of village autonomy, should be called a chiefdom.* Chiefdoms, then, are marked by differences in rank among both individuals and communities.

Fried's third type of society is the *stratified society*. It is based on **social stratification**—the organization of society into sharp social divisions—*strata*—based on unequal access to socially valued resources. The upper classes have privileged access to wealth and power, while the lower classes have inferior access. In stratified societies, class status often is hereditary. In early state-organized societies, the social classes were often nobles, commoners, and slaves. Table 9.1 lists key features and examples of egalitarian, ranked (two types), and stratified societies.

TABLE 9.1    **Egalitarian, Ranked, and Stratified Societies**

| Kind of Status Distinction | Nature of Status | Common Form of Subsistence Economy | Common Forms of Social Organization | Examples |
|---|---|---|---|---|
| Egalitarian | Status distinctions are not inherited. Status is based on age, gender, and individual qualities, talents, and achievements. | Foraging | Bands and tribes | Inuit, Ju/'hoansi San, and Yanomami |
| Ranked | | Horticulture, pastoralism, and some foraging groups | Chiefdoms and some states | |
| Type 1 | Status distinctions are distributed along a continuum and inherited; independent villages. | | | Salish, Kwakiutl (Pacific Northwest) |
| Type 2 | Status distinctions are distributed along a continuum and inherited; loss of village autonomy, ranked villages. | | | Halafian and Ubaid period polities, Olmec, Cauca (Colombia), Natchez (eastern U.S.) |
| Stratified | Status distinctions are inherited and divided sharply between classes. | Agriculture | States | Teotihuacán, Uruk period states, Inca, Shang dynasty, Rome, United States, Great Britain |

The first chiefdoms had developed in the Middle East by 7300 B.P. By that date, the archaeological record confirms behavior typical of chiefdoms, including exotic goods used as markers of status, along with raiding and political instability. Early chiefdoms included both the Halafian culture of northern Iraq and the Ubaid culture of southern Iraq, which spread north. Those chiefdoms left behind cemeteries where high-status people were buried with distinctive items: vessels, statuettes, necklaces, and high-quality ceramics. Such goods were buried with children too young to have earned prestige on their own, who happened to be born into elite families. In the ancient village of Tell es-Sawwan, infant graves show a continuum of richness from six statuettes, to three statuettes, to one statuette, to none. Such signs of slight gradations in social status are exactly what one expects in ranked societies.

These burials demonstrate that hereditary status distinctions were present in the Middle East by 7300 B.P. But had chiefdoms (as opposed to type 1 ranked societies) formed? Had the leaders of large villages extended their authority to the smaller villages nearby? One line of evidence for such loss of village autonomy is that a common canal was used to irrigate several villages. This suggests a way of resolving disputes among farmers over access to water, for example, by appeal to a strong leader—a chief. Further evidence for the loss of village autonomy is the emergence of a two-tier settlement hierarchy, with small villages clustering around a large village, especially one with public buildings. This settlement pattern was present in northern Mesopotamia during the Halafian period.

## The Rise of the State

It's easy for archaeologists to identify early states, which emerged in the Middle East between 6000 and 5500 B.P. Evidence for state organization includes monumental architecture, aqueducts, central storehouses, and written records. By 5700 B.P. in southern Mesopotamia, an expanding population and increased food production from irrigation were drastically altering the social landscape. Irrigation had allowed Ubaid communities to spread along the Euphrates River. Travel and trade were expanding, with water serving as the highway system. Raw materials such as hardwood and stone, which southern Mesopotamia lacked, were imported via river routes. Social and economic networks now linked communities on the rivers in the south and in the foothills to the north. Social differentiation also increased. Priests and political leaders joined expert potters and other specialists. These non–food producers were supported by the larger population of farmers and herders.

Economies were being managed by central leadership. Agricultural villages had grown into cities, some of which were ruled by local kings. Associated with these developments was Uruk pottery (6000–5200 B.P.), which succeeded the Ubaid style. Uruk pottery takes its name from a prominent southern city-state, which by 4800 B.P. had grown into the largest Mesopotamian city (see Table 9.2). The Uruk period established Mesopotamia as "the cradle of civilization."

The first writing, which originated in Sumer, southern Mesopotamia, presumably developed to handle record keeping, for example, of trade transactions. Writing had spread from Mesopotamia to Egypt by 5000 B.P. The earliest writing was pictographic, for example, with pictorial symbols of horses used to represent them. Early Mesopotamian scribes used a stylus (writing implement) to scrawl symbols on raw clay. This writing left

TABLE 9.2    **Archaeological Periods in Middle Eastern State Formation**

| Dates | Period | Advent of |
| --- | --- | --- |
| 3000–2539 B.P. | Neo-Babylonian | Iron Age |
| 3600–3000 B.P. | Kassite | |
| 4000–3600 B.P. | Old Babylonian | Bronze Age |
| 4150–4000 B.P. | Third Dynasty of Ur | |
| 4350–4150 B.P. | Akkadian | |
| 4600–4350 B.P. | Early Dynastic III | |
| 4750–4600 B.P. | Early Dynastic II | |
| 5000–4750 B.P. | Early Dynastic I | |
| 5200–5000 B.P. | Jemdet Nasr | |
| 6000–5200 B.P. | Uruk | Chalcolithic |
| 7500–6000 B.P. | Ubaid (southern Mesopotamia)–Halafian (northern Mesopotamia) | |
| 10,000–7000 B.P. | | Neolithic |

a wedge-shaped impression on the clay, called **cuneiform** writing, from the Latin word for "wedge." Both the Sumerian (southern Mesopotamia) and Akkadian (northern Mesopotamia) languages were written in cuneiform.

Writing and temples played key roles in the Mesopotamian economy. For the historical period after 5600 B.P., when writing was invented, there are temple records of economic activities. States can exist without writing, but literacy facilitates the flow and storage of information. As the economy expanded, trade, manufacture, herding, and grain storage were centrally managed. Temples collected and distributed meat, dairy products, crops, fish, clothing, tools, and trade items. Potters, metalworkers, weavers, sculptors, and other artisans perfected their crafts.

Prior to the invention of **metallurgy** (knowledge of the properties of metals, including their extraction and processing and the manufacture of metal tools), raw copper was shaped by hammering. If copper is hammered too long, it hardens and becomes brittle, with a risk of cracking. But once heated (annealed) in a fire, copper becomes malleable again. Such annealing of copper was an early form of metallurgy. A vital step for metallurgy was the discovery of **smelting**, the high-temperature process by which pure metal is produced from an ore. Ores, including copper ore, have a much wider distribution than does native copper, which initially was traded as a luxury good because of its rarity.

When and how smelting was discovered is unknown. But after 5000 B.P., metallurgy evolved rapidly. The Bronze Age began when alloys of arsenic and copper, or tin and copper (in both cases known as **bronze**), became common and greatly extended the use of metals. Bronze flows more easily than copper does when heated to a similar temperature, so bronze was more convenient for metal casting. Early molds were carved in stone, as shaped depressions to be filled with molten metal. A copper ax cast from such a mold was found in northern Mesopotamia and predates 5000 B.P. Thereafter, other metals came into common use.

Early Mesopotamian scribes used a stylus to scrawl symbols on raw clay. This writing, called *cuneiform*, left a wedge-shaped impression on the clay. What languages were written in cuneiform? LACMA - Los Angeles County Museum of Art.

Iron ore is distributed more widely than is copper ore. Iron, when smelted, can be used on its own; there is no need for tin or arsenic to make a metal alloy (bronze). The Iron Age began once high-temperature iron smelting was mastered. In the Old World after 3200 B.P., iron spread rapidly. Formerly valued as highly as gold, iron crashed in value when it became plentiful.

The Mesopotamian economy, based on intensive agriculture, craft production, and trade, spurred population growth and an increase in urbanism. Sumerian cities were protected by a fortress wall and surrounded by a farming area. By 4800 B.P., Uruk, the largest early Mesopotamian city, had amassed a population of 50,000. As irrigation and the population expanded, communities fought over water. People sought protection in the fortified cities (Adams 2008), which could defend themselves when threatened.

By 4600 B.P., secular authority had replaced temple rule. The office of military coordinator developed into kingship. This change shows up architecturally in palaces and royal tombs. The palace raised armies and supplied them with armor, chariots, and metal armaments. At Ur's royal cemetery, by 4600 B.P., monarchs were being buried with soldiers, charioteers, and ladies in waiting. These subordinates were killed at the time of royal burial to accompany the monarch to the afterworld.

Agricultural intensification made it possible for the number of people supported by a given area to increase. Population pressure on irrigated fields helped create a stratified society. Land became scarce private property that was bought and sold. Some people amassed large estates, and their wealth set them off from ordinary farmers. These landlords joined the urban elite, while sharecroppers and serfs toiled in the fields. By 4600 B.P., Mesopotamia had a well-defined class structure, with complex stratification into nobles, commoners, and slaves.

## Other Early States

The Indus River Valley state takes its name from the river valley along which it extended. Located in what is today northwestern India and adjacent Pakistan, the major cities of that state were Harappa and Mohenjo-daro. (Figure 9.2 maps four great early river valley states of the Old World: Mesopotamia, Egypt, India/Pakistan, and northern China.) Trade and the spread of writing from Mesopotamia may have played a role in the rise of the Indus River Valley state around 4600 B.P. The ruins of the ancient city of Harappa, located in Pakistan's Punjab province, were the first to be identified as part of that civilization. At its peak, the Indus River Valley state incorporated 1,000 cities, towns, and villages and spanned 280,000 square miles (725,000 square kilometers). This state, which flourished between 4600 and 3900 B.P., featured urban planning, social stratification, and an early, and as yet undeciphered, writing system (Meadow and Kenoyer 2000).

FIGURE 9.2    **The Four Great Early River Valley States of the Old World**
By approximately 4000 B.P., urban life had been established along the Tigris and Euphrates Rivers in Mesopotamia, the Nile River in Egypt, the Indus and Ganges Rivers in India/Pakistan, and the Yellow River in China.

Source: A. M., Craig, W. A., Graham, D. M., Kagan, S., Ozment, and F. M.,Turner, *Heritage of World Civilizations, Volume 1 to 1650.* Englewood Cliffs, NJ: Pearson Education, 1997.

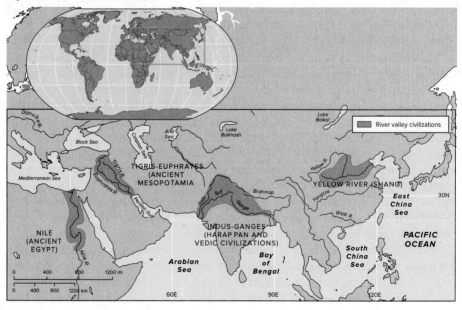

The Indus state collapsed, apparently because of warfare, around 3900 B.P. Its cities were destroyed and abandoned. Skeletons of massacre victims have been found in the streets of Mohenjo-daro. Harappa continued to be occupied but on a much smaller scale (Meadow and Kenoyer 2000). (For more on the Harappa Archaeological Research Project, visit http://www.harappa.com.)

The first Chinese state, dating to 3750 B.P., was that of the Shang dynasty. It arose in the Yellow River area of northern China, where wheat had replaced millet as the dietary staple. This state was characterized by urbanism, palatial (as well as domestic) architecture, human sacrifice, and a sharp division between social classes. Burials of the aristocracy were marked by ornaments of stone, including jade. The Shang had bronze metallurgy and an elaborate writing system. In warfare they used chariots and took prisoners.

As in Mesopotamia and China, many other early civilizations came to rely on metallurgy. A hemisphere away, in the Peruvian Andes, metalworking appeared around 4000 B.P. Ancient Andeans were skilled workers of bronze, copper, and gold. They also are well known for their pottery. Their arts, crafts, and agricultural knowledge compared well with those of Mesoamerica at its height. Note that Andean civilization, like Mesoamerican state formation, was truncated by Spanish conquest. The Aztecs of Mexico were conquered in 1519 C.E. (formerly A.D.); the Inca of Peru, in 1532 (see Marcus and Williams 2009).

Overlooking the Indus River Valley, where an ancient civilization flourished between 4600 and 3900 B.P., ruins of India's Lamayuru Monastery occupy the higher part of a hill, with local houses below, closer to the road. David Samuel Robbins/Getty Images

## State Formation in Mesoamerica

The processes of state formation that took place in the Middle East and Mesoamerica were comparable, beginning with ranked societies and chiefdoms and ending with fully formed states and empires. The first monumental buildings (temple complexes) in the Western Hemisphere were constructed by Mesoamerican chiefdoms in many areas, from the Valley of Mexico to Guatemala (see Evans 2013). These chiefdoms influenced one another as they traded materials, such as obsidian, shells, jade, and pottery. (Figure 9.3 maps major sites in the emergence of Mesoamerican food production, chiefdoms, and states.)

FIGURE 9.3    **Major Sites in the Emergence of Food Production and the State in Mesoamerica**

McGraw-Hill Education

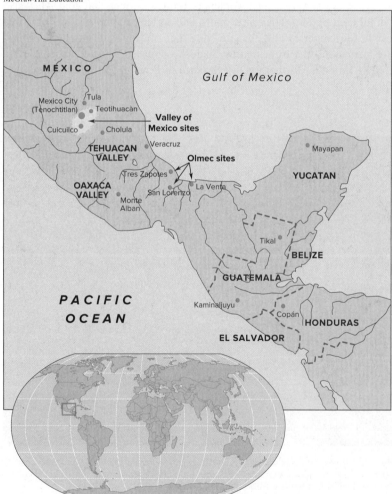

## Early Chiefdoms and Elites

The Olmec built a series of ritual centers on Mexico's southern Gulf Coast between 3,200 and 2,500 years ago. Three of those centers, each from a different century, are known. Earthen mounds were grouped into plaza complexes, presumably for religious use. Such centers show that Olmec chiefs could marshal human labor to construct such mounds. The Olmec also were master sculptors; they carved massive stone heads, perhaps as images of their chiefs.

Regional trade linked the Olmec with other parts of Mesoamerica, including the Oaxaca Valley. By 3000 B.P. (1000 B.C.E.—formerly B.C.), a ruling elite had emerged in Oaxaca (see the next section). The items traded between Oaxaca and the Olmec were for elite consumption. High-status Oaxacans wore mussel-shell ornaments from the coast. In return, the Olmec elites got mirrors and jade made by Oaxacan artisans. Oaxacan chiefdoms developed irrigation systems, exported magnetite mirrors, and were precocious in their use of adobes (mud bricks), stucco, stone masonry, and architecture. Olmec chiefdoms farmed river levees, built mounds of earth, and carved colossal stone heads. Other early Mexican chiefdoms also had skilled artists and builders, who used adobes and plaster and constructed stone buildings precisely oriented 8 degrees north of east—a positioning assumed to have had some sort of ritual significance.

The period between 3200 and 3000 B.P. (1200–1000 B.C.E.) was one of rapid social change in Mesoamerica. Its many chiefdoms were concentrating labor power, intensifying agriculture, exchanging trade goods, and borrowing ideas, including art motifs and styles, from each other. Archaeologists now believe it was the *intensity of competitive interaction*—rather than the supremacy of any one chiefdom—that made social change so rapid. The social and political landscape of Mexico around 3000 B.P. (1000 B.C.E.) was one in which 25 or so chiefly centers were (1) sufficiently separate and autonomous to adapt to local zones and conditions and (2) sufficiently interactive and competitive to borrow and incorporate new ideas and innovations as they arose in other regions (Flannery and Marcus 2000; Kurnick and Baron 2016).

It used to be thought that a single chiefdom could become a state on its own. Archaeologists know now that state formation typically involves one chiefdom's incorporating several others into the emerging state it controls, and making changes in its own infrastructure as it acquires and holds on to new territories, followers, and goods. Waging warfare and attracting followers are two key elements in state formation (see Stanish and Levine 2011). (This chapter's "Anthropology Today" debunks popular pseudo-archaeological theories about the origin of Mesoamerican civilization.)

Many chiefdoms have dense populations, intensive agriculture, and settlement hierarchies that include hamlets, villages, and perhaps towns. These factors pave the way for greater social and political complexity as states begin to form. Political leaders emerge, and military success often solidifies their position. Such figures attract lots of followers, loyal to their leader. Conquest warfare brings in new territories and subjects. Unlike chiefdoms, states can acquire labor and land and hold on to them. States have armies, warfare, developed political hierarchies and law codes.

Olmec and Oaxaca were just two among many early Mexican chiefdoms that thrived in the area from the Valley of Mexico to Guatemala (see Figure 9.3). Oaxaca went on to develop a state a bit earlier than the Teotihuacán state of the Valley of Mexico. Oaxaca and other highland areas came to overshadow the Olmec area and the Mesoamerican lowlands in general. We turn now to the process of state formation that unfolded in Oaxaca among its Zapotec people.

## Warfare and State Formation: The Zapotec Case

The first Mesoamerican state, the **Zapotec state**, arose in the Valley of Oaxaca. The city of Monte Albán served as capital of this Zapotec polity for *1,200 years,* between 500 B.C.E. and 700 C.E. The polity was a chiefdom from about 500 B.C.E. to 100 B.C.E. and after that a state that lasted 800 years—from 100 B.C.E. to 700 C.E.

As has been noted previously, *warfare* plays a key role in primary state formation. In the Valley of Oaxaca, armed conflict began as village-on-village raiding, with killing, burning, and captive taking but no permanent acquisition of territory (Flannery and Marcus 2003b). A monument from the Oaxacan site of San José Mogote, erected no later than 500 B.C.E., is the earliest reliably dated monument with writing in Mesoamerica. It depicts a named, sacrificed captive, likely a rival chief. The first evidence for organized conquest warfare in Oaxaca comes four centuries later, simultaneously with evidence for state formation. This co-occurrence supports the idea of a causal link between conquest warfare and state formation (Spencer 2003, 2010).

As states emerge and grow, they develop an internally specialized, administrative organization—a bureaucracy. Chiefdoms, by contrast, lack such administrative specialization. States have at least four levels of decision making (Wright 1977). The center, or capital, creates subsidiary administrative centers (Elson 2007). The result is a nested structure of secondary, tertiary, and even quaternary centers. Population size tends to follow this administrative structure. A key difference between chiefdoms and states is that states typically have at least a *four-level* hierarchy of settlements according to both administrative functions and population size. Chiefdoms have no more than *three levels* (Spencer 2003, 2010).

Three of more than 300 carved stones depicting slain war captives at the important archaeological site of Monte Albán, Oaxaca, Mexico. Dated to 500–400 B.C.E., these images originally were set in the Prisoner Gallery of Monte Albán's Building L. This huge display of slain enemies was a form of political and military propaganda. The carved stones warned potential rivals what would happen if they defied Monte Albán.
DEA/G. Dagli Orti/Getty Images

Conquest warfare helps the state build its bureaucracy. An expansive state must send delegates, such as soldiers, governors, and other officials, to subjugate and rule in distant territories. Lacking such bureaucrats, chiefdoms can't do this, which means that the geographic range of chiefly authority is smaller than in a state. According to Spencer (2003, 2010), the limit of a chiefdom's range is half a day's travel from its center. States, however, can transcend such limits and carry out long-distance conquests. Archaeological evidence for conquest warfare includes burned and abandoned villages; specialized forts and administrative outposts; and forced changes in the economic, social, and religious behaviors of subjugated peoples.

The conquest of polities in distant regions, coupled with regularized tribute exaction, can bring about a transition from chiefdom to state (Spencer 2003, 2010). For such a strategy to succeed (especially when the conquered polities lie more than a half-day's trip away), the conquering state has to send agents to the subjugated areas. Generals and bureaucrats are needed not only to carry out the subjugation but also to maintain long-term control and to manage tribute collection. Given its need to rely on distant representatives, the state's central leadership promotes internal administrative specialization and loyalty. Tribute provides new resources to support this administrative transformation. The conquest of distant polities and bureaucratic growth were integral parts of the process of Zapotec state formation.

Typically, state bureaucracies occupy a group of administrative buildings, especially at the capital. Thus, surrounding the Main Plaza at Monte Albán were specialized buildings, including palaces, temples, and ball courts. Hieroglyphs on one building in Monte Albán's Main Plaza record how outlying areas were acquired. We learn that although the Zapotec state had managed to conquer distant regions to the north, west, and southwest, certain areas to the east and south managed to resist for centuries.

By 30–20 B.C.E., the Zapotec state, from its capital at Monte Albán, presided over a fully developed four-tier settlement hierarchy (see Elson 2007), which it maintained for several hundred years. Eventually, Monte Albán lost its prominence, as other Zapotec centers successfully challenged its authority. After 700 C.E., the Zapotec state fragmented into a series of smaller centers, or principalities, alternately vying for supremacy through continued warfare and peaceful alliances through marriage (Flannery and Marcus 2003a; Marcus 1989).

## States in the Valley of Mexico

During the first century C.E., the Valley (Basin) of Mexico, located in the highlands where Mexico City now stands, rose to prominence in Mesoamerican state formation. In this large valley, **Teotihuacán** flourished between 100 and 700 C.E.

The valley is actually a large basin surrounded by mountains; it has rich volcanic soils, but rainfall isn't always reliable. The northern valley, where the huge city and state of Teotihuacán eventually arose, is colder and drier than the south. Frosts limited farming in that area until quick-growing varieties of maize were developed. Until 500 B.C.E., most people lived in the southern part of the valley, where rainfall made farming possible. After 500 B.C.E., new maize varieties and small-scale irrigation appeared. The population increased and began to spread north (see Carballo 2016).

By 1 C.E., Teotihuacán was a town of 10,000 people. It presided over a state whose territory spanned a few thousand square kilometers and included some 50,000 people (Cowgill 2015; Parsons 1974). Teotihuacán's growth reflected its agricultural potential. Perpetual springs permitted irrigation of a large alluvial plain. Rural farmers supplied food for the growing urban population. By this time, a clear **settlement hierarchy** had emerged. This is a ranked series of communities that differ in size, function, and building types. The settlements at the top of the hierarchy were political and religious centers. Those at the bottom were rural villages.

Along with state organization went large-scale irrigation, status differentiation, and complex architecture. Teotihuacán developed as a planned city built on a grid pattern, with the Pyramid of the Sun at its center. By 500 C.E., the population of Teotihuacán had reached 130,000, making it larger than imperial Rome. Farmers were one of its diverse specialized groups, along with artisans, merchants, and political, religious, and military personnel.

After 700 C.E., Teotihuacán, like the Zapotec state, declined in size and power. By 900 C.E., its population had shrunk to 30,000. Between 900 and 1200 C.E., the Toltec period, the population scattered, and small cities and towns sprang up throughout the valley. People also left the Valley of Mexico to live in larger cities—like Tula, the Toltec capital—on its edge (see Figure 9.3).

Population increase (including immigration by the ancestors of the Aztecs) and urban growth returned to the Valley of Mexico between 1200 and 1520 C.E. During the **Aztec** period (1325 to 1520 C.E.) there were several cities, the largest of which—Tenochtitlán, the capital—may have surpassed Teotihuacán at its height (see Gonlin and French 2015; Nichols and Rodríguez-Alegría 2017). A dozen Aztec towns had more than 10,000 people. Fueling this population growth was intensification of agriculture, particularly in the southern part of the valley, where the drainage of lake bottoms and swamps added new cultivable land.

The layout of Teotihuacán in the Valley of Mexico. Teotihuacán is one of the most important archaeological sites in the Americas. At its height around 500 C.E., the city was larger than imperial Rome. The mobilization of manual labor to build such a city is one of the costs of state organization.
gerialarchives.com/Alamy Stock Photo

Another factor in the renaissance of the Valley of Mexico was trade. The major towns and markets were located on lakeshores, with easy access to canoe traffic (see Hirth 2016). The Aztec capital stood on an island in the lake. In Tenochtitlán, the production of luxury goods was more prestigious and more highly organized than that of pottery making, basket making, and weaving (Smith 2016). Luxury producers, such as stone workers, feather workers, and gold- and silversmiths, occupied a special position in Aztec society. The manufacture of luxury goods for export was an important part of the economy of the Aztec capital (see Garraty 2013; Nichols and Rodríguez-Alegría 2017).

# Why States Collapse

States can fall apart along the same cleavage lines (e.g., regional political units) that were originally brought together to form the state. Various factors, such as warfare, invasion, disease, famine, or prolonged drought, can threaten their economies and political institutions (see Johnson 2017). Citizens might degrade the environment, usually with economic costs. For example, farmers and smelters might cut down trees. Such deforestation promotes erosion and leads to a decline in the water supply. Overuse of land may deplete the soil of the nutrients needed to grow crops.

## The Maya and Their Fall

Generations of scholars have puzzled over the decline of Maya civilization around 900 C.E. (see, for example, Storey and Storey 2017). Classic Maya culture, featuring several competing states, flourished between 300 and 900 C.E. in parts of what are now Mexico, Honduras, Guatemala, Belize, and El Salvador. Some important Maya cities, now archaeological sites and tourist attractions, included the Mexican sites of Bonampak, Calakmul, Chichen Itzá, Palenque, and Tulum; the Guatemalan sites of Tikal and Uaxactún; and Copán in Honduras. Maya cities had marketplaces, workshops, and community gardens. The ancient Maya probably are best known for their monuments (temples and pyramids), calendars, mathematics, and hieroglyphic writing (see Coe 2011; Edwards 2015).

Today, an inaccessible forest covers the ruins of Maya civilization. That forest has impeded (but never stopped) archaeological exploration of this tropical lowland region. Fortunately, archaeologists now have access to a new way of seeing below that forest cover—the airborne laser scanning system known as LiDAR (as described in Chapter 3). A large-scale LiDAR survey of northern Guatemala in 2016 revealed a landscape dotted with structures (over 60,000 of them); settlements, including urban centers; and extensive infrastructure (waterworks and elevated roads). LiDAR confirms that the Maya presided over a network of densely populated and fortified cities. Sustaining this population was a complex and productive agricultural economy. Based on the number and density of ancient structures in the area surveyed, the research team estimated an overall Maya population of 7 to 11 million. Their settlement pattern was uneven. The mapping revealed (1) sparsely populated rural areas, (2) areas with small towns/cities and surrounding populations, and (3) urban zones featuring a single, large city. Approximately 66 miles (106 km) of causeways (elevated roadways) linked settlements and communities. Sizable defensive features suggest large-scale conflict (see Canuto et al. 2018; Ford and Horn 2018).

## Anthropology Today  *The Fantastic Claims of Pseudo-Archaeology*

Interest in archaeology, particularly in ancient civilizations, has spawned numerous popular-culture creations, including movies, TV programs, and books. In fictional works, the anthropologists don't bear much resemblance to their real-life counterparts. Unlike the most famous pop-culture archaeologist, Indiana Jones, real archaeologists don't go around fighting Nazis, lashing whips, or seizing antiquities. The archaeologist's profession isn't a matter of raiding lost arks, going on crusades, or finding crystal skulls, but of reconstructing ancient lifeways through the careful and systematic analysis of material remains.

The serialized publication of H. G. Wells's *War of the Worlds* (about a Martian invasion of Earth) in 1897 spurred a fascination with Martians and other aliens that has lasted ever since. The year 2018 marked the 50th anniversary of the original publication (in German) of Erich von Däniken's best-known book, *Chariots of the Gods,* in which he proposed that major human achievements of the ancient world were created or assisted by extraterrestrials. Tabloids and television helped make the book a best seller, and its continuing influence is illustrated by the History Channel's series *Ancient Aliens,* of which von Däniken is a producer (see Bond 2018).

The media also have helped propagate the pseudoscientific theories of Thor Heyerdahl and Graham Hancock—neither of them a professional archaeologist. World traveler and adventurer Heyerdahl wanted to prove that developments in one world area (e.g., Mesoamerica) were derived from ideas and techniques brought or borrowed from somewhere else (e.g., Egypt). In *The Ra Expeditions* (1971), he argued that his voyage in a papyrus boat from the Mediterranean to the Caribbean demonstrated that ancient Egyptians could have navigated to the New World. (The boat was modeled on an ancient Egyptian vessel, but Heyerdahl and his crew brought along such modern conveniences as a radio and canned goods.) Heyerdahl maintained that, given the possibility of ancient trans-Atlantic travel, Old World people could have influenced the emergence of civilization in the Americas. *Could have,* however, even if true, is not the same as *did.*

Pseudo-archaeologists often have trouble with chronology. In this chapter, we've seen that ancient civilizations

Sarajevo-born American Sam Semir Osmanagich claims to have discovered a giant pyramid built by an ancient civilization under Visocica Hill, Bosnia. Most scientists doubt his claim. Fehim Demir/epa/Corbis

comparable to those of Mesopotamia and Egypt evolved in the Mexican highlands (e.g., in Oaxaca and the Valley of Mexico). This occurred, however, at least 2,000 years after the major period of Egyptian pyramid building. If Egypt did contribute to Mesoamerican civilization, we would expect this influence to have been exerted during Egypt's heyday as an ancient power—not millennia later. There is, however, no archaeological evidence for trans-Atlantic contact at either time. There is, on the other hand, abundant archaeological evidence for the gradual emergence of food production and the state in Mesoamerica. Fantastic claims to the contrary, changes, advances, and setbacks in ancient American social life were the products of the ideas and activities of Native Americans themselves.

Abundant, well-analyzed archaeological data from the Middle East, Mesoamerica, and Peru tell a clear story. Food production and the state were not brilliant discoveries that humans needed to learn from outsiders. They were gradual processes with down-to-earth causes and effects. They required thousands of years of orderly change, not some chance meeting in the high Andes between an ancient Inca chief and a beneficent Johnny Appleseed from Aldebaran.

Occasionally, fantastic claims about prehistory *exaggerate*, rather than deny, the abilities of ancient humans. Consider Graham Hancock's contention that an Upper Paleolithic civilization, rather than ancient Egyptians, built Egypt's great Sphinx, some 7,000 years earlier than its actual construction date (Hancock 2015). And then there is Sam Semir Osmanagich, a Bosnian-born amateur archaeologist who has been dubbed the Indiana Jones of the Balkans because of his flat-crowned Navajo hat. Osmanagich claims to have identified in Bosnia the world's largest ancient pyramid, which he thinks is "older than the last ice age" (Smith 2006). Archaeologists and geologists, however, say that his "pyramid" is really a large, symmetrical hill formed by buckling of the Earth's crust millions of years ago.

The University of Michigan offers a popular course, Frauds and Fantastic Claims in Archaeology. The course examines and debunks these and other theories that archaeologists view as fringe or pseudoscientific. Available as a course textbook is Kenneth L. Feder's *Frauds, Myths, and Mysteries: Science and Pseudoscience in Archaeology* (2017)—a must for any reader wanting to pursue this topic further. When and where have you heard a fantastic claim about prehistory?

Some important archaeological clues to the Maya decline have been found at Copán, in western Honduras. This classic Maya royal center, the largest site in the southeastern part of the Maya area, covered 29 acres. It was built on an artificial terrace overlooking the Copán River. Its rulers inscribed their monuments with their names and dates, and accounts of their coronation, lineage history, and important battles (see Iannone et al. 2016). One monument at Copán was intended to be the ruler's throne platform, but only one side was ever finished. The monument bears a date, 822 C.E., in a section of unfinished text. Copán has no monuments with later dates. The site probably had been abandoned by 830 C.E.

Environmental factors implicated in Copán's demise may have included erosion and soil exhaustion caused by overfarming. Debris at excavated hillside farms confirms erosion, probably due to unsustainable agricultural intensification beginning around 750 C.E. Eventually, most farm sites were abandoned, some buried by erosion debris. Food stress and malnutrition were clearly present at Copán, where 80 percent of the buried skeletons display signs of anemia, due to iron deficiency. One skull shows anemia severe enough to have caused death. Even the nobles were malnourished. The skull of one member of the nobility, known to be such from its carved teeth and cosmetic deformation, also has telltale signs of anemia: spongy areas at its rear (Annenberg/CPB Exhibits 2000).

Just as the causes of state formation are diverse, so are the reasons for state decline. In the long run, Maya political organization turned out to be vulnerable (see Fojas 2013). Political competition and increased warfare destabilized many of its dynasties and governments. Hieroglyphic texts document a pattern of increasing warfare among many Maya cities (see Houk 2015). From the period just before the collapse, there is archaeological evidence for increased concern with fortifications (moats, ditches, walls, and palisades) and relocation to defensible locations. Archaeologists have evidence of the burning of structures, projectile points from spears, and bodies of some of those killed. Some sites were abandoned, with the people fleeing into the forests to occupy perishable huts. (Copán, as we have seen, was depopulated soon after 822 C.E.) Archaeologists now believe that social, political, and military upheaval had as much to do with the Maya decline and abandonment of its cities as did natural environmental factors (Marcus, personal communication).

Archaeologists formerly tended to seek explanations for state origin and decline almost exclusively in terms of natural environmental factors, such as climate change, habitat destruction, and demographic pressure (see Weiss 2005). They now see state origins and declines more fully—in social and political terms—because we can read the texts. The Maya texts document competition and warfare between dynasties jockeying for position and power. The two explanations (environmental versus sociopolitical) are not necessarily mutually exclusive. Environmental destruction and demographic pressure can create resource shortages that fuel conflict and warfare. Whatever its cause, we know that warfare played a key role in both the rise and the fall of ancient chiefdoms and states. What's its role in today's world?

## Summary

1. States develop to handle regulatory problems as the population grows and the economy gets more complex. Multiple factors, including irrigation, regional trade, warfare, population growth, and environmental circumscription have contributed to state formation.

2. A state is a society with a formal, central government and a division of society into classes. The first cities and states, supported by irrigated farming, developed in southern Mesopotamia between 6000 and 5500 B.P. Evidence for early state organization includes monumental architecture, central storehouses, irrigation systems, and written records.

3. Towns predate pottery in the Middle East. The first towns grew up 10,000 to 9,000 years ago. Before then, Göbekli Tepe was an early ritual center supported by broad-spectrum foraging. The first pottery dates back just over 8,000 years. *Halafian* (7500–6000 B.P.) refers to a pottery style and to the period when the first chiefdoms emerged. Ubaid pottery (7000–6000 B.P.) is associated with advanced chiefdoms and perhaps the earliest states. Most state formation occurred during the Uruk period (6000–5200 B.P.).

4. Based on the status distinctions they include, societies may be classified as egalitarian, ranked, or stratified. In egalitarian societies, status distinctions are not usually inherited. Ranked societies, of which there are two types, have hereditary inequality, but they lack stratification. In type 1 ranked societies, individuals are ranked, but villages are independent (autonomous) of one another. In type 2, both individuals and villages are ranked, and there is loss of village autonomy. Stratified societies have sharp social divisions—social classes or strata—based on unequal access to wealth and power. Ranked societies with loss of village autonomy are chiefdoms.

5. Mesopotamia's economy was based on intensive agriculture, craft production, and trade. Writing, invented by 5600 B.P., was first used to keep accounts for trade. With the invention of smelting, the Bronze Age began just after 5000 B.P.

6. In northwestern India and Pakistan, the Indus River Valley state flourished from 4600 to 3900 B.P. The first Chinese state, dating to 3750 B.P., was that of the Shang dynasty in northern China. The major early states of the Western Hemisphere were in Mesoamerica and Peru.

7. Between 3200 and 3000 B.P., intense competitive interaction among the many chiefdoms in Mesoamerica fueled rapid social change. Some chiefdoms would develop into states (e.g., Oaxaca, Valley of Mexico). Others (e.g., Olmec) would not. In the Valley of Oaxaca, changing patterns of warfare—from village raiding to conquest warfare—played a prominent role in the formation of Mesoamerica's earliest state, the Zapotec state, whose capital was Monte Albán. By 1 C.E. (2000 B.P.), the Valley of Mexico had come to prominence. In this large valley in the highlands, Teotihuacán thrived between 100 and 700 C.E. Tenochtitlán, the capital of the Aztec state (1325 to 1520 C.E.), may have surpassed Teotihuacán at its height.

8. Early states faced various threats: invasion, disease, famine, drought, soil exhaustion, erosion, and the buildup of irrigation salts. States may collapse when they fail to keep social and economic order or to protect themselves against outsiders. The Maya state fell in the face of increased warfare among competing dynasties.

## Think Like an Anthropologist

1. Only those ranked societies with loss of village autonomy should be called chiefdoms. What kinds of evidence could archaeologists search for as clues to this loss of autonomy?

2. Based on the evidence from coastal Peru (near the beginning of this chapter) and Oaxaca (near the end of this chapter), what role did warfare play in early state formation?

## Key Terms

Aztec, *226*
bronze, *218*
chiefdom, *207*
cuneiform, *218*
egalitarian
    society, *215*
empire, *209*
Halafian, *215*

Mesopotamia, *211*
metallurgy, *218*
polities, *207*
primary states, *208*
ranked society, *216*
settlement
    hierarchy, *226*
smelting, *218*

stratification, *216*
state, *207*
Teotihuacán, *225*
Zapotec state, *224*

# Chapter 10

# Language and Communication

## Language

Linguistic anthropology illustrates anthropology's characteristic interests in diversity, comparison, and change—but here the focus is on language (see Ahearn 2017; Bonvillain 2016; Enfield, Kockelman, and Sidnell 2014; Garcia, Flores and Spotti 2017). Language, whether spoken (*speech*) or written (*writing*—which has existed for less than 6,000 years), is our primary means of communication. We can define language more broadly as a communication system based on meaningful signs, sounds, gestures, or marks (e.g., words, letters, and punctuation marks). Like culture in general, of which language is a part, language is transmitted through learning. Language is based on arbitrary, learned associations between words and the things they stand for. Unlike the communication systems of other animals, language allows us to discuss the past and future, share our experiences with others, and benefit from their experiences.

Anthropologists study language in its social and cultural context (see Bonvillain 2013; Salzmann et al. 2015). Some linguistic anthropologists reconstruct ancient languages by comparing their contemporary descendants. Others study languages to discover how worldviews and patterns of thought vary from culture to culture. Sociolinguists examine dialects and styles in a single language to show how speech reflects social differences. Linguistic anthropologists also explore the role of language in colonization and expansion of the world system (Borjian 2017; Trudgill 2010).

## Nonhuman Primate Communication

### Call Systems

No other animal has anything approaching the complexity of language. The communication systems of other primates (monkeys and apes) are **call systems**. These vocal systems consist of a limited number of sounds—*calls*—that are produced only when particular environmental stimuli are encountered. Such calls may be varied in intensity and duration, but they are much less flexible than language because they are automatic and can't be combined. At some point in human evolution, however, our ancestors began to combine calls and to understand the combinations. The number of calls also expanded, eventually becoming too great to be transmitted, from generation to generation, even partly through the genes. Communication came to rely almost totally on learning.

Although wild primates use call systems, the vocal tract of apes is not suitable for speech. Until the 1960s, attempts to teach spoken language to apes suggested that they lack linguistic abilities. In the 1950s, a couple raised a chimpanzee, Viki, as a member of their family and systematically tried to teach her to speak. However, Viki learned only four words ("mama," "papa," "up," and "cup").

### Sign Language

More recent experiments have shown that apes can learn to use, if not speak, true language (see Hanzel 2017). Several apes have learned to converse with people through means other than speech. One such communication system is American Sign Language, or ASL, which is widely used by deaf Americans. ASL employs a limited number of gesture units that are analogous to sounds in spoken language. These units combine to form words and larger units of meaning.

The first chimpanzee to learn ASL was Washoe, a female, who died in 2007 at the age of 42. Captured in West Africa, Washoe was acquired by R. Allen Gardner and Beatrice Gardner, scientists at the University of Nevada in Reno, in 1966, when she was a year old. Four years later, she moved to Norman, Oklahoma, to a converted farm that had become the Institute for Primate Studies. Washoe revolutionized the discussion of the language-learning abilities of apes (Carey 2007). At first she lived in a trailer and heard no spoken language. The researchers always used ASL to communicate with each other in her presence. The chimp gradually acquired a vocabulary of more than 100 signs representing English words (Gardner et al. 1989). At the age of 2, Washoe began to combine as many as five signs into rudimentary sentences such as "you, me, go out, hurry."

Apes, such as these Congo chimpanzees, use call systems to communicate in the wild. Their vocal systems consist of a limited number of sounds—calls—that are produced only when particular environmental stimuli are encountered. Michael Nichols/National Geographic Creative

The second chimp to learn ASL was Lucy, Washoe's junior by one year. Lucy died, or was murdered by poachers, in 1986, after having been introduced to "the wild" in Africa in 1979 (Carter 1988). From her second day of life until her move to Africa, Lucy lived with a family in Norman, Oklahoma. Roger Fouts, a researcher from the nearby Institute for Primate Studies, came twice a week to test and improve Lucy's knowledge of ASL. During the rest of the week, Lucy used ASL to converse with her foster parents. After acquiring language, Washoe and Lucy exhibited several human traits: swearing, joking, telling lies, and trying to teach language to others (Fouts 1997).

When irritated, Washoe called her monkey neighbors at the institute "dirty monkeys." Lucy insulted her "dirty cat." On arrival at Lucy's place, Fouts once found a pile of excrement on the floor. When he asked the chimp what it was, she replied, "dirty, dirty," her expression for feces. Asked whose "dirty, dirty" it was, Lucy named Fouts's coworker, Sue. When Fouts refused to believe her about Sue, the chimp blamed the excrement on Fouts himself.

Fundamental to any language is its **cultural transmission** through learning. People talk to you and around you, and you learn. Washoe, Lucy, and other chimps have tried to teach ASL to other animals, including their own offspring. Washoe taught gestures to other institute chimps, including her son Sequoia, who died in infancy (Fouts, Fouts, and Van Cantfort 1989).

Because of their size and strength as adults, gorillas are less likely subjects than chimps for such experiments. Psychologist Francine "Penny" Patterson's work with gorillas at Stanford University therefore seems more daring than the chimp experiments. Patterson raised the female gorilla Koko (1971–2018) in a trailer next to a Stanford museum. Koko's vocabulary eventually surpassed that of any chimp. She learned more than 1,000 signs, of which she regularly used over 800. She also recognized at least 2,000 spoken words in English when she heard them. Video clips and other documentation of Patterson's work with Koko and Michael, a male gorilla who also learned sign language, are available at http://www.koko.org/sign-language.

Koko and the chimps also show that apes share still another linguistic ability with humans: **productivity**. Speakers use the rules of their language to produce entirely new expressions that are comprehensible to other native speakers. I can, for example, create "baboonlet" to refer to a baboon infant. I do this by analogy with English words in which the suffix *-let* designates the young of a species. Anyone who speaks English immediately understands the meaning of my new word. Apes can also use language productively. Lucy used gestures she already knew to create "drinkfruit" for "watermelon." Washoe, seeing a swan for the first time, coined "waterbird." Koko, who knew the gestures for "finger" and "bracelet," formed "finger bracelet" when she was given a ring.

Although apes have never invented their own meaningful gesture system in the wild, when given such a system, they show many humanlike abilities in learning it. They can employ it productively and creatively, although not with the sophistication of human ASL users.

Apes also have demonstrated linguistic **displacement**. Absent in call systems, displacement is our ability to talk about things that are not present. We don't have to see the objects before we say the words. We can discuss the past and future, share our experiences with others, and benefit from theirs. Patterson has described several examples of Koko's capacity for displacement. The gorilla once expressed sorrow about having bitten Patterson three days earlier. Koko used the sign "later" to postpone doing things she didn't want to do. Table 10.1 summarizes the contrasts between language, whether sign or spoken, and call systems.

**TABLE 10.1**   **Language Contrasted with Call Systems**

McGraw-Hill Education

| Human Language | Primate Call Systems |
|---|---|
| Has the capacity to speak (or gesture) of things and events that are not present (displacement) | Are stimuli dependent (e.g., the food call will be made only in the presence of food); it cannot be faked |
| Has the capacity to generate new expressions by combining other expressions (productivity) | Consist of a limited number of calls that cannot be combined to produce new calls |
| Is group specific in that all humans have the capacity for language, but each linguistic community has its own language, which is culturally transmitted | Tend to be species specific, with little variation among communities of the same species for each call |

No one denies the huge difference between human language and gorilla signs. There is surely a major gap between the ability to write a book or say a prayer and an ape's use of signs. Apes may not be people, but they aren't just animals, either. Let us remember how Koko once expressed it: When asked by a reporter whether she was a person or an animal, Koko signed "fine animal gorilla" (Patterson 1978). Koko died in her sleep at the age of 46 on June 19, 2018, at the Gorilla Foundation's preserve in Woodside, California. Her legacy continues at http://www.koko.org.

## The Origin of Language

Although the capacity to remember and combine linguistic symbols appears to be latent in the apes, human evolution was needed for this seed to sprout into language. A mutated gene known as *FOXP2* helps explain why humans speak and chimps don't (Paulson 2005). The key role of *FOXP2* in speech came to light in a study of a British family, identified only as KE, half of whose members had a severe inherited deficit in speech (Trivedi 2001). The same variant form of *FOXP2* that is found in chimpanzees causes this disorder in humans. Those with the nonspeech version of the gene can't make the tongue and lip movements necessary for clear speech, and their speech is unintelligible (Trivedi 2001). Genomic analysis suggests that the speech-friendly form of *FOXP2* may have taken hold in humans around 150,000 years ago (Paulson 2005). We know now, however, that other genes and a series of anatomical changes were necessary for fully evolved human speech. It would be an oversimplification to call *FOXP2* "the language gene," as was done initially in the popular press, because other genes also determine language development.

# Nonverbal Communication

Language is our principal means of communicating, but it isn't the only one we use. We *communicate* whenever we transmit information about ourselves to others and receive information from them. Our expressions, stances, gestures, and movements, even if unconscious, convey information and are part of our communication styles. Deborah Tannen (1990, 2017) discusses differences in the communication styles of American men and women. She notes that American girls and women tend to look directly at each other when they talk, whereas boys and men do not. Males are more likely to look straight ahead rather than turn and make eye contact with someone, especially another man, seated beside them. Also, in conversational groups, American men tend to relax and sprawl out. Consider the phenomenon known as "manspreading"—the tendency for men using public transportation to open their legs and thus take up more than one place. American women may relax their posture in all-female groups, but when they are with men, they tend to draw in their limbs and assume a tighter stance.

## Kinesics

The study of communication through body movements, stances, gestures, and expressions is known as **kinesics**. Linguists pay attention not only to what is said but also to how it is said. A speaker's enthusiasm is conveyed not only through words but also through facial expressions, gestures, and other signs of animation. We use gestures, such as a jab of the

Manspreading on a New York subway. Why do you think the woman is standing? Hiroko Masuike/
*The New York Times*/Redux Pictures

hand, for emphasis. We vary our intonation and the pitch or loudness of our voices. We communicate through strategic pauses, and even by being silent. An effective communication strategy may include altering pitch, voice level, and grammatical forms such as declaratives ("I am . . ."), imperatives ("Go forth . . ."), and questions ("Are you . . . ?"). Culture teaches us that certain manners and styles should accompany certain kinds of speech.

Much of what we communicate is nonverbal and reflects our emotional states and intentions. This can create problems when we use rapid means of communication such as texting and online messaging. People can use emoticons (☺, ☹, ~/ [confused], :~0 ["hah!" no way!]) and abbreviations (lol—laugh out loud; lmao—laugh my a** off; wtf—what the f***; omg—oh my god) to fill in what might otherwise be communicated by tone of voice, laughter, and facial expression (see Baron 2009; Tannen and Trester 2013). While people still use emoticons, emojis have more recently taken on a similar and growing role in digital communication. An *emoji* is a digital image or pictograph, widely available on smartphones and tablets, used to express an idea or emotion, such as happiness or sadness. This chapter's "Anthropology Today" addresses the growing role of emojis in digital communication.

Although our gestures, facial expressions, and body stances have roots in our primate heritage, and can be glimpsed in the monkeys and the apes, they have not escaped cultural molding (see Salzmann et al. 2015). For humans, culture always plays a role in shaping the "natural." Cross-culturally, nodding does not always mean affirmative, nor does head shaking from side to side always mean negative. Americans say "uh huh" to affirm, whereas in Madagascar a similar sound is made to deny. Americans point with their fingers; the people of Madagascar point with their lips.

Body movements communicate social differences. In Japan, bowing is a regular part of social interaction, but different bows are used depending on the social status of the people who are interacting. In Madagascar and Polynesia, people of lower status should not hold their heads above those of people of higher status. When one approaches someone older or of higher status, one bends one's knees and lowers one's head as a sign of respect. In Madagascar, one always does this, for politeness, when passing between two people.

## Personal Space and Displays of Affection

The world's nations and cultures have strikingly different notions about personal space and displays of affection. Cocktail parties in international meeting places such as the United Nations can resemble an elaborate insect mating ritual as diplomats from different countries advance, withdraw, and sidestep. When Americans talk, walk, and dance, they maintain a certain distance from others. Italians and Brazilians, who need less personal space, may interpret such "standoffishness" as a sign of coldness. In conversational pairs, the Italian or Brazilian typically moves in, while the American "instinctively" retreats from a "close talker." Such bodily movements illustrate culture–behavior programmed by years of exposure to a particular cultural tradition.

Consider, too, some striking contrasts between a national culture (American) that tends to be reserved about (and often even suspicious of) displays of physical affection and a national culture (Brazilian) in which the opposite is true. Brazilians approach, touch, and kiss one another much more frequently than North Americans do. Middle-class Brazilians teach their kids to kiss (on the cheek, two or three times, coming and going) all their adult relatives. Given the size of Brazilian extended families, this can mean hundreds of people. Women continue kissing those people throughout their lives. Until they are adolescents, boys kiss adult relatives. Thereafter, with extended family men and close male friends, they may adopt the characteristic Brazilian hug (abraço). Men typically continue to kiss female relatives and friends, as well as their fathers and uncles, throughout their lives.

Do you kiss your father? Your uncle? Your grandfather? How about your mother, aunt, or grandmother? The answers to these questions may differ between men and women, and for male and female relatives. In the United States, a cultural homophobia (fear of homosexuality) may deter American men from displays of affection with other men.

However, culture is not static. Sarah Kershaw (2009) describes a surge of teenage hugging behavior in American schools. Concerned about potential sexual harassment issues, parents and school officials are suspicious of such public displays of affection, even if the younger generation is more tolerant. Even American boys appear to be more likely nowadays to share nonromantic hugs, as such expressions as "bromance" and "man crush" have entered our vocabulary. What's your experience with, and your opinion about, displays of affection?

# The Structure of Language

**Descriptive linguistics**—the scientific study of a spoken language—involves several interrelated areas of analysis: phonology, morphology, lexicon, and syntax (see Akmajian et al. 2017; McGregor 2015). **Phonology**, the study of speech sounds, considers which sounds are present and meaningful in a given language. **Morphology** studies how sounds combine to form *morphemes*—words and their meaningful parts. Thus, the word *cats* would be

*Syntax* refers to the arrangement and order of words in phrases and sentences. A photo of Yoda from *Star Wars (Revenge of the Sith)* this is. What's odd about Yoda's syntax? Lucas Film/Topham/The Image Works

analyzed as containing two morphemes—*cat,* the name for a kind of animal, and *-s,* a morpheme indicating plurality. A morpheme, therefore, is a minimal unit of meaning. A language's **lexicon** is a dictionary containing all its morphemes and their meanings. **Syntax** refers to the arrangement and order of words in phrases and sentences. For example, do nouns usually come before or after verbs? Do adjectives normally precede or follow the nouns they modify?

From the media, and from meeting foreigners, we know something about foreign accents and mispronunciations. We know that someone with a marked French accent doesn't pronounce *r* as an American does. But at least someone from France can distinguish between "craw" and "claw," which someone from Japan may not be able to do. The difference between *r* and *l* makes a difference in English and in French, but it doesn't in Japanese. In linguistics we say that the difference between *r* and *l* is *phonemic* in English and French but not in Japanese. In English and French *r* and *l* are phonemes but not in Japanese. A **phoneme** is a sound contrast that makes a difference, that differentiates meaning.

We discover the phonemes in a given language by comparing *minimal pairs,* words that resemble each other in all but one sound. The words have different meanings, but they differ in just one sound. The contrasting sounds therefore are phonemes in that language. An example in English is the minimal pair *pit/bit.* These two words are distinguished by a single sound contrast between /p/ and /b/ (we enclose phonemes in slashes). Thus, /p/ and /b/ are phonemes in English. Another example is the different vowel sound of *bit* and *beat* (see Figure 10.1). This contrast distinguishes these two words and the two vowel phonemes written /I/ and /i/ in English.

**FIGURE 10.1** **Vowel Phonemes in Standard American English**

The phonemes are shown according to height of tongue and tongue position at front, center, or back of mouth. Phonetic symbols are identified by English words that include them; note that most are minimal pairs.

Source: Adaptation of Dwight Bolinger, and Donald A. Sears, *Aspects of Language,* Boston, MA: Cengage Learning, 1981.

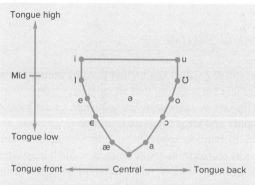

| [i] | as in *beat* | High front (spread) |
|-----|--------------|---------------------|
| [I] | as in *bit* | Lower high front (spread) |
| [e] | as in *bait* | Mid front (spread) |
| [ɛ] | as in *bet* | Lower mid front (spread) |
| [æ] | as in *bat* | Low front |
| [ə] | as in *butt* | Central |
| [a] | as in *pot* | Low back |
| [ɔ] | as in *bought* | Lower mid back (rounded) |
| [o] | as in *boat* | Mid back (rounded) |
| [ʊ] | as in *put* | Lower high back (rounded) |
| [u] | as in *boot* | High back (rounded) |

Standard (American) English (SAE), the "region-free" dialect of TV network newscasters, has about 35 phonemes—at least 11 vowels and 24 consonants. The number of phonemes varies from language to language—from 15 to 60, averaging between 30 and 40. The number of phonemes also varies between dialects of a given language. In North American English, for example, vowel phonemes vary noticeably from dialect to dialect. Readers should pronounce the words in Figure 10.1, paying attention to (or asking someone else) whether they distinguish each of the vowel sounds. Most North Americans don't pronounce them all.

My grandson Lucas thinks it's funny that I make a phonemic distinction he doesn't make. I pronounce words beginning with *wh* as though they began with *hw.* My personal set of phonemes includes both /hw/ and /w/. This enables me to distinguish between *white* and *Wight* (as in the Isle of Wight) and between *where* and *wear.* Lucas pronounces all four of those words as though they begin with [w], so that he does not distinguish between *white* and *Wight* or between *where* and *wear.* How about you?

**Phonetics** is the study of speech sounds in general, what people actually say in various languages or dialects (see the "Sociolinguistics" section of this chapter). **Phonemics** studies only the *significant* sound contrasts (phonemes) of a given language. In English, like /r/ and /l/ (remember *craw* and *claw*), /b/ and /v/ also are phonemes, occurring in minimal pairs like *bat* and *vat.* In Spanish, however, the contrast between [b] and [v] doesn't distinguish meaning, and they therefore are not phonemes (we enclose sounds that are not phonemic in brackets). Spanish speakers normally use the [b] sound to pronounce words spelled with either *b* or *v.*

In any language, a given phoneme extends over a phonetic range. In English the phoneme /p/ ignores the phonetic contrast between the [pʰ] in *pin* and the [p] in *spin.* Most English speakers don't even notice that there is a phonetic difference. The [pʰ] is aspirated, so that a puff of air follows the [p]. The [p] in *spin* is not. (To see the difference, light a match, hold it in front of your mouth, and watch the flame as you pronounce the two words.) The contrast between [pʰ] and [p] *is* phonemic in some languages, such as Hindi (spoken in India). That is, there are words whose meaning is distinguished only by the contrast between an aspirated and an unaspirated [p].

Native speakers vary in their pronunciation of certain phonemes, such as the /e/ phoneme in the midwestern United States. This variation is important in the evolution of language. Without shifts in pronunciation, there could be no linguistic change. The "Sociolinguistics" section later in this chapter considers phonetic variation and its relationship to social differences and the evolution of language.

## Language, Thought, and Culture

The well-known linguist Noam Chomsky (1957, 2014) has argued that the human brain contains a limited set of rules for organizing language, so that all languages have a common structural basis. (Chomsky calls this set of rules *universal grammar*.) That people can learn foreign languages and that words and ideas translate from one language to another support Chomsky's position that all humans have similar linguistic abilities and thought processes. Another line of support comes from creole languages. Such languages develop from *pidgins*, which form during acculturation, when different societies come into contact and must devise a system of communication (see Lim and Ansaldo 2016; Velupillai 2015). After generations of being spoken, pidgins may develop into *creole* languages, which have fully developed grammatical rules and native speakers (people who learn the language as their primary one during enculturation).

Creoles are spoken in several Caribbean societies. Gullah, which is spoken by African Americans on coastal islands in South Carolina and Georgia, is a creole language. Supporting the idea that creoles are based on universal grammar is the fact that such languages all share certain features. Syntactically, all use particles (e.g., *will, was*) to form future and past tenses and multiple negation to deny or negate (e.g., "she don't got none"). Also, all form questions by changing inflection rather than by changing word order—for example, "You're going home for the holidays?" (with a rising tone at the end) rather than "Are you going home for the holidays?"

### The Sapir-Whorf Hypothesis

Other linguists and anthropologists take a different approach to the relation between language and thought. Rather than seeking universal linguistic structures and processes, they believe that different languages produce different ways of thinking. This position sometimes is known as the **Sapir-Whorf hypothesis** after Edward Sapir (1931) and his student Benjamin Lee Whorf (1956), its prominent early advocates. Sapir and Whorf argued that the grammatical categories of different languages lead their speakers to think about things in particular ways. For example, English divides time (tenses) into past, present, and future. Hopi, a language of the Pueblo region of the Native American Southwest, does not. Rather, Hopi distinguishes between events that exist or have existed (what we use present and past to discuss) and those that don't or don't yet (our future events, along with imaginary and hypothetical events). Whorf argued that this difference leads Hopi speakers to think about time and reality in different ways than English speakers do.

Clark Tenakhongva, who was (or is) a candidate to be Hopi tribal chairman, spoke (or speaks) to an audience member during a forum in Flagstaff, Arizona. The Hopi language would not distinguish between *was* and *is* or *spoke* and *speaks* in the previous sentence. For the Hopi, present and past are real and are expressed grammatically in the same way, while the future remains hypothetical and has a different grammatical expression. Felicia Fonseca/AP Images

A similar example comes from Portuguese, which employs a future subjunctive verb form, introducing a degree of uncertainty into discussions of the future. In English we routinely use the future tense to talk about something we think will happen. We don't hesitate to proclaim "I'll see you next summer," even when we can't be absolutely sure we will. The Portuguese future subjunctive qualifies the future event, recognizing that the future can't be certain. Our way of expressing the future as certain is so ingrained that we don't even think about it, just as the Hopi don't see the need to distinguish between present and past, both of which are real, while the future remains hypothetical. Contrary to Sapir-Whorf, however, it would seem that language does not tightly restrict thought, because cultural changes can produce changes in thought and in language, as we shall see in the next section (see McWhorter 2014).

## Focal Vocabulary

A lexicon (vocabulary) is a language's dictionary, its set of names for things, events, and ideas. Lexicon influences perception. Thus, Eskimos (Inuit) have several distinct words for different types of snow that in English are all called *snow*. Eskimos recognize and think about differences in snow that English speakers don't see because our language gives us just one word.

Similarly, the Nuer of South Sudan developed an elaborate vocabulary to describe cattle. Eskimos have several words for snow and Nuer have dozens for cattle because of their particular histories, economies, and environments (Robson 2013). When the need arises, English speakers can also elaborate their snow and cattle vocabularies. For example, skiers describe types of snow with words that are missing from the lexicons of Florida retirees. Similarly, the cattle vocabulary of a Texas rancher is much more ample than that of a salesperson in a New York City department store. Such specialized sets of terms and distinctions that are particularly important to certain groups (those with particular *foci* of experience or activity) are known as **focal vocabulary**.

Vocabulary is the area of language that changes most readily. New words and distinctions, when needed, appear and spread. For example, who would have "texted" or "emailed" anything 40 years ago? Names for items get simpler as they become common and important. A television has become a *TV*, an automobile a *car*, and an application for a smartphone an *app* (see this chapter's "Anthropology Today" for a discussion of recent changes in word use in English).

Language, culture, and thought are certainly interrelated. In opposition to Sapir-Whorf, however, it is probably more accurate to say that changes in *culture* produce changes in language and thought than to say the reverse. Consider differences in the color terms used by American men and women (Lakoff 2004, 2017). Distinctions implied by such terms as *salmon, rust, peach, beige, teal, mauve, cranberry,* and *dusky orange* aren't in the vocabularies of most American men. However, many of them weren't even in American women's lexicons 70 years ago. Color terms and distinctions have increased with the growth of the fashion and cosmetic industries. Thus, cultural contrasts and changes affect lexical distinctions (for instance, *peach* versus *salmon*) within semantic domains (for instance, color terminology). **Semantics** refers to a language's meaning system.

The ways in which people divide the world—the lexical contrasts they perceive as meaningful or significant—reflect their experiences. Anthropologists have discovered that certain sets of vocabulary items evolve in a determined order. For example, after studying more than 100 languages, Berlin and Kay (1969/1992) discovered 10 basic color terms: *white, black, red, yellow, blue, green, brown, pink, orange,* and *purple* (they evolved in more or less that order). The number of terms varied with cultural complexity. Representing one extreme were Papua New Guinea cultivators and Australian hunters and gatherers, who used only two basic terms, which translate as *black* and *white* or *dark* and *light*. At the other end of the continuum were European and Asian languages with all the color terms. Color terminology was most developed in areas with a history of using dyes and artificial coloring.

# Sociolinguistics

## Social and Linguistic Variation

Is there anything distinctive or unusual about the way you talk? If you're from Canada, Virginia, or Savannah, you may say "oot" instead of "out." A southerner might request a "soft drink" rather than a New Yorker's "soda" or someone else's "pop." Can you imagine how a "Valley Girl" or "surfer dude" might talk? Usually when we pay attention to how we talk, it's because someone comments on our speech. It may be only when students move from one state or region to another that they realize how much of a regional accent they have. I moved as a teenager from Atlanta to New York City. Previously I hadn't realized I had a southern accent, but the guardians of linguistic correctness in my new high school did. They put me in a speech class, pointing out linguistic flaws I never knew I had. One was my "dull *s*," particularly in terminal consonant clusters, as in the words *tusks* and *breakfasts*. Apparently I didn't pronounce all three consonants at the ends of those words. Later it occurred to me that these weren't words I used very often. As far as I know, I've never had a conversation about tusks or proclaimed, "I ate seven breakfasts last week."

We all have stereotypes about how people in other regions talk. Some stereotypes, spread by the media, are more generalized than others. Most Americans think they can imitate a "Southern accent." We also stereotype speech in Boston ("I pahked the kah in Hahvahd Yahd") and Canada ("oot" for "out"). Although many people assume, erroneously, that midwesterners don't have accents, people from that region do exhibit significant linguistic variation (see Eckert 1989, 2000). One of the best examples is pronunciation of the *e* vowel sound (called the /e/ phoneme), in such words as *ten, rent, section, lecture, effect, best,* and *test.* In southeastern Michigan, there are four different ways of pronouncing this *e* sound. African Americans and immigrants from Appalachia often pronounce *ten* as "tin," just as Southerners habitually do. Some Michiganders say "ten," the correct pronunciation in Standard English. However, two other pronunciations also are common. Instead of "ten," many Michiganders say "tan" or "tun" (as though they were using the word *ton,* a unit of weight).

I remember, for example, how one of my Michigan-raised teaching assistants appeared deliriously happy one afternoon. When I asked why, she replied, "I've just had the best suction." "What?" I asked, and she replied more precisely. "I've just had the best saction." She considered this a clearer pronunciation of the word *section.* Another TA complimented me, "You luctured to great effuct today." After an exam, a student lamented that she had not done her "bust on the tust" (i.e., "best on the test"). The truth is, regional patterns affect the way we all speak.

Unlike grammarians, linguists and anthropologists are interested in what people do say, rather than what they should say. No language is a uniform system in which everyone talks just like everyone else. The field of **sociolinguistics** investigates relationships between social and linguistic variation (Eckert 2018; Meyerhoff 2018; Simpson 2019; Wardhaugh and Fuller 2015). How do linguistic features correlate with social diversity and stratification, including class, ethnic, and gender differences (Coates 2016; Eckert and McConnell-Ginet 2013)? How is language used to express, reinforce, or resist power (Fairclough 2015; Mooney and Evans 2019; Simpson, Mayer and Statham 2018)? How does language vary in the context of new media (Danesi 2019)? To study variation, sociolinguists must observe, define, and measure variable use of language and speakers in real-world situations.

## The Language of Restaurant Food

*Upscale and Downscale Menus*

In his book *The Language of Food,* linguist Dan Jurafsky (2014) describes some of his studies of sociolinguistic variation as it relates to restaurant food. Jurafsky and his colleagues analyzed the menus of 6,500 contemporary American restaurants. One of their goals was to see how the food vocabularies of upscale restaurants differed from those of cheaper establishments. One key difference they found was that upscale restaurants were much more likely to include on their menus the sources of the foods they served. They

named specific farms, gardens, ranches, pastures, woodlands, and farmers' markets. They were careful to mention, if the season was right, that their tomatoes or peas were heirloom varieties. Very expensive restaurants mentioned the origin of food more than 15 times as often as inexpensive restaurants.

Word length was another differentiator. Menu words averaged half a letter longer in upscale restaurants than in the cheaper establishments. Cheaper eateries, for instance, were more likely to use *decaf,* rather than *decaffeinated,* and *sides* rather than *accompaniments.* Diners had to pay higher prices for those longer words: Every increase of one letter in the average length of words describing a dish meant an average increase of 18 cents in the price of that dish.

Cheaper restaurants were more apt to use linguistic fillers. These included positive but vague words like *delicious, tasty, mouthwatering,* and *flavorful,* or other positive, but impossible to measure, adjectives such as *terrific, wonderful, delightful,* and *sublime.* Each positive vague word for a dish in

Study these menus from two restaurants, one more upscale than the other. Note the use of names of farms (food origin) in one menu and the use of adjectives such as *delicious, fresh,* and *premium* in the other. Which menu is from the more upscale restaurant? (both): Mark Dierker/McGraw-Hill Education

a modest restaurant reduced its average price by 9 percent. Downscale restaurants also were more likely to assure their diners that their offerings were "fresh." Expensive restaurants expected their patrons to assume freshness, without having to say it. Next time you eat out, pay attention to these findings about "the language of food" (see also Karrebæk et al. 2018)

## Southwestern Spanglish

Linguist Jane Hill also examined restaurant menus as reflective of sociolinguistic differences. How is Spanish used on menus of restaurants serving Mexican-themed food in southern Arizona? Hill examined the online menus of every such restaurant south of the Gila River that had a web presence. In a lighthearted article titled "A Linguist Walks into a Mexican Restaurant," Hill (2017) described and explained the mixtures of Spanish and English she encountered.

She noted that many English-speaking Arizonans pepper their speech with occasional Spanish words like "adiós" and "gracias." They also use mock Spanish expressions like "no problemo," "el cheapo," and "bad hombre." Such Spanishisms help them assert their regional identity. "Knowing a little Spanish" might also make them appear a little bit cosmopolitan (but not too much). Ironically, many of these same people view real Spanish as a threat to "America." Some get angry when they hear Spanish spoken in public, or see signs in Spanish, when "English is our national language."

To accommodate such attitudes, menus in Mexican-themed restaurants perform a delicate balancing act. They use just enough Spanish to make the restaurant seem authentic, but not so much as to threaten their nativist customers. They toss in a few small or familiar Spanish words, as in "Green Corn Tamale y Cheese Enchilada" or "deliciously grande." (All examples come from real menus.) It helps if bigger Spanish words look like English words, as in "Elegante style." "Mucho" is good, because it's just English with an *o* tacked on. Mock Spanish is okay, too, as in "Burrito Loco," "Macho Burrito," "Gordo Burrito," and the "Smoky Señorita" cocktail. Hill's study shows how restaurant menus manage a treacherous linguistic environment.

## Linguistic Diversity within Nations

As an illustration of the linguistic variation encountered in all nations, consider the contemporary United States. Ethnic diversity is revealed by the fact that millions of Americans learn first languages other than English. Spanish is the most common. Many of those people eventually become bilingual, adding English as a second language. In many multilingual (including colonized) nations, people use two or more languages on different occasions—one in the home, for example, and the other on the job or in public. In India, where some 22 languages are spoken, a person may need to use three different languages when talking, respectively, with a boss, a spouse, and a parent. Only about one-tenth of India's population speaks English, the colonial language. As they interact today with one of the key instruments of globalization—the Internet—even those English speakers appreciate being able to read, and to find Internet content in, their own regional languages.

Whether bilingual or not, we all vary our speech in different contexts; we engage in **style shifts**. In 2013, I traveled to India with a friend, an India-born American who speaks perfectly good Standard American English (SAE). During the time we spent in India, it was fascinating to watch as he shifted back and forth between Hindi, English with a strong Indian accent (when speaking to Indians in English), and SAE (when speaking to his American fellow travelers).

In certain parts of Europe, people regularly switch dialects. This phenomenon, known as **diglossia**, applies to "high" and "low" variants of the same language, for example, in

Multilingualism on display. In this photo, taken in Los Angeles, the (non-English) languages in the "Vote Here" sign are in alphabetical order according to their English names: Chinese, Hindi, Japanese, Khmer, Korean, Spanish, Tagalog, Thai, and Vietnamese. Monica Almeida/*The New York Times*/Redux Pictures

German and Dutch. People employ the high variant at universities and in writing, professions, and the mass media. They use the low variant for ordinary conversation with family members and friends.

Just as social situations influence our speech, so do geographic, cultural, and socioeconomic differences. Many dialects coexist in the United States with SAE, which itself is a dialect that differs from, say, "BBC English," the preferred dialect in Great Britain. Different dialects are equally effective as systems of communication, which is the main job of language. Our tendency to think of particular dialects as cruder or more sophisticated than others is a social rather than a linguistic judgment. We rank certain speech patterns as better or worse because we recognize that they are used by groups that we also rank. People who say *dese, dem,* and *dere* instead of *these, them,* and *there* communicate perfectly well with anyone who recognizes that the *d* sound systematically replaces the *th* sound in their speech. However, this form of speech has become an indicator of low social rank. We call it, like the use of *ain't,* "uneducated speech." The use of *dese, dem,* and *dere* is one of many phonological differences that Americans recognize and look down on (see Labov 2012).

## Linguistic Diversity in California

Popular stereotypes about how Californians talk reflect media images of White, blonde, Valley girls and White, blond surfers, who say things like "dude," "gnarly," and "Like, totally!" These stereotypes have some accuracy. Among coastal California Whites, a distinctive "Valley girl accent" has been developing since the 1940s. That accent is most evident in vowels. For example, the vowels in *hock* and *hawk,* or *cot* and *caught,* are pronounced the same, so that *awesome* rhymes with *possum.* Second, the vowel sound in *boot* and *dude* has shifted and now is pronounced as in *cute* or *pure* (thus, *boot* becomes "beaut," and *dude* becomes "dewed," rather than "dood") (see Eckert and Mendoza-Denton 2002).

To document this diversity, annually since 2009, Professor Penelope Eckert, a sociolinguist at Stanford University, and her graduate students are engaged in an ongoing research project called Voices of California (see http://www.stanford.edu/dept/linguistics/VoCal/). A team of 10–15 researchers visits a new site each fall, spending about 10 days interviewing about 100 residents who grew up in the area. Much of their research has been done in inland California, which has been less studied than have the main coastal cities. The researchers always test certain words that elicit specific pronunciations. These words include *wash,* sometimes pronounced "warsh," *greasy* ("greezy"), and *pin* and *pen,* which some people pronounce the same. Interviews in Merced and Shasta Counties have revealed ways that Depression-era migrants from Oklahoma's Dust Bowl left their mark on California speech, such as their pronunciation of *wash* and *greasy* (see King 2012).

Another factor contributing to diversity is how people feel about their home community versus the outside world. In California's Central Valley, which is economically depressed, young people must choose whether to stay put or move elsewhere. When people want to stay involved in their home community, they tend to talk like locals. A desire *not* to be perceived as being from a particular place can motivate people to change their speech (King 2012).

## Gender Speech Contrasts

Men and women talk differently (see Coates 2016). I'm sure you can think of examples based on your own experience, although you probably never realized that women tend to peripheralize their vowels (think of the sounds in *weasel* and *whee*), whereas men tend to centralize them (think of *rough* and *ugh*). Men are more likely to speak "ungrammatically" than women are. In their sports vocabularies, men typically know more terms, make more distinctions among them (e.g., *runs* versus *points*), and try to use the terms more precisely than women do. Correspondingly, women use more color terms and attempt to use them more specifically than men do. To make this point when I lecture, I bring an off-purple shirt to class. Holding it up, I first ask women to say aloud what color the shirt is. The women rarely answer with a uniform voice, as they try to distinguish the actual shade (mauve, lilac, lavender, wisteria, or some other purplish hue). I then ask the men, who consistently answer as one, "PURPLE."

According to Robin Lakoff (2004, 2017), the use of certain types of words and expressions has been associated with women's traditional lesser power in American society. For example, *Oh dear, Oh fudge,* and *Goodness!* are less forceful than *Hell* and *Damn.* Watch the lips of a disgruntled athlete in a televised competition, such as a football game. What's the likelihood he's saying "Phooey on you"? Women are more likely to use such adjectives as *adorable, charming, sweet, cute, lovely,* and *divine* than men are. A man may be called out for "mansplaining" when he attempts to "enlighten" a woman about a domain in which he assumes he has superior knowledge. Is there any linguistic practice that might be called "womansplaining"?

Differences in the linguistic strategies and behavior of men and women are examined in several books by the well-known sociolinguist Deborah Tannen (1990, 2017). Tannen uses the terms *rapport* and *report* to contrast women's and men's overall linguistic styles. Women, says Tannen, typically use language and the body movements that accompany it to build rapport, social connections with others. Men, on the other hand, tend to make reports, reciting information to establish a place for themselves in a hierarchy, as they also attempt to determine the relative ranks of their conversation mates.

## Stratification and Symbolic Domination

We use and evaluate speech in the context of *extralinguistic* forces—social, political, and economic. Mainstream Americans evaluate the speech of low-status groups negatively, calling it "uneducated." This is not because these ways of speaking are bad in themselves but because they have come to symbolize low status. Consider variation in the pronunciation of *r*. In some parts of the United States, *r* is regularly pronounced, and in other (*r*less) areas it is not. Originally, American *r*less speech was modeled on the fashionable speech of England. Because of its prestige, *r*lessness was adopted in many areas and continues as the norm around Boston and in the South.

New Yorkers sought prestige by dropping their *r*'s in the 19th century, after having pronounced them in the 18th. However, contemporary New Yorkers are going back to the 18th-century pattern of pronouncing *r*'s. What matters, and what governs linguistic change, is not the reverberation of a strong midwestern *r* but *social* evaluation, whether *r*'s happen to be "in" or "out."

Studies of *r* pronunciation in New York City have clarified the mechanisms of phonological change. William Labov (1972b) focused on whether *r* was pronounced after vowels in such words as *car, floor, card,* and *fourth.* To get data on how this linguistic variation correlated with social class, he used a series of rapid encounters with employees in three New York City department stores, each of which had prices and locations that attracted a different socioeconomic group. Saks Fifth Avenue (68 encounters) catered to the upper middle class, Macy's (125) attracted middle-class shoppers, and S. Klein's (71) had predominantly lower-middle-class and working-class customers. The class origins of store personnel reflected those of their customers.

Having already determined that a certain department was on the fourth floor, Labov approached ground-floor salespeople and asked where that department was. After the salesperson had answered, "Fourth floor," Labov repeated his "Where?" in order to get a second response. The second reply was more considered and emphatic, the salesperson presumably thinking that Labov hadn't heard or understood the first answer. For each salesperson, therefore, Labov had two samples of *r* pronunciation in two words.

Labov calculated the percentages of workers who pronounced *r* at least once during the interview. These were 62 percent at Saks, 51 percent at Macy's, but only 20 percent at S. Klein's. He also found that personnel on upper floors, where he asked, "What floor is this?" (and where more expensive items were sold), pronounced *r* more often than ground-floor salespeople did (see also Labov 2006).

In Labov's study, *r* pronunciation was clearly associated with prestige. Certainly the job interviewers who had hired the salespeople never counted *r*'s before offering employment. However, they did use speech evaluations to make judgments about how effective certain people would be in selling particular kinds of merchandise. In other words, they practiced sociolinguistic discrimination, using linguistic features in deciding who got certain jobs.

Our speech habits help determine our access to employment and other material resources. Because of this, "proper language" itself becomes a strategic resource—and a path to wealth, prestige, and power. Illustrating this, many ethnographers have described the importance of verbal skill and oratory in politics (Lakoff 2008; Lakoff and Wehling 2012). Ronald Reagan, known as a "great communicator," dominated American society in the 1980s as a two-term president. Another twice-elected president, Bill Clinton, despite his Arkansas accent, was known for his verbal skills in certain contexts (e.g., televised debates and town-hall meetings). Communications flaws may have helped doom the presidencies of Gerald Ford, Jimmy Carter, and George Bush the elder.

The speech habits of the 45th U.S. president, Donald J. Trump, have attracted the attention of linguistics. George Lakoff and Gil Duran, in a 2018 article, analyze how "Trump Has Turned Words into Weapons. And He's Winning the Linguistic War." In another 2018 article titled "The Unmonitored President," linguist John McWhorter points out that Trump is the first U.S. president who consistently eschews traditional presidential formal speech and instead just gets up and talks.

The French anthropologist Pierre Bourdieu views linguistic practices as *symbolic capital* that properly trained people may convert into economic and social capital. The value of a dialect—its standing in a "linguistic market"—depends on the extent to which it provides access to desired positions. In turn, this reflects its legitimation by formal institutions—educational institutions, state, church, and prestige media. Even people who don't use the prestige dialect accept its authority and correctness, its "symbolic domination" (Bourdieu 1982, 1984; Labov 2012). Thus, linguistic forms, which lack power in themselves, take on the power of the groups they symbolize (see Mooney and Evans 2019). The education

Certain dialects are stigmatized, not because of actual linguistic deficiencies, but because of a symbolic association between a certain way of talking and low social status. In this scene from the movie *My Fair Lady,* Professor Henry Higgins (Rex Harrison) teaches Eliza Doolittle (Audrey Hepburn), formerly a Cockney flower girl, how to speak "proper English." Warner Brothers/Album/Newscom

system, however (defending its own worth), denies linguistic relativity. It misrepresents prestige speech as being inherently better. The linguistic insecurity often felt by lower-class and minority speakers is a result of this symbolic domination.

## African American Vernacular English (AAVE)

The sociolinguist William Labov (1972a) and several associates, both White and Black, have conducted detailed studies of what they call **African American Vernacular English (AAVE)**. (*Vernacular* means ordinary, casual speech.) AAVE is actually a complex linguistic system with its own rules, which linguists have described. Consider some of the phonological and grammatical differences between AAVE and SAE. One phonological difference is that AAVE speakers are less likely to pronounce *r* than SAE speakers are. Actually, many SAE speakers don't pronounce *r*'s that come right before a consonant (ca*r*d) or at the end of a word (ca*r*). But SAE speakers usually do pronounce an *r* that comes right before a vowel, either at the end of a word (fou*r* o'clock) or within a word (Ca*r*ol). AAVE speakers, by contrast, are much more likely to omit such intervocalic (between vowels) *r*'s. The result is that speakers of the two dialects have different *homonyms* (words that sound the same but have different meanings). AAVE speakers who don't pronounce intervocalic *r*'s have the following homonyms: *Carol/Cal*; *Paris/pass.*

Phonological rules also may lead AAVE speakers to omit *-ed* as a past-tense marker and *-s* as a marker of plurality. However, other speech contexts demonstrate that AAVE speakers do understand the difference between past- and present-tense verbs, and between singular and plural nouns. Confirming this are irregular verbs (e.g., *tell, told*) and irregular plurals (e.g., *child, children*), in which AAVE works the same as SE.

SAE is not superior to AAVE as a linguistic system, but it does happen to be the prestige dialect—the one used in the mass media, in writing, and in most public and professional contexts. SAE is the dialect that has the most "symbolic capital." In areas of Germany where there is diglossia, speakers of Plattdeusch (Low German) learn the High German dialect (originally spoken in the highlands of southern Germany) to communicate appropriately in the national context. High German is the standard literary and spoken form of German. Similarly, upwardly mobile AAVE-speaking students learn SAE.

## Historical Linguistics

Sociolinguists study contemporary variation in speech, which is language change in progress. **Historical linguistics** deals with longer-term change (see Burridge and Bergs 2017). Historical linguists can reconstruct many features of past languages by studying contemporary **daughter languages**. These are languages that descend from the same parent language and that have been changing separately for hundreds or even thousands of years. We call the original language from which they diverge the **protolanguage**. Romance languages such as French and Spanish, for example, are daughter languages of Latin, their common protolanguage. German, English, Dutch, and the Scandinavian languages are daughter languages of proto-Germanic. The Romance languages and the Germanic languages all belong to the Indo-European (IE) language family. Proto-Indo-European (PIE), spoken in the more distant past, was the common protolanguage of Latin, proto-Germanic, and many other ancient languages (see Figure 10.2).

When did PIE originate, and how did it spread? Decades ago, archaeologist Colin Renfrew (1987) traced the origin of PIE to a farming population living in Anatolia, in what is now Turkey, about 9,000 years ago. More recent studies by the evolutionary biologist Quentin Atkinson and his colleagues in New Zealand support this Anatolian origin of PIE (see Bouckaert et al. 2012). Atkinson's team focused on a set of vocabulary items known to be resistant to linguistic change. These include pronouns, parts of the body, and family relations. For 103 IE languages, the researchers compared those words with the PIE ancestral word (as reconstructed by historical linguists). Words that clearly descend from the same ancestral word are known as *cognates*. For example, *mother* (English) is a cognate with all these words for the same relative: *mutter* (German), *mat* (Russian), *madar* (Persian), *matka* (Polish), and *mater* (Latin). All are descendants of the PIE word *mehter*.

For each language, when the word was a cognate, the researchers scored it 1; when it was not (having been replaced by an unrelated word), it was scored 0. With each language represented by a string of 1s and 0s, the researchers could establish a family tree showing the relationships among the 103 languages. Based on those relationships and the geographic areas where the daughter languages are spoken, the computer determined the likeliest routes of movement from an origin. The calculation pointed to Anatolia, southern Turkey. This is precisely the region originally proposed by Renfrew, because it was the

## FIGURE 10.2   PIE Family Tree

Main languages and subgroups of the Indo-European language stock, showing approximate time to their divergence.

McGraw-Hill Education

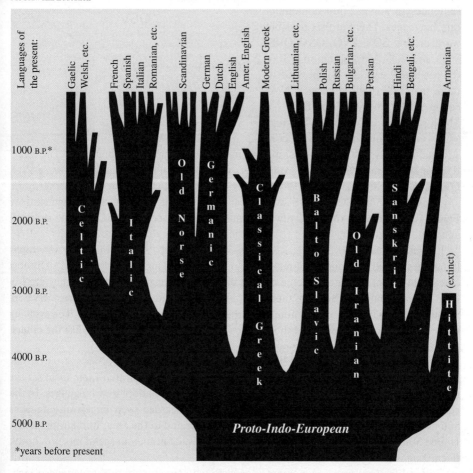

*years before present

area from which farming spread to Europe. Atkinson also ran a computer simulation on a grammar-based IE tree—once again finding Anatolia to be the most likely origin point for PIE (Wade 2012). Several lines of biological and archaeological evidence now indicate that the Neolithic economy spread more through the actual migration of farmers than through the diffusion of crops and ideas. This would seem to offer support to the Renfrew-Atkinson model of PIE origin and dispersal of Neolithic farmers.

Historically oriented linguists suspect that a very early protolanguage, spoken perhaps 50,000 years ago in Africa, gave rise to all contemporary languages. Murray Gell-Mann and Merritt Ruhlen (2011), who co-direct the Evolution of Human Languages project at the Sante Fe Institute, have reconstructed the syntax (word ordering) of this ancient protolanguage (see http://ehl.santafe. edu/intro1.htm). Their study focused on how subject (S), objects (O), and verbs (V) are arranged in phrases and sentences in some 2,000 contemporary languages. There are six possible word orders: SOV, SVO, OSV, OVS, VSO, and VOS. Most common is SOV ("I you like," e.g., Latin), present in more than half of all languages. Next comes SVO ("I like you," e.g., English). Much rarer are OSV, OVS, VSO, and VOS. Gell-Mann and Ruhlen con-

**FIGURE 10.3   Evolution of Word Order from Original SOV (Subject, Object, Verb) in Ancient Ancestral Protolanguage**

McGraw-Hill Education

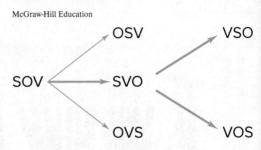

structed a family tree of relationships among 2,000 contemporary languages. The directions of change involving the six word orders were clear. All the languages that were SVO, OVS, and OSV derived from SOV languages—never the other way around. Furthermore, any language with VSO or VOS word order always came from an SVO language (see Figure 10.3). The fact that SVO always comes from SOV confirms SOV as the original, ancestral word order.

Language changes over time. It evolves—varies, spreads, and divides into **subgroups** (languages within a taxonomy of related languages that are most closely related). Dialects of a single parent language become distinct daughter languages, especially if they are isolated from one another. Some of them split, and new "granddaughter" languages develop. If people remain in the ancestral homeland, their speech patterns also change. The evolving speech in the ancestral homeland should be considered a daughter language like the others.

## Language, Culture, and History

A close relationship between languages doesn't necessarily mean that their speakers are closely related biologically or culturally, because people can adopt new languages. In the equatorial forests of Africa, "pygmy" hunters have discarded their ancestral languages and now speak those of the cultivators who have migrated to the area. Immigrants to the United States spoke many different languages on arrival, but their descendants now speak fluent English.

Cultural features may (or may not) correlate with the distribution of language families. Groups that speak related languages may (or may not) be more culturally similar to each other than they are to groups whose speech derives from different linguistic ancestors. Of course, cultural similarities aren't limited to speakers of related languages. Even groups whose members speak unrelated languages have contact through trade, intermarriage, and warfare. Many items of vocabulary in contemporary English, particularly food items such as "beef" and "pork," come from French. Even without written documentation of France's influence after the Norman Conquest of England in 1066, linguistic evidence in contemporary English would reveal a long period of important firsthand contact with France. Similarly, linguistic evidence may confirm cultural contact and borrowing when written history is lacking. By considering which words have been borrowed, we also can make inferences about the nature of the contact.

## Language Loss

One aspect of linguistic history is language loss. According to linguist K. David Harrison, "When we lose a language, we lose centuries of thinking about time, . . . seasons, mathematics, landscapes, myths, music, the unknown and the everyday" (quoted in Maugh 2007). Harrison's book *When Languages Die* (2007) notes that the world's linguistic diversity has been cut in half (measured by number of distinct languages) in the past 500 years, and half of the remaining languages are predicted to disappear during this century. Colonial languages (e.g., English, Spanish, Portuguese, French, Dutch, Russian) have expanded at the expense of indigenous ones. Of approximately 7,000 remaining languages, about 20 percent are endangered, compared with 18 percent of mammals, 8 percent of plants, and 5 percent of birds (Harrison 2010; Maugh 2007).

*National Geographic*'s Enduring Voices Project (https://www.nationalgeographic.org/projects/enduring-voices/) strives to preserve endangered languages by identifying the geographic areas with unique, poorly understood, or threatened languages and by documenting those languages and cultures. The website shows various language hot spots where the endangerment rate ranges from low to severe. The rate is high in an area encompassing Oklahoma, Texas, and New Mexico, where 40 Native American languages are at risk. The top hot spot is northern Australia, where 153 Aboriginal languages are endangered (Maugh 2007). Other hot spots are in central South America, the Pacific Northwest of North America, and eastern Siberia. In all these areas, indigenous tongues have yielded, either voluntarily or through coercion, to a colonial language (see Harrison 2010).

One way of preserving indigenous languages is through translation. Here, in September 2016, the Spanish anthropologist Bartomeu Melia displays his translation into Guarani (Paraguay's principal indigenous language) of Cervantes' *Don Quixote*. This translation is intended to reach young people in rural areas of Paraguay. Noberto Duarte/AFP/Getty Images

## Anthropology Today   *Words of the Year*

Annual lists of "words of the year" provide an excellent illustration of how vocabulary shifts in response to cultural changes. Organizations in various countries routinely publish such lists, from which one increasingly common word or phrase is generally chosen as the winner—the "word of the year." Table 10.2 lists the word of the year chosen by the American Dialect Society for every year between 2000 (*chad*) and 2018 (*tender-age shelter*). The list tells us a lot about recent American history, especially the concerns that have dominated the news and public discourse from year to year. For instance, we see how certain key words—often just one word or phrase—can sum up the presidential elections of 2000 (*chad*), 2004 (*red state, blue state, purple state*), and 2016 (*dumpster fire*). National crises of 2001, 2002, 2007, and 2008 are encapsulated respectively by *9-11, weapons of mass destruction, subprime,* and *bailout.* Years of protest show up in *occupy* (2011) and *#blacklivesmatter* (2014). *Tweet* (2009), *app* (2010), and *hashtag* (2012) summarize changes in technology and communication. Sometimes, the words are more playful, like *metrosexual* (2003), *truthiness* (2005), and *plutoed* (2006)—this last word coined from the demotion of our former ninth planet.

In less exciting years, the Dialect Society may single out a common word that is being used in a new way. In 2015, for example, several organizations chose the singular form of the common pronoun *they* as word of the year (Baron 2015). *They* is a third-person pronoun that is gender neutral; it includes males and females. Although grammatically *they* is a plural pronoun, it also is used informally in speech and writing as a singular pronoun. Someone can use *they* when they want to avoid having to use "he or she" in a sentence—as I just did. Historical documents show that *they* has been used as a singular pronoun for over 600 years (Baron 2015). The popularity of the singular *they* has been growing recently because it fills an important linguistic niche—the need for a gender-neutral third-person singular pronoun.

The word *they* itself was introduced into the English language by Danish immigrants in the ninth century. It gradually replaced the then-existing English third-person plural pronoun. For centuries thereafter, English writers and speakers commonly used both the singular and the plural *they.* Its use as a singular pronoun began to meet resistance around 1800. Grammarians discouraged the use of the singular *they* because of lack of agreement between an apparently plural pronoun and a singular verb (e.g., "They eats dinner."). Those grammatical purists who continue to resist the singular *they* might be reminded that the singular pronoun *you* in English began as a plural pronoun, which eventually replaced *thou* and *thee* as a singular pronoun. According to various "word of the year" lists, the time has come for a similar shift to using *they* instead of the more unwieldy "he or she." If someone wants to do that, they won't get any flak from me.

The same year that the American Dialect Society named *they* as its word of the

The Face with Tears of Joy emoji—a recent "word" of the year. Have you ever used this, or a similar, emoji? MaxTaylors/Shutterstock

year, the Oxford Dictionaries bestowed that honor on the "Face with Tears of Joy" emoji (Oxford University Press 2015). An *emoji* is a digital image used to express an idea or emotion in electronic communication. Despite its similarity to the English word *emoticon* (coined from *emotion* and *icon*), the word *emoji* actually comes from Japanese. Emojis have been around since the late 1990s, but their use, and the use of the term *emoji* itself, have increased substantially. No doubt this reflects the growing availability of these pictographs on smartphones, tablets, computers, and other communication devices we use on a daily basis. According to a study done by Oxford University Press and the mobile technology company SwiftKey, the most popular emoji is the "Face with Tears of Joy" (Northover 2016). The growing role of digital transmission in our everyday lives, including reliance on emojis, illustrates once again how language and communication continue to evolve in our globalizing world.

## TABLE 10.2   Words of the Year, 2000–2018, as Chosen by the American Dialect Society

Source: Adapted from the Words of the Year website of the American Dialect Society. https://www.americandialect.org/woty.

2000: **chad** (from the "hanging chads" on several ballots cast in Florida in the 2000 U.S. presidential election)

2001: **9–11** (for obvious reasons)

2002: **weapons of mass destruction** (used by the George W. Bush administration as a pretense for invading Iraq)

2003: **metrosexual** (a fashion-conscious heterosexual male)

2004: **red state, blue state, purple state** (from the 2004 U.S. presidential election)

2005: **truthiness** (from *The Colbert Report*; preferring concepts or facts one wishes to be true, rather than concepts or facts known to be true)

2006: **plutoed** (demoted or devalued, like the former planet Pluto)

2007: **subprime** (a risky loan, mortgage, or investment)

2008: **bailout** (government rescue of a company on the brink of failure)

2009: **tweet** (a message sent via Twitter)

2010: **app** (short for *application,* as on a smartphone, now extended to any computer program)

2011: **occupy** (as in Occupy Wall Street)

2012: **hashtag** (a word or phrase preceded by a hash symbol, as on Twitter)

2013: **because** (when used to introduce a noun, adjective, or other part of speech, as in "because awesome")

2014: **#blacklivesmatter** (hashtag used to protest killings of African Americans by police)

2015: singular **they** (as a gender-neutral pronoun)

2016: **dumpster fire** (a disastrous or chaotic situation, representing the public discourse and preoccupations surrounding the 2016 U.S. presidential election)

2017: **fake news** (meaning either: [1] disinformation or falsehoods presented as real news or [2] actual news that is claimed to be untrue)

2018: **tender-age shelter** (also *tender-age facility* or *tender-age camp,* are terms used euphemistically to describe the government-run detention centers housing the children of asylum seekers at the U.S./Mexico border

## Summary

1. Wild primates use call systems to communicate. Contrasts between language and call systems include displacement, productivity, and cultural transmission. Over time, our ancestral call systems grew too complex for genetic transmission, and hominin communication began to rely on learning. Humans still use nonverbal communication, such as facial expressions, gestures, and body stances and movements. But language is the main system humans use to communicate. Chimps and gorillas can understand and manipulate nonverbal symbols based on language.

2. Phonology—the study of speech sounds—focuses on sound contrasts (phonemes) that distinguish meaning. Morphology studies how sounds combine to form morphemes—words and their meaningful parts. A language's lexicon is a dictionary containing all its morphemes and their meanings. Syntax refers to the arrangement and order of words in phrases and sentences. The grammar and lexicon of a language can influence how its speakers perceive and think about the world.

3. Linguistic anthropologists share anthropology's general interest in diversity in time and space. Sociolinguistics investigates relationships between social and linguistic variation by focusing on the actual use of language. Sociolinguists study how linguistic features correlate with social diversity and stratification, including class, ethnic, regional, and gender differences; and how language is used to gain, express, and reinforce power and symbolic capital. Only when features of speech acquire social meaning are they imitated. If they are valued, they will spread. People vary their speech, shifting styles, dialects, and languages.

4. As linguistic systems, all languages and dialects are equally complex, rule-governed, and effective for communication. However, speech is used, is evaluated, and changes in the context of political, economic, and social forces. Often the linguistic traits of a low-status group are negatively evaluated. This devaluation is not because of *linguistic* features per se. Rather, it reflects the association of such features with low *social* status. One dialect, supported by the dominant institutions of the state, exercises symbolic domination over the others.

5. One aspect of linguistic history is language loss. The world's linguistic diversity has been cut in half in the past 500 years, and half of the remaining 7,000 languages are predicted to disappear during this century.

## Think Like an Anthropologist

1. What dialects and languages do you speak? Do you tend to use different dialects, languages, or speech styles in different contexts? Why or why not?

2. Consider how changing technologies have affected how you communicate with family, friends, and even strangers. Suppose your best friend decides to study sociolinguistics in graduate school. What ideas about the relationship among changing technologies, language, and social relations could you suggest to him or her as worth studying?

**Key Terms**

# Chapter 11

# Making a Living

## Adaptive Strategies

Communities and societies throughout the world are being incorporated, at an accelerating rate, into larger systems (Caldararo 2014). The first major acceleration in the growth of human social systems can be traced back to 12,000–10,000 years ago, when humans started intervening in the reproductive cycles of plants and animals. **Food production** refers to human control over the reproduction of plants and animals, and it contrasts with the foraging economies that preceded it and that persist in some parts of the world. To make their living, foragers hunt, gather, and collect what nature has to offer. Foragers may harvest, but they don't plant. They may hunt animals, but (except for the dog) they don't domesticate them. Only food producers systematically select and breed for desirable traits in plants and animals. With the advent of food production, which includes plant cultivation and animal domestication, people, rather than nature, become selective agents.

The origin and spread of food production accelerated human population growth and led to the formation of larger and more powerful social and political systems. The pace of cultural transformation increased enormously. This chapter provides a framework for understanding a variety of human adaptive strategies and economic systems.

The anthropologist Yehudi Cohen (1974) used the term *adaptive strategy* to describe a society's main system of economic production. He argued that the most important reason for social and cultural similarities among unrelated societies is their possession of a similar adaptive strategy. In other words, similar economies have similar sociocultural characteristics. For example, there are clear similarities among societies that have a foraging (hunting and gathering) strategy. Cohen developed a classification or *typology* of societies based on correlations between their economies and their social features. His typology includes these five adaptive strategies: foraging, horticulture, agriculture, pastoralism, and industrialism. Industrialism is the focus of the last two chapters of this book. The present chapter focuses on the first four adaptive strategies, which are characteristic of nonindustrial societies.

## Foraging

**Foraging**—an economy and way of life based on hunting and gathering—was humans' only way of making a living until about 12,000 years ago, when people began experimenting with food production. To be sure, environmental differences created substantial contrasts among foragers living in different parts of the world (see Kelly 2013). Some, like the people who lived in Europe during the ice ages, were big-game hunters (see Lemke 2018). Today, foragers in the Arctic still focus on large animals. They also fish, but their diets are much less varied, with fewer plant foods, than those of tropical foragers.

Considering world geography, as one moves from colder to warmer areas, the number of species increases. The tropics contain tremendous biodiversity, and tropical foragers typically hunt and gather a wide range of plant and animal species. Some temperate areas also offer abundant and varied species. For example, on the North Pacific Coast of North America, foragers could draw on varied sea, river, and land species, such as salmon and other fish, sea mammals, mountain goats, and berries. Although their environments may differ, all foraging economies have shared one essential feature: People rely on nature to make their living. They don't grow crops or breed and tend animals.

Animal domestication (initially of sheep and goats) and plant cultivation (of wheat and barley) began 12,000 to 10,000 years ago in the Middle East. Cultivation based on different crops, such as corn (maize), manioc (cassava), and potatoes, arose independently in the Americas. In both hemispheres, most societies eventually turned from foraging to food production. Today most foragers have at least some dependence on food production or on food producers (Codding and Kramer 2016; Kent 1996).

Foraging economies survived into modern times in certain forests, deserts, islands, and very cold areas—places where cultivation was not practicable with simple technology (see Ikeya and Hitchcock 2016; Lee and Daly 1999). Figure 11.1 presents a partial

**FIGURE 11.1**   **Locations of Some Recent Hunter-Gatherers**

Robert L. Kelly, *The Foraging Spectrum: Diversity in Hunter-Gatherer Lifeways,* fig. 1.1. 2007 by Eliot Werner Publications, Inc.
Reprinted by permission of the publisher.

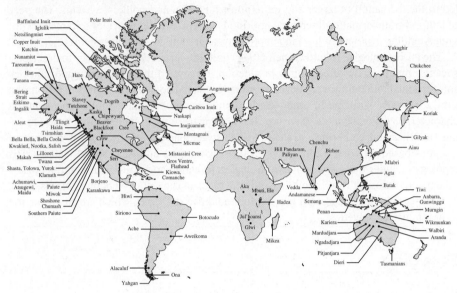

distribution of recent foragers. Their habitats tend to have one thing in common—their marginality. Posing major obstacles to food production, these environments did not attract farmers or herders. The difficulties of cultivating at the North Pole are obvious. In southern Africa, the Dobe Ju/'hoansi San area studied by Richard Lee and others is surrounded by a huge waterless belt (Solway and Lee 1990). Farming could not exist in much of California without irrigation, which is why its native populations were foragers.

We should not assume that foragers will inevitably turn to food production once they learn of its existence. In fact, foragers in many areas have been—and still are—in contact with farmers or herders but have chosen to maintain their hunter-gatherer lifestyle. Their traditional economy supports them well enough, lacks the greater labor requirements associated with farming and herding, and provides an adequate and nutritious diet. In some places, people have tried food production, only to abandon it eventually and return to foraging.

Today all foragers live in nation-states. Typically, they are in contact with food-producing neighbors as well as with missionaries and other outsiders. We should not view contemporary foragers as isolated or pristine survivors of the Stone Age. Modern foragers are influenced by national and international policies and political and economic events in the world system.

## Geographic Distribution of Foragers

It will be helpful to refer to Figure 11.1 throughout this section. Africa contains two broad belts of contemporary or recent foraging. One is the Kalahari Desert of southern Africa.

This is the home of the San ("Bushmen"), who include the Ju/'hoansi (Lee 2012, 2013). The other main African foraging area is the equatorial forest of central and eastern Africa, home of the Mbuti, Efe, and other "pygmies."

People still do, or until recently did, subsistence foraging in certain remote forests in Madagascar, in South and Southeast Asia, in Malaysia, in the Philippines, and on certain islands off the Indian coast (see Ikeya and Hitchcock 2016). In addition, some of the best-known recent foragers are the Aborigines of Australia. Those Native Australians lived on their island continent for perhaps 65,000 years without developing food production.

The Western Hemisphere also had recent foragers. The Eskimos, or Inuit, of Alaska and Canada are well-known hunters. These (and other) northern foragers now use modern technology, including rifles and snowmobiles, in their subsistence activities. The native populations of the North Pacific Coast of North America (northern California, Oregon, Washington, British Columbia, and southern Alaska) all were foragers, as were those of inland subarctic Canada and the Great Lakes. For many Native Americans, fishing, hunting, and gathering remain important subsistence (and sometimes commercial) activities. Considering South America, there were coastal foragers along that continent's southern tip, in Patagonia. Additional foragers inhabited the grassy plains of Argentina, southern Brazil, Uruguay, and Paraguay.

Jana Fortier (2009) summarizes key attributes of foragers in South Asia, which today is home to more full- and part-time hunter-gatherers than any other world area. In India, Nepal, and Sri Lanka, about 40 societies and an estimated 150,000 people continue to derive their subsistence from full- or part-time foraging. The Hill Kharia and the Yanadi are the largest contemporary South Asian foraging populations, with about 20,000 members each. Several other ethnic groups are highly endangered, with fewer than 350 members still engaging in subsistence foraging.

Surviving South Asian foraging societies are those whose members, despite having lost many of their natural resources to deforestation and spreading farming populations, have been unwilling to adopt food cultivation and its cultural correlates. These hunter-gatherers share features with other foragers worldwide: small social groups, mobile settlement patterns, sharing of resources, immediate food consumption, egalitarianism, and decision making by mutual consent (Fortier 2009; Widlock 2017).

As is true elsewhere, specific foraging techniques reflect variations in environment and resource distribution. Foragers living in the hills and mountains of South Asia focus their hunting on medium-sized prey (langur monkey, macaque, porcupine). Other groups pursue smaller species or practice broad-spectrum hunting of bats, porcupines, and deer. Larger groups use communal hunting techniques, such as spreading nets over large fig trees to entangle sleeping bats. Some South Indian foragers focus on wild plant resources such as yams, palms, and taro, in addition to more than 100 other locally available plants. Harvesting honey and beeswax has been prominent in many South Asian foraging societies (Fortier 2009).

Members of these societies cherish their identities as people who forage for a living in biologically rich and diverse environments. They stress their need for continued access to rich forest resources to continue their lifestyles, yet many have been evicted from their traditional habitats. Their best chances for cultural survival depend on national governments that maintain healthy forests, allow foragers access to their traditional resources, and foster cultural survival rather than assimilation (Fortier 2009).

Some governments have done quite the opposite. For example, between 1997 and 2002, the government of Botswana (in southern Africa) carried out a relocation scheme affecting about 3,000 Basarwa San Bushmen (Motseta 2006). The government forced these people to leave their ancestral territory, which became a wildlife reserve. After some of them sued, Botswana's High Court eventually ruled that the Basarwa had been wrongly evicted, and issued a court order allowing them to return, but under very restrictive conditions. Although 3,000 people had been moved out, only the 189 people who actually filed the lawsuit were granted an automatic right to return with their children. The many other Basarwa San who wanted to return to their ancestral territory would need to apply for special permits. Even the 189 favored people would be allowed to build only temporary structures and to use just enough water for subsistence needs. Water would be a major obstacle, because the government had shut down the main well. Furthermore, anyone wishing to hunt would have to apply for a permit. This case illustrates how contemporary governments can limit the independence of indigenous peoples and restrict their traditional lifestyle.

## Correlates of Foraging

Typologies, such as Cohen's adaptive strategies, are useful because they suggest **correlations**—that is, associations or covariations between two or more variables. (Correlated variables are factors that are linked and interrelated, such as food intake and body weight. When one increases or decreases, the other changes as well.) Ethnographic studies in hundreds of societies have revealed many correlations between the economy and social life. Associated (correlated) with each adaptive strategy is a bundle of sociocultural features. Correlations, however, rarely are perfect. Some foragers lack cultural features usually associated with foraging, and some of those features are found in groups with other adaptive strategies.

What are some correlates of foraging? Foragers often, but not always, lived in band-organized societies. Their basic social unit, the **band,** was a small group of fewer than a hundred people, all related by kinship or marriage. Among some foragers, band size stayed about the same year-round. In others, the band split up for part of the year. Families left to gather resources that were better exploited by just a few people. Later, they regrouped for cooperative work and ceremonies.

Typical characteristics of the foraging life are flexibility and mobility. In many San groups, as among the Mbuti of Congo, people shifted band membership several times in a lifetime. One could be born, for example, in a band in which one's mother had kin. Later, one's family could move to a band in which the father had relatives. Because bands were exogamous (people married outside their own bands), one's parents came from two different bands, and one's grandparents could have come from four. People could join any band to which they had kin or marital links. A couple could live in, or shift between, the husband's and the wife's bands.

Foraging societies tend to be *egalitarian.* That is, they make few status distinctions, and the ones they make are based mainly on age, gender, and personal qualities or achievements. For example, old people—elders—may receive respect as guardians of myths, legends, stories, and traditions. Younger people may value the elders' special knowledge of ritual and practical matters. A good hunter, an especially productive gatherer, or a skilled midwife or shaman may be recognized as such. But foragers are known for sharing rather than bragging. Their status distinctions are not associated with differences in wealth and power, nor are they inherited. When considering issues of "human nature," we should remember that the egalitarian society associated with foraging was a basic form of human social life for most of our history. Food production has existed less than 1 percent of the time *Homo* has spent on Earth. However, it has produced huge social differences. We now consider the main economic features of food-producing strategies.

# Adaptive Strategies Based on Food Production

The three adaptive strategies based on food production in nonindustrial societies are horticulture, agriculture, and pastoralism. With horticulture and agriculture, plant cultivation is the mainstay of the economy, whereas with pastoralism, herding is key. All three strategies originated in nonindustrial societies, although they may persist as ways of making a living even after some degree of industrialization reaches the nation-states that include them. In fully industrial societies, such as the United States and Canada, most cultivation has become large-scale, commercial, mechanized, agrochemical-dependent farming. Rather than simple pastoralism, industrial societies use technologically sophisticated systems of ranch and livestock management. These industrial societies, and their global context, are the focus of the last two chapters of this book. This chapter's focus is on the nonindustrial strategies of adaptation.

A society's adaptive strategy (e.g., pastoralism ) refers to its *primary* way of making a living, even though its people may also engage in other economic activities. Pastoralists (herders), for example, consume milk, blood, and meat from their animals as mainstays of their diet. However, they also add plant food to their diet by doing some cultivating or by trading with neighbors.

## Horticulture

The two types of plant cultivation found in nonindustrial societies are **horticulture** (nonintensive, shifting cultivation) and **agriculture** (intensive, continuous cultivation). Both differ from the commercially oriented farming systems of industrial nations, which use large land areas and rely on machinery and agrochemicals.

Horticulture is cultivation that does *not* make intensive use of land, labor, or machinery. When food production arose, both in the Middle East and in the Americas, the earliest cultivators were rainfall-dependent horticulturalists. More recently, horticulture has been—and in many cases still is—the primary form of cultivation in parts of Africa, Southeast Asia, the Pacific islands, Mexico, Central America, and the South American tropical forest.

Horticulturalists use simple tools such as hoes and digging sticks to grow their crops. They typically rely on *slash-and-burn* techniques. Farmers clear land by cutting down (slashing) trees, saplings, and brush. Then they burn that vegetation. They also may set fire directly to grasses and weeds on their farm plots before planting. Slashing and burning

In slash-and-burn horticulture, the land is cleared by cutting down (slashing) and burning trees and brush, using simple technology, as is done here among mountain rice farmers in the hills of Thailand. UniversalImagesGroup/ Universal Images Group/ Getty Images

not only gets rid of unwanted vegetation, but it also kills pests and provides ashes that help fertilize the soil. The farmers then sow, tend, and harvest their crops on the cleared plot. They do not use that plot continuously; often they farm it for only a year or two.

Horticulture also is known as *shifting cultivation*, because farmers shift back and forth between plots, rather than using any one of those plots continuously. With shifting cultivation, horticulturalists farm a plot for a year or two, then abandon it, clear another plot, cultivate it for a year or two, then abandon it, and so on. After the original plot lies fallow for several years (the duration varies in different societies), it can be farmed again.

Shifting cultivation doesn't mean that whole villages must move when plots of land are abandoned. Horticulture can support large, permanent villages. Among the Kuikuru of the South American tropical forest, for example, one village of 150 people remained in the same place for 90 years (Carneiro 1956). Kuikuru houses are large and well made. Because the work involved in building them is great, the Kuikuru preferred to walk farther to their fields, rather than construct a new village. They chose to shift their plots rather than their villages. By contrast, other horticulturalists in the montaña (Andean foothills) of Peru maintained small villages of about 30 people (Carneiro 1961/1968). Their houses were small, simple, and easy to rebuild. They would stay a few years in one place, then move on to a different site near their fields where they would build new homes. They preferred rebuilding to walking even a half-mile to their fields.

## Agriculture

The greater labor demands associated with agriculture, as compared with horticulture, reflect the former's use of domesticated animals, irrigation, or terracing.

### Domesticated Animals

Many agriculturalists use animals as means of production—for transport, as cultivating machines, and for their manure. Asian farmers typically incorporate cattle and/or water buffalo into their agricultural economies. Those rice farmers may use cattle to trample pre-tilled flooded fields, thus mixing soil and water, before transplanting. Many agriculturalists attach animals to plows and harrows for field preparation before planting or transplanting. Also, agriculturalists typically collect manure from their animals, using it to fertilize their plots, thus increasing yields.

## Irrigation

While horticulturalists must await the rainy season, agriculturalists can schedule their planting in advance because they control water—they irrigate their fields. Like other irrigation experts in the Philippines, the Ifugao water their fields with canals that divert water from rivers, streams, springs, and ponds. Irrigation makes it possible to cultivate a plot year after year. Irrigation enriches the soil because the irrigated field is a unique ecosystem with several species of plants and animals, many of them minute organisms, whose wastes fertilize the land.

An irrigated field is a capital investment that usually increases in value. It takes time for a field to start yielding; it reaches full productivity only after several years of cultivation. The Ifugao, like other irrigators, have farmed the same fields for generations. In some agricultural areas, including the Middle East, however, salts carried in the irrigation water can make fields unusable after 50 or 60 years.

## Terracing

Terracing is another agricultural technique the Ifugao have mastered. Their homeland has small valleys separated by steep hillsides. Because the population is dense, people need to farm the hills. However, if they simply planted on the steep hillsides, fertile soil

Agriculture requires longer work hours than horticulture does and uses land intensively and continuously. Labor demands associated with agriculture reflect its use of domesticated animals, irrigation, and terracing. Shown here, rice terraces surround a farming village in Longsheng, Guangxi province, China. KingWu/iStockphoto.com

and crops would be washed away during the rainy season. To prevent this, the Ifugao cut into the hillside and build stage after stage of terraced fields rising above the valley floor. Springs located above the terraces supply their irrigation water. Building and maintaining a system of terraces requires a lot of work. Terrace walls crumble and must be repaired or rebuilt. The canals that bring water down through the terraces also need maintenance.

### Costs and Benefits of Agriculture

Agriculture requires considerable labor to build and maintain irrigation systems, terraces, and other works. People must feed, water, and care for their animals. But agricultural land can yield one or two crops annually for years, or even generations. An agricultural field does not necessarily produce a higher single-year yield than does a horticultural plot. The first crop grown by horticulturalists on long-idle land may be larger than that from an agricultural plot of the same size. Furthermore, because agriculturalists must work more hours than horticulturalists do, agriculture's yield relative to the labor time invested also is lower. Agriculture's main advantage is that the long-term yield per area is far greater and more dependable. Because a single field sustains its owners year after year, there is no need to maintain a reserve of uncultivated land as horticulturalists do. This is why agricultural societies tend to be more densely populated than horticultural ones.

## The Cultivation Continuum

Because some nonindustrial economies have features of both horticulture and agriculture, it is useful to discuss cultivators as being arranged along a **cultivation continuum.** Horticultural systems stand at one end—the "low-labor, shifting-plot" end. Agriculturalists are at the other—the "labor-intensive, permanent-plot" end.

We speak of a continuum because there are intermediate economies, which combine horticultural and agricultural features. In such economies, cultivation is more intensive than with annually shifting horticulture, but less so than with permanent agriculture. The South American Kuikuru, for example, grow two or three crops of manioc, or cassava—an edible tuber—before abandoning their plots. Cultivation is even more intensive in certain densely populated areas of Papua New Guinea, where plots are planted for two or three years, allowed to rest for three to five, and then recultivated. After several of these cycles, the plots are abandoned for a longer fallow period. Such intermediate economies, which support denser populations than does simple horticulture, also can be found in parts of West Africa and in the highlands of Mexico, Peru, and Bolivia.

The one key difference between horticulture and agriculture is that *horticulture always has a fallow period,* whereas agriculture does not.

## Agricultural Intensification: People and the Environment

The range of environments available for cultivation has widened as people have increased their control over nature. Agriculturalists have been able to colonize many areas that are too arid for nonirrigators or too hilly for nonterracers. Agriculture's increased labor intensity and permanent land use have major demographic, social, political, and environmental consequences.

How, specifically, does agriculture affect society and the environment? Because of their permanent fields, agriculturalists tend to be sedentary. People live in larger and more permanent communities located closer to other settlements. Growth in population size and density increases contact between individuals and groups. There is more need to regulate interpersonal relations, including conflicts of interest. Economies that support more people usually require more coordination in the use of land, labor, and other resources (see Chapter 12).

Intensive agriculture has significant environmental effects. Irrigation ditches and paddies (fields with irrigated rice) become repositories for organic wastes, chemicals (such as salts), and disease microorganisms. Intensive agriculture typically spreads at the expense of trees and forests, which are cut down to be replaced by fields. Accompanying such deforestation is a loss of environmental diversity (see Dove and Carpenter 2008). Compared with horticulture, agricultural economies are specialized. They focus on one or a few caloric staples, such as rice, and on the animals that aid the agricultural economy. Because tropical horticulturalists typically cultivate dozens of plant species simultaneously, a horticultural plot mirrors the botanical diversity found in a tropical forest. Agricultural plots, by contrast, reduce ecological diversity by cutting down trees and concentrating on just a few staple foods. Such crop specialization is true of agriculturalists both in the tropics (e.g., Indonesian paddy farmers) and outside the tropics (e.g., Middle Eastern irrigation farmers).

Agriculturalists attempt to reduce risk in production by counting on a reliable annual harvest and long-term production. Tropical foragers and horticulturalists, by contrast, attempt to reduce risk by relying on multiple species and benefiting from ecological diversity. The agricultural strategy is to put all one's eggs in one big and usually very dependable basket. The strategy of tropical foragers and horticulturalists is to have several smaller baskets, a few of which may fail without endangering subsistence. The agricultural strategy makes sense when there are lots of children to raise and adults to be fed. Foraging and horticulture, of course, are associated with smaller, sparser, and more mobile populations.

Agricultural economies also pose a series of regulatory problems. How is water to be managed? How are disputes about access to and distribution of water to be resolved? With more people living closer together on more valuable land, agriculturalists have more opportunities for interpersonal contact and conflict than foragers and horticulturalists do. The social and political implications of food production and intensification are examined more fully in Chapter 12, on political systems.

Anthropologists know that many indigenous groups—especially foragers and nonintensive cultivators—have done a reasonable job of managing their resources and preserving their ecosystems (see Menzies 2006). Such societies had traditional ways of categorizing resources and regulating their use. Increasingly, however, these traditional management systems have been challenged by national and international incentives to exploit and degrade the environment (see Dove, Sajise, and Doolittle 2011). These challenges are the focus of the last two chapters of this book.

## Pastoralism

Herders, or **pastoralists,** are people whose activities focus on such domesticated animals as cattle, sheep, goats, camels, yak, and reindeer. They live in North and sub-Saharan Africa, the Middle East, Europe, and Asia. East African pastoralists, like many others, live in symbiosis with their herds. (*Symbiosis* is an obligatory interaction between groups—

here, humans and animals—that is beneficial to each.) Herders attempt to protect their animals and to ensure their reproduction in return for food (dairy products and meat) and other products, such as leather.

People use livestock in various ways. Natives of North America's Great Plains, for example, didn't eat, but only rode, their horses. (They got those horses after Europeans reintroduced them to the Western Hemisphere; the native American horse had gone extinct thousands of years earlier.) For Plains Indians, horses served as "tools of the trade," means of production used to *hunt* buffalo, the main target of their economies. The Plains Indians were not true pastoralists but hunters who used horses—as many agriculturalists use animals—as means of production.

Pastoralists, by contrast, typically use their herds for food. They consume the animals' meat, blood, and milk, from which they make yogurt, butter, and cheese. Although some pastoralists rely on their herds more completely than others do, it is impossible to base subsistence solely on animals. Most pastoralists therefore supplement their diet by hunting, gathering, fishing, cultivating, or trading.

The Samis (also known as Lapps or Laplanders) of Norway, Sweden, and Finland domesticated the reindeer, which their ancestors had once hunted, in the 16th century. Like other herders, they follow their animals as they make an annual trek, in this case from coast to interior. Today's Samis use modern technology, such as snowmobiles and four-wheel-drive vehicles, to accompany their herds on their annual nomadic trek, and they market reindeer products to outsiders, including tourists. Some of them probably use reindeer management software on their laptops, tablets, personal digital assistants (PDAs), or smartphones. Although their environment is harsher, the Samis, like other herders, live in nation-states and must deal with outsiders, including government officials, as they follow their herds and make their living through animal husbandry, trade, and sales (Hoge 2001; Paine 2009).

Unlike foraging and plant cultivation, which existed throughout the world before the Industrial Revolution, pastoralism was confined almost totally to the Old World. Before European conquest, the only herders in the Americas lived in the Andean region of South America. They used their llamas and alpacas for food and wool and in agriculture and transport. Much more recently, the Navajo of the southwestern United States developed a pastoral economy based on sheep, which were brought to North America by Europeans. The populous Navajo became the major pastoral population in the Western Hemisphere.

Two patterns of movement occur with pastoralism: *nomadism and transhumance.* Both are based on the fact that herds must move to use pasture available in particular places in different seasons. In **pastoral nomadism,** the entire group—women, men, and children—moves with the animals throughout the year. The Middle East and North Africa provide numerous examples of pastoral nomads (see Salzman 2008). In Iran, for example, the Basseri and the Qashqai ethnic groups traditionally followed a nomadic route more than 300 miles (480 kilometers) long (see Salzman 2004).

With **transhumance,** part of the group moves with the herds but most people stay in the home village. There are examples from Europe and Africa. In Europe's Alps it is just the shepherds and goatherds—not the whole hamlet, village, or town—who accompany the flocks to highland meadows in summer. Among the Turkana of Uganda, men and boys take the herds to distant pastures, while much of the village stays put and does some

Reindeer (and bear) products on display at a tourist-oriented market in Helsinki, Finland. (both): Conrad P. Kottak

horticultural farming. During their annual trek, pastoral nomads trade for crops and other products with more sedentary people. Transhumants don't have to trade for crops. Because only part of the population accompanies the herds, transhumants can maintain year-round villages and grow their own crops.

## Economic Systems

An **economy** is a system of production, distribution, and consumption of resources; *economics* is the study of such systems. Economists, however, tend to focus on modern nations and capitalist systems. Anthropologists have broadened understanding of economic principles by gathering data on nonindustrial economies. Economic anthropology brings a comparative, cross-cultural perspective to the study of economics (see Carrier 2012; Chibnik 2011; Gudeman 2016; Hann and Hart 2011; Sahlins 1972/2017).

A **mode of production** is a way of organizing production—"a set of social relations through which labor is deployed to wrest energy from nature by means of tools, skills, organization, and knowledge" (Wolf 1982, p. 75). In the capitalist mode of production, money buys labor, and there is a social gap between the people (bosses and workers) involved in the production process. By contrast, in nonindustrial societies, labor usually is not bought but is given as a social obligation. In such a *kin-based* mode of production, mutual aid in production is one among many expressions of a larger web of social relations (see Marshall 2011). A kin-based mode of production typifies foragers, horticulturalists, pastoralists, and many agriculturalists, especially those lacking state organization.

Societies representing each of the adaptive strategies just discussed (e.g., foraging) tend to have roughly similar modes of production. Variation in the mode of production within a given strategy can reflect differences in the resources they target. Thus, a foraging mode of production may be based on individual hunters or teams, depending on whether the game is solitary, or a herd or flocking animal. Gathering is usually more individualistic than hunting, although collecting teams may assemble when abundant resources ripen and must be harvested quickly. Fishing may be done alone (as in ice fishing or spearfishing) or in crews (as with open-sea fishing and hunting of sea mammals).

## Organization of Production in Nonindustrial Societies

Although some kind of division of economic labor based on age and gender is a cultural universal, the specific tasks assigned to males, females, and people of different ages vary (see Chapter 14). Many horticultural societies assign a major productive role to women, but some make men's work primary. Similarly, among pastoralists, men generally tend large animals, but in some societies women do the milking. Tasks that involve teamwork in some cultivating societies are done in other societies by smaller groups or by individuals working over a longer period.

The Betsileo of Madagascar have two stages of teamwork in rice cultivation: transplanting and harvesting. Both activities feature a traditional division of labor by age and gender that is well known to all Betsileo and is repeated across the generations. The first job in the transplanting process is the trampling of a previously tilled and flooded field by young men driving cattle, in order to mix earth and water. The young men yell at and beat the cattle, striving to drive them into a frenzy, so that they will trample the fields properly. Trampling breaks up clumps of earth and mixes irrigation water with soil to form a smooth mud, into which women will soon transplant seedlings. Once the tramplers leave the field, older men arrive. With their spades, they break up the clumps that the cattle missed. Meanwhile, the owner and other adults uproot rice seedlings and take them to edge of the field, where women will transplant them.

At harvest time, four or five months later, young men cut the rice off the stalks. Young women carry it to a clearing above the field, where older women arrange and stack it. The oldest men and women then stand on the stack, stomping and compacting it. Three days later, young men thresh the rice, beating the stalks against a rock to remove the grain. Older men then beat the stalks with sticks to make sure all the grains have fallen off.

# Means of Production

The relationship between the worker and the means of production is more intimate in nonindustrial societies than it is in industrial nations. **Means (or factors) of production** include land (territory), technology, and the available labor supply.

## Land as a Means of Production

Ties between people and land are less permanent among foragers than among food producers. The borders between foraging territories are neither precisely demarcated nor enforced. A hunter's stake in pursuit of an animal is more important than where that animal finally dies. One acquires the right to use a band's territory by being born in that band or by joining it through a tie of kinship or marriage. On changing bands, one immediately acquires rights to hunt or gather in the new band's territory.

Among food producers, rights to the means of production also come through kinship and marriage. Descent groups (groups whose members claim common ancestry) are common among nonindustrial food producers. Those who descend from the founder share the group's territory and resources. If the adaptive strategy is horticulture, the estate includes gardens and fallow land for shifting cultivation. With pastoralism, descent group members have access to animals to start their own herds, to grazing land, to garden land, and to other means of production.

## Labor, Tools, and Specialization

Like land, the labor supply is a means of production. In nonindustrial societies, access to both land and labor comes through social links such as kinship, marriage, and descent. The labor that is mutually given in production is merely one aspect of ongoing social relations that are expressed on many other occasions.

Nonindustrial societies contrast with industrial nations regarding another means of production—technology. Manufacturing often is linked to age and gender. Women may weave and men may make pottery, or vice versa. Most people of a particular age and gender share the technical knowledge associated with that age and gender. If married women customarily make baskets, most married women know how to make baskets. Neither technology nor technical knowledge is very specialized.

Some tribal societies, however, do promote specialization. Among the Yanomami of Venezuela and Brazil, for instance, certain villages manufacture clay pots and others make hammocks. They don't specialize, as one might suppose, because certain raw materials happen to be available near particular villages. Clay suitable for pots is widely available. Everyone knows how to make pots, but not everybody does so. Craft specialization reflects the social and political environment rather than the natural environment. Such specialization promotes trade, which is the first step in creating an alliance with enemy villages (Chagnon 2013a, 2013b).

# Alienation in Industrial Economies

There are significant contrasts between nonindustrial economies and industrial ones. In the former, economic relations are just one part of a larger, multidimensional social matrix. People don't just work for and with others; they live with those same people, and they pray with, feast with, and care about them. One works for and with people with whom one has long-term personal and social bonds (e.g., kin and in-laws).

In industrial societies, by contrast, workers sell their labor to bosses who can fire them. Work and the workplace are separated—*alienated*—from one's social essence. The term *alienation* is used to describe a situation in which a worker has produced something but sees that product as belonging to someone else, rather than to the man or woman whose labor actually produced it. Rather than expressing an ongoing, mutual social relationship, labor becomes a thing (commodity) to be paid for, bought, and sold—and from which the boss can generate an individual profit. Furthermore, industrial workers usually don't work with their relatives and neighbors. If coworkers are friends, the personal relationship often develops out of their common employment rather than a previous social tie.

In nonindustrial societies, the individual who has made an item can use or dispose of it as he or she sees fit. That maker may feel pride in his or her own product and, if it is given away, a renewed commitment to the social relationship that is reinforced by the gift. On the other hand, when factory workers produce for someone else's profit, their products, as well as their labor, are alienated. Human labor and its products belong to someone other than the individual producer. Unlike assembly-line workers, producers in nonindustrial societies typically see their work through from start to finish and feel a sense of accomplishment.

In nonindustrial societies, the economic relation between coworkers is just one aspect of a more general social relation. They aren't just coworkers but kin, in-laws, or celebrants in the same ritual. In such settings, the relations of production, distribution, and consumption are *social relations with economic aspects*. Economy is not a separate entity but is *embedded* in the society.

## A Case of Industrial Alienation

For decades, the government of Malaysia has promoted export-oriented industry, allowing transnational companies to install manufacturing operations in rural Malaysia. In search of cheaper labor, corporations headquartered in Japan, Western Europe, and the United States have moved labor-intensive factories to developing countries. Malaysia has hundreds of Japanese and American subsidiaries, which produce garments, foodstuffs, and electronics components. Thousands of young Malaysian women from rural families now assemble microchips and microcomponents for transistors and capacitors. Aihwa Ong (1987; Ong and Collier 2010) did a study of electronics assembly workers in an area where 85 percent of the workers were young, unmarried females from nearby villages.

Ong found that, unlike village women, female factory workers had to cope with a rigid work routine and constant supervision by men. The discipline that factories enforce was being taught in local schools, where uniforms helped prepare girls for the factory dress code. Village women wore loose, flowing tunics, sarongs, and sandals, but factory workers had to don tight overalls and heavy rubber gloves, in which they felt constrained. Labor in these factories illustrates the alienation that Karl Marx considered the defining feature of industrial work. One woman said about her bosses, "They exhaust us very much, as if they do not think that we too are human beings" (Ong 1987, p. 202). Nor does factory

A technician displays the circuit board for a compact digital camera at a Canon factory in Petaling Jaya, Malaysia. Throughout Southeast Asia, hundreds of thousands of young women from peasant families now work in factories. Chances are good that you own one of their products. Goh Seng Chong/ Bloomberg/Getty Images

work bring women a substantial financial reward, given low wages, job uncertainty, and family claims on wages. Although young women typically work just a few years, production quotas, three daily shifts, overtime, and surveillance take their toll in mental and physical exhaustion.

One response to factory relations of production has been spirit possession (factory women are possessed by spirits). Ong interprets this phenomenon as the women's unconscious protest against labor discipline and male control of the industrial setting. Sometimes possession takes the form of mass hysteria. Spirits have simultaneously invaded as many as 120 factory workers. Weretigers (the Malay equivalent of the werewolf) arrive to avenge the construction of a factory on local burial grounds. Disturbed earth and grave spirits swarm on the shop floor. First the women see the spirits; then their bodies are invaded. The weretigers send the women into sobbing, laughing, and shrieking fits. To deal with possession, factories employ local medicine men, who sacrifice chickens and goats to fend off the spirits. This solution works only some of the time; spirit possession still happens. Ong argues that spirit possession expresses anguish at, and resistance to, the capitalist mode of production. By engaging in this form of rebellion, however, factory women avoid a direct confrontation with the source of their distress. Ong concludes that spirit possession, while expressing repressed resentment, doesn't do much to modify factory conditions. (Other tactics, such as unionization, would do more.) Spirit possession may even help maintain the current system by operating as a safety valve for accumulated tensions. This chapter's "Anthropology Today" describes a different kind of alienation—that which follows the job loss associated with deindustrialization.)

# Economizing and Maximization

Economic anthropologists have been concerned with two main questions:

* How are production, distribution, and consumption organized in different societies? This question focuses on economic *systems* and their organization.
* What motivates people in different societies to produce, distribute or exchange, and consume? Here the focus is not on systems of behavior but on the *individuals* who participate in those systems.

Anthropologists view economic systems and motivations in a cross-cultural perspective. Motivation is a concern of psychologists, but it also has been a concern of economists and anthropologists. Economists assume that our decisions are guided by the *profit motive*—the desire to make a monetary profit. Although anthropologists know that the profit motive is not universal, the assumption that individuals try to maximize profits is basic to capitalism and to Western economic theory. In fact, the subject matter of economics often is defined as *economizing*, or the rational (profit-oriented) allocation of scarce means (or resources) to alternative ends (or uses) (see Chibnik 2011).

What does that mean? Classical economic theory assumes that our wants are infinite, while our means are limited. People must make choices about how to use their scarce resources—their time, labor, money, and capital. Western economists assume that when confronted with choices and decisions, people tend to make the one that maximizes profit. This is assumed to be the most rational choice.

The idea that individuals choose to maximize profits was a basic assumption of the classical economists of the 19th century and one still held by many contemporary economists. However, certain economists now recognize that individuals may be motivated by many other goals. Depending on the society and the situation, people may try to maximize profit, wealth, prestige, pleasure, comfort, social harmony, or spiritual goals. Individuals may want to realize their personal, family, or community ambitions, or those of some other group to which they belong (see Chibnik 2011; Sahlins 1972/2017).

## Alternative Ends

To what uses do people put their scarce resources? Throughout the world, people devote some of their time and energy to building up a *subsistence fund* (Wolf 1966). In other words, people must work to subsist, to feed themselves, to go on living. People also have to invest in a *replacement fund*. They must maintain their technology and other items essential to production. If a hoe or plow breaks, they must repair or replace it. They also must obtain and replace items that are essential not to production but to everyday life, such as clothing and shelter.

People everywhere also have to invest in a *social fund*. They must help their friends, relatives, in-laws, and neighbors. It is useful to distinguish between a social fund and a *ceremonial fund*. The latter term refers to expenditures on ceremonies or rituals. To prepare a festival honoring one's ancestors, for example, requires time and the outlay of wealth.

Citizens of nation-states also must allocate scarce resources to a *rent fund*. We think of rent as payment for the use of property. However, the term has a wider meaning. It refers to resources that people must render to an individual or agency that is superior politically or economically. Tenant farmers and sharecroppers, for example, either pay rent or give some of their produce to their landlords, as peasants did under feudalism. The rent fund also includes taxes, which people typically pay in state-organized societies.

**Peasants** are small-scale farmers who live in state-organized societies and have rent fund obligations. They produce to feed themselves, to sell their produce, and to pay rent. All peasants have two things in common: (1) They live in state-organized societies, and (2) they produce food without the elaborate technology—chemical fertilizers, tractors, airplanes to spray crops, and so on—of modern farming or agribusiness.

Besides paying rent to landlords, peasants must satisfy government obligations, paying taxes in the form of money, produce, or labor. The rent fund is not simply an *additional* obligation for peasants. Often it becomes their foremost and unavoidable duty. Sometimes their own diets suffer as a result. The demands of social superiors may divert resources from subsistence, replacement, social, and ceremonial funds.

Motivations vary from society to society, and people often lack freedom of choice in allocating their resources. Because of obligations to pay rent, peasants may allocate their scarce means toward ends that are not their own but those of landlords or government officials. Thus, even in societies in which there is a profit motive, people often are prevented from rationally maximizing self-interest by factors beyond their control.

# Distribution and Exchange

The economist Karl Polanyi (1968) was a key early contributor to the comparative study of exchanges (e.g., gift giving, trade), and several anthropologists followed his lead. Polanyi defined three principles that guide exchanges: the market principle, redistribution, and reciprocity. All three principles can be present in the same society, but in that case they govern different kinds of transactions. In any society, one of them usually dominates. The principle that dominates in a given society is the one that determines how the means of production are exchanged (see Chibnik 2011; Hann and Hart 2011).

## The Market Principle

In today's world capitalist economy, the **market principle** dominates. It governs the distribution of the means of production—land, labor, natural resources, technology, knowledge, and capital. With market exchange, items are bought and sold, using money, with an eye to maximizing profit, and value is determined by the *law of supply and demand* (things cost more the scarcer they are and the more people want them). Bargaining is characteristic of market principle exchanges. The buyer and the seller strive to maximize—to get their "money's worth." The bargainers don't need to meet personally, but their offers and counteroffers usually take place within a fairly short time period.

## Redistribution

**Redistribution** occurs when products, such as a portion of the annual harvest, move from the local level to a center, from which they eventually flow back out. That center may be a capital, a regional collection point, or a storehouse near a chief's residence. Redistribution typically occurs in societies that have chiefs. To reach the center, where they will be stored, products often move through a hierarchy of officials. Along the way, those officials and their dependents may consume some, but never all, of the products. After reaching the center, the flow of goods eventually will reverse direction—out from the center, down through the hierarchy, and back to the common people. Redistribution is a way of moving a variety of goods from different areas to a central point, where they are stored and eventually redistributed to the public. The custom of tithing encouraged by many religions is a form of redistribution, because what the church receives can be used (redistributed) to benefit the needy.

One ethnographic example of redistribution comes from the Cherokee, Native Americans who were the original inhabitants of the Tennessee Valley. The Cherokee were productive cultivators of maize, beans, and squash, which they supplemented by hunting and fishing. They also had chiefs. Each of their main villages had a central plaza, where meetings of the chief's council took place and where redistributive feasts were held. According to Cherokee custom, each family farm had an area where the family could set aside part of its annual harvest for the chief. This supply of corn was used to feed the needy, as well as travelers and warriors journeying through Cherokee territory. This store of food was available to all who needed it, with the understanding that it "belonged" to the chief and was available through his generosity. The chief also hosted the redistributive feasts held in the main settlements. On those occasions, ordinary people were able to consume some of the produce they had previously given in the chief's name (Harris 1978).

## Reciprocity

Reciprocity is the act of reciprocating—giving back, returning a favor, repaying a debt. More specifically, economic anthropologists use the term **reciprocity** to refer to exchanges between social equals, people who are related by some kind of personal tie, such as kinship or marriage. Because it occurs between social equals, reciprocity is the dominant exchange principle in the more egalitarian societies—among foragers, cultivators, and pastoralists.

There are three forms of reciprocity: generalized, balanced, and negative (Sahlins 1968, 2017/1972; Service 1966). These may be imagined as areas along a continuum defined by these questions:

- How closely related are the individuals who are doing the exchanging?
- How quickly and unselfishly are the gifts reciprocated?

The exchanges that occur between closely related people illustrate *generalized reciprocity*. There is no expectation of immediate return of a gift or favor. With *balanced reciprocity*, social distance increases, as does the need to reciprocate. In *negative reciprocity*, social distance is greatest and reciprocation is most calculated. This range, from generalized through balanced to negative, is called the **reciprocity continuum.**

With **generalized reciprocity,** someone gives to another person and expects nothing immediate in return. Such exchanges are not primarily economic transactions but expressions of personal relationships. Most parents don't keep accounts of all the time, money, and energy they expend on behalf of their children. They merely hope their children will respect their culture's customs involving obligations to parents.

Among foragers, generalized reciprocity—unselfish giving with no immediate expectation of return—is the norm. People routinely share with other band members. So strong is the ethic of sharing that most foragers lack an expression for "thank you." To offer thanks would imply that a particular act of sharing, which is the keystone of egalitarian society, was unusual. Among the Semai, foragers of central Malaysia (Dentan 2008), to express gratitude would suggest surprise at a hunter's success (see also Widlok 2017; Zhang 2016).

**Balanced reciprocity** characterizes exchanges between people who are more distantly related than are members of the same band or household. In a horticultural society, for example, a man presents a gift to a distant cousin, a trading partner, or a brother-in-law. The giver expects something in return. This may not come immediately, but the social relationship will be strained if there is no eventual and more or less equivalent return gift.

Exchanges in nonindustrial societies also may illustrate **negative reciprocity,** mainly in dealing with people beyond their social systems. To people who live in a world of close personal relations, exchanges with outsiders are full of ambiguity and distrust. Exchange is one way of establishing friendly relations, but when trade begins, the relationship is still tentative. Initially, people want something back immediately. Just as in market economies, but without using money, they try to get the best possible immediate return for their investment (see Clark 2010; Hann and Hart 2009).

Generalized reciprocity and balanced reciprocity are based on trust and a social tie. With negative reciprocity, the goal is to get something immediately and as cheaply as possible, even if it means being cagey or deceitful or even cheating. Among the most extreme and "negative" examples was 19th-century horse thievery by North American Plains Indians. Men would sneak into camps of neighboring tribes to steal horses. Such thefts were likely to be reciprocated. A similar pattern of livestock (cattle) raiding continues today in East Africa, among tribes such as the Kuria (Fleisher 2000). In these cases, the party that starts the raiding can expect reciprocity—a raid on their own village—or worse. The Kuria hunt down cattle thieves and kill them. It's still reciprocity, governed by "Do unto others as they have done unto you."

One way of reducing the tension in situations of potential negative reciprocity is to engage in "silent trade." One example was the silent trade of the Mbuti pygmy foragers of the African equatorial forest and their neighboring horticultural villagers. There was no personal contact during their exchanges. A Mbuti hunter left game, honey, or another forest product at a customary site. Villagers collected it and left crops in exchange. Often the parties bargained silently. If one felt the return was insufficient, he or she simply left it at the trading site. If the other party wanted to continue trade, it was increased.

## Coexistence of Exchange Principles

In contemporary North America, the market principle governs most exchanges, from the sale of property to the sale of consumer goods. We also have redistribution. Some of our tax money goes to support the government, but some comes back to us in the form of social services, education, health care, and infrastructure. We also have reciprocal exchanges. Generalized reciprocity characterizes the relationship between parents and children. However, even here the dominant market mentality surfaces in comments about the high cost of raising children and in the stereotypical statement of the disappointed parent: "We gave you everything money could buy."

Exchanges of gifts, cards, and invitations exemplify reciprocity, usually balanced. Everyone has heard remarks like "They invited us to their daughter's wedding, so when ours gets married, we'll have to invite them" and "They've been here for dinner three times and haven't invited us yet. I don't think we should ask them back until they do." Such precise balancing of reciprocity would be out of place in a foraging band, where resources are communal (common to all) and sharing is normal and essential to social life and survival (see Widlok 2017).

Generalized reciprocity is the most widespread form of exchange, because it exists in every kind of society, from foraging bands to industrial nations. The larger social and economic networks typically found among food producers (compared with foragers) allow for wider and more distant exchanges characterized by balanced and even negative reciprocity. Societies with chiefs have redistribution. The market principle tends to dominate exchanges in state-organized societies, which are examined further in Chapter 12.

## Potlatching

The **potlatch** is a festive event within a regional exchange system among tribes of the North Pacific Coast of North America, including the Salish and Kwakiutl of Washington and British Columbia, and the Tsimshian of Alaska. Historically, at a potlatch, the sponsoring community gave away food and wealth items, such as blankets and pieces of copper, to visitors from other villages. The sponsoring community received prestige in return. That prestige increased with the lavishness of the potlatch. Some North Pacific tribes still practice the potlatch, sometimes as a memorial to the dead (Kan 1986, 1989).

The potlatching tribes were foragers, but very atypical ones. Rather than living in nomadic bands, they were sedentary and even had chiefs. They enjoyed access to a wide variety of land and sea resources. Among their most important foods were salmon, herring, candlefish, berries, mountain goats, seals, and porpoises (Piddocke 1969).

The economist Thorstein Veblen (1934) criticized potlatching, which he saw as an out-of-control form of conspicuous consumption. He emphasized the lavishness and supposed wastefulness, especially of Kwakiutl potlatches, to support his contention that in some societies people strive to maximize prestige at the expense of their material well-being. Anthropologists have challenged his interpretation.

Ecological anthropology, also known as *cultural ecology*, is a theoretical school that attempts to interpret cultural practices, such as the potlatch, in terms of their long-term role in helping humans adapt to their environments (see Haenn, Wilk, and Harnish 2016). Wayne Suttles (1960) and Andrew Vayda (1961/1968) saw potlatching not in terms of its immediate wastefulness but in terms of its long-term role as a cultural adaptive mechanism (see also Trosper 2009). This view also helps us understand similar patterns of lavish feasting throughout the world. Here is the ecological interpretation: *Customs such as the potlatch are cultural adaptations to alternating periods of local abundance and shortage.*

How did this work? Although the natural environment of the North Pacific Coast is favorable, resources fluctuate from year to year. Salmon and herring aren't equally abundant every year in a given locality. One village can have a good year while another is experiencing a bad one. Later, their fortunes reverse. In this context, the potlatch cycle had adaptive value; it was not a competitive display that brought no material benefit.

This historic (1904) photo shows an assembly of guests at a potlatch in Sitka, Alaska.
Source: Sitka National Historical Park/National Park Service/U.S. Department of the Interior

A village enjoying an especially good year had a surplus of subsistence items, which it could trade for more durable wealth items, such as blankets, canoes, or pieces of copper. Such wealth, in turn, could be given away and thereby converted into prestige. Members of several villages were invited to any potlatch and got to take home the resources that were distributed. In this way, potlatching linked villages together in a regional economy—an exchange system that distributed food and wealth from wealthy to needy communities.

The long-term adaptive value of potlatching becomes clear when a formerly prosperous village had a run of bad luck. Its people started accepting invitations to potlatches in villages that were doing better. The tables were turned as the temporarily rich became temporarily poor and vice versa. The newly needy accepted food and wealth items. They were willing to receive rather than bestow gifts and thus to relinquish some of their stored-up prestige. They hoped their luck would eventually improve, so that resources could be recouped and prestige regained.

The potlatch linked local groups along the North Pacific Coast into a regional alliance and exchange network. Potlatching and intervillage exchange had adaptive functions, regardless of the motivations of the individual participants. The anthropologists who stressed rivalry for prestige were not wrong. They were merely emphasizing *motivations* at the expense of an analysis of economic and ecological *systems*.

## Anthropology Today *When the Mills Shut Down: An Anthropologist Looks at Deindustrialization*

Some 5 million American manufacturing jobs have disappeared so far in the 21st century, continuing a trend that started in the 1970s and intensified in the 1980s and thereafter. This industrial decline has affected hundreds of towns and cities, particularly in the Rust Belt states of Illinois, Wisconsin, Michigan, and Pennsylvania. As described by Elizabeth Svoboda (2017), Christine Walley, an anthropology professor at MIT, focuses on the human effects of factory closures on laid-off workers, their families, and communities.

Walley was raised in a steel-working family in Southeast Chicago. As a participant observer of her childhood neighborhood, she has been gathering stories that reveal the trauma that displaced industrial workers have suffered. In her book *Exit Zero: Family and Class in Postindustrial Chicago* (2013) and her film *Exit Zero: An Industrial Family Story* (2014), Walley describes how her father, Chuck, lost his job at Wisconsin Steel when that mill closed in 1980. Other mill closures followed, devastating Walley's family and community.

Southeast Chicago's mills were still churning out steel when Christine Walley was born in 1965. Every morning, her dad headed to his job at Wisconsin Steel, the area's oldest mill. The work was hazardous, but it paid enough to support the Walley family of five, and it promised Chuck a generous pension when he retired.

Along with more than 3,000 other Wisconsin Steel workers, Chuck was laid off in 1980, when Christine Walley was 14 years old. For years, the mill's corporate owners had neglected its upkeep, and its final owner was suspected of deliberately squeezing some terminal profits out of the mill before declaring bankruptcy. Chuck lost not only his job but also his promised pension. Henceforth, the lives of the Walley family would be divided sharply into "before" and "after" the mill shut down.

Following his layoff, Chuck Walley pursued a series of odd jobs, including janitorial work and truck driving. Those jobs paid very little, and Chuck's wife had to start working as well. No longer able to support his family, Chuck suffered chronic depression and despair—lying on his couch and smoking cigarettes. He died of lung cancer in 2005, still shaken by his inability to find satisfactory employment. Of the 3,400 men and women who once worked for Wisconsin Steel, about one-quarter were dead just eight years later. They fell victim to addiction, depression, and suicide. Around them, the layoffs continued. The nearby U.S. Steel South Works production plant, which once employed more than 20,000 Chicagoans, shut down in 1992 (Svoboda 2017).

As an adult and an anthropologist, Christine Walley has sought to understand what happened—not just to her family and community but throughout the Rust Belt. Her Exit Zero Project, which combines film, writing, collaboration with a local historical museum, and a web presence, tells the story of her family's postindustrial demise (see http://www.exitzeroproject.org/). Walley brings in other voices as well; she conversed with and interviewed people in her old neighborhood who shared her family's experience and its sense of displacement and alienation. The social and psychological impacts of industrial closures have been profound. Former workers lost both their livelihoods (financial security) and the work that gave their lives meaning and value. Churches, restaurants, and other local gathering spots closed along with

Bethlehem Steel's massive five furnace industrial complex in Bethlehem, Pennsylvania, produced American steel for 120 years, employing tens of thousands of workers. After it closed for good in 1995, the city redeveloped the area as a tourist attraction, park, and community arts center. Andrew Lichtenstein/Corbis/Getty Images

the mills, depriving laid-off workers of familiar networks of social support.

Deindustrialization continues today for three main reasons: (1) global competition, (2) automation, and (3) corporate decisions and government policies. Some manufacturing jobs have been shifted to other countries or lost to foreign competition. Even more significant is automation, as machines do more and more jobs—a trend that will continue. As automation—increasingly powered by artificial intelligence—continues, white-collar workers, too, will face the same displacement and anxiety that blue-collar workers have experienced for decades. A University of Oxford study estimated that almost half (47 percent) of all U.S. jobs may be lost to automation (Frey and Osborne 2013).

Also important have been federal laws that have facilitated corporate decisions to close factories. A trend toward looser regulation began in the 1970s and accelerated during the 1980s. Corporations could merge, acquire, and dispose of new companies with little interference. Federal laws permitted investors to buy up older factories and milk them for profits while neglecting pension funds and eventually allowing the enterprises to go bankrupt. This is exactly what happened at Wisconsin Steel. With further deregulation under the Trump administration, workers are likely to be even more at the mercy of corporate schemes.

Examples from other countries demonstrate that industrial decline is not an inevitable result of global competition. As

## Anthropology Today   *continued*

American mills and factories were failing, something very different was happening in Canada. Government policies were encouraging companies to modernize and funnel profits back into mill upkeep. As a result, not a single Canadian steel mill closed during this period of American industrial decline. Germany, too, has managed to maintain a robust industrial economy even with global competition (see Svoboda 2017).

During the 2016 U.S. presidential primaries and election, both the eventual winner, Donald Trump, and Vermont senator Bernie Sanders, who has described himself as a democratic socialist, drew significant support from Rust Belt blue-collar workers. Trump mainly faulted trade agreements and immigrants, promising to bring back jobs and "make America great again." Sanders blamed "millionaires and billionaires," including corporations and Wall Street, for the country's ills. Both promised more radical solutions than their rivals. As president, Trump announced in March 2018 that he would impose a 25 percent tariff on imported steel. When Christine Walley analyzed election data from her old neighborhood, she found that the 2016 Trump voters there tended to be swing voters rather than core Trump supporters. She speculates that they may well abandon Trump if his policies fail to bring back jobs. The overriding concern of these Southeast Chicago voters was to challenge an economic system that had failed them (see Svoboda 2017).

From Walley's work, we learn how industrial workers and their families have experienced their loss of, and how they wish to recapture, the sense of dignity and self-worth that comes from work that is productive and meaningful. Walley advocates closer scrutiny of laws and policies that have facilitated the wave of mill closures. Along with social scientists, policy makers need to pay more concerted attention to what future work should look like, and to mitigating laws and policies that favor corporate interests over workers' well-being. Is this a pipe dream, or do you think it might really happen?

## Summary

1. Cohen's adaptive strategies include foraging (hunting and gathering), horticulture, agriculture, pastoralism, and industrialism. Foraging was the only human adaptive strategy until the transition to food production (farming and herding), which began about 12,000 years ago. Food production eventually replaced foraging in most places. Almost all modern foragers have some dependence on food production or food producers.

2. Horticulture doesn't use land or labor intensively. Horticulturalists cultivate a plot for one or two years (sometimes longer) and then abandon it. There is always a fallow period. Agriculturalists farm the same plot of land continuously and use labor intensively. They use one or more of the following: irrigation, terracing, domesticated animals as a means of production, and manure for fertilizer.

3. The pastoral strategy is mixed. Nomadic pastoralists trade with cultivators. Part of a transhumant pastoral population cultivates while another part takes the herds to

pasture. Except for some Peruvians and the Navajo, who are recent herders, the New World lacks native pastoralists.

4. Economic anthropology is the cross-cultural study of systems of production, distribution, and consumption. In nonindustrial societies, a kin-based mode of production prevails. One acquires rights to resources and labor through membership in social groups, not impersonally through purchase and sale. Work is just one aspect of social relations expressed in varied contexts.

5. Economics has been defined as the science of allocating scarce means to alternative ends. Western economists assume the notion of scarcity is universal—which it isn't—and that, in making choices, people strive to maximize personal profit. In nonindustrial societies, indeed as in our own, people often maximize values other than individual profit.

6. In nonindustrial societies, people invest in subsistence, replacement, social, and ceremonial funds. States add a rent fund: People must share their output with their social superiors. In states, the obligation to pay rent often becomes primary.

7. Besides studying production, economic anthropologists study and compare exchange systems. The three principles of exchange are the market principle, redistribution, and reciprocity, which may coexist in a given society. The primary exchange mode is the one that allocates the means of production.

8. Patterns of feasting and exchanges of wealth among villages are common in nonindustrial food-producing societies, and also in the potlatching societies of North America's North Pacific Coast. Such systems help even out the availability of resources over time.

## Think Like an Anthropologist

1. When considering issues of "human nature," why should we remember that the egalitarian band was a basic form of human social life for most of our history?

2. Give examples from your own exchanges of different degrees of reciprocity. Why are anthropologists interested in studying exchange across cultures?

## Key Terms

agriculture, 265
balanced reciprocity, 279
band, 264
correlation, 264
cultivation continuum, 268
economy, 271
food production, 260
foraging, 261
generalized reciprocity, 278
horticulture, 265
market principle, 277
means (factors) of production, 273
mode of production, 272
negative reciprocity, 279
pastoral nomadism, 270
pastoralists, 269
peasants, 277
potlatch, 280
reciprocity, 278
reciprocity continuum, 278
redistribution, 277
transhumance, 270

# Chapter 12

# Political Systems

## What Is "The Political"?

Anthropologists share with political scientists an interest in political systems, power, and politics. Here again, however, the anthropological approach is global and comparative and includes nonstates, whereas political scientists tend to focus on contemporary nation-states (see O'Neil 2018). Anthropological studies have revealed substantial variation in power, authority, and legal systems in different societies (see Goodale 2017; Pirie 2013; Walton and Suarez 2016). (**Power** is the ability to exercise one's will over others; **authority** is the formal, socially approved use of power—e.g., by government officials.)

Morton Fried (1967) offered the following definition of political organization:

> Political organization comprises those portions of social organization that specifically relate to the individuals or groups that manage the affairs of public policy or seek to control the appointment or activities of those individuals or groups. (pp. 20–21)

This definition certainly fits contemporary North America and other nation-states. Under "individuals or groups that manage the affairs of public policy" come various

Seeking to influence public policy, thousands of participants joined the March for Our Lives rally held on March 24, 2018 in Washington, DC. More than 800 March for Our Lives events, originally organized by survivors of the 2018 Parkland, Florida school shooting, were held that day in cities and towns around the world. The marchers called for legislative action to address school safety and gun violence. The Asahi Shimbun/Getty Images

agencies and levels of government. Those who seek to influence public policy include political parties, unions, corporations, consumers, lobbyists, activists, political action committees (including super PACs), religious groups, and nongovernmental organizations (NGOs).

In nonstates, by contrast, it's often difficult to detect any "public policy." For this reason, I prefer to speak of *socio*political organization in discussing the exercise of power and the regulation of relations among groups and their representatives. *Political regulation* includes such processes as decision making, dispute management, and conflict resolution. The study of political regulation draws our attention to those who make decisions and resolve conflicts. Are there formal leaders? If not, who leads and how? (See Rhodes and Hart 2014; Stryker and Gonzalez 2014.)

## Types and Trends

Ethnographic and archaeological studies in hundreds of places have revealed many correlations between the economy and social and political organization. Decades ago, the anthropologist Elman Service (1962) listed four types, or levels, of political organization: band, tribe, chiefdom, and state. Today, none of the first three types can be studied as a self-contained form of political organization, because all now exist within the context of nation-states. There is archaeological evidence for early bands, tribes, and chiefdoms that existed before the first states appeared. However, because anthropology originated long after states did, anthropologists have rarely if ever observed "in the flesh" a band, tribe, or chiefdom outside the influence of some state. There still may be local political leaders (e.g., village heads) and regional figures (e.g., chiefs) of the sort discussed in this chapter, but all now exist and function within the context of state organization.

A **band** is a small, kin-based group (all its members are related by kinship or marriage) found among foragers. **Tribes** typically have economies based on horticulture and pastoralism. Living in villages and organized into kin groups based on common descent, tribes have no formal government and no reliable means of enforcing political decisions. **Chiefdom** refers to a form of sociopolitical organization intermediate between the tribe and the state. In chiefdoms, social relations are based mainly on kinship, marriage, descent, age, generation, and gender—just as in bands and tribes. However, although chiefdoms are kin based, they feature **differential access** to resources (some people have more wealth, prestige, and power than others do) and a permanent political structure. The **state** is a form of sociopolitical organization based on a formal government structure and socioeconomic stratification.

The four labels in Service's typology are much too simple to account for the full range of political diversity and complexity known to anthropologists. We'll see, for instance, that tribes have varied widely in their political systems and institutions. Nevertheless, Service's typology does highlight significant contrasts in political organization, especially those between states and nonstates. For example, in bands and tribes—unlike states, which have clearly visible governments—political organization does not stand out as separate and distinct. In bands and tribes, it is difficult to characterize an act or event as political rather than merely social.

Service's labels "band," "tribe," "chiefdom," and "state" are categories or types within a **sociopolitical typology.** These types are correlated with the adaptive strategies (an *economic typology*) discussed in Chapter 11. Thus, foragers (an economic type) tend to have band organization (a sociopolitical type). Similarly, many horticulturalists and pastoralists live in tribes. Although most chiefdoms have farming economies, herding is important in some Middle Eastern chiefdoms. Nonindustrial states usually have an agricultural base.

Food production led to larger, denser populations and more complex economies than existed among foragers. New forms of sociopolitical organization emerged in response to the increased regulatory demands associated with cultivation, herding, and population increase. Archaeologists have studied these developments through time, and ethnographers have documented a range of sociopolitical forms among recent and contemporary societies (see Shore, Wright, and Però 2011).

## Bands and Tribes

This chapter will discuss, as case studies, a series of societies with different political systems. A common set of questions will be addressed for each one. What kinds of social groups does the society have? How do those groups deal with one another? How are their internal and external relations regulated? To answer these questions, we begin with bands and tribes and then consider chiefdoms and states.

## Foraging Bands

Modern foragers are very different from their Stone Age predecessors (see Lee 2018). They live within nation-states, and in an interlinked world. All foragers now trade with food producers. The pygmies of Congo, for example, for generations have shared a social world and economic exchanges with neighbors who are cultivators. Furthermore, most contemporary hunter-gatherers rely on governments, missionaries, and other outsiders for at least part of what they consume.

### *The San*

In Chapter 11, we saw how the Basarwa San of Botswana have been affected by government policies that relocated them after converting their ancestral lands into a wildlife reserve (Motseta 2006). More generally, San speakers ("Bushmen") of southern Africa have been influenced by Bantu speakers (farmers and herders) for 2,000 years and by Europeans for centuries. Edwin Wilmsen (1989) argues that many San descend from herders who were pushed into the desert by poverty or oppression. He sees the San today as a rural underclass in a larger political and economic system dominated by Europeans and Bantu food producers. Within this system, many San now tend cattle for wealthier Bantu rather than foraging independently. San also have their own domesticated animals, further illustrating their movement away from a foraging lifestyle.

The nature of San life has changed considerably since the 1950s and 1960s, when a series of anthropologists from Harvard University, including Richard B. Lee, embarked on a systematic study of their lives. Studying the San over time, Lee and others have documented many changes (see Lee 2012, 2013; Tanaka 2014). Such longitudinal research monitors variation in time, while fieldwork in many San areas has revealed

An Aboriginal elder stands next to his home in the Anangu Pitjantjatjara lands, South Australia. Like this man, most recent and contemporary foragers and their descendants participate in the modern world system. Susie Bennett/ Alamy Stock Photo

variation in space. One of the most important contrasts is between settled (sedentary) and nomadic groups (Kent and Vierich 1989). Although sedentism has increased substantially in recent years, some San groups (along rivers) have been sedentary for generations. Others, including the Dobe Ju/'hoansi San studied by Lee (2012, 2013) and the Kutse San whom Susan Kent (2002) studied, have retained more of the hunter-gatherer lifestyle.

To the extent that foraging continues to be their subsistence base, groups like the San can illustrate links between a foraging economy and other aspects of life in bands. For example, San groups that still are mobile, or that were so until recently, emphasize social, political, and gender equality, which are traditional band characteristics. A social system based on kinship, reciprocity, and sharing is appropriate for an economy with few people and limited resources. People have to share meat when they get it; otherwise, it rots. The nomadic pursuit of wild plants and animals tends to discourage permanent settlement, wealth accumulation, and social distinctions.

Marriage and kinship create ties between members of different bands. Trade and visiting also link them. Band leaders are leaders in name only. Bands are *egalitarian* societies. That is, they make only a few social distinctions, based mainly on age, gender, and individual talents or achievements. In these egalitarian societies, the "leaders" are merely first among equals. If they give advice or make decisions, they have no sure way to enforce those decisions.

## The Inuit

The Aboriginal Inuit (Hoebel 1954, 2006), another group of foragers, provide a classic example of methods of settling disputes—**conflict resolution**—in stateless societies. All societies have ways of settling disputes (of variable effectiveness) along with cultural rules or norms about proper and improper behavior. **Norms** are cultural standards or guidelines that enable individuals to distinguish between appropriate and inappropriate behavior in a given society (N. Kottak 2002). Although rules and norms are cultural universals, only state societies, those with established governments, have formal *laws* that are formulated, proclaimed, and enforced (see Donovan 2007; Goodale 2017; Pirie 2013).

Foragers lacked formal **law** in the sense of a legal code with trial and enforcement, but they did have methods of social control and dispute settlement. The absence of law did not mean total anarchy. As described by E. A. Hoebel (1954, 2006) in a classic ethnographic study of conflict resolution, a sparse population of some 20,000 Inuit spanned 6,000 miles (9,500 kilometers) of the Arctic region. The most significant social groups were the nuclear family and the band. Some bands had headmen. There also were shamans (part-time religious specialists). However, these positions conferred little power on those who occupied them. Each Inuit had access to the resources he or she needed to sustain life. Every man could hunt, fish, and make the tools necessary for subsistence. Every woman could obtain the materials needed to make clothing, prepare food, and do domestic work. Inuit men could even hunt and fish in the territories of other local groups. There was no notion of private ownership of territory or animals.

Hunting and fishing by men were the primary subsistence activities. The diverse and abundant plant foods available in warmer areas, where female labor in gathering is important, were absent in the Arctic. Traveling on land and sea in a bitter environment, Inuit men faced more dangers than women did. The traditional male role took its toll in lives, so that adult women outnumbered men. This permitted some men to have two or three wives. The ability to support more than one wife conferred a certain amount of prestige, but it also encouraged envy. (*Prestige* is social esteem, respect, or approval.) If a man seemed to be taking additional wives just to enhance his reputation, a rival was likely to steal one of them. Most Inuit disputes were between men and originated over women, caused by wife stealing or adultery.

A jilted husband had several options. He could try to kill the wife thief. However, if he succeeded, one of his rival's kinsmen surely would try to kill him in retaliation. One dispute might escalate into several deaths as relatives avenged a succession of murders. No government existed to intervene and stop such a *blood feud* (a murderous feud between families). However, one also could challenge a rival to a song battle. In a public setting, contestants made up insulting songs about each other. At the end of the match, the audience proclaimed the winner. However, if the winner was the man whose wife had been stolen, there was no guarantee she would return. Often she stayed with her abductor.

## Tribal Cultivators

As is true of foraging bands, there are no totally autonomous tribes in today's world. Still, there are societies, for example, in Papua New Guinea and in South America's tropical forests, in which tribal principles continue to operate. Tribes typically have a horticultural or pastoral economy and are organized into villages and/or *descent groups* (kin groups whose members trace descent from a common ancestor). Tribes lack socioeconomic stratification (i.e., a class structure) and a formal government of their own. A few tribes still conduct small-scale warfare, in the form of intervillage raiding. Tribes have more effective regulatory mechanisms than foragers do, but tribal societies have no sure means of enforcing political decisions (see Gluckman 2012). The main regulatory officials are village heads, "big men," descent-group leaders, village councils, and leaders of pantribal associations (described later in this section). All these figures and groups have limited authority.

Like foragers, horticulturalists tend to be egalitarian, although some have marked *gender stratification:* an unequal distribution of resources, power, prestige, and personal freedom between men and women (see Chapter 14). Horticultural villages usually are small, with low population density and open access to strategic resources. Age, gender, and personal traits determine how much respect people receive and how much support they get from others. Egalitarianism diminishes, however, as village size and population density increase. Horticultural villages usually have headmen—rarely, if ever, headwomen.

## The Village Head

The Yanomami (Chagnon 2013a; Ferguson 1995; Ramos 1995) live in southern Venezuela and an adjacent region of Brazil. When anthropologists first studied them, they numbered about 26,000 people living in 200 to 250 widely scattered villages, each with a population between 40 and 250. The Yanomami are horticulturalists who also hunt and gather. Their staple crops are bananas and plantains (a banana-like crop). The Yanomami have more social groups than exist in a foraging society. They have families, villages, and descent groups. Their descent groups, which span more than one village, are *patrilineal* (ancestry is traced back through males only) and *exogamous* (people must marry outside their own descent group). However, branches of two different descent groups may live in the same village and intermarry.

Traditionally the only leadership position has been that of **village head** (always a man). A village head is chosen based on his personal characteristics (e.g., bravery, persuasiveness) and the support he can muster from fellow villagers. The position is not inherited, and the authority of the village head is severely limited. The headman lacks the right to issue orders. He can only persuade, harangue, and try to influence public opinion. For example, if he wants people to clean up the central plaza in preparation for a feast, he must start sweeping it himself, hoping his covillagers will take the hint and relieve him.

When conflict erupts within the village, the headman may be called on as a mediator who listens to both sides. He will give an opinion and advice. If a disputant is unsatisfied, the headman has no power to back his decisions and no way to impose punishments.

A Yanomami headman also must lead in generosity. Expected to be more generous than any other villager, he cultivates more land. His garden provides much of the food consumed when his village hosts a feast for another village. The headman represents the village in its dealings with outsiders, including Venezuelan and Brazilian government agents.

Napoleon Chagnon (2013a) describes how one village headman, Kaobawa, guaranteed safety to a delegation from a village with which a covillager of his wanted to start a war. Kaobawa was a particularly effective headman. He had demonstrated his mettle in battle, but he also knew how to use diplomacy to avoid offending other villagers. No one in his village had a better personality for the headmanship. Nor (because Kaobawa had many brothers) did anyone have more supporters. Among the Yanomami, when a village is dissatisfied with its headman, its members can leave and found a new village. This happens from time to time and is called *village fissioning*.

With its many villages and descent groups, Yanomami sociopolitical organization is more complicated than that of a band-organized society. The Yanomami face more problems in regulating relations between groups and individuals. Although a headman sometimes can prevent a specific violent act, intervillage raiding has been common in some areas of Yanomami territory, particularly those studied by Chagnon (2013a, 2013b).

The Yanomami are not isolated from outside events. They live in two nation-states, Venezuela and Brazil, and attacks by outsiders, especially Brazilian ranchers and miners, have plagued them (Chagnon 2013a; *Cultural Survival Quarterly* 1989; Ferguson 1995). During a Brazilian gold rush between 1987 and 1991, one Yanomami died each day, on average, from such attacks. By 1991, some 40,000 miners had reached the Brazilian Yanomami homeland. They introduced new diseases, and the swollen population ensured that old diseases became epidemic. Brazilian Yanomami were dying at a rate of 10 percent annually, and their fertility rate had dropped to zero. Since then, one Brazilian president declared a huge Yanomami territory off-limits to outsiders. Unfortunately, local politicians, miners, and ranchers have managed to evade the ban. The future of the Yanomami remains uncertain, especially with the election in 2018 of a new Brazilian president, Jair Bolsonaro, who has shown little interest in preserving indigenous peoples and their territories.

# The "Big Man"

Many societies of the South Pacific, particularly on the Melanesian Islands and in Papua New Guinea, had a kind of political leader that we call the big man. The **big man** (almost always a male) was an elaborate version of the village head, but with one significant difference. Unlike the village head, whose leadership is limited to one village, the big man had supporters in several villages. The big man thus was a regulator of *regional* political organization.

Consider the Kapauku Papuans, inhabitants of Irian Jaya, Indonesia (located on the island of New Guinea). Anthropologist Leopold Pospisil (1963) studied the Kapauku (then 45,000 people), who grew crops (with the sweet potato as their staple) and raised pigs. Their economy was too labor intensive to be described as simple horticulture. It required mutual aid in turning the soil before planting. The digging of long drainage ditches, which a big man often helped organize, was an even more complex endeavor. Kapauku cultivation supported a larger and denser population than does the simpler horticulture of the Yanomami. The Kapauku economy required collective cultivation and political regulation of the more complex tasks. The key political figure was the big man.

Attributes that distinguished the big man from his fellows included wealth, generosity, eloquence, physical fitness, bravery, supernatural powers, and the ability to gain the support and loyalty of others. Men became big men because they had certain personalities; they did not inherit their position but created it through hard work and good judgment. Wealth resulted from successful pig breeding and trading. As a man's pig herd and prestige grew, he attracted supporters. He sponsored pig feasts in which pork (provided by the big man and his supporters) was distributed to guests, bringing him more prestige and widening his network of support (see also O'Connor 2015).

The big man's supporters, acknowledging his past favors and anticipating future rewards, recognized him as a leader and accepted his decisions as binding. The Kapauku big man, known as the *tonowi*, was an important regulator of regional events. He helped determine the dates for feasts and markets. He initiated economic projects requiring the cooperation of a regional community.

The big man persuades people to organize feasts, which distribute pork and wealth. Shown here is a big man from the Huli (or Haroli) tribe of the southern highlands of Papua New Guinea. Does your own society have equivalents of big men? Edward Reeves/Alamy Stock Photo

The Kapauku big man again exemplifies a generalization about leadership in tribal societies: If someone achieves wealth and widespread respect and support, he or she must be generous. The big man worked hard not to hoard wealth but to be able to give away the fruits of his labor, to convert wealth into prestige and gratitude. A stingy big man would lose his support. Selfish and greedy big men sometimes were killed by their fellows (Zimmer-Tamakoshi 1997).

How similar are contemporary politicians to the big man? Big men get their loyalists to produce and deliver pigs, just as modern politicians persuade their supporters to make campaign contributions. And like big men, successful American politicians try to be generous with their supporters. Payback may take the form of a night in the Lincoln bedroom, a strategic dinner invitation, an ambassadorship, or largesse to a place that was particularly supportive. Big men amass wealth, then distribute pigs and their meat. Successful American politicians may give away "pork." As with the big man, communication skills contribute to political success (e.g., Ronald Reagan, Bill Clinton, Barack Obama, Donald Trump), although lack of such skills isn't necessarily fatal (e.g., either President Bush). What about physical fitness? Hair, height, and health are still political advantages. Bravery, in the form of military service, also helps political careers (e.g., John Kerry and John McCain), but it certainly isn't required, nor does it guarantee success. Supernatural powers? Candidates who proclaim themselves atheists are almost as unusual as self-identified witches or warlocks. Almost all political candidates claim to belong to a mainstream religion. Some even present their candidacies as promoting God's will. (How does the current leader of your country fare in terms of the attributes discussed in this paragraph?)

## Pantribal Sodalities

Big men could forge regional political organization, albeit temporarily, by mobilizing supporters from several villages. Other principles in tribal societies—such as a belief in common ancestry, kinship, or descent—could be used to link local groups within a region. The same descent group, for example, might span several villages, and its dispersed members might recognize the same leader.

Principles other than kinship also can link local groups, especially in modern societies. People who live in different parts of the same nation may belong to the same labor union, sorority or fraternity, political party, or religious denomination. In tribes, nonkin groups called *associations* or *sodalities* may serve a similar linking function. Often, sodalities are based on common age or gender, with all-male sodalities more common than all-female ones.

**Pantribal sodalities** are groups that extend across the whole tribe, spanning several villages. Such sodalities were especially likely to develop in situations of warfare with a neighboring tribe. Mobilizing their members from multiple villages within the same tribe, pantribal sodalities could assemble a force to attack, defend, or retaliate against another tribe.

The best examples of pantribal sodalities come from the Central Plains of North America and from tropical Africa. During the 18th and 19th centuries, Native American populations of the Great Plains of the United States and Canada experienced a rapid growth of pantribal sodalities. This development reflected an economic change that followed the spread of horses, which had been reintroduced to the Americas by the Spanish, to the area between the Rocky Mountains and the Mississippi River. Many Plains societies changed their adaptive strategies because of the horse. At first they had been foragers who hunted bison (buffalo) on foot. Later they adopted a mixed economy based on hunting, gathering, and horticulture. Finally they changed to a much more specialized economy based on horseback hunting of bison (eventually with rifles).

As the Plains tribes were undergoing these changes, other groups also adopted horseback hunting and moved into the Plains. Attempting to occupy the same area, groups came into conflict. A pattern of warfare developed in which members of one tribe raided another, usually for horses. The economy demanded that people follow the movement of the bison herds. During the winter, when the bison dispersed, a tribe fragmented into small bands and families. In the summer, when huge herds assembled on the Plains, the tribe reunited. They camped together for social, political, and religious activities, but mainly for communal bison hunting.

Two activities demanded strong leadership: organizing and carrying out raids on enemy camps (to capture horses) and managing the summer bison hunt. All the Plains societies developed pantribal sodalities, and leadership roles within them, to police the summer hunt. Leaders coordinated hunting efforts, making sure that people did not cause a stampede with an early shot or an ill-advised action. Leaders imposed severe penalties, including seizure of a culprit's wealth, for disobedience.

Many tribes that adopted this Plains strategy of adaptation had once been foragers for whom hunting and gathering had been individual or small-group affairs. They never had come together previously as a single social unit. Age and gender were available as social principles that could quickly and efficiently forge unrelated people into pantribal sodalities.

Raiding of one tribe by another, this time for cattle rather than horses, was common in eastern and southeastern Africa, where pantribal sodalities also developed. Among the pastoral Masai of Kenya, men born during the same four-year period were circumcised together and belonged to the same named group, an age set, throughout their lives. The sets moved through *age grades*, the most important of which was the warrior grade. Members of a set felt a strong allegiance to one another. Masai women lacked comparable set organization, but they also passed through culturally recognized age grades: the initiate, the married woman, and the female elder.

In certain parts of western and central Africa, pantribal sodalities are secret societies, made up exclusively of men or women. Like our college fraternities and sororities, these associations have secret initiation ceremonies. Among the Mende of Sierra Leone, men's and women's secret societies were very influential. The men's group, the Poro, trained boys in social conduct, ethics, and religion and supervised political and economic activities. Leadership roles in the Poro often overshadowed village headship and played an important part in social control, dispute management, and tribal political regulation. Age, gender, and ritual can link members of different local groups into a single social collectivity in a tribe and thus create a sense of ethnic identity, of belonging to the same cultural tradition.

## Nomadic Politics

The political systems associated with pastoralism varied considerably, ranging from tribal societies to chiefdoms. The Masai (just discussed) live in a tribal society. The sociopolitical organization of such tribal herders is based on descent groups and pantribal sodalities. Other pastoralists, however, have chiefs and live in nation-states. The scope of political authority among pastoralists expands considerably as regulatory problems

garden. Every three years, a group of boys around the age of 20 were formally initiated into manhood. They went to a secluded mountain lodge, where they were visited and inseminated by several older men.

A code of propriety governed male-male sex among the Etoro. Although sexual relations between older and younger males were considered culturally essential, those between boys of the same age were discouraged. A boy who took semen from other youths was believed to be sapping their life force and stunting their growth. A boy's rapid physical development could suggest he was getting semen from other boys. Like a sex-hungry wife, he could be shunned as a witch.

The sexual practices described in this section rested not on hormones or genes but on cultural beliefs and traditions. The Etoro shared a cultural pattern, which Gilbert Herdt (1984, 2006) calls "ritualized homosexuality," with some 50 other tribes in one area of Papua New Guinea. These societies illustrate one extreme of a male-female avoidance pattern that has been widespread in Papua New Guinea, and in patrilineal-patrilocal societies more generally.

Flexibility in sexual expression seems to be an aspect of our primate heritage. Both masturbation and same-sex sexual activity exist among chimpanzees and other primates. Male bonobos (pygmy chimps) regularly engage in a form of mutual masturbation that has been called "penis fencing." Female bonobos get sexual pleasure from rubbing their genitals against those of other females (De Waal 1997). Our primate sexual potential is molded by culture, the environment, and reproductive necessity. Male-female coitus is practiced in all human societies—which, after all, must reproduce themselves—but alternatives also are widespread (Lyons and Lyons 2011; Rathus, Nevid, and Fichner-Rathus 2018). Like our gender roles, the sexual component of human personality and identity—the ways in which we express our "natural," or biological, sexual urges—is a matter that culture and environment influence and limit.

## Anthropology Today  *Gender, Ethnicity, and a Gold Medal for Fiji*

On August 11, 2016, in Rio de Janeiro, Brazil, the island nation of Fiji won its first-ever Olympic medal. That gold medal, in men's rugby sevens, was awarded after Fiji trounced Great Britain, its former colonial master, by a score of 43 to 7. In Fiji, a Southwest Pacific nation of some 900,000 people, rugby is immensely popular. Specifically, Fijians excel at rugby sevens, a rapid game played by seven participants per side in just 14 minutes.

The addition of rugby to the roster of Olympic sports for the Rio summer games offered Fijians an opportunity to excel in a venue where previously Fiji had been woefully unrepresented. Only two Fijian athletes had qualified to participate in the games between 1956, when Fiji officially entered the Olympics, and 2016, when it won its gold medal.

Rugby is the national sport of Fiji, where its fans include men, women, and Fijians of all ethnic backgrounds. There are, however, dramatic differences in rugby participation between men and women, and between Fiji's two main ethnic groups: indigenous Fijians and Indo-Fijians. The latter are the descendants of

Indian immigrants who came to the island as indentured servants or free migrants during the 19th and 20th centuries, when both Fiji and India were British colonies. As anthropologist Niko Besnier, who has conducted fieldwork in Fiji since 1980, notes, participation in rugby is mainly by men who are indigenous Fijians.

In contrast to the success of the men's rugby team, the Fijian women's team—the Fijiana—managed only an eighth place finish out of 11 teams participating. This less-than-stellar result is not surprising given Fijian attitudes toward female players. Besnier and Brownell (2016) report that many Fijians view female rugby players as "tomboys"—women who act too masculine by being independent, aggressive, and loud, and who often are assumed to be lesbians. Besnier heard stories of female players who had been beaten by their

fathers or expelled from their family homes—an especially unhappy fate in a kin-based society. The Fijiana also receive little official support, with few corporate sponsors, unlike the men's team, which enjoys the sponsorship of the country's major companies. When Besnier visited the Fijiana at their training camp in March 2016, he found the women put up in a Christian camp, five people to a room, while the men's team was lodged at a luxury resort. Prior to the Olympic Games, there was even an attempt to replace some of the actual Fijiana national team with women from netball, who were more "feminine acting" even though they knew little about rugby (Besnier and Brownell 2016).

Women aren't the only Fijians who are discouraged from rugby. Indo-Fijians also face multiple barriers to participation in the sport. Indigenous Fijians contend that

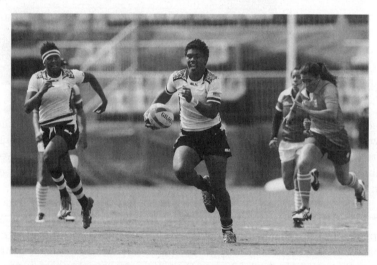

Fijiana player Rusila Nagasau rushes to score against Colombia during a women's rugby match on Day 2 (August 7) of the 2016 summer Olympic Games in Rio de Janeiro, Brazil. David Rogers/Getty Images Sport/Getty Images

*continued*

Citizens of Aitutaki, one of the Cook Islands in Polynesia, celebrate the investiture of Makirau Haurua as one of Aitutaki's four paramount chiefs. Dressed in traditional garb, Makirau Haurua is carried on a makeshift throne as part of his elevation to chiefly status. Marco Pompeo Photography/Alamy Stock Photo

Such a flow of resources to and then from a central place is known as *chiefly redistribution*, which offers economic advantages. If different parts of the chiefdom specialized in particular products, chiefly redistribution made those products available to the entire society. Chiefly redistribution also helped stimulate production beyond the basic subsistence level and provided a central storehouse for goods that might become scarce in times of famine (Earle 1997).

## Status Systems

Social status (one's position in society) in chiefdoms was based on seniority of descent. Polynesian chiefs kept extremely long genealogies. Some chiefs (without writing) managed to trace their ancestry back 50 generations. Everyone in a chiefdom was related to everyone else. Presumably, all were descended from the same founding ancestors.

The chief would be the oldest child (usually son) of the oldest child of the oldest child, and so on. Degrees of seniority were calculated so intricately on some islands that there were as many ranks as people. For example, the third son would rank below the second, who in turn would rank below the first. The children of an eldest brother, however, would rank above the children of the next brother, whose children in turn would outrank those of younger brothers. However, even the lowest-ranking man or woman in a chiefdom was still the chief's relative, and everyone, including the chief, had to share with their relatives. It was difficult to draw a line between elites and common people.

Nevertheless, in chiefdoms as in states, some men, women, and even children had more prestige, wealth, and power than others did. These elites controlled strategic resources such as land and water. Earle (1987) characterizes chiefs as "an incipient aristocracy with advantages in wealth and lifestyle" (p. 290).

Compared with chiefdoms, archaic states drew a much firmer line between elites and masses, distinguishing at least between nobles and commoners. Kinship ties did not extend from the nobles to the commoners because of *stratum endogamy*–marriage within one's own group. Commoners married commoners; elites married elites.

## The Emergence of Stratification

We see that a key difference between chiefdom and state was the chiefdom's kinship basis. However, we know of historical instances in which ambitious chiefs and their closest relatives have launched an attack on their society's kinship basis. In Madagascar they would do this by demoting their more distant relatives to commoner status and banning marriage between nobles and commoners (Kottak 1980). Such moves, if accepted by the society, created separate *social strata*–unrelated groups that differ in their access to wealth, prestige, and power. (A *stratum* is one of two or more groups that contrast in social status and access to strategic resources. Each stratum includes people of both sexes and all ages.) The creation of separate social strata is called *stratification*, and its emergence signified the transition from chiefdom to state. The presence of stratification is one of the key distinguishing features of a state.

The influential sociologist Max Weber (1922/1968) defined three related dimensions of social stratification: (1) Economic status, or **wealth**, encompasses a person's material assets, including income, land, and other types of property. (2) Power, the ability to exercise one's will over others–to get what one wants–is the basis of political status. (3) **Prestige**–the basis of social status–refers to esteem, respect, or approval for acts, deeds, or qualities considered exemplary. Prestige, or "cultural capital" (Bourdieu 1984), gives people a sense of worth and respect, which they may often convert into economic advantage (see Table 12.1).

In archaic states–for the first time in human history–there were contrasts in wealth, power, and prestige between entire groups (social strata) of men and women. The **superordinate** (the higher, or elite) stratum had privileged access to valued resources.

TABLE 12.1    **Max Weber's Three Dimensions of Stratification**

| Wealth | Economic status |
|---|---|
| Power | Political status |
| Prestige | Social status |

# Chapter 15

# Religion

## What Is Religion?

In his book *Religion: An Anthropological View,* Anthony F. C. Wallace (1966) defined **religion** as "belief and ritual concerned with supernatural beings, powers, and forces" (p. 5). By "supernatural," Wallace was referring to a nonmaterial realm beyond (but believed to impinge on) the observable world. The supernatural cannot be verified or falsified empirically. It cannot be explained in ordinary or natural terms. It must be accepted "on faith." Supernatural *beings* (e.g., deities, ghosts, demons, souls, spirits) dwell outside our material world, which they may visit from time to time. There also are supernatural or sacred *forces,* some of them wielded by deities and spirits, others that simply exist. In many societies, people believe they can benefit from, become imbued with, or manipulate such forces (see Bielo 2015; Boddy and Lambek 2013; Bowen 2017; Eller 2015; Sidky 2015; Stein and Stein 2017).

Wallace's definition of religion focuses on beings, powers, and forces within the supernatural realm. Émile Durkheim (1912/2001), one of the founders of the anthropology of religion, focused on the distinction between the sacred (the domain of religion) and the profane (the everyday world). Like the supernatural for Wallace, Durkheim's "sacred" was a domain set off from the ordinary, or the mundane. (Durkheim actually used the word *profane* for the ordinary, natural, non-sacred world). For Durkheim, although every society recognized a sacred domain, the specifics of that domain would vary from society to society. In other words, he saw religion as a cultural universal, while recognizing that specific religious beliefs and practices vary from society to society.

Durkheim believed that Native Australian societies had retained the most elementary, or basic, forms of religion. He noted that their most sacred objects, including plants and animals that served as totems, were not supernatural at all. Rather, they were "real-world" entities (e.g., kangaroos, grubs) that had acquired religious meaning and became sacred objects for the social groups that "worshipped" them. Durkheim saw totemism as the most elementary or basic form of religion.

Durkheim (1912/2001) focused on groups of people—congregants—who gather together for worship, such as a group of Native Australians worshiping a particular totem. He stressed the collective, social, and shared nature of religion; the meanings it embodies; and the emotions it generates. He highlighted religious *effervescence*, the bubbling up of collective emotional intensity generated by worship. As Michael Lambek (2008) remarks, "good anthropology understands that religious worlds are real, vivid, and significant to those who construct and inhabit them" (p. 5).

Congregants who worship together share certain beliefs; they have accepted a particular set of doctrines concerning the sacred and its relationship to human beings. The word *religion* derives from the Latin *religare*—"to tie, to bind"—but it is not necessary for all members of a given religion to meet together as a common body. Subgroups meet regularly at local congregation sites. They may attend occasional meetings with adherents representing a wider region. And they may form an imagined community with people of similar faith throughout the world.

Verbal manifestations of religious beliefs include prayers, chants, myths, texts, and statements about ethics and morality (see Myers-Moro and Myers 2012; Stein and Stein 2017; Winzeler 2012). Other aspects of religion include notions about purity and pollution (including taboos involving diet and physical contact), sacrifice, initiation, rites of passage, vision quests, pilgrimages, spirit possession, prophecy, study, devotion, and moral actions (Lambek 2008, p. 9).

Like ethnicity and language, religion is associated with social divisions within and between societies and nations. Religion both unites and divides. Participation in common rites may affirm, and thus maintain, the solidarity of a group of adherents. As we know from daily headlines, however, religious difference also may be associated with bitter enmity. Contacts and confrontations have increased between so-called world religions, such as Christianity and Islam, and the more localized forms of religion that missionaries typically lump together under the disparaging term "paganism." Increasingly, ethnic, regional, and class conflicts come to be framed in religious terms. Contemporary examples of religion as a social and political force include the rise of the religious right in the United States, the worldwide spread of Pentecostalism, and various Islamic movements (see Lindquist and Handelman 2013).

Armies help states subdue and conquer neighboring nonstates, but conquest isn't the only reason state organization has spread. Although states impose hardships, they also offer advantages. States have formal agencies (e.g., military and police) designed to protect against external threats and to preserve internal order. When they are successful in promoting internal peace, states enhance production. Their economies can support massive, dense populations, which supply armies and colonists to promote expansion.

## Fiscal Support

States rely on financial, or **fiscal**, mechanisms (e.g., taxation) to support the government apparatus and agents just discussed. As in the chiefdom, the state intervenes in production, distribution, and consumption. The state may require a certain area to produce specific things, or ban certain activities in particular places. Like chiefdoms, states have redistribution ("spreading the wealth around"), but less of what comes in from the people actually goes directly back to the people.

In nonstates, people customarily share with their relatives, but people who live in states also have to turn over a significant portion of what they produce to the state. Officials standardize weights and measures and collect taxes on goods passing into or through the state. Of the revenues the state collects, it reallocates part for the general good and keeps another part (often larger) for itself—its agents and agencies.

State organization doesn't bring more freedom or leisure to the common people, who may be conscripted to build monumental public works. Some projects, such as dams and irrigation systems, may be economically necessary, but residents of archaic states also had to build temples, palaces, and tombs for the elites. Those elites reveled in the consumption of sumptuary goods—jewelry, exotic food and drink, and stylish clothing reserved for, or affordable only by, the rich. Peasants' diets suffered as they struggled to meet government demands for produce, currency, or labor (see Scott 2017). Commoners perished in territorial wars that had little relevance to their own needs. To what extent are these observations true of contemporary states?

Although it offers advantages, we should not think of the state as "better" than other forms of sociopolitical organization. Stratification and the state are antithetical to the egalitarian and free-ranging way of life practiced by our foraging ancestors. We have just considered some of the demands that states place on ordinary people. It should not be surprising, then, that populations in various parts of the world have resisted, and tried to avoid or escape, state organization. We saw in Chapter 11 that foragers do not necessarily adopt food production just because they know of its existence. Similarly, certain societies have managed to resist or escape state organization by adopting nomadic lifestyles that are difficult for states to supervise. For example, James C. Scott (2009) discusses how a belt of highland societies with economies based on shifting cultivation in Southeast Asia have survived for generations outside the control of states based in the lowlands of the same countries.

## Social Control

In studying political systems, anthropologists pay attention not only to formal, governmental institutions but also to other forms of social control. The concept of social control is broader than "the political." **Social control** refers to "those fields of the social system (beliefs, practices, and institutions) that are most actively involved in the maintenance of any norms and the regulation of any conflict" (N. Kottak 2002, p. 290). *Norms*, remember, are cultural standards or guidelines that enable individuals to distinguish between appropriate and inappropriate behavior.

Previous sections of this chapter have focused more on formal political organization than on sociopolitical process. We've seen how the scale of political systems has expanded through time and in relation to economic changes. We've examined means of conflict resolution, or their absence, in various types of society. We've looked at political decision making, including leaders and their limits. We've also recognized that all contemporary humans have been affected by states, colonialism, and the spread of the world system (Kaplan 2014; Shore et al. 2011).

*Sociopolitical* was introduced as a key concept at the beginning of this chapter. So far, we've focused mainly on the *political* part of sociopolitical; now we focus on the *social* part. In this section we'll see that political systems have their informal, social, and subtle aspects along with their formal, governmental, and public dimensions.

## Hegemony and Resistance

In addition to the formal mechanisms discussed in the section "State Systems," what techniques do states employ to maintain social order? Antonio Gramsci (1971) developed the concept of **hegemony** for a stratified social order in which subordinates comply with domination by internalizing their rulers' values and accepting the "naturalness" of domination (this is, the way things were meant to be). According to Pierre Bourdieu (1977, p. 164), every social order tries to make its own arbitrariness (including its mechanisms of control and domination) seem natural and in everyone's interest—even when that is not the case. Both Bourdieu (1977) and Michel Foucault (1979) argue that it is easier and more effective to dominate people in their minds than to try to control their bodies. Nonphysical forms of social control include various techniques of persuading and managing people and of monitoring and recording their beliefs, activities, and contacts.

Hegemony, the internalization of a dominant ideology, is one way in which elites curb resistance to their power and privileged position. Another way to discourage resistance is to make subordinates believe they eventually will gain power—as young people usually foresee when they let their elders dominate them. Yet another way to curb resistance is to separate or isolate people while supervising them closely, as is done in prisons (Foucault 1979).

Some contexts enable or encourage public resistance, particularly when people are allowed to assemble. The setting of a crowd offers anonymity, while also reinforcing and encouraging the common sentiments that have brought those people together. The elites, sensing the threat of surging crowds and public rebellion, often discourage such gatherings. They try to limit and control holidays, funerals, dances, festivals, and other occasions that might unite the oppressed. For example, in the American South before the Civil War, gatherings of five or more slaves were prohibited unless a White person was present.

Also working to discourage resistance are factors that interfere with community formation—such as geographic, linguistic, and ethnic separation. Elites want to isolate the oppressed rather than bringing them together in a group. Consequently, southern U.S.

One of these universal questions is what happens in sleep and trance, and with death. Another is the question of why some people prosper, while others fail. A religious explanation might blame unequal success or fortune on such nonmaterial factors as luck, mana, sorcery, or being one of "God's chosen."

The beliefs in spiritual beings (e.g., animism) and supernatural forces (e.g., mana) fit within Wallace's definition of religion given at the beginning of this chapter. Most religions include both spirits and forces. Likewise, the supernatural beliefs of contemporary North Americans include beings (gods, saints, souls, demons) and forces (charms, talismans, crystals, and sacred objects).

## Magic and Religion

**Magic** refers to supernatural techniques intended to accomplish specific goals. Those techniques include actions, offerings, spells, formulas, and incantations used with deities or with impersonal forces. Magicians might employ *imitative magic* to produce a desired effect by imitating it. For example, if magicians wish to harm someone, they may imitate that effect on an image of the victim. Sticking pins in "voodoo dolls" is an example. With *contagious magic*, whatever is done to an object is believed to affect a person who has, or once had, contact with it. Sometimes practitioners of contagious magic use body products from prospective victims—their nails or hair, for example. The spell performed on the body product is believed eventually to reach the person. Magic exists in societies with diverse religious beliefs, including animism, mana, polytheism, and monotheism.

## Uncertainty, Anxiety, Solace

Religion and magic serve emotional needs as well as explanatory ones. Religion can help people face death and endure life crises. Magical techniques can be used when outcomes are beyond human control. According to Malinowski, when people face uncertainty and danger, they often turn to magic. The Trobriand Islanders, whom Malinowski studied, used magic during sailing—a hazardous activity in which people lacked control over wind and weather (Malinowski 1931/1978). Only in situations they could not control did Trobrianders, out of psychological stress, turn to magic.

Despite our improving technical skills, we still cannot control every outcome, so magic persists in contemporary societies. Most of us still draw on magic and ritual in situations of uncertainty, such as before a test or perhaps a plane ride. To enhance their success magically, athletes use personal rituals in many sports, with baseball magic particularly noteworthy. The anthropologist George Gmelch (1978, 2006) describes a series of rituals, taboos, and sacred objects used in the sport. Like Trobriand sailing magic, these behaviors reduce psychological stress, creating an illusion of magical control when real control is lacking. Baseball magic is especially prevalent in pitching and batting (see this chapter's "Anthropology Today").

## Rituals

Several features distinguish **rituals** from other kinds of behavior (Rappaport 1974, 1999). Rituals are formal—stylized, repetitive, and stereotyped. People perform them in special places and at set times. Rituals include liturgical orders—sequences of words and actions invented prior to the current performance of the ritual in which they occur.

These features link rituals to plays, but there are important differences. Actors merely portray something, but ritual performers—who make up congregations—are in earnest. Rituals convey information about the participants and their traditions. Repeated year after year, generation after generation, rituals translate enduring messages, values, and sentiments into action.

Rituals are social acts. Inevitably, some participants are more committed than others are to the beliefs that lie behind the rites. However, just by taking part in a joint public act, the performers signal that they accept a common social and moral order, one that transcends their status as individuals.

## Rites of Passage

Magic and religion, as Malinowski noted, can reduce anxiety, allay fears, and help people deal with life crises. Ironically, beliefs and rituals also can create anxiety and a sense of insecurity and danger (Radcliffe-Brown 1952/1965). Anxiety may arise because a ritual exists. Indeed, participation in a collective ritual (e.g., circumcision of early teen boys, common among East African pastoralists) can produce considerable stress, whose common relief, once the ritual is completed, enhances the solidarity of the participants. Collective circumcision is an example of a ritual, or rite, of passage, as participants transition from one stage of life to another.

**Rites of passage** (rituals associated with the transition from one place, or stage of life, to another) can be individual or collective. The traditional vision quests of Native Americans, particularly the Plains Indians, illustrate individual rites of passage. To move from boyhood to manhood, a youth would temporarily separate from his community. After a period of isolation in the wilderness, often featuring fasting and drug consumption, the young man would see a vision, which would become his guardian spirit. He would return then to his community as an adult.

Contemporary rituals or rites of passage include confirmations, baptisms, bar and bat mitzvahs, initiations, weddings, and application for Medicare. Passage rites involve changes in social status, such as from boyhood to manhood, or from nonmember to sorority sister. More generally, a rite of passage may mark any change in place, condition, social position, or age.

All rites of passage have three phases: separation, liminality, and incorporation. In the first phase, people withdraw from ordinary society. In the third phase, they reenter society, having completed a ritual that changes their status. The second, or liminal, phase is the most critical and interesting. It is the limbo, or "time-out," during which people have left one status but haven't yet entered or joined the next (Downey, Kinane, and Parker 2017; Turner 1967/1974).

**Liminality** always has certain characteristics. Liminal people exist apart from ordinary distinctions and expectations; they are living in a time out of time. A series of contrasts set liminality apart from normal social life. For example, among the Ndembu of Zambia, a new chief underwent a rite of passage before taking office. During the liminal period, his past and future positions in society were ignored, even reversed. He was subjected to a variety of insults, orders, and humiliations.

Often, rites of passage are collective. Several individuals—boys being circumcised, fraternity or sorority initiates, men at military boot camps, football players in summer

Although it isn't part of any formal or official authority structure, shame can be a powerful social sanction. People aren't just citizens of governments; they are members of society, and social sanctions exist alongside governmental ones. Such sanctions exemplify other "weapons of the weak," because they often are wielded most effectively by people, such as women or young people, who have limited access to the formal authority structure.

## The Igbo Women's War

Shame and ridicule—used by women against men—played a key role in a decisive protest movement that took place in southeastern Nigeria in late 1929. This is remembered as the "Aba Women's Riots of 1929" in British colonial history and as the "Women's War" in Igbo history (see Dorward, 1983; Martin 1988; Mba 1982; Oriji 2000; Van Allen 1971). During this two-month "war," at least 25,000 Igbo women joined protests against British officials, their agents, and their colonial policies. This massive revolt touched off the most serious challenge to British rule in the history of what was then the British colony of Nigeria.

In 1914, the British had implemented a policy of indirect rule by appointing local Nigerian men as their agents—known as "warrant chiefs." These chiefs became increasingly oppressive, seizing property, imposing arbitrary regulations, and imprisoning people who criticized them. Colonial administrators further stoked local outrage when they announced plans to impose taxes on Igbo market women. These women were key suppliers of food for Nigeria's growing urban population; they feared being forced out of business by the new tax.

After hearing about the tax in November 1929, thousands of Igbo women assembled in various towns to protest both the warrant chiefs and the taxes on market women. They used a traditional practice of censoring and shaming men through all-night song and dance ridicule (often called "sitting on a man"). This process entailed constant singing and dancing around the houses and offices of the warrant chiefs. The women also followed the chiefs' every moves, forcing the men to pay attention by invading their space (see also Walton and Suarez 2016). Disturbed by the whole process, wives of the warrant chiefs also pressured their husbands to listen to the protesters' demands.

The protests were remarkably effective. The tax was abandoned, and many of the warrant chiefs resigned, some to be replaced by women. Other women were appointed to the Native courts as judges. The position of women improved in Nigeria, where market women especially remain a powerful political force to this day. Many subsequent Nigerian political events were inspired by the Women's War, including additional tax protests. Furthermore, the Igbo Women's War inspired protests all over Africa. It is seen as the first major challenge to British authority in Nigeria and West Africa during the colonial period.

At the beginning of this chapter, *power* was defined as the ability to exercise one's will over others. It was contrasted with *authority*—the formal, socially approved use of power by government officials and others. The case of the Igbo Women's War shows how women effectively used their social power (through song, dance, noise, and "in-your-face" behavior) to subvert the formal authority structure and, in so doing, gained greater influence within that structure. Can you think of other, perhaps recent examples? We see how gossip, ridicule, and shaming can be effective processes of social control, which can even result in governmental change. The Igbo case also shows the importance of community organizing and political mobilization in effective resistance.

## Anthropology Today    *The Illegality Industry: A Failed System of Border Control*

"Secure the border!" has become a familiar refrain in political discussion about undocumented immigrants to the United States. But what exactly does this mean? How can a border be truly secure in today's world, in which tens of millions of people are routinely on the move, and what can anthropologists contribute to the discussion?

Ruben Andersson is a Swedish anthropologist and postdoctoral fellow at the London School of Economics. His 2014 book *Illegality, Inc.* is based on his ethnographic study of actual and would-be migrants to Europe, along with the people and agencies—some supportive, the majority just the opposite—they encounter along the way. The book's title reflects Andersson's contention that the European Union's migration policies have created an "illegality industry," which is fueling, rather than curbing, illegal activity.

The International Organization for Migration (IOM) reports that 111,558 migrants and refugees entered Europe by sea in 2018 (mainly via Italy and Greece, but also Malta, Cyprus, and Spain). This was the fifth straight year during which the arrival of irregular migrants and refugees topped 100,000—although 2018's total was low compared to those recorded for 2017 (167,916) and 2016 (358,018). Europe's migratory crisis year was 2015, when a million migrants and refugees sought asylum. Their journey remains treacherous. Worldwide, IOM's Missing Migrants Project (MMP) recorded the deaths of about 2,000 would-be migrants in 2018, mostly through drowning, as their boats capsized in the Mediterranean. Most migrants are from West Africa, the Middle East, and Afghanistan. Lack of job opportunities at home is the main driver sending young West Africans toward Europe. Political instability and war have been pushing refugees from the Middle East (especially Syria and Iraq) and Afghanistan toward Europe.

Andersson did his fieldwork for the book between 2005 and 2014 and initially focused on would-be migrants from West Africa (mainly Senegal and Mali). Although his study took place before the recent refugee crisis in the Middle East, the lessons he derived can easily be applied to today's refugees.

Andersson began his research by focusing on a small sample of people, with whom he established close personal relationships. He wanted to understand how border controls affect individual migrants. He was particularly struck by his informants' accounts of the various people and organizations they encountered (or tried to avoid) as they moved, and he extended his study to those intermediaries. He discovered an entire "illegality industry" deployed around, and benefiting financially from, migrants and their misfortunes. This industry supports border guards and police; defense, monitoring, and construction companies; nongovernmental aid organizations; journalists; and even academics building their careers on the study of migrants. Benefiting especially are human

*continued*

Members of a sect or cult often wear uniform clothing. They may adopt a common hairstyle (shaved head, short hair, or long hair). Liminal groups submerge the individual in the collective. This may be one reason Americans, whose core values include individuality and individualism, are so fearful and suspicious of "cults."

Not all collective rites are rites of passage. Most societies observe occasions on which people come together to worship or celebrate and, in doing so, affirm and reinforce their solidarity. Rituals such as the totemic ceremonies described in the next section are *rites of intensification*: They intensify social solidarity. The ritual creates communitas and produces emotions—the collective spiritual effervescence described by Durkheim (1912/2001)—that enhance social solidarity.

## Totemism

Totemism was a key ingredient in the religions of the Native Australians. **Totems** could be animals, plants, or geographic features. In each tribe, groups of people had particular totems. Members of each totemic group believed themselves to be descendants of their totem, which they customarily neither killed nor ate. However, this taboo was suspended once a year, when people assembled for ceremonies dedicated to the totem. Only on that occasion were they allowed to kill and eat their totem. These annual rites were believed to be necessary for the totem's survival and reproduction.

Totemism uses nature as a model for society. The totems usually are animals and plants, which are part of nature. People relate to nature through their totemic association with natural species. Because each group has a different totem, social differences mirror natural contrasts. Diversity in the natural order becomes a model for diversity in the social order. However, although totemic plants and animals occupy different niches in nature, on another level they are united because they all are part of nature. The unity of the human social order is enhanced by symbolic association with and imitation of the natural order (Durkheim 1912/2001; Lévi-Strauss 1963; Radcliffe-Brown 1952/1965).

Totems are sacred emblems symbolizing common identity. This is true not just among Native Australians but also among Native American groups of the North Pacific Coast of North America, whose totem poles are well known. Their totemic carvings, which commemorated and told visual stories about ancestors, animals, and spirits, were also associated with ceremonies. In totemic rituals, people gather together to honor their totem. In so doing, they use ritual to maintain the social oneness that the totem symbolizes.

Totemic principles continue to demarcate groups, including clubs, teams, and universities, in modern societies. Think of familiar team mascots and symbols. Badgers, wolverines, and gators are animals, and buckeye nuts come from the buckeye tree. Differences between natural species (e.g., lions, tigers, and bears) distinguish sports teams and even political parties (donkeys and elephants). Although the modern context is more secular, one can still witness, in intense college football rivalries, some of the effervescence Durkheim noted in Australian totemic religion and other rites of intensification.

# Social Control

Religion helps people cope with adversity, fear, tragedy, and uncertainty (lack of control). Religion can offer hope that things will get better. Lives can be transformed through spiritual healing. Sinners can repent and be saved—or they can go on sinning and be damned. If the faithful truly internalize a system of religious rewards and punishments, their religion becomes a powerful influence on their attitudes and behavior, as well as on what they teach their children.

Many people continue to engage in religious activity because it works for them. Prayers get answered. Healers heal. Many Native American people in southwestern Oklahoma use faith healers at high monetary cost, not just because it makes them feel better but also because they believe it works (Lassiter 1998). Each year legions of Brazilians visit a church, Nosso Senhor do Bonfim, in the city of Salvador, Bahia. They vow to repay "Our Lord" (Nosso Senhor) if healing happens. Showing that the vows work, and are repaid, are the thousands of *ex votos*, plastic impressions of every conceivable body part, that adorn the church, along with photos of people who have been cured.

Religion can work by mobilizing emotions—joy, wrath, righteousness. People can feel a deep sense of shared joy, enlightenment, communion, belonging, and commitment to their religion. Religion affects action. When religions meet, they can coexist peacefully, or their differences can be a basis for enmity and disharmony, even battle. Throughout history, political leaders have used religion to promote and justify their views and policies.

Each year legions of Brazilians visit the church of Nosso Senhor do Bonfim, in Salvador, Bahia state, seeking healing or fulfilling their vows to repay "Our Lord" (Nosso Senhor) if healing happens. Testimony to successful cures are the myriad photos of survivors, along with plastic and wooden body parts, representing what has been cured. Gonzalo Azumendi/age fotostock/Alamy Stock Photo

9. *Hegemony* describes a stratified social order in which subordinates comply with domination by internalizing its values and accepting its "naturalness." Situations that appear hegemonic may have resistance that is individual and disguised rather than collective and defiant. "Public transcript" refers to the open, public interactions between the dominators and the oppressed. "Hidden transcript" describes the critique of power that goes on where the power holders can't see it. Discontent also may be expressed in public rituals such as Carnaval.

10. Broader than the political is the concept of social control—those fields of the social system most actively involved in the maintenance of norms and the regulation of conflict. Sanctions are social as well as governmental. Shame and gossip can be effective social sanctions. In the Igbo Women's War, women effectively used their social power (through song, dance, noise, and "in-your-face" behavior) to subvert the formal authority structure and, in so doing, gained greater influence within that structure.

## Think Like an Anthropologist

1. This chapter notes that the labels "band," "tribe," "chiefdom," and "state" are too simple to account for the full range of political diversity and complexity known to archaeologists and ethnographers. Why not get rid of this typology altogether if it does not accurately describe reality? What is the value, if any, of retaining the use of such ideal types to study society?

2. This chapter describes population control as one of the specialized functions found in all states. What are examples of population control? Have you had direct experiences with these controls? (Think of the last time you traveled abroad, registered to vote, paid taxes, or applied for a driver's license.) Do you think these controls are good or bad for society?

## Key Terms

authority, *286*
band, *288*
big man, *293*
chiefdom, *288*
conflict
    resolution, *290*
differential
    access, *288*
fiscal, *302*

hegemony, *303*
law, *290*
norms, *290*
office, *297*
pantribal
    sodality, *294*
power, *286*
prestige, *299*
social control, *303*

sociopolitical
    typology, *288*
state, *288*
subordinate, *300*
superordinate, *299*
tribe, *288*
village
    head, *292*
wealth, *299*

# Chapter 13

# Families, Kinship, and Marriage

## How Anthropologists View Families and Kinship

Although it still is something of an ideal in our culture, the nuclear family (parents and their children) now accounts for a bit less than one-fifth of all American households. What kind of family raised you? Perhaps it was a nuclear family. Or maybe you were raised by a single parent, with or without the help of extended kin. Perhaps your extended kin acted as your parents. Or maybe you had a stepparent and/or step or half siblings in a blended family. Maybe you had two moms or two dads. Given the diversity of families in contemporary North America, your family may not have fit any of these descriptions, or perhaps it varied over time.

and attributed this difference to the values stressed by their religions. Weber viewed Protestants as more entrepreneurial and future-oriented than Catholics. Protestantism placed a premium on hard work, an ascetic life, and profit seeking. Early Protestants saw success on Earth as a sign of divine favor and probable salvation.

Weber also argued that rational business organization required the removal of production from the home. Protestantism made such a separation possible by emphasizing individualism: Individuals, not families or households, would be saved or not. Today, of course, in North America as throughout the world, people of many religions and with diverse worldviews are successful capitalists. Furthermore, traditional Protestant values often have little to do with today's economic maneuvering. Still, there is no denying that the individualistic focus of Protestantism was compatible with the severance of ties to land and kin that industrialism demanded.

## World Religions

Information on the world's major religions in 2015 and projected for 2050 is provided in Figure 15.1, based on the most recent comprehensive studies by the Pew Research Center (2015a, 2015b). Considering data from more than 230 countries, researchers estimated that 84 percent of the world's population had some religious affiliation.

**FIGURE 15.1    Major World Religions by Percentage of World Population, 2015, and Projected for 2050**

Source: Pew Research Center. "2015 Data," The Changing Global Religious Landscape, April 5, 2017; "2050 Projections," The Future of World Religions: Population Growth Projections, 2010–2050, April 2, 2015.

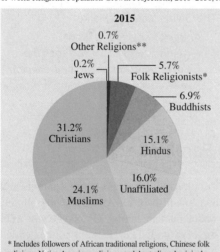

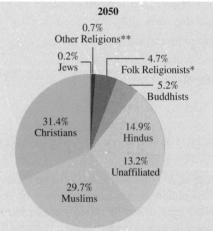

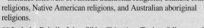

\* Includes followers of African traditional religions, Chinese folk religions, Native American religions, and Australian aboriginal religions.

\*\* Includes Bahai's, Jains, Sikhs, Shintoists, Taoists, followers of Tenrikyo, Wiccans, Zoroastrians, and many other faiths.

Percentage may not add to 100 due to rounding.

\* Includes followers of African traditional religions, Chinese folk religions, Native American religions, and Australian aboriginal religions.

\*\* Includes Bahai's, Jains, Sikhs, Shintoists, Taoists, followers of Tenrikyo, Wiccans, Zoroastrians, and many other faiths.

Percentages may not add to 100 due to rounding.

In 2015, there were approximately 2.3 billion Christians (31.2 percent of the world's population), 1.8 billion Muslims (24.1 percent), 1.1 billion Hindus (15.1 percent), about 500 million Buddhists (6.9 percent), and 14 million Jews (0.2 percent). In addition, about 400 million people (5.7 percent) practiced folk or traditional religions of various sorts. Around 60 million people, a bit less than 1 percent of the world's population, belonged to other religions, including Baha'i, Jainism, Sikhism, Shintoism, Taoism, Tenrikyo, Wicca, and Zoroastrianism.

About 1.2 billion people–16 percent of the world's population–lacked any religious affiliation. The unaffiliated therefore constitute the third-largest group worldwide with respect to religious affiliation, behind Christians and Muslims. There are about as many unaffiliated people as Roman Catholics in the world. Many of the unaffiliated actually hold religious or spiritual beliefs, even if they don't identify with a particular religion (Pew Research Center 2012a, 2012b, 2015a, 2015b).

Worldwide, Islam is growing at a rate of about 2.9 percent annually, compared with 2.3 percent for Christianity. Within Christianity, the growth rate for "born-again" Christians (e.g., Evangelicals/Pentecostals) is much higher than for either Catholics or mainline Protestants. Recent demographic projections by the Pew Research Center (2015b) suggest that by 2050 there will be almost as many Muslims (29.7 percent) as Christians (31.4 percent) in the world (see Figure 15.1). In Europe, Muslims will constitute about 10 percent of the population, compared with about 6 percent today.

# Religion and Change

Like political organization, religion helps maintain social order. And also like political mobilization, religious energy can be harnessed not just for change but also for revolution. Reacting to conquest or to actual or perceived foreign domination, for instance, religious leaders may seek to alter or revitalize their society.

## Revitalization Movements and Cargo Cults

**Revitalization movements** are social movements that occur in times of change, in which religious leaders emerge and undertake to alter or revitalize a society. Christianity originated as a revitalization movement. Jesus was one of several prophets who preached new religious doctrines while the Middle East was under Roman rule. It was a time of social unrest, when a foreign power ruled the land. Jesus inspired a new, enduring, and major religion. His contemporaries were not so successful.

Revitalization movements known as **cargo cults** have arisen in colonial situations in which local people have regular contact with outsiders but lack their wealth, technology, and living standards. Cargo cults attempt to explain European domination and wealth and to achieve similar success magically by mimicking European behavior and manipulating symbols of the desired lifestyle. The cargo cults of Melanesia and Papua New Guinea are hybrid creations that weave Christian doctrine with indigenous beliefs. They take their name from their focus on cargo–European goods of the sort natives have seen unloaded from the cargo holds of ships and airplanes.

In one early cult, members believed that the spirits of the dead would arrive one day in a ship. Those ghosts would bring manufactured goods for the natives and would kill all

A matrilineal extended family of the Khasi ethnic group in India's northeastern city of Shillong. The Khasis trace descent through women, taking their maternal ancestors' surnames. Women choose their husbands, family incomes are pooled, and extended family households are managed by older women. DINODIA/ Dinodia Photo/age fotostock

through females). Nayar lived in matrilineal extended family compounds called *tarawads*. Headed by a senior woman, assisted by her brother, the tarawad housed her siblings, sisters' children, and other matrikin—matrilineal relatives.

Traditional Nayar marriage was barely more than a formality: a kind of coming-of-age ritual. A young woman would go through a marriage ceremony with a man, after which they might spend a few days together at her tarawad. Then the man would return to his own tarawad, where he lived with his mother, aunts, uncles, siblings, and other matrikin. Nayar men belonged to a warrior class, who left home regularly for military expeditions, returning permanently to their tarawad on retirement. Nayar women could have multiple sexual partners. Children became members of the mother's tarawad; they were not considered to be relatives of their biological father. Indeed, many Nayar children didn't even know who their biological father was. Child care was the responsibility of the tarawad. Nayar society therefore reproduced itself biologically without the nuclear family.

A third example of how the extended family can overshadow the nuclear family is provided by the Moso (also spelled Mosuo)—sedentary farmers who live in Yunnan province, southwestern China. Based on his many years of fieldwork among them, anthropologist Chuan-Kang Shih (2010) has described the unique Moso system of kinship and (the insignificance of) marriage. Like the Nayars, the Moso are matrilineal and prefer to live in matrilocal extended family households. Although marriage exists and is practiced in some parts of the Moso territory, the dominant form of sexual and reproductive union is a visiting system called *tisese*, which means "walking back and forth" between the households of the lovers. Tisese relationships are neither binding nor exclusive, and all children produced by such a union belong to their mother's household. As among the

Nayars, the biological father has no role in his child's family and no legal authority over his offspring. The Moso have no kinship terms for relatives on the father's side, or for in-laws (other than husband and wife, for those who are married). Paternity is recognized (only) when Moso marry.

Shih surmises that the tisese system has existed for at least a millennium. Marriage was introduced later, by members of a patrilineal group known as the Pumi, who established themselves as chiefs among the Moso in the 13th century. Tisese is still favored, and marriage remains a marginal practice. Those Moso who do marry live mostly in sparsely populated mountain areas where households are too far apart to make tisese practical. This is yet another example of how a society can reproduce itself biologically without the nuclear family.

## Industrialism and Family Organization

The geographic mobility associated with industrialism works to fragment kinship groups larger than the nuclear family. As people move, often for economic reasons, they are separated from their parents and other kin. Eventually, most North Americans will enter a marriage or domestic partnership and establish a family of procreation. With only about 2 percent of the U.S. population now working in farming, relatively few Americans are tied to the land—to a family farm or estate. A nonfarming nation can be a mobile nation. Americans can move to places where jobs are available, even if they have to leave their hometown to do so. Individuals and married couples often live hundreds of miles from their parents. This pattern of postmarital residence, in which married couples establish a new place of residence away from their parents, is called **neolocality**. The prefix *neo* means new; the couple establishes a new residence, a "home of their own." For middle-class North Americans, neolocality is both a cultural preference and a statistical norm. That is, they both want to, and eventually do, establish homes and nuclear families of their own.

It should be noted, however, that there are significant differences involving kinship between middle-class and poorer North Americans. One example is the association between poverty and single-parent households. Another example is the higher incidence of *expanded family households* among Americans who are less well off financially. An **expanded family household** is one that includes a group of relatives other than, or in addition to, a married couple and their children. Expanded family households take various forms. When the expanded household includes three or more generations, it is an **extended family household**, like the Bosnian zadruga. Another type of expanded family household is the *collateral household*, which includes siblings and their spouses and children. Yet another form is a *matrifocal household*, which is headed by a woman and includes other adult relatives and children. The higher proportion of expanded family households among poorer Americans has been explained as an adaptation to poverty (Stack 1975). Unable to survive economically as independent nuclear family units, relatives band together and pool their resources (see Coles 2016; Hansen 2005).

## Changes in North American Kinship

Even in this age of "modern families," many Americans still think of the traditional nuclear family (mom, dad, and kids) as the ideal family type. However, as we see in

One factor behind the growth in the unaffiliated category may be the decline in religious in-marriage or endogamy. Of the Americans who have married since 2010, 39 percent were in a religiously mixed marriage, compared with 19 percent before 1960. When parents have different religions, it may be easier to raise unaffiliated children than to choose between faiths.

It is increasingly common for Americans to change, or give up, religion. Just over one-third (34 percent) of Americans have a religious identity (or lack thereof) different from the one in which they were raised. If switching from one Protestant church to another, for example, from mainline to Evangelical, is also included, this figure rises to 42 percent.

In the context of this increasing U.S. religious diversity, the established religions themselves are also becoming more diverse. Minorities now constitute 41 percent of American Catholics, 24 percent of Evangelicals, and 14 percent of mainline Protestants. These trends are likely to continue. Have you changed religions?

## New and Alternative Religious Movements

The previous section described religious changes in the United States, including significant growth in the unaffiliated category. This trend toward nonaffiliation, whether as atheist, agnostic, or "nothing in particular," can also be detected in Canada, Western Europe, China, and Japan. In addition to increasing nonaffiliation, contemporary industrial societies also feature new religious trends and forms of spiritualism. The New Age movement, which emerged in the 1980s, draws on and blends cultural elements from multiple traditions. It advocates change through individual personal transformation. In the United States and Australia, respectively, some people who are not Native Americans or Native Australians have appropriated the symbols, settings, and purported religious practices of Native Americans and Native Australians for New Age religions. Native American activists decry the appropriation and commercialization of their spiritual beliefs and rituals, as when "sweat lodge" ceremonies are held on cruise ships, with wine and cheese served. They see the appropriation of their ceremonies and traditions as theft. Some Hindus feel similarly about the popularization of yoga.

Many contemporary nations contain unofficial religions. One example is "Yoruba religion," a term applied to perhaps 15 million adherents in Africa as well as to millions of practitioners of *syncretic*, or blended, religions (with elements of Catholicism and spiritism) in the Western Hemisphere. Forms of Yoruba religion include *santería* (in the Spanish Caribbean and the United States), *candomblé* (in Brazil), and *vodoun* (in the French Caribbean). Yoruba religion, with roots in precolonial nation-states of West Africa, has spread far beyond its region of origin, as part of the African diaspora. It remains an influential, identifiable religion today, despite suppression, such as by Cuba's communist government. There are perhaps 3 million practitioners of santería in Cuba, plus another 800,000 in the United States (Ontario Consultants 2007). Between 5 and 10 million Brazilians participate in candomblé, also known as *macumba* (Garcia-Navarro 2013). Voodoo (*vodoun*) has between 2.8 and 3.2 million practitioners (Ontario Consultants 2011), many (perhaps most) of whom would name something else, such as Catholicism, as their official religion.

# Religion and Cultural Globalization

## Evangelical Protestantism and Pentecostalism

The rapid and ongoing spread of Evangelical Protestantism represents a highly successful form of contemporary cultural globalization. A century ago, more than 90 percent of the 80 million Evangelicals in the world at that time lived in Europe and North America (Pew Research Center 2011). Today, there are more than 600 million Evangelicals worldwide. Most now live in Latin America, Asia, sub-Saharan Africa, and the Middle East and North Africa (see Coleman and Hackett 2015).

The growth and spread of Evangelical Protestantism has been particularly explosive in Brazil—traditionally (and still) the world's most Catholic country. In 1980, when Pope John Paul II visited the country, 89 percent of Brazil's population claimed to be Roman Catholic, compared with less than 65 percent today. This decline is due mainly to Evangelical Protestantism, which has spread like wildfire there. Having made small inroads during the first half of the 20th century, Evangelical Protestantism grew exponentially in Brazil during the second half. Protestants accounted for less than 5 percent of the population through the 1960s. By 2000, Evangelical Protestants constituted more than 15 percent of Brazilians affiliated with a church. The current estimate of the Evangelical share of Brazil's population is around 25 percent and growing. Among the factors that have worked in Brazil against Catholicism are these: a declining and mainly foreign priesthood, sharply contrasting political agendas of many of its clerics, and its reputation as mainly a women's religion.

Evangelical Protestantism stresses conservative morality, biblical authority, and a personal ("born-again") conversion experience. Most Brazilian Evangelicals are Pentecostals, who may also embrace glossolalia (speaking in tongues) and beliefs in faith healing, spirits, exorcism, and miracles. In its focus on ecstatic and exuberant worship, Pentecostalism has been heavily influenced by—and shares features with—African American Protestantism. In Brazil it shares features with candomblé, which also features chanting and spirit possession (Casanova 2001; Meyer 1999).

Peter Berger (2010) thinks that modern Pentecostalism may be the fastest-growing religion in human history and focuses on its social dimensions to explain why. According to Berger, Pentecostalism promotes strong communities while offering practical and psychological support to people whose circumstances are changing. My own experience in Brazil supports Berger's hypothesis; most new Pentecostals I encountered came from underprivileged, poor, and otherwise marginalized groups in areas undergoing rapid social change.

The British sociologist David Martin (1990) argues that Pentecostalism is spreading so rapidly because its adherents embody Max Weber's Protestant ethic—valuing self-discipline, hard work, and thrift. Others see Pentecostalism as a kind of cargo cult, built on the belief that magic and ritual activity can promote material success (Freston 2008; Meyer 1999). Berger (2010) thinks that today's Pentecostals probably include both types—Weberian Protestants working to produce material wealth as a sign of their salvation, along with people who believe that magic and ritual will bring them good fortune.

When I, an anthropologist and a grandfather, first read the list, I was astonished. Grandparents are considered close relatives in every culture I've ever worked in or read about. Why should a stepsibling, who is not a biological relative, have preference over a grandparent, who is? I was not alone in my bewilderment. Lawyers argued in court that fiancés/fiancées, grandparents, grandchildren, brothers-in-law, sisters-in-law, aunts, uncles, nieces, nephews, and cousins of U.S. citizens should also be exempt from the ban.

On July 14, 2017, U.S. district judge Derrick K. Watson agreed, ruling that the government's list was too "narrowly defined." "Common sense . . . dictates that close family members be defined to include grandparents," he wrote. "Indeed, grandparents are the epitome of close family members" (see Zapotosky 2017). The U.S. Supreme Court later reaffirmed Judge Watson's wider definition of kinship. In this way, the social construction of kinship has moved beyond your anthropology textbook into our systems of law and border control. How do you define your close family members?

## The Family among Foragers

Foraging societies are far removed from industrial nations in terms of population size and social complexity, but they do feature geographic mobility, which is associated with nomadic or seminomadic hunting and gathering. Here again, a mobile lifestyle favors the nuclear family as the most significant kin group, although in no foraging society is the nuclear family the only group based on kinship. The two basic social units of traditional foraging societies are the nuclear family and the band. Both are based on kinship ties.

Unlike middle-class couples in industrial nations, foragers don't usually reside neolocally. Instead, they join a band in which either the husband or the wife has relatives. However, couples and families may move freely from one band to another. Although nuclear families are ultimately as impermanent among foragers as they are in any other society, they usually are more stable than bands are.

Many foraging societies lacked year-round band organization. The Native American Shoshone of Utah and Nevada provide an example. The resources available to the Shoshone were so meager that for most of the year nuclear families traveled alone through the countryside, hunting and gathering. In certain seasons, such families came together to hunt cooperatively as a band, but after just a few months together they dispersed.

In neither industrial nor foraging economies are people permanently tied to the land. The mobility and the emphasis on small, economically self-sufficient family units promote the nuclear family as a basic kin group in both types of societies.

## Descent

We've seen that the nuclear family is important in industrial nations and among foragers. The descent group, by contrast, is the key kinship group among nonindustrial farmers and herders. A **descent group** includes people who share common ancestry—they *descend* from the same ancestor(s). Descent groups typically are spread out among several villages, so that all their members do not reside together; only some of them do—those who live in a given village.

Unlike nuclear families, descent groups are permanent. They last for generations. The group endures even as its individual members are born and die, move in and move out. Descent groups may take their names from an ancestor, or from a familiar animal, plant, or natural feature. If a descent group is known as "Children of Abraham," there will be "Children of Abraham" generation after generation. Ditto for "Wolves," "Willow Trees," or "People of the Bamboo Houses." All of these are actual descent group names.

## Attributes of Descent Groups

Descent groups frequently are exogamous: Exogamy means to marry outside one's own group. Members of a descent group must marry someone from another descent group. Often, descent group membership is determined at birth and is lifelong. Two common rules admit certain people as descent-group members while excluding others. With a rule of **patrilineal descent**, people automatically have lifetime membership in their father's group. The children of the group's men join the group, but the children of the group's women are excluded. With **matrilineal descent**, people belong to the mother's group automatically at birth and stay members throughout life. Matrilineal descent groups therefore include only the children of the group's women. (In Figures 13.1 and 13.2, which show patrilineal and matrilineal descent groups, respectively, the triangles stand for males and the circles for females, and lineage members are shown in blue.) Matrilineal and patrilineal descent are types of **unilineal descent**. That means they use only *one* line of descent,

---

**FIGURE 13.1    A Patrilineage Five Generations Deep**
Lineages are based on demonstrated descent from an apical ancestor. With patrilineal descent, children of the group's men (shaded) are included as descent-group members. Children of the group's women are excluded; they belong to *their* father's patrilineage.

**Note:** In this and other kin charts, *triangles* represent *males*; *circles* are *females*; an *equals* sign indicates *marriage*; a *vertical* line shows *descent*; and a *horizontal* line denotes a *sibling* relationship.

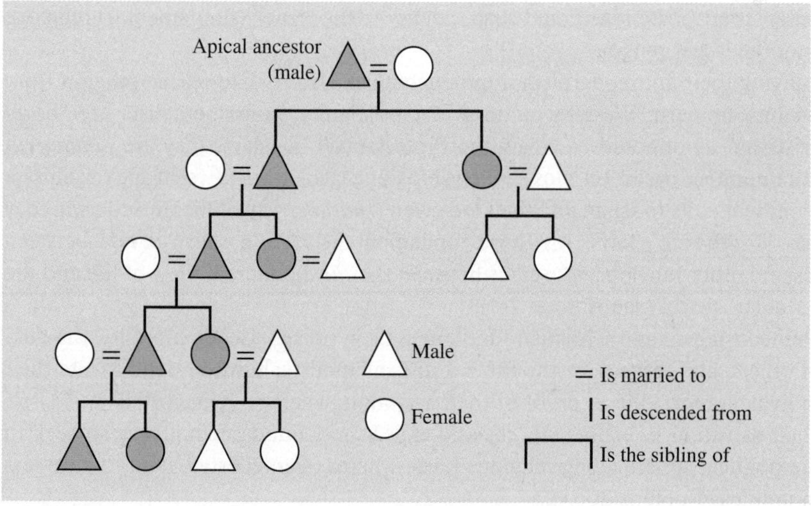

also incorporate architectural and decorative elements from their national settings. Arabic is Islam's liturgical language, used for prayer, but most Muslims' discussion of their faith occurs in their local language. In China, Islamic concepts have been influenced by Confucianism. In India and Bangladesh, the Islamic idea of the prophet has blended with the Hindu notion of the avatar, a deity who takes mortal form and descends to Earth to fight evil and guide the righteous. Islam entered Indonesia by means of Muslim merchants who devised devotional exercises that fit in with preexisting religions—Hinduism and Buddhism in Java and Sumatra and animism in the eastern islands, which eventually became Christian. In Bali, Hinduism survived as the dominant religion.

Both Pentecostalism and Islam, we have learned, hybridize and become locally relevant as they spread globally. Although certain core features endure, local people always assign their own meanings to the messages and social forms they receive from outside, including religion. Such meanings reflect their cultural backgrounds, experiences, and prior belief systems. We must consider the processes of hybridization and indigenization in examining and understanding any form of cultural diffusion or globalization.

## Antimodernism and Fundamentalism

*Antimodernism* is the rejection of the modern in favor of what is perceived as an earlier, purer, and better way of life. This viewpoint first arose out of disillusionment with the Industrial Revolution and with subsequent developments in science, technology, and consumption patterns. Antimodernists consider the use of modern technology to be misguided or think that technology should have a lower priority than religious and cultural values.

Religious *fundamentalism* describes antimodernist movements in various religions, including Christianity, Islam, and Judaism. Not only do fundamentalists feel strongly alienated from modern secular culture, but they also have separated from a larger religious group, whose founding principles, they believe, have been corrupted or abandoned. Fundamentalists advocate return and strict fidelity to the "true" (fundamental) religious principles of the larger religion.

Exemplifying their antimodernism, fundamentalists also seek to rescue religion from absorption into modern, Western culture. In Christianity, fundamentalists are "born-again Christians" as opposed to "mainline Protestants." In Islam, they are *jamaat* (in Arabic, communities based on close fellowship) engaged in *jihad* (struggle) against a Western culture hostile to Islam and the God-given (*shariah*) way of life. In Judaism, they are *Haredi,* "Torah-true" Jews. All these fundamentalists see a sharp divide between themselves and other religions, as well as between their own "sacred" view of life and the modern "secular" world (see Antoun 2008).

Both Pentecostalism and Christian fundamentalism preach ascetic morality, the duty to convert others, and respect for the Bible. Fundamentalists, however, tend to cite their success in living a moral life as proof of their salvation, whereas Pentecostals find assurance of their salvation in exuberant, ecstatic experience. Fundamentalists also seek to remake the political sphere along religious lines, whereas Pentecostals tend to have less interest in politics (Robbins 2004).

Outside the French embassy in London, a group known as "Muslims against Crusades" protests France's introduction of a burka ban. What role have such bans played, either in reducing or in increasing, recent religious radicalization? Cliff Hide News/Alamy Stock Photo

## Religious Radicalization Today

What radicalizes people today? What motivates them to join militant groups like al Qaeda and the Islamic State (also known as IS, ISIS, ISIL, and Daesh)? The growth of such extremist groups is part of a process of political globalization that has accompanied economic globalization. Political globalization reflects the need, in a fragmented world, for some form of attachment to a larger community. Among those most likely to feel this need are displaced and alienated people. Among them are refugees, migrants, and marginalized groups—individuals who feel adrift and apart from, perhaps even despised by, the society or nation-state that surrounds them. One French militant whom anthropologist Scott Atran interviewed traced his radicalization to a childhood incident in which a Frenchman spat at his sister and called her a "dirty Arab" (Atran quoted in Reardon 2015).

Atran is the foremost anthropologist working on the topic of religious radicalization. He and his multinational team of researchers have interviewed members of radical movements in several countries, including members of ISIS in Kirkuk, Iraq, and potential members in Barcelona and Paris. Atran's team also worked in Morocco, in two neighborhoods in Casablanca sympathetic to militant jihad. One of those neighborhoods had produced five of the seven 2004 Madrid train bombers. The other had sent dozens of volunteers, including suicide bombers, to Iraq and Syria. The researchers got to know the families and friends of the militants, learning how they lived and gaining insight into their beliefs.

Atran argues that militants and terrorists are "devoted actors" (Atran 2016; Atran et al. 2014)—individuals who are willing to kill and die for values and beliefs they consider to be sacred and unquestionable. One key value of ISIS has been the need to establish a caliphate ruled by sharia law and led by a successor to the prophet Mohammed. Devoted

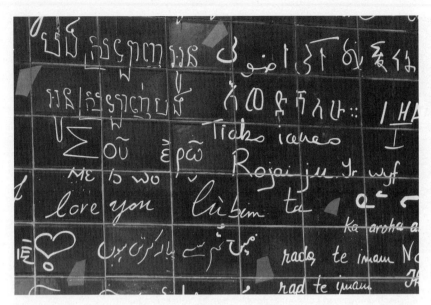

This "I love you" wall is on display in an open area of Monmartre, Paris, France. It shows how to say "I love you" in various languages. Is romantic love a cultural universal?
Conrad P. Kottak

This definition isn't universally valid for several reasons. First, in many societies, marriage unites more than two spouses. Here we speak of *plural marriages*, as when a man weds two (or more) women, or a woman weds a group of brothers—an arrangement called *fraternal polyandry* that is characteristic of certain Himalayan cultures.

Second, some societies (even very traditional ones) recognize various kinds of same-sex marriages. In South Sudan, for example, a Nuer woman could take a wife if her father had no sons, who were necessary for the survival of his patrilineage. That father could ask his daughter to stand as a fictive son in order to take a bride. This daughter would become the socially recognized husband of another woman (her wife). This was a symbolic and social relationship rather than a sexual one. The "wife" had sex with a man or men (whom her female "husband" approved) until she became pregnant. The children born to the wife were accepted as the offspring of both the female husband and the wife. Although the female husband was not the actual *genitor*, the biological father of the children, she was their *pater*, or socially recognized father. What's important in this Nuer case is *social* rather than *biological paternity*. Kinship is socially constructed. The bride's children were considered the legitimate offspring of her female "husband," who was biologically a woman but socially a man, and the patrilineal descent line continued.

A third objection to the definition of marriage offered earlier is that it focuses on the fact that marriage establishes the legitimacy of children. Does this mean that people who marry after childbearing age, or who do not plan to have children, are not actually married (see also this chapter's "Anthropology Today")?

In fact, marriage has several roles in society beyond legitimating children. The British anthropologist Edmund Leach (1955) observed that, depending on the society, several different kinds of rights and benefits are allocated by marriage. According to Leach, marriage can, but doesn't always, accomplish the following:

1. Establish legal parentage
2. Give either or both spouses a monopoly on the sexuality of the other
3. Give either or both spouses rights to the labor of the other
4. Give either or both spouses rights over the other's property
5. Establish a joint fund of property—a partnership—for the benefit of the children
6. Establish a socially significant "relationship of affinity" between spouses and their relatives

## Exogamy and Incest

In nonindustrial societies, a person's social world includes two main categories—friends and strangers. Strangers are potential or actual enemies. Marriage is one of the primary ways of converting strangers into friends, of creating and maintaining personal and political alliances. **Exogamy**—the custom and practice of seeking a mate outside one's own group, has adaptive value, because it links people into a wider social network that can nurture, help, and protect them in times of need. Incest restrictions (prohibitions on sex with relatives) reinforce exogamy by pushing people to seek their mates outside the local group. Most societies discourage sexual contact involving close relatives, especially members of the same nuclear family.

**Incest** refers to sexual contact with a relative, but cultures define their kin, and thus incest, differently. In other words, incest, like kinship, is socially constructed. Some U.S. states, for example, permit marriage, and therefore sex, with first cousins, while others ban it. The social construction of kinship, and of incest, is far from simple.

For example, when unilineal descent is very strongly developed, the parent who belongs to a different descent group from your own isn't considered a relative. Thus, with strict patrilineality, the mother is not a relative but a kind of in-law who has married a member of your own group—your father. With strict matrilineality, the father isn't a relative because he belongs to a different descent group.

The Lakher of Southeast Asia are strictly patrilineal (Leach 1961). Using the male ego (the reference point, the person in question) in Figure 13.3, let's suppose that ego's father and mother get divorced. Each remarries and has a daughter by a second marriage. A Lakher always belongs to his or her father's group, all of whose members (one's *agnates,* or patrikin) are considered relatives, because they belong to the same descent group. Ego cannot have sex with or marry his father's daughter by the second marriage, just as in contemporary North America it's illegal for half siblings to have sex and marry. However, unlike our society, where all half siblings are restricted, sex between our Lakher ego and his maternal half sister would be nonincestuous. She isn't ego's relative because she belongs to her own father's descent group rather than ego's. The Lakher illustrate very well that definitions of relatives, and therefore of incest, vary from culture to culture.

## Anthropology Today *continued*

nor do basketball players, who might slip on the court. No spitting by Roger Federer, Tiger Woods, or Michael Phelps. Not even Mark Spitz (a swimming Olympian turned dentist). But watch any baseball game for a few innings and you'll see spitting galore. Since pitchers appear to be the spitting champions, the custom likely originated on the mound. It continues today as a carryover from the days when pitchers routinely chewed tobacco, believing that nicotine enhanced their concentration and effectiveness. The spitting custom spread to other players, who unabashedly spew saliva from the outfield to the dugout steps.

For the student of custom, ritual, and magic, baseball is an especially interesting game, to which lessons from anthropology are easily applied. The pioneering anthropologist Bronislaw Malinowski (1961/1922), writing about Pacific islanders rather than baseball players, noted they had developed all sorts of magic to use in sailing, a hazardous activity. He proposed that when people face conditions they can't control (e.g., wind and weather), they turn to magic. Magic, in the form of rituals, taboos, and sacred objects, is particularly evident in baseball. Like sailing magic, baseball magic serves to reduce psychological stress, creating an illusion of control when real control is lacking.

In several publications about baseball, the anthropologist George Gmelch (1992) makes use of Malinowski's observation that magic is most common in situations dominated by chance and uncertainty. All sorts of magical behaviors surround pitching and batting, which are full of uncertainty. There are fewer rituals for fielding, over which players have more control. (Batting averages of .350 or higher are very rare after a full season, but a fielding percentage below .900 is a disgrace.) Especially obvious are the rituals (like the spitting) of pitchers, who may tug their cap between pitches, spit in a particular direction, magically manipulate the resin bag, talk to the ball, or wash their hands after giving up a run. Batters have their rituals, too. It isn't uncommon to see outfielder Carlos Gomez kiss his bat, which he also likes to talk to, smell, threaten, try to break—and reward when he gets a hit. Another batter routinely would spit, then ritually touch his gob with his bat, to enhance his success at the place.

Humans use tools to accomplish a lot, but technology still doesn't let us "have it all." To keep hope alive in situations of uncertainty, and for outcomes we can't control, all societies draw on magic and religion as sources of nonmaterial comfort, explanation, and control. What are your rituals?

## Summary

1. Given the varied and worldwide scope of beliefs and behavior labeled "religious," anthropologists recognize the difficulty of defining religion. Religion, a cultural universal, consists of beliefs and behavior concerned with supernatural beings, powers, and forces. Religion also encompasses the feelings, meanings, and congregations associated with such beliefs and behavior. Religious worlds are real, vivid, and significant to those who construct and inhabit them. Anthropological studies have revealed many forms, expressions, and functions of religion.

2. Tylor considered animism—the belief in spirits or souls—to be religion's earliest and most basic form. He focused on religion's explanatory role, arguing that religion would eventually disappear as science provided better explanations. Besides animism, another view of the supernatural also occurs in nonindustrial societies, seeing the supernatural as a domain of raw, impersonal power or force (called mana in Polynesia and Melanesia). People can manipulate and control mana under certain conditions.

3. When ordinary technical and rational means of doing things fail, people may turn to magic. Often they use magic when they lack control over outcomes. Religion offers comfort and psychological security at times of crisis. On the other hand, rites can also create anxiety. Rituals are formal, invariant, stylized, earnest acts in which people subordinate their beliefs to a social collectivity. Rites of passage have three stages: separation, liminality, and incorporation. Such rites can mark any change in social status, age, place, or social condition. Collective rites are often cemented by communitas, a feeling of intense solidarity.

4. Religion establishes and maintains social control through a series of moral and ethical beliefs and real and imagined rewards and punishments, internalized in individuals. Religion also achieves social control by mobilizing its members for collective action.

5. Religions exist in particular societies, and cultural differences show up systematically in religious beliefs and practices. The ecclesiastical and monotheistic religions of stratified, state societies, for example, differ from those of societies that lack hierarchies and specialized officials. The world's major religions vary in their growth rates, with Islam expanding more rapidly than Christianity.

6. Religion helps maintain social order, but it also can promote change. Cargo cults are revitalization movements that hybridize beliefs and that have helped people adapt to changing conditions. Among contemporary "new" religious movements, some have been influenced by Christianity, others by Eastern (Asian) religions, still others by mysticism and spiritualism or by science and technology.

7. The spread of Evangelical/Pentecostal Protestantism worldwide illustrates contemporary cultural globalization. Evangelical Protestantism stresses conservative morality, the authority of the Bible, and a personal ("born-again") conversion experience. To people who feel socially adrift, Pentecostalism offers tightly knit communities and a weblike structure of personal connections. The rapid spread of Islam also illustrates cultural globalization and hybridization. Although certain core features endure, local people always assign their own meanings to the messages and social forms they receive from outside, including religion. Antimodernism is the rejection of the modern, including globalization, in favor of what is perceived as an earlier, purer, and better way of life. Religious fundamentalism describes antimodernist movements in Christianity, Islam, and Judaism. Militant extremism in the name of religion also appeals to people, primarily young men, who feel alienated from, or despised by, the society that surrounds them. These radicals form "bands of brothers" united by common values and willing to kill and die for a cause.

8. There are secular as well as religious rituals. It is possible for apparently secular settings, things, and events to acquire intense meaning for individuals who have grown up in their presence.

A member of India's Dalit ("untouchable") caste (center) holds a placard proclaiming (sarcastically): "In Gujarat, Cow Slaughter is a Sin while Killing Dalits is pardonable." This 2016 rally was organized to protest an attack on Dalit caste members in the town of Una, Gujarat state. The Dalits, who number some 200 million people, are denied access to temples, public wells, even barbershops, and are routinely subjected to violence. Sam Panthaky/AFP/Getty Images

Occupational specialization often sets off one caste from another. A community may include separate castes of agricultural workers, merchants, artisans, priests, and sweepers. The untouchable varna, found throughout India, includes castes whose ancestry, ritual status, and occupations are considered so impure that higher-caste people consider even casual contact with untouchables to be defiling.

The Indian system fosters the belief that sexual relations between members of different castes brings ritual impurity to the higher-caste partner. A man who has sex with a lower-caste woman can restore his purity with a bath and a prayer. However, a woman who has intercourse with a man of a lower caste has no such recourse. Her defilement cannot be undone. Because women have the babies, these differences help ensure the pure ancestry of high-caste children.

Although Indian castes are endogamous groups, many of them are internally subdivided into exogamous lineages. Traditionally this meant that Indians had to marry a member of another descent group from the same caste. This shows that rules of exogamy and endogamy can coexist in the same society.

## Same-Sex Marriage

What about same-sex marriage? Such unions, of various sorts, have been recognized in many different historical and cultural settings (see Ball 2016; Thompson 2015). We saw earlier that the Nuer of South Sudan allowed a woman whose father lacked sons to take a wife and be socially recognized as her husband and as the father (pater, although not genitor) of her children. In situations in which women, such as prominent market women in West Africa, are able to amass property and other forms of wealth, they may take a wife. Such marriages allow the prominent woman to strengthen her social status and the economic importance of her household (Amadiume 1987).

Sometimes, when same-sex marriage is allowed, one of the partners is of the same biological sex as the spouse but is considered to belong to a different, socially constructed

In Australia, Professor Kerryn Phelps speaks to the media as her wife, Jackie Stricker-Phelps, looks on. Along with other supporters of same-sex marriage, they gathered in front of Parliament House in Canberra on December 7, 2017, ahead of the (favorable) parliamentary vote on same-sex marriage. Sean Davey/AFP/Getty Images

gender. Several Native American groups had figures known as "Two-Spirit," representing a gender in addition to male or female (Murray and Roscoe 1998; Roscoe 1998). Sometimes, the Two-Spirit was a biological man who assumed many of the mannerisms, behavior patterns, and tasks of women. Such a Two-Spirit might marry a man and fulfill the traditional wifely role. Also, in some Native American cultures, a marriage of a "manly hearted woman" (a third or fourth gender) to another woman brought the traditional male-female division of labor to their household. The manly woman hunted and did other male tasks, while the wife played the traditional female role (Roscoe 1998).

Beginning in the Netherlands in 2001, the legalization of same-sex marriage in modern nations has snowballed throughout the world. As of this writing, same-sex marriage is legal in 28 countries: Argentina, Australia, Austria, Belgium, Brazil, Canada, Colombia, Denmark, England and Wales, Finland, France, Germany, Greenland, Iceland, Ireland, Luxembourg, Malta, the Netherlands, New Zealand, Norway, Portugal, Scotland, South Africa, Spain, Sweden, Taiwan, the United States, and Uruguay. Twenty-first-century North America has witnessed a rapid and dramatic shift in public and legal opinions about same-sex marriage.

Canada legalized same-sex marriage in 2005, but the United States delayed marriage equality for another decade. The legalization of same-sex marriage throughout the United States in June 2015 was achieved despite considerable opposition. In 1996, the U.S. Congress had approved the Defense of Marriage Act (DOMA), which denied federal recognition and benefits to same-sex couples. Voters in at least 29 U.S. states passed measures defining marriage as an exclusively heterosexual union. On June 26, 2013, the U.S. Supreme Court struck down a key part of DOMA and granted to legally married same-sex couples the same federal rights and benefits received by any legally married couple. In June 2015, the Supreme Court upheld the legality of same-sex marriage throughout the United States. Although opposition continues (often on religious grounds), public opinion has followed the judicial shift toward approval of same-sex marriage. (This chapter's "Anthropology Today" discusses how anthropological knowledge could have informed the 2015 Supreme Court decision legalizing same-sex marriage.)

TABLE 16.1   **Racial/Ethnic Identification in the United States, 2018**

Source: Population Estimates, July 1, 2018. Quick Facts. United States Census Bureau.

| Claimed Identity | Number (millions) | Percentage |
|---|---|---|
| White (non-Hispanic) | 198.6 | 60.7 |
| Hispanic | 59.2 | 18.1 |
| Black | 43.8 | 13.4 |
| Asian | 19.0 | 5.8 |
| Other* | 6.6 | 2.0 |
| Total population | 327.2 | 100.0 |

* Includes American Indian, Alaska Native, and Two or More Races.

Markers of an ethnic group may include a collective name, belief in common descent, a sense of solidarity, and an association with a specific territory, which the group may or may not hold.

**Ethnicity** means identification with, and feeling part of, an ethnic group and exclusion from certain other groups because of this affiliation. Ethnic feelings and associated behavior vary in intensity within ethnic groups and countries and over time. A change in the degree of importance attached to an ethnic identity may reflect political changes (Soviet rule ends—ethnic feeling rises) or individual life-cycle changes (old people relinquish, or young people reclaim, an ethnic background).

## Status and Identity

Ethnicity is only one basis for group identity. Cultural differences also are associated with class, region, religion, and other social variables (see Warne 2015). Individuals often have more than one group identity. In a complex society such as the United States or Canada, people negotiate their social identities continually. All of us "wear different hats," presenting ourselves sometimes as one thing, sometimes as another.

These different social identities are known as statuses. In daily conversation, we hear the term *status* used as a synonym for *prestige*. In this context, "She's got a lot of status" means she's got a lot of prestige; people look up to her. Among social scientists, that's not the only meaning of *status*. Social scientists use **status** more neutrally—for any position, no matter what the prestige, that someone occupies in society. Parent is a social status. So are professor, student, factory worker, Republican, salesperson, homeless person, labor leader, ethnic-group member, and thousands of others. People always occupy multiple statuses (e.g., Hispanic, Catholic, infant, brother). Among the statuses we occupy, particular ones dominate in particular settings, such as son or daughter at home and student in the classroom.

Some statuses are **ascribed:** People have limited choice about occupying them. Age is an ascribed status. We can't choose not to age, although many people, especially wealthy ones, use cultural means, such as plastic surgery, to try to disguise the biological aging process. Race and gender usually are ascribed; most people are born members of a given race or gender and remain so all their lives. **Achieved statuses,** by contrast, aren't automatic; they come through choices, actions, efforts, talents, or accomplishments and may be positive or negative. Examples of achieved statuses include physician, senator, convicted felon, salesperson, union member, father, and college student.

From the media, you will be familiar with recent cases in which gender and race have become achieved rather than ascribed statuses. Transgender individuals, including the media figure Caitlyn Jenner, modify the gender status they were assigned at birth or during childhood. People who were born members of one race have chosen to adopt another. In some cases, individuals who were born African American have passed as White, Hispanic, or Native American. In a case widely reported in 2015, a woman known as Rachel Dolezal, who was born White, changed her racial identity to Black or African American as an adult. In doing this, she modified her phenotype by changing her hairstyle to better fit her new identity. Given what culture can do to biology, few statuses are absolutely ascribed.

Often status is contextual: One identity is used in certain settings, another in different ones. We call this the *situational negotiation of social identity* (Spickard 2013; Tamai 2019; Warne 2015). Members of an ethnic group may shift their ethnic identities. Hispanics, for example, may use different ethnic labels (e.g., *Cuban* or *Latino*) to describe themselves depending on context. In one study, about half (51 percent) of American Hispanics surveyed preferred to identify using their family's country of origin (as in *Mexican, Cuban,* or *Dominican*) rather than *Hispanic* or *Latino.* Just one-quarter (24 percent) chose one of those two pan-ethnic terms, while 21 percent said they use the term *American* most often (Taylor et al. 2012).

Latinos with different national roots may mobilize around issues of general interest to Hispanics, such as a path to citizenship for, or the possible deportation of, undocumented immigrants, while acting as separate interest groups in other contexts. Among Hispanics, Cuban Americans are older and richer on average than Mexican Americans and Puerto Ricans, and their class interests and voting patterns differ. Cuban Americans are more likely to vote Republican than are Puerto Ricans and Mexican Americans. Some Mexican Americans whose families have lived in the

Gender and race are not necessarily ascribed statuses: (Left) Caitlyn Jenner (born Bruce, whose image also is shown in this photo) is interviewed on the *This Morning* TV show in London in May 2017. (Right) Rachel Dolezal poses for a 2017 photo with her son in Spokane, Washington. Dolezal, who was born White, rose to prominence as a Black civil rights leader and has legally changed her name to Nkechi Amare Diallo. (left): Ken McKay/ITV/REX/Shutterstock; (right): Nicholas K. Geranios/AP Images

In such societies, marriage entails an agreement between descent groups. If Sarah and Michael try to make their marriage succeed but fail to do so, both groups may conclude that the marriage can't last. Here it becomes especially obvious that marriages are relationships between groups as well as between individuals. If Sarah has a younger sister or niece (her older brother's daughter, for example), the concerned parties may agree to Sarah's replacement by a kinswoman.

However, incompatibility isn't the main problem that threatens marriage in societies with lobola customs. Infertility is a more important concern. If Sarah has no children, she and her group have not fulfilled their part of the marriage agreement. If the relationship is to endure, Sarah's group must furnish another woman, perhaps her younger sister, who can have children. If this happens, Sarah may choose to stay in her husband's village as his wife. Perhaps she will someday have a child. If she does stay on, her husband will have established a plural marriage, with more than one wife.

## Durable Alliances

Also illustrating the group-alliance nature of marriage is another common practice: continuation of marital alliances when one spouse dies.

### Sororate

What happens if Sarah dies young? Michael's group will ask Sarah's group for a substitute, often her sister. This custom is known as the **sororate** (see Figure 13.5). If Sarah has no sister, or if all her sisters already are married, another woman from her group may be available. Michael marries her, there is no need to return the lobola, and the alliance continues.

**FIGURE 13.5**

**Sororate and Levirate**

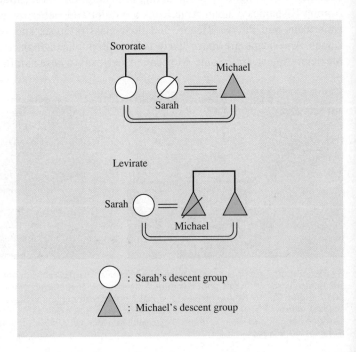

The sororate exists in both matrilineal and patrilineal societies. In a matrilineal society with matrilocal postmarital residence, a widower may remain with his wife's group by marrying her sister or another female member of her matrilineage (see Figure 13.5).

*Levirate*

What happens if the husband dies? In many societies, the widow may marry his brother. This custom is known as the **levirate** (see Figure 13.5). Like the sororate, it is a continuation marriage that maintains the alliance between descent groups, in this case by replacing the husband with another member of his group. The implications of the levirate vary with age. One study found that in African societies the levirate, although widely permitted, rarely involves cohabitation of the widow and her new husband. Furthermore, widows don't automatically marry the husband's brother just because they are allowed to. Often they prefer to make other arrangements.

# Divorce

What factors work for and against divorce cross-culturally? As we've seen, marriages that are political alliances between groups are more difficult to dissolve than are marriages that are more individual affairs. We've seen that a substantial lobola gift may reduce the divorce rate for individuals; replacement marriages (levirate and sororate) also work to preserve group alliances. Furthermore, arranged marriages can be very stable, compared with Western-style individualistic, romance unions.

Divorce tends to be more common in matrilineal than in patrilineal societies. When residence is matrilocal (in the wife's home village), the wife may simply send off a man with whom she's incompatible, or he may choose to leave. Among the Hopi of the American Southwest, houses were owned by matrilineal clans, with matrilocal postmarital residence. The household head was the senior woman of that household, which also included her daughters and their husbands and children. A son-in-law had no important role there; he returned to his own mother's home for his clan's social and religious activities. In this matrilineal society, women were socially and economically secure and the divorce rate was high.

Consider specifically the Hopi of Oraibi pueblo, northeastern Arizona (Levy with Pepper 1992; Titiev 1992). In a study of the marital histories of 423 Oraibi women, Mischa Titiev found that 35 percent had been divorced at least once. Jerome Levy found that 31 percent of 147 adult women had been divorced and remarried at least once. For comparison, of all ever-married women in the United States, only 4 percent had been divorced in 1960, 11 percent in 1980, and around 16 percent today. Much of the instability of Hopi marriages was due to conflicting loyalties to matrikin versus spouse. Most Hopi divorces appear to have been matters of personal choice. Levy generalizes that, cross-culturally, high divorce rates are correlated with a secure female economic position. In Hopi society, women were secure in their homes and land ownership and in the custody of their children. In addition, there were no formal barriers to divorce.

Divorce is more difficult in a patrilineal society, especially when a substantial lobola gift would have to be reassembled and repaid if the marriage failed. A woman residing

An international and multiethnic American family. Joakim Noah, center, is an All-Star professional basketball player, who played in college for the Florida Gators. Also shown are his mother, a former Miss Sweden, and father, a French singer and tennis player who won the French Open in 1983. Joakim's grandfather, Zacharie Noah, was a professional soccer player from the African nation of Cameroon. What is Joakim Noah's race? Matt Marton/ AP Images

The hypodescent rule may be arbitrary, but it is very strong. How else can we explain the common assertion that Barack Obama was the first Black president, rather than the first biracial president, of the United States? (This chapter's "Anthropology Today" focuses on another successful biracial or multiracial American, Tiger Woods, in a discussion of the lack of racial diversity in golf.) American rules for assigning racial status can be even more arbitrary, as the following case illustrates.

Governments (federal or, in this case, the state of Louisiana) can play a decisive role in defining and assigning racial and ethnic identities (see Mullaney 2011). Susie Guillory Phipps, a light-skinned woman with straight black hair, discovered as an adult that she was Black. When Phipps ordered a copy of her birth certificate, she found her race listed as "colored." Since she had been "brought up white and married white twice," Phipps challenged a 1970 Louisiana law declaring anyone with at least one-thirty-second "Negro blood" to be legally Black. Although the state's lawyer admitted that Phipps "looks like a white person," the state of Louisiana insisted that her racial classification as colored was proper (Yetman 1991, pp. 3-4).

## Race in the Census

The U.S. Census Bureau has gathered data by race since 1790. Figure 16.1 shows that the most recent (2010) census asked about both race and Hispanic origin. What do you think of the racial categories included?

Attempts to add a "multiracial" category to the U.S. Census have been opposed by the National Association for the Advancement of Colored People (NAACP) and the National Council of La Raza (a Hispanic advocacy group). Racial classification is a political issue involving access to resources, including federal programs aimed at minorities. The hypodescent rule results in all the population growth being attributed to the minority category. Minorities fear their political clout will be diminished if their numbers go down.

But things are changing. Choice of "some other race" in the U.S. Census tripled from 6.8 to 19 million people between 1980 and 2010—suggesting imprecision in and dissatisfaction with the existing categories. In the 2000 census, 2.4 percent of Americans—almost

FIGURE 16.1    **Questions on Race and Hispanic Origin from the 2010 U.S. Census**

Source: U.S. Census Bureau, Census 2010 questionnaire.

**5.** **Is this person of Hispanic, Latino, or Spanish origin?**

☐ No, not of Hispanic, Latino, or Spanish origin
☐ Yes, Mexican, Mexican Am., Chicano
☐ Yes, Puerto Rican
☐ Yes, Cuban
☐ Yes, another Hispanic, Latino, or Spanish origin — *Print origin, for example, Argentinean, Colombian, Dominican, Nicaraguan, Salvadoran, Spaniard, and so on.* ↗

| | | | | | | | | | | | | | | | | | | | |
|---|---|---|---|---|---|---|---|---|---|---|---|---|---|---|---|---|---|---|---|

**6.** **What is this person's race?**    *Mark* ☒ *one or more boxes.*

☐ White
☐ Black, African Am., or Negro
☐ American Indian or Alaska Native — *Print name of enrolled or principal tribe.* ↗

| | | | | | | | | | | | | | | | | | | | |
|---|---|---|---|---|---|---|---|---|---|---|---|---|---|---|---|---|---|---|---|

☐ Asian Indian      ☐ Japanese        ☐ Native Hawaiian
☐ Chinese           ☐ Korean          ☐ Guamanian or Chamorro
☐ Filipino          ☐ Vietnamese      ☐ Samoan
☐ Other Asian — *Print race, for                    ☐ Other Pacific Islander — *Print*
    example, Hmong, Laotian, Thai,                      *race, for example, Fijian, Tongan,*
    Pakistani, Cambodian, and so on.* ↗                  *and so on.* ↗

| | | | | | | | | | | | | | | | | | | | |
|---|---|---|---|---|---|---|---|---|---|---|---|---|---|---|---|---|---|---|---|

☐ Some other race — *Print race.* ↗

| | | | | | | | | | | | | | | | | | | | |
|---|---|---|---|---|---|---|---|---|---|---|---|---|---|---|---|---|---|---|---|

7 million people—chose a first-ever option of identifying themselves as belonging to two or more races. This figure rose to 2.9 percent in the 2010 census. The group of children who are "two or more races" is projected to more than double between today and 2060, from 5 percent to 11 percent of all Americans under age 18 years (Vespa et al. 2018). An increase in the frequency of interracial marriages and children has implications for the traditional system of American racial classification. "Interracial," "biracial," or "multiracial" children who grow up with both parents undoubtedly identify with particular qualities of either parent. It may be troubling for many of them to have so important an identity as race dictated by the arbitrary rule of hypodescent.

Modern-day polygyny is illustrated by this photo (left) of South Africa's former President (through February 2018) Jacob Zuma and his three wives. In the United States as in South Africa, powerful men often have multiple wives, but legally not at the same time. In the photo on the right, U.S. President Donald Trump and First Lady Melania Trump (his third wife) prepare to board Air Force One on November 9, 2018, for a flight to Paris. (left): Mike Hutchings/AP Images, (right): Saul Loeb/ AFP/Getty Images

## Polyandry

Polyandry is rare and is practiced under very specific conditions. Most of the world's polyandrous peoples live in South Asia—Tibet, Nepal, India, and Sri Lanka. In some of these areas, polyandry seems to be a cultural adaptation to mobility associated with customary male travel for trade, commerce, and military operations. Polyandry ensures there will be at least one man at home to accomplish male activities within a gender-based division of labor. Fraternal polyandry is also an effective strategy when resources are scarce. Brothers with limited resources (in land) pool their resources in expanded (polyandrous) households. They take just one wife. Polyandry restricts the number of wives and heirs. Less competition among heirs means that land can be transmitted with minimal fragmentation.

## The Online Marriage Market

People today shop for everything online, including romantic relationships, in what has been labeled the online "marriage market." There are huge differences in the marriage markets of industrial versus nonindustrial societies. In some of the latter, potential spouses may be limited to certain cousins or members of a specific descent group. Often, marriages are arranged by relatives. In almost all cases, however, there is some kind of preexisting social relationship between any two individuals who marry and their kin groups.

Potential mates still meet in person in modern nations. Sometimes, friends or relatives help arrange such meetings. Besides friends of friends, the marriage market also includes the workplace, bars, clubs, parties, churches, and hobby groups. Add the Internet, which has become a new place to seek out and develop "virtual" relationships, including romantic ones. As part of the "Me, My Spouse, and the Internet" project at the University of Oxford in England, Bernie Hogan, Nai Li, and William Dutton (2011) surveyed cohabiting couples in 18 countries. Their study (conducted online) sampled 12,600 couples

(25,200 individuals aged 18 and older), all with home Internet access. Respondents were asked about how they had met their partners, their dating strategies, how they maintain their current relationships and social networks, and how they use the Internet.

The researchers found that people still seek and find partners in the old, familiar places, even as they look online as well. One-third of the respondents in the study had done online dating, and about 15 percent were in a relationship that had started online. Who benefits most from this technology? Is it young, tech-savvy people, who go online for virtually everything? Or might it be people who are socially isolated in the offline world, including divorced, older, and widowed people? Interestingly, the Oxford researchers found that older people were more likely than younger ones to use online dating. About 36 percent of people over 40 had done so, versus 23 percent of younger adults.

A more recent survey (2015) focusing on the United States found that 15 percent of American adults had used online dating sites and/or mobile dating apps, up from 11 percent two years earlier. Online dating had increased the most for young Americans. The share of 18- to 24-year-olds using online dating almost tripled, from 10 percent in 2013 to 27 percent in 2015. The convenience of mobile dating apps is driving much of this increase. Use of such apps rose from a mere 5 percent in 2013 to 22 percent (of 18- to 24-year-olds) in 2015 (Livingston and Caumont 2017).

In Europe (returning to the Oxford study), the media-saturated nations of northern Europe were most likely to use online dating, which benefits from a critical mass of Internet connectivity (the more people online, the larger the pool of potential contacts). Online Brazilians (who tend to be gregarious both on- and offline) were most likely to know someone who either began a relationship online or married someone first met online. Personal knowledge of an online romantic relationship was reported by 81 percent of the Brazilians in the study, versus only 40 percent of Germans.

## Anthropology Today  *What Anthropologists Could Teach the Supreme Court about the Definition of Marriage*

A majority of Americans today, especially the younger ones, have no trouble accepting the practice and legalization of same-sex marriage. However, opinions on this issue have evolved rapidly. As recently as 2004, then-president George W. Bush was calling for a constitutional amendment banning gay marriage.

Eleven years later, on June 26, 2015, the U.S. Supreme Court issued one of its most socially significant rulings—legalizing same-sex marriage throughout the United States. In the landmark case *Obergefell v. Hodges,* the Court ruled, in a 5–4 decision, that the right to marry is guaranteed to same-sex couples by both the due process clause and the equal protection clause of the 14th Amendment to the U.S. Constitution.

In his strong dissent to that ruling, Chief Justice John Roberts asked, "Just who do we think we are?"—to so enlarge the definition of marriage. Roberts faulted the court for endorsing "the transformation of

*continued*

## Burakumin

In its construction of race, Japanese culture regards certain ethnic groups as having a biological basis, when there is no evidence that they do. The best example is the *burakumin*, a
stigmatized group of some 3 million outcasts, sometimes compared to India's untouchables.
The burakumin are physically and genetically indistinguishable from other Japanese. Many
of them "pass" as (and marry) majority Japanese, but a deceptive marriage can end in
divorce if burakumin identity is discovered (Amos 2011).

Based on their ancestry (and thus, it is assumed, their "blood," or genetics), burakumin
are considered "not us." Majority Japanese try to keep their lineage pure by discouraging mixing. The burakumin are residentially segregated in neighborhoods (rural or
urban) called *buraku*, from which the racial label is derived. Compared with majority
Japanese, the burakumin are less likely to attend high school and college. When
burakumin attend the same schools as majority Japanese, they face discrimination.
Majority children and teachers may refuse to eat with them because burakumin are
considered unclean.

In applying for university admission or a job, and in dealing with the government,
Japanese must list their address, which becomes part of a registry. This list makes
residence in a buraku, and likely burakumin social status, evident. Schools and companies use this information to discriminate. (The best way to pass is to move so often that
the buraku address eventually disappears from the registry.) Majority Japanese also
limit "race" mixture by hiring marriage mediators to check out the family histories of
prospective spouses. They are especially careful to check for burakumin ancestry
(Amos 2011).

The origin of the burakumin lies in a historical tiered system of stratification (from the
Tokugawa period, 1603–1868). The top four ranked categories were warrior-administrators
(*samurai*), farmers, artisans, and merchants. The ancestors of the burakumin were below
this hierarchy. They did "unclean" jobs such as animal slaughter and disposal of the dead.
Burakumin still do similar jobs, including work with leather and other animal products
(see Hankins 2014). They are also more likely than majority Japanese to do manual labor
(including farm work) and to belong to the national lower class. Burakumin and other
Japanese minorities also are more likely to have careers in crime, prostitution, entertainment, and sports.

Like African Americans, the burakumin are internally stratified. In other words,
there are class contrasts within the group. Because certain jobs are reserved for the
burakumin, people who are successful in those occupations (e.g., shoe factory owners)
can be wealthy. Burakumin also have found jobs as government bureaucrats. Successful burakumin can temporarily escape their stigmatized status by travel, including
foreign travel.

Discrimination against the burakumin is similar to the discrimination that Blacks
have experienced in the United States. The burakumin often live in communities with
poor housing and sanitation. They have limited access to education, jobs, amenities, and
health facilities. In response to burakumin political mobilization, Japan has dismantled
the legal structure of discrimination against burakumin and has worked to improve conditions in the buraku. (The Buraku Liberation and Human Rights Research Institute provides the most recent information about the burakumin liberation movement.) However,

On June 12, 2016, in Tokyo, Japan, burakumin protesters seek greater respect and protection from the government and society. The term *burakumin* literally means "hamlet people" and originates from a now-defunct caste system that existed in the Edo Period (1603–1867). Alessandro Di Ciommo/NurPhoto/Getty Images

discrimination against nonmajority Japanese is still the rule in companies. Some employers say that hiring burakumin would give their company an unclean image and thus create a disadvantage in competing with other businesses.

## Phenotype and Fluidity: Race in Brazil

There are more flexible, less restrictive ways of socially constructing race than those used in the United States and Japan. Along with the rest of Latin America, Brazil has less exclusionary categories, which permit individuals to change their racial classification. Brazil shares a history of slavery with the United States, but it lacks the hypodescent rule.

Brazilians use many more racial labels—over 500 were once reported (Harris 1970)—than Americans or Japanese do. In northeastern Brazil, I found 40 different racial terms in use in Arembepe, then a village of only 750 people (Kottak 2018). Through their traditional classification system, Brazilians recognize and attempt to describe the physical variation that exists in their population. The American classification system, which recognizes only a few races, obscures an equivalent range of evident physical contrasts. Brazilian racial classification has other significant features. In the United States, one's race is assigned automatically by hypodescent and usually doesn't change. In Brazil, racial identity is more flexible, more of an achieved status. Brazilian racial classification pays attention to phenotype. *Phenotype* refers to an organism's evident traits, its "manifest biology"—physiology and anatomy, including skin color, hair form, facial features, and eye color. A Brazilian's phenotype and racial label may change because of environmental factors, such as the tanning rays of the sun or the effects of humidity on the hair.

## Think Like an Anthropologist

1. Although the nuclear family may remain a cultural ideal for many Americans, other domestic arrangements now outnumber the "traditional" American household by more than five to one. What are some reasons for this shift? How do the media, including TV sitcoms, reflect changing ideas about family form and function?

2. Depending on the society, several different kinds of rights are allocated by marriage. What are those rights? Which among those rights do you consider more fundamental than others in your definition of marriage? Which ones can you do without? Why?

**Key Terms**

caste system, *325*
clan, *320*
descent group, *318*
dowry, *329*
endogamy, *325*
exogamy, *323*
expanded family
 household, *315*
extended family
 household, *315*
family, *312*

family of
 orientation, *313*
family of
 procreation, *313*
incest, *323*
levirate, *331*
lineage, *320*
lobola, *329*
matrilineal
 descent, *319*
matrilocality, *321*

neolocality, *315*
patrilineal
 descent, *319*
patrilocality, *321*
plural marriages
 (polygamy), *332*
polyandry, *332*
polygyny, *332*
sororate, *330*
unilineal
 descent, *319*

# Chapter

# 14

# Gender

## Sex and Gender

Because anthropologists study biology, society, and culture, they are in a unique position to comment on nature (biological predispositions) and nurture (environment) as determinants of human behavior. Human attitudes, values, and behavior are limited not only by our genetic predispositions—which often are difficult to identify—but also by our experiences during enculturation. Our attributes as adults are determined both by our genes and by our environment during growth and development.

Questions about nature and nurture arise in the discussion of human sex–gender roles and sexuality. Men and women differ genetically. Women have two X chromosomes, and men have an X and a Y. The father determines a baby's sex because only he has the Y chromosome to transmit. The mother always provides an X chromosome.

The chromosomal difference is expressed in hormonal and physiological contrasts. Humans are sexually dimorphic, more so than some primates, such as gibbons (small, tree-living Asiatic apes) and less so than others, such as gorillas and orangutans. **Sexual dimorphism** refers to differences in male and female biology besides the contrasts in breasts and genitals. Women and men differ not just in primary (genitalia and reproductive organs) and secondary (breasts, voice, hair distribution) sexual characteristics, but also in average weight, height, strength, and longevity. Women

the most culturally diverse countries were in Africa. Heading his list were Chad, Cameroon, Nigeria, Togo, and the Democratic Republic of the Congo. African countries tend to rank high on any diversity index because of their multiple ethnic groups and languages. The only Western country among the 20 most diverse was Canada. The United States ranked near the middle, a bit more diverse than Russia but slightly less so than Spain (see Morin 2013).

The world's least diverse countries included Argentina and Uruguay. Although Argentina (like Brazil) has experienced significant German and Italian immigration, Spanish remains its almost universal language, and most Argentines are White and Roman Catholic. Gören also placed Brazil among the least diverse, because virtually all Brazilians speak Portuguese regardless of their racial characteristics or ethnic backgrounds.

Most Latin American and Caribbean countries contain a majority group (speaking a European language, such as Portuguese or Spanish) and a single minority group—indigenous peoples. The latter is a catch-all category encompassing several small Native American tribes or remnants. Exceptions are Guatemala and the Andean countries of Bolivia, Peru, and Ecuador, with large indigenous populations (see Gotkowitz 2011; Wade 2010, 2017).

Most countries in Asia and the Middle East/North Africa have ethnic majorities. The Asian countries of Myanmar, Laos, Vietnam, and Thailand contain a large lowland majority edged by more fragmented mountain folk. Several oil-producing countries in the Middle East, including Saudi Arabia, Bahrain, United Arab Emirates, Oman, and Kuwait, contain an ethnically homogeneous group of citizens who form either a plurality or a bare majority; the rest of the population consists of ethnically diverse noncitizen workers. Several countries in the Middle East/North Africa contain two principal ethnic or ethnoreligious groups: Arabs and Berbers in Morocco, Algeria, Libya, and Tunisia; Muslims and Copts in Egypt; Turks and Kurds in Turkey; Greeks and Turks in Cyprus; and Palestinians and Transjordan Arabs in Jordan (Fearon 2003).

## Nationalities without Nations

Strong central governments, particularly in Europe (e.g., France), have deliberately and actively worked to homogenize their diverse premodern populations to a common national identity and culture (see Beriss 2004). Benedict Anderson (1991/2006) traces Western European *nationalism* (the feeling of belonging to a nation), back to the 18th century. He stresses the crucial role of the printed word in the growth of national consciousness in England, France, and Spain. The novel and the newspaper were "two forms of imagining" communities (consisting of all the people who read the same sources and thus witnessed the same events) that flowered in the 18th century (Anderson 1991/2006, pp. 24–25).

Groups that have, once had, or wish to have or regain, political autonomy (their own country) are called **nationalities.** As a result of political upheavals, wars, and migration, many nationalities have been split and placed in separate nation-states. For example, the German and Korean homelands were artificially divided after wars, according to communist and capitalist ideologies. World War I dispersed the Kurds, who form a majority in no state but exist as minority groups in Turkey, Iran, Iraq, and Syria.

**Colonialism**—the foreign domination of a territory—established a series of multitribal and multiethnic states. The new national boundaries created under colonialism often corresponded poorly with preexisting cultural divisions. However, colonial institutions also helped forge new identities that extended beyond nations and nationalities. A good example is the idea of *négritude* ("Black identity") developed by African intellectuals in Francophone (French-speaking) West Africa. Négritude can be traced to the association and common experience in colonial times of youths from Guinea, Mali, the Ivory Coast, and Senegal at the William Ponty School in Dakar, Senegal (Anderson 1991/2006, pp. 123–124).

# Ethnic Tolerance and Accommodation

Ethnic diversity may be associated either with positive group interaction and coexistence, or with conflict (see the section "Ethnic Conflict"). There are nation-states, including some "less-developed countries," in which multiple cultural groups live together in reasonable harmony.

## Assimilation

**Assimilation** describes the process of change that members of an ethnic group may experience when they move to a country where another culture dominates. In assimilating, the ethnic group members adopt the patterns and norms of the host culture. They are incorporated into the dominant culture to the point that their ethnic group no longer exists as a separate cultural unit. Some countries, such as Brazil, are more assimilationist than others. Germans, Italians, Japanese, Middle Easterners, and East Europeans started migrating to Brazil late in the 19th century. These immigrants have assimilated to a common Brazilian culture, which has Portuguese, African, and Native American roots. The descendants of these immigrants speak the national language (Portuguese) and participate in the national culture. (During World War II, Brazil, which was on the Allied side, forced assimilation by banning instruction in any language other than Portuguese—especially in German.) The United States was much more assimilationist during the early 20th century than it is today, as the multicultural model has become more prominent (see "Multiculturalism" later in this section).

## The Plural Society

Assimilation isn't inevitable, and there can be ethnic harmony without it. Through a study of three ethnic groups in Swat, Pakistan, Fredrik Barth (1958/1968) showed that ethnic groups can be in contact for generations without assimilating. Barth defined **plural society** as a society combining ethnic contrasts, ecological specialization (i.e., use of different environmental resources by each ethnic group), and the economic interdependence of those groups (p. 324).

In Barth's view, ethnic boundaries are most stable and enduring when the groups occupy different ecological niches. That is, they make their living in different ways and don't compete. Ideally, they should depend on each other's activities and exchange with one another. When different ethnic groups exploit the *same* ecological niche, the militarily more powerful group will typically replace the weaker one. If they exploit more or less the same niche, but the weaker group is better able to use marginal environments, they also may coexist (Barth 1958/1968, p. 331). Given such niche specialization, ethnic

TABLE 14.1   **Generalities in the Division of Labor by Gender, Based on Data from 185 Societies**

Murdock, George P., Caterina Provost. Factors in the Division of Labor by Sex: A Cross-Cultural Analysis. Pittsburgh: *Ethnology*, 1973, 203-225.

| Generally Male Activities | Swing (Male or Female) Activities | Generally Female Activities |
| --- | --- | --- |
| Hunting large aquatic animals (e.g., whales, walrus) | Making fire | Gathering fuel (e.g., firewood) |
| Smelting ores | Body mutilation | Making drinks |
| Metalworking | Preparing skins | Gathering wild vegetable foods |
| Lumbering | Gathering small land animals | Dairy production (e.g., churning) |
| Hunting large land animals | Planting crops | Spinning |
| Working wood | Making leather products | Doing the laundry |
| Hunting fowl | Harvesting | Fetching water |
| Making musical instruments | Tending crops | Cooking |
| Trapping | Milking | Preparing vegetable food (e.g., processing cereal grains) |
| Building boats | Making baskets | |
| Working stone | Carrying burdens | |
| Working bone, horn, and shell | Making mats | |
| Mining and quarrying | Caring for small animals | |
| Setting bones | Preserving meat and fish | |
| Butchering* | Loom weaving | |
| Collecting wild honey | Gathering small aquatic animals | |
| Clearing land | Manufacturing clothing | |
| Fishing | Making pottery | |
| Tending large herd animals | | |
| Building houses | | |
| Preparing the soil | | |
| Making nets | | |
| Making rope | | |

*All the activities above "butchering" are almost always done by men; those from "butchering" through "making rope" are usually done by men.

gathering wild vegetable foods ( ), tending crops ( ), fishing ( ), cooking ( ), fetching water ( ), making baskets ( ), making drinks ( ). Now consult Table 14.1 and see how you did. Reflect on your results. Is what's true cross-culturally still true of the division of labor by gender in today's world, including the United States?

The data in Table 14.1 illustrate cross-cultural generalities rather than universals. For example, the table reports a general tendency for men to build boats, but there are societies that contradict the rule. One was the Hidatsa, a Native American group in which the women made the boats used to cross the Missouri River. (Traditionally, the Hidatsa were village farmers and bison hunters on the North American Plains; they now live in North Dakota.) Another exception is that Pawnee women worked wood; this is the only Native American group that assigned this activity to women. (The Pawnee, also traditionally Plains farmers and bison hunters, originally lived in what is now central Nebraska and central Kansas; they now live on a reservation in north central Oklahoma.)

Exceptions to cross-cultural generalizations may involve societies or individuals. That is, a society like the Hidatsa can contradict the cross-cultural generalization that men build boats by assigning that task to women. Or, in a society where men usually build boats, a particular woman or women can contradict that expectation by doing the male activity. Table 14.1 shows that in a sample of 185 societies, certain activities ("swing activities") are assigned to either or both men and women. Among the most important of these swing activities are planting, tending, and harvesting crops. Some societies customarily assign more farming chores to women, whereas others make men the primary farmers. Among the tasks almost always assigned to men, some (e.g., hunting large animals on land and sea) seem clearly related to the greater average size and strength of males. Others, such as working wood and making musical instruments, seem more arbitrary. Women, of course, are not exempt from arduous and time-consuming physical labor, such as gathering firewood and fetching water. In Arembepe, Bahia, Brazil, women routinely transported water in 5-gallon tins, balanced on their heads, from wells and lagoons located long distances from their homes.

The original coding of the data in Table 14.1 probably illustrates a male bias in that extradomestic activities received much more prominence than domestic activities did. Think about how female domestic activities could have been specified in greater detail. One wonders whether collecting wild honey (listed in Table 14.1) is more necessary or time-consuming than nursing a baby (absent from the table). Also, notice that the table does not mention trade and market activity, in which either or both men and women are active.

Both women and men have to fit their activities into 24-hour days. Turn now to Table 14.2, which shows that the time and effort spent in subsistence activities by men and women tend to be about equal. If anything, women do slightly more subsistence work than men do. In domestic activities and child care, however, female labor predominates. In about half the societies studied, men did virtually no domestic work. Even in societies where men did domestic chores, the bulk of such work was done by women. Adding together their subsistence activities and their domestic work, women tend to work more hours than men do. Furthermore, women had primary responsibility for young children in two-thirds of the societies studied.

TABLE 14.2    **Time and Effort Expended on Subsistence Activities by Men and Women (percent)\***

Whyte, Martin King. 1978. Cross-Cultural Codes Dealing with the Relative Status of Women. Pittsburgh: *Ethnology*.

| | |
|---|---|
| More by men | 16 |
| Roughly equal | 61 |
| More by women | 23 |

*Percentage of 88 randomly selected societies for which information was available on this variable.

Politically the two groups—the gray (older) and the brown (younger)—are poles apart. The aging White population appears increasingly resistant to taxes and public spending, while younger people and minorities value government support of education, health, and social welfare. In recent presidential elections, young people, especially minorities, have strongly supported the Democratic candidates, Barack Obama (2008 and 2012) and Hillary Clinton (2016), while White seniors voted solidly for Republicans John McCain, Mitt Romney, and Donald Trump.

The history of U.S. national immigration policy helps us understand how the gap between the gray and the brown arose. Federal policies established in the 1920s severely curtailed immigration from areas other than northern Europe. In 1965, Congress loosened restrictions—resulting in an eventual influx of immigrants from southern Europe, Asia, Africa, the Caribbean, and Latin America (see Vigil 2012).

Non-Hispanic Whites constituted the overwhelming majority of Americans through the mid-20th century, including the post–World War II baby boom (1946-1964). Most baby boomers grew up and have lived much of their lives in White suburbs, residentially isolated from minorities (Brownstein 2010). As they age and retire, many older White Americans are reconstituting such communities in racially homogeneous enclaves in the Southeast and Southwest.

In such communities, except for their yard and construction workers and house cleaners, older White Americans live apart from the minorities who represent a growing share of the national population. Since 1965, expanded immigration and higher fertility rates among minorities have transformed American society. As recently as 1980, minorities made up only 20 percent of the total population (versus 39 percent today), and 25 percent of children under 18 (versus more than 45 percent today, expected to exceed 50 percent by 2020). Similar trends are evident in western Europe and are everyday expressions of globalization.

## The Gray Need the Brown

The gray and the brown are more interdependent economically than either usually realizes. Minority children may benefit disproportionately from public education today, but minority workers will pay a growing share of the payroll taxes needed to sustain Social Security and Medicare in the future. These are government programs that most directly benefit old White people.

The year 2030 will mark a demographic turning point for the United States (Vespa et al. 2018). By that year, all baby boomers will be older than 65 years. By 2035, for the first time in American history, old people will outnumber children. The older (65+) population of the United States is projected to nearly double in size, from 49 million today to 95 million in 2060. In percentage terms, older Americans will constitute 23 percent of the population in 2060 versus about 16 percent today. This demographic shift will affect the ratio of workers to nonworkers.

Furthermore, in coming decades, the youth dependency ratio—the number of children under 18 for every 100 working-age adults (aged 18 to 64)—is projected to shrink. By 2060 there will be only 35 children for every 100 working-age adults, versus 65 children in 1960, when the baby boom was nearing its end. As this youth ratio contracts, the aged ratio will expand. By 2060, the old-age dependency ratio will nearly double, rising from 21 today to 41. In other words, there will be 41 seniors for every 100 adults of working age.

FIGURE 16.3    **The Changing Ethnic Composition of the United States.**
The proportion of the American population that is White and non-Hispanic is declining. The projection for 2060 shown here comes from a 2018 report. Note especially the dramatic rise in the Hispanic and Asian portions of the American population between 2018 and 2060.

2018 data from Population Estimates, Quick Facts, United States Census Bureau, July 1, 2018; 2060 projection from Vespa, J., D. M. Armstrong, and L. Medina. 2018. Demographic Turning Points for the United States: Population Projections for 2020 to 2060, U.S. Census Bureau, Current Population Reports P25-1144, March.

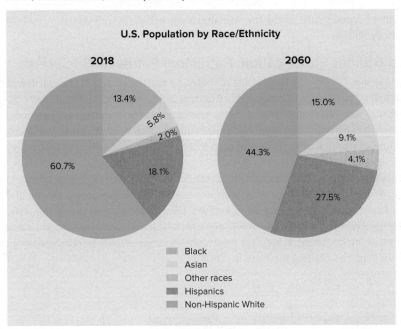

Unless working patterns change substantially, the overall dependency ratio among Americans (35 children + 41 seniors per 100 workers) will be significantly higher than it is today (Vespa et al. 2018).

Immigration will be needed to supply workers for this increasingly dependent population. The aging of America explains why immigration is projected to overtake (probably around 2030) natural increase (the number of births over deaths) as the main engine that drives U.S. population growth. And the "gray" will become increasingly "brown." As its deaths exceed its births, the non-Hispanic White population is projected to shrink from 199 million (60.7 percent) in 2020 to 179 million (44.3 percent) in 2060 (see Figure 16.3), even as the overall U.S. population grows (slowly) (Vespa et al. 2018). Can you speculate about if and how the political orientations of American minorities are likely to change as they, too, age during coming decades?

## The Backlash to Multiculturalism

When Barack Obama was first elected president of the United States in 2008, it seemed to many commentators that the United States had entered a postracial era. It was taken as a sign of progress in racial and ethnic relations that an African American man could

decades. Sanday considers the Minangkabau a matriarchy because women are the center, origin, and foundation of the social order. The oldest village in a cluster is called the "mother village." In ceremonies, women are addressed by the term used for their mythical Queen Mother. Women control land inheritance, and couples reside matrilocally. In the wedding ceremony, the wife collects her husband from his household and, with her female kin, escorts him to hers. If there is a divorce, the husband simply takes his things and leaves. Yet despite the special position of women, the Minangkabau matriarchy is not the equivalent of female rule, given the Minangkabau belief that all decision making should be by consensus.

## Increased Gender Stratification: Patrilineal-Patrilocal Societies

Martin and Voorhies (1975) link the decline of matriliny and the spread of the **patrilineal-patrilocal complex** (consisting of patrilineality, patrilocality, warfare, and male supremacy) to pressure on resources. Faced with scarce resources, patrilineal-patrilocal cultivators such as the Yanomami often raid other villages. This warfare favors patrilocality and patriliny, customs that keep related men together in the same village, where they make strong allies in battle.

The patrilineal-patrilocal complex also characterizes many societies in highland Papua New Guinea. Women work hard growing and processing subsistence crops, raising and tending pigs (the main domesticated animal and a favorite food), and doing domestic cooking, but they are isolated from the public domain, which men control. Men grow and distribute prestige crops, prepare food for feasts, and arrange marriages. The men even get to trade the pigs and control their use in ritual.

In some parts of Papua New Guinea, the patrilineal-patrilocal complex has extreme social repercussions. Regarding females as dangerous and polluting, men may segregate themselves in men's houses (such as this one, located near the Sepik River), where they hide their precious ritual objects from women. Are there places like this in your society? George Holton/Science Source

In densely populated areas of the Papua New Guinea highlands, male-female avoidance has been associated with strong pressure on resources (Lindenbaum 1972). In this context, men fear all contact with females, including sexual acts. They think that sexual contact with women will weaken them. Indeed, men see everything female as dangerous and polluting. They segregate themselves in men's houses and hide their precious ritual objects from women. They delay marriage, and some never marry. By contrast, the sparsely populated areas of Papua New Guinea, such as recently settled areas, lack taboos on male-female contacts. The image of woman as polluter fades, men and women mingle together, and reproductive rates are high.

## Patriarchy and Violence

**Patriarchy** describes a political system ruled by men in which women have inferior social and political status, including basic human rights. Barbara Miller (1997), in a study of systematic neglect of females, describes women in rural northern India as "the endangered sex." Societies that feature a full-fledged patrilineal-patrilocal complex, replete with warfare and intervillage raiding, also typify patriarchy. Such practices as dowry murders, female infanticide, and clitoridectomy exemplify patriarchy, which extends from tribal societies such as the Yanomami to state societies such as India and Pakistan.

The gender inequality spawned by patriarchy and violence, which continues into the 21st century, can be deadly. Anyone who follows current events will have heard of recent cases of blatant abuse of women and girls, particularly in the context of warfare and terrorism, for example, in Bosnia, Syria, and Nigeria. In all of these places, rape has been used as a weapon of war or as punishment for transgressions committed by the victim's male relatives. In Afghanistan, Pakistan, and elsewhere, girls have been prevented from, or punished for, attending school. In 2014, Boko Haram, a jihadist rebel group in northern Nigeria, which also opposes female education, kidnapped nearly 300 schoolgirls, whom they subjected to abuse and forced marriages.

Sometimes, thankfully, such abuse fails in its attempt to silence female voices. Consider Malala Yousafzai (born in 1997 in northern Pakistan), who at the early age of 9 years embarked on her ongoing career as a forceful and persuasive advocate for female education. Her courageous early work, including public speaking and a blog for the BBC (started when she was 11), criticized the Taliban for its efforts to block girls' education and prompted the Taliban to issue a death threat against her. In October 2012, a gunman shot Malala (then age 14) three times on a school bus as she was traveling home from school. She survived and has continued to speak out about the importance of education for girls. In 2014 she became the youngest person ever to receive the Nobel Peace Prize.

Family violence and domestic abuse of women are widespread problems. Domestic violence occurs in nuclear family settings, such as Canada and the United States, as well as in more blatantly patriarchal contexts. Cities, with their impersonality and isolation from extended kin networks, are breeding grounds for domestic violence, as may be certain rural areas where women lead isolated lives.

When a woman lives in her own birth village, she has kin nearby to protect her interests. Even in patrilocal polygynous settings, women often count on the support of their cowives and sons in disputes with potentially abusive husbands. Unfortunately, settings whose numbers, commitment, and effectiveness have been unclear, have been supported by the United States and other Sunni-majority countries in the Middle East. Finally, (4) the Kurds, also supported by the United States, have been particularly effective in the fight against ISIS.

The Syrian conflict has displaced at least half of Syria's population of 23 million. Some 6.3 million people have been uprooted internally, while more than 5 million others have fled Syria as refugees. The latter have sought refuge primarily in other Middle Eastern countries, including Turkey, Lebanon, Jordan, Iraq, and Egypt. Turkey hosts the highest number of Syrians displaced by the conflict—about 3 million people. Other Syrian refugees have traveled by boat across the Aegean Sea to the Greek islands and mainland, and from there into Europe via the Balkans. Others have crossed the Mediterranean into Italy, and some have crossed from North Africa to Spain. Sweden and, particularly, Germany have been the most welcoming European countries, with Germany pledging to accept up to 800,000 Syrian refugees. In Syria itself, if Assad eventually vacates the presidency, Sunni reprisals are likely against Alawites and other religious minorities, including Christians and Shiite Muslims (see Adams 2012).

## Prejudice and Discrimination

Members of an ethnic group may be the targets of prejudice (negative attitudes and judgments) or discrimination (punitive action). **Prejudice** means devaluing (looking down on) a group because of its assumed behavior, values, capabilities, or attributes. People are prejudiced when they hold stereotypes about groups and apply them to individuals. (**Stereotypes** are fixed ideas—often unfavorable—about what the members of a group are like.) Prejudiced people assume that members of the group will act as they are "supposed to act" (according to the stereotype) and interpret a wide range of individual behaviors as evidence of the stereotype. They use this behavior to confirm their stereotype (and low opinion) of the group.

**Discrimination** refers to policies and practices that harm a group and its members. Discrimination may be legally sanctioned (*de jure*, or part of the law), or it may be practiced but not legally sanctioned (*de facto*). An example of de facto discrimination is the harsher treatment that American minorities (compared with other Americans) tend to receive from the police and the judicial system. This unequal treatment isn't legal, but it happens, anyway, as the following section documents.

## Black Lives Matter

Anyone who follows the news regularly will have heard of a series of cases in which African Americans, mostly young men, have been shot dead by White police officers. The "Black Lives Matter" movement arose in the United States in response to these and other incidents in which Black lives have not seemed to matter much to local officials. As described by Elizabeth Day (2015), the movement originated in July 2013, when an African American woman named Alicia Garza reacted to the acquittal of George Zimmerman, a neighborhood watch volunteer, in the shooting of Trayvon Martin, an unarmed Black teenager, in Sanford, Florida. Stunned by Zimmerman's acquittal on charges of second-degree murder and manslaughter, Garza posted the following message on Facebook: "Black people. I love you. I love us. Our lives matter."

The third day of protests against police brutality, which followed the release of security camera footage contradicting the NYPD account of the death of Delrawn Small, a young African American man. Erik McGregor/Pacific Press/LightRocket/Getty Images

Garza's friend, Patrisse Cullors, adopted Garza's words and began to post them online using the hashtag #blacklivesmatter. The two women wanted to raise public awareness about the apparent devaluation of Black lives in the American judicial and enforcement systems. Using Facebook, Tumblr, and Twitter, Garza and Cullors encouraged users to share stories of why #blacklivesmatter. In August 2014, another unarmed African American teenager, 18-year-old Michael Brown, was killed by 12 rounds of ammunition from the gun of a White police officer in Ferguson, Missouri. Garza helped organize a "Freedom Ride" to Ferguson that brought some 500 people to the St. Louis suburb. On arrival, she was astonished to see her own phrase being shouted by protesters and written on their banners. There were additional protests in Ferguson after a grand jury failed to indict the police officer. Thereafter, with a series of additional cases in which unarmed Black men were shot by White police officers, the slogan "Black Lives Matter" rose to national prominence. The American Dialect Society even named #blacklivesmatter as their word of the year for 2015. By 2016, Black Lives Matter chapters had opened throughout the country (Day 2015).

The movement has grown not only in response to police shootings and brutality but also following the mass murder on June 17, 2015, of nine African American churchgoers in Charleston, South Carolina, by a White supremacist domestic terrorist. That tragic event prompted the governor to call for and achieve the removal of a contentious and racially charged symbol, the Confederate battle flag, from prominent display in the state capital, Columbia.

Social media continue to be prominent in linking and organizing the #blacklivesmatter movement. Activists have been able to respond quickly to an ongoing series of widely reported incidents (e.g., in Cleveland, Baltimore, North Charleston, and Chicago, and more recently in Baton Rouge, Louisiana; Falcon Heights, Minnesota; Balch Springs, Texas; and South Bend, Indiana) in which Black people have been killed by police or died in police custody. By 2017, the #blacklivesmatter movement had evolved into the Movement for Black Lives, a coalition that includes the Black Lives Matter Global Network and other groups. Their goal is to cultivate a network of skilled local organizers concerned with issues affecting Black lives, including but also extending beyond police violence (Ransby 2017).

Between 1970 and 2018, the female percentage of the American workforce rose from 38 to 47 percent. About 76 million women now have paid employment, along with about 86 million men. Women today fill more than half (52 percent) of all management and professional jobs (U.S. Bureau of Labor Statistics 2018). And it's not mainly single women working, as once was the case.

## Working Parents

It's mothers, too, including married ones. Among American mothers of children under age 18, labor force participation (people working or looking for work) stood at 71 percent in 2017. About 69 percent of *married* mothers were in the labor force, fewer than the 76 percent of mothers with other marital statuses. As her children get older, a woman is more likely to enter the labor force. Of married mothers with children under age 3, about 60 percent are in the labor force, a figure that rises to 65 percent of mothers with children under age 6. Among women whose youngest child was between 6 and 17 years old, 76 percent were in the labor force in 2017 (U.S. Bureau of Labor Statistics 2018).

That same year, 94 percent of married fathers with children under age 18 were in the labor force. Most of them (about 96 percent) worked full time, compared with 77 percent of employed mothers (U.S. Bureau of Labor Statistics 2018). The median income of American women working full time in 2017 was 80 percent that of a comparably employed male, up from 68 percent in 1989 (Entmacher et al. 2013; Fontenot, Semega, and Kollar 2018) but still a long way from parity.

## Higher Education and Professional Employment

Another important change since the 1960s is the increasing success of women in higher education and professional employment. In the United States today, women are more likely than men to attend and graduate from college. More than 40 percent of women in the U.S. labor force have college degrees, compared with 11 percent in 1970. Women will soon constitute the majority of college-educated workers in the U.S.

Back in 1968, women made up less than 10 percent of the entering classes of MD (medicine), JD (law), and MBA (business) programs. The proportion of female students in these programs has risen to about 50 percent. Nowadays, female college graduates aged 30 to 34 are just as likely to be doctors, dentists, lawyers, professors, managers, and scientists as they are to be working in traditionally female professions as teachers, nurses, librarians, secretaries, or social workers. In the 1960s, women were seven times more likely to be in the latter than in the former series of professions. Women already constitute more than one-third of attorneys, compared with less than a tenth in 1970.

In 1970, over 60 percent of occupations were so male-dominated that 80 percent or more of their workers were male. Today, only about a third of occupations have that degree of overrepresentation by males. At the same time, however, the share of occupations in which women make up 80 percent or more of workers has remained fairly constant at 10 percent.

Despite the many gains, female employment continues to lag noticeably in certain highly paid professions. In computer science and engineering, the percentage of female graduates has actually declined, to below 20 percent, compared with 37 percent in 1980. By midcareer, twice the number of women as men leave their jobs in computer science, often because they perceive an uncomfortable and unsupportive workplace environment. Nearly 40 percent of women leaving jobs in science, engineering, and technology mention a "hostile macho culture" as their primary reason for doing so, versus only 27 percent who cite compensation issues (Council of Economic Advisers Report 2014).

## Work and Family: Reality and Stereotypes

As the workforce has changed, so too have ideas and attitudes about gender roles. Compare your grandparents and your parents. Chances are you have an employed mother, but your grandmother (and especially your great grandmother) was more likely to have been a stay-at-home mom. Your grandfather (and especially your great grandfather) is more likely than your father to have worked in manufacturing and to have belonged to a union. Your father is more likely than any of his male forebears to have participated significantly in child care and housework.

People everywhere have work and family obligations, but ideas about how to balance those responsibilities have changed considerably in recent years. Both men and women increasingly question the cultural assumption that the man should be the breadwinner while the woman assumes domestic and child-care responsibilities. Over 40 percent of American mothers are their household's primary or sole breadwinner. This includes both single mothers and married mothers. Fathers increasingly are assuming caregiving activities traditionally done by mothers. Seven percent of American families with children are father-only families. In general, American fathers spend significantly more time on child care and housework today than they did in the past. American fathers now do 4.6 more hours of child care, and 4.4 more hours of housework, per week than they did in 1965.

However, just as barriers remain to women's progress in the workplace, there are lingering obstacles—both material and cultural—to men's success at home. Women still do much more domestic work than men do, and the average man still works longer hours outside the home and earns more money than the average woman does. There is a cultural lag as well. A persistent stereotype is that of the incompetent male homemaker. For decades, clueless husbands and inept fathers have been a staple of television sitcoms—especially those produced after large numbers of women began to enter the workforce. Women still tend to think of themselves as better homemakers than their husbands are. Former Princeton professor Anne-Marie Slaughter (2013, 2015) cites examples of American women who maintain deeply entrenched stereotypes about men's (lack of) domestic capabilities—from kids to kitchens (Slaughter 2013).

Slaughter discusses how, even when men want to play a prominent domestic role, women may resist. The same woman who says she wants her husband to do more at home may then criticize him for not "doing things right" when he does "pitch in." As Slaughter points out, "Doing things right" means doing things the woman's way. Practice, of course, does make perfect, and if the woman is the one who usually does the domestic work, and if she assumes she can do it better and faster than her husband, she probably will do so. A stereotype can become a self-fulfilling prophecy, often reinforced by material reality.

When women ask their husbands for "help" around the house or with the kids, they are affirming the feminine role as primary homemaker and child-care provider. The

considered a potential target of Russian annexation. In 2014, Russia did annex Crimea, where ethnic Russians (constituting more than 60 percent of the Crimean population) and the Russian language dominate.

The fall of the Soviet Union in 1991 was accompanied by a resurgence of ethnic feeling among formerly dominated groups. The ethnic groups and nationalities once controlled by Moscow have sought, and continue to seek, to forge their own separate and viable nation-states. This celebration of ethnic autonomy is part of an ethnic florescence that—as surely as globalization and transnationalism—has been a trend of the late 20th and early 21st centuries. The new assertiveness of long-resident ethnic groups extends to the Welsh and Scots in the United Kingdom, Bretons and Corsicans in France, and Basques and Catalans in Spain.

## Anthropology Today   Why Are the Greens So White? Race and Ethnicity in Golf

How do race and ethnicity figure in the world of golf, a sport whose popularity has been growing not only in the United States but also in Europe, Asia, and Australia? More than 20 million Americans play golf, an industry that also supports about 400,000 workers. For decades, golf has been the preferred sport of business tycoons and politicians—mainly White. President Dwight D. Eisenhower (1953–1960), whose love for golf was well known, etched a lasting (and accurate) image of golf as a Republican sport (despite the fact that former presidents Bill Clinton and Barack Obama also play the game). A recent survey found that only 2 of the top 125 PGA touring pros identified as Democrats. The most recent Republican president, Donald Trump, is both a business tycoon and an avid golfer.

A glance at golfers in any televised game reveals a remarkable lack of variation in skin color. American golf was the nation's last major sport to desegregate, and minorities traditionally have been relegated to supporting roles. Nowadays, Latinos maintain golf's greens and physical infrastructure. Until the motorized golf cart

replaced them, African Americans had significant opportunities to observe and learn the game by caddying. Indeed, there once was a tradition of African American caddies becoming excellent golfers.

The best example of this trajectory is Dr. Charlie Sifford (1922–2015), who, in 1961, broke the color barrier in American professional golf. Sifford began his golf career as a caddie for White golfers. He went on to dominate the all-Black United Golfers Association, winning five straight national titles, but he wanted to play with the world's best golfers. At the age of 39, Sifford successfully challenged—and ended—the White-only policy of the Professional Golfers' Association (PGA), becoming its first African American member.

Sifford, who had to endure phone threats, racial slurs, and other indignities at the beginning of his PGA career, went on to win the Greater Hartford Open in 1967, the Los Angeles Open in 1969, and the 1975 Senior PGA Championship. In 2004 he became the first African American inducted into the World Golf Hall of Fame. His major regret was that he never got to play in a Masters Tournament. That event, held annually in Augusta, Georgia, did not invite its first Black player until Lee Elder in 1975. Sifford's bitterness about his own exclusion from the Masters was tempered somewhat by his pleasure when Tiger Woods, another African American golfer, won the first of his five green Masters jackets in 1997.

In terms of diversity, golf has actually regressed since the 1970s, when 11 African Americans played on the PGA Tour. As of this writing, there are only 2 African Americans (Tiger Woods and Harold Varner III) among the 125 top players on the PGA Tour. In Britain, only 2 percent of an estimated 850,000 regular golfers are non-White.

Economic factors continue to limit minority access to golf, compared with baseball, football, and especially basketball—all of which offer greater public access. As Harold Varner puts it, "golf is really expensive. Why would I spend $30 a day to play golf when I can spend 30 bucks a month and go to the 'Y' and play basketball" (quoted in Bianchi 2017). Prospective golfers need money for instruction, equipment, access to courses, and travel to tournaments. Asian Americans, who enjoy a relatively high socioeconomic status, are the only minority group in the United States with a growing representation in golf, for both men and women.

For years, Tiger Woods has been the standout non-White individual in this mainly White, affluent, Republican sport. Woods became one of America's most celebrated and popular athletes by combining golfing success with a carefully cultivated reputation as a family man. He presented himself as the hard-working and achievement-oriented son of an Asian mother and an African American father, and as a devoted husband and father (with a Scandinavian wife and two photogenic children). Woods's fall from grace began late in 2009, as a flood of media reports converted his image from family man into serial philanderer. Although his marriage did not survive his transgressions, his golfing career did.

Woods gradually reintegrated into the world of golf, even receiving the 2013 PGA Tour Player of the Year Award. For several years thereafter, however, he struggled with back injuries, surgeries, and other woes. By July 2017, his ranking among the world's golfers had fallen to 1,005th.

Yet Tiger Woods was far from done. In September 2018, he claimed victory in the 2018 Tour Championship at Atlanta's East Lake Golf Club—his first win since the WGC-Bridgestone Invitational in 2013. He had played in 41 PGA Tour events between those two victories. His 2018 win (his 80th) placed him just two victories shy of Sam Snead's record of 82. On April 14, 2019, in Augusta, Georgia, Woods won his fifth Masters title and his 15th major tournament, his first major championship in 11 years.

A resurgent champion at age 43, a decade after his fall from grace, Tiger Woods seemed destined for additional victories. Whatever the future holds, he will be remembered historically as a pioneer among African American golfers, and one of that sport's all-time greats. What role, if any, do you think race, ethnicity, racism, and racial stereotyping have played in the rise, fall, resurgence, and overall career of Tiger Woods?

**Source:** Bianchi (2017); Ferguson (2015); Riach (2013); Starn (2011).

A relationship appears to exist between a country's rate of female labor-force participation and its citizens' feelings of well-being. The *World Happiness Report* (*WHR*), published annually since 2012, is an attempt to measure well-being and happiness in 156 countries (see Helliwell et al. 2019). Its measurements are based on a set of six key variables, and a series of lesser ones. The six variables that are related most strongly to a country's sense of well-being are its per-capita gross domestic product (GDP, an indicator of its economic strength), social support, healthy life expectancy, freedom to make life choices, generosity in giving, and perceptions of corruption. The first five are positive variables: As they increase, so does the sense of well-being. The last one, perceptions of corruption, is a negative variable. That is, the less people perceive corruption, the happier they are. As of this writing, the most recent *World Happiness Report* can be found at the following website: https://worldhappiness.report/ed/2019/changing-world-happiness/.

Four Scandinavian countries—Finland, Denmark, Norway, and Iceland—have occupied the top spots in the *WHR* for several years, with the position of any one of them shifting from year to year within that top group. All four have a female labor-force participation rate of 75 percent or higher. Correlations, of course, are not causes, and one wonders exactly why, as more women work outside the home, citizens might feel a greater sense of well-being. The greater financial security associated with dual-earner households may be part of the explanation. The world's happiest countries not only have more employed women but also have a higher living standard and a more secure government safety net. Can you think of other factors that might explain a relationship between happiness and work outside the home?

## Beyond Male and Female

Gender is socially constructed, and societies can recognize more than two genders (see Nanda 2014). In the contemporary United States, gender classification is in flux, with a proliferation of new options beyond male and female. A growing number of Americans self-identify as *transgender, nonbinary, gender-fluid,* or *gender-nonconforming.* These terms and identities complement and enlarge the traditional binary male-female contrast by recognizing that a person's gender can (1) transition from female to male, (2) transition from male to female, (3) be part male and part female, or (4) be neither male nor female. Someone who is gender-fluid or nonbinary may prefer to be referred to as *they,* rather than *he* or *she.*

**Cisgender** refers to someone who still identifies with the gender assigned to them at birth (usually male or female). The terms *transgender* and *nonbinary* can be used to refer to individuals who do not (see Risman 2018; Wortham 2018). Individuals may become **transgender** when their gender identity differs from their biological sex at birth and the gender identity that society assigned to them in infancy. Feeling that their previous gender assignment was incorrect, they assert, or seek to achieve, a new one.

The distinction between *intersex* and *transgender* is like the distinction between sex and gender. Sex, we have seen, refers to biology—chromosomes and their phenotypical manifestations—whereas gender is constructed socially (see Butler 1988, 1990, 2015). The term *intersex* is used to describe individuals who (usually) contrast biologically with biological males and females. *Both sex and gender, however, go beyond male and female.*

South Africa's Caster Semenya won a gold medal for this race—the final of the women's 800-meter run at the Rio 2016 Summer Olympic Games. Ms. Semenya's eligibility to compete against other women has been challenged (so far unsuccessfully) based on a diagnosis that she has hyperandrogenism, a medical condition characterized by very high levels of male sex hormones such as testosterone. The Asahi Shimbun/Getty Images

The term **intersex** describes a range of conditions resulting from an unusual combination of the X and Y chromosomes, or discrepancies involving the external genitals (penis, vagina, etc.) and the internal genitals (testes, ovaries, etc.). The causes of intersex are varied and complex (Kaneshiro 2009): (1) An XX intersex person has the chromosomes of a woman (XX) and normal ovaries, uterus, and fallopian tubes, but the external genitals appear male. Usually this results from a female fetus having been exposed to an excess of male hormones before birth. (2) An XY intersex person has the chromosomes of a man (XY), but the external genitals are incompletely formed, ambiguous, or female. The testes may be normal, malformed, or absent. (3) A true gonadal intersex person has both ovarian and testicular tissue. The external genitals may be ambiguous or may appear to be female or male. (4) Intersex also can result from an unusual chromosome combination, such as X0 (only one X chromosome, and no Y chromosome), XXY, XYY, and XXX. In the last three cases there is an extra sex chromosome, either an X or a Y.

These chromosomal combinations don't typically produce a discrepancy between internal and external genitalia, but there may be issues involving sex hormone levels and overall sexual development. The XXY configuration, known as *Klinefelter's syndrome,* is the most common of these chromosomal combinations and the second most common condition (after Down syndrome) caused by the presence of extra chromosomes in humans. Klinefelter's syndrome occurs in about 1 of every 1,000 male births, but only about half of them have symptoms, such as small testicles and reduced fertility. With XXX, also known as *triple X syndrome,* there is an extra X chromosome in each cell of a human

# Chapter 17

# Applying Anthropology

## What Is Applied Anthropology?

Applied anthropology is the use of anthropological data, perspectives, theory, and methods to identify, assess, and solve contemporary problems (see Ervin 2005; Nolan 2013; Wasson, Butler, and Copeland-Carson 2012). Applied anthropologists help make anthropology relevant and useful to the world beyond anthropology. Medical anthropologists, for instance, have worked as cultural interpreters in public health programs, helping such programs fit into local culture. Development anthropologists work for or with international development agencies, such as the World Bank and the U.S. Agency for International Development (USAID). The findings of garbology, the archaeological study of waste, are relevant to the Environmental Protection Agency, the paper industry, and packaging and trade associations. Archaeology also is applied in cultural resource management and historic preservation. Biological anthropologists apply their expertise in programs aimed at public health, nutrition, genetic counseling, aging, substance abuse, and mental health. Forensic anthropologists work with the police, medical examiners, the courts, and international organizations to identify victims of crimes, accidents, wars, and terrorism. Linguistic anthropologists study physician-patient communication and show how speech

In Tuzla, Bosnia and Herzegovina, forensic anthropologist Dragana Vucetic displays human bones that have been cut for sampling in the DNA identification process. Vucetic is helping to identity victims of the 1995 Srebrenica genocide. Forensic anthropologists work with the police, medical examiners, the courts, and international organizations to identify victims of crimes, accidents, wars, terrorism, and genocide. David Bathgate/Corbis News/Getty Images

differences influence classroom learning. Most applied anthropologists seek humane and effective ways of helping people (see Nahm and Rinker 2016).

The ethnographic method is a particularly valuable tool in applying anthropology. Remember that ethnographers study societies firsthand, living with, observing, and learning from ordinary people. Nonanthropologists working in social-change programs often are content to converse with officials, read reports, and copy statistics. However, the applied anthropologist's likely early request is some variant of "take me to the local people." Anthropologists know that people must play an active role in the changes that affect them and that "the people" have information that "the experts" lack (see Field and Fox 2007).

Anthropological theory, the body of findings and generalizations of the four subfields, also guides applied anthropology. Just as theory aids practice, application fuels theory (see Pink, Fors, and O'Dell 2017). As we compare social-change programs, our understanding of cause and effect increases. We add new generalizations about culture change to those discovered in traditional and ancient cultures.

## The Role of the Applied Anthropologist

### Early Applications

Anthropology is, and has long been, the primary academic discipline that focuses on non-Western cultures. One example is the role that anthropologists played as advisers to, and even agents of, colonial regimes during the first half of the 20th century. Under colonialism,

as of 2015. With reference specifically to transgender rights, more than 20 U.S. states, along with the District of Columbia, Guam, and Puerto Rico, offer legal protection against employment discrimination based either on sexual orientation or gender identity. As of this writing, one unresolved issue affecting the rights of transgender and nonbinary Americans is whether public restroom and locker room access should be based on gender at birth or current gender identification. What do you think?

## Sexual Orientation

**Gender identity** refers to whether a person feels, acts, and is regarded as male, female, nonbinary, or something else. One's gender identity does not dictate one's sexual orientation. Men who have no doubt about their masculinity can be sexually attracted to women or to other men, as can women with regard to female gender identity and variable sexual attraction. **Sexual orientation**, to which we now turn, refers to a person's sexual attraction to, and habitual sexual activities with, persons of the opposite sex (*heterosexuality*), the same sex (*homosexuality*), or both sexes (*bisexuality*). *Asexuality*, indifference toward or lack of attraction to either sex, also is a sexual orientation. All four of these forms are found throughout the world. But each type of desire and experience holds different meanings for individuals and groups. For example, male-male sexual activity may be a private affair in Mexico, rather than public, socially sanctioned, and encouraged, as it is among the Etoro and several other groups in Papua New Guinea (see below).

Recently in the United States there has been a tendency to see sexual orientation as fixed and biologically based. There is not enough information at this time to determine the extent to which sexual orientation is based on biology. What we can say is that all human activities and preferences, including erotic expression, are at least partially constructed and influenced by culture.

In any society, individuals will differ in the nature, range, and intensity of their sexual interests and urges (see Blackwood 2010; Herdt and Polen 2013; Hyde and DeLamater 2016; Lyons and Lyons 2011; Nanda 2014). No one knows for sure why such individual sexual differences exist. Part of the answer probably is biological, reflecting genes or hormones. Another part may have to do with experiences during growth and development. But whatever the reasons for individual variation, culture tends to direct individual sexual urges toward a collective norm. And such sexual norms vary from culture to culture.

What do we know about variation in sexual norms from society to society and over time? A classic cross-cultural study of 76 societies (Ford and Beach 1951) found wide variation in attitudes about forms of sexual activity. In a single society, such as the United States, attitudes about sex differ over time and with socioeconomic status, region, and rural versus urban residence. However, even in the 1950s, prior to the "age of sexual permissiveness" (the pre-HIV period from the mid-1960s through the 1970s), research showed that almost all American men (92 percent) and more than half of American women (54 percent) admitted to masturbation. In the famous Kinsey report (Kinsey, Pomeroy, and Martin 1948), 37 percent of the men surveyed admitted having had at least one sexual experience leading to orgasm with another male. In a later study of 1,200 unmarried women, 26 percent reported same-sex sexual activities. (Because Kinsey's research relied on nonrandom samples, it should be considered merely illustrative, rather than a statistically accurate representation, of sexual behavior at the time.)

In almost two-thirds (63 percent) of the 76 societies in the Ford and Beach study, various forms of same-sex sexual activity were acceptable. Occasionally sexual relations between people of the same sex involved transvestism on the part of one of the partners (see Kulick 1998). Transvestism did not characterize male-male sex among the Sudanese Azande, who valued the warrior role (Evans-Pritchard 1970). Prospective warriors—young men aged 12 to 20—left their families and shared quarters with adult fighting men, who paid lobola for, and had sex with, them. During this apprenticeship, the young men did the domestic duties of women. Upon reaching warrior status, these young men took their own younger male brides. Later, retiring from the warrior role, Azande men married women. Flexible in their sexual expression, Azande males had no difficulty shifting from sex with older men (as male brides) to sex with younger men (as warriors) to sex with women (as husbands) (see Murray and Roscoe 1998).

Consider also the Etoro (Kelly 1976), then a group of some 400 people who subsisted by hunting and horticulture in the Trans-Fly region of Papua New Guinea. The Etoro illustrate the power of culture in molding human sexuality. The following account, based on ethnographic fieldwork by Raymond C. Kelly in the late 1960s, applies only to Etoro males and their beliefs. Etoro cultural norms prevented the male anthropologist who studied them from gathering comparable information about female attitudes and behavior. Note also that the activities described have been discouraged by missionaries. Because there has been no restudy of the Etoro specifically focusing on these activities, the extent to which these practices continue today is unknown. For this reason, I'll use the past tense in describing them.

Etoro opinions about sexuality were linked to their beliefs about the cycle of birth, physical growth, maturity, old age, and death. Etoro men believed that semen was necessary to give life force to a fetus, which was, they believed, implanted in a woman by an ancestral spirit. A man was required to have sexual intercourse with his wife during her pregnancy to nourish the growing fetus with his semen. The Etoro believed, however, that men had a limited lifetime supply of semen. Any sex act leading to ejaculation was seen as draining that supply, and as sapping a man's vitality. The birth of children, nurtured by semen, symbolized a necessary sacrifice that would lead to the husband's eventual death. Male-female sexual intercourse, required for reproduction, was otherwise discouraged. Women who wanted too much sex were viewed as witches, hazardous to their husbands' health. Furthermore, Etoro culture allowed male-female intercourse only about 100 days a year. The rest of the time it was tabooed. Seasonal birth clustering shows that the taboo was respected.

So objectionable was male-female sex that it was removed from community life. It could occur neither in sleeping quarters nor in the fields. Coitus could happen only in the woods, where it was risky because poisonous snakes, the Etoro believed, were attracted by the sounds and smells of male-female sex.

Although coitus was discouraged, sex acts between males were viewed as essential. Etoro believed that boys would not produce semen on their own. To grow into men and eventually give life force to their children, boys had to acquire semen orally from older men. From the age of 10 until adulthood, boys were inseminated by older men. No taboos were attached to this. This oral insemination could proceed in the sleeping area or

increase in densely populated regions (see Salzman 2008). Consider two Iranian pastoral nomadic tribes—the Basseri and the Qashqai (Salzman 1974). Starting each year from a plateau near the coast, these groups took their animals to grazing land 17,000 feet (5,400 meters) above sea level. The Basseri and the Qashqai shared this route with one another and with several other ethnic groups.

Use of the same pasture land at different times of year was carefully scheduled. Ethnic-group movements were tightly coordinated. Expressing this schedule is *il-rah*, a concept common to all Iranian nomads. A group's il-rah is its customary path in time and space. It is the schedule, different for each group, of when specific areas can be used in the annual trek.

Each tribe had its own leader, known as the *khan* or *il-khan*. The Basseri khan, because he dealt with a smaller population, faced fewer problems in coordinating its movements than did the leaders of the Qashqai. Correspondingly, his rights, privileges, duties, and authority were weaker. Nevertheless, his authority exceeded that of any political figure discussed so far. The khan's authority still came from his personal traits rather than from his office. That is, the Basseri followed a particular khan not because of a political position he happened to fill but because of their personal allegiance and loyalty to him as a man. The khan relied on the support of the heads of the descent groups into which Basseri society was divided.

Among the Qashqai, however, allegiance shifted from the person to the office. The Qashqai had multiple levels of authority and more powerful chiefs or khans. Managing 400,000 people required a complex hierarchy. Heading it was the il-khan, helped by a deputy, under whom were the heads of constituent tribes, under each of whom were descent-group heads.

A case illustrates just how developed the Qashqai authority structure was. A hailstorm prevented some nomads from joining the annual migration at the appointed time. Although everyone recognized that the latecomers were not responsible for their delay, the il-khan assigned them less favorable grazing land, for that year only, in place of their usual pasture. The tardy herders and other Qashqai considered the judgment fair and didn't question it. This is one example of how Qashqai authorities regulated the annual migration. They also adjudicated disputes between people, tribes, and descent groups (see Salzman 2008).

These Iranian cases illustrate the fact that pastoralism often is just one among many specialized economic activities within a nation-state. As part of a larger whole, pastoral tribes are continually pitted against other ethnic groups. Within the context of the modern nation-state, that government becomes a final authority, a higher-level regulator that attempts to limit conflict between ethnic groups. State organization arose not just to manage agricultural economies but also to regulate the activities of ethnic groups within expanding social and economic systems (see Das and Poole, 2004; Saleh 2013).

## Chiefdoms

The first states developed about 5,500 years ago; and the first chiefdoms, a thousand or so years earlier. Today, in a world full of nation-states, there are few, if any, surviving chiefdoms. In many parts of the world, the chiefdom was a transitional form of political organization that emerged during the evolution of tribes into states. State formation began in Mesopotamia (currently Iran and Iraq). It next occurred in Egypt, the Indus Valley of Pakistan and India, and northern China. A few thousand years later, states arose in two parts of the Western Hemisphere—Mesoamerica (Mexico, Guatemala, Belize) and the central Andes (Peru and Bolivia) (see Carneiro et al. 2017). Early states are known as *archaic*, or *nonindustrial*, states, in contrast to modern industrial nation-states. Robert Carneiro (1970) defines the state as "an autonomous political unit encompassing many communities within its territory, having a centralized government with the power to collect taxes, draft men for work or war, and decree and enforce laws" (p. 733).

The chiefdom and the state, like many categories used by social scientists, are *ideal types*. That is, they are labels that make social contrasts seem sharper than they really are. In reality there is a continuum from tribe to chiefdom to state. Some societies had many attributes of chiefdoms but retained tribal features. Some advanced chiefdoms had many attributes of archaic states and thus are difficult to assign to either category. Recognizing this "continuous change" (Johnson and Earle 2000), some anthropologists speak of "complex chiefdoms" (Earle 1997), which are almost states.

## Political and Economic Systems

Geographic areas where chiefdoms once existed include the circum-Caribbean (e.g., Caribbean islands, Panama, Colombia), lowland Amazonia, the southeastern United States, and Polynesia. Chiefdoms created the megalithic cultures of Europe, including the one that built Stonehenge. Bear in mind that chiefdoms and states can fall (disintegrate) as well as rise. Before Rome's expansion, much of Europe was organized at the chiefdom level, to which it reverted for centuries after the fall of Rome in the 5th century C.E.

Much of our ethnographic knowledge about chiefdoms comes from Polynesia, where they were common at the time of European exploration (see Kirch 2010, 2015, 2017). In chiefdoms, social relations are based mainly on kinship, marriage, descent, age, generation, and gender—just as in bands and tribes. This is a fundamental difference between chiefdoms and states. States bring *nonrelatives* together and oblige them to pledge allegiance to a government.

Unlike bands and tribes, however, chiefdoms administer a regional political system that is permanent. Chiefdoms may include thousands of people living in many settlements. Regulation is carried out by the chief and his or her assistants, who occupy political offices. An **office** is a permanent position in a political structure; it must be refilled when it is vacated. The political system that is the chiefdom endures across the generations, thus ensuring permanent political regulation.

Polynesian chiefs were full-time specialists whose duties included managing the economy. They regulated production by commanding or prohibiting (often using religious taboos) the cultivation of certain lands and crops. Chiefs also regulated distribution and consumption. At certain seasons—often on a ritual occasion such as a first-fruit ceremony—people would offer part of their harvest to the chief through his or her representatives. Products moved up the hierarchy, eventually reaching the chief. Conversely, illustrating obligatory sharing with kin, chiefs sponsored feasts at which they gave back some of what they had received (see O'Connor 2015). Unlike big men, chiefs were exempt from ordinary work and had special rights and privileges. Like big men, however, they still returned a portion of the wealth they took in.

Indo-Fijians have slight physiques that make them unsuitable for rugby's roughness. Even Indo-Fijian parents discourage their sons from playing, fearing injury by the larger and rougher indigenous Fijians. In this ostensibly multicultural society, it is not uncommon for indigenous Fijians (57 percent of the population) to resent the Indian-derived minority (38 percent) because of its business success. Indo-Fijians fear physical expressions of this resentment on the playing field. Can you think of comparable barriers to sports participation and success based on gender and ethnic differences in other societies, including your own? Are these barriers physical, cultural, or a combination of the two?

## Summary

1.  *Gender roles* are the tasks and activities that a culture assigns to each sex. *Gender stereotypes* are oversimplified ideas about attributes of males and females. *Gender stratification* describes an unequal distribution of rewards by gender, reflecting different positions in a social hierarchy. Cross-cultural comparison reveals some recurrent patterns involving the division of labor by gender. Gender roles and gender stratification also vary with environment, economy, adaptive strategy, level of social complexity, and degree of participation in the world economy.

2.  When gathering is prominent, gender status is more equal than when hunting or fishing dominates a foraging economy. Gender status also is more equal when the domestic and public spheres aren't sharply separated.

3.  Gender stratification also is linked to descent and residence. Women's status in matrilineal societies tends to be high because overall social identity comes through female links. Women in many societies, especially matrilineal ones, wield power and make decisions. Scarcity of resources promotes intervillage warfare, patriliny, and patrilocality. The localization of related males is adaptive for military solidarity. Men may use their warrior role to symbolize and reinforce the social devaluation and oppression of women. Patriarchy describes a political system ruled by men in which women have inferior social and political status, including basic human rights.

4.  Americans' attitudes toward gender vary with class and region. When the need for female labor declines, the idea that women are unfit for many jobs increases, and vice versa. Factors such as war, falling wages, and inflation help explain female cash employment and Americans' attitudes toward it. The need for flexible employment, permitting a proper balance of work and family responsibilities, is increasingly important to both male and female workers. Despite the increased participation by women in the labor force and higher education, and by men in the domestic realm, including child care, barriers to full equality remain. Countering the economic gains of many American women is the feminization of poverty. This has become a global phenomenon, as impoverished female-headed households have increased worldwide.

5. *Societies* may recognize more than two genders. In the contemporary United States, gender classification is in flux, with a proliferation of new options beyond male and female. A growing number of Americans self-identify as transgender, nonbinary, gender-fluid, or gender-nonconforming. These terms and identities complement and enlarge the traditional binary male-female contrast by recognizing that a person's gender can (1) transition from female to male, (2) transition from male to female, (3) be part male and part female, or (4) be neither male nor female. The term *intersex* describes a group of conditions, including chromosomal configurations, that may produce a discrepancy between external and internal genitals. Transgender individuals may or may not contrast biologically with ordinary males and females.

6. *Gender identity* refers to whether a person feels, and is regarded as, male, female, or something else. One's gender identity does not dictate one's sexual orientation. *Sexual orientation* stands for a person's habitual sexual attraction to, and activities with, persons of the opposite sex (heterosexuality), the same sex (homosexuality), or both sexes (bisexuality). Sexual norms and practices vary widely from culture to culture.

## Think Like an Anthropologist

1. How are sex, gender, and sexual orientation related to one another? What are the differences among these three concepts? Provide an argument about why anthropologists are uniquely positioned to study the relationships among the three.

2. Using your own society, give an example of a gender role, a gender stereotype, and gender stratification. Are these examples likely to apply cross-culturally?

## Key Terms

cisgender, *354*
domestic, *344*
domestic-public dichotomy, *344*
gender identity, *358*
gender roles, *340*
gender stereotypes, *340*
gender stratification, *340*
intersex, *355*
patriarchy, *347*
patrilineal-patrilocal complex, *346*
sexual dimorphism, *339*
sexual orientation, *358*
transgender, *354*

Access to those resources by members of the **subordinate** (lower, or underprivileged) stratum was limited by the privileged group.

## State Systems

Table 12.2 summarizes the information presented so far on bands, tribes, chiefdoms, and states. States, remember, are autonomous political units with social stratification and a formal government. States tend to be large and populous, and certain systems and subsystems with specialized functions are found in all states (see Sharma and Gupta 2006). They include the following:

- Population control: fixing of boundaries, border control, establishment of citizenship categories, and censusing
- Judiciary: laws, legal procedure, and judges
- Enforcement: permanent military and police forces
- Fiscal support: taxation

**TABLE 12.2    Economic Basis of and Political Regulation in Bands, Tribes, Chiefdoms, and States**

| Sociopolitical Type | Economic Type | Examples | Type of Regulation |
|---|---|---|---|
| Band | Foraging | Inuit, San | Local |
| Tribe | Horticulture, pastoralism | Yanomami, Masai, Kapauku | Local, temporary, regional |
| Chiefdom | Intensive horticulture, pastoral nomadism, agriculture | Qashqai, Polynesia, Cherokee | Permanent, regional |
| State | Agriculture, industrialism | Ancient Mesopotamia, contemporary U.S., Canada | Permanent, regional |

In archaic states, these subsystems were integrated by a ruling system—a government composed of civil, military, and religious officials. Let's look at the four subsystems one by one.

## Population Control

To keep track of whom they govern, states enumerate—they conduct censuses. States also demarcate boundaries—borders—that separate that state from other societies. (See this chapter's "Anthropology Today" for a discussion of border control issues in today's world.) Population displacements, within and between states, have increased with globalization and as war, famine, crime, and job seeking churn up migratory currents. Customs agents, immigration officers, navies, and coast guards patrol frontiers. States also regulate population through administrative subdivision: provinces, districts, "states," counties, and parishes. Lower-level officials manage the subdivisions.

States often promote geographic mobility and resettlement, severing long-standing ties among people, land, and kin. Depending on the state, its citizens can identify by region, ethnicity, occupation, political party, religion, and team or club affiliation—rather than only as members of a descent group or an extended family.

States also manage their populations by granting different rights and obligations to citizens and noncitizens. Social distinctions among citizens also are common. Archaic states granted different rights to nobles, commoners, and slaves. In American history before the Emancipation Proclamation, there were different laws for enslaved and free people. In European colonies, separate courts judged cases involving only natives and cases involving Europeans. In contemporary America, a military judiciary coexists alongside the civil system.

## Judiciary

All states have laws based on precedent and legislative proclamations (see Dresch and Skoda 2012; Fikentscher 2016). Without writing, laws may be preserved in oral tradition. Crimes are violations of the legal code ("breaking the law"), with specified types of punishment. To handle crimes and disputes, all states have courts and judges (see Donovan 2007; Goodale 2017; Pirie 2013).

A striking contrast between states and nonstates is intervention in internal and domestic disputes, such as violence within and between families. Governments step in to halt blood feuds and regulate previously private disputes. However, states aren't always successful in their attempts to curb *internal* conflict. Most of the world's armed conflicts since the end of World War II have begun within states—in efforts to overthrow a ruling regime or as disputes over ethnic, religious, or human rights issues.

## Enforcement

How do states enforce laws and judicial decisions? All states have enforcement agents—some kind of police force—whose duties may include apprehending and imprisoning law-breakers. Confinement requires prisons and jailers. If there is a death penalty, executioners are needed. Government officials have the power to collect fines and confiscate property. The government uses its enforcement agents to maintain internal order, suppress disorder, and guard against external threats (with the military and border officials—see Maguire, Frois, and Zurawski 2014).

A man makes a burnt offering as he prays at a Taoist temple, the Jade Emperor Pagoda, in Ho Chi Minh City (formerly Saigon), Vietnam. Established in 1909 by the Cantonese (Chinese) community in Saigon, congregants at the pagoda include Buddhists as well as Taoists; both religions are widely practiced in Vietnam. Conrad P. Kottak

Long ago, Edward Sapir (1928/1956) argued for a distinction between "a religion" and "religion." The former term would apply only to a formally organized religion, such as the world religions just mentioned. The latter—*religion*—is universal; it refers to religious beliefs and behavior, which exist in all societies, even if they don't stand out as a separate and clearly demarcated sphere. Anthropologists agree that religion exists in all human societies; it is a cultural universal. However, we'll see that it isn't always easy to distinguish the sacred from the profane and that different societies conceptualize divinity, the sacred, the supernatural, and ultimate realities very differently.

## Expressions of Religion

When and how did religion begin? No one knows for sure. There are suggestions of religion in Neandertal burials and on European cave walls, where painted stick figures may represent **shamans,** early religious specialists. Nevertheless, any statement about when, where, why, and how religion arose, or any description of its original nature, can be only speculative. Although such speculations are inconclusive, many have revealed important functions and effects of religious behavior. Several theories will be examined in this section.

### Spiritual Beings

Another founder (along with Durkheim) of the anthropology of religion was the Englishman Sir Edward Burnett Tylor (1871/1958; Tremlett, Harvey, and Sutherland 2017). Religion arose, Tylor thought, as people tried to understand phenomena they could not explain by reference to daily experience. Tylor believed that ancient humans—and contemporary nonindustrial peoples—were particularly intrigued with death, dreaming, and trance. People see images they may remember when they wake up or come out of a trance state. Tylor concluded that attempts to explain dreams and trances led early humans to believe that two entities inhabit the body. One is active during the day, and the other—a double, or soul—is active during sleep and in trance states. When the double leaves the body permanently, the person dies. Death is departure of the soul. From *anima*, the Latin for "soul," Tylor named this belief **animism.** The soul was one sort of spiritual entity; people remembered various other entities from their dreams and trances—other spirits. For Tylor, animism, the earliest form of religion, was a belief in spiritual beings.

Tylor proposed that religion evolved through stages, beginning with animism. **Polytheism** (the belief in multiple gods) and then **monotheism** (the belief in a single, all-powerful deity) developed later. Because religion originated to explain things, Tylor thought it would decline as science offered better explanations. To an extent, he was right. We now have scientific explanations for many things that religion once elucidated (see Salazar and Bestard 2015). Of course, many of the "faithful" reject such secular explanations, preferring the nonscientific, religious ones instead. Nevertheless, because religion persists even among those who accept science, it must do something more than explain. It must, and does, have other functions and meanings.

## Powers and Forces

In addition to animism—and sometimes coexisting with it in the same society—is a view of the supernatural as a domain of impersonal power, or force, which people can control under certain conditions. (You'd be right to think of *Star Wars*.) Such a conception has been particularly prominent in Melanesia, the area of the South Pacific that includes Papua New Guinea and adjacent islands. Melanesians traditionally believed in **mana,** a sacred impersonal force existing in the universe. Mana could reside in people, animals, plants, and objects.

Melanesian mana was similar to our notion of luck. Objects with mana could change someone's luck. For example, a charm or an amulet belonging to a successful hunter could transmit that hunter's mana to the next person who held or wore it. A woman could put a rock in her garden, see her yields improve, and attribute the change to the force contained in the rock.

Beliefs in manalike forces have been widespread, although the specifics of the religious doctrines have varied. Consider the contrast between mana in Melanesia and Polynesia (the islands included in a triangular area marked by Hawaii to the north, Easter Island to the east, and New Zealand to the southwest). In Melanesia, anyone could acquire mana by chance, or by working hard to get it. In Polynesia, however, mana wasn't potentially available to everyone but was attached to political offices. Chiefs and nobles had more mana than ordinary people did.

So charged with mana were the highest chiefs that contact with them was dangerous to commoners. The mana of chiefs flowed out of their bodies. It could infect the ground, making it dangerous for others to walk in the chief's footsteps. It could permeate the containers and utensils chiefs used in eating. Because high chiefs had so much mana, their bodies and possessions were **taboo** (set apart as sacred and off-limits to ordinary people). Because ordinary people couldn't bear as much sacred current as royalty could, when commoners were accidentally exposed, purification rites were necessary.

As Horton (1993) and Lambek (2008) point out, there are universals in human thought and experience, common conditions and situations that call out for explanation.

plantation owners sought slaves with diverse cultural and linguistic backgrounds, and limited their rights to assemble. Despite the measures used to divide them, the slaves did resist, developing their own popular culture, linguistic codes, and religious vision. The masters stressed portions of the Bible that emphasized compliance (e.g., the book of Job). The slaves, however, preferred the story of Moses and deliverance. The cornerstone of slave religion became the idea of a reversal in the conditions of Whites and Blacks. Slaves also resisted directly, through sabotage and flight. In many New World areas, slaves managed to establish free communities in the hills and other isolated areas (Price 1973).

## Weapons of the Weak

The study of sociopolitical systems also should consider the sentiments and activity that may be hiding beneath the surface of evident, public behavior. In public, the oppressed may seem to accept their own domination, even when they are questioning it in private. James Scott (1990) uses the term "public transcript" to describe the open, public interactions between oppressed people and their oppressors. He uses "hidden transcript" to describe the critique of the power structure that goes on out of sight of those who hold power. In public, the elites and the oppressed may observe the etiquette of power relations. The dominants act like masters while their subordinates show humility and defer. But resistance often is seething beneath the surface (see Alexandrakis 2016).

Sometimes, the hidden transcript may include active resistance, but it is individual and disguised rather than collective and defiant. Scott (1985) uses Malay peasants, among whom he did fieldwork, to illustrate small-scale acts of resistance—which he calls "weapons of the weak." The Malay peasants used an indirect strategy to resist an Islamic tithe (religious tax). Peasants were expected to pay the tithe, usually in the form of rice, which was sent to the provincial capital. In theory, the tithe would come back as charity, but it never did. Peasants didn't resist the tithe by rioting, demonstrating, or protesting. Instead they used a "nibbling" strategy, based on small acts of resistance. For example, they failed to declare their land or lied about the amount they farmed. They underpaid, or they delivered rice contaminated with water, rocks, or mud, to add weight. Because of this resistance, only 15 percent of what was due actually was paid (Scott 1990, p. 89).

Hidden transcripts tend to be expressed publicly at certain times (festivals and carnavals) and in certain places (such as markets). Because of its costumed anonymity, Carnaval (Mardi Gras in New Orleans) is an excellent arena for expressing feelings that are typically suppressed. Carnavals celebrate freedom through immodesty, dancing, gluttony, and sexuality (DaMatta 1991). Carnaval may begin as a playful outlet for frustrations built up during the year. Over time, it may evolve into a powerful annual critique of stratification and domination and thus a threat to the established order.

## Shame and Gossip

Many anthropologists have noted the importance of such "informal" processes of social control as fear, stigma, shame, and gossip, especially in small-scale societies. Gossip and shame, for example, can function as effective processes of social control when a direct or formal sanction is risky or impossible. Gossip can be used to shame someone who has violated a social norm. Margaret Mead (1937) and Ruth Benedict (1946) distinguished

"Schwellkoepp," or "Swollen Heads," caricature local characters during a Carnaval parade in Mainz, Germany. Because of its costumed anonymity, Carnaval is an excellent arena for expressing feelings that are typically suppressed. Is there anything like Carnaval in your society? Daniel Roland/AP Images

between shame as an external sanction (i.e., forces set in motion by others, for example, through gossip) and guilt as an internal sanction, psychologically generated by the individual. They regarded shame as a more prominent form of social control in non-Western societies and guilt as a more dominant emotional sanction in Western societies. Of course, to be effective as a sanction, the prospect of being shamed or of shaming oneself must be internalized by the individual. In small-scale societies, in a social environment where everyone knows everyone else, most people try to avoid behavior that might harm their reputations and alienate them from their social network.

Bronislaw Malinowski (1927, 2013) described how Trobriand Islanders might climb to the top of a palm tree and dive to their deaths because they couldn't tolerate the shame associated with public knowledge of some stigmatizing action. Nicholas Kottak (2002) heard Makua villagers in northern Mozambique tell the story of a man rumored to have fathered a child with his stepdaughter. The political authorities imposed no formal sanctions (e.g., a fine or jail time) on this man, but gossip about the affair circulated widely. The gossip crystallized in the lyrics of a song that groups of young women would perform. After the man heard his name and behavior mentioned in that song, he hanged himself by the neck from a tree. (Previously we saw the role of song in the social control system of the Inuit. We'll see it again in the case of the Igbo women's war, discussed in the next section.)

**TABLE 15.1   Oppositions between Liminality and Normal Social Life**

Turner, Victor W. 1969. *The Ritual Process: Structure and Anti-Structure*. London: Aldine publishing company.

| Liminality | Normal Social Structure |
| --- | --- |
| transition | state |
| homogeneity | heterogeneity |
| communitas | structure |
| equality | inequality |
| anonymity | names |
| absence of property | property |
| absence of status | status |
| nakedness or uniform dress | dress distinctions |
| sexual continence or excess | sexuality |
| minimization of sex distinctions | maximization of sex distinctions |
| absence of rank | rank |
| humility | pride |
| disregard of personal appearance | care for personal appearance |
| unselfishness | selfishness |
| total obedience | obedience only to superior rank |
| sacredness | secularity |
| sacred instruction | technical knowledge |
| silence | speech |
| simplicity | complexity |
| acceptance of pain and suffering | avoidance of pain and suffering |

training camps, women becoming nuns—pass through the rites together as a group. Table 15.1 summarizes the contrasts, or oppositions, between liminality and normal social life. Most notable is the social aspect of collective liminality called **communitas** (Turner 1967/1974), an intense community spirit, a feeling of great social solidarity, equality, and togetherness. Liminal people experience the same treatment and conditions and must act alike. Liminality may be marked ritually and symbolically by reversals of ordinary behavior. For example, sexual taboos may be intensified; conversely, sexual excess may be encouraged. Liminal symbols, such as special clothing or body paint, mark the condition as extraordinary—beyond ordinary society and everyday life.

Liminality is basic to all rites of passage. Furthermore, in certain societies, including our own, liminal symbols may be used to set off one (religious) group from another and from society as a whole. Such "permanent liminal groups" (e.g., sects, brotherhoods, and cults) are found most characteristically in nation-states. Such liminal features as humility, poverty, equality, obedience, sexual abstinence, and silence (see Table 15.1) may be required for all sect or cult members. Those who join such a group agree to its rules. As if they were undergoing a passage rite—but in this case a never-ending one—they may have to abandon their previous possessions and social ties, including those with family members. Is liminality compatible with Facebook?

Passage rites are often collective. A group passes through the rites as a unit—such as these Maasai warriors in Kenya or these marines in South Korea. Such liminal people experience the same treatment and conditions and must act alike. They share communitas, an intense community spirit, a feeling of great social solidarity or togetherness. (Top): Nigel Pavitt/John Warburton-Lee Photography Ltd/Aurora Photos, (bottom): Chung Sung-Jun/Getty Images News/Getty Images

## Anthropology Today *continued*

smugglers and traffickers, who increase their prices whenever and wherever border control is tightest.

One of Andersson's main conclusions is that the existing system of deterrence is complex and expensive, and is not working as intended. The European Union's costly, militarized, high-tech border control system includes razor-wire fences, naval blockades, drones, and command centers. In the nations through which migrants typically move (e.g., Turkey, Ukraine, Mauritania, Morocco, Libya), the EU subsidizes police officers to seek out and stop would-be migrants. Despite these numerous barriers, migrants and refugees keep coming.

The 1.5 million migrants and refugees who entered Europe by sea in 2015, at the height of the migratory crisis, represent considerably less than 1 percent of Europe's total population of about 740 million. Andersson contends that Europe is wealthy enough to easily absorb this number of arrivals. He also notes that, despite right-wing outrage in Europe and the United States, most refugees today wind up in poorer, rather than wealthier, nations (O'Donnell 2016).

A more effective policy than creating barriers to immigration, Andersson argues, would be to normalize migration and provide people with legal, safe, and efficient ways of moving across national and continental borders. For our 21st-century world, he continues, we need a "political strategy that takes into consideration the globalized nature of human movement." "Ultimately, we need to unfence migration" (both quotes from O'Donnell 2016).

Can you apply lessons from Andersson's study to border control issues in contemporary North America? Is building walls likely to be an effective way to secure the border?

A member of the Spanish NGO Pro Activa extends a hand to seaborne refugees during a rescue in the Mediterranean Sea, Italy on May 6, 2017. Iker Pastor/Anadolu Agency/Getty Images

# Summary

1. Although no ethnographer has been able to observe a polity uninfluenced by some state, many anthropologists use a sociopolitical typology that classifies societies as bands, tribes, chiefdoms, or states. Foragers tended to live in egalitarian, band-organized societies. Personal networks linked individuals, families, and bands. Band leaders were first among equals, with no sure way to enforce decisions. Disputes rarely arose over strategic resources, which were open to all.

2. Political authority increased with growth in population size and density and in the scale of regulatory problems. More people means more relations among individuals and groups to regulate. Increasingly complex economies pose further regulatory problems.

3. Heads of horticultural villages are local leaders with limited authority. They lead by example and persuasion. Big men have support and authority beyond a single village. They are regional regulators, but temporary ones. In organizing a feast, they mobilize labor from several villages. Sponsoring such events leaves them with little wealth but with prestige and a reputation for generosity.

4. Age and gender also can be used for regional political integration. Among North America's Plains tribes, men's associations (pantribal sodalities) organized raiding and buffalo hunting. Such sodalities provide offense and defense when there is inter-tribal raiding for animals. Among pastoralists, the degree of authority and political organization reflects population size and density, interethnic relations, and pressure on resources.

5. The state is an autonomous political unit that encompasses many communities. Its government collects taxes, drafts people for work and war, and decrees and enforces laws. The state is a form of sociopolitical organization based on central government and social stratification. Early states are known as archaic, or nonindustrial, states, in contrast to modern industrial nation-states.

6. Unlike tribes, but like states, chiefdoms had permanent regional regulation and differential access to resources. But chiefdoms lacked stratification. Unlike states, but like bands and tribes, chiefdoms were organized by kinship, descent, and marriage. Chiefdoms emerged in several areas, including the circum-Caribbean, lowland Amazonia, the southeastern United States, and Polynesia.

7. Weber's three dimensions of stratification are wealth, power, and prestige. In early states—for the first time in human history—contrasts in wealth, power, and prestige between entire groups of men and women came into being. A socioeconomic stratum includes people of both sexes and all ages. The superordinate—higher, or elite—stratum enjoys privileged access to resources.

8. Certain systems are found in all states: population control, judiciary, enforcement, and fiscal support. These systems are integrated by a ruling system or government composed of civil, military, and religious officials. States conduct censuses and demarcate boundaries. Laws are based on precedent and legislative proclamations. Courts and judges handle disputes and crimes. A police force maintains internal order, as a military defends against external threats. A financial, or fiscal, system supports rulers, officials, judges, and other specialists and government agencies.

How may leaders mobilize communities and, in so doing, gain support for their own policies? One way is by persuasion; another is by fomenting hatred or fear. Consider witchcraft accusations. Witch hunts can be powerful means of social control by creating a climate of danger and insecurity that affects everyone. No one wants to seem deviant, to be accused of being a witch. Witch hunts often take aim at socially marginal people who can be accused and punished with the least chance of retaliation. During the great European witch craze of the 15th, 16th, and 17th centuries (Harris 1974), most accusations and convictions were against poor women with little social support.

Accusations of witchcraft are ethnographic as well as historical facts. Witchcraft beliefs are common in village and peasant societies, where people live close together and have limited mobility. Such societies often have what anthropologist George Foster (1965) called an "image of limited good"—the idea that resources are limited, so that one person can profit disproportionately only at the expense of others. In this context, the threat of witchcraft accusations can serve as a leveling mechanism if it motivates wealthier villagers to be especially generous or else face shunning and social ostracism. Similarly, in Chapter 14, on gender, we saw that Etoro women who wanted too much sex, as well as boys who grew too rapidly, could be shunned as witches who were depleting a man's limited lifetime supply of semen.

To ensure proper behavior, religions offer rewards (e.g., the fellowship of the religious community) and punishments (e.g., the threat of being cast out or excommunicated). Religions, especially the formal, organized ones typically found in state societies, often prescribe a code of ethics and morality to guide behavior. Moral codes are ways of maintaining order

Witchcraft accusations persist in today's world, with women disproportionately targeted. Hundreds of alleged witches, including these women, are confined to five isolated "witch camps" in northern Ghana. Witchcraft accusations there tend to follow disputes over inheritance rights, or a husband's death that leaves a widow perceived to be a burden on her husband's family or her own. Markus Matzel/ullstein bild/Getty Images

and stability that are reinforced continually in religious sermons, catechisms, and the like. They become internalized psychologically. They guide behavior and produce regret, guilt, shame, and the need for forgiveness, expiation, and absolution when they are not followed.

## Kinds of Religion

Although religion is a cultural universal, religions exist in particular societies, and cultural differences show up systematically in religious beliefs and practices. For example, the religions of stratified, state societies differ from those of societies with less marked social contrasts—societies without kings, lords, and subjects. Churches, temples, and other full-time religious establishments, with their monumental structures and hierarchies of officials, must be supported in some consistent way, such as by tithes and taxes. What kinds of societies can support such hierarchies and architecture?

All societies have religious figures—those believed capable of mediating between humans and the supernatural. More generally, all societies have medico-magico-religious specialists. Modern societies can support both priesthoods and health care professionals. Lacking the resources for such specialization, foraging societies typically have only part-time specialists, who often have both religious and healing roles. *Shaman* is a general term that encompasses curers, mediums, spiritualists, astrologers, palm readers, and other independent diviners. In foraging societies, shamans are usually part-time; that is, they also hunt or gather.

Societies with productive economies (based on agriculture and trade) and large, dense populations (nation-states) can support full-time religious specialists—professional priesthoods. Like the state itself, priesthoods are hierarchically and bureaucratically organized. Anthony Wallace (1966) describes the religions of such stratified societies as "ecclesiastical" (pertaining to an established church and its hierarchy of officials) and "Olympian," after Mount Olympus, home of the classical Greek gods. In such religions, powerful anthropomorphic gods have specialized functions, for example, gods of love, war, the sea, and death. Such *pantheons* (collections of deities) were prominent in the religions of many nonindustrial nation-states, including the Aztecs of Mexico, several African and Asian kingdoms, and classical Greece and Rome. Greco-Roman religions were polytheistic, featuring many deities. In monotheism, all supernatural phenomena are believed to be manifestations of, or under the control of, a single eternal, omniscient, omnipotent, and omnipresent being. In the ecclesiastical monotheistic religion known as Christianity, a single supreme being is manifest in a trinity (see Bellah 2011).

## Protestant Values and Capitalism

Notions of salvation and the afterlife dominate Christian ideologies. However, most varieties of Protestantism lack the hierarchical structure of earlier monotheistic religions, including Roman Catholicism. With a diminished role for the priest (minister), salvation is directly available to individuals, who have unmediated access to the supernatural.

In his influential book *The Protestant Ethic and the Spirit of Capitalism* (1904/1958), the social theorist Max Weber linked the spread of capitalism to the values preached by early Protestant leaders. He saw Protestants as more successful financially than Catholics

Although contemporary American family types are diverse, other cultures offer family alternatives that Americans might have trouble understanding. Imagine a society in which someone doesn't know for sure, and doesn't care much about, who his actual mother was. Consider Joseph Rabe, a Betsileo man who was my field assistant in Madagascar. Illustrating an adoptive pattern common among the Betsileo, Rabe was given as a toddler to his childless aunt, his father's sister. He knew that his birth mother lived far away but did not know which of two sisters in his birth mother's family was his biological mother. His mother and her sister both died in his childhood (as did his father), so he didn't really know them. But he was very close to his father's sister, for whom he used the term for mother. Indeed, he had to call her that, because the Betsileo have only one word, *reny*, that they use for both mother and any blood aunt. (They also use a single term, *ray*, for father and all uncles.) The difference between "real" (biologically based) and socially constructed kinship didn't matter to Rabe.

Contrast this Betsileo case with the common American view that kinship is, and should be, biological. It's increasingly common for adopted children to seek out their birth mothers or sperm donors (which used to be discouraged as disruptive), even after a perfectly satisfactory upbringing in an adoptive family. The American emphasis on biology for kinship is seen also in the recent proliferation of DNA testing. Viewing our beliefs through the lens of cross-cultural comparison helps us appreciate that kinship and biology don't always converge, nor do they need to.

The societies anthropologists traditionally have studied have stimulated a strong interest in families, along with larger systems of kinship and marriage. The wide web of kinship—as vital in daily life in nonindustrial societies as work outside the home is in our own—has become an essential part of anthropology because of its importance to the people we study. We are ready to take a closer look at the systems of kinship and marriage that have organized human life for much of our history.

## Families

One kind of kin group that is widespread among the world's cultures is the *nuclear family,* consisting of parents and children, who normally live together in the same household. Other kin groups include extended families and descent groups. Extended families are those that include three or more generations. Descent groups include people who share common ancestry—they *descend* from the same ancestor(s). Descent groups typically are spread out among several villages, so that all their members do not reside together. Only some of them do—those who live in a given village. Descent groups tend to be found in societies with economies based on horticulture, pastoralism, or agriculture.

The term *family* is basic, familiar (so much so that it even shares its root with *familiar*), and difficult to define in a way that applies to all cultures. A **family** is a group of people (e.g., parents, children, siblings, grandparents, grandchildren, uncles, aunts, nephews, nieces, cousins, spouses, siblings-in-law, parents-in-law, children-in-law) who are considered to be related in some way, for example, by "blood" (common ancestry or descent) or marriage. Some families, such as the nuclear family, are residentially based; its members live together. Others are not; they live apart but come together for family reunions of various sorts from time to time.

## Nuclear and Extended Families

Most people belong to at least two nuclear families at different times in their lives. They are born into a family consisting of their parents and siblings. Reaching adulthood, they may establish a nuclear family that includes their spouse (or domestic partner) and eventually their children. Some people establish more than one family through successive marriages or domestic partnerships.

Anthropologists distinguish between the **family of orientation** (the family in which one is born and grows up) and the **family of procreation** (formed when one marries and has children). From the individual's point of view, the critical relationships are with one's parents and siblings in the family of orientation and with one's spouse and children in the family of procreation.

In most societies, relations with nuclear family members (parents, siblings, and children) take precedence over relations with other kin. Nuclear family organization is widespread but not universal, and its significance varies from one place to another. In a few societies, such as the classic Nayar case described later in this section, nuclear families are rare or nonexistent. In others, the nuclear family plays no special role in social life. Other social units, such as extended families and descent groups, can assume many of the functions otherwise associated with the nuclear family.

The following example from Bosnia illustrates how an extended family can be the most important kinship unit, overshadowing the nuclear family. Among the Muslims of western Bosnia (Lockwood 1975), nuclear families did not exist as independent units. Rather, people lived in an extended family household called a *zadruga*. Heading this household were a senior man and his wife, the senior woman. Also living in the zadruga were their married sons and their wives and children, as well as unmarried sons and daughters. Each married couple had a sleeping room, decorated and partly furnished from the bride's trousseau. However, possessions—even clothing items—were shared freely by zadruga members. Even trousseau items could be used by other zadruga members.

Within the zadruga, social interaction was more usual among its women, its men, or its children than between spouses, or between parents and children. When the zadruga was particularly large, its members ate at three successive sittings: for men, women, and children, respectively. Traditionally, all children over age 12 slept together in boys' or girls' rooms. When a woman wanted to visit another village, she asked permission not from her husband, but from the male zadruga head. Although men may have felt closer to their own children than to those of their brothers, they were obliged to treat all of the zadruga's children equally. Any adult in the household could discipline a child. When a marriage broke up, children under 7 age went with the mother. Older children could choose between their parents. Children were considered part of the household where they were born even if their mother left. One widow who remarried had to leave her five children, all over age 7, in their father's zadruga.

Another example of an alternative to the nuclear family is provided by the Nayars (or Nair), a large and powerful caste on the Malabar Coast of southern India (Gough 1959; Shivaram 1996). Their traditional kinship system was matrilineal (descent traced only

On the island of Tanna, in Vanuatu, Melanesia, members of the John Frum cargo cult stage a military parade. The young men, who carry fake guns and have "USA" painted on their bodies, see themselves as an elite force within the American army.
Thierry Falise/LightRocket/Getty Images

the Whites. Later cargo cults replaced ships with airplanes (Worsley 1959/1985). Many cults have used elements of European culture as sacred objects. The rationale is that Europeans use these objects, have wealth, and therefore must know the "secret of cargo." By mimicking how Europeans (or Americans) use or treat objects, natives hope to come upon the secret knowledge needed to get cargo for themselves.

For example, having seen Europeans' reverent treatment of flags and flagpoles, the members of one cult began to worship flagpoles. They believed the flagpoles were sacred towers that could transmit messages between the living and the dead. Other natives built airstrips to entice planes bearing canned goods, portable radios, clothing, wristwatches, and motorcycles. Some cargo cult prophets proclaimed that success would come through a reversal of European domination and native subjugation. The day was near, they preached, when natives—aided by God, Jesus, or native ancestors—would turn the tables. Native skins would turn white, and those of Europeans would turn brown; Europeans would die or be killed.

Cargo cults blend Aboriginal and Christian beliefs. Melanesian myths told of ancestors shedding their skins and changing into powerful beings and of dead people returning to life. Christian missionaries also preached resurrection. The cults' preoccupation with cargo is related to traditional Melanesian big-man systems. In Chapter 12, on political systems, we saw that a Melanesian big man had to be generous. People worked for the big man, helping him amass wealth, but eventually he had to give a feast and give away all that wealth.

Because of their experience with big-man systems, Melanesians believed that all wealthy people eventually had to give away their wealth. For decades they had attended

Christian missions and worked on plantations. All the while, they expected Europeans to return the fruits of their labor as their own big men did. When the Europeans refused to distribute the wealth or even to let natives know the secret of its production and distribution, cargo cults developed.

Like arrogant big men, Europeans would be leveled, by death if necessary. However, natives lacked the physical means of doing what their traditions said they should do. Thwarted by well-armed colonial forces, natives resorted to magical leveling. They called on supernatural beings to intercede, to kill or otherwise deflate the European big men and redistribute their wealth.

Cargo cults are religious responses to the expansion of the world capitalist economy. However, this religious mobilization had political and economic results. Cult participation gave Melanesians a basis for common interests and activities and thus helped pave the way for political parties and economic interest organizations. Previously separated by geography, language, and customs, Melanesians started forming larger groups as members of the same cults and followers of the same prophets. The cargo cults paved the way for *political* action through which the indigenous peoples eventually regained their autonomy.

## Religious Changes in the United States

Because the U.S. Census doesn't gather information on religion, there are no official statistics on Americans' religious affiliations. To help fill this gap, the Pew Research Center, based in Washington, D.C., carried out "Religious Landscape Studies" in 2007 and 2014. These comprehensive surveys of more than 35,000 adults revealed significant and ongoing changes in Americans' religious affiliations (see Pew Research Center 2015a).

The United States still has the world's largest number of Christians, but the Christian share of the population has been falling. Of the 85 percent of Americans who were raised as Christians, nearly a quarter no longer follow that faith. Catholicism has experienced a particularly steep decline. Of the 32 percent of Americans who were raised Catholic, 41 percent no longer practice.

The absolute number of mainline Protestants—Methodists, Baptists, Lutherans, Presbyterians, and Episcopalians—also fell significantly, from 41 million in 2007 to 36 million in 2014. On the other hand, the number of Americans affiliated with historically Black Protestant churches has remained stable, at around 16 million. America's 62 million Evangelicals represent the only group of Protestants whose numbers have been increasing, but even their share of the U.S. population declined by a percentage point between 2007 and 2014.

In that seven-year period, the percentage of non-Christian faiths within the U.S. population rose from 5 percent to 6 percent. Growth was especially strong for Muslims and Hindus. The most notable increase, however, from 16 percent to 23 percent, has been in the unaffiliated category. These 56 million religious "nones" now outnumber both Catholics and mainline Protestants (Pew Research Center 2012b). They include, but are not limited to, people who identify as atheists, agnostics, and "nothing in particular." (Atheists and agnostics represent just 7 percent of the American population.) Unaffiliated Americans have a median age of 36 years, compared with 52 years for mainline Protestants. Men are much more likely than women to be unaffiliated—27 percent to 19 percent.

TABLE 13.1   **Changes in Family and Household Organization in the United States, 1970 versus 2018**

Sources: Vespa, Jonathan, Jamie M. Lewis, and Rose M. Kreider. "America's Families and Living Arrangements: 2012," *Current Population Reports, P20-570.* Washington: U.S. Census Bureau, 2013; and U.S. Census Bureau, America's Families and Living Arrangements, 2018

| | 1970 | 2018 |
|---|---|---|
| **Numbers:** | | |
| Total number of households | 63 million | 128 million |
| Number of people per household | 3.1 | 2.5 |
| **Percentages:** | | |
| Married couples living with children | 40% | 19% |
| Married couples living without children | 30% | 29% |
| Family households | 81% | 65% |
| Households with five or more people | 21% | 9% |
| People living alone | 17% | 28% |
| Percentage of single-mother families | 5% | 12% |
| Percentage of single-father families | 0% | 5% |
| Households with own children under 18 | 45% | 27% |

Table 13.1, nuclear families now account for only 19 percent of American households. In other words, different domestic arrangements now outnumber nuclear family households more than five to one (see Gamson 2015; Golombok 2015). There are several reasons for this changing household composition. One reason is that women increasingly have joined men in the cash workforce. Often, this removes them from their family of orientation while making it economically feasible to delay (or even forgo) marriage.

The median age at first marriage for American women in 2018 was 28 years, compared with 21 years in 1970. For men the comparable ages were 30 and 23. Currently, more than a third (35 percent) of American men and 30 percent of American women have never married. Fewer than half (47 percent) of American women now live with a husband, compared with 65 percent in 1950. The current percentage of U.S. adults living without a spouse or domestic partner is about 41 percent. Many of them live alone: The proportion of single-person households rose from 17 percent in 1970 to 28 percent in 2018.

Another important trend is the increasing number of single-parent families. Between 1960 and 2018, the percentage of children living with two parents decreased from 88 percent to 69 percent. During that same period, the percentage of children living with only their *mother* nearly tripled from 8 to 22 percent, and the percentage living with only their *father* increased from 1 to 4 percent. The percentage of children not living with either parent also increased slightly, from 3 to 4 percent (U.S. Census Bureau 2018).

Household and family size has declined in both the United States and Canada. Average family size has fallen (since 1980) more noticeably in Canada (from 3.4 to 2.9 persons) than in the U.S. (3.3 to 3.1). The trend toward smaller families also is detectable in Western Europe and other industrial nations. To be sure, contemporary North Americans maintain social lives through school, work, friendship, sports, clubs, religion, and organized social activities. However, the growing isolation from kin that these figures suggest may well be unprecedented in human history.

One among many kinds of American family. This single mother, seen here baking with her daughter, used donor insemination to become pregnant. What do you see as the main differences between nuclear families and single-parent families?
Steve Russell/Toronto Star/Getty Images

What does *family* mean in different cultures? Consider a striking contrast in the meaning of *family* between the United States and Brazil, the two most populous nations of the Western Hemisphere. When asked about their families, married Americans with children usually mention their spouse (or domestic partner) and children. However, when Brazilians talk about their families, they mean their parents, siblings, aunts, uncles, grandparents, and cousins. Later they add their children, but rarely the spouse, who has his or her own family. The children are shared by the two families. Because middle-class Americans are less likely than Brazilians to have access to an extended family support system, marriage assumes more importance. Unlike in Brazil, the spousal relationship is supposed to take precedence over either spouse's relationship with his or her own parents. This places a significant strain on American marriages.

## It's All Relative

The social construction of kinship varies widely among societies. Furthermore, even in a single nation-state, there can be significant disagreement about kinship classification. Consider a travel ban announced by the Trump administration on June 29, 2017. Citizens of six Muslim-majority countries (Iran, Libya, Somalia, Sudan, Syria, and Yemen) would be denied visas to enter the United States as visitors or refugees unless they could demonstrate a "close family relationship" with an American citizen, or a connection with a school or business. Only the following family members of American citizens were considered close enough to enter: parent, spouse, child, adult son or daughter, son-in-law, daughter-in-law, and sibling, as well as their stepfamily counterparts. The administration's definition of "close family member" *excluded grandparents, grandchildren, uncles, aunts, cousins, and fiancés/fiancées.*

Evangelicals, one wearing a T-shirt supporting presidential candidate (and eventual winner) Jair Bolsonaro, attend a mass at an Assembly of God church in Rio de Janeiro, Brazil, on October 18, 2018. Ricardo Moraes/REUTERS/Newscom

Converts to Pentecostalism are expected to separate themselves both from their pasts and from the secular social world that surrounds them. In Arembepe, Brazil, for example, the *crentes* ("true believers," as members of the local Pentecostal community are called) set themselves apart by their beliefs, behavior, and lifestyle (Kottak 2018). They worship, chant, and pray. They dress simply and forgo such worldly temptations (seen as vices) as tobacco, alcohol, gambling, and extramarital sexuality, along with dancing, movies, and other forms of popular culture.

Pentecostalism strengthens family and household through a moral code that respects marriage and prohibits adultery, gambling, drinking, and fighting. These activities were valued mainly by men in preconversion culture. Pentecostalism has appeal for men, however, because it solidifies their authority within the household. Although Pentecostal ideology is strongly patriarchal, with women expected to subordinate themselves to men, women tend to be more active church members than are men. Pentecostalism promotes services and prayer groups by and for women. In such settings women develop leadership skills, as they also extend their social-support network beyond family and kin (Burdick 1998).

## Homogenization, Indigenization, or Hybridization?

Any cultural form that spreads from one society to another—be it a Starbucks, a McDonald's, or a form of religion—has to fit into the country and culture it enters. We can use the rapid spread of Pentecostalism as a case study of the process of adaptation of foreign cultural forms to local settings.

Joel Robbins (2004) has examined the extent to which what he calls Pentecostal/charismatic Christianity preserves its basic form and core beliefs as it spreads and adapts to various national and local cultures. Pentecostalism is a Western invention: Its beliefs, doctrines, organizational features, and rituals originated in the United States, following the European rise and spread of Protestantism. The core doctrines of acceptance of Jesus as one's savior, baptism with the Holy Spirit, faith healing, and belief in the second coming of Jesus have spread across nations and cultures without losing their basic shape.

Scholars have argued about whether the global spread of Pentecostalism is best understood as (1) a process of Western cultural domination and homogenization (perhaps supported by a right-wing political agenda) or (2) one in which imported cultural forms respond to local needs and are differentiated and indigenized. Robbins (2004) takes a middle-ground position, viewing the spread of Pentecostalism as a form of cultural hybridization. He argues that global and local features appear with equal intensity within these Pentecostal cultures. Churches retain certain core Pentecostal beliefs and behaviors while also responding to the local culture and being organized at the local level.

Reviewing the literature, Robbins (2004) finds little evidence that a Western political agenda is propelling the global spread of Pentecostalism. It is true that foreigners (including American pastors and televangelists) have helped introduce Pentecostalism to countries outside North America. There is little evidence, however, that overseas churches are largely funded and ideologically shaped from North America. Pentecostal churches typically are staffed with locals, who run them as organizations that are attentive and responsive to local situations. Conversion is typically a key feature of that agenda. Once converted, a Pentecostal is expected to be an active evangelist, seeking to bring in new members. This evangelization is one of the most important activities in Pentecostal culture and certainly aids its expansion.

Pentecostalism spreads as other forces of globalization displace people and disrupt local lives. To people who feel socially adrift, Pentecostal evangelists offer tightly knit communities and a weblike structure of personal connections within and between Pentecostal communities. Such networks can facilitate access to health care, job placement, educational services, and other resources.

Unlike Catholicism, which is hierarchical, Pentecostalism is egalitarian. Adherents need no special education—only spiritual inspiration—to preach or to run a church. Based on his research in Brazil, John Burdick (1993) notes that many Afro-Brazilians are drawn to the Pentecostal community because others who are socially and racially like them are in the congregation, some serving as preachers. Opportunities for participation and leadership are abundant, for example, as lay preachers, deacons, and leaders of various men's, women's, and youth groups. The churches fund outreach to the needy and other locally relevant social services.

## The Spread of Islam

Islam—whose 1.8 billion followers constitute almost a quarter of the world's population—is another rapidly spreading global religion that can be used to illustrate cultural globalization. The globalization of Islam also illustrates cultural hybridization. Islam has adapted successfully to the many nations and cultures it has entered, adopting architectural styles, linguistic practices, and even religious beliefs from host cultures.

For example, although mosques (Islamic houses of worship) all share certain characteristics (e.g., they face Mecca and have some common architectural features), they

FIGURE 13.2 **A Matrilineage Five Generations Deep**
Matrilineages are based on demonstrated descent from a female ancestor. Only the
children of the group's women (shaded) belong to the matrilineage. The children of
the group's men are excluded; they belong to *their* mother's matrilineage.

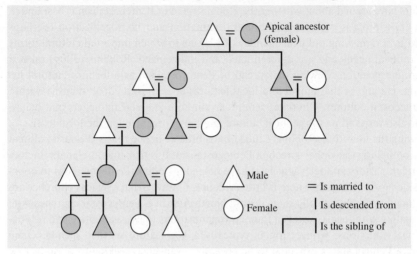

either the male or the female line. Patrilineal descent is much more common than
matrilineal descent is. In a sample of 564 societies (Murdock 1957), patrilineal descent
outnumbered matrilineal descent three to one (247 patrilineal to 84 matrilineal).

Members of any descent group, whether patrilineal or matrilineal, believe that they
are descended from a specific *apical ancestor.* That person stands at the apex, or top, of
their common genealogy. For example, Adam and Eve, according to the Bible, are the
apical ancestors of all humanity. Since Eve is said to have come from Adam's rib, Adam
stands as the original apical ancestor for the patrilineal genealogies laid out in the Bible.

Lineages and clans are two types of descent group. Clans tend to be larger than lineages
and can include lineages. A **lineage** is a descent group based on *demonstrated descent.*
Members can demonstrate how they descend from their common ancestor, by naming their
forebears in each generation from the apical ancestor through the present. (This doesn't
mean the genealogy is accurate, only that lineage members believe it is.) In the Bible the lit-
any of men who "begat" other men demonstrates descent for a large patrilineage that ultimately includes Jews and Arabs (who share Abraham as their last common apical ancestor).

Unlike lineages, members of a clan do not demonstrate how they descend from their
common ancestor. They merely claim, assert, or *stipulate* their common ancestry and
descent. They don't try to specify actual genealogical links generation by generation, as
members of a lineage do. A **clan**, then, is a descent group based on *stipulated descent.*

The Betsileo of Madagascar have both lineages and clans. They can demonstrate descent for the most recent 8 to 10 generations. Going further back than that, however, they
can stipulate their descent only from particular ancestors. The stipulated founders of
Betsileo clans can include vaguely defined foreign royalty or even mythical creatures, such
as mermaids (Kottak 1980). Like the Betsileo, many societies have both lineages and

clans. When this is true, the clan will have more members and cover a larger geographic area than its component lineages do. Sometimes a clan's apical ancestor is not a human at all but an animal or a plant (called a *totem*). Whether human or not, the ancestor symbolizes the social unity and identity of the members, distinguishing them from other groups.

The economic types that usually have descent-group organization are horticulture, pastoralism, and agriculture. A given society usually has multiple descent groups. Any one of them may be confined to a single village, but they usually span more than one village. Any branch of a descent group that lives in one place is a *local descent group*. Two (or more) local branches of different descent groups may live in the same village.

## Lineages, Clans, and Residence Rules

As we've seen, descent groups, unlike families, are permanent and enduring units, with new members added in every generation. Members have access to the lineage estate, where some of them must live, in order to benefit from and manage that estate across the generations. An easy way to keep members at home is to have a rule about who belongs to the descent group and where they should live after they get married. Patrilineal and matrilineal descent, and the postmarital residence rules that usually accompany them, ensure that about half the people born in each generation will spend their lives on the ancestral estate.

With patrilineal descent, the typical postmarital residence rule is **patrilocality**: Married couples reside in the husband's father's community, so that the children will grow up in their father's village. It makes sense for patrilineal societies to require patrilocal postmarital residence. If the group's male members are expected to exercise their rights in the ancestral estate, it's a good idea to raise them on that estate and to keep them there after they marry.

A less common postmarital residence rule, associated with matrilineal descent, is **matrilocality**: Married couples live in the wife's mother's community, and their children grow up in their mother's village. Together, patrilocality and matrilocality are known as *unilocal* rules of postmarital residence. Regardless of where one resides after marriage, one remains a member of one's original unilineal descent group for life. This means that a man residing in his wife's village in a matrilineal society keeps his membership in his own matrilineal descent group, and a woman residing in her husband's village is still a member of her own patrilineal descent group.

# Defining Marriage

"Love and marriage," "marriage and the family": These familiar phrases show how we link the romantic love of two individuals to marriage, and how we link marriage to reproduction and family creation. But marriage is an institution with significant roles and functions in addition to reproduction. What is marriage, anyway?

Marriage is notoriously difficult to define because of the varied forms it can take in different societies. Consider the following definition from *Notes and Queries on Anthropology*:

> Marriage is a union between a man and a woman such that the children born to the woman are recognized as legitimate offspring of both partners. (Royal Anthropological Institute 1951, p. 111).

actors will sacrifice themselves, their families, and all else for their cause. Commitment will be strongest when sacred values are shared, cementing a group identity (Atran 2016). The researchers found that militants, almost always young men, tend to form groups of three to four like-minded friends who forge themselves into a family-like unit, becoming a "band of brothers" in arms, devoted to one another. Like members of a cult, they share a collective sense of righteousness and special destiny. As potential martyrs, they require strong inspiration. Their commitment to a common cause, combined with family-like relationships, provides that inspiration.

Although most recruits to ISIS and al Qaeda are Muslims, many have little prior knowledge of the religious teachings of Islam. What inspires them is not so much religious doctrine as the wish to pursue a thrilling cause—one that promises glory, esteem, respect, and remembrance. ISIS has even attracted "jihad tourists"—people who have visited Syria over school breaks or holidays seeking a brief adventure and then returned to their routine jobs in the West.

These militant groups are not part of an organized global network based on top-down control. Rather, the groups tend to be decentralized and self-organizing. Such locally dispersed groups can, however, connect via the Internet to form a more global community of alienated youth seeking heroic sacrifice.

Atran (2016) suggests that sacred values are fought most successfully with other sacred values, or by undermining the social networks that are held together by those values. He also suggests that the armed forces and sacred ideals needed to defeat ISIS will probably have to come from other Muslim communities, e.g., the Kurds, who are threatened by ISIS.

## Secular Rituals

In concluding this chapter on religion, we may recognize some problems with the definitions of religion given at the beginning of this chapter. The first problem: If we define religion with reference to the sacred and/or supernatural beings, powers, and forces, how do we classify ritual-like behaviors that occur in secular contexts? Some anthropologists believe there are both sacred and secular rituals. Secular rituals include formal, invariant, stereotyped, earnest, repetitive behavior and rites of passage that take place in nonreligious settings (see Bilgrami 2016)

A second problem: If the distinction between the supernatural and the natural is not consistently made in a society, how can we tell what is religion and what isn't? The Betsileo of Madagascar, for example, view witches and dead ancestors as real people who play roles in ordinary life. However, their occult powers are not empirically demonstrable.

A third problem: The behavior considered appropriate for religious occasions varies tremendously from culture to culture. One society may consider drunken frenzy the surest sign of faith, whereas another may inculcate quiet reverence. Who is to say which is "more religious"?

It is possible for apparently secular settings, things, and events to acquire intense meaning for individuals who have grown up in their presence. For example, identities and loyalties based on fandom, football, baseball, and soccer can be powerful, indeed. Rock stars and bands can mobilize many. Long overdue World Series wins led to celebrations across a "Red Sox Nation" in 2004 and among Cubs fans everywhere in 2016. Italians and Brazilians are rarely, if ever, as unified, nationally and emotionally, as they are when their teams are competing in the World Cup. The collective effervescence that Durkheim found so characteristic of religion can equally well describe what Brazilians experience when their country wins a World Cup.

In the context of comparative religion, the idea that the secular can become sacred isn't surprising. Long ago, Durkheim (1912/2001) pointed out that the distinction between sacred and profane doesn't depend on the intrinsic qualities of the sacred symbol. In Australian totemic religion, for example, sacred beings include such humble creatures as ducks, frogs, rabbits, and grubs, whose inherent qualities could hardly have given rise to the religious sentiment they inspire.

Madagascar's tomb-centered ceremonies are times when the living and the dead are joyously reunited, when people get drunk, gorge themselves, and have sexual license. Perhaps the gray, sober, ascetic, and moralistic aspects of many official religious events, in taking the fun out of religion, force some, indeed many, people to find religion (i.e., truth, beauty, meaning, passionate involvement) in fun.

## Anthropology Today  *Great Expectorations*

Secular rituals are apparent in baseball. Have you ever noticed how much baseball players spit? Outside baseball—even among other male sports figures—spitting is considered impolite. Football players, with their customary headgear, don't spit,

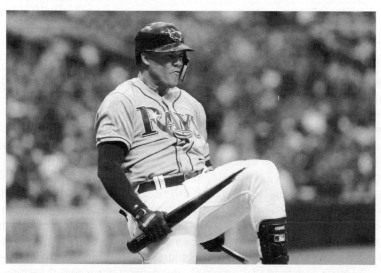

On April 22, 2018, at Tropicana Field in St. Petersburg, Florida, Tampa Bay Rays right fielder Carlos Gomez (27) breaks his bat in disgust after striking out in a game against the Minnesota Twins. Kim Klement/USA TODAY Sports/Newscom

*continued*

FIGURE 13.3    **Patrilineal Descent-Group Identity and Incest among the Lakher**

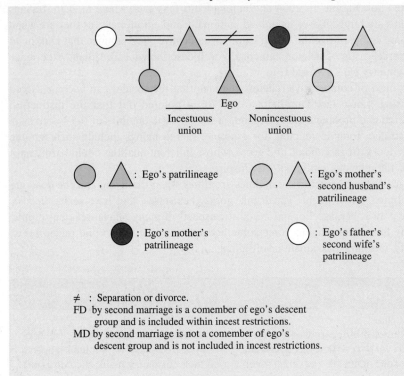

## Incest and Its Avoidance

A century ago, early anthropologists speculated that societies ban incest because humans have an instinctive horror of mating with close relatives (Hobhouse 1915; Lowie 1920/1961). But why, one wonders, if humans really do have an instinctive aversion to incest, would a formal prohibition be necessary? No one would want to have sexual contact with a relative. Yet as social workers, judges, psychiatrists, and psychologists are well aware, incest is more common than we might suppose.

A cross-cultural study of 87 societies (Meigs and Barlow 2002) suggested that incest occurred in several of them (see also Wolf 2014). It's not clear, however, whether the authors of the study controlled for the social construction of incest. They report, for example, that incest occurs among the Yanomami, but they may be considering cross-cousin marriage to be incestuous, when it is not so considered by the Yanomami. Indeed, it is the preferred form of marriage, not just for the Yanomami but in many tribal societies. Another society in their sample is the Ashanti, for whom the ethnographer Meyer Fortes (1950) reports, "In the old days it [incest] was punished by death. Nowadays the culprits are heavily fined" (p. 257). This suggests that there really were violations of Ashanti incest restrictions and that such violations were punished. More strikingly, among 24 Ojibwa individuals from whom he obtained information about incest, A. Irving Hallowell (1955) found 8 cases of parent-child incest and 10 cases of brother-sister incest. Because reported cases of actual parent-child and sibling incest are rare in the ethnographic literature, questions about the possibility of social construction arise here again. In many cultures, including the Ojibwa, people use the same terms for their mother and their aunt, their father and their uncle, and their cousins and siblings. Could the siblings in the Ojibwa case actually have been cousins, and the parents and children uncles and nieces?

In ancient Egypt, sibling marriage apparently was allowed both for royalty and for commoners, in some districts at least. Based on official census records from Roman Egypt (first to third centuries C.E.), 24 percent of all documented marriages in the Arsinoites district were between "brothers" and "sisters." The rates were 37 percent for the city of Arsinoe and 19 percent for the surrounding villages. These figures are much higher than any other documented levels of inbreeding among humans (Scheidel 1997). Again, one wonders if the relatives involved were as close biologically as the kin terms would imply.

According to Anna Meigs and Kathleen Barlow (2002), for Western societies with nuclear family organization, "father–daughter incest" is much more common with stepfathers than with biological fathers. But is it really incest if they aren't biological relatives? American culture is unclear on this matter. Incest also happens with biological fathers, especially those who were absent or did little caretaking of their daughters in childhood. In a carefully designed study, Linda M. Williams and David Finkelhor (1995) found father-daughter incest to be least likely when fathers played a strong role in parenting their daughters. This experience enhanced the father's feelings of nurturance, protectiveness, and identification with his daughter, thus reducing the chance of incest.

## Endogamy

Exogamy pushes social organization outward, establishing and preserving alliances among groups. In contrast, rules of **endogamy** dictate mating or marriage within a group to which one belongs. Endogamic rules are less common but are still familiar to anthropologists. Indeed, most cultures *are* endogamous units, although they usually do not need a formal rule requiring people to marry someone from their own society. In our society, classes and ethnic groups are quasi-endogamous groups. Members of an ethnic or religious group often want their children to marry within that group, although many of them do not do so. Outmarriage rates vary among such groups, with some more committed to endogamy than others.

An extreme example of endogamy is India's **caste system**, which was formally abolished in 1949, although its structure and effects linger. Castes are stratified groups in which lifelong membership is set at birth. Indian castes are grouped into five major categories, or *varna*. Each is ranked relative to the other four, and these categories extend throughout India. Each varna includes a large number of minor castes (*jati*), each of which includes people within a region who may intermarry. All the jati in a single varna in a given region are ranked, just as the varna themselves are ranked.

## Think Like an Anthropologist

1. Describe a rite of passage you (or a friend) have been through. How did it fit the three-phase model given in the text? Now consider a move you have made, such as going away to college. Did it fit the three-phase model? In both cases, describe your experiences with liminality.

2. This chapter notes that many Americans see recreation (e.g., sports) and religion as separate domains. Based on my fieldwork in Brazil and Madagascar and my reading about other societies, I believe that this separation is both ethnocentric and false. Do you agree with me about this? What has been your own experience?

## Key Terms

animism, *367*
cargo cults, *377*
communitas, *370*
liminality, *369*
magic, *368*
mana, *367*

monotheism, *367*
polytheism, *367*
religion, *364*
revitalization
    movements, *377*
rites of passage, *369*

rituals, *368*
shaman, *366*
taboo, *367*
totem, *372*

# Chapter 16

# Ethnicity and Race

## Ethnic Groups and Ethnicity

Ethnicity is based on cultural similarities (with members of the same ethnic group) and differences (between that group and others). Ethnic groups must deal with other such groups in the nation or region they inhabit. Interethnic relations are important in the study of any nation or region—especially so because of the ongoing transnational movement of migrants and refugees (see Marger 2015; Parrillo 2016, 2019). Table 16.1 lists American ethnic groups, based on the most recent U.S. Census Bureau estimates available as of this writing.

Members of an **ethnic group** share certain beliefs, values, habits, customs, and norms because of their common background. They define themselves as different and special because of cultural features. This distinction may arise from language, religion, historical experience, geographic placement, kinship, or "race" (see Spickard 2012).

# Arranged Marriages versus Romance Marriages

In our society, we think of marriage as an individual matter. Although the bride and groom usually seek their parents' approval, the final choice (to live together, to marry, to divorce) lies with the couple. Contemporary Western societies stress the notion that romantic love is necessary for a good marriage. Increasingly, this idea characterizes other cultures as well. The mass media and human migration spread Western ideas about the importance of love for marriage.

Just how widespread is romantic love, and what role should it play in marriage? A study by anthropologists William Jankowiak and Edward Fischer (1992) found romantic ardor to be very common cross-culturally. Previously, anthropologists had tended to ignore evidence for romantic love in other cultures, probably because arranged marriages were so common. Surveying ethnographic data from 166 cultures, Jankowiak and Fischer (1992) found evidence for romantic love in 147 of them—89 percent (see also Jankowiak 1995, 2008).

Furthermore, diffusion of Western ideas about the importance of love for marriage has influenced marital decisions in other cultures. Among villagers in the Kangra valley of northern India, as reported by anthropologist Kirin Narayan (quoted in Goleman 1992; see also Narayan 2016), even in the traditional arranged marriages, the partners might eventually fall in love. In that area nowadays, however, the media have spread the idea that young people should choose their own spouse based on romantic love, and elopements now rival arranged marriages.

Love remains Americans' top reason to marry (see Figure 13.4). In a recent Pew Research Center survey, 88 percent of Americans ranked "love" highest among reasons to get married, ahead of "making a lifelong commitment" (81 percent) and "companionship" (76 percent). Notice that fewer than half (49 percent) of respondents listed "having children" as a very important reason to marry.

**FIGURE 13.4**   **Why Americans Marry**

Source: Pew Research Center, 2019.

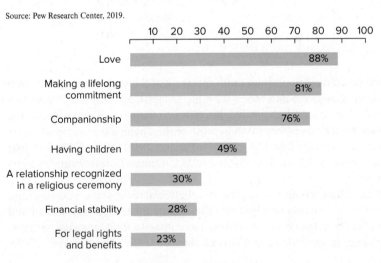

# Marriage: A Group Affair

In nonindustrial societies, although there can be romantic love, marriage is a group concern. People don't just take a spouse; they assume obligations to a group of in-laws. When residence is patrilocal, for example, a woman must leave the community where she was born. She faces the prospect of spending the rest of her life in her husband's village, with his relatives.

## Gifts at Marriage

Gifts at marriage are common among the world's cultures. A marital gift known as **dowry** occurs when the bride's family or kin group provides substantial gifts when their daughter marries. Ernestine Friedl (1962) describes a form of dowry in rural Greece, in which the bride gets a wealth transfer from her mother, to serve as a kind of trust fund during her marriage. More commonly, however, the dowry goes to the husband's family, and the custom is correlated with low female status. In this form of dowry, best known from India, women are perceived as burdens. When a man and his family take a wife, they expect to be compensated for the added responsibility.

In many societies with patrilineal descent, it is customary for the husband's group to present a substantial gift—before, at, or soon after the wedding—to his bride's group. The BaThonga of Mozambique call such a gift *lobola*, and the custom of giving something like **lobola** is widespread in patrilineal societies (Radcliffe-Brown 1924/1952). This gift compensates the bride's group for the loss of her companionship and labor. More important, it makes the children born to the woman full members of her husband's descent group. In matrilineal societies, children are members of the mother's group, and there is no reason for a lobola-like gift.

Lobola-like gifts exist in many more cultures than dowry does, but the nature and quantity of transferred items differ. Among the BaThonga of Mozambique, whose name—lobola—I will extend for this widespread custom, the gift consists of cattle. Use of livestock (usually cattle in Africa, pigs in Papua New Guinea) for lobola is common, but the number of animals given varies from society to society. We can generalize, however, that the larger the gift, the more stable the marriage. Lobola is insurance against divorce.

Imagine a patrilineal society in which a marriage requires the transfer of about 25 cattle from the groom's descent group to the bride's. When Michael, a member of descent group A, marries Sarah from group B, he has to give lobola cattle to her group. His relatives help him assemble that lobola. He gets the most help from his close patrikin—his older brother, father, father's brother, and closest patrilineal cousins. The distribution of the cattle once they reach Sarah's group mirrors the manner in which they were assembled. Sarah's father, or her oldest brother if the father is dead, receives her lobola. He keeps most of the cattle to use as lobola for his sons' marriages. However, a share also goes to everyone who will be expected to help when Sarah's brothers marry.

When Sarah's brother David gets married, many of the cattle go to a third group—C, which is David's wife's group. Thereafter, those same cattle may be transmitted as lobola to still other groups. Men constantly use their sisters' lobola cattle to acquire their own wives. In a decade, the cattle given when Michael married Sarah will have been exchanged widely.

United States for generations have little in common with new Hispanic immigrants, such as those from Central America.

The Hispanic share of the U.S. population grew rapidly, by 68 percent, between 2000 and 2018, from 35.2 million to 59.2 million people. However, the annual Asian growth rate (3 percent) now exceeds that of Hispanics (2 percent). The Hispanic growth rate has slowed because immigration of Mexicans to the United States has leveled off and because the fertility rate among Hispanic women has declined (see Krogstad 2017).

*Hispanic* is a category based mainly on language. It includes Whites, Blacks, and "racially" mixed Spanish speakers and their ethnically conscious descendants. (There also are Native American and even Asian Hispanics.) The label *Hispanic* lumps together people of diverse geographic origin—Mexico, Puerto Rico, El Salvador, Cuba, the Dominican Republic, Guatemala, and other Spanish-speaking countries of Central and South America and the Caribbean. *Latino* is a broader category, which also can include Brazilians (who speak Portuguese). Mexicans constitute about two-thirds of American Hispanics. Next come Puerto Ricans at around 9 percent. Salvadorans, Cubans, Dominicans, and Guatemalans living in the United States all number more than 1 million people per nationality. Of the major racial and ethnic groups in the United States, Hispanics are by far the youngest. At 28 years, their median age is a decade lower than that of the U.S. overall (Flores 2017).

## Minority Groups and Stratification

*Minority groups* are so called because, as a group, they occupy subordinate (lower) positions within a social hierarchy. Minority groups have less power and wealth than *majority groups* do. Minority groups are obvious features of stratification in the United States. The 2017 poverty rate was 9 percent for non-Hispanic Whites, 10 percent for Asian Americans, 18 percent for Hispanics, and 21 percent for African Americans (Fontenot et al. 2018). Inequality shows up consistently in unemployment figures as well as in income and wealth. Median household incomes in 2017 were as follows: $81,331 for Asian Americans, $68,145 for non-Hispanic Whites, $50,486 for Hispanics, and $40,258 for African Americans (Fontenot et al. 2018). The economic gap between Black and Hispanic families, on the one hand, and non-Hispanic Whites, on the other, has been widening in recent years, even among Americans with comparable levels of education. In 2016, the median American White family had a net worth of $140,000, while the median Black family had a net worth of $3,400 (Ingraham 2018).

## Race and Ethnicity

When an ethnic group is assumed to have a biological basis (distinctively shared "blood" or genes), it is called a **race** (see Mukhopadhyay, Henzie, and Moses 2014; Wade 2015, 2017). Discrimination against such a group is **racism** (Scupin 2012). Race, like ethnicity in general, is a cultural category rather than a biological reality. That is, ethnic groups, including "races," derive from contrasts perceived and perpetuated in particular societies, rather than from scientific classifications based on common genes.

In American culture, we hear the words *ethnicity* and *race* frequently, without clear distinctions made between them. For example, the term *race* often is used inappropriately to refer to Hispanics, who, in fact, can be of any race. The following example provides one illustration of the popular confusion about ethnicity and race in American culture. Eight years prior to her appointment to the U.S. Supreme Court, Sonia Sotomayor, then an appeals court judge, gave a talk titled "A Latina Judge's Voice," at the University of California, Berkeley, School of Law. As part of a much longer speech, Sotomayor declared:

> I would hope that a wise Latina woman with the richness of her experiences would more often than not reach a better conclusion than a white male who hasn't lived that life. (Sotomayor 2001/2009)

On hearing about that speech, conservatives, including former House Speaker Newt Gingrich and radio talk show host Rush Limbaugh, seized on this declaration as evidence that Sotomayor was a "racist" or a "reverse racist." Her critics ignored the fact that *Latina* is an ethnic (and gendered-female) rather than a racial category. I suspect that Sotomayor also was using "white male" as an ethnic-gender category, to refer to nonminority men. Our popular culture does not consistently distinguish between ethnicity and race (see Ansell 2013; Banton 2015; Golash-Boza 2019).

## The Social Construction of Race

Most Americans believe (incorrectly) that their population includes *biologically based* races to which various labels are applied. Such racial terms include *White, Black, Yellow, Red, Caucasoid, Negroid, Mongoloid, Amerindian, Euro-American, African American, Asian American,* and *Native American.*

We have seen that races, while assumed to have a biological basis, actually are socially constructed in particular societies. Let's consider now several examples of the social construction of race, beginning with the United States.

### Hypodescent: Race in the United States

Most Americans acquire a racial identity at birth and stick with it throughout their lives, but race isn't based on biology or on simple ancestry. Consider the case of the child of a "racially mixed" marriage involving one Black and one White parent. We know that 50 percent of the child's genes come from one parent and 50 percent from the other. Still, American culture overlooks heredity and classifies this child as Black. This rule is arbitrary. On the basis of genotype (genetic composition), it would be just as logical to classify the child as White.

American rules for assigning racial status can be even more arbitrary. In some states, anyone known to have any Black ancestor, no matter how distant, is classified as Black or African American. This is a rule of **descent** (it assigns social identity on the basis of ancestry), but of a sort that is rare outside the contemporary United States. It is called **hypodescent** (Harris and Kottak 1963), because it automatically places the children of a union between members of different groups in the minority group (*hypo* means "lower"). Hypodescent divides American society into groups that have been unequal in their access to wealth, power, and prestige.

patrilocally (in her husband's household and community) might be reluctant to leave him and her children. In patrilineal, patrilocal societies, the children of divorce would be expected to remain with their father, as members of his patrilineage. From the women's perspective, this is a strong impediment to divorce.

Divorce is fairly common among foragers. Among the Kalahari San, for example, between 25 and 40 percent of all marriages end in divorce (Blurton-Jones et al. 2000). Facilitating divorce is the fact that the group alliance functions of marriage are less important, because descent groups are less common among foragers than among food producers. Also facilitating divorce is the fact that marriages tend to last longer when a couple shares—and would have trouble dissolving—a significant joint fund of property. This usually is not the case among foragers, who have minimal material possessions. On the other hand, marital stability is more likely among foragers when the nuclear family is a fairly autonomous year-round unit with a gender-based division of labor, particularly when the population is sparse, so that few alternative spouses are available.

In contemporary Western societies, we have the idea that romantic love is necessary for a good marriage (see Ingraham 2008). When romance fails, so may the marriage. Or it may not fail, if other benefits associated with marriage are compelling. Economic ties and obligations to children, along with other factors, such as concern about public opinion, or simple inertia, may keep marriages intact after sex, romance, or companionship fades. Also, even in modern societies, leaders and other elites may want to maintain their politically strategic marriages at all costs.

## Plural Marriages

Most nonindustrial food-producing societies, unlike most industrial nations, allow **plural marriages**, or **polygamy**. There are two varieties; one is common, and the other is very rare. The more common variant is **polygyny**, in which a man has more than one wife. The rare variant is **polyandry**, in which a woman has more than one husband. Polyandry is practiced in only a few societies, notably among certain groups in Tibet, Nepal, India, and Sri Lanka. In contemporary North America, where divorce is fairly easy and common, polygamy is against the law. North Americans are allowed, however, to practice *serial monogamy*: Individuals may have more than one spouse but never, legally, more than one at the same time.

### Polygyny

We must distinguish between the social approval of plural marriage and its frequency. Many cultures approve of a man's having more than one wife. However, even when polygyny is allowed or encouraged, most men are monogamous, and polygyny characterizes only a fraction of the marriages.

What factors promote, and discourage, polygyny? Polygyny is much more common in patrilineal than in matrilineal societies. The relatively high status that women enjoy in matrilineal societies tends to grant them a degree of independence from men that makes polygyny less likely. Nor is polygyny characteristic of most foraging societies, where a married couple and nuclear family often function as an economically viable team. Most industrial nations have outlawed polygyny.

An equal sex ratio tends to work against polygyny if marriage is an expectation for both men and women. In the United States, about 105 males are born for every 100 females. In adulthood the ratio of men to women equalizes, and eventually it reverses. The average North American woman outlives the average man. In many nonindustrial societies as well, the male-biased sex ratio among children reverses in adulthood.

The custom of men marrying later than women promotes polygyny. Among Nigeria's Kanuri people (Cohen 1967), for example, men married between the ages of 18 and 30; women, between 12 and 14. The age difference between spouses meant there were more widows than widowers. Most of the widows remarried, some in polygynous unions. Among the Kanuri and in other polygynous societies, such as the Tiwi of northern Australia, widows made up a large number of the women involved in plural marriages (Hart, Pilling, and Goodale 1988). Polygyny is favored in situations in which having plural wives is an indicator of a man's household productivity, prestige, and social position. The more wives, the more workers. Increased productivity means more wealth. This wealth in turn attracts additional wives to the household. Wealth and wives bring greater prestige to the household and its head.

Polygyny also is supported when the existing spouses agree that another one should be added, especially if they are to share the same household. Sometimes, the first wife requests a second one to help with household chores. The second wife's status is lower than that of the first; they are senior and junior wives. The senior wife sometimes chooses the junior one from among her close kinswomen. Polygyny also can work when the cowives live apart. Among the Betsileo of Madagascar, the different wives always lived in different villages. A man's first (senior) wife, called "Big Wife," lived in the village where he cultivated his best rice field and spent most of his time. High-status Betsileo men with multiple rice fields could have a wife and households near each field. Those men spent most of their time with the senior wife, but they visited the others throughout the year.

Polygyny also can be politically advantageous. Plural wives can play important political roles in nonindustrial states. The king of the Merina, a populous society in the highlands of Madagascar, had palaces for each of his 12 wives in different provinces. He stayed with them when he traveled through the kingdom, and they acted as his local agents, overseeing and reporting on provincial matters. The king of Buganda, the major precolonial state of Uganda, took hundreds of wives, representing all the clans in his nation. Everyone in the kingdom became the king's in-law, and all the clans had a chance to provide the next ruler. This was a way of giving the common people a stake in the government.

There is no single explanation for polygyny. Its context and function vary from society to society and even within the same society. Some men are polygynous because they have inherited a widow from a brother. Others have plural wives because they seek prestige or want to increase their household productivity. Men and women with political and economic ambitions cultivate marital alliances that serve their aims. In many societies, including the Betsileo of Madagascar and the Igbo of Nigeria, women arrange the marriages.

FIGURE 16.2    **Visible Minority Population of Canada, 2016, According to Most Recent Census**

2016. Census Profile, 2016 Census. Ottawa: Statistics Canada

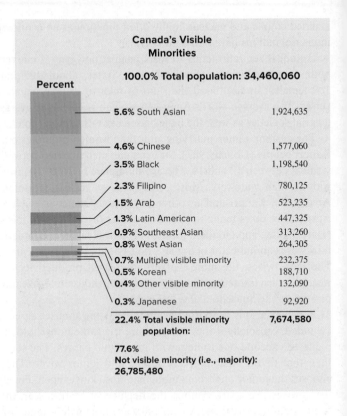

**Canada's Visible Minorities**

**100.0% Total population: 34,460,060**

| Percent | | |
|---|---|---|
| **5.6%** South Asian | 1,924,635 |
| **4.6%** Chinese | 1,577,060 |
| **3.5%** Black | 1,198,540 |
| **2.3%** Filipino | 780,125 |
| **1.5%** Arab | 523,235 |
| **1.3%** Latin American | 447,325 |
| **0.9%** Southeast Asian | 313,260 |
| **0.8%** West Asian | 264,305 |
| **0.7%** Multiple visible minority | 232,375 |
| **0.5%** Korean | 188,710 |
| **0.4%** Other visible minority | 132,090 |
| **0.3%** Japanese | 92,920 |
| **22.4% Total visible minority population:** | **7,674,580** |

**77.6%**
**Not visible minority (i.e., majority):**
**26,785,480**

Rather than race, the Canadian census asks about "visible minorities"—"persons, other than Aboriginal [First Nations] peoples, who are non-Caucasian in race or non-white in colour." Canada's visible minority population consists mainly of the following groups: South Asian, Chinese, Black, Filipino, Latin American, Arab, Southeast Asian, West Asian, Korean, and Japanese (Statistics Canada 2016). "South Asian" and "Chinese" are Canada's largest visible minorities (see Figure 16.2). Canada's visible minority population of 22.4 percent in 2016 (up from 11.2 percent in 1996) contrasts with a figure of 39.3 percent for the United States (in 2018, up from 25 percent in 2000).

As in the United States, Canada's (visible) minority population has been growing much faster than the country's overall population. In 1981, visible minorities accounted for just 4.7 percent of Canadians, versus 22.4 percent in 2016. Visible minorities accounted for 88 percent of Canada's total population growth between 2011 and 2016. If recent immigration trends continue, by 2031 visible minorities will comprise almost one-third (31 percent) of the Canadian population (Statistics Canada 2010).

## Not Us: Race in Japan

Japan presents itself, and is commonly viewed, as a nation that is homogeneous in race, ethnicity, language, and culture (see Toyosaki and Eguchi 2017). Although Japan's population really is less diverse than those of most nations, it does contain significant minority groups (see Graburn 2008; Weiner 2009). Constituting about 10 percent of Japan's total population, those groups include aboriginal Ainu, annexed Okinawans, outcast *burakumin,* children of mixed marriages, and immigrant nationalities, especially Koreans, who number more than 700,000 (Ryang and Lie 2009). The (majority) Japanese define themselves by opposition to others, whether minority groups in their own nation or outsiders—anyone who is "not us." Furthermore, assimilation is discouraged. Cultural mechanisms, including residential segregation and taboos on "interracial" marriage, work to keep minorities "in their place."

To describe racial attitudes in Japan, Jennifer Robertson (1992) used Kwame Anthony Appiah's (1990) term "intrinsic racism"—the belief that a (perceived) racial difference is a sufficient reason to value one person less than another. In Japan the valued group is majority ("pure") Japanese, who are believed to share "the same blood." Thus, the caption to a printed photo of a Japanese American model reads: "She was born in Japan but raised in Hawaii. Her nationality is American but no foreign blood flows in her veins" (Robertson 1992, p. 5). Something like hypodescent also operates in Japan, but less precisely than in the United States, where mixed offspring automatically become members of the minority group. The children of mixed marriages between majority Japanese and others (including Euro-Americans and African Americans) may not get the same "racial" label as their minority parent, but they are still stigmatized for their non-Japanese ancestry (Yamashiro 2017).

## Biracial Japanese

One exception to this stigma is tennis's Naomi Osaka, who beat Serena Williams in the final of the 2018 U.S. Open. Osaka, who is the daughter of a Haitian American father and a Japanese mother, became the first Japanese-born tennis player to win a Grand Slam championship.

Her victory was widely celebrated in Japan as one for that country. Japanese media focused on Osaka's cultural "Japaneseness" rather than her appearance, parentage, or the fact that she had been raised in the United States and spoke halting Japanese. Like a proper Japanese, she did not display excessive joy when she won (in fact, she even apologized), and, despite her aggressive play, she is humble in interviews and bows appropriately (Rich 2018).

This warm reception by the press struck some as hypocritical while Japan's pure-blood definition of ethnicity persists. Many biracial people in Japan still feel undervalued. One term applied to them is *hafu,* derived from the English word "half"—a label that implies "not whole," incomplete, or "less than."

Could Osaka's reception be a sign that things are changing? Other evidence: In 2015 Ariana Miyamoto, a half-Black, half-Japanese woman, was chosen Miss Universe Japan. A year later, another mixed-race woman, Priyanka Yosikawa, won the same crown. In Brazil, it often is said that "Money whitens." In other words, someone who is wealthy will be perceived as having lighter skin color than a physically similar person who is less well off. Media treatment of Osaka, Miyamoto, and Yosikawa suggest that something comparable may be going on in Japan. Can we conclude that "celebrity Japanizes"?

## Anthropology Today *continued*

a social institution that has formed the basis of human society for millennia, for the Kalahari Bushmen and the Han Chinese, the Carthaginians and the Aztecs."

If Roberts knew more about anthropology, he would realize that these four societies don't really support his claim that marriage has universally been a union between one man and one woman. Although the "Kalahari Bushmen" (San peoples) do have exclusively heterosexual marriages, they also divorce and remarry at will. Nor, in Han period China, was marriage a lifetime union between one man and one woman. Han men were allowed to divorce, remarry, and consort with concubines. Within the Roman Empire, Carthaginian women who were Roman citizens were allowed to marry and divorce freely. Many members of the final society cited by Roberts—the Aztecs— were polygamists. The Aztecs used matchmakers to arrange marriages and asked widows to marry a brother of their deceased husband (Joyce 2015). I doubt that Chief Justice Roberts intended to endorse frequent divorce, consorting with mistresses and concubines, and polygamy as aspects of "a social institution that has formed the basis of human society for millennia."

Roberts went on to argue that marriage "arose in the nature of things to meet a vital need: ensuring that children are conceived by a mother and father committed to raising them in the stable conditions of a lifetime relationship." Here the focus is on the role of marriage in procreation and raising children. As we have seen, however, marriage confers socially significant rights and obligations other than raising children. Nor is procreation necessary for or within marriage. Is a childless marriage

any less legitimate than one with children? Is legal adoption of a child less legitimate than conception of the child by a married heterosexual couple? Every day in contemporary societies, men and women marry without expecting to conceive and raise children.

As John Borneman and Laurie Kain Hart (2015) observe, marriage is an elastic institution whose meaning and value vary from culture to culture and evolve over time. Consider the many examples of families, kinship groups, and marriage types considered in this chapter. From the Bosnian *zadruga* to the Nayar *tarawad* to matrilineal and patrilineal clans, lineages, local descent groups, and extended families, children have been raised in, and have managed to survive and even flourish in, all kinds of kin groups. If we go back millennia, as Chief Justice Roberts would like to trace marriage, we would find "love, marriage, and the baby carriage" to be the exception rather than the rule. That is, the combination of romantic love, marriage, procreation, and raising children mainly, or even exclusively, within a nuclear family is a relatively recent—rather than a universal or ages-old—development.

Finally, consider the different forms of marriage that have been considered in this chapter: woman-marriage-to-a-woman among the Nuer, cousin marriage, Lakher marriage to a half sibling, serial monogamy, and other forms that violate the idea that marriage is a lifetime union of one man and one woman.

I would hope, therefore, that the next time a member of the Supreme Court attempts to justify a practice using terms like "for millennia," "ages-old," "universal," or "basic human," he or she will first consult an anthropologist.

# Summary

1. Kinship and marriage organize social and political life in nonindustrial societies. One widespread kin group is the nuclear family, consisting of a married couple and their children. Other groups, such as extended families and descent groups, may assume functions usually associated with the nuclear family. Nuclear families tend to be especially important in foraging and industrial societies.

2. In contemporary North America, the nuclear family is the characteristic kin group for the middle class. Expanded households and sharing with extended family kin occur more frequently among the poor, who may pool their resources in dealing with poverty. Today, however, even in the American middle class, nuclear family households are declining as single-person households and other domestic arrangements increase.

3. The descent group is a basic kin group among nonindustrial food producers (farmers and herders). Unlike families, descent groups have perpetuity, lasting for generations. Descent-group members share and manage an estate. Lineages are based on demonstrated descent; clans, on stipulated descent. Unilineal (patrilineal and matrilineal) descent is associated with unilocal (patrilocal and matrilocal, respectively) postmarital residence.

4. Marriage, which usually is a form of domestic partnership, is difficult to define. Marriage conveys various rights. It establishes legal parentage, and it gives each spouse rights to the sexuality, labor, and property of the other. Marriage also establishes a "relationship of affinity" between each spouse and the other spouse's relatives.

5. Most societies have incest restrictions. Because kinship is socially constructed, such restrictions apply to different relatives in different societies. Exogamy extends social and political ties outward; endogamy does the reverse. Endogamic rules are common in stratified societies. One extreme example is India, where castes are the endogamous units.

6. In societies with descent groups, marriages are relationships between groups as well as between spouses. With lobola, the groom and his relatives transfer wealth to the bride and her relatives. As the value of the lobola gift increases, the divorce rate declines. Lobola customs show that marriages among nonindustrial food producers create and maintain group alliances. So does the sororate, by which a man marries the sister of his deceased wife, and the levirate, by which a woman marries the brother of her deceased husband.

7. The ease and frequency of divorce vary across cultures. When marriage is a matter of intergroup alliance, as is typically true in societies with descent groups, divorce is less common. A large fund of joint property also complicates divorce.

8. Many societies permit plural marriages. The two kinds of polygamy are polygyny and polyandry. The former involves multiple wives; the latter, multiple husbands. Polygyny is much more common than polyandry.

9. The Internet, which reconfigures social relations and networks more generally, is an important addition to the marriage market in contemporary nations.

A Brazilian also can change his or her "race" (say from "Indian" to "mixed") by altering his or her clothing, speech, location (e.g., rural to urban), and even attitude (e.g., by adopting urban behavior). Two racial/ethnic labels used in Brazil are *indio* (indigenous, Native American) and *cabôclo* (someone who "looks *indio*" but wears modern clothing and participates in Brazilian culture, rather than living in an indigenous community). Similar shifts in racial/ethnic classification occur in other parts of Latin America, for example, Guatemala (see Wade 2010). Racial perceptions are influenced not just by one's physical phenotype but also by how one dresses and behaves.

Furthermore, racial differences in Brazil may be so insignificant in structuring community life that people may forget the terms they have applied to others. Sometimes they even forget the ones they've used for themselves. In Arembepe, I made it a habit to ask the same person on different days to tell me the races of others in the village (and my own). In the United States, I am always "White" or "Euro-American," but in Arembepe, I got lots of terms besides *branco* ("White"). I could be *claro* ("light"), *louro* ("blond"), *sarará* ("light-skinned redhead"), *mulato claro* ("light mulatto"), or *mulato* ("mulatto"). The racial term used to describe me or anyone else varied from person to person, week to week, even day to day. My best informant, a man with very dark skin color, changed the term he used for himself all the time—from *escuro* ("dark") to *preto* ("Black") to *moreno escuro* ("dark brunet").

For centuries the United States and Brazil have had mixed populations, with ancestors from Native America, Europe, Africa, and Asia. Although races have mixed in both countries, Brazilian and American cultures have constructed the results differently. The

Phenotypical diversity is evident every day on any Rio de Janeiro Metrò train.
Lazyllama/Alamy Stock Photo

historical reasons for this contrast lie mainly in the different characteristics of the settlers of the two countries. The mainly English early settlers of the United States came as women, men, and families, but Brazil's Portuguese colonizers were mainly men—merchants and adventurers. Many of these Portuguese men married Native American women and recognized their racially mixed children as their heirs. Like their North American counterparts, Brazilian plantation owners had sexual relations with their slaves. But the Brazilian landlords more often freed the children that resulted—for demographic and economic reasons. (Sometimes these were their only children.) Freed offspring of master and slave became plantation overseers and foremen and filled many intermediate positions in the emerging Brazilian economy. They were not classed with the slaves but were allowed to join a new intermediate category. No hypodescent rule developed in Brazil to ensure that Whites and Blacks remained separate (see Degler 1970; Harris 1964).

In today's world system, Brazil's system of racial classification is changing in the context of international identity politics and rights movements. Just as more and more Brazilians claim indigenous (Native Brazilian) identities, an increasing number now assert their Blackness and self-conscious membership in the African diaspora. Particularly in such northeastern Brazilian states as Bahia, where African demographic and cultural influence is strong, public universities have instituted affirmative action programs aimed at indigenous peoples and especially at Blacks. Racial identities firm up in the context of international (e.g., pan-African and pan-Indian) mobilization and access to strategic resources based on race.

## Ethnic Groups, Nations, and Nationalities

The term **nation** once was synonymous with *tribe* or *ethnic group*. All three of these terms have been used to refer to a single culture sharing a single language, religion, history, territory, ancestry, and kinship. Thus, one could speak interchangeably of the Seneca (Native American) nation, tribe, or ethnic group. Now *nation* has come to mean state—an independent, centrally organized political unit, or a government. *Nation* and *state* have become synonymous. Combined in **nation-state,** they refer to an autonomous political entity, a country.

Because of migration, conquest, and colonialism, few nation-states are ethnically homogeneous. In a study of "Ethnic and Cultural Diversity by Country," James Fearon (2003) found that a single ethnic group formed an absolute majority of the population in about 70 percent of all countries. The average population share of that majority group was 65 percent. The average size of the *second* largest group, or largest ethnic minority, was 17 percent. (Notice that the United States today is similar to this distribution, with the majority group [non-Hispanic Whites] at 60.7 percent and the largest minority [Hispanics] at 18.1 percent.) In Fearon's study, only 18 percent of all countries, including Brazil and Japan, had a single ethnic group representing 90 percent or more of its population.

### Ethnic Diversity by Region

There is substantial regional variation in countries' ethnic structures. The German researcher Erkan Gören measured cultural diversity in more than 180 countries, based on each country's degree of diversity in ethnicity, race, and language. In Gören's study,

tend to live longer than men and have excellent endurance capabilities. In a given population, men tend to be taller and to weigh more than women do. Of course, there is a considerable overlap between the sexes in terms of height, weight, and physical strength, and there has been a pronounced reduction in sexual dimorphism during human biological evolution.

Just how far do these biological differences go? And what effects do they have on the way men and women act and are treated in different societies? Anthropologists have discovered both similarities and differences in the roles of men and women in different cultures. The predominant anthropological position on sex–gender roles and biology may be stated as follows:

> The biological nature of men and women [should be seen] not as a narrow enclosure limiting the human organism, but rather as a broad base upon which a variety of structures can be built. (Friedl 1975, p. 6)

Sex differences are biological, but gender encompasses all the traits that a culture assigns to and inculcates in males, females, and in some cases additional genders. *Gender,* in other words, refers to the cultural construction of whether one is female, male, or something else. Susan Bourque and Kay Warren (1987) emphasize the rich and varied constructions of gender among the world's cultures (see also Cornwall and Lindisfarne 2017). Margaret Mead did an early ethnographic study of variation in gender roles. Her book *Sex and Temperament in Three Primitive Societies* (1935/1950) was based on fieldwork in three societies in Papua New Guinea: the Arapesh, Mundugumor, and Tchambuli. The extent of personality variation in men and women in those three societies on the same island amazed Mead. She found that Arapesh men and women both acted as Americans have traditionally expected women to act: in a mild, parental, responsive way. Mundugumor men and women both, in contrast, acted as she believed we expect men to act: fiercely and aggressively. Finally, Tchambuli men were "catty," wore curls, and went shopping, but Tchambuli women were energetic and managerial and placed less emphasis on personal adornment than did the men. (Drawing on their case study of the Tchambuli, whom they call the Chambri, Errington and Gewertz [1987], while recognizing gender malleability, have disputed the specifics of Mead's account.)

There is a well-established field of feminist scholarship within anthropology (Lewin and Silverstein 2016; Rosaldo 1980b; Strathern 1988). Anthropologists have gathered systematic ethnographic data about similarities and differences involving gender in many cultural settings (Brettell and Sargent 2017; Burn 2011; Kimmel 2013; Mascia-Lees 2010; Ward and Edelstein 2014). Before we examine the cross-cultural data, some definitions are in order.

**Gender roles** are the tasks and activities a culture assigns by gender. Related to gender roles are **gender stereotypes**, which are oversimplified but strongly held ideas about the traits associated with different genders. **Gender stratification** describes inequality based on a gender hierarchy. There is differential access to socially valued resources, such as power, prestige, human rights, and personal freedom, based on gender.

In stateless societies, gender stratification often is more obvious in regard to prestige than it is in regard to wealth. In her study of the Ilongots of northern Luzon in the

The realm of cultural diversity contains richly varied expressions of gender roles. In October 2016, in the African nation of Chad, these Wodaabe men prepare for the annual Gerewol celebration, in which young bachelors paint their faces, dress elaborately, and gather in lines to dance and sing, vying for the attentions of marriageable young women. Tariq Zaidi/ZUMA Press/Alamy Stock Photo

Philippines, Michelle Rosaldo (1980a) described gender differences related to the positive cultural value placed on adventure, travel, and knowledge of the external world. More often than women, Ilongot men, as headhunters, visited distant places. They acquired knowledge of the world outside, amassed experiences there, and returned to display their knowledge, adventures, and feelings in public oratory. They received acclaim as a result. Ilongot women had inferior prestige because they lacked external experiences on which to base knowledge and dramatic expression. We must distinguish between prestige systems and actual power in a given society (Ong 1989; see also Hodgson 2016). High male prestige does not necessarily mean that men wield economic or political power. (For more on Rosaldo's contributions to gender studies, see Lugo and Maurer 2000.)

## Recurrent Gender Patterns

You probably had chores when you were growing up. Was there any gender bias in what you were asked to do, compared with your brother or sister? If you were raised by two parents, did any tension arise over your parents' division of labor? Based on cross-cultural data from 185 societies worldwide, Table 14.1 lists activities that are generally male, generally female, or swing (either male or female). Before you look at that table, see if you can assign the following to one gender or the other (M or F): hunting large animals ( ),

boundaries and interdependence can be maintained, although the specific cultural features of each group may change. By shifting the analytic focus from individual cultures or ethnic groups to *relationships* between cultures or ethnic groups, Barth (1958/1968, 1969) made important contributions to ethnic studies (see also Kamrava 2013).

## Multiculturalism

The view of cultural diversity in a country as something good and desirable is called **multiculturalism** (see Kottak and Kozaitis 2012). The multicultural model is the opposite of the assimilationist model, in which minorities are expected to abandon their cultural traditions and values, replacing them with those of the majority population. The multicultural view encourages the practice of cultural-ethnic traditions. A multicultural society socializes individuals not only into the dominant (national) culture but also into an ethnic culture. Thus, in the United States today millions of people speak both English and another language, eat both "American" foods (apple pie, steak, hamburgers) and "ethnic" dishes, and celebrate both national (July 4, Thanksgiving) and ethnic-religious holidays.

Multiculturalism seeks ways for people to interact that don't depend on sameness but rather on respect for differences. Multiculturalism assumes that each ethnic group has something to offer and learn from the others. The United States and Canada have become increasingly multicultural, focusing on their internal diversity. Rather than as "melting pots," they are better described as ethnic "salads" (each ingredient remains distinct, although in the same bowl and with the same dressing).

Several forces have propelled North America away from the assimilationist model toward multiculturalism. First, multiculturalism reflects the fact of recent large-scale migration, particularly from the less-developed countries. The global scale of modern migration introduces unparalleled ethnic variety to host nations (see Marger 2015; Parrillo 2016, 2019). People migrate to nations whose lifestyles they learn about through the media and from tourists who increasingly visit their own countries. Much of the increasing ethnic diversity in Europe's former colonial powers, such as France and the United Kingdom, reflects migration from former colonies.

Migration also is fueled by rapid population growth, coupled with insufficient jobs (for both educated and uneducated people), in the less-developed countries. As traditional rural economies decline or mechanize, displaced farmers move to cities, where they and their children often are unable to find jobs. As people in the less-developed countries get better educations, they seek more skilled employment, often outside their country of origin. Urban migration and unemployment also fuel crime, including the growth of gangs in such countries as El Salvador in Central America. Fear of gangs then becomes a powerful push factor in migration.

## Changing Demographics in the United States

In October 2006, the population of the United States reached 300 million people, just 39 years after reaching 200 million (in 1967) and 91 years after reaching the 100 million mark (in 1915). The country's ethnic composition has changed dramatically in the past 50 years. The 1970 census, the first to attempt an official count of Hispanics, found they represented no more than 4.7 percent of the American population. By 2018, this figure had risen to 18.1 percent—more than 59 million Hispanics. The percentage of African Americans grew from 11.1 percent in 1967 to 13.4 percent in 2018, while (non-Hispanic) whites ("Anglos") declined from 83 to 60.7 percent (Krogstad 207; Quick Facts, United States Census Bureau 2018).

In 1973, 78 percent of students in American public schools were White, and 22 percent were minorities. By 2004, only 57 percent of public school students were White. In fall 2014, for the first time, the overall number of Latino, African American, and Asian students in public K–12 classrooms surpassed the number of non-Hispanic Whites (Maxwell 2014).

## The Gray and the Brown

Drawing on a Brookings Institution (2010) report titled *State of Metropolitan America: On the Front Lines of Demographic Transformation,* Ronald Brownstein (2010) analyzes an intensifying confrontation between groups he describes as "the gray and the brown." Brownstein and demographer William Frey, an author of the Brookings report, focus on two key U.S. demographic trends:

1. Ethnic/racial diversity is increasing, especially among the young.
2. The country is aging, and most of the senior population is White.

Frey sees these trends as creating a "cultural generation gap"—a sharp contrast in the attitudes, priorities, and political leanings of younger and older Americans (Brookings Institution 2010, pp. 26, 63; see also Vespa et al. 2018).

In this recent American photo, contrast the visible ethnic diversity in the line of children with the racially more uniform line of older people. James Marshall/Corbis Historical/Getty Images

TABLE 14.3   **Does the Society Allow Multiple Spouses? (percent)***

Whyte, Martin King. 1978. Cross-Cultural Codes Dealing with the Relative Status of Women. Pittsburgh: *Ethnology*.

| | |
|---|---|
| For males only (polygyny) | 77 |
| For both, but more commonly for males | 4 |
| For neither (monogamy) | 16 |
| For both, but more commonly for females (polyandry) | 2 |

*Percentage of 92 randomly selected societies for which information was available on this variable.

What about access to mates? Table 14.3 shows that polygyny (multiple wives) is much more common than polyandry (multiple husbands). Furthermore, concerning premarital and extramarital sex, men tend to be less restricted than women are, although the restrictions were equal in about half the societies studied (Whyte 1978). Double standards that limit women more than men are one illustration of gender stratification, which we now examine more systematically.

# Gender Roles and Gender Stratification

Economic roles influence gender stratification (the *unequal* distribution of social value by gender). In one cross-cultural study, Sanday (1974) found that gender stratification was least in societies in which men and women made roughly equal contributions to subsistence. Among foragers, gender stratification was most marked when men contributed much *more* to the diet than women did. This was true among the Inuit and other northern hunters and fishers. Among tropical and semitropical foragers, by contrast, gathering usually supplies more food than hunting and fishing do. Gathering is generally women's work. Men are the usual hunters and fishers, but women may do some fishing and hunt small animals, as is true among the Agta of the Philippines (Griffin and Estioko-Griffin 1985). Gender status tends to be more equal when gathering is prominent than it is when hunting and fishing are the main subsistence activities.

Gender status also is more equal when the domestic and public spheres aren't sharply separated. (**Domestic** means within or pertaining to the home.) Strong differentiation between the home and the outside world is called the **domestic-public dichotomy**, or the *private-public contrast*. The outside world can include politics, trade, warfare, or work. Often when domestic and public spheres are sharply separated, public activities have greater prestige than domestic ones do. This can promote gender stratification, because men are more likely to be active in the public domain than women are.

## Reduced Gender Stratification: Matrilineal-Matrilocal Societies

Cross-cultural variation in gender status also is related to rules of descent and postmarital residence. With matrilineal descent and *matrilocality* (residence after marriage with the wife's relatives), female status tends to be high. Matriliny and matrilocality disperse related males, rather than consolidating them. By contrast, patriliny and *patrilocality* (residence after marriage with the husband's kin) keep related males together. Matrilineal-matrilocal systems tend to occur in societies where population pressure on strategic resources is minimal and warfare is infrequent.

Women tend to have high status in matrilineal-matrilocal societies for several reasons. Descent-group membership, succession to political positions, allocation of land, and overall social identity all come through female links. Among the matrilineal Malays of Negeri Sembilan, Malaysia, matriliny gave women sole inheritance of ancestral rice fields (Peletz 1988). Matrilocality created solidary clusters of female kin. These Malay women had considerable influence beyond the household. In such matrilineal contexts, women are the basis of the entire social structure. Although public authority may be assigned nominally to the men, much of the power and decision making may belong to the senior women.

## Matriarchy

If a patriarchy is a political system ruled by men, is a matriarchy necessarily a political system *ruled* by women? Or might we apply the term *matriarchy*, as anthropologist Peggy Reeves Sanday (2002) does, to a political system in which women play a much more prominent role than men do in social and political organization? One example would be the Minangkabau of West Sumatra, Indonesia, whom Sanday (2002) has studied for

A Minangkabau bride and groom in West Sumatra, Indonesia, where anthropologist Peggy Reeves Sanday has conducted several years of ethnographic fieldwork. Lindsay Hebberd/Corbis

be elected to the highest office in the land. The backlash began soon after Obama's election, culminating in Donald Trump's election as president in 2016. The period between 2008 and 2010 saw the growth of the Tea Party wing of the Republican Party and a dramatic reduction in the power of Democrats after the 2010 election. A similar coalition of young people, women, and minorities that backed Obama in 2008 and 2012 enabled Hillary Clinton to win the popular vote in 2016 but was insufficient to propel her to an Electoral College victory and the presidency.

One of the rallying cries of Tea Party voters was to "take our country back." A similar sentiment was prominent in the 2016 presidential campaign. Tycoon and reality TV star Donald Trump rose to prominence as a Republican presidential candidate by promising to "make America great again." Prominent in his campaign was open *ethno-nationalism*, the idea of an association between ethnicity—traditionally and predominantly European derived and Christian—and the right to rule the United States. Trump advocated deportation of undocumented immigrants, focusing on Mexicans. He envisioned a wall along the southern border of the United States to keep out Mexicans and other Latinos. He proposed various bans on Muslim entry into the United States.

Trump and other Republican candidates also decried multiculturalism and "political correctness," which they saw as excessive caution about using language and labels that might offend particular groups. Trump, in particular, used the claim of hypersensitive political correctness to justify his stereotyping of Mexicans as "bad hombres" and of Muslims as terrorists. Anyone who complained about insults was "overreacting"—just being hypersensitive. Trump's successful candidacy harnessed and expressed the backlash against the multicultural model of ethnic relations that has been gaining ground in the United States for the past few decades. Rarely, if ever, does cultural change occur without opposition, and rarely does a backlash not produce a backlash of its own. Sure enough, in the 2018 midterm elections, an Obama-like voting coalition reassembled. Democrats won 24 of 35 open Senate seats, and picked up 40 seats in the House of Representatives, to take control of the latter.

# Ethnic Conflict

Ethnic differences can exist harmoniously, for example, in plural societies or through multiculturalism. However, ethnic differences also can lead to interethnic confrontation and discrimination. The perception of cultural differences can have disastrous effects on social interaction. Why are ethnic differences often associated with conflict and violence? Ethnic groups may compete economically and/or politically. An ethnic group may react if it perceives prejudice or discrimination by another group or society as a whole, or if it feels otherwise devalued or disadvantaged (see "Black Lives Matter" later in this section).

## Sectarian Violence

Much of the ethnic unrest in today's world has a religious component—whether between Christians and Muslims, Muslims and Jews, or different sects within one of the major religions. The Iraqi dictator Saddam Hussein, who was deposed in 2003, favored his own

Sunni Muslim sect while fostering discrimination against other Muslims (Shiites and Kurds). Under Saddam, Sunnis, although a numeric minority within Iraq's population, enjoyed privileged access to power, prestige, and position. After the elections of 2005, which many Sunnis chose to boycott, Shiites gained political control over Iraq and retaliated quickly against prior Sunni privilege. A civil war soon developed out of *sectarian violence* (conflicts among sects of the same religion) as Sunnis (and their foreign supporters) fueled an insurgency against the new government and its foreign supporters, including the United States. Shiites then retaliated further against Sunni attacks and a history of Sunni favoritism. The Sunnis, lacking power in the new Iraqi government, eventually helped form the so-called Islamic State (IS), also known as ISIS, ISIL, and Daesh.

Iraq and Syria each contain substantial Muslim populations of Shiites, Sunnis, and Kurds (along with various ethno-religious minorities). Syria's president, Bashar al-Assad, like his father and predecessor in office, Hafez al-Assad (who ruled from 1971 to 2000), has favored his own minority Muslim group (Alawites—allied with the Shiites) over his country's Sunni majority. Syria has experienced devastating internal warfare since 2011, when, as in other parts of the Middle East, a series of uprisings known collectively as the Arab Spring occurred in opposition to authoritarian governments. The Assad regime fanned the flames of civil war by its violent suppression of the protesters and eventual rebels.

The parties to the conflict in Syria have included (1) the Assad government and its foreign allies, including Russia, Shiite Iran, and the Lebanese militia Hezbollah; (2) Sunni-led ISIS, whose influence (now substantially reduced) was strongest in parts of northern and eastern Syria, adjacent to and extending into Iraq; and (3) "moderate" rebels, presumably including Sunnis opposed to both Assad and ISIS. These rebels,

On December 19, 2016, Syrians wait to be evacuated from the eastern part of the war-ravaged city of Aleppo, as buses and ambulances await them. Mohammed Seyh/Anadolu Agency/Getty Images

In many societies, especially patriarchal ones, women experience, and fear, intimidation as they increasingly enter the public sphere, especially in impersonal, urban settings. "Ladies Only" lines like this one at the Golden Temple in Amritsar, Punjab, India, are designed to help women feel safer and more comfortable in public areas. Conrad P. Kottak

in which women have a readily available support network are disappearing from today's world. Patrilineal social forms and isolated families have spread at the expense of matriliny. Many nations have declared polygyny illegal. More and more women, and men, find themselves cut off from their families and extended kin. This chapter's "Anthropology Today" illustrates how women who depart from cultural stereotypes can suffer domestic abuse, including expulsion from their family homes.

With the spread of the women's rights and human rights movements, attention to abuse of women has increased. Laws have been passed, and mediating institutions established. Brazil's female-run police stations for battered women provide an example, as do shelters for victims of domestic abuse in the United States and Canada. A series of "Ladies Only" facilities, including trains and entry lines, can be found throughout India. But patriarchal institutions do persist in what should be a more enlightened world.

## Gender in Industrial Societies

The economic roles of men and women have changed and changed again over the course of American history. Nineteenth-century pioneer women worked productively in farming and home industry. As production shifted from home to factory, some women, particularly those who were poor or unmarried, turned to factory employment. Young White women typically worked outside the home only for a time, until they married and had children. The experience was different for African American women, many of whom, after abolition, continued working as field hands and domestic workers.

Gender in Industrial Societies   349

## Changes in Gendered Work

Changing attitudes about women's work have reflected economic conditions and world events. In the United States, for example, the idea that "a woman's place is in the home" developed as industrialism spread after 1900. One reason for this change was an influx of European immigrants, providing a male workforce willing to accept low wages for jobs, including factory work, that women previously might have held. Eventually, machine tools and mass production further reduced the need for female labor.

Anthropologist Maxine Margolis (2000) describes how gendered work, attitudes, and beliefs have varied in response to American economic needs. For example, when men are off fighting wars, work outside the home has been presented as women's patriotic duty, and the notion that women are biologically unfit for hard physical labor has faded.

The rapid population growth and business expansion that followed World War II created a demand for women to

During the world wars the notion that women were biologically unfit for hard physical labor faded. Shown here is World War II's famous Rosie the Riveter. Is there a comparable poster woman today? What does her image say about modern gender roles? Source: J. Howard Miller/ National Archives and Records Administration

fill jobs in clerical work, public school teaching, and nursing (traditionally defined as female occupations). Inflation and the culture of consumption also have spurred female employment. When demand and/or prices rise, multiple paychecks help maintain family living standards. Economic changes following World War II also set the stage for a women's movement, marked by the publication of Betty Friedan's influential book *The Feminine Mystique* in 1963 and the founding of NOW, the National Organization for Women, in 1966. Among other things, the movement promoted expanded work opportunities for women, including the goal (as yet unrealized) of equal pay for equal work.

Thanks to automation and robotics, jobs have become less demanding in terms of physical labor. With machines to do the heavy work, the smaller average body size and lesser average strength of women are no longer significant obstacles to blue-collar employment. But the main reason we don't see more modern-day Rosies working alongside male riveters is that the U.S. workforce itself has been abandoning heavy-goods manufacture. In the 1950s, two-thirds of American jobs were blue-collar, compared with less than 15 percent today. The location of those jobs has shifted within the world capitalist economy. Developing countries, with their cheaper labor costs, produce steel, automobiles, and other heavy goods less expensively than the United States can, but the United States excels at services. The American mass education system has many deficiencies, but it does train millions of people for service and information-oriented jobs.

## Anti-ethnic Discrimination

This section considers some of the most extreme forms of anti-ethnic discrimination, including genocide, forced assimilation, ethnocide, ethnic expulsion, and cultural colonialism (see also Lange 2017). The most extreme form is **genocide,** the deliberate elimination of a group (such as Jews in Nazi Germany, Muslims in Bosnia, or Tutsi in Rwanda) through mass murder (see Hinton and O'Neill 2009; Jones 2017). More recently, in the Darfur region of western Sudan, government-supported Arab militias, called the *Janjaweed*, have forced Black Africans off their land. The militias are accused of genocide, of killing up to 30,000 darker-skinned Africans.

**Ethnocide** is the deliberate suppression or destruction of an ethnic culture by a dominant group. One way of implementing a policy of ethnocide is through *forced assimilation*, in which the dominant group forces an ethnic group to adopt the dominant culture. Many countries have penalized or banned the language and customs of an ethnic group (including its religious observances). One example of forced assimilation is the anti-Basque campaign that the dictator Francisco Franco (who ruled between 1939 and 1975) waged in Spain. Franco banned Basque books, journals, newspapers, signs, sermons, and tombstones and imposed fines for using the Basque language in schools. In reaction to his policies, nationalist sentiment strengthened in the Basque region, and a Basque terrorist group took shape.

A policy of *ethnic expulsion* aims at removing from a country groups that are culturally different. There are many examples, including Bosnia-Herzegovina in the 1990s. Uganda expelled 74,000 Asians in 1972. The neofascist parties of contemporary Western Europe advocate repatriation (expulsion) of immigrant workers, such as Algerians in France and Turks in Germany. As of this writing (2019), the United States contains approximately 11 million undocumented immigrants. They are here without documents because they overstayed their visas or work permits, entered unofficially, or were smuggled in. Millions of them work, pay taxes, and have children born in the United States who are American citizens. What are their prospects? The future of undocumented immigrants became a particularly contentious political issue during the 2016 presidential election, with multiple Republican presidential candidates advocating their mass deportation. Such deportation would be a form of forced expulsion, although America's undocumented immigrants come from many countries and lack legal documents granting them the right to remain in the United States.

When members of an ethnic group are expelled, they often become **refugees**—people who have been forced (involuntary refugees) or who have chosen (voluntary refugees) to flee a country, to escape persecution or war. A government policy of ethnic expulsion is only one source of refugees. The Syrian refugees discussed previously have been driven from their homes by civil war and reprisals by various factions and their foreign allies. They are not, by and large, voluntary refugees, but they were not forced out by a government policy of ethnic expulsion.

**Cultural colonialism** refers to the domination by one group and its culture or ideology over others. One example is how Russian people, language, and culture and communist ideology dominated the former Soviet empire. In cultural colonialism, the dominant culture makes itself the official culture. This is reflected in schools, the media, and public interaction. Under Soviet rule, ethnic minorities had very limited self-rule in republics and regions controlled by Moscow. All the republics and their peoples were to be united

by the oneness of "socialist internationalism." A common technique in cultural colonialism is to flood ethnic areas with members of the dominant ethnic group. In the former
Soviet Union, ethnic Russian colonists were sent to many areas, to diminish the cohesion
and clout of the local people.

For example, when Ukraine belonged to the Soviet Union, Moscow promoted a policy of Russian in-migration and Ukrainian out-migration, so that ethnic Ukrainians'
share of the population of Ukraine declined from 77 percent in 1959 to 73 percent in
1991. That trend reversed after Ukraine gained independence, so that, by the turn of the
21st century, ethnic Ukrainians made up more than three-fourths of their country's
population. Russians still constitute Ukraine's largest minority, but they now represent
less than one-fifth of the population. They are concentrated in eastern Ukraine, where
ethnic Russians have rebelled against Ukraine's pro-Western government. Eastern
Ukraine, especially those provinces dominated by the Russian language and ethnicity, is

The author took this photo in August 2017 in a Moscow metro station named for
Kiev, the Ukrainian capital. In it, a group of tourists from the former Soviet Union
pose in front of a colorful mosaic depicting Ukrainian folk life and friendly
Russian soldiers. A common technique in cultural colonialism is to flood ethnic
areas with members of the dominant ethnic group. Conrad P. Kottak

A father and son cooking in the kitchen. In married-couple households, American men have assumed a greater share of domestic and child-care responsibilities, and more single fathers are raising their children than was the case in the past.
Hero/Corbis/Glow Images

husband is viewed as merely a helper rather than as an equal partner. Slaughter (2013, 2015) argues that men and women need to commit to and value a larger male domestic role, and employers need to make it easier for their employees, male and female, to balance work and family responsibilities.

Both fathers and mothers increasingly are seeking jobs that offer flexibility, require less travel, and include paid parental leave (including paternity leave). The United States lags behind other developed nations in providing such benefits, which help workers build long-term careers as they also fulfill family responsibilities. Although a few states and local governments do offer paid parental leave to their employees, only about 11 percent of American private-sector employers offer paid leave specifically for family reasons. Americans, both men and women, increasingly report that work interferes with family—not the other way around. Some 46 percent of working men and women report that job demands sometimes or often interfere with their family lives, up from 41 percent 15 years ago (Parker and Livingston 2017).

A quarter of American workers report actual or threatened job loss because of an illness or family-related absence. The work-family balancing act is particularly challenging for low-wage workers. They tend to have the least workplace flexibility, the most uncertain work hours, and the fewest benefits, and they can least afford to take unpaid leave. The toll is especially hard on single mothers.

## The Feminization of Poverty

Alongside the economic gains of many American women, especially the college educated, stands an opposite extreme: the feminization of poverty. This refers to the increasing representation of women (and their children) among America's poorest people. The 2017 median income of married-couple families ($90,386) was substantially more than twice that of families maintained solely by a woman ($41,703) (Fontenot et al. 2018).

The feminization of poverty isn't just a North American phenomenon. The percentage of single-parent (usually female-headed) households has been increasing worldwide. The figure ranges from about 10 percent in Japan, to between 10 and 20 percent in certain South Asian and Southeast Asian countries, to almost 50 percent in certain African countries and the Caribbean. Among the developed Western nations, the United States maintains the largest percentage of single-parent households (around 30 percent), followed by the United Kingdom, Canada, Ireland, and Denmark (over 20 percent in each).

Globally, female-headed households tend to be poorer than those headed by men. The 2017 U.S. poverty rate was 26 percent for female-headed families with no husband present, compared with 12 percent for male-headed families with no wife present, and 5 percent for married-couple families (Fontenot et al. 2018). More than half of the poor children in the United States live in families headed by women.

## Work and Happiness

Table 14.4 compares a country's rate of female labor-force participation with that country's rank on a list of the world's happiest countries (Helliwell, Hwang, and Wang 2019, Figure 2.7). The highest rate of labor participation, 86 percent, was in Iceland. Of the Western economies listed in the table, the United States had the lowest female labor participation rate, at 71 percent.

TABLE 14.4   **Female Labor Force Participation and Well-Being by Country, 2017–2018**

Source: Organization for Economic Cooperation and Development.

| Country | Percentage of Women in Labor Force (2017) | Rank among World's "Happiest Countries" (2018) |
|---|---|---|
| Iceland | 86 | 4 |
| Sweden | 81 | 7 |
| Switzerland | 79 | 6 |
| Denmark | 76 | 2 |
| New Zealand | 76 | 8 |
| Canada | 75 | 9 |
| Finland | 75 | 1 |
| Netherlands | 75 | 5 |
| Norway | 75 | 3 |
| Germany | 74 | 17 |
| United Kingdom | 74 | 15 |
| Australia | 72 | 11 |
| United States | 71 | 19 |
| Turkey (lowest in table) | 38 | 79 |

## Summary

1. An ethnic group consists of members of a particular culture in a nation or region that contains others. Ethnicity is based on actual, perceived, or assumed cultural similarities (among members of the same ethnic group) and differences (between that group and others). Ethnic distinctions can be based on language, religion, history, geography, kinship, or race. A race is an ethnic group assumed to have a biological basis. Usually, race and ethnicity are ascribed statuses; people are born members of a group and remain so all their lives.

2. Human races are cultural rather than biological categories. Such races derive from contrasts perceived in particular societies, rather than from scientific classifications based on common genes. In the United States, racial labels such as *White* and *Black* designate socially constructed categories defined by American culture. American racial classification, governed by the rule of hypodescent, is based neither on phenotype nor on genes. Children of mixed unions, no matter what their appearance, are classified with the minority group parent.

3. Racial attitudes in Japan illustrate intrinsic racism—the belief that a perceived racial difference is a sufficient reason to value one person less than another. The valued group is majority (pure) Japanese, who are believed to share the same blood. Majority Japanese define themselves by opposition to others, such as Koreans and burakumin. These may be minority groups in Japan or outsiders—anyone who is "not us."

4. Such exclusionary racial systems are not inevitable. Although Brazil shares a history of slavery with the United States, it lacks the hypodescent rule. Brazilian racial identity is more of an achieved status. It can change during someone's lifetime, reflecting phenotypical changes.

5. The term *nation* once was synonymous with *ethnic group*. Now *nation* has come to mean a state—a centrally organized political unit. Because of migration, conquest, and colonialism, most nation-states are not ethnically homogeneous. Ethnic groups that seek autonomous political status (their own country) are nationalities. Political upheavals, wars, and migrations have divided many imagined national communities.

6. Assimilation is the process of change members of an ethnic group may experience when they move to a country where another culture dominates. By assimilating, the minority adopts the patterns and norms of the host culture. Assimilation isn't inevitable, and there can be ethnic harmony without it. A plural society combines ethnic contrasts and economic interdependence between ethnic groups. The view of cultural diversity in a nation-state as good and desirable is multiculturalism. A multicultural society socializes individuals not only into the dominant (national) culture but also into an ethnic one.

7. In the United States, ethnic/racial diversity is increasing, especially among the young. Simultaneously, the country is aging, and most of the senior population is White. These trends are associated with contrasting attitudes, priorities, and political leanings of younger and older Americans. Minorities constitute a growing percentage of the total U.S. population, especially among children under age 18.

8. Ethnicity can be expressed either in peaceful multiculturalism or in discrimination or violent confrontation. Ethnic conflict often arises in reaction to prejudice (attitudes and judgments) or discrimination (action). The most extreme form of ethnic discrimination is genocide, the deliberate elimination of a group through mass murder. A dominant group may try to destroy certain ethnic practices (ethnocide) or to force ethnic group members to adopt the dominant culture (forced assimilation). A policy of ethnic expulsion may create refugees. Cultural colonialism is internal domination—by one group and its culture or ideology over others.

## Think Like an Anthropologist

1. What's the difference between a culture and an ethnic group? In what culture(s) do you participate? To what ethnic group(s) do you belong? What is the basis of your primary cultural identity? Do others readily recognize this basis and identity? Why or why not?

2. Name five social statuses you currently occupy. To what extent are these statuses achieved? Are any of them mutually exclusive? Which are contextual?

## Key Terms

achieved status, *392*
ascribed status, *392*
assimilation, *405*
colonialism, *404*
cultural colonialism, *414*
descent, *395*
discrimination, *412*
ethnic group, *391*
ethnicity, *392*
ethnocide, *414*
genocide, *414*
hypodescent, *395*
multiculturalism, *406*
nation, *403*
nation-state, *403*
nationalities, *404*
plural society, *405*
prejudice, *412*
race, *394*
racism, *394*
refugees, *414*
status, *392*
stereotypes, *412*

female. Triple X occurs in about 1 of every 1,000 female births. There usually is no physically distinguishable difference between triple X women and other women. The same is true of XYY compared with other males. Finally, *Turner syndrome* encompasses several conditions, of which 0X (absence of one sex chromosome) is most common. In this case, all or part of one of the sex chromosomes is absent. Girls with Turner syndrome typically are sterile because of nonworking ovaries and amenorrhea (absence of a menstrual cycle).

Many individuals affected by one of the biological conditions just described see themselves simply as male or female. Others identify as nonbinary, transgender, or even intersex (which then becomes a social as well as a biological term).

The anthropological record confirms that gender diversity beyond male and female exists in many societies and has taken many forms (see Nanda 2014; Peletz 2009). Consider, for example, the eunuch, or "perfect servant" (a castrated man who served as a safe attendant to harems in Byzantium [Tougher 2008]). Hijras, who live mainly in northern India, are culturally defined as "neither men nor women," or as men who become women by undergoing castration and adopting women's dress and behavior. Hijras identify with the Indian mother goddess and are believed to channel her power. They are known for their ritualized performances at births and marriages, where they dance and sing, conferring the mother goddess's blessing on the child or the married couple. Although culturally defined as celibate, some hijras now engage in prostitution (Nanda 1996, 1998). Hijra social movements have campaigned for recognition as a third gender, and in 2005, Indian passport application forms were updated with three gender options: M, F, and E (for male, female, and eunuch [i.e, hijra], respectively) (*Telegraph* 2005). Similarly, in the United States, California and Washington, among other states, now allow people to select "x" as their gender, instead of "male" or "female," on identity documents (Wortham 2018).

Several Native American tribes, including the Zuni of the American Southwest, included gender-variant individuals, described by the term "Two-Spirit." Depending on the society, as many as four genders might be recognized: feminine women, masculine women, feminine men, and masculine men. The Zuni Two-Spirit was a male who adopted social roles traditionally assigned to women and, through performance of a third gender, contributed to the social and spiritual well-being of the community (Roscoe 1991, 1998). Some Balkan societies included "sworn virgins," born females who assumed male gender roles and activities to meet societal needs when there was a shortage of men (Gremaux 1993).

Among the Gheg tribes of North Albania, "virginal transvestites" were biologically female, but locals considered them "honorary men" (Shryock 1988). Some Albanian adolescent girls have chosen to become men, remain celibate, and live among men, with the support of their families and villagers (Young 2000). And consider Polynesia. In Tonga the term *fakaleitis* describes males who behave as women do, thereby contrasting with mainstream Tongan men. Similar to Tonga's fakaleitis, Samoan *fa'afafine* and Hawaiian *mahu* are men who adopt feminine attributes, behaviors, and visual markers.

In the contemporary United States, the terms *transgender* and *nonbinary* encompass varied individuals whose gender performance and identity enlarge an otherwise binary gender structure. Transgender individuals are increasingly visible in the media and our everyday lives. The Amazon television series *Transparent*, whose principal character is a transgender woman, has received several awards. The emergence of Caitlyn (formerly

Neither men nor women, hijras constitute India's third gender. Many hijras get their income from performing at ceremonies, begging, or prostitution. The beauty contest shown here was organized by an AIDS prevention and relief organization that works with the local hijra community. Maciej Dakowicz/Alamy Stock Photo

Bruce) Jenner as a transgender woman received considerable media attention in 2015. In November 2017, 33-year-old Danica Roem became the first transgender person to be elected to Virginia's House of Delegates. She defeated a 13-term Republican who had introduced a bill to bar transgender students from using the bathrooms of their choice.

In 2014, Facebook added a range of nonbinary gender identities and pronouns, offering more than 50 options for users who don't identify as male or female, including *agender*, *gender-questioning*, and *intersex* (Wortham 2018). Social media, especially Instagram and Facebook, provide a vital context for information on, and discussions of, gender identity and nonconformity. Especially for young people who are questioning, exploring, or developing their gender identities, social media sites offer advice, reassurance, and emotional support (see Darwin 2017; Wortham 2018). As a gateway to a wider world, the Internet has become a place where almost anyone can find others like themselves, even if such others are absent or hidden in one's own hometown (Wortham 2018).

In recent years, the lesbian and gay rights movement has expanded to include bisexual, transgender, and "gender-Queer" (including nonbinary) individuals. The resulting LGBTQ community works to promote government policies and social practices that protect its members' civil and human rights. In recent years, this movement and its supporters have achieved many successes, including the repeal of the Defense of Marriage Act and of the "Don't Ask Don't Tell" policy of the U.S. armed services. The most notable achievement has been the legalization of same-sex marriage throughout the United States

some anthropologists worked as administrators in the colonies or held lower-level positions as government agents, researchers, or advisers. The main European colonial powers at that time—Britain, France, Portugal, and the Netherlands—all employed anthropologists. When those colonial empires began to collapse after World War II, as the former colonies gained independence, many anthropologists continued to offer advice to government agencies about the areas and cultures they knew the best.

In the United States, American anthropologists have worked extensively with the subjugated Native American populations within its borders. The 19th-century American anthropologist Lewis Henry Morgan studied the Seneca Iroquois tribe, Native Americans living in New York state, not far from his home in Rochester. Morgan was also a lawyer who represented the Iroquois in their disputes with a company that wanted to seize some of their land. Just as Morgan worked on behalf of the Seneca, there are anthropologists today who work on behalf of the non-Western groups they have studied.

Other anthropologists, working as government employees and agents, have helped to establish and enforce policies developed by ruling classes and aimed at local populations. Bronislaw Malinowski, a Polish-born scholar who spent most of his career teaching in England, was one of the most prominent cultural anthropologists of the early 20th century. Malinowski is well known for his ethnographic fieldwork with the Trobriand Islanders of the South Pacific and for his role in establishing ethnographic field methods. He also is recognized as one of the founders of applied anthropology, which he called "practical anthropology" (Malinowski 1929). Like many other anthropologists of his time, Malinowski worked *with* colonial regimes, rather than opposing the European subjugation of non-Western peoples.

Malinowski, who focused on Britain's African colonies, intended his "practical anthropology" to support and facilitate colonial rule. He believed that anthropologists could play an important role in helping European colonial officials administer non-Western societies. Anthropologists could help answer questions like the following: How was contact with European settlers and colonial officials affecting tribal societies? How much taxation and forced labor could "the natives" tolerate without resisting? Anthropologists could study local land use and ownership in order to determine how much of their land "natives" could keep and how much Europeans could take from them. Malinowski did not question the right of Europeans to rule the societies they had conquered. For him, the anthropologist's job was not to question colonial rule, but to make it work as harmoniously as possible. Other colonial-era anthropologists offered similar advice to the French, Portuguese, and Dutch regimes (see also Duffield and Hewitt 2009; Lange 2009).

During World War II, American anthropologists applied anthropology by trying to gain insights about the motivations and behavior of the enemies of the United States—principally Germany and Japan. Margaret Mead (1977) estimated that during the 1940s, 95 percent of U.S. anthropologists were involved in the war effort. For example, Ruth Benedict (1946) wrote an influential study of Japanese national culture not by doing fieldwork in Japan, but by studying Japanese literature, movies, and other cultural products and by interviewing Japanese in the United States. She called her approach "the study of culture at a distance." After World War II, American anthropologists worked to promote local-level cooperation with American policies on several Pacific islands that had been under Japanese control and were now administered by the United States.

Many of the early applications of anthropology described in this section were problematic because they aided and abetted the subjugation and control of non-Western cultures by militarily stronger societies. Most applied anthropologists today see their work as radically removed from colonial-era applied anthropology. They are likely to view applied anthropology as a helping profession, designed to assist local people. Contemporary applied anthropology draws on the theories, concepts, and methods of anthropology to confront human problems, such as poverty, that often contribute to profound human suffering (Rylko-Bauer, Singer, and van Willigen 2006).

## Academic and Applied Anthropology

The U.S. baby boom, which began in 1946 and peaked in 1957, fueled a tremendous expansion of the American educational system. New junior, community, and four-year colleges opened, and anthropology became a standard part of the curriculum. During the 1950s and 1960s, most American anthropologists were college professors, although some still worked in agencies and museums.

The growth of academic anthropology continued through the early 1970s. Especially during the Vietnam War, undergraduates flocked to anthropology classes to learn about other cultures. Students were especially interested in Southeast Asia, whose indigenous societies were being disrupted by war. Many anthropologists protested the superpowers' apparent disregard for non-Western lives, values, customs, and social systems.

Most anthropologists still worked in colleges and museums during the 1970s and 1980s. However, an increasing number of anthropologists were finding jobs in international organizations, governments, businesses, hospitals, and schools. Today, applied anthropologists work in varied contexts, including economic development organizations, government agencies, nongovernmental organizations (NGOs) and nonprofit organizations, international policy bodies, and private entities, such as unions, social movements, and increasingly businesses and corporations. The American Anthropological Association estimates that well over half of anthropology PhDs today seek nonacademic employment. This shift toward application has benefited the profession. It has forced anthropologists to consider the wider social value and implications of their research.

## Applied Anthropology Today

Although poverty (and its alleviation) has been a key focus of applied anthropology, applied anthropologists also engage with clients who are neither poor nor powerless. An applied anthropologist working as a market researcher may be asked to discover effective ways to increase sales of a particular product. Such commercial goals can pose ethical dilemmas, which also may arise in cultural resource management (CRM). The CRM anthropologist helps decide how to preserve significant remains when development threatens sites. The client that hires a CRM firm may be seeking to build a road or a factory. That client may have a strong interest in a CRM finding that no sites need protection, and the client may pressure the CRM firm in that direction. Among the

Archaeologists Tim Griffith, left, and Ginny Hatfield of Fort Hood's (Texas) Cultural Resources Management Program, sift through sediment collected from an archaeological site. This CRM program manages resources representing more than 10,000 years of occupation of the land around Fort Hood. Scott Gaulin/*Temple Daily Telegram*/AP Images

ethical questions that arise in applied anthropology are these: To whom does the researcher owe loyalty? What problems might be involved in sticking to the truth? What happens when applied anthropologists don't create the policies they have to implement? How does one criticize programs in which one has participated? Anthropology's professional organizations have addressed such questions by establishing codes of ethics and ethics committees.

Anthropologists study, understand, and respect diverse cultural values and ways of living. Because of their knowledge of human problems and social change, anthropologists are highly qualified to suggest, plan, and implement policies affecting people. Proper roles for applied anthropologists include (1) identifying needs for change that local people perceive, (2) collaborating with those people to design culturally appropriate and socially sensitive change, and (3) working to protect local people from harmful policies and projects that may threaten them.

For decades, applied anthropologists have collaborated directly with communities to achieve community-directed change. Applied anthropologists not only work collaboratively with local people, but they may even be hired by such communities to advocate on their behalf. One example is Barbara Rose Johnston's (2005) research on behalf of Guatemalan communities that were adversely affected by the construction of a dam. Johnston's reports documented the dam's long-term impact on these communities. She also offered recommendations and a plan for reparations.

# Development Anthropology

**Development anthropology** is the branch of applied anthropology that focuses on social issues in, and the cultural dimension of, economic development. Development anthropologists don't just carry out development policies planned by others; they also plan and guide policy. (For more detailed discussions of issues in development anthropology, see Crewe and Axelby 2013; Mosse 2011)

Still, ethical dilemmas often confront development anthropologists (Escobar 2012; Venkatesan and Yarrow 2014). Foreign aid, including funds for economic development, usually does not go where need and suffering are greatest. Rather, such aid tends to support political, economic, and strategic priorities that are set by international donors, political leaders, and powerful interest groups. The goals and interests of the planners may ignore or conflict with the best interests of the local people. Although the stated aim of most development projects is to enhance the quality of life, living standards often decline in the affected area.

## Equity

An important stated goal of recent development projects has been to promote equity. **Increased equity** entails (1) reducing poverty and (2) evening out the distribution of wealth. Projects should not benefit only the "haves" but also the "have nots." If people who are already doing well get most of the benefits of a project, then it has not increased equity.

If projects are to increase equity, however, they must have the support of reform-minded governments. Wealthy and powerful people typically resist projects that offer more to the "have nots" than to the "haves." Often, they will actively oppose a project that threatens the status quo.

## Negative Equity Impact

Some projects not only fail to increase equity; they actually widen the gap between the "haves" and "have nots." When this happens, we say they have a *negative equity impact*. I observed firsthand an example of negative equity impact in Arembepe, Bahia, Brazil, a fishing community on the Atlantic Ocean (see Kottak 2018). A development initiative there offered loans to buy motors for fishing boats, but only people who already owned boats ("haves") could get these loans. Nonowners ("have nots") did not qualify. After getting the loans, the boat owners, in order to pay off their debt, increased the percentage of the catch they took from the men who fished in their boats. Their rising profits allowed them to eventually buy larger and more expensive boats. They cited their increased capital expense as a reason to pay their workers less. Over the years, the gap between "haves" and "have nots" widened substantially. The eventual result was socioeconomic stratification—the creation of social classes in a community that had been egalitarian. In the past, Arembepe's fishing boats had been simple sailboats, relying only on wind power, and any enterprising young fisher could hope eventually to own one of his own. In the new economy, the larger motorized boats were so expensive that ambitious young men, who once would have sought careers in fishing, no longer could afford to buy a boat of their own. They sought wage labor on land instead. To avoid this kind of negative equity

A mix of boats harbored in Pucusana, a fishing village in Peru. A boat owner gets a loan to buy a motor. To repay it, he increases the share of the catch he takes from his crew. Later, he uses his rising profits to buy a more expensive boat and takes even more from his crew. Can a more equitable solution be found? Sean Sprague/ The Image Works

impact, credit-granting agencies must seek out and invest in enterprising young fishers, rather than giving loans only to owners and established businesspeople. A lesson here is that the stated goal of increased equity is easier said than done. Because the "haves" tend to have better connections than the "have nots," they are more likely to find out about and take advantage of new programs. They also tend to have more clout with government officials, who often decide who will benefit from a particular program.

## Strategies for Innovation

Development anthropologists should work collaboratively and proactively with local people, especially the "have nots," to assess, and help them realize, their own wishes and needs for change. Too many true local needs cry out for a solution to waste money funding projects in area A that are inappropriate there but needed in area B, or that are unnecessary anywhere. Development anthropology can help sort out the needs of the As and Bs and fit projects accordingly. Projects that put people first by consulting with them and responding to their expressed needs must be identified (Cernea 1991). To maximize social and economic benefits, projects must (1) be culturally compatible, (2) respond to locally perceived needs, (3) involve men and women in planning and carrying out the changes that affect them, (4) harness traditional organizations, and (5) be flexible (see Kottak 1991).

Consider the following example of a development initiative that failed because it ignored local culture. Working in Afghanistan after the fall of the Taliban, ethnographer Noah Coburn (2011) studied Istalif, a village of potters. During his fieldwork there,

Coburn discovered that an NGO had spent $20,000 on an electric kiln that could have greatly enhanced the productivity of local potters. The only problem was that the kiln was donated to a women's center that men could not enter. The misguided donors ignored the fact that Istalif's men did the work—pot-making and firing—that a kiln could facilitate. Women's role in pottery came later—in glazing and decorating.

## Overinnovation

Development projects are most likely to succeed when they avoid the fallacy of **overinnovation** (too much change). People usually are willing to change just enough to maintain, or slightly improve on, what they already have. Motivation to change comes from the traditional culture and the small concerns of ordinary life. Peasants' values are not such abstract ones as "learning a better way," "progressing," "increasing technical know-how," "improving efficiency," or "adopting modern techniques." People want to grow and harvest their crops, amass resources for a ceremony, get a child through school, or have enough cash to pay bills. The goals and values of people who farm and fish for their own subsistence differ from those of people who work for cash, just as they differ from those of development planners.

Development projects that fail usually do so because they are either economically or culturally incompatible (or both). For example, one South Asian project tried to get farmers to start growing onions and peppers, expecting those cash crops to fit into the existing system of rice cultivation—the main local subsistence crop. It turned out, however, that the labor peaks for the new cash crops coincided with those for rice, to which the farmers naturally gave priority. This project failed because it promoted too much change, introducing unfamiliar crops that conflicted with, rather than building on and complementing, an existing system. The planners should have realized that cultivation of the new crops would conflict with that of the main subsistence crop in the area. A good anthropologist could have told them as much.

Recent development efforts in Afghanistan also illustrate the problematic nature of overinnovation. Reporting on social change efforts in Afghanistan after the fall of the Taliban, anthropologists Noah Coburn (2011) and Thomas Barfield (2010) criticize various top-down initiatives that proved incompatible with local culture. Coburn suggests that the best strategy to maintain peace in the Afghan countryside is to work with existing resources, drawing on local beliefs and social organization. To be avoided are overinnovative plans from outside, whether from the national government or foreign donors. Destined for failure, according to Coburn, are attempts to create impersonal bureaucracies based on merit. Also doomed are attempts to impose liberal beliefs about gender at the village level. These are Western ideas that are particularly incompatible in rural areas. Barfield also cites the futility of direct attempts to change rural Afghans' beliefs about such entrenched matters as religion and gender equality. A better strategy, he suggests, is for change agents to work first in urban areas, where innovation is more welcome, and then let those changes spread gradually to the countryside.

In 2014, Afghanistan elected an anthropologist as its president. Ashraf Ghani, who received his doctorate in anthropology from Columbia University in New York, had worked for the World Bank as a development anthropologist. Let us hope that Ghani's background in anthropology and development will eventually lead to more effective development strategies in the conflict-ridden nation he now leads.

# Indigenous Models

Many governments are not genuinely, or realistically, committed to improving the lives of their citizens. Interference by major powers also has kept governments from enacting needed reforms. Occasionally, however, a government does act as an agent of and for its people. One historic example is Madagascar, whose people, the Malagasy, were organized into descent groups prior to indigenous state formation in the 18th century. The Merina, creators of the major precolonial state of Madagascar, wove descent groups into its structure, making members of important groups advisers to rulers—thus giving them authority in government. The Merina state collected taxes and organized labor for public works projects. In return, it redistributed resources to peasants in need. It also granted them some protection against war and slave raids and allowed them to cultivate their rice fields in peace. The government maintained the water works for rice cultivation. It opened to ambitious peasant boys the chance of becoming state bureaucrats, through hard work and study.

Throughout the history of the Merina state—and continuing to some extent in postcolonial Madagascar—there have been strong relationships between the individual, the descent group, and the state. Local Malagasy communities, where residence is based on descent, are more cohesive and homogeneous than are communities in Latin America or North America. Madagascar gained political independence from France in 1960. Its new government implemented an economic development policy aimed at increasing the ability of the Malagasy to feed themselves. Government policy emphasized increased production of rice, a subsistence crop, rather than cash crops. Furthermore, local communities, with their traditional cooperative patterns and solidarity based on kinship and descent, were treated as partners in, not obstacles to, the development process.

In a sense, the descent group is preadapted to equitable national development. In Madagascar, descent groups pooled their resources to educate their most ambitious and talented members. Once educated, those men and women gained economically secure positions in the nation. They then shared the advantages of their new positions with their kin. For example, they gave room and board to rural cousins attending school and helped them find jobs.

This Madagascar example suggests that when government officials are of "the people" (rather than the elites) and have strong personal ties to common folk, they are more likely to promote democratic reform. In Latin America, by contrast, leaders and followers too often have been from different social classes, with no connections based on kinship, descent, marriage, or common background. When elites rule, elites usually prosper. Recently, however, Latin America has elected some nonelite leaders. Brazil's lower class (indeed the entire nation) benefited socioeconomically when one of its own was elected president. Luiz Inácio da Silva, or Lula, a former factory worker with only a fourth-grade education, served two terms (ending in 2011) as one of the Western Hemisphere's most popular leaders. Lula's better educated successor, Dilma Rousseff, from the same Workers' Party, became one of Brazil's least popular presidents and was impeached in 2016. Brazil's most recently elected president is Jair Bolsonaro, a right-wing former army captain and practicing Evangelical, whose substantial victory in the 2018 elections reflected populist disgust with established politicians and corruption.

# Anthropology and Education

Attention to culture also is fundamental to **anthropology and education**, a field whose research extends from classrooms into homes, neighborhoods, and communities (see Anderson-Levitt 2012; Anderson-Levitt and Rockwell 2017; Levinson and Pollock 2011). In classrooms, anthropologists have observed interactions among teachers, students, parents, and visitors. Jules Henry's classic account of the American elementary school classroom (1955; see also Henry 1972) shows how students learn to conform to and compete with their peers. Anthropologists view children as total cultural creatures whose enculturation and attitudes toward education belong to a context that includes family and peers (see also Kontopodis, Wulf, and Fichtner 2011; Reagan 2018; Reyhner et al. 2013).

Sociolinguists and cultural anthropologists have worked side by side in education research. In one classic study of Puerto Rican seventh-graders in the urban Midwest, anthropologists uncovered some key misconceptions held by teachers (Hill-Burnett 1978). The teachers mistakenly had assumed that Puerto Rican parents valued education less than did non-Hispanics, but in-depth interviews revealed that the Puerto Rican parents valued it more. The anthropologists also identified certain practices that were preventing Hispanics from being adequately educated. For example, the teachers' union and the board of education had agreed to teach "English as a foreign language." However, they had provided no bilingual teachers to work with Spanish-speaking students. The school

The NGO Shidhulai Swanirvar Sangstha operates a multi-vessel fleet of floating one-room elementary schools in flood-prone areas of Bangladesh. Here we see a teacher and students in one of those classrooms. Each schoolboat docks each day to pick up and let off about 30 students. The boats have solar panels that power an Internet-linked laptop, library, and electronic resources. Jonas Gratzer/LightRocket via Getty Images

was assigning all students (including non-Hispanics) with low reading scores and behavior problems to the English-as-a-foreign-language classroom. This educational disaster brought together in the classroom a teacher who spoke no Spanish, children who barely spoke English, and a group of English-speaking students with reading and behavior problems. The Spanish speakers were falling behind not just in reading but in all subjects. They could at least have kept up in the other subjects if a Spanish speaker had been teaching them science, social studies, and math until they were ready for English-language instruction in those areas.

# Urban Anthropology

In today's world, media-transmitted images and information play an important role in attracting people to cities. Often, people move to cities for economic reasons, because jobs are scarce at home. Cities also attract people who want to be where the action is. Rural Brazilians routinely cite *movimento*, urban activity and excitement, as something to be valued. International migrants tend to settle in large cities, where a lot is going on and where they can feel at home in ethnic enclaves. Consider Canada, which, after Australia, is the country with the highest percentage of foreign-born population. Three-quarters of immigrants to Canada settle in Toronto, Vancouver, or Montreal. It is estimated that by 2036 immigrants (mostly from Asia) will constitute as much as 30 percent of Canada's population, compared with 21 percent in 2011 (Morency et al. 2017).

More than half (55 percent) of Earth's people now live in cities. That figure first surpassed 50 percent in 2008 and is projected to rise to 68 percent by 2050. Only about 3 percent of people were city dwellers in 1800, compared with 13 percent in 1900, 40 percent in 1980, and 55 percent today. The number of urban residents worldwide has risen rapidly from 751 million in 1950 to 4.2 billion in 2018. Asia contains 54 percent of those city dwellers, followed by Europe and Africa, with 13 percent each (United Nations 2018a).

The degree of urbanization (about 30 percent) in the less-developed countries (LDCs) is well below the world average (55 percent). Even in the LDCs, however, the urban growth rate now exceeds the rural growth rate. By 2030, the percentage of city dwellers in the LDCs is projected to rise to 41 percent. The world had only 16 cities with more than a million people in 1900, versus more than 500 today, including over 100 such cities in China alone (United Nations 2014, 2018b). In 2018, 1.7 billion people—23 per cent of the world's population—lived in a city with at least 1 million inhabitants. This figure is projected to rise to 28 percent by 2030 (United Nations 2018b).

More than one billion people now live in urban slums, mostly without reliable water, sanitation, public services, and legal security. If current trends continue, urban population increase and the concentration of people in slums will continue to be accompanied by rising rates of crime, along with water, air, and noise pollution. These problems will be most severe in the LDCs.

As industrialization and urbanization spread globally, anthropologists increasingly study these processes and the social problems they create. **Urban anthropology**, which has theoretical (basic research) and applied dimensions, is the cross-cultural and ethnographic

In Kolkata (formerly Calcutta), India, girls scavenge garbage for useful artifacts to sell. Almost a third of Kolkata's population live in slums, and an additional 70,000 are homeless. Samir Hussein/ Getty Images News/Getty Images

study of urbanization and life in cities (see Jaffe and De Koning 2016; Nonini 2014; Schwanhäusser, ed. 2016; Zukin, Kasinitz, and Chen 2016). The United States and Canada have become popular arenas for urban anthropological research on topics such as immigration, ethnicity, poverty, class, and urban violence (Vigil 2010).

An early student of urbanization, the anthropologist Robert Redfield contrasted rural communities, where social relations are on a face-to-face basis, with cities, where impersonality reigns. Redfield (1941) proposed that urbanization be studied along a rural-urban continuum. He described differences in values and social relations in four sites that spanned such a continuum. In Mexico's Yucatán peninsula, Redfield compared an isolated Mayan-speaking Indian community, a rural peasant village, a small provincial city, and a large capital. Several studies in Africa (Little 1971) and Asia were influenced by Redfield's view that cities are centers through which cultural innovations spread to rural and tribal areas.

In any nation, urban and rural represent different social systems. However, cultural diffusion or borrowing occurs as people, products, images, and messages move from one to the other. Migrants take rural practices and beliefs to cities and bring urban patterns back home. The experiences and social forms of the rural area affect adaptation to city life. City folk also develop new institutions to meet specific urban needs.

An applied anthropology approach to urban planning begins by identifying key social groups in specific urban contexts—avoiding the fallacy of underdifferentiation.

After identifying those groups, the anthropologist might elicit their wishes for change, convey those needs to funding agencies, and work with agencies and local people to realize those goals. In Africa, relevant urban groups might include ethnic associations, occupational groups, social clubs, religious groups, and burial societies. Through membership in such groups, urban Africans maintain wide networks of personal contacts and support. The groups provide cash support and urban lodging for their rural relatives. Members may call one another "brother" and "sister." As in an extended family, richer members help their poorer relatives. A member's improper behavior, however, can lead to expulsion—an unhappy fate for a migrant in a large, ethnically heterogeneous city.

## Medical Anthropology

**Medical anthropology** is a biocultural field that studies variation in health care systems, including disease, illness, health standards, and disease theories. All societies have **health care systems** consisting of beliefs, customs, specialists, and techniques aimed at ensuring health and diagnosing and curing illness. Medical anthropology is both academic and applied and includes anthropologists from all four subfields (see Brown and Closser 2016; Manderson, Cartwright, and Hardon 2016; Singer et al. 2019). Medical anthropologists examine such questions as which diseases and health conditions affect particular populations (and why) and how illness is socially constructed, diagnosed, managed, and treated in various societies.

**Disease** refers to a scientifically identified health threat caused by genetics or a bacterium, virus, fungus, parasite, or other pathogen. **Illness** is a condition of poor health perceived or felt by an individual (Inhorn and Brown 1990). Perceptions of good and bad health are culturally constructed. Particular cultures and ethnic groups recognize different illnesses, symptoms, and causes and have developed different health care systems and treatment strategies (Womack 2010).

The incidence and severity of *disease* vary as well (see Baer, Singer, and Susser 2013). Group differences are evident in the United States. Consider, for example, health status indicators in relation to U.S. census categories: White, Black, Hispanic, American Indian or Alaska Native, and Asian or Pacific Islander. African Americans' rates for six indicators (total mortality, heart disease, lung cancer, breast cancer, stroke, and homicide) range from 2.5 to 10 times greater than those of the other groups. Other ethnic groups have higher rates for suicide (White Americans) and motor vehicle accidents (American Indians and Alaskan Natives). Overall, Asians have the longest lifespans.

Reviewing the health conditions of the world's surviving indigenous populations (about 400 million people), anthropologists Claudia Vallegia and Josh Snodgrass (2015) found their health risks to be uniformly high. Compared with nonindigenous people, indigenous groups tend to have shorter and riskier lives. Mothers are more likely to die in childbirth; infants and children have lower survival chances. Malnutrition stunts their growth, and they suffer more from infectious diseases. Reflecting their increasing exposure to global forces, they have rising rates of cardiovascular and other chronic diseases, as well as depression and substance abuse. They also have limited access to medical care. An increasing number of anthropologists are working in global health programs at academic and research institutions. This presence should increase understanding of the health concerns of indigenous peoples—but more is needed. Vallegia and Snodgrass (2015) urge medical anthropologists to involve themselves more in community outreach, which could help bring better health care to indigenous populations.

In many areas, the world system and colonialism worsened the health of indigenous peoples by spreading diseases, warfare, servitude, and other stressors. Traditionally and in ancient times, hunter-gatherers, because of their small numbers, mobility, and relative isolation from other groups, lacked most of the epidemic infectious diseases that affect agrarian and urban societies (Cohen and Armelagos 2013; Singer 2015). Epidemic diseases such as cholera, typhoid, and bubonic plague thrive in dense populations, and thus among farmers and city dwellers. The spread of malaria has been linked to population growth and deforestation associated with food production.

## Disease Theory Systems

The kinds and incidence of disease vary among human populations, and cultures perceive and treat illness differently (see Lupton 2012). Still, all societies have what George Foster and Barbara Anderson (1978) call "disease theory systems" to identify, classify, and explain illness. Foster and Anderson identified three basic theories about the causes of illness: personalistic, naturalistic, and emotionalistic. Personalistic disease theories blame illness on agents, such as sorcerers, witches, ghosts, or ancestral spirits.

Naturalistic disease theories explain illness in impersonal terms. One example is Western medicine, or biomedicine, which aims to link illness to scientifically demonstrated agents that bear no personal malice toward their victims (see Lock and Nguyen 2018). Thus, Western medicine attributes illness to organisms (e.g., bacteria, viruses, fungi, or parasites), accidents, toxic materials, or genes. Other naturalistic systems blame poor health on unbalanced body fluids. Many Latin cultures classify food, drink, and environmental conditions as "hot" or "cold." People believe their health suffers when they eat or drink hot or cold substances together or under inappropriate conditions. For example, one shouldn't drink something cold after a hot bath or eat a pineapple (a "cold" fruit) when one is menstruating (a "hot" condition).

Emotionalistic disease theories assume that emotional experiences cause illness (see Kohrt and Mendenhall 2015). For example, Latin Americans may develop *susto*, an illness brought on by anxiety, fright, or tragic news. Its symptoms (lethargy, vagueness, distraction) are similar to those of "soul loss," a diagnosis of similar symptoms made by people in Madagascar.

A society's illness-causation theory is important for treatment. When illness has a personalistic cause, magicoreligious specialists may be effective curers. They draw on varied techniques (occult and practical), which constitute their special expertise. A shaman may cure soul loss by enticing the spirit back into the body. Shamans may ease difficult childbirths by asking spirits to travel up the birth canal to guide the baby out (Lévi-Strauss 1967). A shaman may cure a cough by counteracting a curse or removing a substance introduced by a sorcerer.

If there is a "world's oldest profession" besides hunter-gatherer, it is **curer,** often a shaman. The curer's role has some universal features (Foster and Anderson 1978). Thus, a curer emerges through a culturally defined process of selection (parental prodding, inheritance of the role, visions, dream instructions) and training (apprentice shamanship, medical school). Eventually, the curer is certified by older practitioners and acquires a professional image. Patients believe in the skills of the curer, whom they consult and compensate. Health interventions always have to fit into local cultures. When Western medicine is introduced, people usually preserve many of their old methods while also accepting new ones. Native curers may go on treating certain conditions (e.g., spirit possession), while physicians deal with others. The native curer may get as much credit as the physician for a cure.

## Scientific Medicine versus Western Medicine

We should not lose sight, ethnocentrically, of the difference between scientific medicine and Western medicine per se. **Scientific medicine** relies on advances in technology, genomics, molecular biology, neuroscience, pathology, surgery, diagnostics, and applications. Scientific medicine surpasses tribal treatment in many ways. Although medicines such as quinine, coca, opium, ephedrine, and rauwolfia were discovered in nonindustrial societies, thousands of effective drugs are available today to treat myriad diseases. Today's surgical procedures are much safer and more effective than those of traditional societies. These are strong benefits of scientific medicine, even if they are not always successful

*Western medicine* refers to the practice of medicine in a particular modern Western nation, such as the United States. Of course, the practice of medicine and the quality and availability of heath care vary among Western nations. Some make free or low-cost health care available to all citizens, while other countries are not so generous. Millions of Americans, for example, remain uninsured. Western medicine has both "pros" and "cons." The strongest "pro" of Western medicine is that it incorporates scientific medicine and its many benefits. "Cons" associated with Western medicine include overprescription of drugs (e.g., opioids and antibiotics), unnecessary surgeries, and the impersonality and inequality of the physician-patient relationship. Overuse of antibiotics seems to be triggering an explosion of resistant microorganisms. Another "con" associated with Western medicine is that it tends to draw a rigid line between biomedical and psychological causation. Non-Western theories usually lack this sharp distinction, recognizing that poor health has intertwined physical, emotional, and social causes (see also Brown and Closser 2016; Joralemon 2010).

Treatment strategies that emulate the much more personal non-Western curer-patient-community relationship might benefit Western systems. Physician-patient encounters too often are rushed and truncated. Those who perform a surgical procedure or diagnose a condition often include specialists (e.g., radiologists and lab technicians) whom the patient will never see. Surgeons are not renowned for their "bedside manner." Efforts are being made to improve physician-patient relationships. A recent trend in the United States is the rise of "concierge medicine," in which a physician charges an annual fee to each patient, limits the practice to a certain number of patients, and has ample time to spend with each patient because of the reduced caseload. To an extent, the Internet has empowered patients, who now have access to all kinds of medical information that used to be the sole property of physicians. This access, however, has its drawbacks. Information can make patients more informed as health care consumers, but it also prompts more questions than a physician usually can answer during a brief appointment.

Left: At a market in Yangshuo, China, a woman undergoes a moxibustion treatment, in which mugwort, a small, spongy herb, is burned to facilitate healing. Right: Cupping is a similar ancient Chinese healing and recovery technique that has been adopted by international athletes, most prominently swimmer Michael Phelps at the 2016 Summer Olympics in Rio de Janeiro. Practitioners place specialized cups on the skin, then use either heat or an air pump to suck the skin slightly up and away from the underlying muscles. This causes the capillaries just beneath the surface to rupture, creating circular purple bruises. Note the marks on Phelps's upper body as he celebrates his victory in the Men's 200 m Butterfly and his 20th Olympic Gold medal in Rio. (left): age fotostock/Alamy Stock Photo, (right): Ian MacNicol/Getty Images Sport/Getty Images

## Industrialization, Globalization, and Health

Despite the advances in scientific medicine, industrialization and globalization have spawned many significant health problems. Certain diseases, and physical conditions such as obesity, have spread with economic development and globalization (Inhorn and Wentzell 2012). Schistosomiasis, or bilharzia (liver flukes), is a dangerous and rapidly spreading parasitic threat. People get schistosomiasis from snails living in ponds, lakes, and waterways, often those created by irrigation projects. The applied anthropology approach to reducing such diseases is to see if local people perceive a connection between the vector (e.g., snails in the water) and the disease. If not, local organizations, schools, and the media, including social media, can help spread the relevant information.

HIV/AIDS has been spread through international travel within the modern world system. The world's highest rates of HIV infection and AIDS-related deaths are in Africa, especially southern Africa (Mazzeo, Rödlach, and Brenton 2011). Sexually transmitted infections are spread through prostitution as young men from rural areas seek wage work in cities, labor camps, and mines, often across national borders. When the men return home, they infect their wives (see Baer et al. 2013). By killing productive adults, AIDS leaves behind dependent children and seniors. Cultural factors affect the spread of HIV, which is less likely to spread when men are circumcised.

Other problems associated with industrialization and globalization include the following: poor nutrition; dangerous machinery; impersonal work; isolation; poverty; homelessness; substance abuse; and noise, air, and water pollution (see McElroy and Townsend 2014). With industrialization and globalization, people turn from subsistence work, usually alongside family and neighbors, to cash employment in more impersonal settings such as factories.

Rather than living in villages where everyone knows everyone else, people increasingly live in cities—and often in slums, where they tend to have poorer diets and more exposure to pathogens and crime, poor sanitation, and polluted air. Remember the scares caused by Ebola, H1N1, Zika, and other emergent viruses? Such pathogens, however, are not the only, or perhaps even the primary, cause of health problems associated with industrialization and globalization. Other stressors that endanger our health are economic (e.g., poverty), social (e.g., crowding, homelessness, crime), political (e.g., terrorism, corruption), and cultural (e.g., ethnic conflict). Poverty contributes to many illnesses, including arthritis, heart conditions, back problems, and hearing and vision impairment.

In the United States and other developed countries, good health has become something of an ethical imperative (Foucault 1990). Individuals are expected to regulate their behavior so as to achieve bodies in keeping with new medical knowledge. Those who do so acquire the status of sanitary citizens—people with modern understanding of the body, health, and illness. Such citizens practice hygiene and look to health care professionals when they are sick. People who act differently (e.g., smokers, overeaters, those who avoid doctors) are stigmatized and blamed for their own health problems (Briggs 2005; Foucault 1990).

Nowadays, even getting an epidemic disease such as cholera may be viewed as a moral failure, because people did not take proper precautions. It's assumed that people who act rationally can avoid "preventable" diseases. Individuals are expected to follow scientifically based imperatives (e.g., "boil water," "don't smoke"). People (e.g., smokers, veterans, the homeless) can become objects of avoidance and discrimination simply by belonging to a group seen as having a greater risk of poor health.

Medical anthropology also studies the impact of new scientific and medical techniques on ideas about life, death, and personhood (what it means to be a person). For decades, disagreements about personhood—such as about when life begins and ends—have been part of political and religious discussions of contraception, abortion, and assisted suicide. Recent technological and scientific advances have raised new debates about personhood associated with stem cells, "harvested" embryos, assisted reproduction, genetic screening and editing, cloning, and life-prolonging medical treatments.

Kaufman and Morgan (2005) emphasize the contrast between what they call low-tech and high-tech births and deaths. A desperately poor young mother dies of AIDS in Africa, while half a world away an American child of privilege is born as the result of a $50,000 in-vitro fertilization procedure. Medical anthropologists increasingly are concerned with how the boundaries of life and death are being questioned and negotiated in our globalized world.

## Anthropology and Business

As David Price (2000) has noted, activities encompassed under the label "applied anthropology" are extremely diverse, ranging from research for activist NGOs to workplace studies commissioned by and for management. For decades, anthropologists have used ethnographic procedures to understand organizations and business settings (Briody and Trotter 2008; Cefkin 2009; A. Jordan 2013; B. Jordan 2013; McCabe 2017). Ethnographic research in an automobile factory, for example, might view line workers, managers, and executives as different social categories participating in a common system. Each group has its own characteristic attitudes and behavior patterns. The free-ranging nature of ethnography allows the anthropologist to move across levels and microcultures—from worker through management and back. Having learned the entire system by crossing and recrossing its internal boundaries, the anthropologist can become an effective "cultural broker," translating managers' goals or workers' concerns to the other group (see Ferraro and Briody 2013). A free-ranging ethnographer can be a perceptive oddball in settings where information and decisions typically move through a rigid hierarchy. When allowed to converse freely with, and observe, all types and levels of personnel, the anthropologist gains a unique perspective on organizational conditions and problems.

Business executives, like public policy makers, run organizations that provide goods and services *for people*. The field of market research, which employs an increasing number of anthropologists, is based on the need to know what actual and potential customers do, think, and want. Smart planners study and listen to people to understand what they desire in a product or service and how they use it—the meaningful role it plays in their lives.

Ethnographers can help a business to rethink faulty preconceptions and assumptions about their clients' purchasing habits or service needs, and to *discover* what those clients really are seeking (see Graber and Atkinson 2012). Ethnography relies on in-depth observation of people as they lead their everyday lives. Applying ethnographic techniques, business anthropologists shadow people—actual and potential customers—at home and at work. Researchers observe how those people interact with other people and products. They take notes and video-record behavior and interactions. Eventually, they draw conclusions and make recommendations (see Ha n.d.). Let's consider now a few case studies illustrating the value of anthropology to business.

In an article titled "An Anthropologist Walks into a Bar," Christian Madsbjerg and Mikkel Rasmussen (2014) describe a study commissioned by a beer company, which they call BeerCo. A team of anthropologists studied a dozen bars in Finland and the United Kingdom. The researchers immersed themselves in the life of each bar or pub, observing and getting to know owners, staff, and regulars. The team analyzed 150 hours of video, thousands of still photographs, and massive field notes. Their findings convinced BeerCo to abandon its previous "one-size-fits-all" approach and to launch a more differentiated and targeted campaign. BeerCo started customizing its promotional materials for different types of bars and bar owners. It trained its salesforce to understand and treat each bar owner as an individual. It enhanced loyalty to the brand by offering taxi service for wait staff who had to work late. BeerCo's pub and bar sales rebounded. This case illustrates once again the value of knowing the local culture and, for businesses, of targeting products and services accordingly. (This chapter's "Anthropology Today" provides yet another example of the value of cultural understanding for business expansion.)

Paco Underhill (2009) is a retail anthropologist whose influential book *Why We Buy: The Science of Shopping* has been translated into 27 languages. His market research company, Envirosell, specializes in the study of shopping habits (see Green 1999). Researchers follow shoppers around stores, recording their interactions with merchandise. Underhill's team noted that Americans, on entering a store, tend to gravitate to the right, replicating a pattern used in driving and walking. Australians and Britons, who drive on the left, do the opposite. Based on this observation, Underhill recommended that North American stores place their best merchandise on the right side of the store. He also recommended that stores and departments that cater primarily to women need to give men a place to sit and something to do. (I would add the additional recommendation that Wi-Fi should be easily available, since nowadays "something to do" typically involves a smartphone.) Another Underhill recommendation is that products designed for older people should be placed above the bottom shelf, which gets harder to reach as customers age. Finally, he stresses the key role of the dressing room, as the place where most buying decisions are finalized. Dressing rooms should be clean and well-lit, with places to sit and for children to play (see Green 1999).

One common approach in market research is to assemble a focus group (a small group of people guided by a researcher as they discuss a topic). A limitation of focus groups, surveys, and other common market research techniques is that they elicit only what people *say*, report, or write down, rather than observing real-time, real-life behavior, as anthropologists do. Focus groups also face the danger of groupthink, when one or two very vocal members unduly influence (or hijack) the entire group. A limitation of surveys is that people want to answer the questions as quickly as possible. They have limited patience and imperfect recall. Their answers will be more accurate and complete when they are interviewed in person and probed for additional information.

Business anthropology in action: At the Intel Corporation in Hillsboro, Oregon, anthropologist Alexandra Zafiroglu displays a blanket with a huge photograph of the contents of one automobile. Zafiroglu works on a team directed by anthropologist Genevieve Bell (Intel's director of user experience research) studying objects stored in cars. This research provides insights about how drivers use handheld mobile devices in conjunction with technology built into their cars. Leah Nash/The New York Times/Redux

The ethnographic market research firm Ethnographic Solutions provides qualitative research, including a variety of ethnographic approaches, that has benefited numerous pharmaceutical, biotech, and medical device companies. The firm's website describes the value of several techniques, including *physician-patient dialogue research*. The goal is to understand how physicians and patients decide together to initiate and navigate a course of treatment, including the products to be used. Conducted in physicians' offices, physician-patient dialogue research combines on-site interviewing and observation with later analysis of field notes and video-recorded interactions. The resulting perspective goes beyond traditional market research, which typically takes place in an artificial setting, such as a research facility or via a survey, and which relies on imperfect recall.

Key features of anthropology that are of value to business include (1) ethnography and observation as ways of gathering data, (2) a focus on diversity, and (3) cross-cultural expertise. Businesses have heard that anthropologists are specialists on cultural diversity and the observation of behavior. Hallmark Cards has hired anthropologists to observe parties, holidays, and celebrations of ethnic groups to improve its ability to design cards for targeted audiences (see Denny and Sunderland 2014).

## Can Change Be Bad?

Can change be bad? The idea that innovation is desirable is almost axiomatic and unquestioned in American culture—especially in advertising. "New and improved" is a slogan we hear all the time—a lot more often than "old reliable." Which do you think is best—change or the status quo?

That "new" isn't always "improved" is a painful lesson learned by the Coca-Cola Company (TCCC) in 1985 when it changed the formula of its premier soft drink and introduced "New Coke." After a national brouhaha, with hordes of customers protesting, TCCC brought back old, familiar, reliable Coke under the name "Coca-Cola Classic," which thrives today. New Coke (revived in summer 2019 in Season 3 of the Netflix series "Stranger Things") offers a classic case of how not to treat consumers. TCCC tried a *top-down change* (a change initiated at the top of a hierarchy rather than inspired by the people most affected by the change). Customers didn't ask TCCC to change its product; executives made that decision.

Smart planners (in virtually any field) can benefit when they study and listen to people to try to determine *locally based demand*. In general, what's working well (assuming it's not discriminatory or illegal) should be maintained, encouraged, tweaked, and strengthened. If something's wrong, how can it best be fixed? What changes do the people—and which people—want? How can conflicting wishes and needs be accommodated? Applied anthropologists help answer these questions, which are crucial in understanding whether change is needed, and how it will work.

A key point of this chapter is that innovation succeeds best when it is culturally appropriate. This axiom of applied anthropology should guide the international spread of programs aimed at social and economic change as well as of businesses. Each time an organization expands to a new nation, it must devise a culturally appropriate strategy for fitting into the new setting. In their international expansion, companies as diverse as McDonald's, Starbucks, and Ford have learned that more money can be made by fitting in with, rather than trying to Americanize, local habits (see this chapter's "Anthropology Today").

## Public and Applied Anthropology

Many academic anthropologists, myself included, have worked occasionally as applied anthropologists. Often our role is to advise and consult about the direction of change in places where we originally did "academic" research. In my case, this has meant policy-relevant work on environmental preservation in Madagascar and poverty reduction in northeastern Brazil.

Other academics, while not doing applied anthropology per se, have urged anthropologists to engage more in what they call **public anthropology** (Beck and Maida 2015; Borofsky 2000) or *public interest anthropology* (Sanday 2003). Suggested ways of making anthropology more visible and relevant to the public include nonacademic publishing; testifying at government hearings; consulting; acting as an expert witness; and engaging in citizen activism, electoral campaigns, and political administrations (Sanjek 2004). Public anthropologists work to oppose policies that promote injustice and to reframe discussions of key social issues in the media and by public officials. As Barbara Rylko-Bauer and her colleagues (2006) point out, there is also a long tradition of work guided by such goals in applied anthropology (see also Beck and Maida 2013).

New media are helping to disseminate anthropological knowledge to a wider public. The world of cyberspace, including social media and the blogosphere, constantly grows richer in the resources and communication opportunities available to anthropologists. Anthropology blogs include the following:

Anthrodendum (formerly Savage Minds), a group blog
https://anthrodendum.org/

Living Anthropologically, by Jason Antrosio
http://www.livinganthropologically.com

Neuroanthropology, by Greg Downey and Daniel Lende
http://blogs.plos.org/neuroanthropology/

Anthropologists participate as well in various listservs and networking groups (e.g., on LinkedIn and ResearchGate). A bit of googling on your part will take you to anthropologists' personal websites, as well as to research project websites.

## Careers and Anthropology

Many college students find anthropology interesting and consider majoring in it. However, their parents or friends may discourage them by asking, "What kind of job are you going to get with an anthropology degree?" The first step in answering that question is to consider the more general question "What do you do with any college major?" The answer is "Not much, without a good bit of effort, thought, and planning." One survey of graduates of the University of Michigan's College of Literature, Science, and the Arts showed that few had jobs that were obviously linked to their majors. Most professions, including medicine and law, require advanced degrees. Although many colleges offer bachelor's degrees in engineering, business, accounting, and social work, master's degrees often are needed to get the best jobs in those fields. Anthropologists, too, need an advanced degree, usually a PhD, to find gainful employment as an anthropologist.

A broad college education, and even a major in anthropology, can be an excellent foundation for success in many fields (see Golub 2017). One survey of women executives showed that most had not majored in business but in the social sciences or humanities. Only after graduating from college did they study business, leading to a master's degree in business administration (MBA). Those executives felt that the breadth of their college educations had contributed to their business careers. Anthropology majors go on to medical, law, and business schools and find success in many professions that often have little explicit connection to anthropology.

Anthropology's breadth provides knowledge and an outlook on the world that are useful in many kinds of work. For example, an anthropology major combined with a master's degree in business is excellent preparation for work in international business. Breadth is anthropology's hallmark. Anthropologists study people biologically, culturally, socially, and linguistically, across time and space, in various countries, in simple and complex settings. Most colleges offer anthropology courses that compare cultures, along with others that focus on particular world areas, such as Latin America, Asia, Africa, the Middle East, and Eastern Europe. The knowledge of foreign areas acquired in such courses can be useful in many jobs. Anthropology's comparative outlook and its focus on diverse lifestyles combine to provide an excellent foundation for overseas employment (see Ellick and Watkins 2011; Nolan 2017; Omohundro 2001).

For work in contemporary North America as well, anthropology's focus on culture and diversity is increasingly relevant. Every day we hear about cultural differences and about problems whose solutions require an ability to recognize and reconcile differences related to social variables such as race, ethnicity, gender, and class. Government, schools, hospitals, and businesses constantly deal with people from different social classes, ethnic groups, and cultural backgrounds. Physicians, attorneys, social workers, police officers, judges, teachers, and students can all do a better job if they understand cultural differences in a nation that is one of the most ethnically diverse in history.

Knowledge of the traditions and beliefs of the groups that make up a modern nation is important in planning and carrying out programs that affect those groups. Experience in planned social change—whether community organization in North America or economic development overseas—shows that a proper social study should be done before a project or policy is implemented. When local people want the change and it fits their lifestyle and traditions, it has a better chance of being successful, beneficial, and cost effective.

People with anthropology backgrounds do well in many fields (see https://savageminds .org/2014/05/05/who-majors-in-anthropology/ for some famous people who have studied anthropology). Even if one's job has little or nothing to do with anthropology in a formal or obvious sense, a background in anthropology provides a useful orientation when we work with our fellow human beings. For most of us, this means every day of our lives.

## Anthropology Today    *Culturally Appropriate Marketing*

Innovation succeeds best when it is culturally appropriate. This axiom of applied anthropology could guide the international spread not only of development projects but also of businesses, such as fast food. Each time McDonald's or Burger King expands to a new nation, it must devise a culturally appropriate strategy for fitting into the new setting.

McDonald's has been very successful internationally. Almost 70 percent of its current annual revenue comes from sales outside the United States. As one of, if not the, world's most successful restaurant chain, McDonald's has more than 36,000 restaurants in some 120 countries. One place where McDonald's has expanded successfully is Brazil, where 100 million middle-class people, most living in densely packed cities, provide a concentrated market for a fast-food chain. Still, it took McDonald's some time to find the right marketing strategy for Brazil.

In 1980 when I visited Brazil after a seven-year absence, I first noticed, as a manifestation of Brazil's growing participation in the world economy, the appearance of two McDonald's restaurants in Rio de Janeiro. There wasn't much difference between the Brazilian McDonald's and an American one. The restaurants looked alike. The menus were more or less the same, as was the taste of the quarter-pounders. I picked up an artifact, a white paper bag with yellow lettering, exactly like the take-out bags then used in American McDonald's. An advertising device, it carried several messages about how Brazilians could bring McDonald's into their lives. However, it seemed to me that McDonald's Brazilian ad campaign was missing some important points about how fast food should be marketed in a culture that valued large, leisurely lunches.

The bag proclaimed, "You're going to enjoy the [McDonald's] difference," and listed several "favorite places where you can enjoy McDonald's products." This list confirmed that the marketing people were trying to adapt to Brazilian middle-class culture, but they were making some mistakes. "When you go out in the car with the kids" transferred the uniquely developed North American cultural combination of highways, affordable cars, and suburban living to the very different context of urban Brazil. A similar suggestion was "traveling to the country place." Even Brazilians who owned country places could not find McDonald's, still confined to the cities then, on the road. The ad creator had apparently never attempted to drive up to a fast-food restaurant in a neighborhood with no parking spaces.

Several other suggestions pointed customers toward the beach, where *cariocas* (Rio natives) do spend much of their leisure time. One could eat McDonald's products "after a dip in the ocean," "at a picnic at the beach," or "watching the surfers." These suggestions ignored the Brazilian custom of consuming cold things, such as beer, soft drinks, ice cream, and ham and cheese sandwiches, on the beach. Brazilians don't consider a hot, greasy hamburger proper beach food. They view the sea as "cold" and hamburgers as "hot"; they avoid "hot" foods at the beach.

Also culturally dubious was the suggestion to eat McDonald's hamburgers "lunching at the office." Brazilians prefer their main meal at midday, often eating at a leisurely pace with business associates. Many firms serve ample lunches to their employees. Other workers take advantage of a two-hour lunch break to go home to eat with the spouse and children. Nor did it make sense to suggest that children should eat hamburgers for lunch, since most kids attend school for half-day sessions and have lunch at home. Two other suggestions—"waiting for the bus" and "in the beauty parlor"—did describe common aspects of daily life in a Brazilian city. However, these settings have not proved especially inviting to hamburgers or fish fillets.

The homes of Brazilians who can afford McDonald's products often have cooks and maids to do many of the things that fast-food restaurants do in the United States. The suggestion that McDonald's products be eaten "while watching your favorite television program" is culturally appropriate, because Brazilians watch TV a lot. However, Brazil's consuming classes can ask the cook to make a snack when hunger strikes. Indeed, much televiewing occurs during the light dinner served when the husband gets home from the office.

Most appropriate to the Brazilian lifestyle was the suggestion to enjoy McDonald's "on the cook's day off." Throughout Brazil, Sunday is that day. The Sunday pattern for middle-class families who live on the coast is a trip to the beach, liters of beer, a full midday meal around 3:00 P.M., and a light evening snack. McDonald's found its niche in the Sunday evening meal, when families flock to the fast-food restaurant.

McDonald's has expanded rapidly in Brazil, where, as in North America, young appetites have fueled the fast-food explosion. McDonald's outlets now dot urban neighborhoods throughout Brazil, and the cost of hiring in-home help has skyrocketed. Given these changes, Brazilian teenagers increasingly use McDonald's for after-school snacks, and whole families have evening meals there. As an anthropologist could have predicted, the fast-food industry has not revolutionized Brazilian food and meal customs. Rather, McDonald's is succeeding because it has adapted to preexisting Brazilian cultural patterns. Once McDonald's realized that more money could be made by fitting in with, rather than trying to Americanize, Brazilian meal habits, it started aiming its advertising at that goal. As of this writing (2019), McDonald's has about 900 outlets in Brazil.

## Summary

1. Applied anthropology uses anthropological perspectives, theory, methods, and data to identify, assess, and solve problems. Applied anthropologists have a range of employers. Examples are government agencies; development organizations; NGOs; tribal, ethnic, and interest groups; businesses; hospitals; social services; and educational agencies. Applied anthropologists come from all four subfields. Ethnography is one of applied anthropology's most valuable research tools.

2. Development anthropology focuses on social issues in, and the cultural dimension of, economic development. Not all governments seek to increase equality and end poverty. Resistance by elites to reform is typical. At the same time, local people rarely cooperate with projects requiring major and risky changes in their daily lives. Many projects seek to impose inappropriate property notions and incompatible

social units on their intended beneficiaries. The best strategy for change is to base the social design for innovation on traditional social forms in each target area.

3. Anthropology and education researchers work in classrooms, homes, and other settings relevant to education and make policy recommendations based on their findings. Both academic and applied anthropologists study migration from rural areas to cities and across national boundaries. North America has become a popular arena for urban anthropological research on migration, ethnicity, poverty, and related topics. Although rural and urban are different social systems, there is cultural diffusion from one to the other.

4. Medical anthropology is a biocultural field that studies variation in health care systems, including disease, illness, health standards, and disease theories. In a given setting, the characteristic diseases reflect diet, population density, economy, and social complexity. Native theories of illness may be personalistic, naturalistic, or emotionalistic. In applying anthropology to business, the key features are (1) ethnography and observation as ways of gathering data, (2) a focus on diversity, and (3) cross-cultural expertise. Public anthropology attempts to extend anthropological knowledge of social problems and issues to a wider and more influential audience.

5. A broad college education, including anthropology and foreign-area courses, offers an excellent background for many fields. Anthropology's comparative, cross-cultural outlook provides an excellent basis for overseas employment. Even for work in North America, a focus on culture and cultural diversity is valuable. Anthropology majors attend medical, law, and business schools and succeed in many fields, some of which have little explicit connection with anthropology.

## Think Like an Anthropologist

1. This chapter uses the association between early anthropology and colonialism to illustrate some of the dangers of early applied anthropology. We also learn how American anthropologists studied Japanese "culture at a distance" to predict the behavior of the enemies of the United States during World War II. Political and military conflicts continue today. What role, if any, could and/or should applied anthropologists play in these conflicts?

2. This chapter describes some of the applications of anthropology in educational settings. Think back to your grade school or high school classroom. Were there any social issues that might have interested an anthropologist? Were there any problems that an applied anthropologist might have been able to help solve? How so?

3. Indicate your career plans, if known, and describe how you might apply the knowledge learned through introductory anthropology in your future vocation. If you have not yet chosen a career, pick one of the following: economist, engineer, diplomat, architect, or elementary school teacher. Why is it important to understand the culture and social organization of the people who will be affected by your work?

# Chapter 18

# The World System, Colonialism, and Inequality

## The World System

Although fieldwork in small communities has been anthropology's hallmark, isolated groups are impossible to find today. Truly isolated human societies probably never have existed. For thousands of years, human groups have been in contact with one another. Local societies always have participated in a larger system, which today has global dimensions. We call it the *modern world system*, by which we mean a world in which nations are economically and politically interdependent.

A huge increase in international trade during and after the 15th century led to the **capitalist world economy** (Wallerstein et al. 2013), a single world system committed to

Illustrating the contemporary global spread of capitalism is this photo of Hong Kong's perpetually crowded Sai Yeung Choi Street, where throngs of people shop, sightsee, and search for restaurants. What international brands (an important component of today's world capitalist economy) can you identify in the photo? Alex Woo/Getty Images

production for sale or exchange, with the object of maximizing profits rather than supplying domestic needs. The world system and the relations among the countries within it are shaped by the capitalist world economy. **Capital** refers to wealth or resources invested in a business, with the intent of making a profit.

## World-System Theory

World-system theory can be traced to the French social historian Fernand Braudel. In his three-volume work *Civilization and Capitalism, 15th–18th Century* (1981, 1982, 1992), Braudel argued that societies consist of interrelated parts assembled into a system. Societies themselves are subsystems of larger systems, with the world system the largest. The key claim of **world-system theory** is that all the countries of the world belong to a global system that is marked by differences in wealth and power. This world system, based on capitalism, has existed at least since the late 15th century, when the Old World established regular contact with the Americas.

World-system theory assigns particular countries to one of three different positions, based on their economic and political clout: core, semiperiphery, and periphery. The **core** consists of the strongest and most powerful nations, which have the most productive economies and the greatest concentration of capital. The core monopolizes the most profitable activities, especially the control of world finance (Arrighi 2010). The **semiperiphery** is intermediate between the core and the periphery. Nations of the semiperiphery are industrialized. Like core nations, they produce and export both industrial goods and commodities, but they lack the power and economic dominance of core nations. Thus, Brazil, a semiperiphery nation, exports automobiles to Nigeria (a periphery nation) and auto engines, orange juice extract, coffee, and shrimp to the United States (a core nation). The **periphery** includes the world's poorest and least privileged countries. Economic activities

Jobs continue to migrate from core nations to places in the semiperiphery, such as this call center in India. Fredrik Renander/Alamy Stock Photo

there are less mechanized than in the semiperiphery, although some degree of industrialization has reached even periphery nations. The periphery produces mainly raw materials, agricultural commodities, and, increasingly, human labor for export to the core and the semiperiphery.

In the United States and Western Europe today, immigration—documented and undocumented—from the periphery and semiperiphery supplies cheap labor, especially for agriculture, construction, and paid domestic labor. U.S. states as distant as California, Michigan, and South Carolina make significant use of farm labor from Mexico. The availability of relatively cheap workers from noncore nations such as Mexico (in the United States) and Turkey (in Germany) benefits farmers and business owners in core countries while supplying remittances to families in the semiperiphery and periphery. As a result of 21st-century telecommunications technology, cheap labor doesn't even need to migrate to the United States. Thousands of families in India are being supported as American companies outsource jobs—from telephone assistance to software engineering—to nations outside the core (see Nadeem 2011).

## The Emergence of the World System

International trade is much older than the capitalist world economy. As early as 600 B.C.E., the Phoenicians/Carthaginians sailed around Britain on regular trade routes and circumnavigated Africa. Likewise, Indonesia, the Middle East, and Africa have been linked in Indian Ocean trade for at least 2,000 years. By the 15th century, advances in navigation, mapmaking, and shipbuilding fueled the geographic expansion of trading networks. Europe established regular contact with Asia, Africa, and eventually the New World (the Caribbean and the Americas). Christopher Columbus's first voyage from Spain to the Bahamas and the Caribbean in 1492 was soon followed by additional voyages. These journeys opened the way for sustained contact and major exchanges between the hemispheres, as the Old and New Worlds were forever linked (Crosby 2003, 2015; Diamond 1997/2017; Mann 2012; Marks 2015). The *Columbian exchange* is the term for the spread of people, resources, products, ideas, and diseases between Eastern and Western Hemispheres after contact.

Previously in Europe, as throughout the world, rural people had produced mainly for their own needs, growing their own food and making clothing, furniture, and tools from local products. People produced beyond their immediate needs in order to pay taxes and to purchase trade items such as salt and iron. As late as 1650, the English diet was based on locally grown starches. In the 200 years that followed, however, the English became extraordinary consumers of imported goods. One of the earliest and most popular of those goods was sugar (Mintz 1985).

Sugarcane, originally domesticated in Papua New Guinea, was first processed in India. Reaching Europe via the eastern Mediterranean, it was carried to the Americas by Columbus (Mintz 1985). The climate of Brazil and the Caribbean proved ideal for growing sugarcane, and Europeans built plantations there to supply the growing demand for sugar. This led to the development in the 17th century of a plantation economy based on a single cash crop—a system known as *monocrop* production.

The demand for sugar spurred the development of the transatlantic slave trade and New World plantation economies based on the labor of enslaved people. By the 18th century, an increased English demand for raw cotton led to rapid settlement of what is now the southeastern United States and the emergence there of another slave-based monocrop production system. Like sugar, cotton was a key trade item that fueled the growth of the world system.

# Industrialization

By the 18th century the stage had been set for the **Industrial Revolution**—the historical transformation of "traditional" into "modern" societies through industrialization. The Industrial Revolution began, in Europe, around 1750. However, the seeds of industrial society had been planted well before then (Gimpel 1988). For example, a knitting machine invented in England in 1589 was so far ahead of its time that it played a profitable role in factories two and three centuries later.

The Industrial Revolution required capital for investment, and that capital came from transoceanic commerce, which generated enormous profits. Wealthy people invested in machines and engines to drive machines. New technology and techniques increased production in both farming and manufacturing.

European industrialization eventually replaced the *domestic system* of production, also known as the home-handicraft system. In this system, an organizer-entrepreneur supplied raw materials to workers in their homes and collected finished products from them. This entrepreneur, whose sphere of operations might span several villages, owned the materials, paid for the work, and arranged the distribution of the final product.

In the home-handicraft, or domestic, system of production, an organizer supplied raw materials to workers in their homes and collected their products. Family life and work were intertwined, as in this English scene. Is there a modern equivalent to the domestic system of production?
Source: Library of Congress [LC-USZ62-4801]

## Causes of the Industrial Revolution

The Industrial Revolution began with machines that manufactured cotton products, iron, and pottery. These were widely used items whose manufacture could be broken down into simple routine motions that machines could perform. As manufacturing moved from homes into factories, where machinery replaced handwork, agrarian societies evolved into industrial ones. The Industrial Revolution led to a dramatic increase in production, initially of cheap staple goods. Industrialization also fueled urban growth and created a new kind of city, with factories crowded together in places where coal and labor were cheap.

The Industrial Revolution began in England for several reasons. More than other nations, England needed to innovate in order to meet a demand for staples—at home and from its far-flung colonies. As industrialization proceeded, Britain's population began to increase dramatically. It doubled during the 18th century (especially after 1750) and did so again between 1800 and 1850. This demographic explosion fueled consumption, but British entrepreneurs could not meet the increased demand with traditional production methods. This spurred experimentation, innovation, further industrialization, and rapid technological change.

Also supporting early English industrialization were Britain's advantages in natural resources. Britain was rich in coal and iron ore and had navigable coasts and waterways. It was a seafaring island-nation located at the crossroads of international trade. These features gave Britain a favored position for importing raw materials and exporting manufactured goods. Another factor in England's industrial growth was the fact that much of its 18th-century colonial empire was occupied by English settler families, who looked to the mother country as they tried to replicate European civilization abroad. These colonies bought large quantities of English staples.

It also has been argued that particular cultural and religious factors contributed to industrialization. Many members of the emerging English middle class were Protestants, whose beliefs and values encouraged industry, thrift, the dissemination of new knowledge, inventiveness, and willingness to accept change (Weber 1904/1958). These cultural values were eminently compatible with the spirit of entrepreneurial innovation that propelled the Industrial Revolution.

## Socioeconomic Changes Associated with the Industrial Revolution

The socioeconomic changes that accompanied industrialization were mixed. English national income tripled between 1700 and 1815 and increased 30 times more by 1939. Standards of comfort rose, but prosperity was uneven. Initially, factory workers got decent wages, until owners started recruiting workers in areas where labor (including that of women and children) was cheap. By the 19th century, cities were polluted by factory smoke, and housing was crowded and unsanitary. People faced disease outbreaks and rising death rates. This was the world of Ebenezer Scrooge, Bob Cratchit, Tiny Tim—and Karl Marx.

## Industrial Stratification

The Industrial Revolution created a new form of socioeconomic stratification. Based on his observations of 19th-century industrial capitalism in England, Karl Marx saw this stratification as a sharp and simple division between two opposed classes: the bourgeoisie (capitalists) and the proletariat (propertyless workers) (Marx and Engels 1848/1976). The bourgeoisie traced its origins to overseas commerce, which had created a wealthy commercial class (White 2009).

Industrialization had shifted production from farms and cottages to mills and factories, where mechanical power was available and where workers could be assembled to operate heavy machinery. The **bourgeoisie** owned the factories, mines, estates, and other means of production. Members of the **working class, or proletariat,** had to sell their labor to survive.

By promoting rural-to-urban migration, industrialization hastened the process of *proletarianization*—the separation of workers from the means of production. The bourgeoisie controlled not only factories but also schools, the press, and other key institutions. *Class consciousness* (personal identification and solidarity with one's economic group) was a vital part of Marx's view of class. He saw bourgeoisie and proletariat as having radically opposed interests. Marx viewed classes as powerful collective forces that could mobilize human energies to influence the course of history. Based on their common experience and interests, workers, he thought, would develop class consciousness, which could lead to revolutionary change.

Although England never experienced a proletarian revolution, workers did organize to protect their interests and increase their share of industrial profits. During the 19th century, trade unions and socialist parties emerged, expressing a rising anticapitalist spirit. This early English labor movement worked to remove young children from factories and limit the hours during which women and children could work. The profile of stratification in industrial core nations gradually took shape. Capitalists controlled production, but labor was organizing for better wages and working conditions. By 1900, many govern-ments had factory regulation and social welfare programs. Mass living standards in core nations rose as population grew.

Today, the existence of publicly traded companies complicates the division between capitalists and workers. Through pension plans and personal investments, some workers have become part-owners rather than propertyless workers. Today's key capitalist isn't the factory owner, who may have been replaced by stockholders, but the CEO or the chair of the board of directors, neither of whom may actually own the corporation.

The social theorist Max Weber faulted Karl Marx for an overly simple and exclusively economic view of stratification (see Kalberg 2017). Weber (1922/1968) looked beyond class and identified three (separate but correlated) dimensions of social stratification: wealth, power, and prestige. Weber believed that social identities based on nationality, ethnicity, and religion could take priority over class (social identity based on economic status). Supporting Weber's view, today's world system *is* crosscut by collective identities based on nationality, ethnicity, and religion. Class conflicts tend to occur within nations, and nationalism has impeded global class solidarity, particularly of proletarians.

Although the capitalist class dominates politically in most countries, growing wealth has made it easier for core nations to offer benefits to their workers. However, this im-provement in core workers' living standards would not have occurred without the world system. The wealth that flows from periphery and semiperiphery to core has helped core capitalists maintain their profits while satisfying the demands of core workers. In the periphery and semiperiphery, wages and living standards are lower. The current *world stratification system* features a substantial contrast between both capitalists and workers in the core nations, on the one hand, and workers in the periphery, on the other.

# The Persistence of Inequality

Modern stratification systems are not simple and dichotomous. They include (particu-larly in core and semiperiphery nations) a middle class of skilled and professional work-ers. Gerhard Lenski (1966) argued that social equality tends to increase in advanced industrial societies. The masses improve their access to economic benefits and political power. In Lenski's scheme, the shift of political power to the masses reflects the growth of the middle class, which reduces the polarization between owning and working classes. The proliferation of middle-class occupations creates opportunities for social mobility and a more complex stratification system (Carrier and Kalb 2015; Giddens 1981).

## Wealth Distribution in the United States

Most contemporary Americans claim to belong to the middle class, which they tend to perceive as a vast, undifferentiated group. There are, however, significant, and growing, socioeconomic contrasts within the middle class, and especially between the richest and the poorest Americans. Table 18.1 shows how income varied from the top to the bottom fifths (quintiles) of American households in 2017. We see that the top fifth earned more than half (51.5 percent) of all income generated in the United States. Income has been rising much more significantly for the richest Americans than for everyone else. The top

TABLE 18.1  **U.S. National Income by Quintile, 2017**

Source: Fontenot, Kayla, Semega, Jessica, and Kollar, Melissa, "Table A-2. Selected Measures of Household Income Dispersion: 1967 to 2017. Income and Poverty in the United States: 2017," U.S. Census Bureau, *Current Population Reports*, P60-263. Washington, DC: U.S. Government Printing Office.

| Segment of Population | % Share of National Income | Mean Household Income |
|---|---|---|
| Top 5 percent | 22.3 | $385,289 |
| Top 20 percent | 51.5 | 221,846 |
| Second 20 percent | 23.0 | 99,030 |
| Third 20 percent | 14.3 | 61,564 |
| Fourth 20 percent | 8.2 | 35,401 |
| Bottom 20 percent | 3.1 | 13,258 |

Alexandria Ocasio-Cortez ("AOC"), a media-savvy congresswoman from New York, kicks off the 3rd Annual Woman's March in Manhattan on January 19, 2019. Among the causes championed by AOC are poverty reduction, immigration reform, and a Green New Deal to combat climate change.
Ira L. Black/Corbis News/Getty Images

quintile earned 17 times the share of the bottom quintile in 2017, compared with a ratio of 14:1 in 2000 and 11:1 in 1970. Even more dramatically, the top 5 percent of Americans earned 29 times the share of the bottom fifth in 2017, compared with ratios of 24:1 in 2000 and 17:1 in 1970.

When we consider wealth (investments, property, possessions, and the like) rather than income, the contrast is even more striking. As of 2016, the wealthiest *1 percent* of American households owned 40 percent of the country's total wealth—a higher share than at any point since at least 1962. That top 1 percent has more total wealth than the bottom 90 percent combined (Ingraham 2018; Wolff 2017). The share of national wealth held by the top 1 percent of Americans is twice that of the top 1 percent in France, the United Kingdom, and Canada (Ingraham 2017). In those countries, the top 1 percent owns about 20 percent of all national wealth. Recognition of such disparities, and that the rich continue to get rich as the poor get poorer, led to the Occupy movement of 2011 and fueled Bernie Sanders's 2016 and 2020 presidential campaigns (see also Galbraith 2016).

## Risky Living on the American Periphery

The nations on the periphery of the world system have the least economic development and political clout. Furthermore, within any given nation, certain regions and communities are similarly disadvantaged. One expression of this inequality is exposure to pollution and environmental hazards. Communities that are poorer and predominantly minority are more likely to be the victims of toxic waste exposure than are more affluent or even average (middle-class) communities.

### Environmental Hazards

News reports in 2015 and 2016 highlighted the plight of Flint, Michigan, whose water supply was seriously contaminated following a 2014 cost-cutting switch in its water source. The state of Michigan, which had seized control of Flint's city administration and budget, temporarily switched Flint's water source from Lake Huron and the Detroit River to the Flint River. The switch, which took place in April 2014, was to last until completion, in an estimated three years, of a new supply line from Lake Huron. The Flint River had a reputation for nastiness. Soon after the switch, residents started noticing that their water looked, smelled, and tasted funny (McLaughlin 2016).

Residents experienced myriad health problems, including skin rashes, hair loss, nausea, dizziness, and pain. A local pediatrician found that lead levels in Flint toddlers had doubled, and in some cases tripled, since the switch. After researchers confirmed the toxicity of Flint's water supply, officials finally abandoned the Flint River (Kozlowski 2016), switching back to the Detroit River and Lake Huron in October 2015. By this time, however, irreparable damage had been done, not only to public health but also to the lead water pipes, which the Flint River water had corroded. The state responded by handing out filters and bottled water (McLaughlin 2016).

On January 5, 2016, then Michigan governor Rick Snyder declared Flint to be in a state of emergency. Soon thereafter, President Barack Obama declared the city to be in a federal state of emergency, authorizing additional help from FEMA (the Federal Emergency Management Agency) and the Department of Homeland Security. Residents of Flint have filed more than a dozen lawsuits, faulting various agencies and individuals, including the city of Flint, the state's Department of Environmental Quality, and Governor Snyder, for violating the U.S. Safe Drinking Water Act.

In ruling on one of those lawsuits—a class action—U.S. district judge Judith E. Levy, on August 1, 2018, recognized that "lead poisoning caused plaintiffs to suffer from severe medical problems with their hair, skin, digestive system, and organs, as well as brain and other developmental injuries including cognitive deficits . . ." (quoted in Kvetenadze 2018). The judge found that certain government officials (not, however, including the governor and the mayor of Flint) had "disregarded the risk the water posed, denied the increasingly

At a public meeting called to address her city's water crisis, Flint resident LeeAnne Walters displays water samples from her home to the city's new emergency manager. Detroit Free Press/ZUMA Press/Alamy Stock Photo

clear threat the public faced, protected themselves with bottled water, and rejected solutions that would have ended this crisis sooner" (quoted in Kvetenadze 2018).

A legally mandated settlement reached in 2017 required the City of Flint to take specific steps to address the water crisis. The state of Michigan must pay for and the city of Flint must finish thousands of lead service-line (water-pipe) replacements within three years at no cost to Flint residents. The settlement also required the state to provide filters and filter-installation services to residents, and to monitor Flint's tap water above and beyond the requirements of federal regulations. As a result of the actions mandated by the settlement, the proportion of lead in Flint's tap water has been declining steadily (Kelly 2019).

Many Flint residents wonder if the fact that they live in one of the poorest cities in the nation is a reason why the process has moved so slowly, especially when they see the rapid recovery efforts carried out in places like Florida and Texas after hurricanes hit. They are right to wonder. That this story of toxic endangerment happened in one of Michigan's least affluent cities is no accident. Throughout the United States (as in many other nations), environmental hazards disproportionately endanger poor and minority communities. Flint's population is 57 percent African American. Almost 40 percent of its residents live below the poverty line, compared with state and national rates of 14 percent and 13 percent, respectively. One doubts that similar events would have played out in one of Michigan's affluent communities.

Research demonstrates that industries typically target minority and low-income neighborhoods when deciding where to locate polluting facilities (Erickson 2016). Environmental researchers Paul Mohai and Robin Saha (2015) analyzed 30 years of data on the placement of hazardous waste facilities in the United States. Their sample included 319 commercial hazardous waste treatment, storage, and disposal facilities built between 1966 and 1995. Their analysis revealed a clear pattern of racial and socio-economic bias in the location of environmental hazards. Polluting facilities and other locally unwanted land uses were, and still are, located disproportionately in non-White and poor neighborhoods. These communities have fewer resources and political clout to oppose the location of such facilities. Flint's story has garnered headlines, but there are hundreds more stories waiting to be told about environmental threats on the American periphery.

## Life Expectancy

Another expression of inequality is exposure to risks that reduce life expectancy. Once again, areas whose populations are poorer and predominantly minority are at greatest risk. On average, the poorest 1 percent of American women die 10 years younger than the richest 1 percent. The comparable gap for men is 15 years (*Economist* 2018). Researchers have confirmed that lower incomes and educational levels are associated with obesity, smoking, hypertension, diabetes, and limited exercise. All these are risk factors that shorten lives (*Economist* 2018; Escobedo et al. 2018).

Researchers at the National Center for Health Statistics have estimated life expectancy for every census tract in the United States. These 65,662 tracts cover the entire country, each containing a few thousand people (*Economist* 2018; Escobedo et al. 2018). Overall, median estimated life expectancy was 78.5 years. However, 25 percent of the census tracts had a life expectancy below age 70, while 38 percent had an expectancy above age 85. At the extremes, 64 tracts had an estimated life expectancy above age 90, while in seven census tracts, people could expect to die at least 30 years younger than that.

One of the more fortunate tracts is home to Fearrington, North Carolina, a planned community modeled on an English village. Representing the other extreme is Stilwell, Oklahoma, a farming community that claims to be strawberry capital of the world. Fearrington's average life expectancy is 97.5 years. In Stilwell, it is 56—more than 40 years younger. Someone in Fearrington can expect to live 13 years longer than someone in Japan—the country with the world's most long-lived people. Stilwell's life expectancy is the same as in Somalia, one of the world's most impoverished and war-ravaged countries.

Fearrington's median household income is $81,900, compared with $25,000 in Stilwell. None of Fearrington's children are impoverished, compared with over half of Stilwell's children. Most Fearringtonians are non-Hispanic White. Stilwell's residents are Native Americans who belong to the Cherokee Nation; their ancestors were forcibly relocated to Oklahoma in 1830.

# Colonialism and Imperialism

The major forces influencing cultural interactions during the past 500 years have been commercial expansion, capitalism, and the dominance of colonial and core nations (Wallerstein 2004; Wolf 1982). **Colonialism** is the political, social, economic, and cultural domination of a territory and its people by a foreign power for an extended time. The colonial power establishes and maintains a presence in the dominated territory, in the form of colonists and administrative personnel (see Stoler, McGranahan, and Perdue 2007). **Imperialism** refers to a conscious policy of extending the rule of a country or an empire over foreign nations and of taking and holding foreign colonies (see Burbank and Cooper 2010). Imperialism goes back to early states, including Egypt in the Old World and the Incas in the New. A Greek empire was forged by Alexander the Great, and Julius Caesar and his successors spread the Roman empire. More recent examples include the British, French, and Soviet empires (see Burbank and Cooper 2010).

If imperialism is almost as old as the state, then colonialism can be traced back to the Phoenicians, who established colonies along the eastern Mediterranean 3,000 years ago. The ancient Greeks and Romans were avid colonizers as well as empire builders (see Pagden 2015; Stearns 2016).

## The First Phase of European Colonialism: Spain and Portugal

The first phase of modern colonialism began with the European "Age of Discovery"—of the Americas and of a sea route to the Far East. During the 16th century, Spain, having conquered Mexico (the Aztec empire) and Peru-Bolivia (the Incas), explored and colonized widely in the Caribbean, the southern portions of what was to become the United States, and Central and South America. In the Pacific, Spain extended its rule to the Philippines and Guam. The Portuguese colonial empire included Brazil, South America's largest colonial territory; Angola and Mozambique in Africa; and Goa in South Asia.

Rebellions and wars aimed at independence ended this first phase of European colonialism by the early 19th century. Brazil declared independence from Portugal in 1822. By 1825 most of Spain's colonies had gained their political independence. Spain held on to Cuba and the Philippines until 1898 but otherwise withdrew from the colonial field.

During the first phase of colonialism, Spain and Portugal, along with Britain and France, were the major colonizing nations (see Herzog 2015). The last two (Britain and France) dominated the second phase of colonialism.

## Commercial Expansion and European Imperialism

A second phase of European colonialism occurred between 1875 and 1914. Europe's capitalists sought new markets and its nations competed for colonies and extended their imperial reach to Africa, Asia, and Oceania. During the second half of the 19th century, European imperial expansion was aided by improved transportation, which facilitated the colonization of vast areas of sparsely settled lands, e.g., in Australia. The new colonies purchased goods from Europe's industrial centers and shipped back wheat, cotton, wool, mutton, beef, and leather.

## The British Colonial Empire

Like several other European nations, Britain had two stages of colonialism (see Darwin 2013). The first began with the Elizabethan voyages of the 16th century. During the 17th century, Britain acquired most of the eastern coast of North America, Canada's St. Lawrence basin, islands in the Caribbean, ports in Africa, and interests in India.

The British shared the exploration and early settlement of the New World with the Spanish, Portuguese, French, and Dutch. The British by and large left Mexico, along with Central and South America, to the Spanish and the Portuguese. The end of the Seven Years' War in 1763 forced a French retreat from most of Canada and India, where France previously had competed with Britain (Cody 1998). The American Revolution ended the first stage of British colonialism. India, Canada, and various Caribbean islands remained under British control.

The second stage of British colonialism—the British empire, on which the "sun never set," rose from the ashes of the first (see Black 2015). Beginning in 1788, but intensifying after 1815, the British settled Australia. Britain had acquired Dutch South Africa by 1815. By 1819 Singapore anchored a British trade network that extended to much of South Asia and along the coast of China. By this time, the empires of Britain's traditional rivals, particularly Spain, had been severely diminished in scope. Britain's position as imperial power and the world's leading industrial nation was unchallenged.

Britain's colonial expansion continued during the Victorian Era (1837–1901). Under Queen Victoria, Prime Minister Benjamin Disraeli guided a foreign policy justified by a view of imperialism as shouldering "the white man's burden"—a phrase coined by the poet Rudyard Kipling. People in the empire were seen as incapable of governing, so British guidance was needed to civilize and Christianize them. This paternalistic and racist doctrine was used to legitimize Britain's acquisition and control of parts of central Africa and Asia (Cooper 2014).

The British empire reached its maximum extent around 1914, when it covered a fifth of the world's land surface and ruled a fourth of its population (see Figure 18.1). After World War II, the British empire began to fall apart, with the rise of nationalist movements for independence. India gained its independence in 1947, as did the Republic of Ireland in 1949. The independence movement accelerated in Africa and Asia during the late 1950s (see Buettner 2016). Today, the ties that remain between Britain and its former colonies are mainly linguistic or cultural rather than political (Cody 1998).

## French Colonialism

French colonialism also had two phases. The first began with the explorations of the early 1600s. Prior to the French revolution in 1789, missionaries, explorers, and traders carved out niches for France in Canada, the Louisiana territory, several Caribbean islands, and parts of India, which were lost along with Canada to Great Britain in 1763 (Harvey 1980).

The foundations of the second French empire were established between 1830 and 1870. In Great Britain the drive for profit led expansion, but French colonialism was spurred more by the state, church, and armed forces than by pure business interests. France acquired Algeria and part of what eventually became Indochina (Cambodia, Laos, and Vietnam). By 1914 the French empire covered 4 million square miles and

FIGURE 18.1 Map of the British Empire in 1765 and 1914

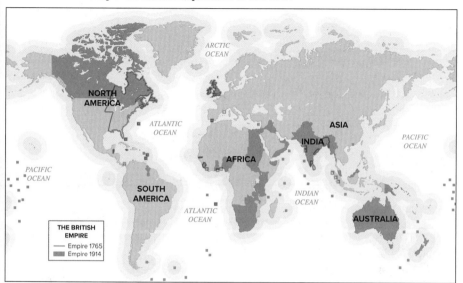

On January 1, 1900, a British officer in India receives a pedicure from a servant. What does this photo say to you about colonialism? Who gives pedicures in your society? Hulton Archive/ Getty Images

**FIGURE 18.2**   Map of the French Empire at Its Height around 1914

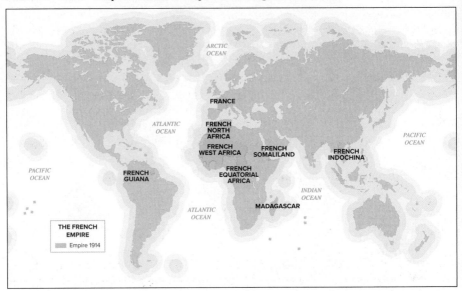

included some 60 million people (see Figure 18.2). By 1893, French rule had been fully established in Indochina. Tunisia and Morocco became French protectorates in 1883 and 1912, respectively (see Conklin, Fishman, and Zaretsky 2015).

To be sure, the French, like the British, had substantial business interests in their colonies, but they also sought, again like the British, international glory and prestige. The French promulgated a *mission civilisatrice*, their equivalent of Britain's "white man's burden." The goal was to implant French culture and language throughout the colonies.

The French used two forms of colonial rule: *indirect rule*, governing through local leaders and existing political structures, in areas with long histories of state organization, such as Morocco and Tunisia; and *direct rule* by French officials in many areas of Africa, where the French imposed new government structures to control diverse societies, many of them previously stateless. Like the British empire, the French empire began to disintegrate after World War II. France fought long—and ultimately futile—wars to keep its empire intact in Indochina and Algeria.

## Colonialism and Identity

Many geopolitical labels in the news today had no equivalent meaning before colonialism. Whole countries, along with social groups and divisions within them, were colonial inventions. In West Africa, for example, by geographic logic, several adjacent countries could be one (Togo, Ghana, Ivory Coast, Guinea, Guinea-Bissau, Sierra Leone, Liberia). Instead, they are separated by linguistic, political, and economic contrasts promoted under colonialism.

Hundreds of ethnic groups and "tribes" are colonial constructions (see Ranger 1996). The Sukuma of Tanzania, for instance, were first registered as a single tribe by the colonial administration. Then missionaries standardized a series of dialects into a single Sukuma language, into which they translated the Bible and other religious texts, and which they taught in missionary schools. Over time this standardized the Sukuma language and ethnicity (Finnstrom 1997).

In the East African countries of Rwanda and Burundi, farmers and herders live in the same areas and speak the same language. Historically they have shared the same social world, although their social organization is "extremely hierarchical," almost "castelike" (Malkki 1995, p. 24). There has been a tendency to see the pastoral Tutsis as superior to the agricultural Hutus. Tutsis have been presented as nobles, Hutus as commoners. Yet when distributing identity cards in Rwanda, the Belgian colonizers simply identified all people with more than 10 head of cattle as Tutsi. Owners of fewer cattle were registered as Hutu (Bjuremalm 1997). Years later, these arbitrary colonial registers were used systematically for "ethnic" identification during the mass killings (genocide) that took place in Rwanda in 1994 (see Totten and Ubaldo 2011).

## Postcolonial Studies

In anthropology, history, and literature, the field of postcolonial studies has gained prominence since the 1970s (see Ashcroft, Griffiths, and Tiffin 2013; Nayar 2016; Stoler 2013). **Postcolonial** studies focus on the past and present interactions between European nations and the societies they colonized (mainly after 1800). In 1914, European empires ruled more than 85 percent of the world (see Streets-Salter and Getz 2016). The term *postcolonial* also has been used to describe the second half of the 20th century in general,

A postcolonial woman on the Mekong River in southern Vietnam, February 2018. Which European empire once ruled Vietnam?
Conrad P. Kottak

the period following colonialism. Even more generically, *postcolonial* may be used to signify a position against colonialism, imperialism, and Eurocentrism (Buettner 2016; Petraglia-Bahri 1996; Stoler 2013). Eurocentrism refers to interpretations of the world that rely mainly or entirely on European or Anglo-American perspectives.

The former colonies (*postcolonies*) can be divided into settler, nonsettler, and mixed (Petraglia-Bahri 1996). The settler countries, with large numbers of European colonists and sparser native populations, include Australia and Canada. Examples of nonsettler countries include India, Pakistan, Bangladesh, Sri Lanka, Malaysia, Indonesia, Nigeria, Senegal, Madagascar, and Jamaica. All these had substantial native populations and relatively few European settlers. Mixed countries include South Africa, Zimbabwe, Kenya, and Algeria. Such countries had significant European settlement despite having sizable native populations.

Given the varied experiences of such countries, *postcolonial* has to be a loose term. The United States, for instance, was colonized by Europeans and fought a war for independence from Britain. Is the United States a postcolony? It usually isn't perceived as such, given its current world power position, its treatment of Native Americans (sometimes called internal colonialism), and its annexation of other parts of the world. Research in postcolonial studies is growing, permitting a wide-ranging investigation of power relations in varied contexts. Broad topics in the field include the formation of empires, the impact of colonization, and the state of the postcolony today.

## Development

During the Industrial Revolution, a strong current of thought viewed industrialization as a beneficial process of organic development and progress. Many economists still assume that industrialization increases production and income. They seek to create in today's "developing" countries a process like the one that first occurred spontaneously in 18th-century Great Britain.

We have seen that Britain used the notion of "the white man's burden" to justify its imperialist expansion and that France claimed to be engaged in a *mission civilisatrice*, a civilizing mission, in its colonies. Both these ideas illustrate an **intervention philosophy,** an ideological justification for outsiders to guide native peoples in specific directions. Economic development plans also have intervention philosophies. John Bodley (2012) argues that the basic belief behind interventions—whether by colonialists, missionaries, governments, or development planners—has been the same for more than a century. This belief is that industrialization, Westernization, and individualism are desirable evolutionary advances that will bring long-term benefits to local people.

### Neoliberalism

One currently influential intervention philosophy is neoliberalism. This term encompasses a set of assumptions that gained influence during the past 30 years. Neoliberal policies are being implemented in many developing nations, including postsocialist societies (e.g., those of the former Soviet Union). **Neoliberalism** is the current form of the classic economic liberalism laid out in Adam Smith's famous capitalist manifesto, *The Wealth of Nations,* published in 1776, soon after the Industrial Revolution. Smith advocated

An engraving of Scottish political philosopher and economist Adam Smith (1723–1790) made by a contemporary artist of his time. In his famed capitalist manifesto, *The Wealth of Nations,* published in 1776, Smith advocated "free" enterprise and competition, with the goal of generating profits. Source: Library of Congress [LC-USZ62-101759]

laissez-faire (hands-off) economics as the basis of capitalism: The government should stay out of its nation's economic affairs. Free, unregulated trade, Smith argued, is the best way for a nation's economy to develop. There should be no restrictions on manufacturing, no barriers to commerce, and no tariffs. This philosophy is called "liberalism" because it aims at liberating, or freeing, the economy from government controls. Economic liberalism encouraged "free" enterprise and competition, with the goal of generating profits. (Ironically, Adam Smith's liberalism is similar to today's capitalist "conservatism.")

Economic liberalism prevailed in the United States until President Franklin Roosevelt's New Deal during the 1930s. The Great Depression produced a turn to Keynesian economics, which challenged liberalism. John Maynard Keynes (1927, 1936) insisted that full employment was necessary for capitalism to grow, that governments and central banks should intervene to increase employment, and that government should promote the common good.

Especially since the fall of Communism (1989–1991), there has been a widespread revival of neoliberalism. Around the world, neoliberal policies have been imposed by powerful financial institutions such as the International Monetary Fund (IMF), the World Bank, and the Inter-American Development Bank (see Edelman and Haugerud 2005). Neoliberalism entails open (tariff- and barrier-free) international trade and investment. Profits are increased by lowering costs, whether by improving productivity, automating, laying off workers, or seeking workers who accept lower wages. In exchange for loans, the governments of postsocialist and developing nations have been required to accept the neoliberal premise that deregulation leads to economic growth, which will eventually benefit everyone through a process sometimes called "trickle down." Accompanying the belief in free markets and the idea of cutting costs is a tendency to impose austerity measures that cut government expenses. This can entail reduced public spending on education, health care, and other social services.

In the United States, the Trump administration has departed from neoliberal policies traditionally favored by his Republican Party. Trump's suspicion of unfettered trade and "unfair trade deals" led his administration to (1) impose tariffs on goods imported from China and other countries and (2) abandon or modify trade agreements designed to facilitate freer trade among partners to the pact. One example of such a pact is NAFTA, the North American Free Trade Agreement. Signed in 1992, NAFTA was to gradually eliminate most tariffs and other trade barriers on products and services passing between the United States, Canada, and Mexico.

## Neoliberalism and NAFTA's Economic Refugees

Most Americans know about large-scale Mexican migration to the United States since the 1990s. Most are unaware, however, that the direction of migration has shifted in recent years. Since 2008, more Mexicans have returned to Mexico than have entered the United States. Americans also are familiar with rhetoric (e.g., during the 2016 presidential campaigns and thereafter under President Trump) about negative effects of trade agreements on American workers.

Much less common is knowledge about how NAFTA has been harmful to Mexico. Anthropologist Ana Aurelia López (2011) has argued convincingly that international forces, including new technologies and NAFTA, have destroyed traditional Mexican farming systems, degraded agricultural land, and displaced Mexican farmers and small-business people—thereby fueling the migration of millions of undocumented Mexicans to the United States. The following account summarizes her findings.

For thousands of years, Mexican farmers grew corn (maize) in a sustainable manner. Generation after generation, farmers selected diverse strains of corn well adapted to a huge variety of specific microclimates. Mexico became a repository of corn genetic diversity for the world. When corn grown elsewhere developed disease or pest susceptibility or was of poor quality, Mexico provided other countries with genetically superior plants.

Before NAFTA, Mexico supported its farmers by buying a portion of their harvest each year at an elevated cost through price supports. This corn went to a countrywide chain of successful CONASUPO (Compañia Nacional de Subsistencias Populares) stores, which sold corn and other staple foodstuffs below market price to the urban and rural poor. Tariffs protected Mexican farmers from the entrance of foreign corn, such as that grown in the United States.

The first assault on Mexico's sustainable farming culture began in the 1940s when "Green Revolution" technologies were introduced, including seeds that required chemical inputs (e.g., fertilizers). The Mexican government encouraged farmers to replace their traditional, genetically diverse *maíz crillo* ("creole corn") with the genetically homogenized *maíz mejorado* ("improved corn"), a hybrid from the United States. Agrochemical companies initially supplied the required chemical inputs free of charge.

Company representatives visited rural villages and offered free samples of seeds and agrochemicals to a few farmers. As news of unusually large first-year crops spread, other farmers abandoned their traditional corn strains for the "improved," chemically dependent corn. As the transition accelerated, the price of both the new seeds and the associated chemical inputs began to rise and kept on rising. Eventually farmers no longer could afford either the seeds or the required agrochemicals. When cash-strapped farmers tried to return to planting their former *maíz criollo* seeds, the plants would grow but corn would not appear. Only the hybrid seeds from the United States would produce corn on the chemically altered soils. Over 60 percent of Mexico's farmland has been degraded by the spread of agrochemicals—chemical fertilizers and pesticides. (This chapter's "Anthropology Today" describes another case of environmental degradation due to chemical pollution, with mining as the culprit.)

NAFTA, which went into effect in 1994, proved to be another major assault on the Mexican farming system. The agreement forced Mexico to restructure its economy along neoliberal lines. The government had to end its price supports for corn grown by small-scale farmers. Also ended were Mexico's CONASUPO food stores, which had benefited the rural and urban poor.

These terminations caused considerable harm to Mexico's farmers and its urban and rural poor. American agricultural industries, by contrast, have benefited from NAFTA. Prior to NAFTA, Mexico's tariffs made the sale of U.S. corn in Mexico unprofitable.

In Mexico City, on January 2, 2008, Mexican farmers protest the end of import protections for their country's corn and bean crops. Corn, beans, sugar, and milk had been granted 15-year import protections when the North American Free Trade Agreement, or NAFTA, was negotiated in 1993. Eduardo Verdugo/AP Images

Under NAFTA, Mexico's corn tariffs were phased out, and corn from the United States began flooding the Mexican markets.

The NAFTA economy offered Mexico's small-scale corn farmers few options: (1) stay in rural Mexico and suffer, (2) look for work in a Mexican city, or (3) migrate to the United States in search of work. NAFTA did not create a common labor market (i.e., the ability of Mexicans, Americans, and Canadians to move freely across each country's borders and work legally anywhere in North America). Nor did NAFTA make provisions for the predicted 15 million Mexican corn farmers who would be forced off the land as a result of the trade agreement. As could have been expected (and planned for), millions of Mexicans seeking a livelihood migrated to the United States.

As a result of NAFTA, Mexican corn farmers have fled the countryside, and U.S.-subsidized corn has flooded the Mexican market. A declining number of traditional farmers remain to plant and conserve Mexico's unique corn varieties. Between one-third and one-half of Mexico's corn now is imported from the United States, much of it by U.S.-based Archer-Daniels-Midland, the world's largest corporate corn exporter. NAFTA also has facilitated the entrance of other giant U.S. corporations into Mexico: Walmart, Dow Agribusiness, Monsanto, and Coca-Cola. These multinationals, in turn, have displaced many small Mexican businesses, creating yet another wave of immigrants—former shopkeepers and their employees—to the United States.

We can summarize the impact of NAFTA on the Mexican economy: destroying traditional small-scale farming, degrading farmland, displacing farmers and small-business people, and fueling massive migration to the United States. In migrating, these millions of economic refugees have faced daunting challenges, including separation from their families and homeland, dangerous border crossings, and the ever-present possibility of deportation from the United States. As of this writing, under President Trump, their fate has become even more uncertain. In 2018 the United States, Mexico, and Canada agreed to modify NAFTA, renaming it the United States–Mexico–Canada Agreement, or USMCA. This modified trade pact must still be ratified by the legislatures of the three partner countries. Until it is finalized and implemented, its costs and benefits to Mexico, the United States, and Canada remain unclear.

As contemporary forces transform rural landscapes worldwide, rural-to-urban and transnational migration have become global phenomena. Over and over again, Green Revolution technologies have converted subsistence into cash economies, fueling a need for money to acquire foreign inputs while hooking the land on chemicals, reducing genetic diversity and sustainability, and forcing the poorest farmers off the land. Few Americans are aware, specifically, of NAFTA's role in ending a 7,000-year-old sustainable farming culture and displacing millions of Mexicans and, more generally, that comparable developments are happening all over the world.

## Communism, Socialism, and Postsocialism

The labels *First World, Second World,* and *Third World* represent a common, although ethnocentric, way of categorizing nations. The *First World* refers to the "democratic West"—traditionally conceived in opposition to a *Second World* ruled by Communism.

The *Second World* refers to the former Soviet Union and the socialist and once-socialist countries of Eastern Europe and Asia. Proceeding with this classification, the "less-developed countries," or "developing nations," make up the *Third World*.

## Communism

The two meanings of communism involve how it is written, whether with a lowercase (small) or an uppercase (large) *c*. Small-*c* **communism** describes a social system in which property is owned by the community and in which people work for the common good. Large-*C* **Communism** was a political movement and doctrine seeking to overthrow capitalism and to establish a form of Communism such as that which prevailed in the Soviet Union (USSR) from 1917 to 1991. The heyday of Communism was a 40-year period from 1949 to 1989, when more Communist regimes existed than at any time before or after. Today only 5 Communist states remain—China, Cuba, Laos, North Korea, and Vietnam, compared with 23 in 1985.

Communism, which originated with Russia's Bolshevik Revolution in 1917 and took its inspiration from Karl Marx and Friedrich Engels, was not uniform over time or among countries. All Communist systems were *authoritarian* (promoting obedience to authority rather than individual freedom). Many were *totalitarian* (banning rival parties and demanding total submission of the individual to the state). The Communist Party monopolized power in every Communist state, and relations within the party were highly centralized and strictly disciplined. Communist nations had state ownership, rather than private ownership, of the means of production. Finally, all Communist regimes, with the goal of advancing communism, cultivated a sense of belonging to an international movement (Brown 2001).

## Postsocialist Transitions

**Socialism** is a sociopolitical organization and economic system in which the means of production are owned and controlled by the government, rather than by individuals or corporations. Because of their state ownership, Communist nations were also socialist, and their successors are referred to as postsocialist. Neoliberal economists assumed that dismantling and privatizing the Soviet Union's planned economy would raise gross domestic product (GDP) and living standards. The goal was to enhance production by substituting a free market system and providing incentives through privatization. In October 1991, Boris Yeltsin, who had been elected president of Russia that June, announced a program of radical market-oriented reform, pursuing a postsocialist changeover to capitalism. Yeltsin's program of "shock therapy" cut subsidies to farms and industries and ended price controls.

During the 1990s, postsocialist Russia endured a series of disruptions, leading to declines in its GDP, average life expectancy, and birth rate, as well as increased poverty. In 2008–2009, Russia shared in the global recession after 10 years of economic growth, but its economy recuperated rapidly and was growing again by 2010, as were its birth rate and average life expectancy. The poverty rate has fallen substantially since the late 1990s, and Moscow is said to be home to more billionaires than New York City or London (Rapoza 2012). In recent years, rising wages have been offset by rising living costs and galloping inflation.

## The World System Today

The spread of industrialization continues today, although nations have shifted their positions within the world system. By 1900, the United States had become a core nation, having overtaken Great Britain in iron, coal, and cotton production. In a few decades (1868–1900), Japan changed from a medieval handicraft economy to an industrial one, joining the semiperiphery by 1900 and moving to the core between 1945 and 1970. India and China have joined Brazil as leaders of the semiperiphery. The map in Figure 18.3 shows the world system today.

Twentieth-century industrialization added hundreds of new industries and millions of new jobs. Production increased, often beyond immediate demand, spurring strategies, such as advertising, to sell everything industry could churn out. Mass production gave rise to a culture of consumption, which valued acquisitiveness and conspicuous consumption (see Meneley 2018).

How do things stand today? Worldwide, young people are abandoning traditional subsistence pursuits and seeking cash. A popular song once queried, "How're you gonna keep 'em down on the farm after they've seen Paree?" Nowadays most people *have* seen Paree—Paris, that is—along with other world capitals, maybe not in person but in print or on screen. Young people today are better educated and wiser in the ways of the world than ever before. Increasingly they are exposed to the material and cultural promises of a better life away from the farm. They seek paying jobs, but work is scarce, spurring migration within and across national boundaries. If they can't get cash legally, they seek it illegally.

**FIGURE 18.3    The World System Today**

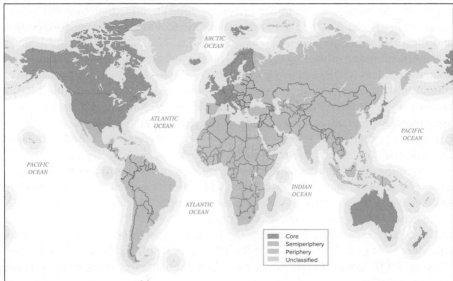

In the aftermath of the global recession of 2007–2009, job opportunities diminished in core nations, including the United States and Western Europe. In a global economy, profitability doesn't necessarily come from hiring workers who are fellow citizens. Jobs continue to be outsourced from core nations to the semiperiphery and the periphery. Machines and information technology continue to replace people. Corporations, from airlines to banks, offer their customers incentives to bypass humans. Even outside the industrial world, but especially within it, the Internet allows an increasing number of people to buy plane tickets, print boarding passes, rent cars, reserve hotel rooms, move money, or pay bills online. Amazon has become a virtual department store that has sent, or threatens to send, not only "mom and pop" shops but even national chains such as Barnes and Noble, Office Depot, and Sears into oblivion. Nowadays, when one does manage to speak by phone to a human, that person is as likely to be in Mumbai or Manila as Minneapolis or Miami.

Companies claim, with some justification, that labor unions limit their flexibility, adaptability, and profitability. American corporations (and the politicians who represent them) have become more ideologically opposed to unions and more aggressive in discouraging unionization. Unions still bring benefits to their workers. Median weekly earnings for union members—$1,051 in 2018—remain higher than those of nonunion workers—$860. Still, union membership in the United States keeps falling. The unionized percentage of the American workforce was 10.5 percent in 2018, down from 20.1 percent in 1983 and a high of 35 percent during the mid-1950s. The number of unionized private-sector workers increased from 7.1 million in 2010 to 7.6 million in 2018, while the number of public-sector union members declined from 7.6 million to 7.2 million. This mainly reflected growth in private-sector jobs, while jobs in the public sector were being reduced. The union membership rate of public-sector workers (33.9 percent) remains more than five times higher than that of private-sector workers (6.4 percent) (All 2018 figures are from the U.S. Bureau of Labor Statistics [2019]). What jobs do you know that are unionized? How likely is it that you will join a union?

## Anthropology Today  Mining Giant Compatible with Sustainability Institute?

The spread of industrialization has contributed to the destruction of indigenous economies, ecologies, and populations. Riverine discharges from the Ok Tedi mine, described here, have severely harmed about 50,000 people living in more than 100 villages downstream. Today, multinational corporations, along with the governments of nations such as Papua New Guinea (PNG), are accelerating the process of resource depletion that began with the Industrial Revolution. Fortunately, however, today's world also contains environmental watchdogs, including concerned anthropologists, lawyers, and NGOs (see Kirsch 2006, 2018). Described here is a conundrum faced by a major public university. Are multinational corporations, whose operations have destroyed the landscapes and livelihoods of indigenous peoples, proper advisers for an institute devoted to ecological sustainability?

*continued*

## Anthropology Today *continued*

In the 1990s, the giant mining company now known as BHP Billiton drew worldwide condemnation for the environmental damage caused by its copper and gold mine in Papua New Guinea. Its mining practices destroyed the way of life of thousands of farming and fishing families who lived along and subsisted on the rivers polluted by the mine, and it was only after being sued in a landmark class-action case that the company agreed to compensate them.

Today several activists and academics who work on behalf of indigenous people around the world say the company continues to dodge responsibility for the problems its mines create. . . .

Yet at the University of Michigan at Ann Arbor, BHP Billiton . . . is one of 14 corporate members of an External Advisory Board for the university's new Graham Environmental Sustainability Institute.

Critics at and outside the university contend that Michigan's decision to enlist BHP Billiton as an adviser to an institute devoted to sustainability reflects badly on the institution and allows the company to claim [an undeserved] mantle of environmental and social responsibility. . . .

The arguments echo the discussions about corporate "greenwashing" that have arisen at Stanford University and the University of California at Berkeley over major research grants from ExxonMobil and BP, respectively. . . .

For one BHP Billiton critic at Michigan, the issue is personal. Stuart Kirsch, a professor of anthropology, has spent most of his academic career documenting the damage caused by BHP Billiton's Ok Tedi mine in Papua New Guinea. . . .

Mr. Kirsch, who first visited some of the affected communities as a young ethnographer in 1987, became involved in the class-action lawsuit brought against the company and helped villagers participate in the 1996 legal settlement. "I put my career on hold while being an activist," he says.

He subsequently published several papers related to his work with the Yonggom people as they fought for recognition and compensation from mine operators—scholarship that helped him win tenure. . . . He remains involved with the network of activists and academics who follow mining and its impact on undeveloped communities around the world. . . .

The company's practices polluted the Ok Tedi and Fly Rivers and caused thousands of people to leave their homes because the mining-induced flooding made it impossible for them to grow food to feed themselves, says Mr. Kirsch.

BHP Billiton, based in Australia, later acknowledged that the mine was "not compatible with our environmental values," and spun it off to an independent company that pays all of its mining royalties to the government of Papua New Guinea.

But Mr. Kirsch says that in doing so, the company skirted responsibility for ameliorating the damage it caused. BHP Billiton says it would have preferred to close the mine, but the Papua New Guinea government, in need of the mine revenues, pressed to keep it open. The deal freed BHP Billiton from any future liabilities for environmental damage. . . .

Illtud Harri, a BHP Billiton spokesman, says the company regrets its past with Ok Tedi but considers its pullout from the mine "a responsible exit" that left in place a system that supports educational, agricultural, and social programs for the people of the community. . . .

BHP Billiton, a company formed from the 2001 merger of the Australian mining enterprise Broken Hill Proprietary Company with London-based Billiton, is now the world's largest mining company, with more than 100 operations in 25 countries. . . .

The BHP Billiton charter includes a statement that the company has "an over-riding commitment to health, safety, environmental responsibility, and sustainable development." But its critics say the company continues to play a key role in mining projects with questionable records on environmental and human rights, even though in many of those cases, it is not directly responsible. . . .

BHP Billiton has the resources to present itself as the "golden boy," but, says Mr. Kirsch, "it's much harder to see the people on the Ok Tedi and Fly rivers."

A forum could help to right that imbalance, he says. "Let the students and faculty decide whether this is an appropriate company to advise the University of Michigan," says Mr. Kirsch. "It would be an educational process for everyone involved."

**Update:** *As of this writing (2019), BHP Billiton has become the world's largest mining company. It no longer is listed as a member of the advisory board of Michigan's Graham Institute. And in Papua New Guinea, after BHP Billiton transferred its ownership of the mine to Ok Tedi Mining Limited, that company has spent more than a billion dollars on environmental remediation. The 1996 settlement (finalized in 2002) decreed that BHP would be spared future legal claims in return for giving all its shares to the people of PNG. Those shares funded a trust (now valued at over $1.4 billion, and growing) held by a*

A demonstration at the mouth of the Fly River, Papua New Guinea, on April 1, 2010. The protesters called attention not only to pollution, but to the loss of their homes due to soil erosion. The Asahi Shimbun/Getty Images

*continued*

**Anthropology Today** *continued*

Singapore-based entity, PNG Sustainable Development Program Limited. The mission of that trust is to promote development in PNG's Western Province, where the mine is located, and across PNG. As of 2019, 67 percent of Ok Tedi Mining Limited is owned by the PNG State, with the balance held by landowners and the government of PNG's Western Province. For hundreds of miles down the Fly River, fishers and farmers still complain about the destruction of their habitat, even as the Ok Tedi mine supplies about 16 percent of PNG's national revenue.

**Sources:** Blumenstyk, Goldie, "Mining Company Involved in Environmental Disaster Now Advises Sustainability Institute at U. of Michigan," *Chronicle of Higher Education*, December 7, 2007. Copyright 2007. All rights reserved. Used with permission

## Summary

1. Local societies increasingly participate in wider systems—regional, national, and global. The capitalist world economy depends on production for sale, with the goal of maximizing profits. The key claim of world-system theory is that an identifiable social system, based on wealth and power differentials, extends beyond individual countries. That system is formed by a set of economic and political relations that has characterized much of the globe since the 16th century. World capitalism has political and economic specialization at the core, semiperiphery, and periphery.

2. Columbus's voyages opened the way for a major exchange between the Old and New Worlds. Seventeenth-century plantation economies in the Caribbean and Brazil were based on sugar. In the 18th century, plantation economies based on cotton arose in the southeastern United States.

3. The Industrial Revolution began in England around 1760. Transoceanic commerce supplied capital for industrial investment. Industrialization hastened the separation of workers from the means of production. Marx saw a sharp division between the bourgeoisie and the proletariat. Class consciousness was a key feature of Marx's view of this stratification. Weber believed that social solidarity based on ethnicity, religion, race, or nationality could take priority over class. Today's capitalist world economy maintains the contrast between those who own the means of production and those who don't, but the division is now worldwide. There is a substantial contrast between not only capitalists but also workers in the core nations and workers on the periphery.

4. Inequality in measures of income and wealth has been increasing in the United States. Another aspect of inequality is in exposure to environmental risks such as pollution and hazardous waste facilities. Communities that are poorer and predominantly minority, such as Flint, Michigan, are most likely to be the victims of toxic waste exposure.

5. Imperialism is the conscious policy of extending the rule of a nation or an empire over other nations and of taking and holding foreign colonies. Colonialism is the domination of a territory and its people by a foreign power for an extended time. European colonialism had two main phases. The first started in 1492 and lasted through 1825. For Britain this phase ended with the American Revolution. For France it ended when Britain won the Seven Years' War, forcing the French to abandon Canada and India. For Spain, it ended with Latin American independence. The second phase of European colonialism extended approximately from 1850 to 1950. The British and French empires were at their height around 1914, when European empires controlled 85 percent of the world. Britain and France had colonies in Africa, Asia, Oceania, and the New World.

6. Many geopolitical labels and identities were created under colonialism that had little or nothing to do with existing social demarcations. The new ethnic or national divisions were colonial inventions, sometimes aggravating conflicts.

7. Like colonialism, economic development has an intervention philosophy that provides a justification for outsiders to guide native peoples toward particular goals. Development usually is justified by the idea that industrialization and modernization are desirable evolutionary advances. Neoliberalism revives and extends classic economic liberalism: the idea that governments should not regulate private enterprise and that free market forces should rule. This intervention philosophy currently dominates aid agreements with postsocialist and developing nations.

8. Spelled with a lowercase c, *communism* describes a social system in which property is owned by the community and in which people work for the common good. Spelled with an uppercase C, *Communism* indicates a political movement and doctrine seeking to overthrow capitalism and to establish a form of Communism such as that which prevailed in the Soviet Union from 1917 to 1991. The heyday of Communism was between 1949 and 1989. The fall of Communism can be traced to 1989–1990 in Eastern Europe and 1991 in the Soviet Union. Postsocialist states have followed the neoliberal agenda, through privatization, deregulation, and democratization.

9. By 1900 the United States had become a core nation. Mass production gave rise to a culture that valued acquisitiveness and conspicuous consumption. As subsistence economies yield increasingly to cash, job seeking and unemployment have become global problems. One effect of industrialization has been an accelerated rate of resource depletion.

## Think Like an Anthropologist

1. According to world-system theory, societies are subsystems of bigger systems, with the world system as the largest. What are the various systems, at different levels, in which you participate?

2. To what extent is the following statement still true: "The wealth that flows from periphery and semi-periphery to core has helped core capitalists maintain their profits while satisfying the demands of core workers." Are core workers still satisfied? What factors might diminish their level of satisfaction?

**Key Terms**

bourgeoisie, *451*
capital, *447*
capitalist world
    economy, *446*
colonialism, *457*
communism, *467*
Communism, *467*
core, *447*

imperialism, *457*
Industrial
    Revolution, *449*
intervention
    philosophy, *462*
neoliberalism, *462*
periphery, *447*
postcolonial, *461*

semiperiphery, *447*
socialism, *467*
working class, or
    proletariat, *451*
world-system
    theory, *447*

# Chapter 19

# Anthropology's Role in a Globalizing World

## Globalization and Global Issues

This chapter applies an anthropological perspective to contemporary global issues. Let's begin by reviewing two different meanings of the term *globalization*. As used in this book, the primary meaning of globalization is worldwide connectedness. Modern systems of transportation, communication, and finance are global in scope. There are interlinked systems of production, distribution, and consumption that extend across all nations and regions. A second meaning of globalization is political; it has to do with ideology, policy, and neoliberalism (see Kotz 2015). In this more limited sense, globalization refers to efforts by international financial powers to create a global free market for goods and services. This second, political meaning of globalization has generated and continues to generate significant opposition. In this book, *globalization* is a neutral term for the fact of global connectedness and linkages, rather than any kind of political position (see also Eriksen 2014; Ervin 2014).

The fact that certain practices and risks have global implications warrants a discussion of energy consumption and environmental degradation, including climate change, or global warming. Also considered in this chapter are the threats that deforestation and emerging diseases pose to global biodiversity and human life. The second half of this chapter turns from ecology to the contemporary flows of people, technology, finance, information, messages, images, and ideology that contribute to a global culture of consumption. Part of globalization is intercultural communication, through the media, travel, and migration, which increasingly bring people from different societies into direct contact. Finally, we'll consider how such contacts and external linkages affect indigenous peoples, as well as how those groups have organized to confront and deal with national and global issues.

It would be impossible in a single chapter (or even book) to do a complete review of all the global issues that are salient today and that anthropologists have studied. Many such issues (e.g., war, terrorism, displacement, transnational migration and refugees, nongovernmental organizations, the media) have been considered in previous chapters. For timely anthropological analysis of a range of global issues, see recent books by John Bodley (2012, 2015, 2017), Shirley Fedorak (2014), and Richard Robbins (2014).

## Energy Consumption and Industrial Degradation

Industrialization entailed a shift from reliance on renewable resources to the use of fossil fuels. Earth's supply of oil, gas, and coal is being depleted to support a previously unknown level of consumption. The average American, for example, consumes about 35 times as much energy as the average forager or tribesperson (Bodley 2015).

Table 19.1 compares energy consumption in the United States and selected other countries—the top 12 consumers of energy. Overall the United States, which ranks second among the countries, accounts for over 16 percent of the world's annual energy consumption. China ranks first at 23 percent. Notice that North Americans—Canadians and Americans—rank high in per-capita consumption. The average American consumes 3 times the energy used by the average Chinese and 11 times the energy used by the average inhabitant of India. Consumption has been increasing faster, however, in China and India than in the United States, Canada, and Europe.

Many contemporary nations are repeating—at an accelerated rate—the process of resource depletion that began in Europe and the United States during the Industrial Revolution. Fortunately, however, today's world has some environmental watchdogs that did not exist during the Industrial Revolution. Given the appropriate political will, leading to national and international cooperation and sanctions, the modern world may benefit from the lessons of the past (see Hornborg, McNeill, and Martinez-Alier 2007).

There are, however, new dangers in today's world, some of which have become worldwide in scope. Accompanying globalization are significant risks that can spread rapidly beyond individual countries. Thanks to modern transportation systems, diseases that break out in one part of the world can quickly become global threats, such as Ebola in 2014 and Zika in 2015–2016. Furthermore, accompanying the actual threat that a disease might go global is the heightened risk perception, augmented by the media, that makes people think that anyone anywhere might succumb to a disease that is confined almost

TABLE 19.1    **Energy Consumption for the Top 12 Countries, 2017**

Source: BP. 2018. BP Statistical Review of World Energy, 67th ed.

| | Total (MTOE) | Share of World Energy Consumption (percent) | Rate of Annual Increase (percent) | Per-Capita Energy Consumption (MTOE) |
|---|---|---|---|---|
| World | 13,511 | 100.0 | 2.2 | 1.8 |
| China | 3,132 | 23.2 | 3.1 | 2.2 |
| United States | 2,235 | 16.5 | 0.6 | 6.9 |
| India | 754 | 5.6 | 4.6 | 0.6 |
| Russia | 698 | 5.2 | 1.5 | 4.8 |
| Japan | 456 | 3.4 | 1.4 | 3.6 |
| Canada | 349 | 2.6 | 3.2 | 9.5 |
| Germany | 335 | 2.5 | 2.4 | 4.0 |
| South Korea | 296 | 2.2 | 1.6 | 5.7 |
| Brazil | 294 | 2.2 | 0.8 | 1.4 |
| Iran | 275 | 2.0 | 6.3 | 3.4 |
| Saudi Arabia | 268 | 2.0 | 1.7 | 8.1 |
| France | 238 | 1.8 | −0.1 | 3.5 |

Note: MTOE–million tons of oil equivalent.

entirely to a particular region. Another global threat, which can spread even faster than a disease, is a cyberattack. We should fear cyber viruses as well as real ones. We have become so reliant on the Internet that anything that might seriously impede the flow of information in cyberspace would have worldwide repercussions.

Dangers that can affect people anywhere and everywhere on the planet are part of a *globalization of risk*. Risks are no longer merely local, like the Flint, Michigan, water crisis, or regional, like a drought or devastating wildfires in California. They have become global in scope. People tend to worry more about short-term threats, such as toxic water or Ebola, and middle-term dangers, such as terrorism, than about long-term threats such as global climate change.

## Global Climate Change

Each consumer of fossil fuels makes his or her personal contribution (that consumer's "carbon footprint") to global climate change. The fact that there are now about 7.6 billion of those "footprints" has major global significance. Globally, the last five years (2014–2018) have been the warmest on record. This increase is not due to increased solar radiation. The causes are mainly **anthropogenic**—caused by humans and their activities. Who can reasonably doubt that 7.6 billion people, along with their animals, crops, machines, and increasing use of fossil fuels, have a greater environmental impact than the 5 million or so pre-Neolithic hunter-gatherers estimated to have lived on our planet 12,000 years ago?

## Emissions and Global Warming

The year 2016 surpassed 2015 as the world's hottest year on record. One reason for the extreme heat in 2016 was an unusually large El Niño weather pattern, which pumped a substantial amount of heat into the atmosphere. Even more significant has been the long-term planetary warming caused by human emissions of greenhouse gases (Gillis 2016b). NASA scientists ranked 2017, which was not an El Niño year, as the second-warmest year since reliable record-keeping began in 1880, trailing only 2016. The National Oceanic and Atmospheric Administration (NOAA), which uses a different analytical method, ranked 2017 third, behind 2016 and 2015 (Fountain, Patel, and Popovich 2018). (The year 2018 ranked fourth, and 2019 seemed destined to become the warmest year on record because of a projected El Niño event exacerbated by overall global warming.)

The **greenhouse effect** is a natural phenomenon that keeps the Earth's surface warm. The greenhouse gases include water vapor ($H_2O$), carbon dioxide ($CO_2$), methane ($CH_4$), nitrous oxide ($N_2O$), halocarbons, and ozone ($O_3$). Without those gases, life as we know it wouldn't exist. Like a greenhouse window, those gases allow sunlight to enter the atmosphere and then trap heat, preventing it from escaping.

The amount of carbon dioxide in the atmosphere has fluctuated naturally in the past. When $CO_2$ emissions increase, the Earth heats up, ice melts, and sea levels rise. Since the Industrial Revolution, humans have been pumping carbon dioxide (and other greenhouse gases) into the air faster than nature ever did (Gillis 2015). The global atmospheric carbon dioxide ($CO_2$) concentration has now passed 400 parts per million. The last time this happened was 3 million years ago, when global temperatures and sea levels were significantly higher than today. Continued growth in $CO_2$ emissions could produce an atmospheric concentration not experienced in tens to hundreds of millions of years (Wuebbles 2017). This buildup continues and has even accelerated (Pierre-Louis 2018). China produces 27 percent of global emissions, followed by the United States at 15 percent, the European Union at 10 percent, and India at 7 percent (Pierre-Louis 2018).

## Climate Change

Scientists prefer the more general and inclusive term **climate change** to *global warming*, as the phenomenon involves both warming and cooling processes. Contemporary manifestations of global climate change include rising temperatures (surface, atmospheric, and oceanic); melting glaciers; reduced snow cover; shrinking sea ice; rising sea levels; ocean acidification; increasing atmospheric water vapor; and changing storm patterns.

Oceans are particularly sensitive to small fluctuations in the Earth's temperature. During the 19th century, as industrialization proceeded, sea levels began to rise, and they continue to do so. Globally, the average sea level has risen 7–8 inches since 1900. About 3 inches of that rise has occurred since 1993. Tidal flooding has accelerated in more than 25 Atlantic and Gulf Coast cities. In the decade between 1955 and 1964, a tide gauge at Annapolis, Maryland, measured 32 days of flooding. Fifty years later, between 2005 and 2014, that figure jumped to 394 days. In Charleston, South Carolina, flood days increased from 34 in the earlier decade to 219 between 2005 and 2014 (Gillis 2016a). Sea levels are projected to rise by several more inches in the next 15 years, and by 1–4 feet by 2100 (Wuebbles 2017). Sea-level rise is projected to be higher than the global average on the East and Gulf Coasts of the United States.

Flooding in downtown Charleston, South Carolina, on October 15, 2015: A resident surveys his flooded street. Mladen Antonov/AFP/Getty Images

When Hurricane Harvey inundated parts of Houston, Texas, with over 4 feet of water in August 2017, the National Weather Service needed two new colors for its rainfall maps. Areas of dark purple and lavender now show amounts of rain from 20 to 30 inches, and above. The weather service labeled Harvey "historic and unusual." More than 80 people died as streets and homes were flooded with muddy, toxic water (Graef 2017).

The intensity and destructiveness of the 2017 hurricane season (Hurricanes Harvey, Irma, and Maria) suggests the immediacy of climate change. Previous predictions of extreme events have become a reality: In just a few weeks, the United States and the Caribbean experienced rapidly intensifying storms and record-breaking rainfall. Writing for Climate.gov, meteorologist Tom Di Liberto (2017) notes that climate change "does not, by itself, *cause* hurricanes . . . but it can certainly make a hurricane's impacts worse," because warmer seas and air increase the strength and intensity of storms (quoted in Graef 2017).

Global energy demand is the single greatest obstacle to slowing down climate change. Worldwide, energy consumption continues to grow with economic and population expansion. China and India, in particular, continue their rapidly increasing use of fossil fuels and, consequently, their emissions. New Delhi has become one of the world's most polluted cities. Pollution has been a significant problem in Chinese cities as well.

China currently accounts for about 23 percent of world energy consumption, compared with 9 percent in 2000. The U.S. share has fallen from 25 percent in 2000 to 16.5 percent today (refer back to Table 19.1). Among the alternatives to fossil fuels are nuclear power and renewable energy technologies such as solar, wind, and biomass generators.

In the global economy, India (shown here) and China in particular have increased their use of fossil fuels and, consequently, their emissions of $CO_2$. This photo shows school children in New Delhi on November 3, 2016, when a blanket of heavy smog sent air pollution to dangerous levels. Some 16 million people had to breathe this toxic air. Experts warned of severe health problems for children forced to attend school. What's the most polluted place you've ever been to?
Arvind Yadav/Hindustan Times/Getty Images

In 2015, the American Anthropological Association (AAA) issued a "Statement on Humanity and Climate Change," which can be found at http://s3.amazonaws.com/rdcms-aaa/files/production/public/anthropology_and_climate_change.pdf. That statement makes several key points, including the following:

- Human cultures and actions are the most important causes of the dramatic environmental changes that have taken place during the last 100 years. Two key factors influencing climate change are (1) reliance on fossil fuels as the primary energy source, and (2) an ever-expanding culture of consumption.

- Climate change will accelerate migration, destabilize communities, and exacerbate the spread of infectious diseases.

- Most affected will be people living on coasts, in island nations, and in high-latitude (e.g., far north) and high-altitude (e.g., very mountainous) areas (see also Tehan 2017).

- The tendency has been to address climate change at the international and national levels. We also need planning at the regional and local levels, because the impacts of climate change vary in specific locales. Affected communities, perhaps working with anthropologists, must be active participants in planning how to adapt to climate change—and in implementing those plans (see also Baer and Singer 2018; Singer 2019).

# Environmental Anthropology

Anthropology always has been concerned with how environmental forces influence humans and how human activities affect the environment. The 1950s–1970s witnessed the emergence of an area of study known as cultural ecology, or **ecological anthropology** (see Haenn et al. 2016). That field focused on how cultural beliefs and practices helped human populations adapt to their environments, as well as how people used elements of their culture to maintain their ecosystems. Ecological anthropologists showed that many indigenous groups had traditional ways of categorizing resources and using them sustainably (see Blewitt 2018; Dagne 2015). The term **ethnoecology** describes a society's set of environmental perceptions and practices (see Vinyeta and Lynn 2013).

Outside forces increasingly challenge indigenous ethnoecologies. Given national and international incentives to exploit and degrade, ethnoecological systems that once preserved local and regional environments increasingly are ineffective or irrelevant (see Dove et al. 2011). Anthropologists routinely witness threats to the people they study and their environments. Among such threats are commercial logging, mining, industrial pollution, and the imposition of external management systems on local ecosystems (see Johnston 2009). Today's ecological anthropology, *environmental anthropology*, attempts not only to understand but also to find solutions to environmental problems. Such problems must be tackled at the national and international levels (e.g., global warming).

Local people and their landscapes, ideas, values, and traditional management systems face attacks from all sides (see Hornborg, Clark, and Hermele 2011). Outsiders attempt to remake native landscapes and cultures in their own image. The aim of many agricultural development projects, for example, seems to be to make the world as much like a midwestern American agricultural state as possible (see Giugale 2017). Often there is an attempt to impose mechanized farming and nuclear family ownership, even though these institutions may be inappropriate in areas far removed from the midwestern United States. Anthropologists know that development projects usually fail when they try to replace indigenous institutions with culturally alien concepts.

## Global Assaults on Local Autonomy

A clash of cultures related to environmental change may occur when development threatens indigenous peoples and their environments (see this chapter's "Anthropology Today"). A different kind of culture clash related to environmental change may occur when external regulation aimed at conservation impinges on indigenous peoples and their ethnoecologies. Like development projects, conservation schemes may ask people to change their ways in order to satisfy planners' goals rather than local goals. In places as different as Madagascar, Brazil, and the Pacific Northwest of the United States, people have been asked, told, or forced to abandon basic economic activities because to do so is good for "nature" or "the globe." "Good for the globe" has not played very well in Brazil, whose Amazon region has been a focus of international environmentalist attention. Brazilians complain that outsiders (e.g., Europeans and North Americans) promote "global needs" and "saving the Amazon" after having destroyed their own primary forests for economic growth. Conservation efforts always face local opposition when they promote radical changes without involving local people in planning and carrying out the policies that affect them. When people are asked to give up the basis of their livelihood, they usually resist.

The spread of environmentalism may reveal radically different notions about the "rights" and value of plants and animals versus humans. In Madagascar, many intellectuals and officials complain that foreigners seem more concerned about lemurs and other endangered species than about the people of Madagascar (the Malagasy). As a geographer there remarked to me, "The next time you come to Madagascar, there'll be no more Malagasy. All the people will have starved to death, and a lemur will have to meet you at the airport." Most Malagasy perceive human poverty as a more pressing problem than animal and plant survival.

On the other hand, who can doubt that conservation, including the preservation of biodiversity, is a worthy goal? The challenge for applied ecological anthropology is to devise culturally appropriate strategies to conserve biodiversity in the face of unrelenting population growth and commercial expansion. How does one get people to support conservation measures that may, in the short run at least, diminish their access to resources? Like development plans in general, the most effective conservation strategies pay attention to the needs and wishes of the local people.

## Deforestation

Generations of anthropologists have studied how human economic activities (ancient and modern) affect the environment. Anthropologists know that food producers (farmers and herders) typically do more to degrade the environment than foragers do. Population increase and the need to expand farming caused deforestation in many parts of the ancient Middle East and Mesoamerica (see Cairns 2015; Hornborg and Crumley, 2007). Even today, many farmers think of trees as giant weeds to be removed and replaced with productive fields.

Often, deforestation is demographically driven—caused by population pressure. For example, Madagascar's population has been growing at a rate of 3 percent annually, doubling every generation. Population pressure leads to migration, including rural-to-urban migration. Madagascar's capital city, Antananarivo, had only 100,000 people in 1967. Its metropolitan population today is around 3 million. Urban growth promotes deforestation if city dwellers rely on fuelwood from the countryside, as is true in Madagascar. As forested watersheds disappear, crop productivity declines. Madagascar is known as the "great red island," after the color of its soil. On that island, the effects of soil erosion and water runoff are visible to the naked eye. Looking at its rivers, Madagascar might seem to be bleeding to death. Increasing runoff of water no longer trapped by trees causes erosion of low-lying rice fields near swollen rivers, as well as siltation in irrigation canals (Kottak 2007).

Globally, the causes of deforestation include demographic pressure (from births or immigration) on subsistence economies, commercial logging, road building, cash cropping, fuelwood needs associated with urban expansion, and clearing and burning associated with livestock and grazing. The fact that forest loss has several causes has a policy implication: Different deforestation scenarios require different conservation strategies.

What can be done? On this question, applied anthropology weighs in, spurring policy makers to think about new conservation strategies. The traditional approach has been to restrict access to forested areas designated as parks, then employ park guards and punish violators. More recent strategies are more likely to consider the needs, wishes, and abilities of the people (often impoverished) living in and near the forest. Since effective conservation depends on the cooperation of the local people, their concerns must be addressed in devising conservation strategies.

Reasons to change behavior must make sense to local people (see Sillitoe 2007). In Madagascar, the economic value of the forest for agriculture (as an antierosion mechanism and reservoir of potential irrigation water) provides a much more powerful incentive against forest degradation than do such global goals as "preserving biodiversity." Most Malagasy have no idea that lemurs and other endemic species exist only in Madagascar. Nor would such knowledge provide much of an incentive for them to conserve the forests if doing so jeopardized their livelihoods.

To curb the global deforestation threat, we need conservation strategies that will work. Laws and enforcement may help reduce commercially driven deforestation caused by burning and clear-cutting. But local people also use and abuse forested lands. A challenge for the environmentally oriented applied anthropologist is to find ways to make forest preservation attractive to local people and ensure their cooperation. Applied anthropologists must work to make "good for the globe" good for the people (see Jodoin 2017; Wasson et al. 2012).

Applied anthropology uses anthropological perspectives to identify and solve contemporary problems that affect humans. Deforestation is one such problem. Here, women take part in a reforestation project in coastal Tanzania near Dar es Salaam. Ed Parker/Alamy Stock Photo

## Emerging Diseases

A number of potentially lethal infectious diseases have emerged and spread in the past few decades. These *emerging diseases* include HIV/AIDS, Ebola, West Nile, SARS (severe acute respiratory syndrome), Lyme disease, Zika, and various strains of influenza. Human activity has helped these diseases emerge and spread. Driven by factors including population increase, changing settlement patterns, and commercial expansion, humans have been encroaching on wild lands, particularly forests, and creating conditions that favor the spread of disease pathogens. In the Amazon, for example, one study showed that an increase in deforestation of just 4 percent produced a 50 percent increase in the incidence of malaria. This is because the mosquitoes that transmit malaria thrive in the right mix of sunlight and water in recently deforested areas (Robbins 2012).

A majority of emerging diseases are *zoonotic*—they spread from animals to humans. The transmission of diseases from wild to domesticated animals and then to humans has been going on since the Neolithic, when animals first were domesticated. Zoonotic diseases pose a huge threat today because of human population increase and forces of globalization.

Among the diseases that have jumped from woods and wildlife to humans through their domesticated animals is the Nipah virus, which began its migration from fruit bats to humans in South Asia. Because fruit bats have co-evolved with the Nipah virus for millions of years, it does little damage to their health. When the virus moves from bats into other species, however, it can be lethal. Fruit bats eat the pulp of fruit and spit out the residue. In rural Malaysia in 1999, an infected bat appears to have dropped a piece of chewed fruit into the food supply of a swine herd (a scenario depicted in the movie *Contagion*). The virus then spread from those pigs to humans. Of 276 people infected in Malaysia, 106 died. Eleven more people died in Singapore, when the virus was exported there via live pigs. South Asia has experienced a dozen smaller Nipah outbreaks in recent years.

Spillovers from wildlife to humans have quadrupled in the past half-century, reflecting increasing human encroachment on disease hotspots, especially in the tropics (Robbins 2012). HIV/AIDS originally jumped from chimpanzees to humans through bush-meat hunters in Africa, who kill and butcher chimps. Modern air travel contributes to the potential for a transnational outbreak or even a pandemic. (A *pandemic* is an epidemic with global scope.)

Biologists and doctors are acutely aware of the threat posed by zoonotic diseases. One international project, called PREDICT, funds teams of veterinarians, conservation biologists, medical doctors, and epidemiologists to identify disease-causing organisms in wildlife before they spread to humans (see http://www.vetmed.ucdavis.edu/ohi/predict/index.cfm). PREDICT, which is financed by the United States Agency for International Development (USAID), attempts to "predict," spot, and prevent the spread of zoonotic diseases from world areas with high potential for disease transmission. Some 24 countries in Africa, Latin America, and Asia participate in the program. PREDICT scientists monitor areas where deadly viruses are known to exist and where humans are encroaching.

PREDICT scientists also gather blood, saliva, and other samples from wildlife species to create a "library" of viruses, to facilitate identification when a threat is imminent. This library focuses on the animals most likely to carry diseases to people, such as primates, rats, and bats. PREDICT scientists also study ways of preventing disease transmission. Sometimes solutions can be remarkably simple. In Bangladesh, for example, outbreaks of the Nipah virus were contained by placing bamboo screens (which cost 8 cents each) over the containers used to collect date palm sap (Robbins 2012). Because humans, by modifying the environment, create the conditions that allow diseases to emerge and spread, anthropologists can contribute by studying the cultural (including economic) causes of environmental encroachment and by suggesting culturally appropriate and workable solutions. PREDICT is now part of USAID's larger https://www.usaid.gov/news-information/fact-sheets/emerging-pandemic-threats-program (EPT) program and is led by the One Health Institute at the University of California, Davis.

## Interethnic Contact

Since at least the 1920s, anthropologists have been interested in changes that take place where there is sustained contact between industrial and nonindustrial societies. The term *acculturation* refers to the cultural changes that occur when different societies come into continuous firsthand contact (Redfield, Linton, and Herskovits 1936). Most acculturation studies have focused on contact between Western and non-Western cultures. Often, this contact reflects Western domination over a non-Western society. In that case, the cultural patterns of the dominant Western society are more likely to be forced upon or accepted by the non-Western society than vice versa. However, the westerners who take up residence in a non-Western setting will also be affected by the cultural practices of that setting. In postcolonial times, people have been migrating from the former colonies to the former colonial nations. Inevitably, these migrants bring along their own cultural practices. It is not uncommon for their foods, music, art, and clothing styles to influence the cultural practices of the former colonial nation. If contact is sustained long enough, acculturation will be reciprocal—influencing both groups, even if one is influenced more than the other.

Although *acculturation* can be applied to any case of cultural contact and change, the term most often described **Westernization**—the influence of Western expansion on indigenous peoples and their cultures. Thus, local people who wear store-bought clothes, learn Indo-European languages, and otherwise adopt Western customs are called "acculturated." Acculturation may be voluntary or forced, and there may be considerable resistance to the process.

Different degrees of destruction, domination, resistance, survival, adaptation, and modification of native cultures may follow interethnic contact. In the most destructive encounters, native and subordinate cultures face obliteration. When contact with powerful outsiders seriously threatens an indigenous culture, a "shock phase" often follows the initial encounter (Bodley 2012). Outsiders may attack or exploit the native people. Such exploitation may increase mortality, disrupt subsistence, fragment kin groups, damage social support systems, and inspire new religious movements. During the shock phase, there may be civil repression backed by military force. Such factors may lead to the group's cultural collapse (*ethnocide*) or physical extinction (*genocide*).

## Cultural Imperialism and Indigenization

**Cultural imperialism** refers to the spread or advance of one culture at the expense of others, or its imposition on other cultures, which it modifies, replaces, or destroys—usually because of differential economic or political influence. Thus, children in the French colonial empire learned French history, language, and culture from standard textbooks also used in France. Tahitians, Malagasy, Vietnamese, and Senegalese learned the French language by reciting from books about "our ancestors the Gauls."

Some commentators see the mass media as erasing cultural differences by spreading dominant products and brands globally. Others focus on how particular groups and cultures use media to express themselves, survive, and even spread (see Lule 2018; Pace 2018). Across time and space, the Internet can and does transmit local and national happenings and expressions to a larger, perhaps global, audience. Think, for example, of YouTube's role in globalizing "Gangnam Style," a song and video originating in South Korea—and, more recently, in making Korean popular music (Kpop) and especially the hugely popular boy band BTS the global phenomena they are today.

A potter plies his trade for a group of observers (including the author) in Fez, Morocco, in February 2015. Increasingly, local communities perform "traditional" activities, especially ceremonies, celebrations, and arts and crafts for TV and tourists. Conrad P. Kottak

In Brazil, local practices, celebrations, and performances have changed in the context of outside forces, including the mass media and tourism. In the town of Arembepe (Kottak 2018), TV coverage stimulated increased participation in a traditional annual performance, the Chegança. This is a danceplay that reenacts the Portuguese discovery of Brazil. Arembepeiros have traveled to the state capital to perform the Chegança before television cameras, for a nationally televised program featuring traditional performances from many rural communities, and cameras have gone to Arembepe to record it. To see it, follow this link: https://www.youtube.com/watch?v=I6wpwW-Ofbc.

In several towns along the Amazon River, annual folk ceremonies now are staged more lavishly for TV and video cameras. In the Amazon town of Parantíns, for example, boatloads of tourists arriving any time of year are shown video-recorded images of the town's annual Bumba Meu Boi festival. This is a costumed performance mimicking bull-fighting, parts of which have been shown on national TV. This pattern, in which local communities preserve, revive, and intensify the scale of traditional ceremonies to perform for the media and tourists, is expanding. To see whether I could, I just managed to watch snippets of these two annual events in Arembepe and Parantíns on YouTube! (for the Parantíns festival, see https://www.youtube.com/watch?v=3WBO1y5EoT8).

In the process of globalization, people continually make and remake culture as they assign their own meanings to the information, images, and products they receive from outside. One example of such a process of **indigenization**—how a globally spreading

Illustrating indigenization, because of the Hindu taboo against beef consumption, the American Big Mac has, in India, become Chicken Maharaja Mac, advertised here in February, 2017.
Homeland photos/Alamy Stock Photo

Evangelical Protestantism adapts to local circumstances—was discussed in Chapter 15. Indigenization occurs in cultural domains as varied as fast food, music, housing styles, science, religion, terrorism, celebrations, and political ideas and institutions (Ellen, Lycett, and Johns 2013; Fiske 2011; Wilk 2006).

## A Global System of Images

With globalization, more people in many more places imagine "a wider set of 'possible' lives than they ever did before. One important source of this change is the mass media . . ." (Appadurai 1991, p. 197). The United States as a global media center has been joined by Canada, Japan, Western Europe, Brazil, Mexico, Nigeria, Egypt, India, and Hong Kong. Like print, the electronic mass media can diffuse the cultures of different countries within (and often beyond) their own boundaries, thus enhancing national cultural identity. For example, millions of Brazilians who formerly were cut off (by geographic isolation or illiteracy) from urban, national, and international events and information now participate in a larger "mediascape" (Appadurai 1991) through mass media and the Internet (Kottak 2009; Pace and Hinote 2013).

Brazil's most popular network (Rede Globo) relies heavily on its own productions, especially news and telenovelas (nightly serial programs often compared to American soap operas). Globo plays each night to one of the world's largest and most devoted audiences. The programs that attract this horde are made by Brazilians, for Brazilians.

On August 21, 2017, for example, 49 million Brazilians watched Globo's one-hour national newscast, *Jornal Nacional.* That is the typical audience size for this program, which is broadcast nightly at 8:30, in a country with 66.5 million TV homes. By contrast, the *combined* nightly viewership of the three network news broadcasts (ABC, CBS, and NBC) in the United States that same year was around 22 million, in a country with twice the number of TV homes as Brazil (Ariens 2017).

Television and the Internet also play a prominent role in maintaining ethnic and national identities among people who lead transnational lives. Arabic-speaking Muslims, including migrants in several countries, follow the TV network Al Jazeera, based in Qatar. As groups move, they can stay linked to each other and to their homeland through global media. **Diasporas** (people who have spread out from an original, ancestral homeland) have enlarged the markets for media, communication, brands, and travel services targeted at specific ethnic, national, or religious groups that now live in various parts of the world.

## A Global Culture of Consumption

Besides the media, other key global forces are production, commerce, and finance. As Arjun Appadurai (1991, p. 194) puts it, "money, commodities, and persons unendingly chase each other around the world." Residents of many Latin American communities now rely financially on outside cash, which their relatives who have migrated send back home. Also illustrating finance as a global force, the U.S. economy is increasingly influenced by foreign investment, especially from Britain, Canada, Germany, the Netherlands, Japan, and China. The American economy also has increased its dependence on foreign labor—through both the immigration of laborers and the outsourcing of jobs.

Business and the media have fueled a global culture of consumption, based on a craving for certain lifestyles and the products that go along with them. People also crave and consume knowledge and information, available through the media and the gadgets that allow media access (see Kennedy 2015). The media also provide connectivity and a forum for expressing shared sentiments. In the Middle East, for example, social media use exploded during the Arab Spring of 2011. In cyberspace, Middle Easterners found something missing from their ordinary, offline worlds: platforms permitting social connectivity and the collective airing of grievances. Since then, social media have entered the region commercially, in a big way. At least 60 percent of Middle Easterners have Internet access, and about 90 percent of them use social media regularly. WhatsApp is the number-one social media site, used by 67 percent of Middle Easterners, followed by Facebook at 63 percent and YouTube at 50 percent (see Northwestern University in Qatar, 2017).

This rapidly rising Middle Eastern Internet presence is occurring in an area where youths (younger than 24 years) make up between 50 and 65 percent of the population. The smartphone is another key element in the Middle Eastern marketing mediascape. The United Arab Emirates leads the world in smartphone penetration. A global survey by Google found that 93 percent of smartphone users notice mobile ads, and 39 percent of those follow up with an online purchase.

As further illustration of the global reach of the consumer culture, consider that few people have never seen a T-shirt advertising a Western product (see Gould 2016). American and English rock stars' recordings blast through the streets of Rio de Janeiro, while taxi drivers from Toronto to Antananarivo listen to Brazilian music. The popularity of Korean pop singers spreads internationally via the Internet. Peasants and tribal people participate in the modern world system not only because they have been hooked on cash but also because their products and images are appropriated by world capitalism. They are commercialized by others (like the Quileute nation in the *Twilight* series of books and movies). Furthermore, indigenous peoples also market their own images and products, through outlets like Cultural Survival.

## People in Motion

Globalization has both enlarged and erased old boundaries and distinctions. Arjun Appadurai (1990, p. 1) characterizes today's world as a "translocal" "interactive system" that is "strikingly new." Whether as refugees, migrants, tourists, pilgrims, proselytizers, laborers, businesspeople, development workers, politicians, terrorists, soldiers, sports figures, or media-borne images, people travel more than ever.

The scale of human movement has expanded dramatically. Migrants maintain their ties with home through social media, by phoning, emailing, texting, Skyping, WhatsApping, Facebooking, and FaceTiming. Frequently, they send money home; when possible, they also visit. In a sense, they live multilocally—in different places at once. Dominicans in New York City, for example, have been characterized as living "between two islands": Manhattan and the Dominican Republic (Grasmuck and Pessar 1991).

With so many people "in motion," the unit of anthropological study expands from the local community to the diaspora (see Wilson and Stierstorfer 2017). Anthropologists increasingly follow descendants of the villages we have studied as they move from rural to urban areas and across national boundaries. For an annual meeting of the American Anthropological Association held in Chicago, the anthropologist Robert Kemper once organized a session of presentations about long-term ethnographic fieldwork. Kemper's own longtime research focus was the Mexican village of Tzintzuntzan, which, with his mentor George Foster, he studied for decades. Eventually, their database expanded to include not only Tzintzuntzan but also its descendants all over the world. Given the Tzintzuntzan diaspora, Kemper was even able to use some of his time in Chicago to visit people from Tzintzuntzan who had established a colony there. In today's world, as people move, they take their traditions and their anthropologists along with them.

**Postmodernity** describes our time and situation: today's world in flux, these people on the move who have learned to manage multiple identities depending on place and context. In its most general sense, **postmodern** refers to the blurring and breakdown of established canons (rules or standards), categories, distinctions, and boundaries. The word is taken

With so many people on the move, the unit of anthropological study has expanded from the local community to the diaspora. This refers to the offspring of an area who have spread to many lands, such as the owners of this falafel shop in Paris, France. Lionel Derimais/VISUM/The Image Works

from **postmodernism**—a style and movement in architecture that succeeded modernism, beginning in the 1970s. Postmodern architecture rejected the rules, geometric order, and austerity of modernism. Modernist buildings were expected to have a clear and functional design. Postmodern design is "messier" and more playful. It draws on a diversity of styles from different times and places—including popular, ethnic, and non-Western cultures. Postmodernism extends "value" globally—well beyond classic, elite, and Western cultural forms. *Postmodern* now is used to describe comparable developments beyond architecture—in music, literature, and visual art. From this origin, postmodernity describes a world in which traditional standards, contrasts, groups, boundaries, and identities are opening up, reaching out, and breaking down.

New kinds of political and ethnic units have emerged along with globalization. In some cases, cultures and ethnic groups have banded together in larger associations. There is a growing pan–Native American identity as well as an international pantribal movement. Thus, in June 1992, the World Conference of Indigenous Peoples met in Rio de Janeiro concurrently with UNCED (the United Nations Conference on the Environment and Development). Along with diplomats, journalists, and environmentalists came 300 representatives of the tribal diversity that survives under globalization—from Lapland to Mali (see Maybury-Lewis et al. 2009).

## Indigenous Peoples

All too often, conquest, annexation, and development have been associated with genocide—the deliberate extermination of a specific ethnic group. Examples of genocide include the Holocaust, Rwanda in 1994, and Bosnia in the early 1990s. Bodley (2015) estimates that an average of 250,000 indigenous people perished annually between 1800 and 1950. The causes included warfare, outright murder, introduced diseases, slavery, land grabbing, and other forms of dispossession and impoverishment.

Remaining in the world today are more than 5,000 distinct groups of indigenous peoples, located in some 90 countries. Called Tribal Peoples, First Peoples, Native Peoples, and Indigenous Peoples, these original inhabitants call themselves by many names in their more than 4,000 languages. They constitute more than 5 percent of the world's population, numbering about 370 million people. They remain among the world's most disadvantaged and vulnerable populations. Many of them struggle to hold on to their lands and natural resources (see this chapter's "Anthropology Today").

All the indigenous groups that survive today live within nation-states. Often, they maintain a distinct ethnic identity, even if they have lost their ancestral languages and cultures to varying degrees. Many such groups aspire to autonomy. To describe these original inhabitants of their territories, the term *indigenous people* entered international law in 1982 with the creation of the United Nations Working Group on Indigenous Populations (WGIP). This group meets annually and has members from six continents. The UN General Assembly adopted its Declaration on the Rights of Indigenous Peoples in 2007. Convention 169, a document supporting cultural diversity and indigenous empowerment, was approved by the International Labor Organization (ILO) in 1989. Such documents, along with the global work of the WGIP, have influenced governments,

Representatives of indigenous people from around the world attended this meeting in Paris, France, on December 12, 2015. The larger event held that day was a march for climate justice, which threatens many indigenous groups. Monika Skolimowska/picture alliance/Getty Images

NGOs, and international agencies to adopt policies favorable to indigenous peoples. In May 2012, the United Nations sponsored a high-level commemoration of the fifth anniversary of the adoption of the UN Declaration on the Rights of Indigenous Peoples (see Doyle 2015; Drahos 2014). In September 2014, the United Nations hosted a World Conference on Indigenous Peoples, to reiterate the UN's ongoing role in promoting and protecting the rights of indigenous peoples (see http://www.un.org/en/ga/69/meetings/indigenous/#&panel1-1). Social movements worldwide use *indigenous people* as a self-identifying label in their quests for social, cultural, and political rights (Brower and Johnston 2007; de la Peña 2005).

In Spanish-speaking Latin America, social scientists and politicians favor the term *indígena* (indigenous person) over *indio* (Indian), the colonial term that European conquerors used for Native Americans (de la Peña 2005). Until the mid to late 1980s, Latin American public policy emphasized assimilation, rather than maintenance of indigenous identities. Since then, the emphasis has shifted dramatically from biological and cultural assimilation—*mestizaje*—to identities that value difference, especially as indigenous peoples.

In Ecuador, for example, groups seen previously as Quichua-speaking peasants are classified now as indigenous communities with their own territories. Brazil has recognized 30 new indigenous communities in the northeast, a region previously seen as having lost its native population. Guatemala, Nicaragua, Brazil, Colombia, Mexico, Paraguay, Ecuador, Argentina, Bolivia, Peru, and Venezuela now are officially multicultural (Jackson and Warren 2005). Several national constitutions recognize the rights of indigenous peoples to cultural distinctiveness and political representation.

Ceuppens and Geschiere (2005) comment on an upsurge, in multiple world areas, of the notion of *autochthony* (being native to, or formed in, the place where found), with an implicit call for excluding strangers. The terms *autochthony* and *indigenous* go back to classical Greek history, with similar implications. *Autochthony* refers to self and soil. *Indigenous* literally means "born inside," with the connotation in classical Greek of being born "inside the house." Both notions stress the rights of first-comers to privileged status and protection versus later immigrants—legal or illegal (Ceuppens and Geschiere 2005; Hornborg et al. 2011).

During the 1990s, autochthony became an issue in many parts of Africa, inspiring violent efforts to exclude (European and Asian) "strangers." Simultaneously, autochthony became a key notion in debates about immigration and multiculturalism in Europe. European majority groups have claimed the label *autochthon*. This term highlights the prominence that the exclusion of strangers has assumed in day-to-day politics worldwide (Ceuppens and Geschiere 2005). One familiar example is the United States, as represented in ongoing debates over undocumented immigration.

**Essentialism** describes the process of viewing an identity (e.g., an ethnic or indigenous label) as established, real, and frozen, thus ignoring the historical processes within which that identity was forged. Identities, however, are not fixed. We saw in Chapter 16 that identities can be fluid and multiple. People draw on particular, sometimes competing, self-labels and identities. Some Peruvian groups, for instance, self-identify as *mestizos* but still see themselves as indigenous. Identity is a fluid, dynamic process, and there are multiple ways of being indigenous. Neither speaking an indigenous language nor wearing "native" clothing is required (Jackson and Warren 2005).

## Anthropology's Lessons

Anthropology teaches us that the adaptive responses of humans are more flexible than those of other species because our main adaptive means are sociocultural. However, in the face of globalization, the cultural institutions of the past always influence subsequent adaptation, producing continued diversity in the actions and reactions of different groups as they indigenize global inputs. Anthropology offers a people-centered vision of social change for today's world. The existence of anthropology is itself a tribute to the continuing need to understand similarities and differences among human beings throughout the world.

Anthropology offers relevant, indeed powerful, ways of understanding how the world works. To benefit humanity, lessons of the past can and should be applied to the present and future. Anthropologists know that civilizations and world powers rise and fall, and that social transformations typically follow major innovations, such as the Neolithic and the Industrial Revolution. There is little chance that the current world system and the power relations within it will last forever. Whatever it may be, our social future will trace its origins to our social present. That is, future developments will need to build on, modify, and perhaps discard preexisting practices and institutions. What trends observable in the world today are most likely to transform society in the long run? Using your new knowledge of anthropology, try to imagine possible futures for humanity.

## Anthropology Today   *Diversity under Siege: Global Forces and Indigenous Peoples*

Around the globe, diversity is under siege. In Alaska, which has been warming twice as fast as the rest of the United States, displaced villagers have become climate change refugees—forced to move as rising sea levels have eroded and flooded their settlements. In the South Pacific, Marshall Islanders also face rising seas, which render their villages increasingly uninhabitable and their land too salty for productive agriculture (Davenport and Haner 2015). In the Brazilian Amazon, outside settlers, including farmers, cattle herders, gold prospectors, and commercial loggers, are illegally encroaching on areas reserved for indigenous groups. A combination of forces at work globally, including climate change and development, are threatening the lifestyles, livelihoods, and even the lives of indigenous peoples.

We focus now on the Norwegian Arctic, where a Sami (Lapp) population of about 100,000 traditional reindeer herders extends over a vast territory—northern areas of Norway, Sweden, Finland, and Russia's Kola Peninsula. Sami nomads once moved their herds seasonally across this expanse, paying little attention to national borders. Today, a mere one-tenth of the total Sami population, Western Europe's only indigenous Arctic group, continues to herd reindeer for a living (Wallace 2016).

Sami herder Johann Anders Oskal and his brother tend their reindeer herd in Troms County, Norway (January 27, 2016). Scott Wallace/Hulton Archive/Getty Images

The Sami way of life is being destroyed incrementally rather than by a major project or event. The cumulative effects of a series of smaller constructions, including roads and pipelines, have reduced Norway's undisturbed reindeer habitat by 70 percent in the past century. Like so many other indigenous peoples, the Sami must compete with powerful external interests for use of their traditional (grazing) lands. For generations, the Sami have lived under state organization. The state allows the Sami to graze their herds, but the land belongs to the national government. The Sami must deal with decisions made at the national level by planners, legislators, and the courts. What is good for the nation and business interests often takes precedence over what may be best for local people.

External inputs have been both positive and negative. The group benefits from the use of GPS collars and smartphone apps to track their animals, and snowmobiles and all-terrain vehicles to round them up. On the negative side, the steady encroachment of industrial infrastructure has reduced their range and freedom of movement. Current threats include dams, roads, live-fire military drills, high-voltage power lines, wind farms, and a copper mine. Many Sami now have to move their herds by truck and boat between summer and winter pastures—a costly operation. When courts approved large-scale projects that negatively affected the Sami, the herders received only a one-time payment as compensation for their losses (Wallace 2016).

Norway is proceeding with plans to extract more resources and build more industry in the Arctic. The Sami fear that their languages and culture, largely sustained by herding, will ultimately be sacrificed to benefit the larger society. The government has ambitious targets for renewable energy, including more hydroelectric and wind power projects. These projects, although possibly "good for the globe," negatively affect reindeer herding, as well as Arctic biodiversity, wilderness landscapes, and traditional subsistence activities. A proposed wind farm (now under judicial review) and associated power lines would encroach substantially on the summer grazing lands of a group of herders who still speak South Sami, a language listed by UNESCO as endangered (Wallace 2016).

In addition to the threats from development, the Sami have an ongoing conflict with the military. Since the Cold War, Norwegian soldiers have been a regular presence in Sami country, preparing for a possible Russian incursion across northern Scandinavia. These troops stage regular, often daily, war exercises, including live gunfire. Herders must be vigilant to avoid flying bullets as they go about their activities. (The information about contemporary Sami in this feature comes mainly from Wallace 2016.)

Even the most enlightened governments pursue policies that are incompatible with preserving the traditional activities and lifestyles of indigenous peoples. Like certain conservation schemes aimed at preserving biodiversity, efforts that are good for the globe, such as the development of green energy sources, may not be best for local people. Planners must be attentive to the need to seek a delicate balance between what's good for the globe and what's good for the people.

## Summary

1. As used in this book, the primary meaning of globalization is *worldwide connectedness*, through contemporary systems of production, distribution, consumption, finance, transportation, and communication (including the Internet and other media). A second meaning of globalization is political, referring to efforts by international financial powers to create a global *free market* for goods and services.

2. Fueling global climate change are human population growth and use of fossil fuels, which produce greenhouse gases. The atmospheric concentration of those gases has increased since the Industrial Revolution, and especially since 1978. Climate change encompasses global warming along with changing sea levels, precipitation, storms, and ecosystem effects.

3. Anthropology always has been concerned with how environmental forces influence humans and how human activities affect the biosphere. Many indigenous groups did a reasonable job of preserving their ecosystems. An ethnoecology is any society's set of environmental practices and perceptions. Indigenous ethnoecologies increasingly are being challenged by global forces that work to exploit and degrade—and that sometimes aim to protect—the environment. The challenge for applied ecological anthropology is to devise culturally appropriate strategies for conservation in the face of unrelenting population growth and commercial expansion.

4. Deforestation is a major factor in the loss of global biodiversity. Causes of deforestation include demographic pressure (from births or immigration) on subsistence economies; commercial logging; road building; cash cropping; fuelwood needs associated with urban expansion; and clearing and burning associated with livestock and grazing. The fact that forest loss has several causes has a policy implication: Different deforestation scenarios require different conservation strategies. Applied anthropologists must work to make "good for the globe" good for the people.

5. The recent emergence and spread of infectious diseases like HIV/AIDS, Ebola, West Nile, SARS, Zika, and Lyme disease are the result of things people have done to their environments. The spread of zoonotic diseases from wild to domesticated animals and then to humans has been going on since the Neolithic. Because human groups create the conditions that allow zoonotic pathogens to jump species and to spread, anthropologists have a key role to play in studying the causes of environmental encroachment and in suggesting culturally appropriate solutions.

6. Cultural imperialism is the spread of one culture and its imposition on other cultures, which it modifies, replaces, or destroys—usually because of differential economic and political power. Some observers worry that modern technology, including the mass media, is destroying traditional cultures. But others see an important role for new technology in allowing local cultures to express themselves. As the forces of globalization spread, they are modified (indigenized) to fit local cultures. The mass media can help diffuse a national culture within and beyond its own boundaries. The media, including the Internet, also play a role in preserving ethnic and national identities among people who lead transnational lives.

7. People travel more than ever. But migrants also maintain ties with home, so they live multilocally. With so many people "in motion," the unit of anthropological study expands from the local community to the diaspora. *Postmodernity* describes this world in flux, with people on the move who manage multiple social identities depending on place and context. With globalization, new kinds of political and ethnic units are emerging as others break down or disappear.

8. Governments, NGOs, and international agencies have adopted policies designed to recognize and benefit *indigenous peoples*. Social movements worldwide have adopted this term as a self-identifying and political label based on past oppression but now signaling a search for social, cultural, and political rights. In Latin America, several national constitutions now recognize the rights of indigenous peoples. Identity is a fluid, dynamic process, and there are multiple ways of being indigenous.

## Think Like an Anthropologist

1. What does it mean to apply an anthropological perspective to contemporary global issues? Can you come up with an anthropological research question that investigates a global issue? Imagine you had a year (and the money!) to carry out this project. How would you spend your time and your resources?

2. The topic of global climate change has been hotly debated during the past few years. Why is there so much debate? Are you concerned about global climate change? Do you think everyone on the planet should be equally concerned and share the responsibility for doing something about it? Why or why not?

3. Consider majority and minority rights in the context of contemporary events involving religion, ethnicity, politics, and law. What kinds of rights should be granted based on religious beliefs? What kinds of groups, if any, within a nation should have special rights? How about indigenous peoples?

## Key Terms

anthropogenic, *477*
climate
  change, *478*
cultural
  imperialism, *486*
diaspora, *488*

ecological
  anthropology, *481*
essentialism, *493*
ethnoecology, *481*
greenhouse
  effect, *478*

indigenization, *487*
postmodern, *490*
postmodernism,
  *491*
postmodernity, *490*
Westernization, *485*

# Glossary

## A

**absolute dating** Dating techniques that establish dates in numbers or ranges of numbers; examples include the radiometric methods of $^{14}$C, K/A, $^{238}$U, TL, and ESR dating.

**acculturation** The exchange of cultural features that results when groups come into continuous firsthand contact; the original cultural patterns of either or both groups may be altered, but the groups remain distinct.

**Acheulean** Derived from the French village of St. Acheul, where these tools were first identified; Lower Paleolithic tool tradition associated with *H. erectus*.

**achieved status** Social status that comes through talents, actions, efforts, activities, and accomplishments, rather than ascription.

**adaptation** The process by which organisms cope with environmental stresses.

**adaptive** Favored by natural selection in a particular environment.

**African American Vernacular English (AAVE)** A rule-governed dialect of American English spoken by some African Americans in their casual, intimate speech.

**agriculture** A nonindustrial system of plant cultivation characterized by continuous and intensive use of land and labor.

**allele** A biochemical difference involving a particular gene.

**analogies** Similarities arising as a result of similar selective forces; traits produced by convergent evolution.

**anatomically modern humans (AMHs)** Including the Cro-Magnons of Europe (31,000 B.P.) and the older fossils from Jebel Irhoud (300,000 B.P.), Omo Kibish (195,000 B.P.), Misliya Cave (194,000–177,000 B.P.), Herto (160,000–154,000 B.P.), Skhūl (100,000 B.P.), and Qafzeh (92,000 B.P.); continuing through the present.

**ancient Beringians** Cousins to ancestral Native Americans, from whom they branched around 20,000 B.P. Ancient Beringians remained in Beringia and Alaska and left no living descendants.

**animism** Belief in souls or doubles.

**anthropogenic** Caused by humans and their activities.

**anthropoids** Monkeys, apes, and humans.

**anthropological archaeology** The branch of anthropology that reconstructs, describes, and interprets human behavior and cultural patterns through material remains; best known for the study of prehistory.

**anthropology** The study of the human species and its immediate ancestors.

**anthropology and education** Anthropological research in classrooms, homes, and neighborhoods, viewing students as total cultural creatures whose enculturation and attitudes toward education belong to a larger context that includes family, peers, and society.

**anthropometry** The measurement of human body parts and dimensions, including skeletal parts (*osteometry*).

**applied anthropology** The application of anthropological data, perspectives, theory, and methods to identify, assess, and solve contemporary social problems.

**arboreal** Tree-dwelling.

*Ardipithecus* The earliest widely accepted hominin genus (5.8–4.4 m.y.a.); includes species *kadabba* (earlier) and *ramidus* (later).

**ascribed status** Social status (e.g., race or gender) that people have little or no choice about occupying.

**assimilation** The process of change that a minority group may experience when it moves to a country where another culture dominates; the minority is incorporated into the dominant culture to the point that it no longer exists as a separate cultural unit.

***Au. (Australopithecus) afarensis*** Early form of *Australopithecus*, found in Ethiopia at Hadar ("Lucy") and in Tanzania at Laetoli; dating to the period between 3.8 and 3.0 m.y.a.

***Au. (Australopithecus) africanus*** First *Australopithecus* discovered, in South Africa; dating to 3.5–2.5 m.y.a.

***Au. (Australopithecus) anamensis*** Earliest form of *Australopithecus* yet discovered; found in Kenya and dating to 4.2 m.y.a.

***Au. (Australopithecus) garhi*** Found in Ethiopia in association with tools and dating to 2.6–2.5 m.y.a.

**australopiths** Varied group of Pliocene-Pleistocene hominins that includes the genera *Australopithecus* and *Paranthropus*.

**authority** The formal, socially approved use of power, e.g., by government officials.

**Aztec** The last independent state in the Valley of Mexico; the capital was Tenochtitlan. It thrived between 1325 C.E. and the Spanish conquest in 1520.

# B

**balanced polymorphism** Two or more forms, such as alleles of the same gene, that maintain a constant frequency in a population from generation to generation.

**balanced reciprocity** See *generalized reciprocity*.

**band** The basic unit of social organization among foragers. A band includes fewer than one hundred people; it often splits up seasonally.

**behavioral modernity** The advent of modern human behavioral capabilities based on symbolic thought and language, in addition to modern anatomy.

**big man** Figure often found among tribal horticulturalists and pastoralists. The big man occupies no office but creates his reputation through entrepreneurship and generosity to others. Neither his wealth nor his position passes to his heirs.

**biocultural** Referring to the inclusion and combination (to solve a common problem) of both biological and cultural approaches—one of anthropology's hallmarks.

**biological anthropology** The branch of anthropology that studies human biological diversity in time and space—for instance, hominid evolution, human genetics, human biological adaptation; also includes primatology (behavior and evolution of monkeys and apes). Also called *physical anthropology*.

**bipedal** Upright two-legged locomotion, the key feature differentiating early hominins from the apes.

**blade tool** The basic Upper Paleolithic tool type, hammered off a prepared core.

**bone biology** The study of bone as a biological tissue, including its genetics; cell structure; growth, development, and decay; and patterns of movement (biomechanics).

**bourgeoisie** One of Karl Marx's opposed classes; owners of the means of production (factories, mines, large farms, and other sources of subsistence).

**brachiation** Swinging, hand-over-hand movement through trees, characteristic of arboreal apes and some New World monkeys.

**broad-spectrum revolution** The period beginning around 20,000 B.P. in the Middle East and 12,000 B.P. in Europe, during which a wider range, or broader spectrum, of plant and animal life was hunted, gathered, collected, caught, and fished; considered revolutionary because it led to food production.

**bronze** An alloy of arsenic and copper or of tin and copper.

# C

**call systems** Systems of communication among nonhuman primates, composed of a limited number of sounds that vary in intensity and duration; tied to environmental stimuli.

**capital** Wealth or resources invested in business, with the intent of producing a profit.

**capitalist world economy** The single world system, which emerged in the 16th century, committed to production for sale, with the object of maximizing profits rather than supplying domestic needs.

**cargo cults**   Postcolonial, acculturative, religious movements common in Melanesia that attempt to explain European domination and wealth and to achieve similar success magically by mimicking European behavior.

**caste system**   A closed, hereditary system of stratification, often dictated by religion; hierarchical social status is ascribed at birth, so that people are locked into their parents' social position.

**catastrophism**   The view that extinct species were destroyed by fires, floods, and other catastrophes. After each destructive event, God created again, leading to contemporary species.

**chiefdom**   A form of sociopolitical organization intermediate between the tribe and the state; kin-based with differential access to resources and a permanent political structure. A ranked society in which relations among villages as well as among individuals are unequal, with smaller villages under the authority of leaders in larger villages; has a two-level settlement hierarchy.

**chromosomes**   Basic genetic units, occurring in matching (homologous) pairs; lengths of DNA made up of multiple genes.

**cisgender**   A person who still identifies with the gender assigned to them at birth.

**clan**   A unilineal descent group based on stipulated descent.

**climate change**   Global warming, plus changing sea levels, precipitation, storms, and ecosystem effects.

**Clovis tradition**   Stone technology based on a projectile point that was fastened to the end of a hunting spear; it flourished between 13,250 B.P. and 12,800 B.P. in North America.

**colonialism**   The political, social, economic, and cultural domination of a territory and its people by a foreign power for an extended time.

**communism**   Spelled with a lowercase c, describes a social system in which property is owned by the community and in which people work for the common good.

**Communism**   Spelled with a capital C, a political movement and doctrine seeking to overthrow capitalism and to establish a form of Communism such as that which prevailed in the Soviet Union (USSR) from 1917 to 1991.

**communitas**   An intense community spirit, a feeling of great social solidarity, equality, and togetherness; characteristic of people experiencing liminality together.

**conflict resolution**   The means by which disputes are socially regulated and settled; found in all societies, but the resolution methods tend to be more formal and effective in states than in nonstates.

**convergent evolution**   Independent operation of similar selective forces; the process by which analogies are produced.

**core**   The dominant structural position in the world system; consists of the strongest and most powerful states with advanced systems of production.

**core values**   Key, basic, or central values that integrate a culture and help distinguish it from others.

**correlation**   An association between two or more variables such that when one changes (varies), the other(s) also change(s) (covaries)—for example, temperature and sweating.

**creationism**   The explanation for the origin of species given in Genesis: God created the species during the original six days of Creation.

**cultivars**   Domesticated plants.

**cultivation continuum**   A continuum of land and labor use, with horticulture at one end and agriculture at the other.

**cultural anthropology**   The study of human society and culture; describes, analyzes, interprets, and explains social and cultural similarities and differences.

**cultural appropriation**   Taking or using, without permission or recompense, an aspect of someone else's heritage in inappropriate, harmful, or unwelcome ways.

**cultural colonialism**   Within a nation or an empire, domination by one ethnic group or nationality and its culture/ideology over others—e.g., the dominance of Russian people, language, and culture in the former Soviet Union.

**cultural consultant**   Someone the ethnographer gets to know in the field, who teaches him or her about the consultant's society and culture; also called an *informant.*

**cultural imperialism**   The rapid spread or advance of one culture at the expense of others, or its imposition on other cultures, which it modifies, replaces, or destroys—usually because of differential economic or political influence.

**cultural relativism**   The position that the values and standards of cultures differ and deserve respect. Anthropology is characterized by methodological rather than moral relativism: In order to understand another culture fully, anthropologists try to understand its members' beliefs and motivations. Methodological relativism does not preclude making moral judgments or taking action.

**cultural resource management (CRM)**   The branch of applied archaeology aimed at preserving sites threatened by dams, highways, and other projects. (CRM)

**cultural rights**   The doctrine that certain rights are vested not in individuals but in identifiable groups, such as religious and ethnic minorities and indigenous societies.

**cultural transmission**   A basic feature of language; transmission through learning.

**culture**   Traditions and customs that govern behavior and beliefs; distinctly human; transmitted through learning.

**cuneiform**   Early Mesopotamian writing that used a stylus (writing implement) to write wedge-shaped impressions on raw clay; from the Latin word for "wedge."

**curer**   A specialized role acquired through a culturally appropriate process of selection, training, certification, and acquisition of a professional image; the curer is consulted by patients, who believe in his or her special powers, and receives some form of special consideration; a cultural universal.

# D

**daughter languages**   Languages developing out of the same parent language; for example,

French and Spanish are daughter languages of Latin.

**Denisovans**   Cousins of the Neandertals who lived in Asia from roughly 400,000 to 50,000 B.P.

**descent**   A rule assigning social identity on the basis of some aspect of one's ancestry.

**descent group**   A permanent social unit whose members claim common ancestry; fundamental to tribal society.

**descriptive linguistics**   The scientific study of a spoken language, including its phonology, morphology, lexicon, and syntax.

**development anthropology**   The branch of applied anthropology that focuses on social issues in, and the cultural dimension of, economic development.

**diaspora**   The offspring of an area who have spread to many lands.

**differential access**   Unequal access to resources; a basic attribute of chiefdoms and states. Superordinates have favored access to such resources, while the access of subordinates is limited by superordinates.

**diffusion**   Borrowing between cultures either directly or through intermediaries.

**diglossia**   The existence of "high" (formal) and "low" (familial) dialects of a single language, such as German.

**discrimination**   Policies and practices that harm a group and its members.

**disease**   A scientifically identified health threat caused by genetics or a bacterium, virus, fungus, parasite, or other pathogen.

**displacement**   A linguistic capacity that allows humans to speak of things and events that are not present.

**domestic**   Within or pertaining to the home.

**domestic-public dichotomy**   The contrast between women's role in the home and men's role in public life, with a corresponding social devaluation of women's work and worth.

**dominant**   An allele that masks another allele in a heterozygote.

**dowry**   A marital exchange in which the wife's group provides substantial gifts to the husband's family.

# E

**ecological anthropology**   The study of cultural adaptations to environments.

**economy**   A population's system of production, distribution, and consumption of resources.

**egalitarian society**   A type of society, most typically found among foragers, that lacks status distinctions except for those based on age, gender, and individual qualities, talents, and achievements.

**emic**   The research strategy that focuses on native explanations and criteria of significance.

**empire**   A mature state that is large, multiethnic, militaristic, and expansive.

**enculturation**   The social process by which culture is learned and transmitted across the generations.

**endogamy**   Marriage between people of the same social group.

**essentialism**   The process of viewing an identity as established, real, and frozen, so as to hide the historical processes and politics within which that identity developed.

**estrus**   The period of maximum sexual receptivity in female baboons, chimpanzees, and other primates, signaled by vaginal area swelling and coloration.

**ethnic group**   A group distinguished by cultural similarities (shared among members of that group) and differences (between that group and others); ethnic group members share beliefs, values, habits, customs, norms, and a common language, religion, history, geography, kinship, and/or race.

**ethnicity**   Identification with, and feeling part of, an ethnic group and exclusion from certain other groups because of this affiliation.

**ethnocentrism**   The tendency to view one's own culture as best and to judge the behavior and beliefs of culturally different people by one's own standards.

**ethnocide**   Destruction by a dominant group of the culture of an ethnic group.

**ethnoecology**   A culture's set of environmental practices and perceptions.

**ethnography**   Fieldwork in a particular culture.

**ethnology**   The theoretical, comparative study of society and culture; compares cultures in time and space.

**etic**   The research strategy that emphasizes the observer's rather than the natives' explanations, categories, and criteria of significance.

**evolution**   Descent with modification; change in form over generations.

**excavation**   Digging through the layers of deposits that make up an archaeological site.

**exogamy**   Mating or marriage outside one's kin group; a cultural universal.

**expanded family household**   A household that includes a group of relatives other than, or in addition to, a married couple and their children.

**extended family household**   An expanded household that includes three or more generations.

# F

**family**   A group of people (e.g., parents, children, siblings, grandparents, grandchildren, uncles, aunts, nephews, nieces, cousins, spouses, siblings-in-law, parents-in-law, children-in-law) who are considered to be related in some way, for example, by "blood" (common ancestry or descent) or marriage.

**family of orientation**   The nuclear family in which one is born and grows up.

**family of procreation**   The nuclear family established when one marries and has children.

**fiscal**   Pertaining to finances and taxation.

**focal vocabulary**   A set of words and distinctions that are particularly important to certain groups (those with particular foci of experience or activity), such as types of snow to Eskimos or skiers.

**food production**   Cultivation of plants and domestication (stockbreeding) of animals; first developed in the Middle East 10,000 to 12,000 years ago.

**foraging**   An economy and way of life based on hunting and gathering.

**fossils**   Remains (e.g., bones), traces, or impressions (e.g., footprints) of ancient life.

# G

**gender identity** Identity based on whether a person feels, and is regarded as, male, female, or something else.

**gender roles** The tasks and activities that a culture assigns to each sex.

**gender stereotypes** Oversimplified but strongly held ideas about the characteristics of males and females.

**gender stratification** Unequal distribution of rewards (socially valued resources, power, prestige, and personal freedom) between men and women, reflecting their different positions in a social hierarchy.

**gene** The area in a chromosome pair that determines, wholly or partially, a particular biological trait, such as whether one's blood type is A, B, AB, or O.

**gene flow** The exchange of genetic material between populations of the same species through direct or indirect interbreeding.

**gene pool** All the alleles and genotypes within a breeding population—the "pool" of genetic material available.

**genealogical method** Procedures by which ethnographers discover and record connections of kinship, descent, and marriage, using diagrams and symbols.

**general anthropology** The field of anthropology as a whole, consisting of cultural, archaeological, biological, and linguistic anthropology.

**generality** A culture pattern or trait that exists in some but not all societies.

**generalized reciprocity** The principle that characterizes exchanges between closely related individuals: As social distance increases, reciprocity becomes balanced and finally negative.

**genetic evolution** Change in gene frequencies within a breeding population.

**genocide** Policies aimed at, and/or resulting in, the physical extinction (through mass murder) of a people perceived as a racial group, that is, as sharing defining physical, genetic, or other biological characteristics.

**genotype** An organism's hereditary makeup.

**glacials** The four or five major advances of continental ice sheets in northern Europe and North America.

**globalization** The accelerating interdependence of nations in a world system linked economically and through mass media and modern transportation systems.

**gracile** Small, slight; opposite of *robust*.

**greenhouse effect** Warming from trapped atmospheric gases.

# H

**H. (Homo) erectus** Hominin type that lived from approximately 1.9 to 500,000 m.y.a.; widely distributed throughout the Old World; immediate predecessor of *Homo sapiens*.

**H. (Homo) floresiensis** Diminutive small-brained hominins that inhabited the isolated Indonesian island of Flores between at least 700,000 B.P. and 60,000 B.P.

**H. (Homo) habilis** Early hominin species (1.9-1.44 m.y.a.), first discovered by L. S. B. and Mary Leakey in 1960; named *habilis*, meaning "able," for their presumed ability to make tools.

**H. (Homo) heidelbergensis** Hominin group that lived in Europe, Africa, and Asia from about 800,000 to about 200,000 B.P.

**Halafian** An early (7500-6500 B.P.) and widespread pottery style, first found in northern Syria; refers to a delicate ceramic style and to the period when the first chiefdoms emerged.

**haplogroup** A lineage or branch of a genetic tree marked by one or more specific genetic mutations.

**Haplorrhini** The primate suborder that includes lemurs, lorises, and their ancestors.

**health care systems** Beliefs, customs, and specialists concerned with ensuring health and preventing and curing illness; a cultural universal.

**hegemony** The internalization of a dominant ideology.

**Herto** Very early (160,000-154,000 y.a.) AMH fossils, found in Ethiopia.

**heterozygous** Having dissimilar alleles of a given gene.

**hilly flanks**   A woodland zone that flanks the Tigris and Euphrates Rivers to the north; a zone of wild wheat and barley and of sedentism (settled, nonmigratory life) preceding food production.

**historical linguistics**   The subdivision of linguistics that studies languages over time.

**holistic**   Interested in the whole of the human condition: past, present, and future; biology, society, language, and culture.

**Holocene**   The geological epoch beginning around 11,700 B.P.; the transition from foraging to food production took place during the early Holocene.

**hominid**   A member of the taxonomic family that includes humans and the African apes and their immediate ancestors.

**hominin**   A member of the human lineage after its split from ancestral chimps; used to describe all the human species that ever have existed, including the extinct ones, but excluding chimps and gorillas.

**hominoid**   The zoological superfamily that includes all fossil and living apes and hominins.

**homologies**   Traits that organisms have jointly inherited from their common ancestor.

**homozygous**   Possessing identical alleles of a particular gene.

**horticulture**   A nonindustrial system of plant cultivation in which plots lie fallow for varying lengths of time.

**human rights**   The doctrine that invokes a realm of justice and morality beyond and superior to particular countries, cultures, and religions. Human rights, usually seen as vested in individuals, include the rights to speak freely, to hold religious beliefs without persecution, and not to be enslaved.

**hypodescent**   A rule that automatically places the children of a union or mating between members of different socioeconomic groups in the less privileged group.

# I

**illness**   A condition of poor health perceived or felt by an individual.

**imperialism**   A policy of extending the rule of a nation or an empire over foreign nations and of taking and holding foreign colonies.

**incest**   Sexual relations with a close relative.

**increased equity**   A reduction in absolute poverty and a fairer (more even) distribution of wealth.

**independent assortment (Mendel's law of)**   Chromosomes are inherited independently of one another.

**independent invention**   Development of the same culture trait or pattern in separate cultures as a result of comparable needs and circumstances.

**indigenization**   The process by which cultural items introduced from outside are modified to fit the local culture.

**Industrial Revolution**   The historical transformation (in Europe, after 1750) of "traditional" into "modern" societies through industrialization of the economy.

**informed consent**   An agreement to take part in research, after the people being studied have been told about that research's purpose, nature, procedures, and potential impact on them.

**intellectual property rights (IPR)**   Each society's cultural base—its core beliefs and principles. IPR is claimed as a group right—a cultural right, allowing indigenous groups to control who may know and use their collective knowledge and its applications.

**interglacials**   Extended warm periods between such major glacials as Riss and Würm.

**international culture**   Cultural traditions that extend beyond national boundaries.

**intersex**   Pertaining to a group of conditions resulting from an unusual combination of the X and Y chromosomes, or discrepancies involving the external genitals (penis, vagina, etc.) and the internal genitals (testes, ovaries, etc.).

**intervention philosophy**   A guiding principle of colonialism, conquest, missionization, or development; an ideological justification for outsiders to guide native peoples in specific directions.

**interview schedule**   An ethnographic tool for structuring a formal interview. A prepared form (usually printed) that guides interviews with households or individuals being compared systematically. Contrasts with a questionnaire because the researcher has personal contact and records people's answers.

## K

**key cultural consultant**   An expert on a particular aspect of local life who helps the ethnographer understand that aspect. Also called *key informant.*

**kinesics**   The study of communication through body movements, stances, gestures, and facial expressions.

## L

**law**   A legal code, including trial and enforcement; characteristic of state-organized societies.

**levirate**   A custom by which a widow marries the brother of her deceased husband.

**lexicon**   Vocabulary; a dictionary containing all the morphemes in a language and their meaning.

**life history**   Of a cultural consultant; provides a personal cultural portrait of existence or change in a culture.

**liminality**   The critically important marginal or in-between phase of a rite of passage.

**lineage**   A unilineal descent group based on demonstrated descent.

**linguistic anthropology**   The branch of anthropology that studies linguistic variation in time and space, including interrelations between language and culture; includes *historical linguistics* and *sociolinguistics.*

**lobola**   A customary gift before, at, or after marriage from the husband and his kin to the wife and her kin.

**longitudinal research**   The long-term study of a community, society, culture, or other unit, usually based on repeated visits.

## M

**m.y.a.**   Million years ago.

**magic**   The use of supernatural techniques to accomplish specific aims.

**maize**   Corn; domesticated in highland Mexico.

**mana**   A sacred impersonal force in Melanesian and Polynesian religions.

**manioc**   Cassava; a tuber domesticated in the South American lowlands.

**market principle**   The profit-oriented principle of exchange that dominates in states, particularly industrial states. Goods and services are bought and sold, and values are determined by supply and demand.

**matrilineal descent**   A unilineal descent rule in which people join the mother's group automatically at birth and stay members throughout life.

**matrilocality**   Customary residence with the wife's relatives after marriage, so that children grow up in their mother's community.

**means (or factors) of production**   Land, labor, technology, and capital—major productive resources (or factors).

**medical anthropology**   A field that unites biological and cultural anthropologists in the study of disease, health problems, health care systems, and theories about illness in different cultures and ethnic groups.

**meiosis**   The special process by which sex cells are produced; four cells are produced from one, each with half the genetic material of the original cell.

**melanin**   A substance manufactured in specialized cells in the lower layers of the epidermis (outer skin layer); melanin cells in dark skin produce more melanin than do those in light skin.

**Mesoamerica**   "Middle America," including Mexico, Guatemala, and Belize.

**Mesolithic**   The tool-making tradition between the Upper Paleolithic and the Neolithic, based on very small stone tools—*microliths.*

**Mesopotamia**   The area between the Tigris and Euphrates Rivers in what is now southern Iraq and southwestern Iran; location of the first cities and states.

**metallurgy**   Knowledge of the properties of metals, including their extraction and processing and the manufacture of metal tools.

**mitosis**   Ordinary cell division; DNA molecules copy themselves, creating two identical cells out of one.

**mode of production**   Way of organizing production—a set of social relations through which labor is deployed to wrest energy from nature by means of tools, skills, and knowledge.

**molecular anthropology**   Genetic analysis, involving comparison of DNA sequences, to determine evolutionary links and distances among species and among ancient and modern populations.

**monotheism**   Worship of an eternal, omniscient, omnipotent, and omnipresent supreme being.

**morphology**   The study of form; used in linguistics (the study of morphemes and word construction) and for form in general—for example, biomorphology relates to physical form.

**Mousterian**   A Middle Paleolithic tool-making tradition associated with Neandertals.

**multiculturalism**   The view of cultural diversity in a country as something good and desirable; a multicultural society socializes individuals not only into the dominant (national) culture but also into an ethnic culture.

**mutation**   Change in the DNA molecules from which genes and chromosomes are built.

# N

**nation**   Once a synonym for *ethnic group,* designating a single culture sharing a language, religion, history, territory, ancestry, and kinship; now usually a synonym for *state* or *nation-state.*

**nation-state**   An autonomous political entity; a country like the United States or Canada.

**national culture**   Cultural experiences, beliefs, learned behavior patterns, and values shared by citizens of the same nation.

**nationalities**   Ethnic groups that once had, or wish to have or regain, autonomous political status (their own country).

**Natufians**   A widespread Middle Eastern culture, dated to between 15,000 and 11,700 B.P.; subsisted on intensive wild cereal collecting and gazelle hunting and had year-round villages.

**natural selection**   Originally formulated by Charles Darwin and Alfred Russel Wallace; the process by which nature selects the forms most fit to survive and reproduce in a given environment, such as the tropics.

**Neandertals**   Distinctive group of hominins that inhabited Europe (through Siberia) and the Middle East from 130,000 to 28,000 B.P.

**negative reciprocity**   See *generalized reciprocity.*

**neoliberalism**   A revival of Adam Smith's classic economic liberalism, the idea that governments should not regulate private enterprise and that free market forces should rule; a currently dominant intervention philosophy.

**Neolithic**   Referring to the "New Stone Age," a term coined to describe techniques of grinding and polishing stone tools; the first cultural period in a region in which the first signs of domestication are present.

**neolocality**   A postmarital residence pattern in which a couple establishes a new place of residence rather than living with or near either set of parents.

**norms**   Cultural standards or guidelines that enable individuals to distinguish between appropriate and inappropriate behavior in a given society.

# O

**office**   A permanent political position.

**Oldowan tools**   Early (2.6–1.8 m.y.a.) stone tools; first discovered in 1931 by L. S. B. and Mary Leakey at Olduvai Gorge.

**opposable thumb**    A thumb that can touch all the other fingers.

**overinnovation**    A characteristic of development projects that require major changes in people's daily lives, especially ones that interfere with customary subsistence pursuits.

# P

**paleoanthropology**    The study of hominin evolution and human life as revealed by the fossil record.

**Paleolithic**    Old Stone Age (from Greek roots meaning "old" and "stone"); divided into Lower (early), Middle, and Upper (late).

**paleontology**    Study of ancient life through the fossil record.

**paleopathology**    The study of disease and injury in skeletons from archaeological sites.

**pantribal sodality**    A non-kin-based group that exists throughout a tribe, spanning several villages.

***Paranthropus boisei***    Hyperrobust form of *Paranthropus*, found in East Africa and dating to the period between 2.3 and 1.4 m.y.a.

***Paranthropus robustus***    Robust early hominin, found in South Africa and dating to the period between 1.9 and 1.0 m.y.a.

**participant observation**    A characteristic ethnographic technique; taking part in the events one is observing, describing, and analyzing.

**particularity**    A distinctive or unique culture trait, pattern, or integration.

**pastoral nomadism**    Movement throughout the year by the whole pastoral group (men, women, and children) with their animals; more generally, such constant movement in pursuit of strategic resources.

**pastoralists**    People who use a food-producing strategy of adaptation based on care of herds of domesticated animals.

**patriarchy**    A political system ruled by men in which women have inferior social and political status, including basic human rights.

**patrilineal descent**    A unilineal descent rule in which people join the father's group automatically at birth and stay members throughout life.

**patrilineal-patrilocal complex**    An interrelated constellation of patrilineality, patrilocality, warfare, and male supremacy.

**patrilocality**    Customary residence with the husband's relatives after marriage, so that children grow up in their father's community.

**peasant**    A small-scale agriculturist living in a state, with rent fund obligations.

**periphery**    The weakest structural position in the world system.

**phenotype**    An organism's evident traits; its "manifest biology"—anatomy and physiology.

**phenotypical adaptation**    Adaptive biological changes that occur during the individual's lifetime, made possible by biological plasticity.

**phoneme**    A significant sound contrast in a language that serves to distinguish meaning, as in minimal pairs.

**phonemics**    The study of the sound contrasts (phonemes) of a particular language.

**phonetics**    The study of speech sounds in general; what people actually say in various languages.

**phonology**    The study of sounds used in speech.

**Pleistocene**    Epoch of *Homo*'s appearance and evolution; began 2 million years ago; divided into Lower, Middle, and Upper.

**plural marriage**    Marriage of a man to two or more women (polygyny) or marriage of a woman to two or more men (polyandry) at the same time; see also *polygamy*.

**plural society**    A society that combines ethnic contrasts, ecological specialization (i.e., use of different environmental resources by each ethnic group), and the economic interdependence of those groups.

**polities**    Political entities or systems.

**polyandry**    Variety of plural marriage in which a woman has more than one husband.

**polygamy**    Marriage with three or more spouses, at the same time; see also *plural marriage*.

**polygyny**    Variety of plural marriage in which a man has more than one wife.

**polytheism**    The belief in several deities who control aspects of nature.

**popular culture**   Aspects of culture that have meaning for many or most people within the same national culture, including media, fast-food restaurant chains, sports, and games.

**population genetics**   The field that studies causes of genetic variation, maintenance, and change in breeding populations.

**postcolonial**   Referring to interactions between European nations and the societies they colonized (mainly after 1800); more generally, *postcolonial* may be used to signify a position against imperialism and Eurocentrism.

**postmodern**   In its most general sense, describes the blurring and breakdown of established canons (rules, standards), categories, distinctions, and boundaries.

**postmodernism**   A style and movement in architecture that succeeded modernism. Compared with modernism, postmodernism is less geometric, less functional, less austere, more playful, and more willing to include elements from diverse times and cultures; *postmodern* now describes comparable developments in music, literature, and visual art.

**postmodernity**   The condition of a world in flux, with people on the move, in which established groups, boundaries, identities, contrasts, and standards are reaching out and breaking down.

**potlatch**   A competitive feast among Indians on the North Pacific Coast of North America.

**power**   The ability to exercise one's will over others—to do what one wants; the basis of political status.

**prejudice**   Devaluing (looking down on) a group because of its assumed behavior, values, capabilities, or attributes.

**prestige**   Esteem, respect, or approval for acts, deeds, or qualities considered exemplary.

**primary states**   States that arise on their own (through competition among chiefdoms), and not through contact with other state societies.

**primates**   Apes, monkeys, tarsiers, lemurs, lorises; members of the zoological order that includes humans.

**primatology**   The study of the biology, behavior, social life, and evolution of monkeys, apes, and other nonhuman primates.

**productivity**   The ability to use the rules of one's language to create new expressions comprehensible to other speakers; a basic feature of language.

**protolanguage**   A language ancestral to several daughter languages.

**public anthropology**   Efforts to extend anthropology's visibility beyond academia and to demonstrate its public policy relevance.

# R

**race**   An ethnic group assumed to have a biological basis.

**racial classification**   The attempt to assign humans to discrete categories (purportedly) based on common ancestry.

**racism**   Discrimination against an ethnic group assumed to have a biological basis.

**random genetic drift**   Changes in gene frequency that result not from natural selection but from chance; most common in small populations.

**ranked society**   A type of society with hereditary inequality but lacking social stratification.

**recessive**   A genetic trait masked by a dominant trait.

**reciprocity**   One of the three principles of exchange; governs exchange between social equals; major exchange mode in band and tribal societies.

**reciprocity continuum**   Regarding exchanges, a range running from generalized reciprocity (closely related/deferred return) through balanced reciprocity to negative reciprocity (strangers/immediate return).

**redistribution**   The major exchange mode of chiefdoms, many archaic states, and some states with managed economies.

**refugees**   People who have been forced (involuntary refugees) or who have chosen (voluntary refugees) to flee a country, to escape persecution or war.

**relative dating** A dating technique (e.g., stratigraphy) that establish a time frame in relation to other strata or materials, rather than absolute dates in numbers.

**religion** Beliefs and rituals concerned with supernatural beings, powers, and forces.

**revitalization movements** Movements that occur in times of change, in which religious leaders emerge and undertake to alter or revitalize a society.

**rites of passage** Culturally defined activities associated with the transition from one place or stage of life to another.

**ritual** Behavior that is formal, stylized, repetitive, and stereotyped, performed earnestly as a social act; rituals are held at set times and places and have liturgical orders.

**robust** Large, strong, sturdy; said of skull, skeleton, muscle, and teeth; opposite of *gracile*.

# S

**sample** A smaller study group chosen to represent a larger population.

**Sapir-Whorf hypothesis** The theory that different languages produce different ways of thinking.

**science** A "systematic field of study or body of knowledge that aims, through experiment, observation, and deduction, to produce reliable explanations of phenomena, with reference to the material and physical world."

**scientific medicine** As distinguished from Western medicine, a health care system based on scientific knowledge and procedures, encompassing such fields as pathology, microbiology, biochemistry, surgery, diagnostic technology, and applications.

**sedentism** Settled (sedentary) life; preceded food production in the Old World and followed it in the New World.

**semantics** A language's meaning system.

**semiperiphery** The structural position in the world system intermediate between core and periphery.

**settlement hierarchy** A ranked series of communities differing in size, function, and type of building; a three-level settlement hierarchy indicates state organization.

**sexual dimorphism** Marked differences in male and female biology, besides the contrasts in breasts and genitals, and temperament.

**sexual orientation** A person's habitual sexual attraction to and activities with persons of the opposite sex (*heterosexuality*), the same sex (*homosexuality*), or both sexes (*bisexuality*).

**sexual selection** Based on differential success in mating, the process in which certain traits of one sex (e.g., color in male birds) are selected because of advantages they confer in winning mates.

**shaman** A part-time religious practitioner who mediates between ordinary people and supernatural beings and forces.

**smelting** The high-temperature process by which pure metal is produced from an ore.

**social control** Those fields of the social system (beliefs, practices, and institutions) that are most actively involved in the maintenance of any norms and the regulation of any conflict.

**social stratification** The organization of society into sharp social divisions—strata—based on unequal access to socially valued resources.

**socialism** A form of sociopolitical organization in which major industries are state owned and controlled.

**society** Organized life in groups; typical of humans and other animals.

**sociolinguistics** The study of relationships between social and linguistic variation; the study of language in its social context.

**sociopolitical typology** A classification scheme based on the scale and complexity of social organization and the effectiveness of political regulation; includes band, tribe, chiefdom, and state.

**sororate** A custom by which a widower marries the sister of the deceased wife.

**speciation**   The formation of new species; occurs when subgroups of the same species are separated for a sufficient length of time.

**species**   A population whose members can interbreed to produce offspring that can live and reproduce.

**state**   A complex sociopolitical system that administers a territory and populace with substantial contrasts in occupation, wealth, prestige, and power. An independent, centrally organized political unit; a government. A form of social and political organization with a formal, central government and a division of society into classes.

**status**   Any position that determines where someone fits in society; may be ascribed or achieved.

**stereotypes**   Fixed ideas—often unfavorable— about what members of a group are like.

**stratigraphy**   The science that examines the ways in which earth sediments are deposited in demarcated layers known as strata (singular, *stratum*).

**Strepsirrhini**   The primate suborder that includes tarsiers, monkeys, apes, and humans.

**style shifts**   Variations in speech in different contexts.

**subcultures**   Different cultural symbol-based patterns and traditions associated with subgroups in the same complex society.

**subgroups**   Languages within a taxonomy of related languages that are most closely related.

**subordinate**   The lower, or underprivileged, group in a stratified system.

**superordinate**   The upper, or privileged, group in a stratified system.

**survey research**   A characteristic research procedure among social scientists other than anthropologists. Studies society through sampling, statistical analysis, and impersonal data collection.

**symbol**   Something, verbal or nonverbal, that arbitrarily and by convention stands for something else, with which it has no necessary or natural connection.

**syntax**   The arrangement and order of words in phrases and sentences.

**systematic survey**   Information gathered on patterns of settlement over a large area; provides a regional perspective on the archaeological record.

# T

**taboo**   Prohibition backed by supernatural sanctions.

**taphonomy**   The study of the processes— biological and geological—by which dead animals become fossils; from the Greek *taphos*, which means "tomb."

**taxonomy**   Classification scheme; assignment to categories (*taxa;* singular, *taxon*).

**teosinte**   Wild grass; apparent ancestor of maize; also called *teocentli.*

**Teotihuacán**   The first state in the Valley of Mexico and the earliest major Mesoamerican empire, 100 to 700 C.E.

**terrestrial**   Ground-dwelling.

**theory**   An explanatory framework, containing a series of statements, that helps us understand why (something exists); theories suggest patterns, connections, and relationships that may be confirmed by new research.

**totem**   An animal, plant, or geographic feature associated with a specific social group, to which that totem is sacred or symbolically important.

**transgender**   A category of varied individuals whose gender identity differs from their biological sex at birth and the gender identity that society assigned to them in infancy.

**transhumance**   One of two variants of pastoralism; part of the population moves seasonally with the herds while the other part remains in home villages.

**tribe**   A form of sociopolitical organization usually based on horticulture or pastoralism. Socioeconomic stratification and centralized rule are absent in tribes, and there is no means of enforcing political decisions.

# U

**uniformitarianism**  The belief that explanations for past events should be sought in ordinary forces that continue to work today.

**unilineal descent**  Matrilineal or patrilineal descent.

**universal**  Something that exists in every culture.

**Upper Paleolithic**  Blade-tool-making traditions associated with AMHs; named for their location in upper, or more recent, layers of sedimentary deposits.

**urban anthropology**  The anthropological study of life in and around world cities, including urban social problems, differences between urban and other environments, and adaptation to city life.

# V

**variables**  Attributes (e.g., age, occupation, income) that differ from one person or case to the next.

**village head**  Leadership position in a village (as among the Yanomami, where the head is always a man); has limited authority; and leads by example and persuasion.

# W

**wealth**  All a person's material assets, including income, land, and other types of property; the basis of economic status.

**Westernization**  The acculturative influence of Western expansion on other cultures.

**working class (or proletariat)**  Those who must sell their labor to survive; the antithesis of the bourgeoisie in Marx's class analysis.

**world-system theory**  An argument for the historic and contemporary social, political, and economic significance of an identifiable global system, based on wealth and power differentials, that extends beyond individual countries.

# Z

**Zapotec state**  Mesoamerica's earliest state, which developed in Mexico's Valley of Oaxaca from a chiefdom by about 100 B.C.E. and lasted until its overthrow by Spain in the 1500s.

**Zapotec state**  The first Mesoamerican state, in the Valley of Oaxaca.

# Bibliography

Adams, R. M. 2008. An Interdisciplinary Overview of a Mesopotamian City and Its Hinterlands. *Cuneiform Digital Library Journal.*

Adams, S. 2012. The World's Next Genocide. *New York Times,* November 15.

Ahearn, L. M. 2017. *Living Language: An Introduction to Linguistic Anthropology,* 2nd ed. Malden, MA: Wiley-Blackwell.

Aiello, L., and M. Collard. 2001. Our Newest Oldest Ancestor? *Nature* 410 (March 29): 526–527.

Akazawa, T. 1980. *The Japanese Paleolithic: A Techno-Typological Study.* Tokyo: Rippo Shobo.

Akazawa, T., and C. M. Aikens, eds. 1986. *Prehistoric Hunter-Gatherers in Japan: New Research Methods.* Tokyo: University of Tokyo Press.

Akmajian, A., et al. 2017. *Linguistics: An Introduction to Language and Communication,* 7th ed. Cambridge, MA: MIT Press.

Aldred, J. 2012. Mountain Gorilla Numbers Rise by 10%. *The Guardian,* November 13. https://www.theguardian.com/environment/ 2012/nov/13/mountain-gorilla-population-rises.

Alexandrakis, O., ed. 2016. *Impulse to Act: A New Anthropology of Resistance and Social Justice.* Indianapolis: Indiana University Press.

Amadiume, I. 1987. *Male Daughters, Female Husbands.* Atlantic Highlands, NJ: Zed.

Amos, T. D. 2011. *Embodying Difference: The Making of the Burakumin in Modern Japan.* Honolulu: University of Hawaii Press.

Anderson, B. 2006 (orig. 1991). *Imagined Communities: Reflections on the Origin and Spread of Nationalism,* rev. ed. New York: Verso.

Anderson-Levitt, K. M. 2012. *Anthropologies of Education: A Global Guide to Ethnographic Studies of Learning and Schooling.* New York: Berghahn Books.

Anderson-Levitt, K. M., and E. Rockwell, eds. 2017. *Comparing Ethnographies: Local Studies of Education across the Americas.* Washington, DC: American Educational Research Association.

Andersson, R. 2014. *Illegality Inc.: Clandestine Migration and the Business of Bordering Europe.* Berkeley: University of California Press.

Anemone, R. L. 2011. *Race and Human Diversity: A Biocultural Approach.* Upper Saddle River, NJ: Prentice Hall/Pearson.

Annenberg/CPB Exhibits. 2000. Collapse, Why Do Civilizations Fall? http://www.learner. org/exhibits/collapse/.

Ansell, A. E. 2013. *Race and Ethnicity: The Key Concepts.* New York: Routledge.

Antoun, R. T. 2008. *Understanding Fundamentalism: Christian, Islamic, and Jewish Movements,* 2nd ed. Lanham, MD: AltaMira.

Appadurai, A. 1990. Disjuncture and Difference in the Global Cultural Economy. *Public Culture* 2(2):1–24.

———. 1991. Global Ethnoscapes: Notes and Queries for a Transnational Anthropology. In *Recapturing Anthropology: Working in the Present,* R. G. Fox, ed., pp. 191–210. Santa Fe, NM: School of American Research Advanced Seminar Series.

Appiah, K. A. 1990. Racisms. In *Anatomy of Racism,* David Theo Goldberg, ed., pp. 3–17. Minneapolis: University of Minnesota Press.

Arcadi, A. C. 2018. *Wild Chimpanzees: Social Behavior of an Endangered species.* New York: Cambridge University Press.

Archibald, J. M. 2018. *Genomics: A Very Short Introduction.* New York: Oxford University Press.

Ariens, C. 2017. Jornal Nacional Is the Flagship Program of Brazil's Globo TV. Adweek, August 29. http://www.adweek.com/tv-video/ this-tv-news-show-gets-more-viewers-than-the- academy-awards-and-it-does-every-night/.

Arnold, C. 2015. New Clues on How and When Wolves Became Dogs. *National*

*Geographic,* December 17. http://news. nationalgeographic.com/2015/12/151217-dogs-domestication-asia-china-genetics-animals-science/.

Arrighi, G. 2010. *The Long Twentieth Century: Money, Power, and the Origins of Our Times,* new and updated ed. New York: Verso.

Asfaw, B., T. White, and O. Lovejoy. 1999. Australopithecus garhi: A New Species of Early Hominid from Ethiopia. *Science* 284 (April 23):629.

Ashcroft, B., G. Griffiths, and H. Tiffin. 2013. *Postcolonial Studies: The Key Concepts,* 3rd ed. New York: Routledge, Taylor and Francis.

Associated Press. 2017. NY State Appeals Court Rules That Chimpanzees Don't Have Rights of People. June 8. http://www.syracuse.com/state/index.ssf/2017/06/ny_state_appeals_court_rules_that_chimpanzees_dont_have_rights_of_people.html.

Atran, S. 2016. The Devoted Actor: Unconditional Commitment and Intractable Conflict across Cultures. *Current Anthropology* 57 (Supplement 13):S192–S203.

Atran, S., et al. 2014. The Devoted Actor, Sacred Values, and Willingness to Fight: Preliminary Studies with ISIL Volunteers and Kurdish Frontline Fighters. University of Oxford, United Kingdom: ARTIS Research. http://johnjayresearch.org/ct/files/2015/05/The-Devoted-Actor-Sacred-Values-and-Willingness-to-Fight.pdf.

Baer, H. A., and M. Singer. 2018. *The Anthropology of Climate Change: An Integrated Critical Perspective,* 2nd ed. New York: Routledge, Taylor & Francis.

Baer, H. A., M. Singer, and I. Susser. 2013. *Medical Anthropology and the World System,* 3rd ed. Santa Barbara, CA: Praeger.

Ball, C. A., ed. 2016. *After Marriage Equality: The Future of LGBT Rights.* New York: New York University Press.

Balter, M. 2010. Romanian Cave Art May Boast Central Europe's Oldest Cave Art. *Science Now,* June 21. http://news.sciencemag.org/sciencenow/2010/06/romanian-cave-may-boast-central.html.

Banton, M. 2015. *What We Now Know about Race and Ethnicity.* New York: Berghahn Books.

Barfield, T. J. 2010. *Afghanistan: A Cultural and Political History.* Princeton, NJ: Princeton University Press.

Barker, A. 2018. Looting, the Antiquities Trade, and Competing Valuations of the Past. *Annual Review of Anthropology* 47:455–474.

Barnaby, F., ed. 1984. *Future War: Armed Conflict in the Next Decade.* London: M. Joseph.

Baron, D. E. 2009. *A Better Pencil: Readers, Writers, and the Digital Revolution.* New York: Oxford University Press.

———. 2015. Singular They Is Word of the Year. The Web of Language, November 19. University of Illinois. https://illinois.edu/blog/view/25/280996.

Barth, F. 1968 (orig. 1958). Ecologic Relations of Ethnic Groups in Swat, North Pakistan. In *Man in Adaptation: The Cultural Present,* Yehudi Cohen, ed., pp. 324–331. Chicago: Aldine.

———. 1969. *Ethnic Groups and Boundaries: The Social Organization of Cultural Difference.* London: Allen and Unwin.

Bar-Yosef, O. 1987. Pleistocene Connections between Africa and Southwest Asia: An Archaeological Perspective. *African Archaeological Review* 5:29–38.

Bar-Yosef, O., and F. R. Valla, eds. 2013. *Natufian Foragers in the Levant: Terminal Pleistocene Social Changes in Western Asia.* Ann Arbor, MI: International Monographs in Prehistory.

Beall, C. M. 2014. Adaptation to High Altitudes: Phenotypes and Genotypes. *Annual Review of Anthropology* 43:251–272.

Beck, S., and C. A. Maida, eds. 2013. *Toward Engaged Anthropology.* New York: Berghahn Books.

———. 2015. *Public Anthropology in a Borderless World.* New York: Berghahn Books.

Becker, K. 2013. 400 Research Chimpanzees to Be Retired. *Healthy Pets,* March 18. http://healthypets.mercola.com/sites/healthypets/archive/2013/03/18/research-chimpanzees.aspx.

Beckett, C. 2019. *Human Growth and Development,* 4th ed. Thousand Oaks, CA: Sage.

Bellah, R. N. 2011. *Religion in Human Evolution: From the Paleolithic to the Axial Age.* Cambridge, MA: Belknap Press of Harvard University Press.

Bellwood, P. S. 2005. *The First Farmers: Origins of Agricultural Societies.* Malden, MA: Blackwell.

Benazzi, S., et al. 2011. Early Dispersal of Modern Humans in Europe and Implications for Neanderthal Behaviour. *Nature* 479 (November 24):525–528. doi:10.1038/nature10617.

Benedict, R. F. 1946. *The Chrysanthemum and the Sword.* Boston: Houghton Mifflin.

Bennett, J. W. 1969. *Northern Plainsmen: Adaptive Strategy and Agrarian Life.* Chicago: Aldine.

Bergendorff, S. 2016. *Kinship and Human Evolution: Making Culture, Becoming Human.* Lanham, MD: Lexington Books.

Berger, L. R., and J. Hawks. 2017. Almost Human: The Astonishing Tale of Homo naledi and the Discovery That Changed Our Human Story. Washington, DC: National Geographic.

Berger, P. 2010. Pentecostalism–Protestant Ethic or Cargo Cult? *Peter Berger's blog,* July 29. http://blogs.the-american-interest.com/berger/2010/07/29/pentecostalism-%E2%80%93-protestant-ethic-or-cargo-cult/.

Beriss, D. 2004. *Black Skins, French Voices: Caribbean Ethnicity and Activism in Urban France.* Boulder, CO: Westview Press.

Berlin, B., and P. Kay. 1992 (orig. 1969). *Basic Color Terms: Their Universality and Evolution,* 2nd ed. Berkeley: University of California Press.

Berna, F., et al. 2012. Microstratigraphic Evidence of in Situ Fire in the Acheulean Strata of Wonderwerk Cave, Northern Cape Province, South Africa. Proceedings of the National Academy of Sciences. doi:10.1073/pnas.1117620109.

Bernard, H. R. 2013. *Social Science Research Methods: Qualitative and Quantitative Approaches,* 2nd ed. Los Angeles: Sage.

———. 2018. *Research Methods in Anthropology: Qualitative and Quantitative Approaches,* 6th ed. Lanham, MD: Rowman & Littlefield.

Bernard, H. R., and C. C. Gravlee, eds. 2014. *Handbook of Methods in Cultural Anthropology,* 2nd ed. Lanham, MD: Rowman & Littlefield.

Besnier, N., and S. Brownell. 2016. The Untold Story behind Fiji's Astonishing Gold Medal. SAPIENS, August 19. http://www.sapiens.org/culture/fiji-rugby-racial-sexual-politics/.

Bianchi, M. 2017. Harold Varner III Walks Alone in Desert of Golf Divesity. *Orlando Sentinel,* March 17. https://www.orlandosentinel.com/sports/golf/os-sp-arnold-palmer-invitational-mike-bianchi-0318-story.html.

Bielo, J. S. 2015. *Anthropology of Religion: The Basics.* New York: Routledge.

Bilgrami, A. 2016. *Beyond the Secular West.* New York: Columbia University Press.

Binford, L. R. 1968. Post-Pleistocene Adaptations. In *New Perspectives in Archeology,* S. R. Binford and L. R. Binford, eds., pp. 313–341. Chicago: Aldine.

Bizumic, B. 2018. *Ethnocentrism: Integrated Perspectives.* New York: Routledge.

Bjuremalm, H. 1997. Rattvisa kan skiruppas i Rwanda: Folkmordet 1994 gar attt forklara och analysera pa samma satt som forintelsen av judarna. *Dagens Nyheter* [06-03-1977, p. B3].

Black, J. 2015. *The British Empire: A History and a Debate.* Burlington, VT: Ashgate.

Blackwood, E. 2010. *Falling into the Lesbi World: Desire and Difference in Indonesia.* Honolulu: University of Hawaii Press.

Blewitt, J. 2018. *Understanding Sustainable Development,* 3rd ed. New York: Routledge, Taylor & Francis.

Blurton-Jones, N. G., et al. 2000. Paternal Investment and Hunter-Gatherer Divorce Rates. In *Adaptation and Human Behavior: An Anthropological Perspective.* L. Cronk, N. Chagnon, and W. Irons, eds., pp. 69–90. New York: Aldine.

Boas, F. 1966 (orig. 1940). *Race, Language, and Culture.* New York: Free Press.

Boddy, J., and M. Lambek, eds. 2013. *A Companion to the Anthropology of Religion.* Hoboken, NJ: Wiley.

Bodley, J. H. 2012. *Anthropology and Contemporary Human Problems,* 6th ed. Lanham, MD: AltaMira.

————. 2015. *Victims of Progress,* 6th ed. Lanham, MD: Rowman & Littlefield.

————. 2017. *Cultural Anthropology: Tribes, States, and the Global System,* 6th ed. Lanham, MD: Rowman & Littlefield.

Bond, S. E. 2018. Pseudoarchaeology and the Racism behind Ancient Aliens. Hyperallergic, November 12. https://hyperallergic.com/470795/pseudoarchaeology-and-the-racism-behind-ancient-aliens/.

Bonvillain, N. 2013. *Language, Culture, and Communication: The Meaning of Messages,* 7th ed. Boston: Pearson Prentice Hall.

————. 2016. *The Routledge Handbook of Linguistic Anthropology.* New York: Routledge.

Borjian, M. 2017. *Language and Globalization: An Autoethnographic Approach.* New York: Routledge.

Borneman, J., and L. K. Hart. 2015. The Institution of Marriage Our Society Needs: Anthropological Investigations over the Last Century Have Shown That Marriage Is an Elastic Institution. *Aljazeera America,* July 12. http://america.aljazeera.com/opinions/2015/7/the-institution-of-marriage-our-society-needs.html.

Borofsky, R. 2000. Public Anthropology: Where To? What Next? *Anthropology Newsletter* 41(5):9-10.

Bouckaert, R., et al. 2012. Mapping the Origins and Expansion of the Indo-European Language Family. *Science* 337:957-960.

Bouquet-Appel, J.-P., and O. Bar-Yosef, eds. 2008. *The Neolithic Demographic Transition and Its Consequences.* New York: Springer.

Bourdieu, P. 1977. *Outline of a Theory of Practice.* R. Nice (trans.). Cambridge, UK: Cambridge University Press.

————. 1982. *Ce Que Parler Veut Dire.* Paris: Fayard.

————. 1984. *Distinction: A Social Critique of the Judgment of Taste.* R. Nice (trans.). Cambridge, MA: Harvard University Press.

Bourque, S. C., and K. B. Warren. 1987. Technology, Gender and Development. *Daedalus* 116(4):173-197.

Bowen, J. R. 2017. *Religions in Practice: An Approach to the Anthropology of Religion,* 7th ed. New York: Routledge.

Bower, B. 2013. Fossils Point to Ancient Ape-Monkey Split. *Science News* 183(12):9. http://www.sciencenews.org/view/generic/id/350410/description/Fossils_point_to_ancient_ape-monkey_split.

Bowles, S. 2011. Cultivation of Cereals by the First Farmers Was Not More Productive Than Foraging. *Proceedings of the National Academy of Sciences* 108(12):4760-4765.

Bowles, S., and J.-K. Choi. 2013. Coevolution of Farming and Private Property during the early Holocene. *Proceedings of the National Academy of Sciences* 110(22):8830-8835.

Braga, J., and J. F. Thackeray. eds. 2016. *Kromdraai: A Birthplace of Paranthropus in the Cradle of Humankind.* South Africa: Sun Press.

Braidwood, R. J. 1975. *Prehistoric Men,* 8th ed. Glenview, IL: Scott, Foresman.

Braudel, F. 1981. *Civilization and Capitalism, 15th-18th Century,* Volume I, *The Structure of Everyday Life: The Limits.* S. Reynolds (trans.). New York: Harper and Row.

————. 1982. *Civilization and Capitalism, 15th-18th Century,* Volume II, *The Wheels of Commerce.* New York: Harper and Row.

————. 1992. *Civilization and Capitalism, 15th-18th Century,* Volume III, *The Perspective of the World.* Berkeley: University of California Press.

Brettell, C. B., and C. F. Sargent, eds. 2017. *Gender in Cross-Cultural Perspective,* 7th ed. New York: Routledge.

Brickley, M. 2018. How Cutting-Edge Archaeology Can Improve Public Health. SAPIENS, July 18. https://www.sapiens.org/archaeology/rickets-vitamin-d-deficiency/.

Briggs, C. L. 2005. Communicability, Racial Discourse, and Disease. *Annual Review of Anthropology* 34:269-291.

Briody, E. K., and R. T. Trotter II. 2008. *Partnering for Organizational Performance: Collaboration and Culture in the Global Workplace.* Lanham, MD: Rowman & Littlefield.

Brooker, R. J. 2019. *Concepts of Genetics,* 3rd ed. New York: McGraw-Hill Education.

Brookings Institution. 2010. *State of Metropolitan America: On the Front Lines of Demographic Transition.* The Brookings Institution Metropolitan Policy Program. http://www.brookings.edu/~/media/Files/Programs/Metro/state_of_metro_america/metro_america_report1.pdf.

Brower, B., and B. R. Johnston. 2007. *Disappearing Peoples? Indigenous Groups and Ethnic Minorities in South and Central Asia.* Walnut Creek, CA: Left Coast Press.

Brown, A. 2001. Communism. *International Encyclopedia of the Social & Behavioral Sciences,* pp. 2323–2326. New York: Elsevier.

Brown, M. F. 2003. *Who Owns Native Culture?* Cambridge, MA: Harvard University Press.

Brown, P. J., and S. Closser. 2016. *Understanding and Applying Medical Anthropology: Biosocial and Cultural Approaches,* 3rd ed. Walnut Creek, CA: Left Coast Press.

Brownstein, R. 2010. The Gray and the Brown: The Generational Mismatch. *National Journal,* July 24. http://www.nationaljournal.com/njmagazines/cs_20100724_3946php.

Bryant, V. M. 1999. Review of Piperno, D. R., and D. M. Pearsall, *The Origins of Agriculture in the Lowland Neotropics* (1998). *North American Archaeologist* (26):245–246.

———. 2003. Invisible Clues to New World Domestication. *Science* 299 (February 14): 1029–1030.

———. 2007a. Artifact: Maize Pollen. *Archaeology* 60(4). www.archaeology.org/0707/etc/artifact.html.

———. 2007b. Little Things Mean a Lot: The Search for Starch Grains at Archaeological Sites. *Mammoth Trumpet* 22(4):3–4, 16.

———. 2013. Please Don't Wash the Artifacts. *General Anthropology* 20(2):1–7.

Buettner, E. 2016. *Europe after Empire: Decolonization, Society, and Culture.* Cambridge, UK: Cambridge University Press.

Buikstra, J. E., and C. A. Roberts, eds. 2012. *The Global History of Paleopathology: Pioneers and Prospects.* Oxford, UK: Oxford University Press.

Burbank, J., and F. Cooper. 2010. *Empires in World History: Power and the Politics of Difference.* Princeton, NJ: Princeton University Press.

Burdick, J. 1993. *Looking for God in Brazil: The Progressive Catholic Church in Urban Brazil's Religious Arena.* Berkeley: University of California Press.

———. 1998. *Blessed Anastácia: Women, Race, and Popular Christianity in Brazil.* New York: Routledge.

Burger, J., M. Kirchner, B. Bramanti, W. Haak, and M. G. Thomas. 2007. Absence of the Lactase-Persistence Associated Allele in Early Neolithic Europeans. *Proceedings of the National Academy of Sciences* 104(10):3736–3741.

Burke, H., et al. 2008. *Kennewick Man: Perspectives on the Ancient One.* Walnut Creek, CA: Left Coast Press.

Burn, S. M. 2011. *Women Across Cultures,* 3rd ed. New York: McGraw-Hill.

Burridge, K., and A. Bergs. 2017. *Understanding Language Change.* New York: Routledge.

Butler, J. 1988. Performative Acts and Gender Constitution: An Essay in Phenomenology and Feminist Theory. *Theatre Journal* 40(4): 519–531.

———. 1990. *Gender Trouble: Feminism and the Subversion of Identity.* New York: Routledge.

———. 2015. *Notes toward a Performative Theory of Assembly.* Cambridge, MA: Harvard University Press.

Byers, S. N. 2017. *Introduction to Forensic Anthropology,* 5th ed. New York: Routledge, Taylor & Francis.

Cairns, M. F. 2015. *Shifting Cultivation and Environmental Change: Indigenous People, Agriculture and Forest Conservation.* New York: Routledge.

Caldararo, N. L. 2014. *The Anthropology of Complex Economic Systems: Inequality, Stability, and Cycles of Crisis.* Lanham, MD: Lexington Books.

———. 2016. Human Remains Found in Hobbit Cave: Ancient Teeth Make *Homo sapiens* the Lead Suspect in the Extinction of *Homo floresiensis. Nature News,* September 21.

Cambridge, University of. 2015. Millet: The Missing Piece in the Puzzle of Prehistoric Humans' Transition from Hunter-Gatherers to Farmers. *Research News,* December 14. http://www.cam.ac.uk/research/news/millet-the-missing-piece-in-the-puzzle-of-prehistoric-humans-transition-from-hunter-gatherers-to-farmers.

Cameron, N., and B. Bogin, eds. 2012. *Human Growth and Development,* 2nd ed. London: Elsevier/AP.

Campbell, C. J., ed. 2011. *Primates in Perspective,* 2nd ed. New York: Oxford University Press.

Cann, R. L., M. Stoneking, and A. C. Wilson. 1987. Mitochondrial DNA and Human Evolution. *Nature* 325:31–36.

Carballo, D. M. 2016. *Urbanization and Religion in Ancient Central Mexico.* New York: Oxford University Press.

Carey, B. 2007. Washoe, a Chimp of Many Words Dies at 42. *New York Times,* November 1.

Carneiro, R. L. 1956. Slash-and-Burn Agriculture: A Closer Look at Its Implications for Settlement Patterns. In *Men and Cultures.* Selected Papers of the Fifth International Congress of Anthropological and Ethnological Sciences, pp. 229–234. Philadelphia: University of Pennsylvania Press.

———. 1968 (orig. 1961). Slash-and-Burn Cultivation among the Kuikuru and Its Implications for Cultural Development in the Amazon Basin. In *Man in Adaptation: The Cultural Present,* Y. A. Cohen, ed., pp. 131–145. Chicago: Aldine.

———. 1970. A Theory of the Origin of the State. *Science* 69:733–738.

———. 1990. Chiefdom-Level Warfare as Exemplified in Fiji and the Cauca Valley. In *The Anthropology of War,* J. Haas, ed., pp. 190–211. Cambridge, UK: Cambridge University Press.

———. 1991. The Nature of the Chiefdom as Revealed by Evidence from the Cauca Valley of Colombia. In *Profiles in Cultural Evolution,* A. T. Rambo and K. Gillogly, eds. Anthropological Papers 85, pp. 167–190. Ann Arbor: University of Michigan Museum of Anthropology.

Carneiro, R. L., et al., eds. 2017. *Chiefdoms: Yesterday and Today.* Clinton Corners, NY: EWP, Eliot Werner Publications.

Cambridge, University of. 2015. Millet: The Missing Piece in the Puzzle of Prehistoric Humans' Transition from Hunter-Gatherers to Farmers. *Research News,* December 14. http://www.cam.ac.uk/research/news/millet-the-missing-piece-in-the-puzzle-of-prehistoric-humans-transition-from-hunter-gatherers-to-farmers.

Canuto, M. A., et al. 2018. Ancient Lowland Maya Complexity as Revealed by Airborne Laser Scanning of Northern Guatemala. *Science* 361(6409), September 28. http://science.sciencemag.org/content/361/6409/eaau0137.

Carrier, J. G. 2012. *A Handbook of Economic Anthropology.* Cheltenham, UK: Edward Edgar.

Carrier, J. G., and D. Kalb, eds. 2015. *Anthropologies of Class: Power, Practice, and Inequality.* Cambridge, UK: Cambridge University Press.

Carroll, R. 2008. Chimps 90 Percent Gone in a "Final Stronghold." *National Geographic News,* October 13. http://news.nationalgeographic.com/news/pf/69848470.html.

Carter, J. 1988. Freed from Keepers and Cages, Chimps Come of Age on Baboon Island. *Smithsonian,* June, pp. 36–48.

Casanova, J. 2001. Religion, the New Millennium, and Globalization. *Sociology of Religion* 62:415–441.

Cefkin, M., ed. 2009. *Ethnography and the Corporate Encounter: Reflections on Research in and of Corporations.* New York: Berghahn Books.

Cernea, M., ed. 1991. *Putting People First: Sociological Variables in Rural Development,* 2nd ed. New York: Oxford University Press (published for the World Bank).

Ceuppens, B., and P. Geschiere. 2005. Autochthony: Local or Global? New Modes in the Struggle over Citizenship and Belonging in Africa and Europe. *Annual Review of Anthropology* 34:385–407.

Chagnon, N. A. 2013a. *Yanomamö*, 6th ed. Australia: Wadsworth Cengage.

―――. 2013b. *Noble Savages: My Life among Two Dangerous Tribes—The Yanomamo and the Anthropologists*. New York: Simon & Schuster.

Chambers, E. 1987. Applied Anthropology in the Post-Vietnam Era: Anticipations and Ironies. *Annual Review of Anthropology* 16:309–337.

Chapais, B. 2008. *Primeval Kinship: How Pair Bonding Gave Birth to Human Society*. Cambridge, MA: Harvard University Press.

Cheney, D. L., and R. M. Seyfarth. 1990. In the Minds of Monkeys: What Do They Know and How Do They Know It? *Natural History*, September, pp. 38–46.

Chibnik, M. 2011. *Anthropology, Economics, and Choice*. Austin: University of Texas Press.

Choi, C. Q. 2011. Savanna, Not Forest, Was Human Ancestors' Proving Ground. *Live Science*, August 3. http://www.livescience.com/15377-savannas-human-ancestors-evolution.html.

―――. 2012. Ancient Foot Suggests How Man Gave Up Treehouses. *Live Science*, March 28. http://www.livescience.com/19333-hominin-foot-humanity-bipedalism.html.

Chomsky, N. 1957. *Syntactic Structures*. The Hague: Mouton.

―――. 2014. *Aspects of the Theory of Syntax*, 50th Anniversary ed. Cambridge, MA: MIT Press.

Chow, P. Y. S. 2018. *Cultural Rights in International Law and Discourse: Contemporary Challenges and Interdisciplinary Perspectives*. Boston: Brill Nijhoff.

Clark, G. 2010. *African Market Women: Seven Life Stories from Ghana*. Indianapolis: Indiana University Press.

Clarkson, C., et al. 2017. Human Occupation of Northern Australia by 65,000 Years Ago. *Nature* 547:306–310. https://www.nature.com/articles/nature22968.

Clynes, T. 2018. Exclusive: Laser Scan Reveals Maya "Megalopolis" below Guatemalan Jungle. *National Geographic*, February 1. https://news.nationalgeographic.com/2018/02/maya-laser-lidar-guatemala-pacunam/.

Coates, J. 2016. *Women, Men, and Language: A Sociolinguistic Account of Gender Differences in Language*. New York: Routledge.

Coburn, N. 2011. *Bazaar Politics: Power and Pottery in an Afghan Market Town*. Stanford, CA: Stanford University Press.

Codding, B. F., and K. L. Kramer, eds. 2016. *Why Forage? Hunters and Gatherers in the Twenty-First Century*. Albuquerque: University of New Mexico Press.

Cody, D. 1998. British Empire. The Victorian Web. http://www.victorianweb.org/history/empire/Empire.html.

Coe, M. D. 2011. *The Maya*, 8th ed. New York: Thames and Hudson.

Cohen, J. H. 2015. *Eating Soup without a Spoon: Anthropological Theory and Method in the Real World*. Austin: University of Texas Press.

Cohen, M. N., and G. J. Armelagos, eds. 2013. *Paleopathology at the Origins of Agriculture*, 2nd ed. Gainesville: University of Florida Press.

Cohen, P. 2008. The Pentagon Enlists Social Scientists to Study Security Issues. *New York Times*, June 18.

Cohen, R. 1967. *The Kanuri of Bornu*. New York: Holt, Rinehart & Winston.

Cohen, Y. 1974. Culture as Adaptation. In *Man in Adaptation: The Cultural Present*, 2nd ed., Y. A. Cohen, ed., pp. 45–68. Chicago: Aldine.

Coleman, S., and R. I. J. Hackett, eds. 2015. *The Anthropology of Global Pentecostalism and Evangelicalism*. New York: New York University Press.

Coles, R. L. 2016. *Race and Family: A Structural Approach*, 2nd ed. Lanham, MD: Rowman & Littlefield.

Collins, F. S. 2015. NIH Will No Longer Support Biomedical Research on Chimpanzees. The NIH Director. November 17. https://www.nih.gov/about-nih/who-we-are/nih-director/statements/nih-will-no-longer-support-biomedical-research-chimpanzees.

Colson, E., and T. Scudder. 1988. *For Prayer and Profit: The Ritual, Economic, and Social Importance of Beer in Gwembe District, Zambia, 1950–1982.* Stanford, CA: Stanford University Press.

Colwell, C. 2017. What Has the Ancient One's Epic Journey Taught Us? *Counterpunch,* January 3. http://www.counterpunch.org/2017/01/03/what-has-the-ancient-ones-epic-journey-taught-us/.

Conard, N. J. 2011. *Neanderthal Lifeways, Subsistence, and Technology.* New York: Springer.

Conklin, A. L., S. Fishman, and R. Zaretsky. 2015. *France and Its Empire since 1870.* New York: Oxford University Press.

Cooper, F. 2014. *Africa in the World: Capitalism, Empire, Nation-State.* Cambridge, MA: Harvard University Press.

Cornwall, A., and N. Lindisfarne, eds. 2017. *Dislocating Masculinity: Comparative Ethnographies,* rev. ed. New York: Routledge, Taylor & Francis.

Costa, J. T. 2014. *Wallace, Darwin, and the Origin of Species.* Cambridge, MA: Harvard University Press.

Council of Economic Advisers. 2014. *Nine Facts about American Families and Work.* Executive Office of the President of the United States. https://www.whitehouse.gov/sites/default/files/docs/nine_facts_about_family_and_work_real_final.pdf.

Cowgill, G. L. 2015. *Ancient Teotihuacan: Early Urbanism in Central Mexico.* New York: Cambridge University Press.

Craig, O. 2013. Earliest Evidence for the Use of Pottery. *Nature* 496:351–354. http://www.nature.com/nature/journal/v496/n7445/full/nature12109.html.

Crewe, E., and R. Axelby. 2013. *Anthropology and Development: Culture, Morality, and Politics in a Globalised World.* Cambridge, UK: Cambridge University Press.

Crosby, A. W., Jr. 2003. *The Columbian Exchange: Biological and Cultural Consequences of 1492.* Westport, CT: Praeger.

———. 2015. *Ecological Imperialism.* New York: Cambridge University Press.

*Cultural Survival Quarterly.* Quarterly journal. Cambridge, MA: Cultural Survival, Inc.

Curry, A. 2008. Gobekli Tepe: The World's First Temple? *Smithsonian,* October 31. http://www.smithsonianmag.com/ist/?next=/history/gobekli-tepe-the-worlds-first-temple-83613665/.

———. 2009. Climate Change: Sites in Peril. *Archaeology* 62(2). http://archive.archaeology.org/0903/etc/climate_change.html.

———. 2016. World's Oldest Temple to Be Restored. *National Geographic News,* January 20. https://www.sapiens.org/archaeology/ancient-footprints/.

———. 2018. As Seas Rise, Ancient Footprints Are Revealed. SAPIENS, August 2. http://news.nationalgeographic.com/2016/01/150120-gobekli-tepe-oldest-monument-turkey-archaeology/.

Dagne, T. W. 2015. *Intellectual Property and Traditional Knowledge in the Global Economy: Translating Geographical Indications for Development.* New York: Routledge.

DaMatta, R. 1991. *Carnivals, Rogues, and Heroes: An Interpretation of the Brazilian Dilemma.* Translated from the Portuguese by John Drury. Notre Dame, IN: University of Notre Dame Press.

D'Andrade, R. 1984. Cultural Meaning Systems. In *Culture Theory: Essays on Mind, Self, and Emotion,* R. A. Shweder and R. A. Levine, eds., pp. 88–119. Cambridge, UK: Cambridge University Press.

Danesi, M. 2018. *Language, Society, and New Media: Sociolinguistics Today.* New York: Routledge.

Darwin, C. 2018 (orig. 1859). *On the Origin of Species.* Minneapolis, MN: First Avenue Editions.

Darwin, H. 2017. Doing Gender Beyond the Binary: A Virtual Ethnography. Symbolic Interaction. https://helanadarwindotcom.files.wordpress.com/2016/11/doing-gender-beyond-the-binary.pdf.

Darwin, J. 2013. *Unfinished Empire: The Global Expansion of Britain.* New York: Bloomsbury Press.

Das, V., and D. Poole, eds. 2004. *Anthropology in the Margins of the State.* Santa Fe, NM: School of American Research Press.

Davenport, C., and J. Haner. 2015. The Marshall Islands Are Disappearing. *New York Times,* December 1. http://www.nytimes.com/interactive/2015/12/02/world/The-Marshall-Islands-Are-Disappearing.html.

Day, E. 2015. #BlackLivesMatter: The Birth of a New Civil Rights Movement. *The Guardian,* July 19. http://www.theguardian.com/world/2015/jul/19/blacklivesmatter-birth-civil-rights-movement.

Degler, C. 1970. *Neither Black nor White: Slavery and Race Relations in Brazil and the United States.* New York: Macmillan.

de la Peña, G. 2005. Social and Cultural Policies toward Indigenous Peoples: Perspectives from Latin America. *Annual Review of Anthropology* 34:717–739.

De Leon, J. 2015. *The Land of Open Graves: Living and Dying on the Migrant Trail.* Oakland: University of California Press.

deLumley, H. 1976 (orig. 1969). A Paleolithic Camp at Nice. In *Avenues to Antiquity, Readings from Scientific American,* B. M. Fagan, ed., pp. 36–44. San Francisco: W. H. Freeman.

Denny, R. M., and P. L. Sunderland, eds. 2014. *Handbook of Anthropology in Business.* Walnut Creek, CA: Left Coast Press.

Dentan, R. K. 2008  *Overwhelming Terror: Love, Fear, Peace and Violence among the Semai of Malaysia.* Lanham, MD: Rowman & Littlefield.

DeSalle, R., and I. Tattersall. 2018. *Troublesome Science: The Misuse of Genetics and Genomics in Understanding Race.* New York: Columbia University Press.

Détroit, F., Mijares, A. S., et al. 2019. A New Species of *Homo* from the Late Pleistocene of the Philippines. *Nature* 568: 181-186. https://www.nature.com/articles/s41586-019-1067-9.

De Waal, F. B. M. 1997. *Bonobo: The Forgotten Ape.* Berkeley: University of California Press.

————. 2013. *The Bonobo and the Atheist: In Search of Humanism among the Primates.* New York: W. W. Norton.

Diamond, J. M. 1990. A Pox upon Our Genes. *Natural History,* February, pp. 26–30.

————. 2017 (orig. 1997). *Guns, Germs, and Steel: The Fates of Human Societies,* 20th anniversary ed. New York: W. W. Norton.

Di Liberto, T. 2017. Reviewing Hurricane Harvey's Catastrophic Rain and Flooding. Climate.gov. September 18. https://www.climate.gov/news-features/event-tracker/reviewing-hurricane-harveys-catastrophic-rain-and-flooding.

Donnelly, J. 2013. *Universal Human Rights in Theory and Practice,* 3rd ed. Ithaca, NY: Cornell University Press.

Donovan, J. M. 2007. *Legal Anthropology.* Lanham, MD: Altamira.

Dorward, D. C., ed. 1983. *The Igbo "Women's War" of 1929: Documents Relating to the Aba Riots in Eastern Nigeria.* Wakefield, England: East Ardsley.

Dove, M. R., and C. Carpenter, eds. 2008. *Environmental Anthropology: A Historical Reader.* Malden, MA: Blackwell.

Dove, M. R., P. E. Sajise, and A. A. Doolittle, eds. 2011. *Beyond the Sacred Forest: Complicating Conservation in Southeast Asia.* Durham, NC: Duke University Press.

Downey, D., I. Kinane, and E. Parker, eds. 2017. *Landscapes of Liminality: Between Space and Place.* Lanham, MD: Rowman & Littlefield.

Doyle, C. M. 2015. *Indigenous Peoples, Title to Territory, Rights, and Resources: The Transformative Role of Free Prior and Informed Consent.* New York: Routledge.

Drahos, P. 2014. *Intellectual Property, Indigenous People, and Their Knowledge.* Cambridge, UK: Cambridge University Press.

Dresch, P., and H. Skoda. 2012. *Legalism: Anthropology and History.* Oxford, UK: Oxford University Press.

Duffield, M., and V. Hewitt, eds. 2009. *Empire, Development, and Colonialism: The Past in the Present.* Rochester, NY: James Currey.

Durkheim, E. 1951 (orig. 1897). *Suicide: A Study in Sociology*. Glencoe, IL: Free Press.

———. 2001 (orig. 1912). *The Elementary Forms of the Religious Life*. Translated by Carol Cosman. Abridged with an introduction and notes by Mark S. Cladis. New York: Oxford University Press.

Earle, T. K. 1987. Chiefdoms in Archaeological and Ethnohistorical Perspective. *Annual Review of Anthropology* 16:279–308.

———. 1997. *How Chiefs Come to Power: The Political Economy in Prehistory*. Stanford, CA: Stanford University Press.

Eckert, P. 1989. *Jocks and Burnouts: Social Categories and Identity in the High School*. New York: Teachers College Press, Columbia University.

———. 2000. *Linguistic Variation as Social Practice: The Linguistic Construction of Identity in Belten High*. Malden, MA: Blackwell.

———. 2018. *Meaning and Linguistic Variation: The Third Wave in Sociolinguistics*. New York: Cambridge University Press.

Eckert, P., and S. McConnell-Ginet. 2013. *Language and Gender,* 2nd ed. Cambridge, UK: Cambridge University Press.

Eckert, P., and N. Mendoza-Denton. 2002. Getting Real in the Golden State. *Language,* March 29.

Economist (The). 2018. How life expectancy varies across America, September 26. https://www.economist.com/democracy-in-america/2018/09/26/how-life-expectancy-varies-across-america.

Edelman, M., and A. Haugerud. 2005. *The Anthropology of Development and Globalization: From Classical Political Economy to Contemporary Neoliberalism*. Malden, MA: Blackwell.

Edwards, S. B. 2015. *Ancient Maya*. Minneapolis, MN: Abdo.

Eldred, S. M. 2013. Chimp Research Curtailed: Will Science Suffer? *Discovery News,* January 23. http://news.discovery.com/animals/zoo-animals/chimp-research-curtailed-will-science-suffer-130123.htm.

Eldredge, N., and S. Pearson. 2010. *Charles Darwin and the Mystery of Mysteries*. New York: Rb Flash Point/Roaring Brook Press.

Ellen, R., S. J. Lycett, and S. E. Johns, eds. 2013. *Understanding Cultural Transmission in Anthropology: A Critical Synthesis*. New York: Berghahn Books.

Eller, J. D. 2015. *Introducing Anthropology of Religion,* 2nd ed. New York: Routledge.

Ellick, C. J., and J. E. Watkins. 2011. *The Anthropology Graduate's Guide: From Student to a Career*. Walnut Creek, CA: Left Coast Press.

Elson, C. 2007. *Excavations at Cerro Tilcajete: A Monte Alban II Administrative Center in the Valley of Oaxaca*. Memoir 42 of the Museum of Anthropology, University of Michigan, Ann Arbor.

Enfield, N. J., P. Kockelman, and J. Sidnell, eds. 2014. *The Cambridge Handbook of Linguistic Anthropology*. New York: Cambridge University Press.

Entmacher, J., et al. 2013. *Insecure and Unequal: Poverty and Income among Women and Families 2000–2012*. Washington, DC: National Women's Law Center. http://www.nwlc.org/resource/insecure-unequal-poverty-among-women-and-families-2000-2012.

Erickson, J. 2016. Minority, Low-Income Neighborhoods Targeted for Hazardous Waste. University of Michigan, *The University Record,* January 20.

Eriksen, T. H. 2014. *Globalization: The Key Concepts,* 2nd ed. New York: Bloomsbury Academic.

Errington, F., and D. Gewertz. 1987. *Cultural Alternatives and a Feminist Anthropology: An Analysis of Culturally Constructed Gender Interests in Papua New Guinea*. New York: Cambridge University Press.

Ervin, A. M. 2005. *Applied Anthropology: Tools and Perspectives for Contemporary Practice,* 2nd ed. Boston: Pearson/Allyn & Bacon.

———. 2014. *Cultural Transformations and Globalization: Theory, Development and Social Change*. Boulder, CO: Paradigm.

Escobar, A. 2012. *Encountering Development: The Making and Unmaking of the Third World.* Princeton, NJ: Princeton University Press.

Escobedo, A. E., et al. 2018. U.S. Small-Area Life Expectancy Estimates Project: Methodology and Results. National Center for Health Statistics. Vital Health Statistics 2(181).

Evans, S. T. 2013. *Ancient Mexico and Central America: Archaeology and Culture History,* 3rd ed. New York: Thames and Hudson.

Evans-Pritchard, E. E. 1970. Sexual Inversion among the Azande. *American Anthropologist* 72:1428–1433.

Fagan, B. M. 1996. *World Prehistory: A Brief Introduction,* 3rd ed. New York: HarperCollins.

Fairbanks, D. J. 2015. *Everyone Is African: How Science Explodes the Myth of Race.* New York: Prometheus Books.

Fairclough, N. 2015. *Language and Power.* New York: Routledge.

Fawcett, K. 2014. To Decode the Mystery of Corn, Smithsonian Scientists Recreate Earth as It Was 10,000 Years Ago. *Smithsonian,* February 11. http://www.smithsonianmag.com/smithsonian-institution/to-decode-mystery-corn-smithsoniain-scientists-recreate-earth-ten-thousand-years-ago-180949708/.

Fearon, J. D. 2003. Ethnic and Cultural Diversity by Country. *Journal of Economic Growth* 8:195–222.

Feder, K. L. 2017. *Frauds, Myths, and Mysteries: Science and Pseudoscience in Archaeology,* 9th ed. New York: Oxford University Press.

Fedorak, S. 2014. Global Issues: A Cross-Cultural Perspective. Toronto: University of Toronto Press.

Ferguson, D. 2015. First Black Player on PGA Tour Dies. *Associated Press, Post and Courier.* Charleston, SC, February 5.

Ferguson, R. B. 1995. *Yanomami Warfare: A Political History.* Santa Fe, NM: School of American Research Press.

Ferraro, G., and E. Briody. 2013. *The Cultural Dimension of Global Business,* 7th ed. Boston: Pearson.

Ferraro, J. V., et al. 2013. Earliest Archaeological Evidence of Persistent Hominin Carnivory. *PLOS ONE Online,* April 5. http://www.plosone.org/article/info%3Adoi%2F10.1371%2Fjournal.pone.0062174.

Field, L. W., and R. G. Fox. 2007. *Anthropology Put to Work.* New York: Berg.

Fikentscher, W. 2016. *Law and Anthropology.* München, Germany: C. H. Beck.

Finnan, C. 2016. Residential Schooling Brings Opportunity to India's Poorest Indigenous Children. SAPIENS, October 12. http://www.sapiens.org/culture/india-indigenous-education/.

Finnstrom, S. 1997. Postcoloniality and the Postcolony: Theories of the Global and the Local. http://www.postcolonialweb.org/poldiscourse/finnstrom/finnstrom2.html.

Fiske, J. 2011. *Reading the Popular,* 2nd ed. New York: Routledge.

Flannery, K. V. 1969. Origins and Ecological Effects of Early Domestication in Iran and the Near East. In *The Domestication and Exploitation of Plants and Animals,* P. J. Ucko and G. W. Dimbleby, eds., pp. 73–100. Chicago: Aldine.

———. 1973. The Origins of Agriculture. *Annual Review of Anthropology* 2:271–310.

———. 1999. Chiefdoms in the Early Near East: Why It's So Hard to Identify Them. In *The Iranian World: Essays on Iranian Art and Archaeology,* A. Alizadeh, Y. Majidzadeh, and S. M. Shahmirzadi, eds. Tehran: Iran University Press.

Flannery, K. V., and J. Marcus. 2000. Formative Mexican Chiefdoms and the Myth of the "Mother Culture." *Journal of Anthropological Archaeology* 19:1–37.

———. 2003a. *The Cloud People: Divergent Evolution of the Zapotec and Mixtec Civilizations.* Clinton Corners, NY: Percheron Press.

———. 2003b. The Origin of War: New $^{14}$C Dates from Ancient Mexico. *Proceedings of the National Academy of Sciences* 100(20): 11801–11805.

———. 2012. *The Creation of Inequality: How Our Prehistoric Ancestors Set the Stage for Monarchy, Slavery, and Empire.* Cambridge, MA: Harvard University Press.

Fleagle, J. G. 2013. *Primate Adaptation and Evolution,* 3rd ed. San Diego, CA: Elsevier.

Fleisher, M. L. 2000. *Kuria Cattle Raiders: Violence and Vigilantism on the Tanzania/ Kenya Frontier.* Ann Arbor: University of Michigan Press.

Flores, A. 2017. How the U.S. Hispanic Population Is Changing. Pew Research Center, September 18. http://www.pewresearch.org/ fact-tank/2017/09/18/how-the-u-s-hispanic-population-is-changing/.

Fojas, A. E. 2013. *Ancient Maya Political Dynamics.* Gainesville: University Press of Florida.

Fontenot, K., J. Semega, and M. Kollar. 2018. Income and Poverty in the United States: 2017. U.S. Census Bureau, Current Population Reports, P60-263. Washington, DC: U.S. Government Printing Office. https://www. census.gov/content/dam/Census/library/ publications/2018/demo/p60-263.pdf.

Ford, A., and S. Horn. 2018. Above and Below the Maya Forest. *Science* 361(6409):1313-1314, September 28. http://science.sciencemag.org/ content/361/6409/1313.

Ford, C. S., and F. A. Beach. 1951. *Patterns of Sexual Behavior.* New York: Harper Torchbooks.

Fortes, M. 1950. Kinship and Marriage among the Ashanti. In *African Systems of Kinship and Marriage,* A. R. Radcliffe-Brown and D. Forde, eds., pp. 252-284. London: Oxford University Press.

Fortier, J. 2009. The Ethnography of South Asian Foragers. *Annual Review of Anthropology* 39:99-114.

Fossey, D. 1983. *Gorillas in the Mist.* Boston: Houghton Mifflin.

Foster, G.M. 1965. Peasant Society and the Image of Limited Good. *American Anthropologist* 67:293-315.

Foster, G. M., and B. G. Anderson. 1978. *Medical Anthropology.* New York: McGraw-Hill.

Foucault, M. 1979. *Discipline and Punish: The Birth of the Prison.* A. Sheridan (trans.). New York: Vintage Books.

———. 1990. *The History of Sexuality,* Volume 2, *The Use of Pleasure.* R. Hurley (trans.). New York: Vintage.

Fountain, H., J. K. Patel, and N. Popovich. 2018. 2017 Was One of the Hottest Years on Record. And That Was without El Niño. *New York Times,* January 18. https://www.nytimes. com/interactive/2018/01/18/climate/hottest-year-2017.html.

Fouts, R. S. 1997. *Next of Kin: What Chimpanzees Have Taught Me about Who We Are.* New York: William Morrow.

Fouts, R. S., D. H. Fouts, and T. E. Van Cantfort. 1989. The Infant Loulis Learns Signs from Cross-Fostered Chimpanzees. In *Teaching Sign Language to Chimpanzees,* R. A. Gardner, B. T. Gardner, and T. E. Van Cantfort, eds., pp. 280-292. Albany: State University of New York Press.

Fowler, C. 2015. *The Oxford Handbook of Neolithic Europe.* New York: Oxford University Press.

Fowler, S. 2011. Into the Stone Age with a Scalpel: A Dig with Clues on Early Urban Life. *New York Times,* September 7. http://www.nytimes. com/2011/09/08/world/europe/08iht-M08C-TURKEY-DIG.html.

Freston, P., ed. 2008. *Evangelical Christianity and Democracy in Latin America.* New York: Oxford University Press.

Frey, C. B., and M. A. Osborne. 2013. The Future of Employment: How Susceptible Are Jobs to Computerisation? Oxford Martin School Working Paper. Oxford, UK: University of Oxford. https://www.oxfordmar-tin.ox.ac.uk/downloads/academic/future-of-employment.pdf.

Fricke, T. 1994. *Himalayan Households: Tamang Demography and Domestic Processes,* 2nd ed. New York: Columbia University Press.

Fried, M. H. 1960. On the Evolution of Social Stratification and the State. In *Culture in History,* S. Diamond, ed., pp. 713-731. New York: Columbia University Press.

———. 1967. *The Evolution of Political Society: An Essay in Political Anthropology.* New York: McGraw-Hill.

Friedl, E. 1962. *Vasilika: A Village in Modern Greece.* New York: Holt, Rinehart, and Winston.

———. 1975. *Women and Men: An Anthropologist's View.* New York: Holt, Rinehart & Winston.

Friedman, K. E., and J. Friedman. 2008. *Historical Transformations: The Anthropology of Global Systems.* Lanham, MD: AltaMira.

Fry, R. 2017. The Share of Americans Living without a Partner Has Increased, Especially among Young Adults. Pew Research Center, October 11. http://www.pewresearch.org/fact-tank/2017/10/11/the-share-of-americans-living-without-a-partner-has-increased-especially-among-young-adults.

Fuchs, C., and M. Sandoval, eds. 2014. *Critique, Social Media, and the Information Society.* New York: Routledge/Taylor and Francis.

Galbraith, J. K. 2016. *Inequality: What Everyone Needs to Know.* New York: Oxford University Press.

Galdikas, B. M. 2007. The Vanishing Man of the Forest. *International Herald Tribune,* January 7. http://www.nytimes.com/2007/01/07/opinion/07iht-edgald.4127210.html.

Galman, S. C. 2018. *Shane, the Lone Ethnographer: A Beginner's Guide to Ethnography.* Lanham: Rowman & Littlefield.

Gamson, J. 2015. *Modern Families: Stories of Extraordinary Journeys to Kinship.* New York: New York University Press.

Garcia, O., Flores, N., and M. Spotti, eds. 2017. *The Oxford Handbook of Language and Society.* New York: Oxford University Press.

Garcia-Navarro, L. 2013. Brazilian Believers of Hidden Religion Step Out of Shadows, September 16. National Public Radio. http://www.npr.org/blogs/parallels/2013/09/16/216890587/brazilian-believers-of-hidden-religion-step-out-of-shadows.

Gardner, R. A., B. T. Gardner, and T. E. Van Cantfort, eds. 1989. *Teaching Sign Language to Chimpanzees.* Albany: State University of New York Press.

Garraty, C. P. 2013. Market Development and Pottery Exchange under Aztec and Spanish Rule in Cerro Portezuelo. *Ancient Mesoamerica* 24(1):151–176.

Geertz, C. 1973. T*he Interpretation of Cultures.* New York: Basic Books.

Gell-Mann, M., and M. Ruhlen. 2011. The Origin and Evolution of Word Order. *Proceedings of the National Academy of Sciences* 108(42):17290–17295. http://www.pnas.org/content/early/2011/10/04/1113716108.

Gibbens, S. 2018. Syphilis DNA Pulled from Colonial-Era Bones. *National Geographic,* June 21. https://news.nationalgeographic.com/2018/06/syphilis-genomes-dna-mexico-skeletons-science/.

Gibbons, A. 2012. A New Face Reveals Multiple Lineages Alive at the Dawn of Our Genus *Homo. Science* 337:635.

Giddens, A. 1981. *The Class Structure of the Advanced Societies,* 2nd ed. London: Hutchinson.

Gillis, J. 2015. Short Answers to Hard Questions about Climate Change. *New York Times,* November 28. http://www.nytimes.com/interactive/2015/11/28/science/what-is-climate-change.html.

———. 2016a. 2015 Was Hottest Year in Historical Record, Scientists Say. *New York Times,* January 20. http://www.nytimes.com/2016/01/21/science/earth/2015-hottest-year-global-warming.html.

———. 2016b. Seas Are Rising at Fastest Rate in Last 28 Centuries. *New York Times,* February 22. http://www.nytimes.com/2016/02/23/science/sea-level-rise-global-warming-climate-change.html.

Gimpel, J. 1988. *The Medieval Machine: The Industrial Revolution of the Middle Ages,* 2nd ed. Aldershot, Hants, UK: Wildwood House.

Giugale, M. 2017. *Economic Development: What Everyone Needs to Know,* 2nd ed. New York: Oxford University Press.

Gluckman, M. 2012. *Politics, Law, and Ritual in Tribal Society.* New Brunswick, NJ: Transaction.

Gmelch, G. 1978. Baseball Magic. *Human Nature* 1(8):32–40.

———. 1992. Superstition and Ritual in American Baseball. *Elysian Fields Quarterly* 11(3):25–36. https://meissinger.com/uploads/3/4/9/1/34919185/gmelch_baseball_magic.pdf.

————. 2006. *Inside Pitch: Life in Professional Baseball.* Lincoln: University of Nebraska Press.

Gmelch, G., and S. B. Gmelch. 2018. *In the Field: Life and Work in Cultural Anthropology.* Oakland: University of California Press.

Golash-Boza, T. M. 2019. *Race & Racisms: A Critical Approach,* 2nd ed. New York: Oxford University Press.

Goleman, D. 1992. Anthropology Goes Looking for Love in All the Old Places. *New York Times,* November 24, p. B1.

Golombok, S. 2015. Modern Families: Parents and Children in New Family Forms. New York: Cambridge University Press.

Golub, A. 2017. What You Can REALLY Do with an Anthropology Degree. Savage Minds, September 8. https://savageminds. org/2017/09/08/what-you-can-really-do-with-an-anthropology-degree/.

Gomez, J. Filipinos Plan More Diggings Where New Human Species Found. Associated Press, *APNews,* April 11. https://www.apnews.com/b0bb10d1d8cd4b3f90f58f617cc05788.

Gonlin, N., and K. D. French, eds. 2015. *Human Adaptation in Ancient Mesoamerica.* Boulder: University Press of Colorado.

Gonzalez-Ruibal, A. 2018. Ethics of Archaeology. *Annual Review of Anthropology* 47:345–360.

Goodale, M. 2017. *Anthropology and Law: A Critical Introduction.* New York: New York University Press.

Goodall, J. 2009. *Jane Goodall: 50 Years at Gombe, a Tribute to Five Decades of Wildlife Research, Education, and Conservation.* New York: Stewart, Tabori, and Chang.

————. 2010. *In the Shadow of Man,* new ed. Boston: Mariner Books.

Gotkowitz, L., ed. 2011. *Histories of Race and Racism: The Andes and Mesoamerica from Colonial Times to the Present.* Durham, NC: Duke University Press.

Gough, E. K. 1959. The Nayars and the Definition of Marriage. *Journal of the Royal Anthropological Institute* 89:23–34.

Gould, T. H. P. 2016. *Global Advertising in a Global Culture.* Lanham, MD: Rowman & Littlefield.

Graber, M., and J. Atkinson. 2012. Business Anthropology Unlocks Opportunities. *Memphis Daily News* 127(185), September 21. https://www.memphisdailynews.com/news/2012/sep/21/business-anthropology-unlocks-opportunities/.

Graburn, N. H. H., et al., eds. 2008. *Multiculturalism in the New Japan: Crossing the Boundaries Within.* New York: Berghahn Books.

Graef, D. J. 2017. Natural Disasters Are Social Disasters. SAPIENS, December 13. https://www.sapiens.org/column/the-climate-report/hurricane-harvey-inequality/.

Gramsci, A. 1971. *Selections from the Prison Notebooks.* Q. Hoare and G. N. Smith, ed. and trans. London: Wishart.

Grasmuck, S., and P. R. Pessar. 1991. *Between Two Islands : Dominican International Migration.* Berkeley: University of California Press.

Green, G. M., and R. W. Sussman. 1990. Deforestation History of the Eastern Rain Forests of Madagascar from Satellite Images. *Science* 248 (April 13):212–215.

Green, P. 1999. Mirror, Mirror: The Anthropologist of Dressing Rooms. *New York Times,* May 2. http://www.nytimes.com/1999/05/02/style/mirror-mirror-the-anthropologist-of-dressing-rooms.html.

Green, T. 2006. *Archaeologist Makes the Case for Burying Dominant Theory of First Americans.* Austin: University of Texas Research. http://www.utexas.edu/research/features/story.php?item/2006/01/collins16.xml.

Gremaux, R. 1993. Woman Becomes Man in the Balkans. In *Third Sex, Third Gender: Beyond Sexual Dimorphism in Culture and History, G. Herdt,* ed. Cambridge, MA: MIT Press.

Griffin, P. B., and A. Estioko-Griffin, eds. 1985. *The Agta of Northern Luzon: Recent Studies.* Cebu City, Philippines: University of San Carlos.

Grimm, D. 2016. Prehistoric Japanese Graves Provide Best Evidence Yet That Dogs Were Our Ancient Hunting Companions. *Science* 353 (September 16):6306. http://www.sciencemag.org/news/2016/09/prehistoric-japanese-graves-provide-best-evidence-yet-dogs-were-our-ancient-hunting.

Gudeman, S. F. 2016. *Anthropology and Economy.* New York: Cambridge University Press.

Gugliotta, G. 2002. Earliest Human Ancestor? Skull Dates to When Apes, Humans Split. *Washington Post,* July 11, p. A01.

Gupta, A., and J. Ferguson. 1997a. Culture, Power, Place: Ethnography at the End of an Era. In *Culture, Power, Place: Explorations in Critical Anthropology,* A. Gupta and J. Ferguson, eds., pp. 1–29. Durham, NC: Duke University Press.

———. 1997b. Beyond "Culture": Space, Identity, and the Politics of Difference. In *Culture, Power, Place,* A. Gupta and J. Ferguson, eds., pp. 33–51. Durham, NC: Duke University Press.

Ha, K. O. n. d. Anthropologists Dig into Business: Researchers Observe Consumer Habits to Design New Products. *Mercury News.* http://www.antropologi.info/antromag/corporate/kopi/business.html.

Habu, J., A. Matsui, N. Yamamoto, and T. Kanno. 2011. Shell Midden Archaeology in Japan: Aquatic Food Acquisition and Long-Term Change in the Jomon Culture. *Quaternary International* 239(1–2):19–27.

Haenn, N., R. R. Wilk, and A. Harnish, eds. 2016. *The Environment in Anthropology: A Reader in Ecology, Culture, and Sustainable Living.* New York: New York University Press.

Hallowell, A. I. 1955. *Culture and Experience.* Philadelphia: University of Pennsylvania Press.

Hancock, G. 2011. *Fingerprints of the Gods.* New York: MJF Books.

———. 2015. *Magicians of the Gods: The Forgotten Wisdom of Lost Civilization.* New York: Thomas Dunne Books.

Handwerker, W. P. 2009. *The Origins of Cultures: How Individual Choices Make Cultures Change.* Walnut Creek, CA: Left Coast Press.

Hankins, J. D. 2014. *Working Skin: Making Leather, Making a Multicultural Japan.* Oakland: University of California Press

Hann, C., and K. Hart. 2011. *Economic Anthropology: History, Ethnography, Critique.* Malden, MA: Polity Press.

Hann, C., and K. Hart, eds. 2009. *Market and Society: The Great Transformation Today.* New York: Cambridge University Press.

Hansen, K. V. 2005. *Not-So-Nuclear Families: Class, Gender, and Networks of Care.* New Brunswick, NJ: Rutgers University Press.

Hanzel, I. 2017. *50 Years of Language Experiments with Great Apes.* New York: Peter Lang Edition.

Hare, B., and Yamamoto, S. 2017. *Bonobos: Unique in Mind, Brain and Behavior.* New York: Oxford University Press.

Harlan, J. R., and D. Zohary. 1966. Distribution of Wild Wheats and Barley. *Science* 153: 1074–1080.

Harper, K. N., M. K. Zuckerman, and G. J. Armelagos. 2014. Syphilis Then and Now. *The Scientist,* February 1. http://www.the-scientist.com/?articles.view/articleNo/38985/title/Syphilis–Then-and-Now/.

Harris, M. 1964. *Patterns of Race in the Americas.* New York: Walker.

———. 1974. *Cows, Pigs, Wars, and Witches: The Riddles of Culture.* New York: Random House.

———. 1978. *Cannibals and Kings.* New York: Vintage Books.

Harris, M., and C. P. Kottak. 1963. The Structural Significance of Brazilian Racial Categories. *Sociologia* 25:203–209.

Harrison, G. G., W. L. Rathje, and W. W. Hughes. 1994. Food Waste Behavior in an Urban Population. In *Applying Anthropology: An Introductory Reader,* 3rd ed., A. Podolefsky and P. J. Brown, eds., pp. 107–112. Mountain View, CA: Mayfield.

Harrison, K. D. 2007. *When Languages Die: The Extinction of the World's Languages and the Erosion of Human Knowledge.* New York: Oxford University Press.

———. 2010. *The Last Speakers: The Quest to Save the World's Most Endangered Languages.* Washington, DC: National Geographic.

Hart, C. W. M., A. R. Pilling, and J. C. Goodale. 1988. *The Tiwi of North Australia,* 3rd ed. Fort Worth, TX: Harcourt Brace.

Hart, D., and R. W. Sussman. 2009. *Man the Hunted: Primates, Predators, and Human Evolution,* expanded ed. Boulder, CO: Westview.

Hartigan, J., ed. 2013. *Anthropology of Race: Genes, Biology, and Culture.* Santa Fe, NM: School for Advanced Research Press.

Hartl, D. L. 2014. *Essential Genetics: A Genomics Perspective,* 6th ed. Burlington, MA: Jones and Bartlett.

Harvey, D. J. 1980. French Empire. *Academic American Encyclopedia,* Volume 8, pp. 309–310. Princeton, NJ: Arete.

Haugerud, A., M. P. Stone, and P. D. Little, eds. 2011. *Commodities and Globalization: Anthropological Perspectives.* Lanham, MD: Rowman & Littlefield.

Helliwell, J., H. Hwang, and S. Wang. 2019. Chapter 2, Changing World Happiness. World Happiness Report 2019. https://worldhappiness. report/ed/2019/changing-world-happiness/.

Henry, J. 1 955. Docility, or Giving the Teacher What She Wants. *Journal of Social Issues* 2:33–41.

——. 1972. *Jules Henry on Education.* New York: Random House.

Herdt, G. H. 2006. *The Sambia: Ritual, Sexuality, and Change in Papua New Guinea.* Belmont, CA: Thomson/Wadsworth.

Herdt, G. H., ed. 1984. *Ritualized Homosexuality in Melanesia.* Berkeley: University of California Press.

Herdt, G. H., and N. Polen. 2013. *Sexual Literacy: Sexuality in Human Nature, Culture and Society.* New York: McGraw-Hill.

Hershkovitz, I., et al. 2015. Levantine Cranium from Manot Cave (Israel) Foreshadows the First European Modern Humans. *Nature,* January 28. http://www.nature.com/nature/journal/vaop/ncurrent/full/nature14134.html.

——. 2018. The Earliest Modern Humans outside Africa. *Science* 359 (6374): 456-459 (January 26). http://science.sciencemag.org/content/359/6374/456.

Herzog, T. 2015. *Frontiers of Possession: Spain and Portugal in Europe and the Americas.* Cambridge, MA: Harvard University Press.

Heyerdahl, T. 1971. *The Ra Expeditions.* P. Crampton (trans.). Garden City, NY: Doubleday.

Hickel, J. 2017. *The Divide: A Brief Guide to Global Inequality and its Solutions.* London: William Heinemann.

Higham, T., et al. 2011. The Earliest Evidence for Anatomically Modern Humans in Northwestern Europe. *Nature* 479 (November 24):521–524. doi:10.1038/nature10484.

Hill, J. H. 2017. A Linguist Walks into a Mexican Restaurant. Edible Baja Arizona 5(25). http://ediblebajaarizona.com/linguist-walks-mexican-restaurant.

Hill, K. R., et al. 2011. Co-residence Patterns in Hunter-Gatherer Societies Show Unique Human Social Structure. *Science* (March 11): 1286–1289.

Hill-Burnett, J. 1978. Developing Anthropological Knowledge through Application. In *Applied Anthropology in America,* E. M. Eddy and W. L. Partridge, eds., pp. 112–128. New York: Columbia University Press.

Hinton, A. L., and K. L. O'Neill, eds. 2011. *Genocide: Truth, Memory, and Representation.* Durham, NC: Duke University Press.

Hirth, K. G. 2016. *The Aztec Economic World: Merchants and Markets in Ancient Mesoamerica.* New York: Cambridge University Press.

Hirth, K. G., and J. Pillsbury, eds. 2013. *Merchants, Markets, and Exchange in the Pre-Columbian World.* Washington, DC: Dumbarton Oaks Research Library and Collection.

Hobhouse, L. T. 1915. *Morals in Evolution,* rev. ed. New York: Holt.

Hodder, I. 2006. *The Leopard's Tale: Revealing the Mysteries of Çatalhöyük.* New York: Thames & Hudson.

Hodgson, D. L. 2016. *The Gender, Culture, and Power Reader.* New Brunswick, NJ: Rutgers University Press.

Hoebel, E. A. 1954. *The Law of Primitive Man.* Cambridge, MA: Harvard University Press.

——. 2006. *The Law of Primitive Man: A Study in Comparative Legal Dynamics.* Cambridge, MA: Harvard University Press.

Hoffecker, J. F., ed. 2017. *Modern Humans: Their African Origin and Global Dispersal.* New York: Columbia University Press.

Hogan, B., N. Li, and W. H. Dutton. 2011. *A Global Shift in the Social Relationships of Networked Individuals: Meeting and Dating Online Comes of Age* (February 14). Oxford Internet Institute, University of Oxford. http://ssrn.com/abstract=1763884 or http://dx.doi.org/10.2139/ssrn.1763884.

Hoge, W. 2001. Kautokeino Journal: Reindeer Herders, at Home on a (Very Cold) Range. *New York Times,* March 26, p. A4.

Hole, F., K. V. Flannery, and J. A. Neely. 1969. *The Prehistory and Human Ecology of the Deh Luran Plain.* Memoir No. 1. Ann Arbor: Museum of Anthropology, University of Michigan.

Holst, I., J. E. Moreno, and D. R. Piperno. 2007. The Identification of Teosinte, Maize, and *Tripsacum* in Mesoamerica by Using Pollen, Starch Grains, and Phytoliths. *Proceedings of the National Academy of Sciences* 104:17608–17613.

Hornborg, A., B. Clark, and K. Hermele, eds. 2011. *Ecology and Power: Struggles over Land and Material Resources in the Past, Present and Future.* New York: Routledge.

Hornborg, A., and C. L. Crumley, eds. 2007. *The World System and the Earth System: Global Socioenvironmental Change and Sustainability since the Neolithic.* Walnut Creek, CA: Left Coast Press.

Hornborg, A., J. R. McNeill, and J. Martinez-Alier, eds. 2007. *Rethinking Environmental History: World-System History and Global Environmental Change.* Lanham, MD: AltaMira.

Horton, R. 1993. *Patterns of Thought in Africa and the West: Essays on Magic, Religion, and Science.* Cambridge, UK: Cambridge University Press.

Houk, B. A. 2015. *Ancient Maya Cities of the Eastern Lowlands.* Gainesville: University Press of Florida.

Hublin, J.-J. 2012. The Earliest Modern Human Colonization of Europe. *Proceedings of the National Academy of Sciences* 109 (34): 13471–13472.

Hunt, R. C. 2007. *Beyond Relativism: Comparability in Cultural Anthropology.* Lanham, MD: AltaMira.

Hyde, J. S., and J. D. DeLamater. 2016. *Understanding Human Sexuality,* 13th ed. New York: McGraw-Hill Education.

Iannone, G., B. A. Houk, and S. A. Schwake, eds. 2016. *Ritual, Violence, and the Fall of the Classic Maya Kings.* Gainesville: University Press of Florida.

Ikeya, K., and R. K. Hitchcock, eds. 2016. *Hunter-Gatherers and Their Neighbors in Asia, Africa, and South America.* Suita, Osaka: National Museum of Ethnology.

Ingraham, Christopher. 2017. The Richest 1 Percent Now Owns More of the Country's Wealth Than at Any Time in the Past 50 years. *Washington Post,* December 6. https://www.washingtonpost.com/news/wonk/wp/2017/12/06/the-richest-1-percent-now-owns-more-of-the-countrys-wealth-than-at-any-time-in-the-past-50-years/?utm_term=.d58e3d0c156f.

———. 2018. How White Racism Destroys Back Wealth. *Washington Post,* November 28. https://www.washingtonpost.com/business/2018/11/28/how-white-racism-destroys-black-wealth/?utm_term=.cab98f3afe12.

Ingraham, Chrys. 2008. *White Weddings: Romancing Heterosexuality in Popular Culture,* 2nd ed. New York: Routledge.

Inhorn, M. C., and P. J. Brown. 1990. The Anthropology of Infectious Disease. *Annual Review of Anthropology* 19:89–117.

Inhorn, M. C., and E. A. Wentzell, eds. 2012. *Medical Anthropology at the Intersections: Histories, Activisms, and Futures.* Durham, NC: Duke University Press.

Iqbal, S. 2002. A New Light on Skin Color. *National Geographic Online Extra.* http://magma.nationalgeographic.com/ngm/0211/feature2/online_extra.html.

Iqbal, Saadia, A New Light on Skin Color, *National Geographic* Online Extra, 2002, 2.

Isaacson, A. 2012. A Mini-Eden for Endangered Orangutans. *New York Times,* January 6.

Jablonski, N. G. 2006. *Skin: A Natural History.* Berkeley: University of California Press.

———. 2012. *Living Color: The Biological and Social Meaning of Skin Color.* Berkeley: University of California Press.

Jablonski, N. G., and G. Chaplin. 2000. The Evolution of Human Skin Coloration. *Journal of Human Evolution* 39:57–106.

Jackson, J., and K. B. Warren. 2005. Indigenous Movements in Latin America, 1992–2004: Controversies, Ironies, New Directions. *Annual Review of Anthropology* 34:549–573.

Jaffe, R., and A. De Koning. 2016. *Introducing Urban Anthropology.* New York: Routledge, Taylor & Francis.

Jankowiak, W. R., ed. 1995. *Romantic Passion: A Universal Experience?* New York: Columbia University Press.

———. 2008. Intimacies: *Love and Sex across Cultures.* New York: Columbia University Press.

Jankowiak, W. R., and E. F. Fischer. 1992. A Cross-Cultural Perspective on Romantic Love. *Ethnology* 31(2):149–156.

Jaschik, S. 2015. Embedded Conflicts. Army Shuts Down Controversial Human Terrain System, Criticized by Many Anthropologists. Inside Higher Ed, July 7. https://www.insidehighered.com/news/2015/07/07/army-shuts-down-controversial-human-terrain-system-criticized-many-anthropologists.

Jenkins, D. L., et al. 2012. Clovis Age Western Stemmed Projectile Points and Human Coprolites at the Paisley Caves. *Science* 13(July):223–228. doi:10.1126/science.1218443.

Jiao, T. 2007. *The Neolithic of Southeast China: Cultural Transformation and Regional Interaction on the Coast.* Youngstown, NY: Cambria Press.

Jodoin, S. 2017. Forest Preservation in a Changing Climate: REDD+ and Indigenous and Community Rights in Indonesia and Tanzania. New York: Cambridge University Press.

Johnson, A. W., and T. K. Earle. 2000. *The Evolution of Human Societies: From Foraging Group to Agrarian State,* 2nd ed. Stanford, CA: Stanford University Press.

Johnson, S. A. 2017. *Why Did Ancient Civilizations Fail?* New York: Routledge/Taylor & Francis.

Johnston, B. R. 2009. *Life and Death Matters: Human Rights, Environment, and Social Justice,* 2nd ed. Walnut Creek, CA: Left Coast Press.

Jolly, C. J., and R. White. 1995. *Physical Anthropology and Archaeology,* 5th ed. New York: McGraw-Hill.

Jones, N. 2019. First Confirmed Denisovan Skull Piece Found. SAPIENS, March 1. https://www.sapiens.org.

Joralemon, D. 2010. *Exploring Medical Anthropology,* 3rd ed. Boston: Pearson.

Jordan, A. 2003. *Business Anthropology.* Prospect Heights, IL: Waveland.

Jordan, B., ed. 2013. *Advancing Ethnography in Corporate Environments: Challenges and Emerging Opportunities.* Walnut Creek, CA: Left Coast Press.

Joyce, R. 2015. Aztec Marriage: A Lesson for Chief Justice Roberts. *Psychology Today,* June 26. https://www.psychologytoday.com/blog/what-makes-us-human/201506/aztec-marriage-lesson-chief-justice-roberts.

Jurafsky, D. 2014. *The Language of Food: A Linguist Reads the Menu.* New York: Norton.

Kahn, J. 2011. Chimpanzees in Biomedical and Behavioral Research: Assessing the Necessity. Institute of Medicine (of the National Academies). December 15. http://iom.edu/Reports/2011/Chimpanzees-in-Biomedical-and-Behavioral-Research-Assessing-the-Necessity.aspx.

Kalberg, S. 2017. *Social Thought of Max Weber.* Los Angeles: Sage.

Kamrava, M. 2011. *The Modern Middle East: A Political History since the First World War,* 2nd ed. Berkeley: University of California Press.

Kan, S. 1986. The 19th-Century Tlingit Potlatch: A New Perspective. *American Ethnologist* 13:191–212.

———. 1989. *Symbolic Immortality: The Tlingit Potlatch of the Nineteenth Century.* Washington, DC: Smithsonian Institution Press.

Kaneshiro, N. K. 2009. Intersex. Medline Plus. National Institutes of Health, U.S. National Library of Medicine. http://www.nlm.nih.gov/medlineplus/ency/article/001669.htm.

Kaplan, H. R. 2014. *Understanding Conflict and Change in a Multicultural World.* Lanham, MD: Rowman & Littlefield.

Kappelman, J. 2016. Perimortem Fractures in Lucy Suggest Mortality from Fall out of Tall Tree. *Nature* 537: 503–507, September 22. https://www.nature.com/articles/nature19332.

Karrebæk, M. S., K. C. Riley, and J. R. Cavanaugh. 2018. Food and Language: Production, Consumption, and Circulation of Meaning and Value. *Annual Review of Anthropology* 47:17–32.

Kaufman, S. R., and L. M. Morgan. 2005. The Anthropology of the Beginnings and Ends of Life. *Annual Review of Anthropology* 34:317–341.

Keim, B. 2014. An Orangutan Has (Some) Basic Human Rights, Argentine Court Rules. *Wired,* December 22. http://www.wired.com/2014/12/orangutan-personhood/.

Kellenberger, J. 2008. *Moral Relativism: A Dialogue.* Lanham, MA: Rowman & Littlefield.

Kelly, R. C. 1976. Witchcraft and Sexual Relations: An Exploration in the Social and Semantic Implications of the Structure of Belief. In *Man and Woman in the New Guinea Highlands,* P. Brown and G. Buchbinder, eds., pp. 36–53. Special Publication No. 8. Washington, DC: American Anthropological Association.

Kelly, R. L. 2013. *The Lifeways of Hunter-Gatherers: The Foraging Spectrum.* New York: Cambridge University Press.

Kennedy, M. D. 2015. *Globalizing Knowledge: Intellectuals, Universities, and Publics in Transformation.* Stanford, CA: Stanford University Press.

Kent, S. 1996. *Cultural Diversity among Twentieth-Century Foragers: An African Perspective.* New York: Cambridge University Press.

Kent, S., ed. 2002. *Ethnicity, Hunter-Gatherers, and the "Other": Association or Assimilation in Africa.* Washington, DC: Smithsonian Institution Press.

Kent, S., and H. Vierich. 1989. The Myth of Ecological Determinism: Anticipated Mobility and Site Organization of Space. In *Farmers as Hunters: The Implications of Sedentism,* S. Kent, ed., pp. 96–130. New York: Cambridge University Press.

Kershaw, S. 2009. For Teenagers, Hello Means "How about a Hug?" *New York Times,* May 28.

Keynes, J. M. 1927. *The End of Laissez-Faire.* London: L. and Virginia Woolf.

———. 1936. *General Theory of Employment, Interest, and Money.* New York: Harcourt Brace.

Kimmel, M. S. 2013. *The Gendered Society,* 5th ed. New York: Oxford University Press.

King, E. 2012. Stanford Linguists Seek to Identify the Elusive California Accent. *Stanford Report,* August 6. http://news.stanford.edu/news/2012/august/california-dialect-linguistics-080612.html.

King, G. E. 2016. *Primate Behavior and Human Origins.* New York: Routledge, Taylor and Francis.

King, T. F., ed. 2011. *A Companion to Cultural Resource Management.* Malden, MA: Wiley-Blackwell.

Kinsey, A. C., W. B. Pomeroy, and C. E. Martin. 1948. *Sexual Behavior in the Human Male.* Philadelphia: W. B. Saunders.

Kirch, P. V. 2010. *How Chiefs Became Kings: Divine Kingship and the Rise of Archaic States in Ancient Hawai'i.* Berkeley: University of California Press.

———. 2015. *Unearthing the Polynesian Past: Explorations and Adventures of an Island Archaeologist.* Honolulu: University of Hawaii Press.

———. 2017. *On the Road of the Winds: An Archaeological History of the Pacific Islands before European Contact.* rev. and expanded ed. Berkeley: University of California Press.

Kirsch, S. 2006. *Reverse Anthropology: Indigenous Analysis of Social and Environmental Relations in New Guinea.* Stanford, CA: Stanford University Press.

——. 2018. *Engaged Anthropology: Politics beyond the Text.* Berkeley: University of California Press.

Kjaerulff, J. 2010. *Internet and Change: An Ethnography of Knowledge and Flexible Work.* Walnut Creek, CA: Left Coast Press.

Klein, J. 2016. Study Suggests 3.2 Million-Year-Old Lucy Spent a Lot of Time in Trees. *New York Times,* November 30. https://www.nytimes.com/2016/11/30/science/lucy-bones-trees.html.

Klein, R. G. 2013. Modern Human Origins. *General Anthropology* 20(1):1–4.

Kluckhohn, C. 1944. *Mirror for Man: A Survey of Human Behavior and Social Attitudes.* Greenwich, CT: Fawcett.

Kohrt, B., and E. Mendenhall, eds. 2015. Global Mental Health: Anthropological Perspectives. Walnut Creek, CA: Left Coast Press.

Konopinski, N., ed. 2014. *Doing Anthropological Research: A Practical Guide.* New York: Routledge.

Kontopodis, M., C. Wulf, and B. Fichtner, eds. 2011. *Children, Development, and Education: Cultural, Historical, and Anthropological Perspectives.* New York: Springer.

Kottak, C. P. 1980. *The Past in the Present: History, Ecology, and Social Organization in Highland Madagascar.* Ann Arbor: University of Michigan Press.

——. 1990. *Prime-Time Society: An Anthropological Analysis of Television and Culture.* Belmont, CA: Wadsworth.

——. 1991. When People Don't Come First: Some Lessons from Completed Projects. In *Putting People First: Sociological Variables in Rural Development,* 2nd ed., ed. M. Cernea, pp. 429–464. New York: Oxford University Press.

——. 1999. The New Ecological Anthropology. *American Anthropologist* 101(1):23–35.

——. 2007. Return to Madagascar: A Forty Year Retrospective. *General Anthropology: Bulletin of the General Anthropology Division of the American Anthropological Association* 14(2):1–10.

——. 2009. *Prime-Time Society: An Anthropological Analysis of Television and Culture,* updated ed. Walnut Creek, CA: Left Coast Press.

——. 2018. *Assault on Paradise: The Globalization of a Little Community in Brazil,* 4th ed. Long Grove, IL: Waveland.

Kottak, C. P., and K. A. Kozaitis. 2012. *On Being Different: Diversity and Multiculturalism in the North American Mainstream,* 4th ed. New York: McGraw-Hill.

Kottak, N. C. 2002. *Stealing the Neighbor's Chicken: Social Control in Northern Mozambique.* PhD dissertation. Department of Anthropology, Emory University, Atlanta, GA.

Kotz, D. M. 2015. *The Rise and Fall of Neoliberal Capitalism.* Cambridge, MA: Harvard University Press.

Kozlowski, K. 2016. Virginia Tech Expert Helped Expose Flint Water Crisis. *Detroit News,* January 24. http://www.detroitnews.com/story/news/politics/2016/01/23/virginia-tech-expert-helped-expose-flint-water-crisis/79251004/.

Kretchmer, N. 1975 (orig. 1972). Lactose and Lactase. In *Biological Anthropology, Readings from Scientific American,* S. H. Katz, ed., pp. 310–318. San Francisco: W. H. Freeman.

Krogstad, J. M. 2017. U.S. Hispanic Population Growth Has Leveled Off. Pew Research Center, August 3. http://www.pewresearch.org/fact-tank/2017/08/03/u-s-hispanic-population-growth-has-leveled-off/.

Kuhn, S. L., M. C. Stiner, and D. S. Reese. 2001. Ornaments of the Earliest Upper Paleolithic: New Insights from the Levant. *Proceedings of the National Academy of Sciences* 98(13):7641–7646.

Kulick, D. 1998. *Travesti: Sex, Gender, and Culture among Brazilian Transgendered Prostitutes.* Chicago: University of Chicago Press.

Kurnick, S., and J. Baron, eds. 2016. *Political Strategies in Pre-Columbian Mesoamerica.* Boulder: University Press of Colorado.

Kvetenadze, T. 2018. Michigan Governor and State Dismissed from Flint Water Lawsuit. Reuters, August 1. https://www.reuters.com/article/us-michigan-water/michigan-governor-and-state-dismissed-from-flint-water-lawsuit-idUSKBN1KM66Y.

Labov, W. 1972a. *Language in the Inner City: Studies in the Black English Vernacular.* Philadelphia: University of Pennsylvania Press.

——. 1972b. *Sociolinguistic Patterns.* Philadelphia: University of Pennsylvania Press.

——. 2006. *The Social Stratification of English in New York City.* New York: Cambridge University Press.

——. 2012. *Dialect Diversity in America: The Politics of Language Change.* Charlottesville: University of Virginia Press.

Lakoff, G. P. 2008. *The Political Mind: Why You Can't Understand 21st-Century Politics with an 18th-Century Brain.* New York: Viking.

Lakoff, G. P., and G. Duran. 2018. Trump Has Turned Words into Weapons. And He's Winning the Linguistic War. *The Guardian,* June 13. https://www.theguardian.com/commentisfree/2018/jun/13/how-to-report-trump-media-manipulation-language.

Lakoff, G. P., and E. Wehling. 2012. *The Little Blue Book: The Essential Guide to Thinking and Talking Democratic.* New York: Free Press.

Lakoff, R. T. 2004. *Language and Women's Place: Text and Commentaries,* rev. ed., M. Bucholtz, ed. New York: Oxford University Press.

——. 2017. *Context Counts: Papers on Language, Gender, and Power.* New York: Oxford University Press.

Lambek, M., ed. 2008. *A Reader in the Anthropology of Religion.* Malden, MA: Blackwell.

Lange, M. 2009. *Lineages of Despotism and Development: British Colonialism and State Power.* Chicago: University of Chicago Press.

——. 2017. *Killing Others: A Natural History of Ethnic Violence.* Ithaca, NY: Cornell University Press.

Langley, N. R., and M. T. A. Tersigni-Tarrant, eds. 2017. *Forensic Anthropology: A Comprehensive Introduction.* New York: CRC Press.

Largent, F. 2007a. Clovis Dethroned: A New Perspective on the First Americans, Part 1. *Mammoth Trumpet* 22(3):1–3, 20.

——. 2007b. Clovis Dethroned: A New Perspective on the First Americans, Part 2. *Mammoth Trumpet* 22(4):1–2, 13.

Larsen, C. S. 2015. *Bioarchaeology: Interpreting Behavior from the Human Skeleton,* 2nd ed. New York: Cambridge University Press.

——. 2018. The Bioarchaeology of Health Crisis: Infectious Disease in the Past. *Annual Review of Anthropology* 47:295–313.

Lassiter, L. E. 1998. *The Power of Kiowa Song: A Collaborative Ethnography.* Tucson: University of Arizona Press.

Laughlin, J. C. H. 2006. *Fifty Major Cities of the Bible.* New York: Routledge.

Leach, E. R. 1955. Polyandry, Inheritance and the Definition of Marriage. *Man* 55: 182–186.

——. 1961. *Rethinking Anthropology.* London: Athlone Press.

Leakey, M. G., et al. 2012. New Fossils from Koobi Fora in Northern Kenya Confirm Taxonomic Diversity in Early *Homo. Nature* (August 9) 488:201–204.

Lee, R. B. 2012. The !Kung and I: Reflections on My Life and Times with the Ju/Hoansi People. *General Anthropology* 19(1):1–4.

——. 2013. *The Dobe Ju/'hoansi.* 4th ed. Belmont, CA: Wadsworth Cengage.

——. 2018. Hunter-Gatherers and Human Evolution: New Light on Old Debates. *Annual Review of Anthropology* 47:513–531.

Lee, R. B., and R. H. Daly. 1999. *The Cambridge Encyclopedia of Hunters and Gatherers.* New York: Cambridge University Press.

Lemke, A. K. ed. 2018. *Foraging in the Past: Archaeological Studies of Hunter-Gatherer Diversity.* Boulder: University Press of Colorado.

Lenski, G. 1966. *Power and Privilege: A Theory of Social Stratification.* New York: McGraw-Hill.

Levinson, B. A. U., and M. Pollock, eds. 2011. *A Companion to the Anthropology of Education.* Malden, MA: Blackwell.

Lévi-Strauss, C. 1963. *Totemism.* R. Needham (trans.). Boston: Beacon Press.

——. 1967. *Structural Anthropology.* New York: Doubleday.

Levy, J. E., with B. Pepper. 1992. *Orayvi Revisited: Social Stratification in an "Egalitarian" Society*. Santa Fe, NM: School of American Research Press, and Seattle: University of Washington Press.

Lewellen, T. C. 2010. Groping toward Globalization: In Search of Anthropology without Boundaries. *Reviews in Anthropology* 31(1):73–89.

Lewin, E., and L. M. Silverstein, eds. 2016. *Mapping Feminist Anthropology in the Twenty-First Century*. New Brunswick, NJ: Rutgers University Press.

Lim, L., and U. Ansaldo. 2016. *Languages in Contact*. New York: Cambridge University Press.

Lindenbaum, S. 1972. Sorcerers, Ghosts, and Polluting Women: An Analysis of Religious Belief and Population Control. *Ethnology* 11:241–253.

Lindquist, G., and D. Handelman, eds. 2013. *Religion, Politics, and Globalization: Anthropological Approaches*. New York: Berghahn Books.

Little, K. 1971. *Some Aspects of African Urbanization South of the Sahara*. Reading, MA: Addison-Wesley, McCaleb Modules in Anthropology.

Livingston, G., and A. Caumont. 2017. 5 Facts on Love and Marriage in America. Pew Research Center, February 13. http://www.pewresearch.org/fact-tank/2017/02/13/5-facts-about-love-and-marriage/

Lock, M., and V.-K. Nguyen. 2018. *An Anthropology of Biomedicine*. Hoboken, NJ: Wiley.

Lockwood, W. G. 1975. *European Moslems: Economy and Ethnicity in Western Bosnia*. New York: Academic Press.

Loomis, W. F. 1967. Skin-Pigmented Regulation of Vitamin-D Biosynthesis in Man. *Science* 157:501–506.

López, A. A. 2011. New Questions in the Immigration Debate. *Anthropology Now* 3(1):47–53.

Lowie, R. H. 1961 (orig. 1920). *Primitive Society*. New York: Harper & Brothers.

Lugo, A. 1997. Reflections on Border Theory, Culture, and the Nation. *Border Theory: The Limits of Cultural Politics,* Scott Michaelsen and David Johnson, eds., pp. 43–67. Minneapolis: University of Minnesota Press.

Lugo, A., and B. Maurer. 2000. *Gender Matters: Rereading Michelle Z. Rosaldo*. Ann Arbor, University of Michigan Press.

Lukas, D., and T. H. Clutton-Brock. 2013. The Evolution of Social Monogamy in Mammals. *Science* 341:526–530. http://www.sciencemag.org/content/341/6145/526.

Lule, J. 2018. *Globalization and Media: Global Village of Babel*. Lanham, MA: Rowman & Littlefield.

Lupton, D. 2012. *Medicine as Culture: Illness, Disease, and the Body*. Los Angeles: Sage.

Lyell, C. 1969 (orig. 1830–1837). *Principles of Geology*. New York: Johnson.

Lyons, A. P., and H. D. Lyons. 2011. *Sexualities in Anthropology: A Reader*. Walden, MA: Wiley Blackwell.

Madsbjerg, C., and M. B. Rasmussen. 2014. An Anthropologist Walks into a Bar. *Harvard Business Review,* March. https://hbr.org/2014/03/an-anthropologist-walks-into-a-bar.

Maguire, M., C. Frois, and N. Zurawski, eds. 2014. *The Anthropology of Security: Perspectives from the Frontline of Policing, Counter-terrorism, and Border Control*. Sterling, VA: Pluto Press.

Malaspinas, A.-S., et al. 2016. A Genomic History of Aboriginal Australia. *Nature,* September 21. doi:10.1038/nature18299.

Malinowski, B. 1927. Sex and Repression in Savage Society. London and New York: International Library of Psychology, Philosophy and Scientific Method.

——. 1929. Practical Anthropology. *Africa* 2:23–38.

——. 1961 (orig. 1922). *Argonauts of the Western Pacific*. New York: Dutton.

——. 1978 (orig. 1931). The Role of Magic and Religion. In *Reader in Comparative Religion: An Anthropological Approach,* 4th ed., W. A. Lessa and E. Z. Vogt, eds., pp. 37–46. New York: Harper and Row.

———. 2013. *Crime and Custom in Savage Society*. New Brunswick, NJ: Transaction.

Malkki, L. H. 1995. *Purity and Exile: Violence, Memory, and National Cosmology among Hutu Refugees in Tanzania*. Chicago: University of Chicago Press.

Mallick, S., et al. 2016. The Simons Genome Diversity Project: 300 Genomes from 142 Diverse Populations. *Nature*. doi:10.1038/nature18964.

Manderson, L., Cartwright, E., and A. Hardon, eds. 2016. *The Routledge Handbook of Medical Anthropology*. New York: Routledge.

Mann, C. C. 2012. *1493: Uncovering the New World Columbus Created*. New York: Vintage Books.

Marcus, G. E., and M. M. J. Fischer. 1986. *Anthropology as Cultural Critique: An Experimental Moment in the Human Sciences*. Chicago: University of Chicago Press.

Marcus, J. 1989. From Centralized Systems to City-States: Possible Models for the Epiclassic. In *Mesoamerica after the Decline of Teotihuacan: A.D. 700-900*, R. A. Diehl and J. C. Berlo, eds., pp. 201-208. Washington, DC: Dumbarton Oaks.

Marean, C. W. 2017. Early Signs of Human Presence in Australia. *Nature* 547 (July 20): 285-287. https://www.nature.com/articles/547285a.

Marger, M. 2015. *Race and Ethnic Relations: American and Global Perspectives*, 10th ed. Stamford, CT: Cengage.

Margolis, M. L. 2000. *True to Her Nature: Changing Advice to American Women*. Prospect Heights, IL: Waveland.

Marks, R. 2015. *The Origins of the Modern World: A Global and Environmental Narrative from the Fifteenth to the Twenty-First Century*, 3rd ed. Lanham, MD: Rowman & Littlefield.

Marshall, R. C., ed. 2011. *Cooperation in Economy and Society*. Lanham, MD: Rowman & Littlefield.

Martin, D. 1990. *Tongues of Fire: The Explosion of Protestantism in Latin America*. Cambridge, MA: Blackwell.

Martin, D. L., R. P. Harrod, and V. R. Perez. 2013. *Bioarcheology: An Integrated Approach to Working with Human Remains*. New York: Springer.

Martin, K., and B. Voorhies. 1975. *Female of the Species*. New York: Columbia University Press.

Martin, S. M. 1988. *Palm Oil and Protest: An Economic History of the Ngwa Region, South-Eastern Nigeria, 1800-1980*. New York: Cambridge University Press.

Marx, K., and F. Engels. 1976 (orig. 1848). *Communist Manifesto*. New York: Pantheon.

Mascia-Lees, F. 2010. *Gender & Difference in a Globalizing World: Twenty-First Century Anthropology*. Long Grove, IL: Waveland.

Masters, J., M. Gamba, and F. Génin. 2013. What's in a Name? Higher Level Taxonomy of the Prosimian Primates. In *Leaping Ahead*, J. Masters et al., eds., pp. 3-9. New York: Springer.

Matsuzawa, T., ed. 2011. *The Chimpanzees of Bossou and Nimba*. New York: Springer.

Maugh, T. H., III. 2007. One Language Disappears Every 14 Days; About Half of the World's Distinct Tongues Could Vanish This Century, Researchers Say. *Los Angeles Times*, September 19.

Maxwell, J. 2012. *Piltdown Man and Other Hoaxes: A Book about Lies, Legends, and the Search for the Missing Link*. Salt Lake City, UT: American University and College Press.

Maxwell, L. A. 2014. U.S. School Enrollment Hits Majority-Minority Milestone. *Education Week*, August 19. https://www.edweek.org/ew/articles/2014/08/20/01demographics.h34.html

Maybury-Lewis, D., T. Macdonald, and B. Maybury-Lewis, eds. 2009. *Manifest Destinies and Indigenous Peoples*. Cambridge, MA: David Rockefeller Center for Latin American Studies and Harvard University Press.

Mazzeo, J., A. Rödlach, and B. P. Brenton. 2011. Introduction: Anthropologists Confront HIV/AIDS and Food Insecurity in Sub-Saharan Africa. American Anthropological Association, *Annals of Anthropological Practice* 35(1-7).

Mba, N. E. 1982. *Nigerian Women Mobilized: Women's Political Activity in Southern Nigeria, 1900-1965*. Berkeley: University of California Press.

McBrearty, S., and A. S. Brooks. 2000. The Revolution That Wasn't: A New Interpretation of the Origin of Modern Human Behavior. *Journal of Human Evolution* 39:453-563.

McCabe, M., ed. 2017. *Collaborative Ethnography in Business Environments*. New York: Routledge, Taylor & Francis.

McDougall, I., F. H. Brown, and J. G. Fleagle. 2005. Stratigraphic Placement and Age of Modern Humans from Kibish, Ethiopia. *Nature* 433:733-736.

McElroy, A., and P. K. Townsend. 2009. *Medical Anthropology in Ecological Perspective*, 5th ed. Boulder, CO: Westview Press.

McGregor, W. 2015. *Linguistics: An Introduction*. New York: Bloomsbury Academic.

McLaughlin, E. C. 2016. 5 Things to Know about Flint's Water Crisis. CNN, January 21. http://www.cnn.com/2016/01/18/us/flint-mich-igan-water-crisis-five-things/.

McManamon, F. P., ed. 2017. *Perspectives in Cultural Resource Management*. New York: Routledge.

McWhorter, J. H. 2014. *The Language Hoax: Why the World Looks the Same in Any Language*. New York: Oxford University Press.

———. 2018. The Unmonitored President. Trump Is the First President Who, Rather Than Striding Forward and Speaking, Just Gets Up and Talks. *The Atlantic*, July 20. https://www.theatlantic.com/ideas/archive/2018/07/trump-speech/565646/.

Mead, M. 1937. *Cooperation and Competition among Primitive Peoples*. New York: McGraw-Hill.

———. 1950 (orig. 1935). *Sex and Temperament in Three Primitive Societies*. New York: New American Library.

———. 1977. Applied Anthropology: The State of the Art. In *Perspectives on Anthropology, 1976*. Washington, DC: American Anthropological Association.

Meadow, R. H., and J. M. Kenoyer. 2000. The Indus Valley Mystery: One of the World's First Great Civilizations Is Still a Puzzle. *Discovering Archaeology*, March/April 2000.

Meigs, A., and K. Barlow. 2002. Beyond the Taboo: Imagining Incest. *American Anthropologist* 104(1):38-49.

Meneley, A. 2018. Consumption. *Annual Review of Anthropology* 47:117-132.

Menez, B. H., and J. A. Ur. 2012. Mapping Patterns of a Long-Term Settlement in Northern Mesopotamia at a Large Scale. *Proceedings of the National Academy of Sciences* 109(14):E778-E787.

Menzies, C. R., ed. 2006. *Traditional Ecological Knowledge and Natural Resource Management*. Lincoln: University of Nebraska Press.

Mercader, J., M. Panger, and C. Boesch. 2002. Excavation of a Chimpanzee Stone Tool Site in the African Rainforest. *Science* 296 (May 24):1452-1455.

Merriam-Webster, *Webster's New World Encyclopedia*. Englewood Cliffs, NJ: Prentice Hall,1993.

Meyer, B. 1999. *Translating the Devil: Religion and Modernity among the Ewe in Ghana*. Trenton, NJ: Africa World Press.

Meyerhoff, M. 2018. *Introducing Sociolinguistics*. New York: Routledge.

Mielke, J. H., L. W. Konigsberg, and J. H. Relethford. 2011. *Human Biological Variation*, 2nd ed. New York: Oxford University Press.

Millaire, J. F. 2010. Primary State Formation in the Viru Valley, North Coast of Peru. *Proceedings of the National Academy of Sciences* 107(14):6186-6191.

Miller, B. D. 1997. *The Endangered Sex: Neglect of Female Children in Rural North India*. New York: Oxford University Press.

Miller, N. F., M. A. Zeder, and S. R. Arter. 2009. From Food and Fuel to Farms and Flocks: The Integration of Plant and Animal Remains in the Study of Ancient Agro-Pastoral Economies. *Current Anthropology* 50:915-924.

Mintz, S. 1985. *Sweetness and Power: The Place of Sugar in Modern History*. New York: Viking Penguin.

Mirrlees, T. 2013. *Global Entertainment Media: Between Cultural Imperialism and Cultural Globalization.* New York: Routledge.

Mitani, J. C. 2011. Fearing a Planet without Apes. *New York Times,* August 20.

Mitani, J. C., J. Call, P. M. Kappeler, R. A. Palombit, and J. B. Silk, eds. 2012. *The Evolution of Primate Societies.* Chicago: University of Chicago Press.

Mitani, J. C., and D. P. Watts. 1999. Demographic Influences on the Hunting Behavior of Chimpanzees. *American Journal of Physical Anthropology* 109:439–454.

Mohai, P., and R. Saha. 2015. Which Came First, People or Pollution? Assessing the Disparate Siting and Post-Siting Demographic Change Hypotheses of Environmental Injustice. *Environmental Research Letters* 10:1–17. http://iopscience.iop.org/article/10.1088/1748-9326/10/11/115008/pdf.

Mooney, A., and B. Evans. 2019. *Language, Society and Power: An Introduction,* 2nd ed. New York: Routledge.

Moore, J. D. 2012. *Visions of Culture: An Introduction to Anthropological Theories and Theorists,* 4th ed. Lanham, MD: AltaMira.

Moran, L. 1993. *Evolution Is a Fact and a Theory.* The Talk Origins Archive. http://www.talkorigins.org/faqs/evolution-fact.html.

Morency, J-D., E. C. Malenfant, and S. MacIsaac. 2017. Immigration and Diversity: Population Projections for Canada and its Regions, 2011 to 2036. Statistics Canada, January 25. https://www150.statcan.gc.ca/n1/pub/91-551-x/91-551-x2017001-eng.htm.

Moreno-Mayar, J. V., et al. 2018a. Terminal Pleistocene Alaskan Genome Reveals First Founding Population of Native Americans. *Nature,* January 3. https://www.nature.com/articles/nature25173.

Moreno-Mayar, J. V., et al. 2018b. Early Human Dispersals within the Americas. *Science,* November 8. http://science.sciencemag.org.proxy.lib.umich.edu/content/early/2018/11/07/science.aav2621.

Morin, M. 2013. Evidence Points Toward Solving Evolutionary "Missing Link." *Los Angeles Times,* April 11. http://articles.latimes.com/2013/apr/11/science/la-sci-australopithecus-20130412.

Morin, R. 2013. The Most (and Least) Culturally Diverse Countries in the World. Pew Research Center, July 18. http://www.pewresearch.org/fact-tank/2013/07/18/the-most-and-least-culturally-diverse-countries-in-the-world/.

Morley, M. W., et al. 2016. Initial Micromorphological Results from Liang Bua, Flores (Indonesia): Site Formation Processes and Hominin Activities at the Type Locality of Homo floresiensis. *Journal of Archaeological Science.* doi:10.1016/j.jas.2016.06.004.

Mosse, D., ed. 2011. *Adventures in Aidland: The Anthropology of Professionals in International Development.* New York: Berghahn Books.

Motseta, S. 2006. Botswana Gives Bushmen Tough Conditions. *Washington Post,* December 14. http://www.washingtonpost.com/wp-dyn/content/article/2006/12/14/.

Mounier, A., S. Condemi, and G. Manzi. 2011. The Stem Species of Our Species: A Place for the Archaic Human Cranium from Ceprano, Italy. *PLOS ONE* 6(4):e18821. doi:10.1371/journal.pone.0018821.

Mukhopadhyay, C. C., R. Henzie, and Y. T. Moses. 2014. *How Real Is Race?: A Sourcebook on Race, Culture, and Biology,* 2nd ed. Lanham, MD: Altamira.

Muller, M. N., R. W. Wrangham, and D. R. Pilbeam, eds. 2017. *Chimpanzees and Human Evolution.* Cambridge, MA: Belknap Press of Harvard University Press.

Murchison, J. M. 2010. *Ethnography Essentials: Designing, Conducting, and Presenting Your Research.* San Francisco: Jossey Bass.

Murdock, G. P. 1957. World Ethnographic Sample. *American Anthropologist* 59:664–687.

Murdock, G. P., and C. Provost. 1973. Factors in the Division of Labor by Sex: A Cross-Cultural Analysis. *Ethnology* 12(2):203–225.

Murray, S. O., and W. Roscoe, eds. 1998. *Boy-wives and Female Husbands: Studies in African Homosexualities.* New York: St. Martin's Press.

Myers-Moro, P. A., and J. E. Myers. 2012. *Magic, Witchcraft, and Religion: A Reader in the Anthropology of Religion,* 9th ed. New York: McGraw-Hill.

Nadeem, S. 2011. *Dead Ringers: How Outsourcing Is Changing the Way Indians Understand Themselves.* Princeton, NJ: Princeton University Press.

Nafte, M. 2016. *Flesh and Bone: An Introduction to Forensic Anthropology.* Durham, NC: Carolina Academic Press.

Nahm, S., and C. H. Rinker, eds. 2016. *Applied Anthropology: Unexpected Spaces, Topics, and Methods.* New York: Routledge.

Nanda, S. 1996. Hijras: An Alternative Sex and Gender Role in India. *Third Sex Third Gender: Beyond Sexual Dimorphism in Culture and History,* G. Herdt, ed., pp. 373–418. New York: Zone Books.

———. 1998. *Neither Man nor Woman: The Hijras of India.* Belmont, CA: Thomson/ Wadsworth.

———. 2014. *Gender Diversity: Crosscultural Variations,* 2nd ed. Long Grove, IL: Waveland.

Narayan, K. 2016. *Everyday Creativity: Singing Goddesses in the Himalayan Foothills.* Chicago: University of Chicago Press.

Nayar, P. K., ed. 2016. *Postcolonial Studies: An Anthology.* Malden, MA: Wiley.

Nengo, I., et al. 2017. New Infant Cranium from the African Miocene Sheds Light on Ape Evolution. *Nature* 548 (7666):169, August 10. https://www.nature.com/articles/nature23456.

Ni, X., et al. 2013. The Oldest Known Primate Skeleton and Early Haplorhine Evolution. *Nature* 498:60–64. https://www.nature.com/articles/nature12200.

Nicholas, G. 2018. Confronting the Specter of Cultural Appropriation. SAPIENS, October 5. https://www.sapiens.org/culture/cultural-appropriation-halloween/.

Nichols, D. L., and E. Rodríguez-Alegría. 2017. The Oxford Handbook of the Aztecs. New York: Oxford University Press.

Nielsen, R., and M. Slatkin. 2013. *An Introduction to Population Genetics: Theory and Applications.* Sunderland, MA: Sinauer Associates.

Nishida, T. 2012. *Chimpanzees at the Lakeshore: Natural History and Culture at Mahale.* New York: Cambridge University Press.

Nolan, R. W. 2017. *Using Anthropology in the World: A Guide to Becoming an Anthropological Practitioner.* New York: Routledge.

———, ed. 2013. *The Handbook of Practicing Anthropology.* Malden, MA: Wiley-Blackwell.

Nononi, D. M, ed. 2014. *A Companion to Urban Anthropology.* Malden, MA: Wiley-Blackwell.

Northover, A. 2016. Words of 2015 Round-Up. Oxford Dictionaries, January 16. Oxford University Press. http://blog.oup.com/2016/01/words-2015-round-up/.

Northwestern University in Qatar. 2017. Overview: Media Use in the Middle East, 2017. http://mideastmedia.org/survey/2017/overview/.

O'Connor, K. 2015. *The Never-Ending Feast: The Anthropology and Archaeology of Feasting.* New York: Bloomsbury Academic.

O'Donnell, J., 2016. The Big Business of Europe's Migration Crisis. SAPIENS, June 21. http://www.sapiens.org/culture/migration-crisis-illegality-industry/.

Okely, J. 2012. *Anthropological Practice: Fieldwork and the Ethnographic Method.* New York: Berg.

Omohundro, J. T. 2001. *Careers in Anthropology,* 2nd ed. New York: McGraw-Hill.

O'Neil, P. H. 2018. Essentials of Comparative Politics. New York: W. W. Norton.

Ong, A. 1987. *Spirits of Resistance and Capitalist Discipline: Factory Women in Malaysia.* Albany: State University of New York Press.

———. 1989. Center, Periphery, and Hierarchy: Gender in Southeast Asia. In *Gender and Anthropology: Critical Reviews for Research and Teaching,* S. Morgen, ed., pp. 294–312. Washington, DC: American Anthropological Association.

———. 2010. *Spirits of Resistance and Capitalist Discipline: Factory Women in Malaysia,* 2nd ed. Albany: State University of New York Press.

Ontario Consultants on Religious Tolerance. 2007. Santeria: A Syncretistic Caribbean Religion. http://www.religioustolerance.org/santeri2.htm.

———. 2011. Religions of the World: Number of Adherents of Major Religions, Their Geographical Distribution, Date Founded, and Sacred Texts. http://www.religioustolerance.org/worldrel.htm.

Opie, C., et al. 2013. Male Infanticide Leads to Social Monogamy in Primates. *Proceedings of the National Academy of Sciences* 110(33): 13328–13332.

Oriji, J. N. 2000. Igbo Women from 1929–1960. *West Africa Review* 2:1.

Ortner, S. B. 1984. Theory in Anthropology since the Sixties. *Comparative Studies in Society and History* 126(1):126–166.

Owen, J. 2006. "Lucy's Baby"—World's Oldest Child—Found by Fossil Hunters. *National Geographic News,* September 20. http://news.nationalgeographic.com/news/2006/09/060920-lucys-baby.html.

———. 2012. "Lucy's Baby" a Born Climber, Hinting Human Ancestors Lingered in Trees. *National Geographic News,* October 26. http://news.nationalgeographic.com/news/2012/10/121026-australopithecus-afarensis-human-evolution-lucy-scapula-science/.

Owsley, D. W., and R. L. Jantz, eds. 2014. *Kennewick Man: The Scientific Investigation of an Ancient American Skeleton.* College Station, TX: Texas A&M University Press.

Oxford University Press. 2015. Oxford Dictionaries Word of the Year 2015 Is . . . . http://blog.oxforddictionaries.com/2015/11/word-of-the-year-2015-emoji.

Özdoğan, M., N. Başgelen, and P. Kuniholm. 2011. *The Neolithic in Turkey: New Excavations and New Research.* Galatasaray, Istanbul: Archaeology and Art Publications.

Pace, R., ed. 2018. *From Filmmaker Warriors to Flash Drive Shamans: Indigenous Media Production and Engagement in Latin America.* Nashville: Vanderbilt University Press.

Pace, R., and B. P. Hinote. 2013. *Amazon Town TV: An Audience Ethnography in Gurupá, Brazil.* Austin: University of Texas Press.

Pagden, A. 2015. *The Burdens of Empire: 1539 to the Present.* New York: Cambridge University Press.

Paine, R. 2009. *Camps of the Tundra: Politics through Reindeer among Saami Pastoralists.* Oslo: Instituttet for sammenlignende kulturforskning.

Parker, K., and G. Livingston. 2017. 6 Facts about American Fathers. FactTank. Pew Research Center. http://www.pewresearch.org/fact-tank/2017/06/15/fathers-day-facts/

Parrillo, V. N. 2016. *Understanding Race and Ethnic Relations,* 5th ed. New York: Pearson.

———. 2019. *Strangers to These Shores: Race and Ethnic Relations in the United States,* 12th ed. New York: Pearson.

Parsons, J. R. 1974. The Development of a Prehistoric Complex Society: A Regional Perspective from the Valley of Mexico. *Journal of Field Archaeology* 1:81–108.

Patterson, F. 1978. Conversations with a Gorilla. *National Geographic,* October, pp. 438–465.

Paulson, T. E. 2005. Chimp, Human DNA Comparison Finds Vast Similarities, Key Differences. *Seattle Post-Intelligencer Reporter,* September 1. http://seattlepi.nwsource.com/local/238852_chimp01.html.

Peletz, M. 1988. *A Share of the Harvest: Kinship, Property, and Social History among the Malays of Rembau.* Berkeley: University of California Press.

——— 2009. *Gender Pluralism: Southeast Asia since Early Modern Times.* New York: Routledge.

Perry, M. A., ed. 2012. *Bioarchaeology and Behavior: The People of the Ancient Near East.* Gainesville: University of Florida Press.

Petraglia-Bahri, D. 1996. *Introduction to Postcolonial Studies.* http://www.emory.edu/ENGLISH/Bahri/.

Pew Research Center. 2011. Global Christianity—A Report on the Size and Distribution of the World's Christian Population, December 19. *The Pew Forum on Religion and Public Life.* http://www.pewforum.org/2011/12/19/global-christianity-exec/.

——. 2012a. *The Global Religious Landscape: A Report on the Size and Distribution of the World's Major Religious Groups as of 2010, Analysis,* December 18. http://www.pewforum.org/global-religious-landscape-exec.aspx#src=global-footer.

——. 2012b. *"Nones" on the Rise, One-in-Five Adults Have No Religious Affiliation,* October 9. http://www.pewforum.org/unaffiliated/nones-on-the-rise.aspx.

——. 2015a. *America's Changing Religious Landscape,* May 12. http://www.pewforum.org/2015/05/12/americas-changing-religious-landscape/.

——. 2015b. *The Future of World Religions: Population Growth Projections, 2010–2050,* April 2. http://www.pewforum.org/files/2015/03/PF_15.04.02_ProjectionsFullReport.pdf.

Piddocke, S. 1969. The Potlatch System of the Southern Kwakiutl: A New Perspective. In *Environment and Cultural Behavior,* A. P. Vayda, ed., pp. 130–156. Garden City, NY: Natural History Press.

Pierre-Louis, K. 2018. Greenhouse Gas Emissions Accelerate Like a "Speeding Freight Train" in 2018. *New York Times,* December 5. https://www.nytimes.com/2018/12/05/climate/greenhouse-gas-emissions-2018.html.

Pink, S., V. Fors, and T. O'Dell, eds. 2017. *Theoretical Scholarship and Applied Practice.* New York: Berghahn Books.

Piperno, D. R., and D. M. Pearsall. 1998. *The Origins of Agriculture in the Lowland Neotropics.* San Diego, CA: Academic Press.

Piperno, D. R., and K. E. Stothert. 2003. Phytolith Evidence for Early Holocene *Cucurbita* Domestication in Southwest Ecuador. *Science* 299(5609):1054–1105.

Pirie, F. 2013. *The Anthropology of Law.* New York: Oxford University Press.

Polanyi, K. 1968. *Primitive, Archaic and Modern Economies: Essays of Karl Polanyi,* G. Dalton, ed. Garden City, NY: Anchor Books.

Pospisil, L. 1963. *The Kapauku Papuans of West New Guinea.* New York: Holt, Rinehart & Winston.

Posth, C., et al. 2017. Deeply Divergent Archaic Mitochondrial Genome Provides Lower Time Boundary for African Gene Flow into Neanderthals. Nature Communications 8 (16046). doi:10.1038/ncomms16046.

——. 2018. Reconstructing the Deep Population History of Central and South America. Cell. November 8. https://doi.org/10.1016/j.cell.2018.10.027.

Potts, D. T. 2015. *The Archaeology of Elam: Formation and Transformation of an Ancient Iranian State.* New York: Cambridge University Press.

Price, D. 2000. Anthropologists as Spies. Nation, November 20, 24–27.

Price, R., ed. 1973. *Maroon Societies.* New York: Anchor Press/Doubleday.

Radcliffe-Brown, A. R. 1965 (orig. 1952). *Structure and Function in Primitive Society.* New York: Free Press.

Radcliffe-Brown, A. R. 1952 (orig. 1924). The Mother's Brother in South Africa. In A. R. Radcliffe-Brown, *Structure and Function in Primitive Society,* pp. 15–31. London: Routledge & Kegan Paul.

Radin, J. 2018. Ethics in Human Biology: A Historical Perspective on Present Challenges. *Annual Review of Anthropology* 47:263–278.

Ramachandran, S., and N. Rosenberg. 2011. A Test of the Influence of Continental Axes of Orientation on Patterns of Human Gene Flow. *Journal of Physical Anthropology* 146(4):515–529.

Ramos, A. R. 1995. *Sanumá Memories: Yanomami Ethnography in Times of Crisis.* Madison: University of Wisconsin Press.

Ranger, T. O. 1996. Postscript. In *Postcolonial Identities,* R. Werbner and T. O. Ranger, eds. London: Zed.

Ransby, B. 2017. Black Lives Matter Is Democracy in Action. *New York Times,* October 21. https://www.nytimes.com/2017/10/21/opinion/sunday/black-lives-matter-leadership.html.

Rapoza, K. 2012. Disturbing Trend for Putin, Russian Poverty Rising. *Forbes,* April 12. http://www.forbes.com/sites/kenrapoza/2012/04/12/disturbing-trend-for-putin-russian-poverty-rising/.

Rappaport, R. A. 1974. Obvious Aspects of Ritual. *Cambridge Anthropology* 2:2–60.

——. 1999. *Holiness and Humanity: Ritual in the Making of Religious Life.* New York: Cambridge University Press.

Rathje, W. L., and C. Murphy. 2001. *Rubbish! The Archaeology of Garbage.* Tucson: University of Arizona Press.

Rathus, S. A., J. S. Nevid, and J. Fichner-Rathus. 2018. *Human Sexuality in a Changing World,* Hoboken, NJ: Pearson.

Reagan, T. 2018. *Non-Western Educational Traditions: Local Approaches to Thought and Practice,* 4th ed. New York: Routledge.

Reardon, S. 2015. Psychologists Seek Roots of Terror: Studies Raise Prospect of Intervention in the Radicalization Process. *Nature* 517 (421). http://www.nature.com/polopoly_fs/1.16756!/menu/main/topColumns/topLeftColumn/pdf/517420a.pdf.

Redfield, R. 1941. *The Folk Culture of Yucatan.* Chicago: University of Chicago Press.

Redfield, R., R. Linton, and M. Herskovits. 1936. Memorandum on the Study of Acculturation. *American Anthropologist* 38:149–152.

Relethford, J. 2009. Race and Global Patterns of Phenotypic Variation. *American Journal of Physical Anthropology* 139(1):16–22.

——. 2012. *Human Population Genetics.* Hoboken, NJ: Wiley-Blackwell.

Renfrew, C. 1987. *Archaeology and Language: The Puzzle of Indo-European Origin.* London: Pimlico.

Renfrew, C., and P. Bahn. 2016. *Archaeology Essentials: Theories, Methods, and Practice,* 7th. ed. London: Thames and Hudson.

Reyhner, J., et al., eds. 2013. *Honoring Our Children: Culturally Appropriate Approaches for Teaching Indigenous Students.* Flagstaff: Northern Arizona University.

Rhodes, R. A. W., and P. 't Hart. 2014. *The Oxford Handbook of Political Leadership.* Oxford, UK: Oxford University Press.

Riach, J. 2013. Golf's Failure to Embrace Demographics across Society Is Hard to Stomach. *The Guardian,* May 22. http://www.theguardian.com/sport/blog/2013/may/22/uk-golf-clubs-race-issues.

Rich, M. 2018. In U.S. Open Victory, Naomi Osaka Pushes Japan to Redefine Japanese. New York Times, September 9. https://www.nytimes.com/2018/09/09/world/asia/japan-naomi-osaka-us-open.html.

Richter, T., and A. Arranz-Otaegui. 2018. Following a New Trail of Crumbs to Agriculture's Origins. SAPIENS, July 16. https://www.sapiens.org/archaeology/oldest-known-bread-crumbs-discovered/.

Riley, E. P., and M. Bezanson. 2018. Ethics of Primate Fieldwork: Toward an Ethically-Engaged Primatology. *Annual Review of Anthropology* 47:493–521.

Risman, B. J. 2018. *Where the Millennials Will Take Us: a New Generation Wrestles with the Gender Structure.* New York: Oxford University Press.

Ritter, M. 2019. Bones from Philippine Cave Reveal a New Human Cousin. Associated Press, *APNews,* April 10. https://www.apnews.com/723369cfaf2745e1ab8d25fe0bb4de0d.

Robbins, Jim. 2012. The Ecology of Disease, *New York Times,* July 14. http://www.nytimes.com/2012/07/15/sunday-review/the-ecology-of-disease.html.

Robbins, Joel. 2004. The Globalization of Pentecostal and Charismatic Christianity. *Annual Review of Anthropology* 33:17–143.

Robbins, R. 2014. *Global Problems and the Culture of Capitalism,* 6th ed. Boston: Pearson.

Robertson, J. 1992. Koreans in Japan. Paper presented at the University of Michigan Department of Anthropology, Martin Luther King Jr. Day Panel, January. Ann Arbor: University of Michigan Department of Anthropology (unpublished).

Robson, D. 2013. There Really Are 50 Eskimo Words for Snow. *Washington Post,* January 14. http://articles.washingtonpost.com/2013-01-14/national/36344037_1_eskimo-words-snow-inuit.

Romm, C. 2016. A New Skeleton and an Old Debate about Syphilis. *The Atlantic,* February 18. https://www.theatlantic.com/health/archive/2016/02/the-neverending-story-of-the-origins-of-syphilis/463401/.

Rosaldo, M. Z. 1980a. *Knowledge and Passion: Notions of Self and Social Life.* Stanford, CA: Stanford University Press.

———. 1980b. The Use and Abuse of Anthropology: Reflections on Feminism and Cross-Cultural Understanding. *Signs* 5(3):389–417.

Roscoe, W. 1991. *Zuni Man-Woman.* Albuquerque: University of New Mexico Press.

———. 1998. *Changing Ones: Third and Fourth Genders in Native North America.* New York: St. Martin's Press.

Rothman, J. M., D. Raubenheimer, and C. A. Chapman. 2011. Nutritional Geometry: Gorillas Prioritize Non-Protein Energy While Consuming Surplus Protein. *Biology Letters* 7:847–849.

Rothstein, E. 2006. Protection for Indian Patrimony That Leads to a Paradox. *New York Times,* March 29.

Ruff, C. B., et al. 2016. Limb Bone Structural Proportions and Locomotor Behavior in A. L. 288-1 ("Lucy"). PLOS One, November 30. http://journals.plos.org/plosone/article/authors?id=10.1371/journal.pone.0166095.

Ryang, S., and J. Lie. 2009. *Diaspora without Homeland: Being Korean in Japan.* Berkeley: University of California Press.

Rylko-Bauer, B., M. Singer, and J. Van Willigen. 2006. Reclaiming Applied Anthropology: Its Past, Present, and Future. *American Anthropologist* 108(1):178–190.

Sabloff, J. A. 2008. *Archaeology Matters: Action Archaeology in the Modern World.* Walnut Creek, CA: Left Coast Press.

Sadig, A. M. 2010. *The Neolithic of the Middle Nile Region: An Archeology of Central Sudan and Nubia.* East Lansing: Michigan State University Press.

Sahlins, M. D. 1968. *Tribesmen.* Englewood Cliffs, NJ: Prentice Hall.

———. 2017 (orig. 1972). *Stone Age Economics.* New York: Routledge Classics.

Salazar, C., and J. Bestard, eds. 2015. *Religion and Science as Forms of Life: Anthropological Insights into Reason and Unreason.* New York: Berghahn Books.

Saleh, A. 2013. *Ethnic Identity and the State in Iran.* New York: Palgrave Macmillan.

Salzman, P. C. 1974. Political Organization among Nomadic Peoples. In *Man in Adaptation: The Cultural Present,* 2nd ed., Y. A. Cohen, ed., pp. 267–284. Chicago: Aldine.

———. 2004. *Pastoralists: Equality, Hierarchy, and the State.* Boulder, CO: Westview Press.

———. 2008. *Culture and Conflict in the Middle East.* Amherst, NY: Humanity Books.

Salzmann, Z., J. M. Stanlaw, and N. Adachi. 2015. *Language, Culture, and Society: An Introduction to Linguistic Anthropology,* 6th ed. Boulder, CO: Westview Press.

Sample, I. 2018. Dramatic Decline in Borneo's Orangutan Population as 150,000 Lost in 16 Years. *Guardian,* February 15. https://www.theguardian.com/environment/2018/feb/15/dramatic-decline-in-borneos-orangutan-population-as-150000-lost-in-16-years.

Sanday, P. R. 1974. Female Status in the Public Domain. In *Woman, Culture, and Society,* M. Z. Rosaldo and L. Lamphere, eds., pp. 189–206. Stanford, CA: Stanford University Press.

———. 2002. *Women at the Center: Life in a Modern Matriarchy.* Ithaca, NY: Cornell University Press.

———. 2003. Public Interest Anthropology: A Model for Engaged Social Science. http://www.sas.upenn.edu/anthro/CPIA/PAPERS/SARdiscussion%20paper.65.html.

Sanjek, R. 2004. Going Public: Responsibilities and Strategies in the Aftermath of Ethnography. *Human Organization* 63(4):444–456.

Sapir, E. 1931. Conceptual Categories in Primitive Languages. *Science* 74:578–584.

———. 1956 (orig. 1928). The Meaning of Religion. In *Culture, Language and Personality: Selected Essays,* E. Sapir. Berkeley: University of California Press.

Saville, A., ed. 2012. *Flint and Stone in the Neolithic Period.* Oakville, CT: Oxbow Books.

Scarre, C., and B. Fagan. 2016. *Ancient Civilizations,* 4th ed. Milton Park, Abingdon, Oxon: Routledge.

Schaik, C. V. 2004. *Among Orangutans: Red Apes and the Rise of Human Culture.* Tucson: University of Arizona Press.

——. 2016 . *The Primate Roots of Human Nature.* Hoboken, NJ: Wiley.

Scheidel, W. 1997. Brother-Sister Marriage in Roman Egypt. *Journal of Biosocial Science* 29(3):361–371.

Schultz, S., C. Opie, and Q. D. Atkinson. 2011. Stepwise Evolution of Stable Sociality in Primates. *Nature* 479:229–222, November 11. http://www.nature.com/nature/journal/v479/n7372/full/nature10601.html.

Schwanhäusser, A., ed. 2016. *Sensing the City: A Companion to Urban Anthropology.* Gütersloh: Bauverlag.

Scott, James C. 1985. *Weapons of the Weak.* New Haven, CT: Yale University Press.

——. 1990. *Domination and the Arts of Resistance.* New Haven, CT: Yale University Press.

——. 2017. *Against the Grain: A Deep History of the Earliest States.* New Haven, CT: Yale University Press.

Scott, S., and C. Duncan. 2004. *Return of the Black Death: The World's Greatest Serial Killer.* Hoboken, NJ: Wiley.

Scudder, T., and E. Colson. 1980. *Secondary Education and the Formation of an Elite: The Impact of Education on Gwembe District, Zambia.* London: Academic Press.

Scupin, R. 2012. *Race and Ethnicity: An Anthropological Focus on the United States and the World,* 2nd ed. Upper Saddle River, NJ: Prentice Hall.

Senut, B., M. Pickford, D. Gommery, P. Mein, K. Cheboi, and Y. Coppens. 2001. First Hominid from the Miocene (Lukeino Formation, Kenya). *Comptes Rendus de l'Academie des Sciences, Series IIA—Earth and Planetary Science* 332 (January 30):137–144.

Service, E. R. 1962. *Primitive Social Organization: An Evolutionary Perspective.* New York: McGraw-Hill.

Sharma, A., and A. Gupta, eds. 2006. *The Anthropology of the State: A Reader.* Malden, MA: Blackwell.

Shermer, M. 2011. *In Darwin's Shadow: The Life and Science of Alfred Russel Wallace: A Biographical Study on the Psychology of History.* New York: Oxford University Press.

Shih, C.-K. 2010. *Quest for Harmony: The Moso Traditions of Sexual Union and Family Life.* Stanford, CA: Stanford University Press.

Shivaram, C. 1996. Where Women Wore the Crown: Kerala's Dissolving Matriarchies Leave a Rich Legacy of Compassionate Family Culture. *Hinduism Today.* http://www.spiritweb.org/HinduismToday/96_02_Women_Wore_Crown.html.

Shore, C., S. Wright, and D. Però, eds. 2011. *Policy Worlds: Anthropology and the Analysis of Contemporary Power.* New York: Berghahn Books.

Shryock, A. 1988. Autonomy, Entanglement, and the Feud: Prestige Structures and Gender Values in Highland Albania. *Anthropological Quarterly* 61(3):113–118.

Sidky, H. 2015. *Religion: An Anthropological Perspective.* New York: Peter Lang Publishing.

Sillitoe, P., ed. 2007. *Local Science versus Global Science: Approaches to Indigenous Knowledge in International Development.* New York: Berghahn Books.

Simmons, A. H. 2007. *The Neolithic Revolution in the Near East: Transforming the Human Landscape.* Tucson: University of Arizona Press.

Simpson, A. 2019. *Language and Society: An Introduction.* New York: Oxford University Press.

Simpson, P., A. Mayer, and S. Statham. 2018. *Language and Power: A Resource Book for Students,* 2nd ed. New York: Routledge.

Sims, C. 2016. Academics in Foxholes: The Life and Death of the Human Terrain System. Foreign Affairs, February 4. https://www.foreignaffairs.com/articles/afghanistan/2016-02-04/academics-foxholes.

Singer, M. 2015. *Anthropology of Infectious Disease.* Walnut Creek, CA: Left Coast Press.

——. 2019. *Climate Change and Social Inequality: The Health and Social Costs of Global Warming.* New York: Routledge.

Singer, M., H. Baer, et al. 2019. *Introducing Medical Anthropology: A Discipline in Action,* 3rd ed. Lanham, MD: Rowman & Littlefield.

Skeates, R., ed. 2017. *Museums and Archaeology*. New York: Routledge.

Skoglund, P., et al. 2012. Origins and Genetic Legacy of Neolithic Farmers and Hunter-Gatherers in Europe. *Science* 336(466–469).

Slaughter, A.-M. 2013. Women Are Sexist, Too: If Women Are Equal at the Office, Why Can't Men Be Equal at Home? *Time*. http://time.com/women-are-sexist-too/.

———. 2015. *Unfinished Business: Men, Women, Work, Family*. New York: Random House.

Smith, C. H., and G. Beccaloni, eds. 2010. *Natural Selection and Beyond: The Intellectual Legacy of Alfred Russel Wallace*. New York: Oxford University Press.

Smith, C. S. 2006. Some See a "Pyramid" to Hone Bosnia's Image. Others See a Big Hill. *New York Times*, May 15.

Smith, M. E. 2016. *At Home with the Aztecs: An Archaeologist Uncovers Their Daily Life*. New York: Routledge.

Solway, J., and R. Lee. 1990. Foragers, Genuine and Spurious: Situating the Kalahari San in History (with CA Treatment). *Current Anthropology* 31(2):109–146.

Sotomayor, S. 2009 (orig. 2001). A Latina Judge's Voice. Judge Mario G. Olmos Memorial Lecture, University of California, Berkeley School of Law. Reprinted by the *New York Times*, http://www.nytimes.com/2009/05/15/us/politics/15judge.text.html.

Spencer, C. S. 2003. War and Early State Formation in Oaxaca, Mexico. *Proceedings of the National Academy of Sciences* 100(20): 11185–11187.

Spencer, E. T. 2010. *Sociolinguistics*. Hauppauge, NY: Nova Science.

Spickard, P., ed. 2012. *Race and Immigration in the United States: New Histories*. New York: Routledge.

———. 2013. *Multiple Identities: Migrants, Ethnicity, and Membership*. Bloomington: Indiana University Press.

Spoor, F., M. G. Leakey, P. N. Gathongo, F. H. Brown, S. C. Anton, I. McDougall, C. Kiarie, F. K. Manthi, and L. N. Leakey. 2007. Implications of New Early *Homo* Fossils from Ileret,

East of Lake Turkana, Kenya. *Nature* 448 (7154):688–691.

Stack, C. B. 1975. *All Our Kin: Strategies for Survival in a Black Community*. New York: Harper Torchbooks.

Stanish, C., and A. Levine. 2011. War and Early State Formation in the Northern Titicaca Basin, Peru. *Proceedings of the National Academy of Sciences* 108(34): 13901–13906.

Starn, O. 2011. *The Passion of Tiger Woods: An Anthropologist Reports on Golf, Race, and Celebrity Scandal*. Durham, NC: Duke University Press.

Statistics Canada. 2010. *Study: Projections of the Diversity of the Canadian Population*. http://www.statcan.gc.ca/daily-quotidien/100309/dq100309a-eng.htm.

———. 2016. Census Profile, 2016 Census. http://www12.statcan.gc.ca/census-recensement/2016/dp-pd/prof/details/page.cfm?Lang=E&Geo1=PR&Code1=01&Geo2=&Code2=&Data=Count&SearchText=Canada&SearchType=Begins&SearchPR=01&B1=All&TABID=1.

Staudt, K. A. 2018. *Border Politics in the Global Era: Comparative Perspectives*. Lanham, MD: Rowman & Littlefield.

Stearns, P. N. 2016. *Globalization in World History*, 2nd ed. New York: Routledge.

Stein, R. L., and P. L. Stein. 2017. *The Anthropology of Religion, Magic, and Witchcraft*, 4th ed. New York: Routledge.

Stevens, N. J., et al. 2013. Palaeontological Evidence for an Oligocene Divergence between Old World Monkeys and Apes. *Nature* 497:611–614. http://www.nature.com/nature/journal/v497/n7451/full/nature12161.html.

St. Fleur, N. 2017. Humans First Arrived in Australia 65,000 Years Ago, Study Suggests. *New York Times*, July 19. https://www.nytimes.com/2017/07/19/science/humans-reached-australia-aboriginal-65000-years.html.

———. 2018. In an Israeli Cave, Scientists Discover Jawbone of Earliest Modern Human Out of Africa. *New York Times*, January 25. https://www.nytimes.com/2018/01/25/science/jawbone-fossil-israel.html.

Stoddard, E., and J. M. Collins, eds. 2017. *Social and Cultural Foundations in Global Studies*. New York: Routledge/Taylor and Francis.

Stoler, A. L., ed. 2013. *Imperial Debris: On Ruins and Ruination*. Durham, NC: Duke University Press.

Stoler, A. L., C. McGranahan, and P. C. Perdue, eds. 2007. *Imperial Formations*. Santa Fe, NM: School for Advanced Research Press.

Stoneking, M. 2015. *An Introduction to Molecular Anthropology*. Hoboken, NJ: Wiley.

Storey, R., and G. R. Storey. 2017. *Rome and the Classic Maya: Comparing the Slow Collapse of Civilizations*. New York: Routledge/Taylor & Francis.

Strathern, M. 1988. *Dealing with Inequality: Analysing Gender Relations in Melanesia and Beyond: Essays by Members of the 1983/1984 Anthropological Research Group at the Research School of Pacific Studies, the Australian National University*. New York: Cambridge University Press.

Streets-Salter, H., and T. Getz. 2016. *Empires and Colonies in the Modern World: A Global Perspective*. New York: Oxford University Press.

Strier, K. B., ed. 2014. *Primate Ethnographies*. Boston: Pearson.

Stringer, C. 2012a. *Lone Survivors: How We Came to Be the Only Humans on Earth*. New York: Henry Holt.

———. 2012b. Palaeontology: The 100-Year Mystery of Piltdown Man. *Nature* 492:177–179.

Stryker, R., and R. J. Gonzalez, eds. 2014. *Up, Down, and Sideways: Anthropologists Trace the Pathways of Power*. New York: Berghahn Books.

Subbaraman, N. 2013. Earliest Fish Stews Were Cooked in Japan during Last Ice Age, Experts Say. NBC News, June 22. http://science.nbcnews.com/_news/2013/04/10/17687754-earliest-fish-stews-were-cooked-in-japan-during-last-ice-age-experts-say?lite.

Sunstein, B. S., and E. Chiseri-Strater. 2012. *Fieldworking: Reading and Writing Research*, 4th ed. Upper Saddle River, NJ: Prentice Hall.

Sussman, R. W., D. T. Rasmussen, and P. H. Raven. 2013. Rethinking Primate Origins Again. *American Journal of Primatology* 75(2):95–106.

Suttles, W. 1960. Affinal Ties, Subsistence, and Prestige among the Coast Salish. *American Anthropologist* 62:296–305.

Svoboda, E. 2017. Life and Death after the Steel Mills. SAPIENS, October 18. https://www.sapiens.org/culture/postindustrial-world-chicago-steel/.

Tamai, L. A. Y. W., et al., eds. 2019. *Shape-Shifters: Journeys across Terrains of Race and Identity*. Lincoln: University of Nebraska Press.

Tanaka, J. 2014. *The Bushmen: A Half-Century Chronicle of Transformations in Hunter-Gatherer Life and Ecology*. Kyoto, Japan: Kyoto University Press.

Tannen, D. 1990. *You Just Don't Understand: Women and Men in Conversation*. New York: Ballantine Books.

———. 2017. *You're the Only One I Can Tell Inside the Language of Women's Friendships*. New York: Ballantine.

Tattersall, I., and R. De Salle. 2011. *Race? Debunking a Scientific Myth*. College Station: Texas A&M University Press.

Tavernise, S. 2012. Whites Account for Under Half of Births in U.S. *New York Times,* May 17. http://www.nytimes.com/2012/05/17/us/whites-account-for-under-half-of-births-in-us.html.

Taylor, P., M. H. Lopez, J. H. Martinez, and G. Velasco. 2012. *When Labels Don't Fit: Hispanics and Their Views of Identity*. Pew Research Hispanic Center, April 4. http://www.pewhispanic.org/2012/04/04/when-labels-dont-fit-hispanics-and-their-views-of-identity/.

Tehan, M. 2017. *The Impact of Climate Change Mitigation on Indigenous and Forest Communities: International, National, and Local Law Perspectives on REDD+*. New York: Cambridge University Press.

*Telegraph.* 2005. Third Sex Finds a Place on Indian Passport Forms. March 10. http://infochangeindia.org/human-rights/news/third-sex-finds-a-place-on-indian-passport-forms.html.

Templeton, A. 2019. Human Population Genetics and Genomics. San Diego, CA: Elsevier.

The Week. 2013. Should Apes Have Legal Rights? August 3. http://theweek.com/articles/461480/should-apes-have-legal-rights.

Thompson, T., ed. 2015. Same-Sex Marriage. Farmington Hills, MI: Greenhaven Press.

Tishkoff, S. A., et al. 2007. Convergent Adaptation of Human Lactase Persistence in Africa and Europe. Nature Genetics 39(1):1–40.

Titiev, M. 1992. Old Oraibi: A Study of the Hopi Indians of Third Mesa. Albuquerque: University of New Mexico Press.

Tobler, R., et al. 2017. Aboriginal Mitogenomes Reveal 50,000 Years of Regionalism in Australia. Nature 544 (April 13):180–184. https://www.nature.com/articles/nature21416.

Totten, S., and R. Ubaldo, eds. 2011. We Cannot Forget: Interviews with Survivors of the 1994 Genocide in Rwanda. New Brunswick, NJ: Rutgers University Press.

Tougher, S. 2008. The Eunuch in Byzantine History and Society. New York: Routledge.

Toyosaki, S., and S. Eguchi, eds. 2017. Intercultural Communication in Japan: Theorizing Homogenizing Discourse. New York: Routledge.

Tremlett, P.-F., G. Harvey, and L. T. Sutherland, eds. 2017. Edward Burnett Tylor, Religion, and Culture. New York: Bloomsbury Academic.

Trivedi, B. P. 2001. Scientists Identify a Language Gene. National Geographic News, October 4. http://news.nationalgeographic.com/news/2001/10/1004_Tvlanguagegene.html.

Trosper, R.L. 2009. Resilience, Reciprocity and Ecological Economics: Northwest Coast Sustainability. New York: Routledge.

Trudgill, P. 2010. Investigations in Sociohistorical Linguistics: Stories of Colonisation and Contact. New York: Cambridge University Press.

Tucci, S., and J. M. Akey. 2016. Population Genetics: A Map of Human Wanderlust. Nature September 21. doi:10.1038/nature19472.

Turner, V. W. 1974 (orig. 1967). The Ritual Process. Harmondsworth, England: Penguin Press.

Tuttle, R. H. 2014. Apes and Human Evolution. Cambridge, MA: Harvard University Press.

Tylor, E. B. 1958 (orig. 1871). Primitive Culture. New York: Harper Torchbooks.

Underhill, P. 2009. Why We Buy? The Science of Shopping. New York: Random House.

Ungar, P. S. 2017. Evolution's Bite: A Story of Teeth, Diet, and Human Origins. Princeton, NJ: Princeton University Press.

U.S. Bureau of Labor Statistics. 2018. Employment Characteristics of Families—2017. April 19. https://www.bls.gov/news.release/pdf/famee.pdf.

——. 2019. Union Members Summary. January 18. https://www.bls.gov/news.release/union2.nr0.htm.

U.S. Census Bureau. 2019. America's Families and Living Arrangements: 2018. https://www.census.gov/data/tables/2018/demo/families/cps-2018.html.

United Nations, Department of Economic and Social Affairs. 2014. World Urbanization Prospects, The 2014 Revision. https://esa.un.org/unpd/wup/publications/files/wup2014-highlights.pdf.

——. 2018a. 68% of the World Population Projected to Live in Urban Areas by 2050, says UN. May 16. https://www.un.org/development/desa/en/news/population/2018-revision-of-world-urbanization-prospects.html.

——. 2018b. The World's Cities in 2018. http://www.un.org/en/events/citiesday/assets/pdf/the_worlds_cities_in_2018_data_booklet.pdf

Vallegia, C. R., and J. J. Snodgrass. 2015. Health of Indigenous Peoples. Annual Review of Anthropology 44:117–135.

Van Allen, J. 1971. "Aba Riots" or "Women's War"? British Ideology and Eastern Nigerian Women's Political Activism. Waltham, MA: African Studies Association.

Vayda, A. P. 1968 (orig. 1961). Economic Systems in Ecological Perspective: The Case of the Northwest Coast. In Readings in Anthropology, 2nd ed., Volume 2, M. H. Fried, ed., pp. 172–178. New York: Crowell.

Veblen, T. 1934. The Theory of the Leisure Class: An Economic Study of Institutions. New York: The Modern Library.

Vekua, A., D. Lordkipanidze, and G. P. Rightmire. 2002. A Skull of Early *Homo* from Dmanisi, Georgia, *Science,* July 5, pp. 85–89.

Velupillai, V. 2015. *Pidgins, Creoles, and Mixed Languages: An Introduction.* Philadelphia: John Benjamins.

Venkatesan, S., and T. Yarrow, eds. 2014. *Differentiating Development: Beyond an Anthropology of Critique.* New York: Berghahn Books.

Vespa, J., D. M. Armstrong, and L. Medina. Demographic Turning Points for the United States: Population Projections for 2020 to 2060. U.S. Census Bureau, Current Population Reports, P25-1144. Washington, DC: U.S. Government Printing Office. https://www.census.gov/content/dam/Census/library/publications/2018/demo/P25_1144.pdf

Vigil, J. D. 2010. *Gang Redux: A Balanced Anti-Gang Strategy.* Long Grove, IL: Waveland.

———. 2012. *From Indians to Chicanos: The Dynamics of Mexican-American Culture,* 3rd ed. Boulder, CO: Westview Press.

Vigne, J.-D., et al. 2012. First Wave of Cultivators Spread to Cyprus at Least 10,600 Years Ago. *Proceedings of the National Academy of Sciences* 109(22):8445–8449.

Villmoare, B., et al. 2015. Early *Homo* at 2.8 Ma from Ledi-Geraru, Afar, Ethiopia. *Science* (March 4) 347:1352–1355. http://science.sciencemag.org/content/early/2015/03/03/science.aaa1343.

Vinyeta, K., and K. Lynn. 2013. *Exploring the Role of Traditional Ecological Knowledge in Climate Change Initiatives.* Portland, OR: U. S. Department of Agriculture, Forest Service, Pacific Northwest Research Station.

Vivanco, L. A. 2017. *Field Notes: A Guided Journal for Doing Anthropology.* New York: Oxford University Press.

von Cramon-Taubadel, N. 2011. Global Human Mandibular Variation Reflects Differences in Agricultural and Hunter-Gatherer Subsistence Strategies. *Proceedings of the National Academy of Sciences* 108(49):19546–19551.

Wade, L. 2018a. To Overcome Decades of Mistrust, A Workshop Aims to Train Indigenous Researchers to Be Their Own Genome Experts. *Science,* September 27. https://www.sciencemag.org/news/2018/09/overcome-decades-mistrust-workshop-aims-train-indigenous-researchers-be-their-own.

Wade, L. 2018b. Ancient DNA Tracks Migrations around Americas. Science 362 (6415):627–628.http://science.sciencemag.org.proxy.lib.umich.edu/content/sci/362/6415/627.full.pdf.

Wade, N. 2004. New Species Revealed: Tiny Cousins of Humans. *New York Times,* Ω 28, national edition, pp. Al, A6.

———. 2012. Earliest Americans Arrived in Waves, DNA Study Finds. *New York Times,* July 11. http://www.nytimes.com/2012/07/12/science/earliest-americans-arrived-in-3-waves-not-1-dna-study-finds.html.

Wade, P. 2010. *Race and Ethnicity in Latin America,* 2nd ed. New York: Pluto Press.

———. 2015. *Race: An Introduction.* New York: Cambridge University Press

———. 2017. *Degrees of Mixture, Degrees of Freedom: Genomics, Multiculturalism, and Race in Latin America.* Durham, NC: Duke University Press.

Walker, S. M., and D. W. Owsley. 2012. *The Skeletons Speak: Kennewick Man and the Paleoamerican World.* Minneapolis: Carolrhoda Books.

Wallace, A. F. C. 1966. *Religion: An Anthropological View.* New York: McGraw-Hill.

Wallace, S. 2016. Dodging Wind Farms and Bullets in the Arctic. *National Geographic,* March 1. http://news.nationalgeographic.com/2016/03/160301-arctic-sami-norway-reindeer/.

Wallerstein, I. M. 2004. *World-Systems Analysis: An Introduction.* Durham, NC: Duke University Press.

———. 2013. *Does Capitalism Have a Future?* New York: Oxford University Press.

Walley, C. J. 2013. *Exit Zero: Family and Class in Postindustrial Chicago.* Chicago: University of Chicago Press.

Walton, D., and J. A. Suarez, eds. 2016. *Culture, Space, and Power: Blurred Lines.* Lanham, MD: Lexington Books.

Ward, C. V., W. H. Kimbel, and D. C. Johanson. 2011. Complete Fourth Metatarsal and Arches in the Foot of *Australopithecus afarensis*. *Science* 331(6018):750–753.

Ward, M. C., and M. Edelstein. 2014. *A World Full of Women*, 6th ed. Upper Saddle River, NJ: Pearson.

Wardhaugh, R., and J. Fuller. 2015. *An Introduction to Sociolinguistics,* 7th ed. Malden, MA: Wiley-Blackwell.

Warne, A. D., ed. 2015. *Ethnic and Cultural Identity: Perceptions, Discrimination, and Social Challenges*. Hauppauge, NY: Nova Science.

Wasson, C., M. O. Butler, and J. Copeland-Carson, eds. 2012. *Applying Anthropology in the Global Village*. Walnut Creek, CA: Left Coast Press.

Waters, M. R., and T. W. Stafford, Jr. 2007. Redefining the Age of Clovis: Implications for the Peopling of the Americas. *Science* (February 23) 315:1122–1126.

Waters, M. R., et al. 2011 Pre-Clovis Mastodon Hunting 13,800 Years Ago at the Manis Site, Washington. *Science* 334(6054):351–353. doi:10.1126/science.1207663.

Weber, M. 1958 (orig. 1904). *The Protestant Ethic and the Spirit of Capitalism*. New York: Scribner.

———. 1968 (orig. 1922). *Economy and Society*. E. Fischoff et al. (trans.). New York: Bedminster Press.

Weiner, J. S. 2003. *The Piltdown Forgery*. New York: Oxford University Press.

Weiner, M. 2009. *Japan's Minorities: The Illusion of Homogeneity,* 2nd ed. New York: Routledge.

Weiss, E. 2015. *Paleopathology in Perspective: Bone Health and Disease through Time*. Lanham, MD: Rowman & Littlefield.

Weiss, H. 2005. *Collapse*. New York: Routledge.

Wendorf, F., and R. Schild. 2000. Late Neolithic Megalithic Structures at Nabta Playa (Sahara), Southwestern Egypt. http://www.comp-archaeology.org/WendorfSAA98.html.

Wenke, R. J., and D. I. Olszewski. 2007. *Patterns in Prehistory: Mankind's First Three Million Years,* 5th ed. New York: Oxford University Press.

White, L. A. 2009. *Modern Capitalist Culture,* abridged ed. Walnut Creek, CA: Left Coast Press.

White, T. D., M. T. Black, and P. A. Folkens. 2012. *Human Osteology,* 3rd ed. San Diego: Academic Press.

Whyte, M. F. 1978. Cross-Cultural Codes Dealing with the Relative Status of Women. *Ethnology* 12(2):203–225.

Widlok, T. 2017. Anthropology and the Economy of Sharing. New York: Routledge.

Wilford, J. N. 2007a. Fossils in Kenya Challenge Linear Evolution, *New York Times,* August 9, p. A6.

———. 2007b. Fossils Reveal Clues on Human Ancestors. *New York Times,* September 20. https://www.nytimes.com/2007/09/20/science/20fossil.html.

———. 2010. In Syria, a Prologue for Cities. *New York Times,* April 6. http://www.nytimes.com/2010/04/06/science/06archeo.html.

———. 2011a. Fossil Teeth Put Humans in Europe Earlier Than Thought. *New York Times,* November 3, p. A4.

———. 2011b. In African Cave, Signs of an Ancient Paint Factory. *New York Times,* October 13, p. A14.

———. 2011c. Earliest Signs of Advanced Tools Found. *New York Times,* August 31.

———. 2012. Artifacts Revive Debate on Transformation of Human Behavior. *New York Times,* July 30. http://www.nytimes.com/2012/07/31/science/cave-findings-revive-debate-on-human-behavior.html.

———. 2013. Palm-Size Fossil Resets Primates' Clock, Scientists Say. *New York Times,* June 5. http://www.nytimes.com/2013/06/06/science/palm-size-fossil-resets-primates-clock-scientists-say.html.

———. 2015. Stone Tools from Kenya Are Oldest Yet Discovered. *New York Times,* May 20. https://www.nytimes.com/2015/ 05/21/science/stone-tools-from-kenya-are-oldest-yet-discovered.html.

Wilk, R. R. 2006. *Fast Food/Slow Food: The Cultural Economy of the Global Food System*. Lanham, MD: AltaMira.

Williams, L. M., and D. Finkelhor. 1995. Paternal Caregiving and Incest: Test of a Biosocial Model. *American Journal of Orthopsychiatry* 65(1):101–113.

Williams, S. A., et al. 2018. Special Issue: Australopithecus sediba. PaleoAnthropology 2018: 49–55. http://www.paleoanthro.org/media/journal/content/PA20180049.pdf.

Wilmsen, E. N. 1989. *Land Filled with Flies: A Political Economy of the Kalahari.* Chicago: University of Chicago Press.

Wilson, J., and K. Stierstorfer, eds. 2017. *The Routledge Diaspora Studies Reader.* New York: Routledge.

Wilson, M. L., and R. W. Wrangham. 2003. Intergroup Relations in Chimpanzees. *Annual Review of Anthropology* 32:363–392.

Winzeler, R. L. 2012. *Anthropology and Religion,* 2nd ed. Lanham, MD: Rowman & Littlefield.

Wittfogel, K. A. 1957. *Oriental Despotism: A Comparative Study of Total Power.* New Haven, CT: Yale University Press.

Wolcott, H. F. 2008. *Ethnography: A Way of Seeing,* 2nd ed. Lanham, MD: AltaMira.

Wolf, A. P. 2014. *Incest Avoidance and the Incest Taboos: Two Aspects of Human Nature.* Stanford, CA: Stanford Briefs.

Wolf, E. R. 1966. *Peasants.* Englewood Cliffs, NJ: Prentice Hall.

——. 1982. *Europe and the People without History.* Berkeley: University of California Press.

Wolff, E. N. 2017. *A Century of Wealth in America.* Cambridge, MA: Belknap Press of Harvard University Press.

Womack, M. 2010. *The Anthropology of Health and Healing.* Lanham, MD: AltaMira.

Wong, K. 2014. Tiny Genetic Differences between Humans and Other Primates Pervade the Genome. *Scientific American,* September 1. https://www.scientificamerican.com/article/tiny-genetic-differences-between-humans-and-other-primates-pervade-the-genome/.

Worsley, P. 1985 (orig. 1959). Cargo Cults. In *Readings in Anthropology* 85/86. Guilford, CT: Dushkin.

Wortham, J. 2018. On Instagram, Seeing between the (Gender) Lines. *New York Times Magazine,* November 16. https://www.nytimes.com/interactive/2018/11/16/magazine/tech-design-instagram-gender.html.

Wright, H. T. 1977. Recent Research on the Origin of the State. *Annual Review of Anthropology* 6:379–397.

——. 1994. Prestate Political Formations. In *Chiefdoms and Early States in the Near East: The Organizational Dynamics of Complexity,* G. Stein and M. S. Rothman, eds., *Monographs in World Archaeology* 18:67–84. Madison, WI: Prehistory Press.

Wu, X., et al. 2012. Early Pottery at 20,000 Years Ago in Xianrendong Cave, China. *Science* 336:1696.

Wuebbles, D. J., et al., eds. 2017. Executive Summary. Climate Science Special Report: Fourth National Climate Assessment, 1:12–34. Washington, DC: U.S. Global Change Research Program.

Yamashiro, J. H. 2017. *Redefining Japaneseness: Japanese Americans in the Ancestral Homeland.* New Brunswick, NJ: Rutgers University Press.

Yetman, N., ed. 1991. *Majority and Minority: The Dynamics of Race and Ethnicity in American Life,* 5th ed. Boston: Allyn & Bacon.

Young, A. 2000. *Women Who Become Men: Albanian Sworn Virgins.* New York: Berg.

Zapotosky, M. 2017. Grandparents, Other Extended Relatives Exempt from Trump Travel Ban, Federal Judge Rules. *Washington Post,* July 14. https://www.washingtonpost.com/world/national-security/grandparents-other-extended-relatives-exempt-from-trump-travel-ban-federal-judge-rules/2017/07/14/ce67aa72-6888-11e7-8eb5-cbccc2e7bfbf_story.html.

Zeder, M. A. 2008. Domestication and Early Agriculture in the Mediterranean Basin: Origins, Diffusion, and Impact. *Proceedings of the National Academy of Sciences* 105(33): 11597–11604. http://www.pnas.org/content/early/2008/08/11/0801317105.

Zhang, Y. 2016. *Trust and Economics: The Co-evolution of Trust and Exchange Systems.* New York: Routledge.

Zimmer, C. 2010. Siberian Fossils Were Neanderthals' Eastern Cousins, DNA Reveals. *New York Times,* December 22. http://www.nytimes.com/2010/12/23/science/23ancestor.html.

———. 2013. Monogamy and Human Evolution. *New York Times,* August 2. http://www.nytimes.com/2013/08/02/science/monogamys-boost-to-human-evolution.html.

———. 2015. Agriculture Linked to DNA Changes in Ancient Europe. *New York Times,* November 23. http://www.nytimes.com/2015/11/24/science/agriculture-linked-to-dna-changes-in-ancient-europe.html.

———. 2016a. A 3.2-Million-Year-Old Mystery: Did Lucy Fall from a Tree? *New York Times,* August 29. https://www.nytimes.com/2016/08/30/science/lucy-hominid-fossils-fall.html.

———. 2016b. A Single Migration from Africa Populated the World, Studies Find. *New York Times,* September 21. https://www.nytimes.com/2016/09/22/science/ancient-dna-human-history.html.

———. 2017a. How Did Aboriginal Australians Arrive on the Continent? DNA Helps Solve a Mystery. *New York Times,* March 8. https://www.nytimes.com/2017/03/08/science/aboriginal-australians-dna-origins-australia.html.

———. 2017b. In Neanderthal DNA, Signs of a Mysterious Human Migration. *New York Times,* July 4. https://www.nytimes.com/2017/07/04/science/neanderthals-dna-homo-sapiens-human-evolution.html.

———. 2017c. Oldest Fossils of Homo Sapiens Found in Morocco, Altering History of Our Species. *New York Times,* June 7. https://www.nytimes.com/2017/06/07/science/human-fossils-morocco.html.

———. 2018. In the Bones of a Buried Child, Signs of a Massive Human Migration to the Americas. *New York Times,* January 3. https://www.nytimes.com/2018/01/03/science/native-americans-beringia-siberia.html.

Zimmer-Tamakoshi, L. 1997. The Last Big Man: Development and Men's Discontents in the Papua New Guinea Highlands. *Oceania* 68(2):107–122.

Zimring, C. A., ed. 2012. *Encyclopedia of Consumption and Waste: The Social Science of Garbage.* Thousand Oaks, CA: Sage.

Zukin, S., P. Kasinitz, and X. Chen, eds. 2015. *Global Cities, Local Streets: Everyday Diversity from New York to Shanghai.* New York: Routledge.

# Index